P9-ECY-981

Henry FIELDING

a reference guide

A
Reference
Guide
to
Literature

Arthur Weitzman
Editor

Henry FIELDING

a reference guide

L. J. MORRISSEY

G.K.HALL &CO.

70 LINCOLN STREET, BOSTON, MASS.

Library of Congress Cataloging in Publication Data

Morrissey, L J
Henry Fielding, a reference guide.

(Reference guides to literature)
Includes index.
1. Fielding, Henry, 1707-1754—Bibliography.
I. Title. II. Series.
Z8293.72.M67 [PR3456] 016.823'5
ISBN 0-8161-8139-X 80-16396

This publication is printed on permanent/durable acid-free paper
MANUFACTURED IN THE UNITED STATES OF AMERICA

To Edward and Edith Morrissey

Contents

Introduction

Fielding had several successful careers: fashionable playwright, journalist, novelist, and magistrate. He lived all his adult life in vigorous, brawling eighteenth century London, and most of his plays, as well as the novel Amelia, were about London sharpers, fakes, and malicious contrivers. But Fielding's sharks were not limited to urban settings. Because he had grown up in the country, he knew that the sentimentalist's "pastoral" England was filled with pretentious, uncharitable hypocrites who were also parsons, innkeepers, squires, maids, doctors, highwaymen, gypsies, itinerant preachers, lawyers, hermits, and court gentlemen. Self-interest reigned; rapes were attempted, people beaten. One needed a stout heart and a strong oak stick to make one's way through Fielding's England: his good parson prays as he cracks open heads; his "fallen women" cheerfully continue falling. Despite this rowdy realism, the protagonists of his major novels (Joseph, Tom and Amelia) share a comic mythic experience: each is taken away from, or cast out of, a rural 'Paradise Hall'; each returns to the security of the rural parish (see 1968.B12).

Fielding's own life shows none of that "mythic experience," even though he probably was born near the legendary Camelot in April 1707, at the Gould estate, Sharpham Park, Somerset. His father was a lieutenant in the army who spent a great deal of time on half-pay. His mother was the daughter of a judge of King's bench. His father was cousin to the Desmonds, and his mother cousin to the Montagues. In a society based on first sons, Henry's father, Edmund Fielding, third son of the fifth son of the Earl of Desmond, was not a glittering prize. Sarah Fielding, née Gould, was. She came from a rich, distinguished family of judges and magistrates, while Edmund was only the son of a canon of Salisbury Cathedral. The discrepancy in rank and money led to a bitter dispute between Edmund and the Goulds soon after Sarah's death.

The family moved from the Gould estate to East Stout, Dorset, when Henry was three. He was the first of a number of children (perhaps six) which included Sarah Fielding, also a novelist. Henry's mother died in 1718, and his father married again within months, the second of four marriages. One of Fielding's half-brothers, John, also became a distinguished London magistrate, and the two jointly created the famous "Bow Street Runners."

About the time Henry was sent to Eton (1719), Lady Gould brought Edmund Fielding to court over her daughter's dowry and the custody of the children (see 1940.B14). The custody suit was bitter, and, largely on the evidence of a bribed servant, Lady Gould won. Among the charges were that Edmund and the second Mrs. Fielding were not feeding the children properly, were giving them small beer rather than good ale, and were bringing them up papists. Despite the obvious differences between the families, Henry continued to move easily between the two households, visiting them in turns on school holidays.

By the time he left Eton (probably in 1724), Henry Fielding was a finished young gentleman with a classical education and a servant of his own. His first attempt at choosing a wife ended disastrously. After wooing a provincial heiress, Sarah Andrews (1931.B4), and attempting an elopement, Fielding, with his manservant, was thrashed by her mercenary family. Henry Fielding, Esquire then moved to London and became a clever young man about town. By 1728, he had written a fashionably sophisticated comedy, Love in Several Masques, which was produced with the help of an important relative, Lady Mary Wortley Montagu. Shortly after its production, Henry enrolled at, or perhaps was sent to, the University of Leyden in Holland to continue his formal education.

Considered one of the great European universities of its day and a center of the Enlightenment, Leyden was probably the source of Fielding's healthy contempt for pedantry. Joining the Scriblerus tradition begun by Swift and Pope, Fielding later mocked academics and critics in The Tragedy of Tragedies' preface and footnotes, giving himself a plug and Dutch lack of humor a kick by reporting that Pieter Burmann, a professor at Leyden, "hath stiled Tom Thumb, Heroum omnium Tragicorum facilé Principem" or, of all the tragic heroes, easily the foremost. After less than a year, Fielding considered his formal education ended, returned to England and began his stage career in earnest. Twenty Fielding plays were produced between 1730 and 1737, and several, like Tom Thumb (later The Tragedy of Tragedies) and The Welsh Opera (later The Grub-Street Opera), were extensively revised for separate production. He also managed the Little Haymarket Theatre. Although he attempted most of the comic dramatic forms popular in his age (sentimental comedy, humorous comedy, ballad opera and witty comedy), his unique talent lay in a kind of satiric theatrical review best exemplified by Pasquin and The Historical Register for the Year 1736. These sharp satiric attacks helped provoke Robert Walpole's ministry to bring in the Theatre Licensing Act (1737) that closed the Little Haymarket Theatre and ended Fielding's career as an active dramatist. Although he wrote The Fathers, never produced in his lifetime, and The Wedding Day, produced in 1743, his career as a dramatist was over. Fielding, who had never made more than a precarious living in the theater, had to find a new career. He went on writing, becoming a journalist to support his wife and two children (he had married Charlotte Cradock in 1737). He also began a career that the Goulds would have approved.

He began reading law at the Middle Temple and was called to the bar in 1740. In November 1739, while he was reading law, he and an old friend from the theater, James Ralph, began a periodical called The Champion. He must have thought that the hard work of writing a semi-weekly or weekly essay was a temporary expedient. He was wrong. He never made enough money at law to give up periodical journalism. In 1745 he edited The True Patriot, in 1747 The Jacobite's Journal, in 1752 The Covent-Garden Journal. In all of these he continued the attacks on artistic, social and political corruption for which he had become famous in his satiric plays (in The Lottery, for example, he had attacked the chicanery of the public lotteries). His shift from attacker to supporter of Robert Walpole and his satire made him a fair target for contemporary writers and journalists. Alexander Pope may have encouraged, or at least countenanced, an attack in The Grub-Street Journal; Tobias Smollett also vigorously attacked him. These early attacks on Fielding helped create the Fielding myth of the hard-drinking profligate (1918.B1), and scholars are still attempting to untangle his political alliances (see 1950.B4).

In 1741 he was provoked into his real career by the bad sexual ethics and worse art of Samuel Richardson's Pamela. He wrote a delicious anonymous parody called Shamela (see 1916.B1 and 1953.A1) and then his first novel, Joseph Andrews (1742), about Pamela's "brother," also intent on preserving his virginity until marriage. These two works created an animosity between Richardson and Fielding in life (see 1936.B7) and a critical opposition that continues today (see 1950.B6 or 1965.B7). In 1743, partly for money and partly to assert his existence as a major literary figure, he published three volumes of his Miscellanies. Among poetic dross and interesting essays was his excellent sustained political irony, The Life of Mr. Jonathan Wild the Great. He would never again attempt such sustained irony, but it is a constant and complicating rhetorical device in his final novels, Tom Jones (1749) and Amelia (1751), and it continues to obsess critics (e.g., 1965.A15 and 1971.B25).

His wife died in 1744. Fielding had only ten more years to live. In these ten years he married again (1747), fathered five children, wrote two major novels, became a London magistrate and justice of the peace for Westminster (1748), established a primitive police force for London, and edited three journals (one semi-weekly for 52 issues and weekly for 20 more issues), and issued a flood of pamphlets against crime and for better order, among them "A Proposal for Making an Effectual Provision for the Poor" (see 1966.A26) and several vigorous attacks on the Jacobite rebels (1934.A2, 1945.B3, B4, B5, 1956.B5).

He died on 8 October 1754 in Lisbon, where he had gone for the sun, hoping to escape the pain and wasting of what his doctors called dropsy, but what was probably cancer (1925.B6). With witty irascibility he records this last voyage in The Journal of a Voyage to Lisbon.

Fielding's critical reputation, outlined from 1742 to 1925 in F. T. Blanchard's Fielding the Novelist (1926.A1), has always been secure. He has suffered at the hands of his friends, however. His first "editor," Arthur Murphy (1762.A10), did not publish the complete works of Fielding, nor did he edit them (collate and attempt to establish the best text). Yet he established the Fielding canon and the texts for several centuries. His edition was thoughtlessly followed by Alexander Chalmers (1806.A3), Thomas Roscoe (1840.A3), James Browne (1871.A6), Leslie Stephen (1882.A6), George Saintsbury (1893. A4), and Edmund Gosse (1898-99.A1). Only W. E. Henley (1902.A4) added works and thought again about some of the texts. His is still the most comprehensive edition of the works, although the novels have been intelligently, if not quite reliably, edited since then (1926. A8). Fielding's complete works are now being carefully edited for the Wesleyan Edition (1967.A2, 1972.A3, 1974.A7, A9). Several of his plays have been properly edited in the Regents Restoration series (e.g., 1966.A5, 1967.A5, 1968.A7) and in the Fountainwell Drama series (1970.A11 and 1973.A11). There are also reasonably reliable editions of The True Patriot (1964.A17) and The Covent-Garden Journal (1915.A1), of Shamela (1953.A1), and of The Journal of a Voyage to Lisbon (1892.A2 or 1963.A6).

Arthur Murphy was also Fielding's first biographer. He was not a careful biographer; instead he passed on some of the Fielding myth. In the late nineteenth and early twentieth century, scholars like Dobson, de Castro, Lawrence, Godden, and Keightley began to untangle the truth about Fielding. Their research culminated in Wilbur Cross's three volume History of Henry Fielding (1918.A1), still the standard biography despite a more recent one by F. Holmes Dudden (1952.A1).

Almost immediately after his death, friendly critics and scholars felt that it was necessary to defend his novels, particularly Tom Jones, against charges of "lowness" (the commonness of his characteristic episodes). "Lowness" no longer bothers us. In the nineteenth century and later, others defended him against criticism of his breaches of the sexual ethic (as late as 1907 Thomas Seccombe thought that Tom Jones was a great book but inappropriate for the classroom, and to be read by boys only by stealth; in 1896 Fielding's great-granddaughter bowdlerized Tom Jones, eliminating its "grossnesses"). To set aside unfriendly criticism, his admirers praised him for his realism, his mimetic truth to life, and for his downright Englishness. While such defense of his art continued for a surprisingly long time (1955.B3), H. A. Taine had pointed out its shortcomings in 1863. After accepting such a defense as truth, Taine demonstrated the aesthetic limits of such John Bullishness (1863.B4). Only a few critics were wise enough either to dismiss the charges of sexual grossness as a shift in culture (1858.B2) or to treat the "grossness" as an aesthetic virtue (1894.B2).

Two of Fielding's professed admirers who were also novelists may have done Fielding the greatest disservice. Thackeray (1853.B1) and Maugham (1947.B3) both accepted the myth of Henry Fielding and then read Fielding's supposed dissolute life into his novels. For Maugham there was no excuse. In 1913 Frederick S. Dickson had explained a fundamental truth of literary criticism (1913.B3): it is extremely dangerous to read fiction as autobiography. Maugham's lack of aesthetic sense also prompted him to put out a shortened version of Tom Jones (with all the introductory chapters cut out) for easy modern reading (1948.A4).

Two modern critics have repeated Taine's charges that Fielding's work lacks moral and mythopoeic complexity. The first attacked him as a moralist. In 1948 F. R. Leavis excluded Fielding from The Great Tradition of the English novel in an aside: "Fielding's attitudes, and his concern with human nature are simple, and not such as to produce an effect of anything but monotony (on a mind, that is, demanding more than external action)." A year later the defense of Fielding as a Christian moralist began. James A. Work's "Henry Fielding, Christian Censor" (1949.B6) corrected the assumption that Fielding was a rather thoughtless Deist and Neostoic, who drifted towards Christianity (1923.A1). William Empson (1958.B6) redefined the nature of irony to accommodate Fielding's high-minded but abstruse gospel Christianity. By the time Martin C. Battestin had carefully established Fielding's debt to rational latitudinarian Anglicanism (1959.A1), first articulated, but less well worked out, by Charles Whittuck (1901.B4), one critic felt that Fielding was in danger of being thought of as an exclusively serious writer (1959.B8). Nevertheless the flood of major works on Fielding, devoted to the notion that his ideas or the traditions from which he grew were morally complex, continued. Fielding was set up in the epistemological debate about self and the nature of reality (1966.A16); he was called a non-Cartesian realist (1975.A5) or a reactionary pioneer standing between eras (1975.A6). He was shown to have drawn seriously on classical notions and generic traditions (1961.A13) and to have developed those generic types he inherited (1964.A24). Alternatively he was seen to have created his novels from historiographic practice (1970.B4). While his deeper moral convictions were being explained, his precise shifts in political loyalty and morality were also under examination (see 1967.B2, 1972.B7). He has been seen as a political liberal articulating constitutional freedom (1951.B7), as a profound social critic partially aware of the limits of bourgeois liberalism (1958.B12), and as a conservative reformer who only attracts other conservatives (1919.B6). Both Hugh Amory (1971.B2) and C. J. Rawson (1972.A9) have recently examined Fielding's conservative political morality, Rawson arguing for the modernity of his radical insecurity.

The second attacked his mythic shallowness. Frank Kermode (1950.B6) repeated, and expanded, Taine's comparison between the artfully subtle and mythopoeic Richardson and the allegorically simple Fielding. While Robert Alter directly answered Kermode, accusing him of post-puritanism (1966.B1), and William Park (1966. B15) suggested that Richardson and Fielding shared more than most imagine, Kermode had done more than renew the Fielding-Richardson debate. He prompted critics to find a new subjective, mythopoeic dimension in Fielding. Sophia's muff was seen as a complex sexual symbol (1959.B10; see also 1967.B26); Fielding's symbolic comedy and Freudian use of incest were explained (1960.B7); it was argued that Tom Jones archetypally reembodied Hamlet and Jesus (1974.B23; see also 1971.B28). Again major works emphasized Fielding's complexity, this time his complex artifice (e.g., 1965.A20 and 1968.A1).

For many, Fielding's technical competence had been taken as proven since Coleridge, in Table Talk (1834), had observed that "the Oedipus Tyrannus, The Alchemist, and Tom Jones [were] the three most perfect plots ever planned." Yet some critics were disturbed by what they saw as technical flaws in his novels. One of the most articulate and persuasive attacks on Tom Jones was written in 1860 by G. H. Lewes (1860.B1). Using the new concept of organic unity, later articulated by Henry James, Lewes attacked the novel as episodic rather than carefully plotted, marred by digressions and intrusions, and made up of caricatures rather than characters. No critic answered Lewes, but modern criticism is dominated by attempts to explain the technical rightness of Fielding's interpolated tales (see for example 1973.B34), the intrusive narrator (1961.B4 and 1970.B18), the plot of Tom Jones, Fielding's mixing of character and caricature (1972.A11), and the design of Fielding's novels (finding unity in architectural metaphor, 1968.B21 and 1968.B2, or in numerology, 1973.B6, B7). Although this attempt at technical justification has led to R. S. Crane's brilliant Neoaristotelian definition of the nature of the comic plot and its perfect working out in Tom Jones (1950.B2), not all critics have been convinced (see David Goldknopf, "The Failure of Plot in Tom Jones," 1969.B7). Several have suggested that the solution to the problem may simply be that Fielding was writing in a genre different from the realistic novels of Defoe and Richardson. Ian Watt suggested that the epic was Fielding's real tradition (1957.B17), Henry Knight Miller that the romance was (1976.A7), Thomas Maresca (1974.B16) that he used both traditions.

These various shifts in Fielding studies have been ably summed up by McKillop (1956.B8 and 1959.B16) and Battestin (1974.B1). Specific critical positions--on Fielding's narrator, on the moral basis of Fielding's art, on Fielding's use of symbolic nakedness (1953.B10)--

have been effectively dissected and attacked by John R. Baker (1973.B2) and Arthur Sherbo (1969.B29, B27, etc.).

Because Fielding was a dramatist, journalist, and a reforming magistrate, as well as being one of the first English novelists *and* one of the first aestheticians of the novel, he is mentioned in nearly every twentieth century book or article written about the novel, from Sidney Lanier's *The English Novel: A Study in the Development of Personality* (New York, 1908) through George Lukács's *The Historical Novel* (London, 1962). He is also often briefly mentioned in studies of burlesque (e.g., George Kitchin, *Burlesque and Parody in English*), of drama (e.g., Ernest Bernbaum's *The Drama of Sensibility*), criticism (e.g., J. W. H. Atkins's *English Literary Criticism: Seventeenth and Eighteenth Centuries*), and of theories of the epic (e.g., H. T. Swedenberg, *The Theory of the Epic in England, 1650-1800*). Few histories of the period, from Tobias Smollett's *Continuation of the Complete History of England* (1761) to J. H. Plumb's *Walpole* (1956-60) fail to mention him. With such plenty, no bibliography of Fielding can either pretend to be "complete" or even wish it. I *have* attempted to abstract every article and book (or chapter of a book) that has been written directly about Fielding. I have included general studies only when Fielding is significantly and substantially discussed. Thus, I have omitted several of the most interesting observations, or asides, on Fielding--Dr. Johnson on *Tom Jones*, George Bernard Shaw's observation about Fielding as a dramatist in his preface to *Plays, Pleasant and Unpleasant* (1904), Coleridge's notes in his copy of *Tom Jones* (c. 1809-10), André Gide's "Notes en Manière de Préface" to *Tom Jones* (c. 1924), and F. R. Leavis's dismissal in *The Great Tradition* (1948), among many others. I have excluded them despite the fact that several, notably Leavis's, are controversial. Two books included in this bibliography (Paulson and Lockwood, *Henry Fielding: The Critical Heritage*, 1969.A18, and Rawson, *Henry Fielding*, 1973.A19) admirably extract these brief allusions, as well as some more sustained discussions of Fielding.

For my finding list I have relied on the standard bibliographies --Martin Battestin's *New Cambridge Bibliography of English Literature* (1971.B5), the Modern Humanities Research Assocation's *Annual Bibliography of English Language and Literature*, the *PMLA* annual bibliography, the *Philological Quarterly* annual bibliography, *Restoration and Eighteenth Century Theatre Research: A Bibliographical Guide, 1900-1968*, ed. Carl J. Stratman, D. G. Spencer and M. E. Devine (1971.B36), and an excellent dissertation by T. Humphrey (1972.A7)--as well as checking the individual indexes of various periodicals. For dissertations I have relied on Lawrence McNamee's three volume *Dissertations in English and American Literature from 1865 to 1973* (1968.B25, 1969.B11 and 1974.B15), on *Dissertation Abstracts* (after 1969 called *Dissertation Abstracts International*), and on T. Humphrey's dissertation. The following short forms have been used in the citation of dissertations: *McNamee's, 1865-1964*, *1964-1968*, or *1969-1973*, T. Humphrey, and finally, *Dissertation*

Abstracts, even after 1969. I have not read all reviews. Any items that I have not personally examined are marked with an asterisk.

I have relied on the catalogues of the Bodleian Library, the British Museum (National Library), and the National Union Catalogue for editions of Fielding's work. In addition, Professor Hugh Amory has been kind enough to let me use his working bibliography of editions of Fielding's works. I have also relied on these catalogues for the dating of undated editions. I have attempted to record each edition of a work by Fielding only once. For instance, if the same publisher issued Tom Jones as part of the Works of Fielding and as a separate edition in the same year (many Collected Works were printed with separate title pages for each work), I have merely listed the Works and not each separate part of the Works. I have not included in this bibliography any of the many adaptations of Fielding's works, such as Joseph Reed's comic opera Tom Jones (1769), J. H. Steffens's five act German comedy Thomas Jones (1765), or the Richardson/Osborn film script (1965), nor have I included dramatic expansions like The Opera of Operas; or, Tom Thumb the Great (1733), with music by Arne and alterations by Eliza Haywood and William Hatchett, or Kane O'Hara's burletta Tom Thumb (1780). (See 1975.B3 for film reviews of Tom Jones and similar lists for reviews of Richardson's Joseph Andrews.) I have not included every reprint of every modern paperback; I have merely tried to indicate in the annotation how often each has been reissued. Finally, I have included single illustrators and translators as part of the title even when their names have not appeared on the title page. And I have occasionally used "edited by" as a handy short form when in fact "selected" or "introduced" might have been a more accurate description (e.g., 1762.A10, 1893.A4).

The bibliography is arranged chronologically. The entries for each year are divided into two sections--one for books (including both books about Fielding and editions of his works) and one for articles or chapters in books. Each of these sections is alphabetized. The index includes each author who has written about Fielding, each of Fielding's works (every unique edition is entered), and some selected topics (e.g., French influence on, French reaction to, French theatrical adaptations of Tom Jones).

I would like to thank Yvette Kagis, who assisted me invaluably in abstracting books and articles in German, Italian, and French, and Janice Dales, who has carefully edited and helped prepare the manuscript for publication. I would also like to thank the Canada Council for financial support.

Journal Abbreviations

ABC	American Book Collector
AHR	American Historical Review
Ang. Bbl.	Anglia Beiblatt
AUMLA	Journal of the Australasian Universities Language and Literature Association
BA	Books Abroad
Beiblatt	Beiblatt zur Anglia
BJA	British Journal of Aesthetics
Can.F	Canadian Forum
Cath.HR	Catholic Historical Review
CE	College English
CR	The Critical Review
Crit. Q	Critical Quarterly
CW	Classical Weekly
DR	Dalhousie Review
Drama S	Drama Survey
DUJ	Durham University Journal
EA	Etudes Anglaises
ECS	Eighteenth-Century Studies
EE	Enlightenment Essays
EHR	English Historical Review
EIC	Essays in Criticism
ELN	English Language Notes
ES	English Studies (Spain)
E. St	Englische Studien

Journal Abbreviations

E. Studies	English Studies (Netherlands)
ETJ	Educational Theatre Journal
EUQ	Emory University Quarterly
GaR	Georgia Review
GRM	Germanisch-romanische Monatsschrift
Holb. Rev	Holborn Review
HSL	Hartford Studies in Literature
HT	History Today
Hud. Rev.	Hudson Review
JA	Journal of Aesthetics and Art Criticism
JEGP	Journal of English and Germanic Philology
JGE	Journal of General Education
JMH	Journal of Modern History
JNL	Johnsonian Newsletter
KR	Kenyon Review
Leuv.Bijdr.	Leuvense Bijdragen
LGRP	Literaturblatt für germanische und romanische Philologie
LJ	The Library Journal
LL	Language Learning
London Mag.	London Magazine
Lond.Merc/ Mercury	London Mercury
MFS	Modern Fiction Studies
MHRA	Modern Humanities Research Association Annual Bibliography
MLN	Modern Language Notes
MLQ	Modern Language Quarterly
MLR	Modern Language Review
MP	Modern Philology
MQR	Michigan Quarterly Review
N&Q	Notes and Queries
NCF	Nineteenth-Century Fiction
New Rep/NR	New Republic
NS	Neueren Sprachen

NSN	New Statesman and Nation
N.ST	New Statesman
NYHTB	New York Herald Tribune Book Review
NYRB	New York Review of Books
NYTBR	New York Times Book Review
Obs	Observer
PQ	Philological Quarterly
PR	Partisan Review
QJS	Quarterly Journal of Speech
QQ	Queen's Quarterly
RAA	Revue Anglo-Americaine
RBPH	Revue belge de philologie et d'histoire
RELV	Revue de l'Enseignement des Langues Vivantes
RES	Review of English Studies
RLC	Revue de Littérature Comparée
SAQ	South Atlantic Quarterly
Sat.Rev.	Saturday Review
SCN	Seventeenth-Century News
SEL	Studies in English Literature
So.HR	Southern Humanities Review
So.RA	Southern Review
SQ	Shakespeare Quarterly
SR	Sewanee Review
St.N	Studies in the Novel
TC	Twentieth Century
Th.	Thought
TLS	Times Literary Supplement
TN	Theatre Notebook
UTQ	University of Toronto Quarterly
VQR	Virginia Quarterly Review
WMQ	William and Mary Quarterly
YES	Yearbook of English Studies
ZAA	Zeitschrift für Anglistik und Amerikanistik

Writings by and about Fielding 1755-1977

1755 A BOOKS

1 ANON. A Catalogue of the Entire and Valuable Library of Books of the Late Henry Fielding. London: Catalogue to be had Gratis at the Place of Sale, of Mr. Miller in the Strand; Mr. Dodsley's Pall-Mall; Mr. Meadows in Cornhill; and Mr. Owen's Temple-Bar, 20pp.

Fielding's extensive library was sold in four nights (10-13 Feb. 1755) by "Samuel Baker, At his House in York-Street, Covent-Garden."

2 FIELDING, HENRY. A Plan of the Universal Register-Office in the Strand. Eighth edition. London: [?], 23 pp.

Reprint of the 1752 pamphlet by John Fielding Esq. and Co.

*3 _____. Don Quixote in England. Glasgow: [?], 52 pp.

Source: National Union Catalogue: Pre-1956 Imprints. Vol. 171, p. 672.

4 _____. The Dramatic Works. 3 vols. London: A. Miller.

This collection, issued by Fielding's principal publisher after 1749, is made up of plays printed by the earlier publishers of Fielding's plays, J. Roberts and J. Watts. Vol. 1 includes Love in Several Masques, Temple Beau, The Author's Farce, The Coffee-house Politician, Tom Thumb, and The Letter Writers. Vol. 2 includes The Grub-Street Opera, "The Masquerade" (a poem), The Lottery, The Modern Husband, The Mock Doctor, Covent-Garden Tragedy, The Debauchee, and The Miser. Vol. 3 includes Intriguing Chambermaid, Don Quixote in England, The Virgin Unmasked, The Universal Gallant, Pasquin, The Historical Register, Tumble-down Dick, and Miss Lucy in Town.

These volumes were actually issued in 1761. See appendix 1973.A11.

*5 _____. The History of the Life of Mr. Jonathan Wild the Great. To which is added A Journey from This World to the Next. London: J. Bell, 339 pp.
Said to be the same plates used to print Vol. 5 of Bell's edition of Fielding's works (1775.A7).
Source: National Union Catalogue: Pre-1956 Imprints. Vol. 171, p. 693.

6 _____. The Journal of a Voyage to Lisbon and A Fragment of a Comment on L. Bolingbroke's Essays. London: A. Miller, 245 pp.
The longer version of The Journal . . . (1755.A7). See 1963.A6 for textual history.

7 _____. The Journal of a Voyage to Lisbon. London: A. Miller, 228 pp.
Contains "A Fragment of a Comment on Lord Bolingbroke's Essays" and the shorter version of The Journal . . . . See 1963.A6 for textual history.

8 _____. The Miser. Glasgow: [?], 76 pp.
Includes contemporary cast list; said to be "As it is acted . . . ."

*9 _____. The Virgin Unmask'd; or, An Old Man Taught Wisdom. Glasgow: [?], 22 pp.
Without music; "As it is performed at the Theatre-Royal, by His Majesty's servants."
Source: National Union Catalogue: Pre-1956 Imprints. Vol. 172, p. 4.

1755 B SHORTER WRITINGS

1 ANON. Review of Journal of a Voyage to Lisbon, by Henry Fielding, Esq. Gentleman's Magazine, 25 (March), 129.
Briefly describes the events of the book and then recommends it for its humor, "in which he is confessed to have excelled every other writer of his age," and for "the instruction which it contains." Calls attention to Fielding's public-spiritedness, his attempt to correct the "many intolerable inconveniences which arise either from the defect of our laws, or the ignorance of those by whom they should be executed" (cites passage about availability of fish as proof).
Reprinted 1969.A18.

2 _____. Review of Journal of a Voyage to Lisbon. London Magazine, 24 (Feb.), 54-56.

A brief extract from the Journal of a Voyage to Lisbon is reprinted, and the work is said to be "a Specimen of the Strength even of an expiring Genius" that will "give it an extraordinary Relish to Persons of Benevolence and Humanity" (p. 54).

Reprinted 1969.A18.

3 _____. Review of The Journal of a Voyage to Lisbon. By the late Henry Fielding, esq. . . . Miller. Monthly Review, 12 (March), 234-35.

Appeals to Fielding's weakened state to excuse the imperfections; says that although it is "not greatly abounding with incidents . . . the reflections interspersed in it, are worthy of a writer, than whom few, if any, have been more justly celebrated for a thorough insight into human nature" (p. 234). Hopes that there are more "posthumous volume[s] of an author, who long hath been, and will continue to be, the delight of his readers" (p. 235).

Reprinted 1969.A18.

1756 A BOOKS

*1 FIELDING, HENRY. A Journal of a Voyage to Lisbon. With A Fragment of a Comment on Lord Bolingbroke's Essays. Dublin: James Hoey, 190 pp.

Source: National Union Catalogue: Pre-1956 Imprints. Vol. 171, p. 685.

2 _____. La Storia di Tom Jones. Translated by Pietro Chiari. 2 vols. Venice: Presso Gio. Battista Regozza, 654 (348 & 306) pp.

According to the title page, this Italian translation is taken from the French translation of Mr. de la Place.

3 _____. Miss Lucy in Town. A Sequel to The Virgin Unmasqued. London: A. Miller, 44 pp.

The "second" edition by the major publisher of Fielding's works in his lifetime; printed without music.

4 _____. Tom Thumb the Great. An Opera. Set to Music after the Italian Manner, By Mr. Arne. Dublin: Richard Watts, 28 pp.

Arne simply set some of the verse speeches to "airs."

1756 B SHORTER WRITINGS - NONE

1757

1757 A BOOKS

1 FIELDING, HENRY. Leevensbeschryving van wylen den heere Jonathan Wild, den Grooten. Amsterdam: Pieter Meyer, 414 pp.
Dutch translation of Jonathan Wild.

2 _____. The Intriguing Chambermaid. Glasgow: [?], 36 pp.
No music; no indication of copy text.

1757 B SHORTER WRITINGS - NONE

1758 A BOOKS

1 FIELDING, HENRY. Amelia, of de Rampspoedige Deugd, Uitblinkende in alle Gevallen van het Huwelyks Leven, en Zegepralende over al het Natuurlyk en Zedelyk Kwaad. Translated by P. A. Verwer. 3 vols. Amsterdam: Fredrik de Kruyff and Albert van der Kroe.
Dutch translation.

*2 _____. La Storia di Tom Jones. 2 vols. Napoli: [?]. Illustrations. Italian translation.
Source: National Union Catalogue: Pre-1956 Imprints. Vol. 171, p. 691.

3 _____. The Intriguing Chambermaid. Dublin: Sarah Cotter, 24 pp.
Includes a cast list, apparently from Dublin.

*4 _____. The Life of Mr. Jonathan Wild the Great. To which is added, A Journey from This World to the Next. Dublin: W. Williamson, 408 pp.
Source: National Union Catalogue: Pre-1956 Imprints. Vol. 171, p. 693.

5 _____. The Lottery. Glasgow: [?], 28 pp.
No indication of copy text; music not included.

1758 B SHORTER WRITINGS

1 ANON. Review of An Account of the Origin and Effect of a Police, set on foot by his Grace the Duke of Newcastle in the [year] 1753, upon a plan presented to his Grace by the late Henry Fielding, Esq. To which is added, A Plan for

preventing those deserted Girls in this town, who became prostitutes from necessity by John Fielding. Monthly Review, 18 (March), 267-68.

Quotes approvingly from this pamphlet, agreeing that prostitutes ought to be put to work and magistrates paid better; commends the Fieldings for cleaning up the Covent-Garden area.

1759 A BOOKS

1 FIELDING, HENRY. Der Hochzeitstag . . . und Eurydice. Copenhagen: Rothensche Buchhandlung, 192 pp.

German translation of The Wedding Day and Eurydice Hiss'd.

*2 _____. History of Tom Jones, a Foundling. 6 vols. London: A. Miller.

Source: National Union Catalogue: Pre-1956 Imprints. Vol. 171, p. 682.

3 _____. Reise nach der andern Welt. Copenhagen: Rothensche Buchhandlung, 270 pp.

German translation of Journey from This World to the Next.

4 _____. The History of Tom Jones, A Foundling. 3 vols. Dublin: W. Smith, P. Wilson, et al.

Appears to reprint the first edition.

5 _____. The Lottery. Dublin: P. Wilson, 27 pp.

Title page calls this the "fifth edition."

6 _____. The Lover's Assistant; or, New Year's Gift; Being, A New Art of Love, Adapted to the Present Times. Dublin: [?], 95 pp.

Title page calls it "Ovid's Art of Love Paraphrased." No indication of copy text.

7 _____. The Miser, in A Select Collection of English Plays from the Best Authors. Vol. 3. Edinburgh: A. Donaldson, 87 pp.

Collection title page date 1760; each play separately paged. No indication of copy text.

1759 B SHORTER WRITINGS - NONE

1760

1760 A BOOKS

1 FIELDING, HENRY. Don Quixote in England. Edinburgh: A. Donaldson, 23 pp.
Title page says "As it is now acted." No indication of copy text.

*2 _____. The History of Amelia. London: R. Snagg. [1760].
This abridgment, called the fourth edition, is missing from the British Museum.

3 _____. The Intriguing Chambermaid. London: "Printed for the Proprietors," 44 pp. [1760].
Title page says "As it is Acted at the Theatre Royal in Drury-Lane"; includes a cast list.

4 _____. The Miser. London: H. Garland, 88 pp. [1760].
Includes cast list with Mr. Yates as Lovegold; title page says "Exactly agreeable to the Representation."

*5 _____. The Miser. London: R. Butters, 50 pp. [1760?].
Said to be "Taken from the manager's book at the Theatre Royal, Covent-Garden."
Source: National Union Catalogue: Pre-1956 Imprints. Vol. 172, p. 1.

1760 B SHORTER WRITINGS - NONE

1761 A BOOKS

1 FIELDING, HENRY. Geschichte des Joseph Andrews, Bruders der Pamela. Engravings by Glassbach. Berlin and Leipzig: Johann H. Rüdiger, 472 pp.
No indication of translator but a brief introduction dated 1761. German translation.

2 _____. The Intriguing Chambermaid. London: A. Miller, 52 pp.
This "new edition," by Fielding's principal publisher, includes woodcuts of the music for the song.

3 _____. The Lottery. London: A. Miller, 34 pp.
The "fifth edition" by Fielding's principal publisher. Printed with the music.

4 _____. The Miser. London: A. Miller, 95 pp.
The title page of this edition, by Fielding's principal publisher, calls it the "fourth edition."

5 _____. The Mock Doctor: or, The Dumb Lady Cur'd. London: A. Miller, 40 pp.
Printed by Fielding's publisher and friend; includes the music.

1761 B SHORTER WRITINGS

1 FIELDING, HENRY. "Preface," in The Adventures of David Simple. By Sarah Fielding. Dublin: Peter Wilson, pp. iii-x.
Reproduced whenever this novel was reprinted; not cited hereafter.

1762 A BOOKS

1 FIELDING, HENRY. Amélie, Histoire Angloise. [Translated by P. F. de Puisieux.] 4 vols. London and Paris: Chez Charpentier.
French translation of Amelia.

2 _____. Amélie. Translated by Madame Riccoboni. 3 parts (1 vol.). Paris: Brocas & Humblot, 655 pp.
Each part separately paged. French translation.

3 _____. An Old Man Taught Wisdom: or, The Virgin Unmask'd. Cork: [?], 28 pp.
Title page says as performed "in London and Dublin." No indication of copy text.

*4 _____. An Old Man Taught Wisdom; or, The Virgin Unmask'd. Dublin: G. and A. Ewing.
Called the sixth edition; reissue of 1747.
Source: National Union Catalogue: Pre-1956 Imprints. Vol. 172, p. 4.

*5 _____. Histoire de Tom Jones, ou L'Enfant Trouvé. Translated by M. de la Place. 2 vols. France: [?].
Called the fourth edition revised and corrected. French translation.
Source: National Union Catalogue: Pre-1956 Imprints. Vol. 171, p. 690.

1762

6 _____. The History of the Adventures of Joseph Andrews and His Friend Mr. Abraham Adams. 2 vols. London: A. Miller 478 (246 & 232) pp.
Printed by the principal publisher of Fielding's works in his lifetime. According to the title page, it is "the Sixth Edition, revised and corrected." Twelve "plates" by James Hulett.

7 _____. The Miser. Dublin: G. and A. Ewing, W. Smith, et al., 84 pp.
No indication of copy text.

8 _____. The Virgin Unmask'd: or An Old Man taught Wisdom. Glasgow: [?], 24 pp.
Contemporary cast list (Macklin as Wormwood); said to be "As it is performed at the Theatre Royal."

9 _____. The Works of Henry Fielding, Esq. with The Life of the Author. 8 vols. London: A. Miller.
The "second" edition of the Arthur Murphy/Andrew Miller edition of Fielding's works.

10 _____. The Works of Henry Fielding, Esq., with The Life of the Author. 4 vols. London: A. Miller.
The "first" edition of the Arthur Murphy/Andrew Miller edition of Fielding's Works. Vol. 1 includes Arthur Murphy's "Essay on the Life and Genius of Henry Fielding, Esq." and the following plays: Love in Several Masks, The Temple Beau, The Author's Farce, The Lottery, The Coffee-House Politician, The Tragedy of Tragedies, The Letter-Writers, The Grub-Street Opera, The Modern Husband, The Mock Doctor, The Covent-Garden Tragedy, The Debauchees, The Miser, The Intriguing Chambermaid, Don Quixote in England, and An Old Man Taught Wisdom. Vol. 2 includes The Universal Gallant, Pasquin, The Historical Register, Eurydice, Eurydice Hiss'd, Tumble-Down Dick, Miss Lucy in Town, The Wedding Day, The Life of Mr. Jonathan Wild the Great, A Journey from this World to the Next, The History of the Adventures of Joseph Andrews, "The Preface to David Simple," and "The Preface to the Familiar Letters . . . ." Vol. 3 includes The History of Tom Jones, "Philosophical Transactions for the Year 1742-3," "The First Olynthiac of Demosthenes," "Of the Remedy of Affliction for the Loss of Our Friends," "A Dialogue Between Alexander the Great, and Diogenes the Cynic," "An Interlude," and The True Patriot. Vol. 4 includes Amelia, "An Essay on Conversation," "An Essay on the Knowledge of the Characters of Men," Covent-Garden Journal, A Charge Delivered to the Grand Jury, The

Journal of a Voyage to Lisbon, and "A Fragment of a Comment on Lord Bolingbroke's Essay." Although Murphy's essay has been vigorously attacked by Cross (1918.A1), it is a surprisingly good (though superficial) essay on Fielding. Murphy quickly and inaccurately sketches Fielding's life (including the anecdote about Fielding writing a scene of a play on a tobacco paper and the one about a lady cutting out a profile of Fielding for Hogarth to sketch, see 1891.B3), emphasizing Fielding's early life of dissipation. His essay touches what have become the conventional ways of defending Fielding: his work is said to be strongly moral (1959.A1); the perfect comic unity of the fable of Tom Jones is recognized (1950.B2); Fielding is commended for his ability to shift tone rapidly (1970.B19); the mimetic strength of characters like Adams is commented on (1923.A1); Fielding's perception of a morally developing character (1958.B6) is seen as extraordinary. Murphy considers Fielding a satirist like Congreve and Wycherley, even though he dismisses Fielding's plays, considering them too quickly written and lacking in moral refinement. Murphy thinks Amelia a weak novel. These last two value judgments have become less widely accepted.

1762 B SHORTER WRITINGS

1 ANON. "Amélie, Histoire Angloise traduite fidèlement de l'Angloise de M. Fielding" ("Lettre 7"). L'Année littéraire, 4 (3 July), 145-75.

Sharply critical of Mme. Riccoboni's version of Amelia, " a proscrits ou qu'elle a totalement defigures" (p. 146). Amelia is said to have passages comparable to Tom Jones but is generally thought to be monotonous and full of disquieting problems with its characterizations. In French.

Reprinted Geneva: Slatkine Reprints, 1966 and in part in 1969.A18.

2 G[RIFFITHS]. "Conclusion of the Account of the Life and Writings of Henry Fielding, Esq.; See our last Appendix, published this Month." Monthly Review, 27 (July), 49-56.

Continuation of 1762.B3.

3 [____]. Review of The Works of Henry Fielding Esq., with the Life of the Author, [by Mr. Murphy] . . . Miller. Monthly Review, 26 (May), 364-75.

After calling Fielding a "favourite Author" (p. 364), he extensively quotes Murphy, summing up his argument as he goes. Disagreeing slightly with Murphy, he sees "an exact correspondency in Joseph Andrews, Tom Jones, and Amelia" (p. 490). He discusses Fielding's debt to Cervantes; sees his dramas as the work of an English Aristophanes (influenced by Wycherley and Congreve). See 1762.B4, B2.

4 [_____]. "The Quarto and Octavo Editions of the Works of Henry Fielding, Esq.; with the Life of the Author, by Mr. Murphy, continued." Monthly Review, 26, Appendix (June), 481-94.

Continuation of 1762.B3.

1763 A BOOKS

1 FIELDING, HENRY. Amélie. Translated by Madame Riccoboni. 3 parts (2 vols.). Paris: J. F. Bassompierre; Brussels: J. Van den Berghen, 655 pp.

Reprint of 1762.A2. French translation.

2 _____. Histoire de Jonathan Wild Le Grand. 2 vols. London [and Paris]: Duchesne, 514 (231 & 283) pp.

Translated into French, probably by C. Picquet.

3 _____. Histoirie van den Vondeling Tomas Jones. Translated by P. Clercq. Illustrations by H. Gravelot. 3 vols. Amsterdam: Gerrit de Groot en Zoon.

Reprint of the 1749 Dutch translation.

4 _____. The History of Tom Jones, A Foundling. 4 vols. London: A. Miller.

Published by the principal publisher of Fielding's works in his lifetime.

5 _____. The Mock Doctor; or The Dumb Lady Cur'd. Belfast: James Magee, 30 pp.

Title page says "as it is acted at the Theatre-Royal in Drury-lane," but it also says "done from Voliere" [sic]. Called the "fifth edition." No indication of copy text.

1763 B SHORTER WRITINGS

1 ANON. "Histoire de Jonathan Wild le Grand" ("Lettre 1"). L'Année littéraire, 2 (23 Feb.), 3-27.

Concludes that Jonathan Wild is a weak work by a brilliant author, written to satisfy the English taste for low life. In French.

Reprinted Geneva: Slatkine Reprints, 1966 and in part in 1969.A18.

2 FIELDING, HENRY. "A Letter to Sir Robert Walpole," in A Collection of Poems in Six Volumes by Several Hands. London: R. and J. Dodsley, pp. 117-18.
Reprints the poem.

3 _____. "Plain Truth," in A Collection of Poems in Six Volumes by Several Hands. London: R. and J. Dodsley, pp. 302-305.
Reprints the poem.

1764 A BOOKS

1 FIELDING, HENRY. Amélie. Translated by Madame Riccoboni. 3 parts (1 vol.). Paris: J. F. Bassompierre; Brussels: J. Van den Berghen, 655 pp.
French translation.
Reprint of 1762.A2.

2 _____. Der Hochzeittag, oder der Feind des Ehestandes. Wien: Kraussischer Buchladen, 112 pp.
German translation of The Wedding-Day.

*3 _____. Examples of the Interposition of Providence in the detection and punishment of Murder. Containing above thirty cases . . . With an introduction and conclusion, both written by H. F. Dublin: [?].
The British Museum has lost its copy.

4 _____. Miss Lucy in Town. A Sequel to the Virgin Unmasqued. London: A. Miller, 44 pp.
Reissue of 1756.A3 and called the "third" edition.

5 _____. Reise nach Lissabon. Von ihm selbst beschrieben. Altona: David Iversen, 262 pp.
Brief anonymous "life" prefaces this German translation of Journal of a Voyage to Lisbon and "A Fragment of a Comment . . . ."

6 _____. The History of the Adventures of Joseph Andrews and his Friend Mr. Abraham Adams. Illustrated by J. Hulett. 2 vols. London: A. Miller, 478 (246 & 232) pp.
Reissue of 1762.A6; now called "the Seventh Edition."

1764

1764 B SHORTER WRITINGS

1 [BAKER, D. E.]. "Henry Fielding," in The Companion to the Playhouse: or, An Historical Account of all the Dramatic Writers (and their Works) that have appeared in Great Britain and Ireland, from the Commencement of our Theatrical Exhibitions, down to the Present Year 1764. Vol. 2. London: T. Becket, et al.
Condensation of Murphy (1762.A10).

1765 A BOOKS

1 FIELDING, HENRY. An Old Man Taught Wisdom: or, the Virgin Unmask'd. London: A. Miller, 39 pp.
Published by Fielding's principal publisher in his lifetime and called the "fifth edition."

2 _____. Fieldings komischer Roman in vier Theilen. Mit Kupfern. Berlin: Johann Heinrich Rüdigern, 472 pp.
A loose German translation of Joseph Andrews based on a French translation.

3 _____. The Dramatic Works of Henry Fielding, Esq. 3 vols. London: A. Miller.
Reissue of 1755.A4.

4 _____. The Intriguing Chambermaid. Cork: Thomas Wilkinson, 24 pp.
Title page says "As it is acted at the Theatre-Royal in London and Dublin." No indication of copy text.

5 _____. The Tragedy of Tragedies; or the Life and Death of Tom Thumb the Great. London: A. Miller, 56 pp.
The "fifth edition," issued by the principal publisher of Fielding's works in his lifetime.

6 _____. Tom Jones Eller Hitte-Barnet. Translated by Lärten Eklund. Wästeräs: Joh. Laur. Horrn, 744 pp.
Danish translation.

1765 B SHORTER WRITINGS - NONE

1766 A BOOKS

1 FIELDING, HENRY. Don Quixote in England. Glasgow: [?], 49 pp.
Said to be "as it is acted at the New Theatre in the Hay-Market"; no music. No indication of copy text.

2 _____ et al. The Champion: Containing A Series of Papers, Humorous, Moral, Political and Critical. Third edition. 2 vols. London: T. Waller, 773 (396 & 377) pp.
Reprinting of The Champion with an index for each volume. Vol. 1 from 15 Nov. 1739 to 13 March 1739-40; Vol. 2 from 15 March 1739-40 to 19 June 1740. No indication of copy text.

3 _____. The History of Tom Jones, A Foundling. Life of the author by Arthur Murphy. 3 vols. Dublin: W. and W. Smith, P. Wilson, J. Exshaw, and H. Bradley.
Reprints Murphy's edition of the novel (1762.A10).

4 _____. The Works of Henry Fielding, Esq.; with The Life of the Author. The Third Edition. 12 vols. London: A. Miller.
A reprint of 1762.A10 following the same order.

1766 B SHORTER WRITINGS - NONE

1767 A BOOKS

1 FIELDING, HENRY. The History of the Adventures of Joseph Andrews, and his Friend Mr. Abraham Adams. Dublin: D. Chamberlaine and J. Potts, 431 pp.
Title page calls it "the Fourth Edition." Reprints Murphy's "Life" (1762.A10).

2 _____. The History of the Adventures of Joseph Andrews, and his Friend Mr. Abraham Adams. Edinburgh: Martin & Wotherspoon, 355 pp.
No indication of copy text.

3 _____. The History of Tom Jones, A Foundling. Engravings by H. Gravelot. 3 vols. Dublin: James Hoey, D. Chamberlaine, et al.
Appears to reprint the "1750" edition followed by Murphy (1762.A10).

4 _____. The History of Tom Jones, A Foundling. 3 vols. Edinburgh: Martin & Wotherspoon.
Appears to reproduce the "1750" edition followed by Murphy (1762.A10).

5 _____. The Works of Henry Fielding, Esq. 12 vols. Edinburgh: Martin & Wotherspoon.
Vol. 1 includes a "life" taken from Companion to the Playhouse (1764.B1). The texts appear to be reprints of Murphy (1762.A10); the title page calls this the "fourth edition."

*6 _____. Tom Jones, ou l'Enfant Trouvé. [Translated by de la Place.] 2 vols. London and Paris: Duchesne.
Called the fourth edition corrected and augmented with a life of the author. French translation.
Source: National Union Catalogue: Pre-1956 Imprints. Vol. 171, p. 690.

7 _____. Tom Jones ou L'Enfant Trouvé. Translated into French by Pierre Antoine de la Place. Illustrations by Gravelot. 4 vols. London and Paris: Chez Valleyre.
Reprint of 1750 Amsterdam edition. Called the fourth edition revised, corrected, and augmented.

1767 B SHORTER WRITINGS - NONE

1768 A BOOKS

1 FIELDING, HENRY. A Treatise on the Office of Constable, in Extracts from such of the Penal Laws, as Particularly relate to the Peace and Good Order of this Metropolis. Edited by John Fielding. London: H. Woodfall and W. Strahan, pp. 321-67.
Reprint of this pamphlet. No indication of copy text.

2 _____. Julien L'Apostat, ou Voyage Dans L'Autre Monde. Translated by le Sieur Kauffmann. 2 vols. Amsterdam and Paris: Le Jay Libraire, 418 (211 & 207) pp.
French translation of Journey from This World to the Next.

3 _____. The History of the Adventures of Joseph Andrews, and his Friend Mr. Abraham Adams. Engravings by J. Hulett. 2 vols. London: A. Miller, 478 (246 & 232) pp.

Published by the principal publisher of Fielding's works in his lifetime and called the eighth edition "revised and corrected."

4 _____. The History of Tom Jones, A Foundling. 4 vols. London: T. Cadell.
Printed "for A. Miller," the principal publisher of Fielding's works in his lifetime. No indication of copy text.

5 _____. The Miser, in The Theatre: or, Select Works of the British Dramatic Poets. Vol. 3. Edinburgh: Martin & Wotherspoon, 107 pp.
Prefaced by a brief "life" of Fielding taken from Murphy (1762.A10). No indication of copy text; separately paged.

1768 B SHORTER WRITINGS - NONE

1769 A BOOKS

1 FIELDING, HENRY. Reyse til den anden Verden. Copenhagen: J. C. and G. C. Berling, 207 pp.
Danish translation of Journey from this World to the Next.

2 _____. The History of the Adventures of Joseph Andrews, And His Friend Mr. Abraham Adams. London: F. Newberry, 160 pp.
A severely abridged edition with anonymous plates. No indication of copy text.

3 _____. The History of the Adventures of Joseph Andrews, And his Friend Mr. Abraham Adams. Illustrations by J. Hulett. 2 vols. London: J. and F. Rivington, W. Strahan, et al., 478 (246 & 232) pp.
Called the "Ninth Edition, revised and corrected"; reproduces the illustrations for the first edition. No indication of copy text.

4 _____. The Miser. Glasgow: [?], 66 pp.
Said to be "As it is acted at the Theatre Royal"; includes contemporary cast list.

5 _____. The Miser. London: A. Miller, 95 pp.
Reissue of 1761.A4.

1769

1769 B SHORTER WRITINGS - NONE

1770 A BOOKS

1 FIELDING, HENRY. An Old Man Taught Wisdom; or, The Virgin Unmask'd. London: Printed for the Proprietor, 24 pp.
Called the "seventh edition"; no indication of copy text but said to be as "perform'd at the Theatre Royal in Drury Lane" with a cast list for that theater. Music not included.

2 _____. Histoire de Tom Jones, ou L'Enfant Trouvé. Translated by M. de la Place. 4 vols. London and Paris: Rollin, Fils.
Reprint of the 1750 French translation.

*3 _____. The History of the Adventures of Joseph Andrews, and His Friend Mr. Abraham Adams. Edinburgh: A. Donaldson, 403 pp.
Source: National Union Catalogue: Pre-1956 Imprints. Vol. 171, p. 675.

4 _____. The Intriguing Chambermaid. London: Sadler, 24 pp. [177?].
Includes cast list (Goodall - Mr. Quick; Valentine - Mr. Lewis). Said to be "taken from the Manager's Books at the Theatre Royal, Covent-Garden."

1770 B SHORTER WRITINGS

1 ANON. Review of The Memoirs of a Man of Quality, Cleveland, and the Dean of Coleraine. . . . Gentleman's Magazine, 40 (Oct.), 454-56.
Reprints the Abbé Prévost's evaluation of Fielding and Richardson. Fielding "is more simple, more instructive" and Richardson "more grand, more framed on models which will live throughout all ages." Fielding's characters "seized the manners of the people" (p. 455).

1771 A BOOKS

1 FIELDING, HENRY. Amelia. 2 vols. London: S. Crowder, C. Ware and T. Payne, 618 (296 & 322) pp.
No indication of copy text.

2 _____. *Geschichte des Thomas Jones, eines Fündlings.* Translated into German by M. A. Wodarch. 4 vols. Hamburg and Leipzig: Friedrich Ludwig Gleditsch.

3 _____. *The History of Tom Jones, A Foundling.* 3 vols. Edinburgh: A. Donaldson.
Appears to reprint "1750" edition followed by Murphy (1762.10).

4 _____. *The Mock Doctor: or, The Dumb Lady Cur'd.* London: T. Caslon, T. Lowndes, T. Davies, et al., 34 pp.
Includes woodcuts of the music. No indication of copy text.

5 _____. *The Works of Henry Fielding, Esq.* 8 vols. London: W. Strahan, J. & F. Rivington, et al.
A complete reprint of Murphy (1762.A10).

6 _____. *The Works of Henry Fielding, Esq.* 12 vols. Edinburgh: A. Donaldson.
Appears to be printed from 1767.A5. Title page calls this the "fifth edition."

7 _____. *The Works of Henry Fielding, Esq.* 12 vols. Edinburgh: Martin & Wotherspoon.
Reissue of 1767.A5.

8 _____. *The Works of Henry Fielding, Esq.* 12 vols. London: S. Crowder, et al.
London issue of 1771.A7.

1771 B SHORTER WRITINGS - NONE

1772 A BOOKS

*1 FIELDING, HENRY. *Dièi͡anii͡a gospodina Ionafåna Vilda Velikago, izdannyià gospodinom.* Translated from the German by Ivan Sytenskoĭ. St. Petersburg: Imperatarskoĭ Akademii nauk.
Russian translation of "The Life of Mr. Jonathan Wild the Great." Two volumes in one.
Source: *National Union Catalogue: Pre-1956 Imprints.* Vol. 171, p. 696.

1772 B SHORTER WRITINGS - NONE

1773

1773 A BOOKS

1 FIELDING, HENRY. The History of the Adventures of Joseph Andrews, And his Friend Mr. Abraham Adams. 2 vols. London: B. Long and T. Pridden, 607 (312 & 295) pp.
No indication of copy text.

2 _____. The History of Tom Jones, A Foundling. 4 vols. London: W. Strahan, J. & F. Rivington, et al.
Appears to be a reprint of the "1750" edition followed by Murphy (1762.A10).

1773 B SHORTER WRITINGS - NONE

1774 A BOOKS

*1 FIELDING, HENRY. Leben Jonathan Wilds, eines englischen Spitzbuben und seiner Kameraden. Newgate: [?], 156 pp.
German translation.
Source: National Union Catalogue: Pre-1956 Imprints. Vol. 171, p. 696.

2 _____. The History of Tom Jones, A Foundling. 3 vols. Dresden: G. C. Walther.
Reprint (in English) of what appears to be the "1750" edition.

3 _____. The History of Tom Jones, A Foundling. 3 vols. Edinburgh: Alexander Donaldson.
Appears to be a reprint of the "1750" edition followed by Murphy (1762.A10).

4 _____. The Humorous and Diverting History of Tom Jones, A Foundling: Containing A pleasant and delightful Account of the Goodness and Hospitality of the benevolent Mr. Allworthy; The Humors of Squire Western, The Famous Fox Hunter . . . . London: R. Snagg, 93 pp. [1774].
A severely abridged version that is little more than plot summary. The title page calls this the "Second Edition."

5 _____. The Miser. Edinburgh: John Robertson, 98 pp.
No indication of copy text. A brief anonymous "life" based on Murphy 1762.A10 is "prefixed."

1774 B SHORTER WRITINGS - NONE

1775 A BOOKS

1 FIELDING, HENRY. Amelia. 3 vols. London: W. Strahan, J. & F. Rivington, et al.
No indication of copy text.

2 _____. Avantures de Joseph Andrews, et de son ami Abraham Adams. [Translated by Pierre Francois Guyot Desfontaines.] 2 vols. Amsterdam: Barthelemi Vlam, 493 (261 & 232) pp.
Title page claims that this French translation was made by "une Dame Angloise," but it was actually by Desfontaines. Unsigned illustrations.

*3 _____. The History of Tom Jones, a Foundling. 3 vols. London: Printed for J. Bell.
Source: National Union Catalogue: Pre-1956 Imprints. Vol. 171, p. 683.

4 _____. The History of Tom Jones, A Foundling. 3 vols. Paisley: Alex Weir.
Appears to reproduce the first edition.

5 _____. The Lottery. London: W. Oxlade and J. Bradshaw, 34 pp.
No indication of copy text.

*6 _____. The Miser. London: T. Lowndes, 82 pp.
Called the "6th edition"; reissued 1776.
Source: National Union Catalogue: Pre-1956 Imprints. Vol. 172, p. 1.

7 _____. The Works of Henry Fielding, Esq. 12 vols. London: John Bell.
Appears to reprint the "works" from Murphy (1762.A10) and a "Life of the Author" from the 1767.A5 Edinburgh edition. The two volumes of Joseph Andrews and the one of Jonathan Wild and A Journey from this World to the Next were separately issued by Bell in 1775.

8 _____. The Works of Henry Fielding, Esq. 12 vols. London: W. Strahan, et al.
Reprint of 1771.A5.

1775 B SHORTER WRITINGS - NONE

1776

1776 A BOOKS

1 FIELDING, HENRY. De Historie of Gev Allen van Joseph Andriessen, Broeder van Pamela, en zyn Vriend den Heer Abraham Adams. Engravings by C. de Putter. 2 vols. Amsterdam: Steven van Esveldt, 564 (277 & 287) pp.
Reprint of 1774 Dutch translation of Joseph Andrews.

2 _____. The Intriguing Chambermaid. London: W. Oxlade, 37 pp.
No indication of copy text.

3 _____. The Miser, in Bell's British Theatre. Vol. 6. London: John Bell; York: C. Etherington, 84 pp.
No indication of copy text; separately paged.

4 _____. The Miser, in The New English Theatre. Vol. 1. London: J. Rivington & Sons, W. Strahan, et al., 82 pp.
This separately paged play was actually printed by T. Lowndes, T. Caslon, et al. and bound into this collection.

5 _____. The Miser. London: T. Lowndes, T. Caslon, T. Davies, et al., 82 pp.
Title page says "Marked with the Variations in the Manager's Books, at the Theatre Royal in Drury Lane." Omitted passages are marked with inverted commas and added passages are in italics. Includes the 1776 cast list and a plate by Parkinson of Mr. Yates as Lovegold.

6 _____. The Tragedy of Tragedies. London: T. Davies, T. Lowndes, et al., 56 pp.
Title page calls this the "fifth edition." No indication of copy text.

7 _____. The Works of Henry Fielding, Esq. 12 vols. London: John Bell.
Reissue of 1775.A7.

1776 B SHORTER WRITINGS

1 [BURNET, J. (LORD MONBODDO)]. Of the Origin and Progress of Language. Edinburgh: J. Balfour; London: T. Cadell, pp. 296-98.
Objects to Fielding's use of the mock-heroic in Tom Jones on two grounds: first, the shift in style is too great for a "regular" work such as Fielding's; second, it destroys the verisimilitude of a mimetic work which is to represent reality.

1777 A BOOKS

*1 FIELDING, HENRY. Amelia. 2 vols. Dublin: [?].
Called the fifth edition.
Source: National Union Catalogue: Pre-1956 Imprints. Vol. 171, p. 667.

2 _____. Don Quixote in England. London: J. Wenman, 17 pp.
Issued as part of the Theatrical Magazine. No indication of copy text.

3 _____. Don Quixote in England. London: W. Oxlade, 48 pp.
No indication of copy text.

4 _____. The Virgin Unmask'd; or An Old Man Taught Wisdom. London: J. Wenman, 7 pp. [1777].
Issued as part of the Theatrical Magazine. No indication of copy text.

5 _____. The Virgin Unmask'd; or, An Old Man taught Wisdom. London: W. Oxlade, 24 pp.
No indication of copy text; music not included.

6 _____. Tom Jones, ou L'Enfant Trouvé. Translated by M. de la Place. 4 vols. London and Paris: Bauche, Libraire.
Reprint of the 1750 Amsterdam edition with the Gravelot illustrations. French translation.

1777 B SHORTER WRITINGS - NONE

1778 A BOOKS

*1 FIELDING, HENRY. Histoire de Tom Jones, ou, L'Enfant Trouvé. Translated by M. de la Place. 4 vols. Amsterdam: Changuion.
French translation.
Source: National Union Catalogue: Pre-1956 Imprints. Vol. 171, p. 690.

2 _____. The Fathers: or, The Good-Natur'd Man. London: T. Cadell, 119 pp.
Includes the "advertisement" describing the discovery of the manuscript and John Fielding's dedication to the Duke of Northumberland.

1778

3 ______. The History of the Adventures of Joseph Andrews and His Friend Mr. Abraham Adams. 2 vols. London: [?], 427 (223 & 204) pp.

No indication of copy text; title page calls it "A New Edition, revised and corrected."

4 ______. The History of Tom Jones, A Foundling. Abridged. London: E. Newbery, 194 pp.

An elaborate plot summary with engravings by Lodge.

5 ______. The Humorous and Diverting History of Tom Jones . . . . Second edition. London: R. Snagg, 93 pp. [1778].

Reprint of 1774.A4.

1778 B SHORTER WRITINGS

1 ANON. Review of The Fathers. St. James's Chronicle, no. 2764 (1 Dec.), column 5.

Fielding is called "one of the first Geniuses that ever adorned this Island," and this play is praised for its delineation of nature and its easy and witty dialogue.

Reprinted 1969.A18.

1779 A BOOKS

1 FIELDING, HENRY. Joseph Andrews och hans Mån Abrahams Adams håndelser. 2 vols. Stockholm: Johan Christoph Holmberg, 580 (288 & 292) pp.

Anonymous engravings. Swedish translation.

2 ______. The Fathers: or The Good-Natur'd Man. Dublin: Printed by W. Boucher for the United Company of Booksellers, 80 pp.

Includes the "advertisement" describing the discovery of the manuscript and John Fielding's dedication to the Duke of Northumberland.

3 ______. The History of the Adventures of Joseph Andrews, and His Friend Mr. Abraham Adams. 2 vols. Paris: J. Fr. Valade, 561 (286 & 275) pp.

English edition; no indication of copy text.

4 ______. The Lottery. London: J. Harrison and J. Wenman, 8 pp.

No music; no indication of copy text.

5 _____. The Mock Doctor. London: J. Harrison and J. Wenman, 8 pp. [1779].
No music; no indication of copy text.

1779 B SHORTER WRITINGS

1 ANON. Review of The Fathers; or, The Good Natur'd Man . . . . By the late Henry Fielding . . . Cadell, 1778. Monthly Review, 60 (Jan.), 56-59.
The reviewer is upset by the suggestion in the "advertisement" that the play, discovered among the papers of Sir Charles Williams, was given the "very liberal and friendly assistance of Mr. Sheridan." He feels that "in strict justice to the deceased Author, and to the Public, the added and altered passages, if there be any such, should have been fairly pointed out to the reader" (p. 57). Although he sees the character of Valence "very much in the best manner of the admirable Fielding," he feels that the others "are scarce more than sketches," that the "dialogue, notwithstanding many masterly strokes, is unfinished . . . and the fable is most grossly defective." There are many undigested borrowings from Terence; in short "The Fathers, may be rather said to contain some crude materials towards the erection of a comedy, than the regular fabric" (p. 57).

1780 A BOOKS

1 FIELDING, HENRY. Amelia, in the Novelists' Magazine. Vol. 1. London: Harrison, 299 pp.
A separate, continuously paged "4 volume" printing, engravings by Walker. No indication of copy text.

2 _____. Geschichte des Tom Jones eines Fündlings. Engravings by Geyser. 4 vols. Nürnberg: J. G. Lochner und Grattenauer.
German translation.

3 _____. The Adventures of Joseph Andrews, in the Novelists' Magazine. Vol. 1. London: Harrison, 179 pp.
Said to be two volumes in one (continuously paged); engravings by Walker. No indication of copy text. Bound together with 1780.A1; separately paged.

4 _____. The Covent-Garden Tragedy. [London: Harrison and J. Wenman], 6 pp. [1780].

1780

Appears to have been sold bound together with Shakespeare's Timon of Athens. At the same time, Harrison was also reprinting bombastic tragedies by Nicholas Rowe and others. Issued as part of the Theatrical Magazine. No indication of copy text.

5 _____. The Debauchees: or, the Jesuit Caught. London: Harrison and J. Wenman, 11 pp.
Title page says "as it is acted at the Theatres Royal in Drury Lane and Covent Garden." Issued as part of the Theatrical Magazine. No indication of copy text.

*6 _____. The History of the Adventures of Joseph Andrews, and of His Friend Mr. Abraham Adams. London: Harrison, 186 pp.
Source: National Union Catalogue: Pre-1956 Imprints. Vol. 171, p. 675.

7 _____. The History of the Adventures of Joseph Andrews, And his Friend Mr. Abraham Adams. London: J. Davies, T. Smith, et al., 358 pp.
No indication of copy text.

8 _____. The History of the Adventures of Joseph Andrews and His Friend Mr. Abraham Adams. 2 vols. London: W. Cavell, 334 (168 & 166) pp.
Called the "seventh edition, revised and corrected"; omits Fielding's preface. No indication of copy text.

9 _____. The History of Tom Jones, A Foundling. 4 vols. London: Joseph Wenman.
No indication of copy text; illustrations by Dodd.

10 _____. The History of Tom Jones, A Foundling. 4 vols. Paris: J. N. Pissot and Barrois junior.
Reprint (in English) of what appears to be the "1750" edition followed by Murphy (1762.A10).

11 _____. The History of Tom Jones, A Foundling, in the Novelists' Magazine. Vol. 3. London: Harrison, 491 pp.
This "4 volume" edition, continuously paged and part of vol. 3 of the Novelists' Magazine, appears to reprint the first edition of the novel. Engravings by various hands. No indication of copy text.

*12 _____. The History of Tom Jones, a Foundling. 3 vols. Edinburgh: W. Darling, et al.

Source: National Union Catalogue: Pre-1956 Imprints. Vol. 171, p. 683.

13 ____. The Humorous and Diverting History of Tom Jones . . . . London: R. Snagg, 93 pp. [1780].
Reprint of 1774.A4.

14 ____. The Intriguing Chambermaid. London: Harrison and J. Wenman, 9 pp. [1780].
Issued as part of the Theatrical Magazine, vol. 4. No indication of copy text.

15 ____. The Lottery. London: Harrison and J. Wenman, 8 pp. [1780].
Issued as part of the Theatrical Magazine. No indication of copy text.

16 ____. The Mock Doctor: or, The Dumb Lady Cur'd. London: H. D. Symonds, 24 pp.
Title page says "taken from The Manager's Book, at the Theatre Royal, Drury-Lane."

17 ____. The Tragedy of Tragedies. London: Harrison and J. Wenman, 10 pp.
This reprint in the Theatrical Magazine does not include the preface or notes added by Fielding. No indication of copy text.

1780 B SHORTER WRITINGS - NONE

1781 A BOOKS

1 FIELDING, HENRY. Amelia, in the Novelists' Magazine. Vol. 1. London: Harrison, 299 pp.
Reissue of 1780.A1.

2 ____. Der Ehemann nach der Mode. Strasburg: Franz Levrault, 173 pp.
German translation of The Modern Husband.

3 ____. Der Hochzeitstag, ein Schauspiel, in Mannheimer Schaubühne. Edited by Anton von Klein. Vol. 1. Mannheim: [?], 176 pp.
German translation of The Wedding Day.

1781

4 _____. Die Briefschreiber oder neues Mittel eine Frau zu Hause zu halten, in Mannheimer Schaubühne. Edited by Anton von Klein. Vol. 2. Mannheim: [?], 99 pp.
German translation of The Letter Writers; or, A New Way to Keep a Wife at Home. Each play in the collection is separately paged.

5 _____. Oeuvres de M. Fielding. 10 vols. Geneva: Nouffer de Rodon.
Vols. 1-3 Amelia Booth, translated by Riccoboni; vol. 4-5 Avantures de Joseph Andrews; vol. 6 Jonathan Wild le Grand; vol. 7-9 Tom Jones ou L'Enfant Trouvé, translated by de la Place; vol. 10 Julien l'Apostat, ou Voyage Dans l'Autre Monde, translated by Kauffmann. Vols. 7-10 were published in 1782. French translation.

6 _____. The Adventures of Joseph Andrews, in the Novelists' Magazine. Vol. 1. London: Harrison, 179 pp.
Reissue of 1780.A3.

7 _____. The History of the Adventures of Joseph Andrews, And his Friend Mr. Abraham Adams. Illustrated by J. Hulett. 2 vols. London: W. Strahan, J. Rivington and Sons, et al., 478 (246 & 232) pp.
No indication of copy text, but called the "tenth edition" and includes the engravings Miller had made for the first edition.

8 _____. The History of the Adventures of Joseph Andrews, And his Friend Mr. Abraham Adams. 2 vols. London: A. Miller, J. & R. Tonson, J. Hinton, and J. Hodges, 414 (214 & 200) pp.
Another edition by the principal publisher of Fielding's works in his lifetime, with illustrations by J. Hulett.

9 _____. The History of Tom Jones a Foundling, in the Novelists' Magazine. Vol. 3. London: Harrison, 491 pp.
This continuously paged "4 volume" printing has illustrations by Stothard and appears to reprint the first edition of the text.

1781 B SHORTER WRITINGS - NONE

1782 A BOOKS

1 FIELDING, HENRY. Amelia. 4 vols. London: Harrison.
Originally issued as part of vol. 1 of the Novelists' Magazine (1780.A1). No indication of copy text.

2 _____. Amélie Booth. Histoire Angloise. 3 vols. Geneva: Nouffer de Rodon.
Probably translated into French by Philippe Florent de Puisieux.

*3 _____. Das verschlagene Kammermädchen. Mannheim: [?], 62 pp.
German translation of The Intriguing Chambermaid.
Source: National Union Catalogue: Pre-1956 Imprints. Vol. 171, p. 693.

4 _____. Der akademische Stutzer. Mannheim: [?], 176 pp.
German translation of The Temple Beau.

5 _____. Die Liebe unter verschiedenen Larven. Strasburg: Franz Levrault, 172 pp.
German translation of Love in Several Masks. No indication of translator.

6 _____. Histoire de Tom Jones, ou L'Enfant Trouvé. Translated by M. D[e] L[a] P[lace]. 3 vols. Geneva: Chez Jean Samuel Cailler.
Includes Gravelot's engravings and a translated selection from Murphy's "Essay . . ." (1762.A10), as well as an extract from Fielding's "Dedicatory Epistle" and the open letter from la Place to Fielding. French translation.

7 _____. Julien L'Apostat, ou Voyage Dans L'Autre Monde. [Translated into French by Kauffmann.] Geneva: Nouffer de Rodon, 249 pp.
Reprint of 1768.A2.

8 _____. The Beauties of Fielding. London: G. Kearsley, 203 pp.
A brief biography taken from Murphy (1762.A10) is followed by selections from Fielding's works organized under various headings (e.g., flattery, knowledge, news, promises, liberty).
On the evidence of title pages this went through three editions in 1782.

9 _____. The History of Jonathan Wild the Great, in the Novelists' Magazine. Vol. 9. London: Harrison, 101 pp.

This separately paged printing has engravings from designs by Stothard. No indication of copy text.

10 _____. The History of Tom Jones, A Foundling. 4 vols. London: Harrison.
Originally issued as part of volume 3 of the Novelists' Magazine (1780.A11). No indication of copy text.

11 _____. The History of Tom Jones, A Foundling. 4 vols. London: W. Strahan, et al.
Reissue of 1773.A2.

12 _____. The Miser. Bell's Characteristical Edition. Edinburgh: Bell, 76 pp.
Said to be "regulated" from the prompt book. No indication of copy text.

*13 _____. The Virgin Unmask'd and The Lottery. Edinburgh: [?].
Source: National Union Catalogue: Pre-1956 Imprints. Vol. 172, p. 4.

1782 B SHORTER WRITINGS - NONE

1783 A BOOKS

1 FIELDING, HENRY. A Journey from This World to the Next, in the Novelists' Magazine. Vol. 12. London: Harrison, 67 pp.
This printing has plates designed by Stothard. No indication of copy text.

2 _____. Journal d'un Voyage de Londres à Lisbonne. Lausanne: François Grasset, 297 pp.
This French translation also includes a catalogue of Fielding's works and a brief life.

3 _____. L'Enfant Trouvé, ou Histoire de Tom Jones. 5 vols. London: [?].
The title pages record neither the publisher nor the translator, although it appears to be a reissue of the 1751 French translation by M. de la Place.

4 _____. The Beauties of Fielding. Dublin: James and William Porter, 200 pp.
Reissue of 1782.A8.

5 _____. The History of the Adventures of Joseph Andrews, and His Friend Mr. Abraham Adams. 2 vols. Dresden: C. and F. Walther, 514 (274 & 240) pp.

Two volumes bound as one. Anonymous engravings; English text.

6 _____. The History of the Adventures of Joseph Andrews, and of His Friend Mr. Abraham Adams. 2 vols. London: Harrison, 179 pp.

Originally issued as part of vol. 1 of the Novelists' Magazine (1780.A3). No indication of copy text.

7 _____. The History of Tom Jones, A Foundling. 4 vols. London: Harrison.

Reprint of 1780.A11.

8 _____. The Works of Henry Fielding, Esq. 12 vols. London: W. Strahan, J. Rivington, et al.

A complete reprint of Murphy (1762.A10), adding The Fathers; or, the Good Natured Man to the last volume of plays (vol. 4).

*9 _____. Tom Jones; ou, L'Enfant Trouvé. 4 vols. Paris: Bauche.

French translation.

Source: National Union Catalogue: Pre-1956 Imprints. Vol. 171, p. 69.

1783 B SHORTER WRITINGS

1 BEATTIE, JAMES. "On Fable and Romance," in his Dissertations Moral and Critical. London: W. Strahan and T. Cadell; Edinburgh: W. Creech, pp. 571-73.

Commends Fielding as the creator of the Comic Romance "which, in the arrangement of events, follows the poetical order; and which may properly enough be called the Epick Comedy, or rather the Comick Epic poem" (p. 571). He finds this epic control in Tom Jones and Amelia; "the latter is entirely poetical . . . beginning in the middle of the action . . . and introducing the previous occurrences, in the form of a narrative episode." Tom Jones becomes "strictly poetical . . . immediately after the sickness of Allworthy" (pp. 572-73). Thinks Fielding has Shakespeare's knowledge of men and Homer's ability to construct, but objects to his circumstantial description of Tom's behavior and to Fielding's rewarding the dishonorable Mr. Wilson in Joseph Andrews.

1784

1784 A BOOKS

1 FIELDING, HENRY. Amélie, Histoire Angloise. [Translated into French by P. F. de Puisieux.] 5 vols. Reims: Cazin.

*2 _____. Avantures de Joseph Andrews, et de son ami Abraham Adams. 3 vols. Reims: Cazin.
French translation.
Source: National Union Catalogue: Pre-1956 Imprints. Vol. 171, p. 681.

3 _____. Jonathan Wild le Grand. Petite Bibliothèque de Campagne, ou Collection de Romans. Paris: J. Fr. Bastien, 222 pp.
French translation of Jonathan Wild.

4 _____. Julien L'Apostat ou Voyage Dans L'Autre Monde. [Translated into French by Kauffmann.] Petite Bibliothèque de Campagne. Reims: Cazin, 313 pp.

*5 _____. Julien L'Apostat, ou, Voyage dans l'Autre Monde. [Translated into French by M. Kauffmann.] Petite Bibliothèque de Campagne, ou Collection de Romans. Paris: J. Fr. Bastien, 313 pp.
Probably the same issue as 1784.A4.
Source: National Union Catalogue: Pre-1956 Imprints. Vol. 171, p. 697.

6 _____. The History of the Adventures of Joseph Andrews, And His Friend Mr. Abraham Adams. London: E. Newberry, 173 pp.
Reprint of 1769.A2.

7 _____. The Intriguing Chambermaid, in Supplement to Bell's British Theatre. Vol. 3. London: John Bell, pp. 138-68.
Music not included, but gives the cast list for a 1781 Edinburgh performance. No indication of copy text.

8 _____. The Lottery, in Supplement to Bell's British Theatre. Vol. 2. London: John Bell, pp. 292-316.
No indication of copy text and no music.

9 _____. The Virgin Unmask'd, in Supplement to Bell's British Theatre. Vol. 2. London: John Bell, pp. 120-41.
No indication of copy text, but 1782 Edinburgh cast list given. No music included.

10 _____. The Works of Henry Fielding, Esq. 10 vols. London: W. Strahan, J. Rivington, et al.
Reprint of 1783.A8.

11 _____. Tom Jones, ou L'Enfant Trouvé. [Translated by de la Place.] Petite Bibliothèque de Campagne. 5 vols. Reims: Cazin.
Brief anonymous "essai" on the genius of Henry Fielding, including biographical details and commending him for his natural imagery and character and for the structural regularity of his novels. In French.

12 _____. Tom Jones, ou L'Enfant Trouvé. [Translated by de la Place.] 4 vols. Paris: Didot l'Ainé.
Four volumes actually bound as eight (each volume has two parts); printed on vellum for the Count d'Artois. Reprint of de la Place's 1750 French translation.

1784 B SHORTER WRITINGS - NONE

1785 A BOOKS

1 FIELDING, HENRY. Amelia. 4 vols. London: Harrison.
Originally issued as part of vol. 1 of the Novelists' Magazine (1780.A1). No indication of copy text.

2 _____. A Journal of a Voyage to Lisbon. London: J. Wenman, 149 pp.
No indication of copy text.

3 _____. The History of the Adventures of Joseph Andrews, and of His Friend Mr. Abraham Adams. 2 vols. London: Harrison, 179 pp.
Originally issued as part of vol. 1 of the Novelists' Magazine (1780.A3). No indication of copy text.

1785 B SHORTER WRITINGS

1 REEVE, CLARA. "Fielding," in The Progress of Romance, Through Times, Countries, and Manners; with Remarks on the Good and Bad Effects of it, on Them Respectively; in a Course of Evening Conversations. Vol. 1. Colchester: W. Keymer; London: G. G. J. and J. Robinson, pp. 139-41.
In the course of a conversation between Hortensius, Sophronia and Euphrasia on the "romance," Euphrasia attacks

Fielding's "mixed characters" (p. 139), particularly Tom Jones, as leading young men astray, and Hortensius defends Fielding by saying that with him "virtue has always the superiority she ought to have" (p. 140) even in these characters.

1786 A BOOKS

1 FIELDING, HENRY. *A New Way to Keep a Wife at Home*. Dublin: H. Chamberlaine, 24 pp.

The title page says "with considerable Alterations and Additions by Walley Chamberlain Oulton" and "performed at the Theatre Royal, Smock-Alley" Dublin.

*2 _____. *D͡ie͡ianii͡a gospodina Ionaf̊ana Vilda Velikago, izdannyi͡a gospodinom*. Translated from the German by Ivan Sytenskoĭ. St. Petersburg: Imperatarskoĭ Akademii nauk.

Reissue of 1772-73.A1.

Source: *New York Public Library Slavonic Catalog*. Vol. 7, p. 06493.

3 _____. *Geschichte des Thomas Jones eines Findelkindes*. 6 vols. Leipzig: Georg Joachim Göschen.

Vols. 3 and 4 of this German translation of *Tom Jones* were issued in 1787; vols. 5 and 6 in 1788.

4 _____. *The Intriguing Chambermaid*, in *A Collection of the Most Esteemed Farces and Entertainments Performed on the British Stage*. Vol. 3. Edinburgh: C. Elliot, pp. 138-68.

Reissue of 1784.A7.

5 _____. *The Lottery*, in *A Collection of the Most Esteemed Farces and Entertainments Performed on the British Stage*. Vol. 2. Edinburgh: C. Elliot, pp. 292-315.

No indication of copy text; music not included.

6 _____. *The Mock Doctor; or, The Dumb Lady Cur'd*, in *A Collection of the Most Esteemed Farces and Entertainments Performed on the British Stage*. Vol. 1. Edinburgh: C. Elliot, pp. 135-61.

No indication of copy text but the cast list for the 1781 Edinburgh performance is given. No music.

7 _____. *The Mock Doctor: or, The Dumb Lady Cur'd*, in *Supplement to Bell's British Theatre*. Vol. 1 (farces and entertainments). London: John Bell, pp. 135-61.

Music not included. No indication of copy text, but prints 1781 Edinburgh cast list.

8 _____. The Virgin Unmask'd, in A Collection of the Most Esteemed Farces and Entertainments Performed on the British Stage. Vol. 2. Edinburgh: C. Elliot, pp. 120-41.
No indication of copy text, but does print 1782 Edinburgh cast list. Music not included.

9 _____. The Virgin Unmasked. London: R. Butters, 22 pp.
The title page says "taken from the Manager's Book at the Theatre Royal, Drury Lane." Printed without music.

10 _____. The Virgin Unmasked. London: T. Payne and Son, J. Nichols, G. G. J. and J. Robinson, et al., 28 pp.
Includes the 1786 cast list and the alterations made for its performance at the Theatre Royal. No music. No indication of copy text.

1786 B SHORTER WRITINGS

1 S., G. "Facetious Anecdote of the Late Harry Fielding." Gentleman's Magazine, 56, no. 2 (Aug.), 659-60.
An anecdote without source passed on: the generous Fielding, dunned for his taxes, borrowed from Jacob Tonson and then over a bottle gave all he had borrowed to a friend.

1787 A BOOKS

1 FIELDING, HENRY. Geschichte des Thomas Jones eines Findelkindes. 6 vols. Carlsruhe: Schmielers Verlag.
Six volumes bound as three. German translation.

2 _____. The History of Tom Jones, A Foundling. 4 vols. London: J. Davies, T. Smith, N. Taylor and W. Thompson.
Appears to reproduce the "1750" text followed by Murphy (1762.A10).

3 _____. The History of Tom Jones, A Foundling. 4 vols. London: W. Cavill and J. Taylor.
Appears to reprint the "1750" edition followed by Murphy (1762.A10).

4 _____. The Virgin Unmask'd. London: G. Lister, 12 pp.
Music not included; said to be "with alterations as it is performed at the Theatre Royal."

*5 _____. The Virgin Unmasked. London: R. Randall, 22 pp.
Without music.
Source: National Union Catalogue: Pre-1956 Imprints. Vol. 172, p. 4.

1787 B SHORTER WRITINGS

1 ANON. "Novels and Romances, with Characters and Anecdotes of Writers." Country Magazine, 1, no. 15 (March), 235.
A sharp attack on Fielding for sapping "the foundation of that morality which it is the duty of parents and all public institutions to inculcate in the minds of young people" and for inventing "that cant phrase, goodness of heart."

2 FIELDING, HENRY. "An Original Song, Written on the first Appearance of the Beggar's Opera." Country Magazine, 1, no. 15 (March), 239.
The song begins "Now Sally Salisbury's dead and gone, / Up starts fav'rite Polly Peachum."

1788 A BOOKS

1 FIELDING, HENRY. Geschichte des Thomas Jones eines Findelkindes. [Translated into German by J. J. C. Bode.] 6 vols. Vienna: [?].

2 _____. Julien L'Apostat, ou Voyage Dans L'Autre Monde. [Translated by M. Kauffmann.] In Voyages Imaginaires, Songes, Visions, et Romans Cabalistiques. Vol. 24. Amsterdam: Rue et Hôtel Serpente, pp. 1-238.
French translation.

3 _____. Julien L'Apostat, ou Voyage Dans L'Autre Monde. Translated by M. Kauffmann. Paris: [?], pp. 1-238. [1788].
This French translation of Journey from this World to the Next is printed together with Les Aventures de Jacques Sadeur Dans la Découverte et le Voyage de la Terre Australe. Same issue as 1788.A2.

4 _____. The History of Jonathan Wild the Great. London: Harrison, 101 pp.

Originally issued as part of the Novelists' Magazine (1782.A9). No indication of copy text.

5 _____. The History of the Adventures of Joseph Andrews, And His Friend Mr. Abraham Adams. 2 vols. London: J. Davis, T. Smith, N. Taylor and W. Thompson.
No indication of copy text. Harvard has vol. 1 only (279 pp.).

6 _____. The Lottery. London: M. Lister, 15 pp.
No indication of copy text.

7 _____. The Miser. Dublin: G. Perrin, 76 pp.
Title page designates this as "Bell's Edition." No indication of copy text.

8 _____. The Miser. London: T. Payne and Sons, J. Nichols, G. G. J. and J. Robinson, et al., 66 pp.
Title page says "With the Variations in the Manager's Book at The Theatre Royal Covent Garden." Cast lists for Drury Lane (incomplete) and Covent Garden.

1788 B SHORTER WRITINGS - NONE

1789 A BOOKS

1 FIELDING, HENRY. Eurydice. Ein Lustspiel. Mannheim: [?], 39 pp.
Anonymous German translation.

*2 _____. La Storia di Tom Jones. 2 vols. Roma: L. Vescovi e F. Neri.
Italian translation; three volumes bound as two.
Source: National Union Catalogue: Pre-1956 Imprints. Vol. 171, p. 691.

3 _____. The History of Tom Jones, A Foundling. 3 vols. London: J. Wenman.
Reprint of 1780.A9.

1789 B SHORTER WRITINGS - NONE

1790

1790 A BOOKS

1 FIELDING, HENRY. Amelia. 4 vols. London: Harrison.
Originally issued as part of vol. 1 of the Novelists' Magazine (1780.A1). No indication of copy text.

2 _____. Amélie. Translated by Madame Riccoboni. 3 parts (2 vols.). [Paris]: [?], 648 pp.
French translation.

3 _____. Geschichte Jonathan Wilds des Grossen, in Thaten und Feinheiten renomirter Kraft- und Kniffgenies. Part I. Berlin: Christian Friedrich Himburg, pp. 1-322.
German translation of Jonathan Wild.

4 _____. The History of the Adventures of Joseph Andrews, and of His Friend Abraham Adams. 2 vols. London: Harrison, 179 pp.
Originally issued as part of vol. 1 of the Novelists' Magazine (1780.A3).

5 _____. The Intriguing Chambermaid. London: J. Debrett, 23 pp.
The title page says "altered from Fielding, First performed at the Theatre Royal, Drury Lane, on Wednesday, November 3, 1790."

6 _____. The Virgin Unmasked. London: R. Butters, 22 pp. [1790].
Includes a cast list in which Mrs. Jordan plays Lucy.

1790 B SHORTER WRITINGS

1 FIELDING, HENRY. "An Essay on Nothing," in The Repository: A Select Collection of Fugitive Pieces of Wit and Humor, in Prose and Verse. Second edition. Vol. 4. London: C. Dilly, pp. 131-49.
No indication of copy text.

2 _____. "Some Papers Proper to be Read Before the Royal Society, Concerning the Terrestrial Chrysipus, Golden-Foot, or Guinea . . . By Petrus Gualterus," in The Repository: A Select Collection of Fugitive Pieces of Wit and Humor, in Prose and Verse. Second edition. Vol. 4. London: C. Dilly, pp. 151-70.
No indication of copy text.

1791 A BOOKS

1 ANON. The Remarkable History of Tom Jones, a Foundling. Boston: Samuel Hall, 28 pp.
Chapbook plot summary for children with six crudely executed illustrations.

2 FIELDING, HENRY. The History of the Adventures of Joseph Andrews, and His Friend Mr. Abraham Adams. 2 vols. London: Harrison, 179 pp.
Originally issued as part of vol. 1 of the Novelists' Magazine (1780.A3). No indication of copy text.

3 _____. The History of the Adventures of Joseph Andrews, and His Friend Mr. Abraham Adams. 2 vols. Philadelphia: Henry Taylor, 431 (223 & 208) pp.
No indication of copy text.

4 _____. The History of Tom Jones, A Foundling. 4 vols. Basel: J. L. Legrand.
A Swiss reprinting in English of what appears to be the first edition.

5 _____. The History of Tom Jones, a Foundling. Illustrations by Rowlandson. 3 vols. Edinburgh: J. Sibbald.
Appears to reprint the "1750" edition followed by Murphy (1762.A10).

6 _____. The Miser. London: John Bell, 126 pp.
Part of Bell's "British Library" series. No indication of copy text.

7 _____. The Virgin Unmasked. London: T. Payne and Son, J. Nichols, et al., 24 pp.
Said to have "the Variations in the Manager's Books at the Theatres Royal Drury Lane and Covent Garden." Includes cast lists from those two theaters and the Haymarket. Music not included. Reprint of 1786.A10.

1791 B SHORTER WRITINGS

1 "HINC INDE." "Tom Jones." Gentleman's Magazine, 61, no. 1 (May), 434.
A note pointing out the chronological errors in Tom Jones, which moves from June to winter in 3 weeks, 5 days and 12 hours. See 1863.B1.

1792

1792 A BOOKS

1 FIELDING, HENRY. The Adventures of Joseph Andrews, and His Friend Mr. Abraham Adams. Illustrations by T. Rowlandson. Edinburgh: Printed by Stewart, Ruthven for W. Coke, Leith, 351 pp.

Same issue as 1792.A2.

2 _____. The Adventures of Joseph Andrews, and his Friend Mr. Abraham Adams. Illustrations by T. Rowlandson. London: J. Murray; Edinburgh: J. Sibbald, 351 pp.

No indication of copy text.

3 _____. The Beauties of Fielding. Philadelphia: M. Carey, 143 pp.

A brief but sympathetic "life," taken largely from Murphy (1762.A10), prefaces this selection of snippets from plays, journalism and novels organized under various headings (avarice, beau, charity, drunkenness, etc.). Called the "first American edition." See 1782.A8.

*4 _____. The History of the Adventures of Joseph Andrews, and of his friend Mr. Abraham Adams. 2 vols. London: A. Miller.

Source: National Union Catalogue: Pre-1956 Imprints. Vol. 171, p. 676.

5 _____. The History of Tom Jones, A Foundling. Cooke's Edition of Select British Novels. 4 vols. London: C. Cooke. [1792].

Illustrations by Corbould, Singleton, and Hamilton; a brief anonymous "life" that accepts the myth of a dissolute Fielding, amusing himself writing Tom Jones. Appears to reprint the first edition of the novel.

6 _____. The History of Tom Jones, A Foundling. Illustrations by A. Bonnor. 3 vols. London: T. Longman, B. Law and Son, J. Nichols, et al.

Appears to reprint the "1750" edition followed by Murphy (1762.A10). Three excellent illustrations.

7 _____. The History of Tom Jones, a Foundling. Illustrations by Rowlandson. 3 vols. London: J. Murray; Edinburgh: J. Sibbald.

Reissue of 1791.A5.

8 _____. The History of Tom Jones, A Foundling, in The Novelist: or, A Choice Selection of the Best Novels. Abridged

by J. H. Emmett. Vol. 1. Göttingen: Vandenhoeck and Ruprecht, pp. 179-360.
English abridgment printed along with Richardson's Sir Charles Grandison. No indication of copy text.

9 ____. The Intriguing Chambermaid, in A Collection of the Most Esteemed Farces and Entertainments Performed on the British Stage. Vol. 3. Edinburgh: C. Elliot, pp. 138-68.
Reissue of 1784.A7. Also issued in 1792 by Silvester Doig in Edinburgh and William Anderson in Stirling. Includes 1781 Edinburgh cast list.

10 ____. The Miser, in Bell's British Theatre. Vol. 11. London: John Bell, 103 pp.
Said to be "regulated from the prompt books" of Drury Lane and Covent Garden. Cast lists from both theaters included. No indication of copy text.

11 ____. The Miser. London: Scatcherd and Whitaker, 43 pp.
Said to be "now first published in three acts" and "corrected from the [Covent Garden] prompt copy by James Wild." No indication of copy text.

12 ____. The Virgin Unmask'd, in A Collection of the Most Esteemed Farces and Entertainments Performed on the British Stage. Vol. 2. Edinburgh: C. Elliot, pp. 120-41.
Reissue of 1786.A8.

1792 B SHORTER WRITINGS - NONE

1793 A BOOKS

1 FIELDING, HENRY. Amelia. Cooke's Pocket Edition of Select Novels. 3 vols. London: C. Cooke.
No indication of copy text. Illustrations by J. De Wilde and R. Corbould. Anonymous "life" based largely on Murphy (1762.A10).

*2 ____. Julien l'Apostat, ou Voyages dans l'autre monde; et les aventures de Jacques Sadeur, dans la découverte et le voyage de la Terre Australe. Paris: Gay and Gide, 416 pp.
Kauffman French translation of A Journey from this World to the Next (1782.A7) and a revision by F. Raguenet of G. de Forgny's La Terre Australe. See 1788.A3.

1793

Source: National Union Catalogue: Pre-1956 Imprints. Vol. 171, p. 697.

3 _____. Podrzutek Czyli Historya Tom-Dźona. [Translated by F. Zablocki.] 2 vols. Warsaw: M. Grölla and J. K. Mości, 798 (406 & 392) pp.
Polish translation of Tom Jones from the French translation of la Place.

4 _____. The Adventures of Joseph Andrews, And His Friend Mr. Abraham Adams. Illustrated by R. Corbould. Cooke's Select British Novels. 2 vols. London: C. Cooke, 414 (213 & 201) pp.
Vols. 6 and 7 of Cooke's Select British Novels. No indication of copy text.

5 _____. The History of Jonathan Wild the Great. Engraving by C. Warren. Cooke's Pocket Edition of Select Novels. London: C. Cooke, 208 pp. [1793].
No indication of copy text.

6 _____. The History of Joseph Andrews, and his Friend Mr. Abraham Adams, in The Novelist: or, A Choice Selection of The Best Novels. Abridged by J. H. Emmett. Vol. 2. Göttingen: Vandenhoeck and Ruprecht, pp. 1-150.
English abridgment printed along with Richardson's Clarissa. No indication of copy text.

1793 B SHORTER WRITINGS - NONE

1794 A BOOKS

1 FIELDING, HENRY. The Adventures of Joseph Andrews, And His Friend Mr. Abraham Adams. Illustrated by R. Corbould. Cooke's edition. 2 vols. London: C. Cooke, 348 (178 & 170) pp. [1794].
Called "two volumes in one," separately paged but bound together. Reissue of 1793.A4.

2 _____. The History of the Adventures of Joseph Andrews, and his Friend Mr. Abraham Adams. 2 vols. London: H. D. Symonds; Paris: The English Press and Barrois, senior, 490 (247 & 233) pp.
No indication of copy text; vol. 2 has Paris imprint.

3 _____. The History of Tom Jones, A Foundling. Illustrations by R. Corbould. Cooke's Edition of Select British Novels. 3 vols. London: C. Cooke. [1794].
Reissue of 1792.A5.

*4 _____. The History of Tom Jones, a Foundling. 3 vols. Philadelphia: Printed for Jacob Johnson and Alexander M'Kenzie.
Source: National Union Catalogue: Pre-1956 Imprints. Vol. 171, p. 683.

5 _____. The Humorous and Diverting History of Tom Jones . . . . London: R. Barsam, 82 pp.
Reprint of 1774.A4.

6 _____. The Mock Doctor; or, The Dumb Lady Cur'd. London: J. Jarvis, 53 pp.
Said to be "as performed at . . . Covent-garden and Haymarket." Music not included. A contemporary cast list included, as well as a brief uncomplimentary life by "T. B." No indication of copy text.

*7 _____. Tom Jones, ou L'Enfant Trouvé. Translated by la Place. 4 vols. Paris: [?]. [1794].
French translation.
Source: National Union Catalogue: Pre-1956 Imprints. Vol. 171, p. 690.

1794 B SHORTER WRITINGS - NONE

1795 A BOOKS

1 FIELDING, HENRY. Historia de Amelia Booth. Translated by D. R. A. D. Q. 5 vols. Madrid: Imprenta de la Viuda de Ibarra.
Vols. 4 and 5 of this Spanish translation were issued i 1796.

2 _____. The History of Tom Jones, A Foundling. London: E. Newbery, 201 pp.
Reissue of 1778.A4.

*3 _____. The History of Tom Jones, a Foundling. 3 vols. New York: Robertson and Gowan. [1795?].
Source: National Union Catalogue: Pre-1956 Imprints. Vol. 171, p. 683.

1795

1795 B SHORTER WRITINGS

1 FIELDING, HENRY. "True Examples of the Interposition of Providence, in the Discovery and Punishment of Murder," in Cheap Repository Tracts. Vol. 1. London: J. Marshall; Bath: S. Hazard, 12 pp.

Printed along with moral exemplars like "Two Wealthy Farmers," and sermons and tracts like "The Plague in London, 1665," designed to strike fear into the hearts of readers. No indication of copy text.

1796 A BOOKS

*1 FIELDING, HENRY. Histoire de Tom-Jones, ou L'Enfant Trouvé. Translated by M. de la Place. 4 vols. Geneva and Bruxelles: Chez B. Le France.

French translation, said to be revised and corrected by M. Le Tourneur.

Source: National Union Catalogue: Pre-1956 Imprints. Vol. 171, p. 690.

2 _____. Tom Jones Ó El Expósito. Translated by D. Ignacio de Ordejon. 4 vols. Madrid: D. Benito Cano.

This Spanish translation is taken from the French translation of M. de la Place (1767.A6).

3 _____. Tom Jones, ou L'Enfant Trouvé. Translated by Le Citoyen Davaux. 4 vols. Paris: Chez Maison.

This post-revolution French translation, issued in the year 4 by citizen Davaux, promises on the title page to be more reliable than la Place's.

1796 B SHORTER WRITINGS - NONE

1797 A BOOKS

*1 FIELDING, HENRY. Amelia. 3 vols. London: [?].

Source: National Union Catalogue: Pre-1956 Imprints. Vol. 171, p. 667.

2 _____. Emelie Booth. Ein Muster ehelicher Liebe. 2 vols. Leipzig: Schwickertscher Verlag, 1075 (498 & 577) pp.

Four volumes printed as two. German translation.

*3 _____. Oeuvres Complettes. 23 vols. Paris: Perlet.
Vols. 1-5 Amélie Booth; vols. 6-10 Tom Jones, ou l'Enfant Trouvé; vols. 15-17 Aventures de Joseph Andrews et de son ami Abraham Adams; vols. 21-22 Jonathan Wild le grand; vol. 23 Voyage dans l'autre monde, ou Julien l'Apostat. French translation.
Source: National Union Catalogue: Pre-1956 Imprints. Vol. 171, pp. 667, 681, 690, 695 and 698.

4 _____. The History of Tom Jones, a Foundling. Boston: S. Hall, 131 pp.
"Abridged from the Works of Henry Fielding"; a severe abridgment with six crudely executed illustrations (although the illustrations are different from 1791.A1, they appear to be by the same illustrator).

5 _____. Tom Jones, ou L'Enfant Trouvé. [Translated by M. de la Place.] Illustrated by Challiou. 4 vols. Paris: André.
French translation.

1797 B SHORTER WRITINGS - NONE

1798 A BOOKS

1 FIELDING, HENRY. Amelia. Engravings by R. Corbould. Cooke's Edition of Select British Novels. 3 vols. London: C. Cooke. [1798].
Reissue of 1793.A1.

2 _____. The History of Tom Jones, A Foundling. Cooke's Edition of Select British Novels. 3 vols. London: C. Cooke. [1798].
Reprint of 1792.A5.

3 _____. The Remarkable History of Tom Jones, a Foundling. Boston: Samuel Hall, 28 pp.
Reissue of 1791.A1.

1798 B SHORTER WRITINGS - NONE

1799

1799 A BOOKS

1 ANON. The Remarkable History of Tom Jones, A Foundling. Fourth Edition. Worcester, Massachusetts: Isaiah Thomas, 28 pp.

A chap book plot summary with woodcuts. Reprint of 1791.A1.

2 FIELDING, HENRY. Amelia. Engravings by R. Corbould. 3 vols. London: C. Cooke.

Reissue of 1793.A1.

3 _____. Aventures de Joseph Andrews, et de son ami Abraham Adams, in Nouvelle Bibliothèque Universelle des Romans. Vol. 6. Paris: [?], pp. 52-117.

A French plot summary of the novel.

4 _____. The History of Jonathan Wild The Great. Cooke's Pocket Edition of Select Novels. London: C. Cooke, 208 pp. [1799].

Reissue of 1793.A5.

5 _____. The Remarkable History of Tom Jones, A Foundling. Salem: N. & J. Coverly, 29 pp.

Reprint of 1791.A1.

1799 B SHORTER WRITINGS - NONE

1800 A BOOKS

1 FIELDING, HENRY. A Journey From This World to the Next. Illustrations by R. Corbould. Cooke's edition. London: C. Cooke, 144 pp. [1800].

No indication of copy text.

2 _____. Jonathan Wild, Rinaldo Rinaldini's Antipode. 2 vols. Ronneburg and Leipzig: Schumannsche Buchhandlung, 500 (230 & 270) pp.

German translation.

3 _____. The History of Tom Jones, A Foundling. Henshall's Ornamental Library of Classic Novels. 4 vols. Dublin: T. Henshall. [1800?].

Illustrations by R. Corbould and Singleton; a brief anonymous life, emphasizing early dissipation. Appears to reprint the first edition.

*4 _____. The History of Tom Jones, a Foundling. 3 vols. New York: B. Gomez. [1800?].
Source: National Union Catalogue: Pre-1956 Imprints. Vol. 171, p. 684.

1800 B SHORTER WRITINGS - NONE

1801 A BOOKS

1 FIELDING, HENRY. The History of the Adventures of Joseph Andrews and His Friend Mr. Abraham Adams. 2 vols. Philadelphia: William Duane, 490 (257 & 233) pp.
No indication of copy text.

*2 _____. Tom Jones, ou L'Enfant Trouvé. Translated by M. de la Place. 4 vols. London: [?].
French translation.
Source: National Union Catalogue: Pre-1956 Imprints. Vol. 171, p. 690.

3 _____. Tom Jones, ou L'Enfant Trouvé. [Translated by M. de la Place.] Illustrations by Borel. 4 vols. Paris: Imbert.
French translation.

1801 B SHORTER WRITINGS - NONE

1802 A BOOKS

1 FIELDING, HENRY. The Miser. London: N. Scarlett, 126 pp.
Said to be "regulated from the prompt books" of Drury Lane.

1802 B SHORTER WRITINGS - NONE

1803 A BOOKS - NONE

1803 B SHORTER WRITINGS

1 AIKIN, JOHN, THOMAS MORGAN, and WILLIAM JOHNSTON. "Henry Fielding," in General Biography; or, Lives, Critical and

Historical, of the Most Eminent Persons of All Ages, Countries, Conditions, and Professions, Arranged According to Alphabetical Order. Vol. 4. London: J. Johnson, et al.; Edinburgh: Bell and Bradfute; Dublin: Colbert, pp. 89-91.
The usual scandalous biography based on Murphy (1762. A10). Dismisses his dramas, emphasizes the "low" nature of much of his work, worries over the morality of Tom Jones and the weakness of Amelia, and praises him for his work as a magistrate. See 1918.B1.

1804 A BOOKS

1 FIELDING, HENRY. Oeuvres de Fielding. 12 vols. Paris: L. Duprat-Duverger.
This French translation in twelve volumes and twenty-three parts includes Amelia (vols. 1-3), Tom Jones (vols. 4-5), Joseph Andrews (vols. 8-9), Jonathan Wild (vol. 11), and Voyage from this World to the Next (vol. 12). Volumes 9 and 10 also contain David Simple, which is attributed to Henry rather than Sarah Fielding. Volumes 6 and 7 are translations of Smollett's Roderick Random, also inaccurately attributed to Fielding. Translation by P. Hernández and P. F. de Puisieux.

2 _____. The History of Tom Jones, A Foundling. English Library. Authors in Prose. Vols. 1-4. Gotha: Steudel and Keil.
Four volumes printed as two; German printing in English of the first edition.

*3 _____. The Intriguing Chambermaid, in The British Drama; Comprehending the Best Plays in the English Language. Vol. 3. London: W. Millar, pp. 67-74.
Source: National Union Catalogue: Pre-1956 Imprints. Vol. 171, p. 693.

4 _____. Tom Jones, ou Histoire d'un Enfant Trouvé. Translated by L. C. Chéron. 6 vols. Paris: Giguet et Michaud.
French translation of Tom Jones.

1804 B SHORTER WRITINGS - NONE

1805 A BOOKS

1 FIELDING, HENRY. The Adventures of Joseph Andrews, and His Friend Mr. Abraham Adams. Engravings by Rowlandson. Edinburgh: Bell & Bradfute, W. Creech, et al., 351 pp.

No identification of copy text.

2 _____. The History of Tom Jones, A Foundling. Illustrations by Rowlandson. 3 vols. Edinburgh: Bell & Bradfute, W. Creech, et al.; London: Longman, Rees, et al.

Appears to reprint the "1750" edition followed by Murphy (1762.A10).

3 _____. The Mock Doctor; or, The Dumb Lady Cur'd, in Sharpe's British Theatre. Vol. 12. London: John Sharpe, 31 pp.

No music; no indication of copy text; separately paged.

4 _____. The Tragedy of Tragedies; or, the Life and Death of Tom Thumb the Great. London: John Cawthorn, 118 pp.

Includes the play, Kane O'Hara's musical adaptation, and Fielding's notes to the play (separate from the text). No indication of copy text.

5 _____. Tom Thumb. Fairburn's Complete Edition of Tom Thumb . . . with the Alterations to the Present Time. London: John Fairburn, 40 pp. [1805].

Includes a slightly altered version of Fielding's Tom Thumb but not his annotated Tragedy of Tragedies. Does include Kane O'Hara's popular musical adaptation. An afterword describes the current Haymarket production. No indication of copy text.

*6 _____. Tom Thumb. Roach's Minor Theatre. No. 6. London: J. Roach, 36 pp.

Said to be "adapted for theatrical representation . . . regulated from the prompt books."

Source: National Union Catalogue: Pre-1956 Imprints. Vol. 172, p. 8.

1805 B SHORTER WRITINGS

1 MURRAY, H. "Henry Fielding," in Morality of Fiction: or An Inquiry into The Tendency of Fictitious Narratives, with Observations on Some of the Most Eminent. Edinburgh: A. Constable and J. Anderson; London: Longman, Hurst, Rees, and Orme, pp. 101-105.

1806

Praises Fielding for "the structure of his fables" (p. 101), for the "noble and beautiful vein of morality [benevolence, generosity, disinterestedness]" (p. 102) which runs through his fiction, and for his pure heroines and his completely good men like Allworthy and Dr. Harrison. Blames him for the narrative intrusions, his "pedantry and ostentation of learning" (p. 101), and for his heroes, particularly Tom and Booth, whose "truly estimable qualities, with a very considerable degree of profligacy . . . [are] confounded together" (p. 103). He also thinks that the character of Blifil makes "evident [the] tendency to represent regularity and prudence as intimately connected with deceit and malignity" (p. 105).

1806 A BOOKS

1 FIELDING, HENRY. The Intriguing Chambermaid, in Cawthorn's Minor British Theatre. Vol. 6. London: John Cawthorn, 53 pp.

Said to be "regulated from the prompt-book . . . as performed at the Theatre Royal, Covent Garden" and includes a nineteenth-century cast list, in which Macready played Valentine. Separately paged.

2 _____. The Mock Doctor; or, The Dumb Lady Cur'd, in Cawthorn's Minor British Theatre. Vol. 3. London: John Cawthorn, 48 pp.

No music but said to be "regulated from the prompt book" of the manager of Drury Lane and includes a Drury Lane cast list. Separately paged.

3 _____. The Works of Henry Fielding, Esq. With an Essay on His Life and Genius, by Arthur Murphy. Edited by Alexander Chalmers. 10 vols. London: J. Johnson, et al.

Adds only "The Essay on Nothing" to 1762.A10.

1806 B SHORTER WRITINGS - NONE

1807 A BOOKS

1 FIELDING, HENRY. A Journey from This World to the Next. English Library. Authors in Prose. Vol. 13. Gotha: Steudel and Keil, 216 pp.

German printing; text in English. No indication of copy text.

2 _____. Select Works of Henry Fielding, Esq. An Account of the Life and Writings of the Author [by William Watson]. 5 vols. Edinburgh: Mundell, Doig, & Stevenson; London: J. Murray and T. Ostell.

Vol. 1 Joseph Andrews; vols. 2-4 Tom Jones; vols. 4-5 Amelia; vol. 5 Jonathan Wild.

The preface borrows from Murphy and then embroiders the myth of the dissolute Fielding. Each of Fielding's works is briefly discussed in chronological order; Watson spends longest on Fielding's political writing and journalism and the controversy they stirred. As a novelist, Fielding is preferred to Smollett because he creates character rather than caricature and because he enforces moral reward and punishment. Various commentators (including Lady Mary Wortley Montagu, Godwin, Warburton, Beattie and Murphy) are quoted, and a bibliography of his works is included.

Appears to reprint the Murphy (1762.A10) texts. Preface a reprint of 1807.A5.

3 _____. The History of Tom Jones, A Foundling. Engravings by James Heath. 4 vols. London: J. Hunt, C. Reynell and C. Chapple.

Appears to reproduce the "1750" edition followed by Murphy (1762.A10).

4 _____. The Tragedy of Tragedies; or, the Life and Death of Tom Thumb the Great. Boston: B. True, 36 pp.

Reproduces the text and a few of Fielding's notes but not his preface.

5 WATSON, WILLIAM. The Life of Henry Fielding, Esq. Edinburgh: Mundell, Doig, et al., 176 pp.

Based on Murphy (1762.A10) and the Biographia Dramatica; sets Fielding's works in the "natural order" of his life, briefly commenting on each (all of his poetry is dismissed in a brief paragraph). A bibliography of Fielding's works "so far as they are known in the present day" (p. 173) is appended.

1807 B SHORTER WRITINGS - NONE

1808

1808 A BOOKS

1 FIELDING, HENRY. The Adventures of Joseph Andrews, And His Friend Mr. Abraham Adams. 2 vols. St. Andrews: R. Tullis, 503 (260 & 243) pp.
No indication of copy text.

2 _____. The History of Amelia. 3 vols. London: J. Johnson, J. Nichols and Son, R. Baldwin, et al.
No indication of copy text.

3 _____. The History of the Adventures of Joseph Andrews, and His Friend Mr. Abraham Adams. 2 vols. London: J. Johnson, J. Nichols and Son, et al., 445 (228 & 217) pp.
No indication of copy text.

4 _____. The History of Tom Jones, A Foundling. 4 vols. London: J. Johnson, J. Nichols and Son, et al.
Appears to reprint the "1750" edition followed by Murphy (1762.A10).

5 _____. The Works of Henry Fielding, Esq. With an Essay on His Life and Genius, by Arthur Murphy. Edited by Alexander Chalmers. 14 vols. London: J. Johnson, et al.
Reprint of 1806.A3.

6 ROWLANDSON, THOMAS. Thirteen Etchings Illustrative of Striking Passages in Tom Jones and Joseph Andrews. Edinburgh: Cornelius Elliot; London: John Murray, 27 pp.
Rowlandson illustrates Mrs. Waters' rescue, Square in Molly's chamber, Tom and Molly in the woods, the battle of Upton, Sophia's fall from her horse, etc.

1808 B SHORTER WRITINGS - NONE

1809 A BOOKS

1 FIELDING, HENRY. The History of the Adventures of Joseph Andrews, And His Friend Mr. Abraham Adams. Illustrations by T. Unwins. 2 vols. London: C. Chapple, 524 (269 & 255) pp.
No indication of copy text.

2 _____. The History of Tom Jones, A Foundling. 2 vols. London: J. Walker, J. Johnson, et al., 1095 (555 & 540) pp.

Appears to reprint the "1750" edition followed by Murphy (1762.A10), and provides a brief anonymous life.

3 _____. The Journal of a Voyage to Lisbon, in General Collection of Voyages and Travels. Edited by W. F. Mavor. Vol. 11. London: Richard Phillips, pp. 201-52.
No indication of copy text.

*4 _____. The Tragedy of Tragedies, or, The Life and Death of Tom Thumb, the Great. Dublin: James Charles, 38 pp.
Source: National Union Catalogue: Pre-1956 Imprints. Vol. 172, p. 8.

1809 B SHORTER WRITINGS

1 DRAKE, NATHAN. "The Champion," in his Essays, Biographical, Critical, and Historical, Illustrative of the Rambler, Adventurer and Idler, and of the Various Periodical Papers which In Imitation of the Writings of Steele and Addison, have been Published Between the Close of the eighth volume of the Spectator, and the Commencement of the year, 1809. Vol. 1. London: W. Suttaby, pp. 79-91.
After a brief sensational biography, Drake discusses the run of the Champion and the authorship (says that Fielding's contributions are "superior to any that we have noticed since the close of the . . . Spectator, p. 85), gives a sample of the papers on the Vinegar family, and identifies and briefly discusses the humorous and critical essays, as opposed to the political ones.

1810 A BOOKS

*1 FIELDING, HENRY. The History of the Adventures of Joseph Andrews, and His Friend Abraham Adams. London: J. Walker, J. Johnson, et al.
Source: National Union Catalogue: Pre-1956 Imprints. Vol. 171, p. 676.

2 _____. The History of the Adventures of Joseph Andrews, and His Friend Mr. Abraham Adams, in The British Novelists. Preface by Mrs. A. L. Barbauld. Vol. 18. London: F. C. and J. Rivington, et al., 434 pp.
Reprints Joseph Andrews without indicating copy text. The preface sets out the usual sensational Fielding biography and discusses Fielding's intrusiveness ("not only in his digressive chapters, but in the representations

of the characters and secret views of his personages" (p. v). Barbauld also discusses lively characters in Joseph Andrews (particularly Adams, who is comic without being contemptible). She discusses effective contrasting emotions in Tom Jones, as well as its plot, characters (Sophia demonstrates that "a yielding easiness of disposition is what he seems to lay the greatest stress upon" in his women [p. xxv]), and morality ("A young man may imbibe from it sentiments of humanity, generosity, and all the more amiable virtues . . . but he is not likely to gain from it firmness to resist temptation" [p. xxvii]). She comments on the contrast between the yielding Amelia and the spirited Miss Matthews in Amelia and on the strength of several other characters in that novel.

3 _____. The History of Tom Jones, A Foundling. Cooke's Edition of Select British Novels. 3 vols. London: C. Cooke.
Reprint of 1792.A5.

4 _____. The History of Tom Jones, A Foundling. 4 vols. Philadelphia: Birch and Small.
Brief anonymous life based on Murphy; appears to reproduce the "1750" edition.

5 _____. The History of Tom Jones, A Foundling, in The British Novelists. With An Essay, and Prefaces Biographical and critical, by Mrs. A. L. Barbauld. Vols. 19-21. London: F. C. and J. Rivington, et al.
See 1810.A2 for Preface. Text appears to be the same as 1762.A10.

6 _____. The Miser, in English Comedy: A Collection of the Most Celebrated Dramas, Since the Commencement of the Reformation of the Stage. Vol. 6. Selected by Sir Richard Steele and Colley Cibber. London: John Sharpe, pp. 75-154.
No indication of copy text.

1810 B SHORTER WRITINGS - NONE

1811 A BOOKS

1 FIELDING, HENRY. The History of Amelia, Joseph Andrews, and Journey from this World to the Next. Introductions by William Mudford. Illustrations by H. Corbould. The British Novelists. Vol. 5. London: W. Clarke, Goddard, et al., 563 pp.

No indication of copy text; each novel separately paged. Mudford thinks Amelia seriously weak in theme (Booth's behavior is either shocking or boring), plot, and character (Mrs. Bennett's behavior implies the degradation of a woman's mind). Praises Fielding for the reality of the characters in Joseph Andrews (although Fanny is not good because "Fielding is never successful in his portraits of women," p. 2), but he thinks the plot weak (particularly the ending) and the "introductory chapters . . . tedious" (p. 4). A Journey . . . he thinks boldly conceived and badly executed, both its satire and irony failing. Thinks him indebted to Cyrano de Bergerac and Swift in it.

2 _____. The History of Tom Jones, A Foundling and The History of Mr. Jonathan Wild the Great. Introductions by William Mudford. The British Novelists. Vol. 4. London: W. Clarke, Goddard, et al., 619 and 106 pp.

No indication of copy text; each novel separately paged. Illustrations by Clennel and others. Mudford provides a brief life, taken from Murphy (1762.A10), and an appreciation of each work. Mudford admires the craftsmanship of Tom Jones, though he fears that Tom's immoral behavior (which artistically forms a good balance) may sway impressionable minds. He then offers an appreciation of the other characters in the novel, pointing out Fielding's habit of balancing characters. He says, surprisingly, that Fielding's style "has no harmony, no flow, no grace" (p. 10). He mentions the irony in Jonathan Wild, thinks Mrs. Heartfree too free in telling her tale of woe, and provides details of the real Wild's life.

3 _____. The Intriguing Chambermaid, in The Modern British Drama. Vol. 5 (operas and farces). London: William Miller, pp. 70-77.

No indication of copy text; music not included.

4 _____. The Miser, in The Modern British Drama. Vol. 4 (comedies). London: William Miller, pp. 335-64.

No indication of copy text.

5 _____. The Mock Doctor, in The Modern British Drama. Vol. 5 (operas and farces). London: William Miller, pp. 59-69.

No indication of copy text; music not included.

1811 B SHORTER WRITINGS - NONE

1812

1812 A BOOKS

1 FIELDING, HENRY. Select Works of Henry Fielding, Esq. An Account of the Life and Writings of the Author by William Watson. 2nd edition. 5 vols. Edinburgh: P. Hill, S. Doig, A. Stirling, et al.; London: Lackington, et al.
Reprint of 1807.A2.

2 _____. Tom Jones, ou O Engeitado. Translated by A. J. da S. C. 4 vols. Lisbon: Na Impressão Regia.
Vol. 1 of this Portuguese translation was issued in 1812, vol. 2 in 1814, vol. 3 in 1815, and vol. 4 in 1816.

1812 B SHORTER WRITINGS

1 NICHOLS, JOHN. "Henry Fielding, Esq.," in his Literary Anecdotes of the Eighteenth Century. Vol. 3. London: Nichols, Son, and Bentley, pp. 356-85.
A critical biography drawing heavily on Murphy (1762.A10), and supplemented by the Biographia Dramatica; notes that had appeared in the Gentleman's Magazine; allusions to Fielding in Blair's Lectures on Rhetoric and Belles Lettres, Knox's Essays, Moral and Literary, etc.

1813 A BOOKS

1 FIELDING, HENRY. The Humorous and Diverting History of Tom Jones . . . . Baltimore: F. Lucas, 105 pp.
Appears to reprint 1774.A4.

2 _____. The Works of Henry Fielding, Esq. With an Essay on His Life and Genius, by Arthur Murphy. Edited by Alexander Chalmers. 14 vols. New York: William Durell.
Reprint of 1806.A3. The first five volumes were also separately issued in 1813 and 1816 as The Dramatic Works of Henry Fielding.

1813 B SHORTER WRITINGS

1 A CONSTANT READER. "Mr. Urban." Gentleman's Magazine, 83, no. 2 (Oct.), 337.
Calls attention to Fielding's pamphlet on Elizabeth Canning, overlooked by Nichols' "Literary Anecdotes of the Eighteenth Century."

1814 A BOOKS

*1 FIELDING, HENRY. The History of Tom Jones, a Foundling. 3 vols. Philadelphia: M. Carey.
Source: National Union Catalogue: Pre-1956 Imprints. Vol. 171, p. 684.

1814 B SHORTER WRITINGS

1 CHALMERS, ALEXANDER. "Henry Fielding," in The General Biographical Dictionary: containing An Historical and Critical Account of the Lives and Writings of the Most Eminent Persons in Every Nation; Particularly the British and Irish; From the Earliest Accounts to the Present Time. Vol. 14. London: J. Nichols and Son, et al., pp. 283-92.
Lifted from Baker (1764.B1) with two added anecdotes from the Gentleman's Magazine for 1786.

1815 A BOOKS

*1 FIELDING, HENRY. Amelia; or, The Interesting History of a Lovely Female in Married Life. Epitomized by Sarah S. Wilkinson. London: Dean and Munday, 30 pp. [1815].
Source: National Union Catalogue: Pre-1956 Imprints. Vol. 171, p. 667.

*2 _____. The History of the Adventures of Joseph Andrews, and His Friend Mr. Abraham Adams, in The British Novelists. Vol. 5, no. 2. Edited by William Mudford. London: Published for the Proprietors by W. Clarke, Goddard, et al., 187 pp.
Probably a reissue of 1810.A2.
Source: National Union Catalogue: Pre-1956 Imprints. Vol. 171, p. 677.

*3 _____. The History of Tom Jones, a Foundling. British Classics. Vols. 71-73. New York: W. Durell.
Source: National Union Catalogue: Pre-1956 Imprints. Vol. 171, p. 684.

4 _____. The Mock Doctor; or, The Dumb Lady Cur'd, in A Collection of Farces and Other Afterpieces. Selected by Mrs. Inchbald. Vol. 5. London: Longman, Hurst, et al., pp. 73-106.
No indication of copy text; no music.

5 _____. The Mock Doctor; or, The Dumb Lady Cur'd, in The London Theatre. Edited by Thomas Dibdin. Vol. 20. London: Whittingham and Arliss, 27 pp.
Omits the songs but is said to be "correctly given, from copies used in the theatres." No other indication of copy text.

6 _____. Wonderboek of Avonturen op eene reis in de Andere Wereld. Dordrecht: A. Blussé & Zoon, 286 pp.
Dutch translation of Journey from This World to the Next.

1815 B SHORTER WRITINGS

1 [HAZLITT, W.]. "Standard Novels and Romances." Edinburgh Review, 24, no. 48 (Feb.), 320-38.
In this review of Madame D'Arblay's The Wanderer: or, Female Difficulties, Hazlitt surveys the novel, discussing Fielding, Richardson, Sterne, Smollett, Cervantes, Lesage and Miss Burney. He treats the novel as nearly perfect mimesis; about Joseph Andrews he says "this work, indeed, we take to be a perfect piece of statistics in its kind; and do not know from what other quarter we could have acquired the solid information it contains" (p. 320). He praises Fielding as an "observer of human nature [only a] little inferior to Shakespeare, though without any of the genius and poetical qualities of his mind" (p. 326). He is offended by "want of refinement and elegance in the two principal characters" (p. 327) in Tom Jones, but he is full of general praise of Fielding's characters (particularly the naive Adams who flatters our "superior sagacity," p. 328).
With very little change this becomes Lecture VI of "Lectures on the Comic Writers"; see 1819.B1.

1816 A BOOKS

*1 FIELDING, HENRY. Amelia. New York: W. Durell.
Source: National Union Catalogue: Pre-1956 Imprints. Vol. 171, p. 667.

*2 _____. The History of the Adventures of Joseph Andrews, and his friend Mr. Abraham Adams. 2 vols. New York: J. Forbes.
Source: National Union Catalogue: Pre-1956 Imprints. Vol. 171, p. 690.

*3 _____. The History of Tom Jones, a Foundling. 3 vols. New York: George F. Hopkins.

Source: National Union Catalogue: Pre-1956 Imprints. Vol. 171, p. 684.

1816 B SHORTER WRITINGS - NONE

1817 A BOOKS

*1 FIELDING, HENRY. Eurydice hissed; or A Word to the Wise. Dramatic pamphlets. Vol. 29, no. 8. New York: D. Longworth, 12 pp.

Source: National Union Catalogue: Pre-1956 Imprints. Vol. 171, p. 673.

2 _____. The History of Tom Jones, A Foundling. Select Novels. Vol. 3. London: Thomas Kelly, 624 pp.

Anonymous illustrations. Appears to reproduce the "1750" edition followed by Murphy (1762.A10).

3 _____. The Miser, in The British Drama. Edited by R. Cumberland. Vol. 5. London: C. Cooke, 108 pp.

Separately paged; no indication of copy text but title page says "as performed at the Theatre-Royal Covent-Garden and Drury-Lane, Regulated from the Prompt Books." The lines omitted are marked "by inverted commas." Cumberland provides a life, based on Murphy, and includes a list of plays. His discussion of the play briefly analyzes the difference between French and English comedy, Fielding's alteration of Molière, and Fielding's limits as a dramatist. Sees Fielding and the English as crude and coarse compared to the French.

4 _____. The Virgin Unmasked, in The London Theatre. Edited by Thomas Dibdin. Vol. 23. London: Sherwood, Neely, and Jones, 24 pp.

No indication of copy text, but said to be "given from copies used in the theatres." No music; separately paged.

1817 B SHORTER WRITINGS - NONE

1818

1818 A BOOKS

1 FIELDING, HENRY. Select Works of Henry Fielding, Esq. An Account of the Life and Writings of the Author by William Watson. 3rd edition. 5 vols. Edinburgh: Doig, Stirling and Slade, et al.; London: Lackington et al.; York: Wilson & Sons; Dublin: Johnston & Deas.
Reprint of 1807.A2.

2 _____. The History and Adventures of Joseph Andrews, and His Friend Mr. Abraham Adams. Walker's British Classics. London: J. Walker, F. C. and J. Rivington, et al., 405 pp.
No indication of copy text. The brief anonymous introduction compares the novel to Don Quixote, discusses the parody of Pamela, and sets out Fielding's use of the Rev. Young as a model for Adams (wishing that the novel had subjected him to fewer low adventures).

3 _____. The History of Tom Jones, A Foundling. 4 vols. Philadelphia: A. Small.
Reissue of 1810.A4.

4 _____. The History of Tom Jones, a Foundling. Illustrations by Clennel. 3 vols. London: Sherwood, Neely, and Jones.
Appears to reprint the "1750" edition followed by Murphy (1762.A10).

5 _____. The Miser, in The London Theatre. Edited by Thomas Dibdin. Vol. 24. London: Sherwood, Neely, and Jones, 41 pp.
Said to be "given from copies used in the theatres." No other information on copy text. Separately paged.

1818 B SHORTER WRITINGS - NONE

1819 A BOOKS

1 FIELDING, HENRY. The History of Tom Jones, A Foundling. Walker's British Classics. 2 vols. London: J. Walker, et al., 1095 (555 & 540) pp.
Reissue of 1809.A2.

2 _____. The Works of Henry Fielding, Esq. With an Essay on His Life and Genius, by Arthur Murphy. Edited by Alexander Chalmers. 14 vols. New York: William Durell. [1819].
Reprint of 1806.A3.

1819 B SHORTER WRITINGS

*1 HAZLITT, WILLIAM. "Lecture VI. On the English Novelists," in Lectures on the English Comic Writers. London: [?].
Reprints 1815.B1.
Available in several other editions: in vol. 8 of the 1903 Collected Works, edited by Waller and Glover (London: J. M. Dent); in vol. 6 of the 1931 Complete Works, edited by P. P. Howe (London: J. M. Dent); and in an Everyman's Library edition, 1955.

1820 A BOOKS

1 FIELDING, HENRY. Le Tom-Jones Des Enfants. [Translated by Bertin.] Paris and Berlin: La Prieur Libraire, 216 pp. [1820?].
Anonymous engravings. French translation.

2 _____. The History of the Adventures of Joseph Andrews, and His Friend Mr. Abraham Adams, in The British Novelists. Preface by Mrs. A. L. Barbauld. Vol. 18. London: F. C. and J. Rivington, et al., 434 pp.
Reissue of 1810.A2.

3 _____. The History of Tom Jones, A Foundling, in The British Novelists. With Preface by Mrs. A. L. Barbauld. Vols. 19-21. London: F. C. and J. Rivington, et al.
Reissue of 1810.A5.

1820 B SHORTER WRITINGS

1 ANON. "William Fielding, Esq." Gentleman's Magazine, 90, no. 2 (Oct.), 373-74.
Obituary for Henry Fielding's eldest son (a senior magistrate at Westminster); supplies family history.

2 FIELDING, HENRY. "Murders. True Examples of the Interposition of Providence in the Discovery and Punishment of Murder." Bath: S. Hazard; London: J. Marshall and R. White, 12 pp. [1820].
Put out by a religious tract society. No indication of copy text.

1821

1821 A BOOKS

1 FIELDING, HENRY. The Miser, in The New English Drama. Edited by W. Oxberry. Vol. 11. London: W. Simpkin, R. Marshall, and C. Chapple, 31 pp.

This edition "is faithfully marked with the stage business, and stage directions. As it is performed at the Theatre Royal." This "editing" was done by the actor William Oxberry. Each play separately paged.

2 _____. The Novels of Henry Fielding, Esq. [Preface by Sir Walter Scott.] Ballantyne's Novelist's Library. Vol. 1. London: Hurst, Robinson; Edinburgh: John Ballantyne, 822 pp.

Commends the utter Englishness of Fielding's novels, passes on the traditional sensational biography based on Murphy (1762.A10), attempts to understand the weakness of the dramas (intelligently distinguishes between the novel and drama, emphasizing the importance of the narrator in the reader's recreation of a novel), and reviews Fielding's career as a writer. Tom Jones is seen as the first English novel, and Scott particularly commends the mimetic qualities of its characters. Although a bit upset by the Man of the Hill digression and Tom's immoral behavior with Lady Bellaston, Scott defends the narrative strength of the novel and finds its coarseness a result of its milieu (in any case, he does not think literature either corrupts or purifies). Appears to reprint the Murphy edition (1762.A10) of Joseph Andrews, Tom Jones, Amelia, and Jonathan Wild. Includes a bibliography of Fielding's known works (to that time).

3 _____. The Works of Henry Fielding, Esq. With an Essay on His Life and Genius, by Arthur Murphy. Edited by Alexander Chalmers. 10 vols. London: F. C. and J. Rivington, et al.

Reprint of 1806.A3.

1821 B SHORTER WRITINGS - NONE

1822 A BOOKS

*1 FIELDING, HENRY. The Adventures of Joseph Andrews, and his Friend Mr. Abraham Adams. London: John Bumpus, et al., 405 pp.

Source: National Union Catalogue: Pre-1956 Imprints. Vol. 171, p. 677.

2 _____. The Tragedy of Tragedies; or the Life and Death of Tom Thumb the Great. Philadelphia: Thomas H. Palmer, 36 pp.

Prints the text and a few of the notes Fielding added to The Tragedy of Tragedies but not the preface. No indication of copy text.

1822 B SHORTER WRITINGS

1 FIELDING, HENRY. "The Preface of Fielding to the Increase of Robbers." Exeter: T. Besley, 15 pp.

Reprints the Enquiry into the Causes of the Late Increase of Robbers for "the Magistrates and Gentlemen of the County of Devon."

1823 A BOOKS

1 FIELDING, HENRY. The Adventures of Joseph Andrews, and His Friend Mr. Abraham Adams. London: C. S. Arnold, Simpkin and Marshall, et al., 372 pp.

No indication of copy text; printed in Chiswick by C. Whittingham.

2 _____. The History of Tom Jones, A Foundling. 4 vols. London: Samuel Richards.

Appears to reprint the third edition (12 April 1749). Illustrations by T. U. J. Stothard, A. W. Davis, and R. Westall.

3 _____. The History of Tom Jones, A Foundling. 2 vols. Chiswick: C. Whittingham, et al., 712 (352 & 360) pp.

Appears to reproduce the first edition.

4 _____. The Miser, in Oxberry English Drama. Edited by W. Oxberry. Boston: Wells and Lilly; New York: A. T. Goodrich, 52 pp.

Appears to reprint 1821.A1.

5 _____. Tom Jones, ou L'Enfant Trouvé. Translated by M. de la Place; illustrations by Choquet. 4 vols. Paris: Dalibon Parmantier.

Reprint of 1750 French translation.

1823 B SHORTER WRITINGS - NONE

1824

1824 A BOOKS

1 FIELDING, HENRY. The Miser, in The London Stage. Vol. 1. London: G. Balne, 16 pp. [1824].
No indication of copy text; separately paged.

2 _____. The Mock Doctor, in British Drama; A Collection of the Most Esteemed Tragedies, Comedies, Operas, and Farces, in the English Language. Vol. 1. London: Jones, pp. 700-708.
Omits the songs; no indication of copy text.

3 _____. The Works of Henry Fielding. 12 vols. London: Otridge and Rackham, Bult, et al.
Vol. 1 has a brief anonymous life taken from Murphy (1762.A10). Vol. 1: Love in Several Masques, The Temple Beau, The Author's Farce, The Pleasures of the Town, The Lottery, The Justice Caught in His Own Trap. Vol. 2: Tom Thumb, A New Way to Keep a Wife at Home, The Grub-Street Opera, The Modern Husbands, The Mock Doctor, The Covent-Garden Tragedy, The Debauchees. Vol. 3: The Miser, The Intriguing Chambermaid, Don Quixote in England, An Old Man Taught Wisdom, The Universal Gallant. Vol. 4: Historical Register, Eurydice, Eurydice Hissed, Tumble-Down Dick, Miss Lucy in Town, The Wedding Day, History of Jonathan Wild. Vol. 5: Journey to the Next World, Joseph Andrews. Vol. 6: Joseph Andrews, Tom Jones. Vols. 7-8: Tom Jones. Vol. 9: Tom Jones. Vol. 10: Tom Jones, "Philosophical Transactions for 1742-43," "First Olynthiac of Demosthenes," "Remedy of Affliction . . .," "Dialogue Between Alexander and Diogenes," "Interlude Between Jupiter . . .," The True Patriot, The Jacobite's Journal. Vols. 10-11: Amelia. Vol. 12: "Inquiry into the Causes of the Late Increase of Robbers," "An Essay on Conversation," "An Essay on the Characters of Men," The Covent-Garden Journal, "A Charge Delivered to the Grand Jury . . .," Journal of a Voyage to Lisbon, "Fragment of a Comment on Lord Bolingbroke's Essay . . .," "Preface to David Simple," "Preface to Familiar Letters."

4 _____. The Works of Henry Fielding. 12 vols. London: Richards.
Reprint of Murphy (1762.A10).

1824 B SHORTER WRITINGS - NONE

1825 A BOOKS

1 FIELDING, HENRY. The History of Joseph Andrews. The English Classics. London: Printed by J. F. Dove, 359 pp. [1825].
No indication of copy text.

2 _____. The History of Tom Jones, A Foundling. 2 vols. London: Baynes and Son, et al., 873 (443 & 430) pp.
Appears to reproduce the first edition.

3 _____. The Mock Doctor; or, The Dumb Lady Cur'd, in The London Stage. Vol. 2. London: G. Balne, pp. 11-16. [1825].
Paged together with Lodoiska, a melodrama in three acts. Omits the songs, although these plays are said to be "accurately printed from the acting copies, as performed at the Theatre Royal."

4 HOWARD, ALFRED, ed. The Beauties of Fielding. London: Thomas Tegg; Glasgow: R. Griffin; Dublin: J. Cumming, 192 pp. [1825].
Selections from Fielding arranged under various headings (game preserves, a proper choice of books, Miss Allworthy, Molly Seagrim's battle, etc.).

1825 B SHORTER WRITINGS

1 SCOTT, SIR WALTER. "Fielding," in his Lives of the Novelists. Paris: A. and W. Galignani, pp. 1-45.
Reprint of Preface to 1821.A2.
This collection has been reprinted several times and is also available in an Everyman's Library edition (1910 and 1928).

1826 A BOOKS

1 FIELDING, HENRY. Geschichte Tom Jones, eines Findlings. Translated by Wilhelm von Lüdemann. 4 vols. Leipzig: F. A. Brockhaus.
Part of the "Bibliothek classischer Romane und Novellen des Auslandes" series. German translation.

2 _____. The History of Tom Jones, A Foundling. London: Thomas Kelly, 624 pp.
Nine unsigned illustrations; appears to reprint the "1750" edition followed by Murphy (1762.A10).

1826

3 _____. The Intriguing Chambermaid, in The British Drama; A Collection of the Most Esteemed Tragedies, Comedies, Operas, and Farces, in the English Language. Vol. 2. London: Jones, pp. 1242-53.
Music not included. No indication of copy text, but a cast list from Covent Garden included.

4 _____. The Virgin Unmasked, in The London Stage. Vol. 3. London: G. Balne, pp. 11-16. [1826].
Paged together with The First Floor, a farce. Said to be printed "from the acting copies, as performed at the Theatre Royal."

1826 B SHORTER WRITINGS - NONE

1828 A BOOKS

*1 FIELDING, HENRY. The History of the Adventures of Joseph Andrews and his Friend Mr. Abraham Adams. Philadelphia: [?].
Source: National Union Catalogue: Pre-1956 Imprints. Vol. 171, p. 677.

2 _____. The History of Tom Jones, A Foundling. 4 vols. Philadelphia: J. J. Woodward.
Includes a brief biography and appears to reprint the "1750" edition followed by Murphy (1762.A10).

3 _____. Tom Jones, ou L'Enfant Trouvé. 6 vols. Paris: Chez Dauthereau.
French translation, introduced by a proposal for a translation by "E. T." and a preface attacking the de la Place translation. Also translates Sir Walter Scott's preface.

1828 B SHORTER WRITINGS - NONE

1829 A BOOKS

1 FIELDING, HENRY. The Miser, in Cumberland's British Theatre. Vol. 35. London: John Cumberland, 36 pp.
"Printed from the acting copy, with remarks, biographical and critical, by D. -----G." Like the Oxberry edition

(1821.A1), this includes stage business. One illustration of a stage set by Cruikshank. Separately paged.

2 HOWARD, ALFRED, ed. The Beauties of Fielding. Howard's Beauties of Literature. Vol. 29. London: Thomas Tegg; Glasgow: R. Griffin; Dublin: J. Cumming, 188 pp. [1829].
Reissue of 1825.A4.

1829 B SHORTER WRITINGS - NONE

1831 A BOOKS

*1 FIELDING, HENRY. The History of Joseph Andrews, and his friend Mr. Abraham Adams. Philadelphia: [?].
Probably a reissue of 1828.A1.
Source: National Union Catalogue: Pre-1956 Imprints. Vol. 171, p. 677.

2 _____. The History of Tom Jones, A Foundling. Life of the author by Sir Walter Scott. Baudry's Collection of Ancient and Modern British Authors. Vols. 4-5. Paris: Baudry's Foreign Library, 1053 (547 & 506) pp.
Appears to reprint the "1750" edition followed by Murphy (1762.A10), and Scott's introduction (1821.A2).

3 _____. The History of Tom Jones, A Foundling. Memoir by Thomas Roscoe and illustrations by George Cruikshank. The Novelist's Library. Vols. 5-6. London: James Cochrane and J. Andrews, 925 (477 & 448) pp.
"Memoir" based on Murphy (1762.A10); no indication of copy text.

4 _____. The History of Tom Jones a Foundling. With a portrait and illustrations by George Cruikshank. 2 vols. London: Hutchinson, 952 (477 & 475) pp.
Appears to reprint "1750" edition of Tom Jones, the same text Murphy (1762.A10) used.

1831 B SHORTER WRITINGS - NONE

1832 A BOOKS

1 FIELDING, HENRY. Select Works of Henry Fielding. "Memoir of the Life of the Author" by Sir Walter Scott and "Essay

on His Life and Genius" by Arthur Murphy. 2 vols. Philadelphia: Carey and Lea, 880 (424 & 456) pp.
Appears to reprint 1821.A2, adding Murphy's "Essay."

2 _____. The Adventures of Joseph Andrews. Illustrations by George Cruikshank. London: J. Cochrane, et al., 347 pp.
Appears to be the same printing as 1832.A4.

3 _____. The History of Amelia. Edited by Thomas Roscoe and illustrated by George Cruikshank. The Novelist's Library. Vols. 8-9. London: James Cochrane and J. Andrews, 659 (313 and 346) pp.
No indication of copy text.

4 _____. The History of Joseph Andrews and His Friend Mr. Abraham Adams. Illustrations by George Cruikshank. London: Hutchinson, 347 pp.
Appears to be a reprint of Murphy's text (1762.A10).

5 _____. Tom Jones, ou L'Enfant Trouvé. [Translated by de la Place.] Bibliothèque des Amis des Lettres. 4 vols. Paris: A. Hiard.
French translation.

1832 B SHORTER WRITINGS

1 CRUIKSHANK, GEORGE. "Fielding," in Illustrations of Smollett, Fielding, and Goldsmith, in a Series of Forty-One Plates. London: Charles Tilt, pp. 35-74.
Eight illustrations to Tom Jones, four to Joseph Andrews, and eight to Amelia, each with an accompanying extract to explain the subject.

2 PLANCHE, GUSTAVE. "Henry Fielding." Revue des deux mondes, 5, 339-358.
Attacks the de la Place (1750) translation of Tom Jones, which corrects the novel and adjusts it to French taste, recommending instead the more exact and complete translations by Laveaux or Cheron. In a biographical-critical appreciation of Fielding, Planche discusses Fielding's dramatic career (contrasting the qualities of a novelist with those of a dramatist), thinks Fielding generous to Richardson, praises Tom Jones for being as witty as Don Quixote and better organized, compares Blifil and Iago, defends Tom against charges of immorality, thinks Amelia a weak novel. Finally Planche compares Fielding's life with Goethe's. In French.

1833 A BOOKS

1 FIELDING, HENRY. Amélie Booth, Histoire Anglaise. 4 vols. Paris: A. Hiard.
Appears to be a reprint of the P. F. de Puisieux French translation.

2 _____. Jonathan Wild Le Grand. Paris: A. Hiard, 313 pp.
French translation.

3 _____. Julien L'Apostat, ou Voyage Dans L'Autre Monde. Paris: A. Hiard, 224 pp.
French translation of Journey from This World to the Next.

4 _____. Tom Jones, ou Histoire d'un Enfant Trouvé. [Translated by Count N. F. H. de Hucet de La Bédoyère.] Illustration by J. N. Moreau. 4 vols. Paris: Didot Frères.
French translation.

5 HOWARD, ALFRED, ed. The Beauties of Fielding. The Beauties of Literature. Vol. 6. London: Thomas Tegg; Glasgow: R. Griffin; Dublin: J. Cumming, 188 pp.
Reissue of 1825.A4.

1833 B SHORTER WRITINGS - NONE

1834 A BOOKS

1 FIELDING, HENRY. Amélie Booth. 4 vols. Paris: Lebigre Frères.
French translation.
Reissue of 1833.A1.

2 _____. A Journey from This World to the Next. London: J. Limbird, 51 pp.
No indication of copy text.

3 _____. Aventures de Joseph Andrews. 2 vols. Paris: Lebigre Frères, 508 (264 & 244) pp.
French translation.

4 _____. Jonathan Wild le Grand. Paris: Lebigre Frères, 313 pp.
French translation.
Reissue of 1833.A2.

1834

5 _____. Julien L'Apostat, ou Voyage Dans L'Autre Monde. Paris: Lebigre Frères, 224 pp.
French translation.
Reissue of 1833.A3.

6 _____. Select Works of Henry Fielding. "Memoir of the Life of the Author" by Sir Walter Scott and "Essay on His Life and Genius" by Arthur Murphy. 2 vols. Philadelphia: Carey and Lea, 880 pp.
Reissue of 1832.A1.

7 _____. The History of Tom Jones, A Foundling. 2 vols. London: Charles Daly, 987 (502 & 485) pp.
Brief anonymous life; appears to reprint "1750" edition followed by Murphy (1762.A10).

1834 B SHORTER WRITINGS - NONE

1836 A BOOKS

1 FIELDING, HENRY. Select Works of Henry Fielding. "Memoir of the Life of the Author" by Sir Walter Scott and "Essay on His Life and Genius" by Arthur Murphy. 2 vols. Philadelphia: Carey, Lea and Blanchard, 880 pp.
Reissue of 1832.A1.

2 _____. The History of the Adventures of Joseph Andrews, and His Friend Mr. Abraham Adams. Illustrations by George Cruikshank and biography by Thomas Roscoe. London: George Bell and Sons, 438 pp.
Reprints "the fifth edition, which appeared in the year 1751" and includes the memoir Roscoe later expanded as the preface to his edition of Fielding's Works (1840.A3).

*3 _____. The History of the Adventures of Joseph Andrews. Philadelphia: [?].
Source: National Union Catalogue: Pre-1956 Imprints. Vol. 171, p. 677.

4 _____. The History of Tom Jones, A Foundling. Memoir by Thomas Roscoe and illustrations by George Cruikshank. 2 vols. New York: Harper & Brothers, 841 (434 and 407) pp.
Roscoe's "memoir" was later expanded for 1840.A3. Same edition and illustrations as 1845.A2.

1836 B SHORTER WRITINGS

1 CUNNINGHAM, GEORGE G. "Henry Fielding," in his Lives of Eminent and Illustrious Englishmen from Alfred the Great to the Latest Times. Vol. 5. Glasgow: A. Fullarton, pp. 221-27.
The usual scandalous biography based on Murphy (1762.A10). More than usual attention is paid to his "ten years" as a playwright, but the plays are said to have been unpopular and undramatic ("practical stage effect appears not to have been his study," p. 223). Cunningham worries about his "lowness" and excuses some of his immorality by blaming the age in which he lived. See 1918.B1 and 1961.B13.

1837 A BOOKS

1 FIELDING, HENRY. The History of Amelia. Illustrations by George Cruikshank. New York: Harper & Brothers, 524 pp.
No indication of copy text.

1837 B SHORTER WRITINGS - NONE

1838 A BOOKS

1 FIELDING, HENRY. Select Works of Henry Fielding. "Memoir of the Life of the Author" by Sir Walter Scott and "Essay on His Life and Genius" by Arthur Murphy. 2 vols. Philadelphia: Lea and Blanchard, 880 pp.
Reissue of 1832.A1.

1838 B SHORTER WRITINGS - NONE

1840 A BOOKS

1 FIELDING, HENRY. The History of the Life of Jonathan Wild, The Great. Illustrations by "Phiz" [H. K. Browne]. London: Charles Daly, 391 pp.
No indication of copy text, but includes "Henry Humbug's" long "Contemporary Life of Jonathan Wild," as well as "Jonathan Wild's Advice to His Successor and Proposals for a Hospital for Decayed and Infirm Thief-

Takers." Also includes a note about Wild's skeleton from the Weekly Dispatch 22 March 1840.

2 _____. The History of the Life of Jonathan Wild, The Great. Illustrations by "Phiz" [H. K. Browne]. London: E. Churton, 391 pp.

Another issue of 1840.A1.

3 _____. The Works of Henry Fielding. Edited by Thomas Roscoe; illustrations by Cruikshank. London: Henry Washbourne, et al.; Glasgow, R. Griffin, 1144 pp.

Follows Murphy's (1762.A10) edition, adding "Essay on Nothing" and selections from Fielding's poems (quoted in the preface). The introduction is a critical biography based on Murphy, Chalmers (1806.A3), and Aikin (1803.B1) with a brief discussion of Fielding's poetry, which Roscoe compares with Swift's and Prior's. Throughout the preface Roscoe insists on the religious and moral basis of Fielding's art and on the "air of philanthropy through his work" (p. xxii). In Roscoe's softened view of Fielding, it is "the happy union, the rich contrast of lights and shadows which renders this great artist's works (for they are splendid emanations of art, and artistical, as the critic Goethe correctly expresses it, in the true sense of the word) so enduring in reputation" (p. v). For Roscoe, "many situations and sentiments [in Tom Jones] are touched with a delicate hand" (p. xxii).

1840 B SHORTER WRITINGS

1 [THACKERAY, W. M.]. Review of Fielding's Works in One Volume, With a Memoir of Thomas Roscoe." The Times (2 Sept.), p. 6.

Suggests that "boys and virgins" must read Fielding with caution but that he is "full of benevolence, practical wisdom, and generous sympathy with mankind." He defends Fielding's and Hogarth's satires (stronger than Dickens' and Cruikshank's) as the products of a "more free-spoken" age; he does not think his age better, only more discreet. "He tries to give you, as far as he knows it, the whole truth about human nature: the good and the evil of his characters are both practical." Throughout, Thackeray accepts the legend of the careless and hard-living man. He also dismisses his dramas as carelessly written, but points out the care with which Tom Jones was written (he sees no incident as superfluous--"not an incident ever so trifling but advances the story"--which is more than he can say for Cervantes, Smollett, or Scott). Thackeray is especially fond of Amelia; he praises it for its Christianity, its unequivocal attitude toward vice, its rich characterization (even the morally doubtful characters are given touches of goodness).

1841 A BOOKS

1 FIELDING, HENRY. Geschichte des Tom Jones, eines Findlings. Translated by A. Diezmann. 4 vols. Braunschweig: Verlag von Georg Westermann.

Four volumes separately paged, bound as two. Volume 4 dated 1842. Printed in Leipzig by E. Polz. German translation.

2 _____. The Works of Henry Fielding. Edited by Thomas Roscoe; illustrations by Cruikshank. London: Henry Washbourne, et al., 1144 pp.

Reissue of 1840.A3.

3 _____. Tom Jones, ou L'Enfant Trouvé. Translated by M. Léon de Wailly. 2 vols. Paris: Charpentier, 949 (485 & 464) pp.

Walter Scott's "life" is also translated into French and included in the first volume.

1841 B SHORTER WRITINGS

1 BARNES, W. "Fielding's House, at East Stower, Co. Dorset." Gentleman's Magazine, n.s. 15 (Feb.), 152-53.

Reprints a drawing of and describes the house at East Stower where Fielding "is supposed to have written his Joseph Andrews" (p. 152), although he did not "occupy it very long [after 1718], as he seems to have lived too much in the style of the Hunting Squire" (p. 152). See Cross 1918.A1.

1843 A BOOKS

1 FIELDING, HENRY. Select Works of Henry Fielding. "Memoir of the Life of the Author" by Sir Walter Scott and "Essay on His Life and Genius" by Arthur Murphy. Philadelphia: Lea and Blanchard, 880 pp.

Two-volume-in-one reissue of 1832.A1.

1843

2 _____. The History of the Life of Jonathan Wild, The Great. Illustrations by "Phiz." Halifax: W. Milner, 391 pp.
Reprint of 1840.A1.

*3 _____. The History of Tom Jones. Philadelphia: Lea and Blanchard, 424 pp.
Preface by Sir Walter Scott. Reissue of vol. 1 of 1832.A1.
Source: National Union Catalogue: Pre-1956 Imprints. Vol. 171, p. 685.

4 _____. The Works of Henry Fielding. Edited by Thomas Roscoe; illustrations by Cruikshank. London: Henry G. Bohn, 1144 pp.
Reissue of 1840.A3.

1843 B SHORTER WRITINGS - NONE

1844 A BOOKS

1 FIELDING, HENRY. The History of Tom Jones, A Foundling. Collection of British Authors. Vols. 60-61. Leipzig: Bernhard Tauchnitz, 899 (456 & 443) pp.
Includes a brief anonymous life that accepts the myth of the dissolute Fielding and appears to reprint the "1750" edition followed by Murphy (1762.A10).

1844 B SHORTER WRITINGS - NONE

1845 A BOOKS

1 FIELDING, HENRY. The History of the Life of Jonathan Wild, The Great. Illustrations by "Phiz." Halifax: W. Milner, 391 pp.
Reprint of 1840.A1.

2 _____. The Works of Henry Fielding. Edited by Thomas Roscoe and illustrated by George Cruikshank. London: Henry G. Bohn, 1144 pp.
Reissue of 1840.A3.

1845 B SHORTER WRITINGS - NONE

1846 A BOOKS

1 FIELDING, HENRY. Amelia. London: J. S. Pratt, 443 pp.
No indication of copy text.

1846 B SHORTER WRITINGS

1 PHILORÈTE, CHARLES. "Fielding et Richardson considérés dans leurs rapports avec le mouvement politique de l'Angleterre et due XVIIIe siècle," in Le XVIIIe siècle en Angleterre. Paris: Amyot, pp. 363-82.
A comparative study of their lives, suggesting that Fielding satirically protested against the puritanical manners and morals defended by Richardson. In French.

1848 A BOOKS

*1 FIELDING, HENRY. Eine Auswahl der Werke Fieldings. 3 vols. Braunschweig: Westermann.
Part of "Bibliothek der classischen Romantiker Altenglands." In German.
Source: National Union Catalogue: Pre-1956 Imprints. Vol. 171, p. 662.

2 _____. The Works of Henry Fielding. Edited by Thomas Roscoe and illustrated by George Cruikshank. London: H. G. Bohn, 1144 pp.
Reissue of 1840.A3.

*3 _____. Tom Džons. Roman v os'mnadtsati knigakh. 2 vols. St. Petersburg: [?].
Russian translation.
Source: Hugh Amory's working bibliography.

1848 B SHORTER WRITINGS - NONE

1849 A BOOKS

1 FIELDING, HENRY. Tom "Džhons": Roman. Translated by A. Kroneberg. St. Petersburg: V" Tipografii Eduarda Prada, 768 pp.
Russian translation of Tom Jones.

1849

1849 B SHORTER WRITINGS

1 [WHIPPLE, E. P.]. Review of The Works of Henry Fielding, with a Life of the Author. By Thomas Roscoe. London: Henry G. Bohn. 1843. 8 ov. pp. 1116." North American Review (Jan.), pp. 41-81.

Long review of a book originally published in 1840 (see 1840.A3). This early intelligent appreciation of Fielding discusses literature as historical artifact, compares Fielding to satirists of his time (commending him for his lack of spleen and egotism, despite his wide experience of the world), and provides a detailed biography interspersed with critical comments on his works (emphasizing his ability to create character). While accepting the myth of the dissipated Fielding, Whipple defends him against charges of artistic immorality (he was better than the "imbecile indecency" of many of his contemporaries; Tom Jones's "tone" is never sensual or malicious). He commends him for his philanthropy, for the weight and range of his intellectual perceptions, for his psychological subtlety (far greater than Addison's or Goldsmith's), and for his moral toleration.

1850 A BOOKS

1 FIELDING, HENRY. The History of the Life of Jonathan Wild, The Great. Illustrations by "Phiz." London: W. Tweedie, 391 pp. [1850].

Reprint of 1840.A1.

2 _____. The Intriguing Chambermaid, in The British Drama: A Collection of the Most Esteemed Tragedies, Comedies, Operas, and Farces, in the English Language. Philadelphia: Thomas Davis, pp. 435-45.

No music; no indication of copy text.

1850 B SHORTER WRITINGS - NONE

1851 A BOOKS

1 FIELDING, HENRY. The Works of Henry Fielding. Edited by Thomas Roscoe and illustrated by George Cruikshank. London: H. G. Bohn, 1144 pp.

Reissue of 1840.A3.

1851 B SHORTER WRITINGS - NONE

1852 A BOOKS

*1 FIELDING, HENRY. The Adventures of Joseph Andrews. New York: Stringer and Townsend, 142 pp.
Source: National Union Catalogue: Pre-1956 Imprints. Vol. 171, p. 677.

*2 _____. The History of Amelia. New York: Stringer and Townsend.
Source: National Union Catalogue: Pre-1956 Imprints. Vol. 171, p. 667.

3 _____. The Works of Henry Fielding. Edited by Thomas Roscoe and illustrated by George Cruikshank. London: H. G. Bohn, 1144 pp.
Reissue of 1840.A3.

1852 B SHORTER WRITINGS - NONE

1853 A BOOKS

1 FIELDING, HENRY. Geschichte Tom Jones, eines Findlings. Translated by Moriz Gans. Presth: Gustav Heckenast, 158 pp. [1853].
An abridged German translation for "Neues Lesekabinet für die reifere Jugend."

2 _____. The History of Joseph Andrews, and His Friend Mr. Abraham Adams. New York: Richard Marsh, 167 pp.
Printed together with The Voyage and Adventures of Capt. Robert Boyle; Also, The Extraordinary Trials of Miss Villars, and Their Wonderful Escape from Slavery In Barbary. Separately paged, Joseph Andrews is vol. 1 of this "two volumes in one" book. No indication of copy text.

*3 _____. The History of Joseph Andrews and his Friend Mr. Abraham Adams. Philadelphia: Leary & Gets.
Source: National Union Catalogue: Pre-1956 Imprints. Vol. 171, p. 677.

*4 ____. The History of the life of the late Mr. Jonathan Wild, the Great and A Journey from this world to the next.

New York: Stringer and Townsend.
Source: National Union Catalogue: Pre-1956 Imprints. Vol. 171, p. 694.

5 _____. The Works of Henry Fielding. Edited by Thomas Roscoe and illustrated by George Cruikshank. London: H. G. Bohn, 1144 pp.
Reissue of 1840.A3.

1853 B SHORTER WRITINGS

1 THACKERAY, W. M. "Hogarth, Smollett, and Fielding," in his English Humorists of the Eighteenth Century (5th lecture). London: Smith, Elder, pp. 219-68.
Sees the age as cruder than his own (fond of hangman's morality and downright Englishness) and Fielding as a manly but dissipated man of his age. Thackeray sees him in all his male heroes; "he is wild Tom Jones, he is wild Captain Booth" (p. 251). Thackeray's admiration for Fielding's natural love of truth and antipathy to hypocrisy is modified by his conviction that Fielding's ethical and moral sense was blunted by his life. Thus Tom Jones is Thackeray's least favorite Fielding hero, and Booth's repentance and Amelia's goodness "pleads for her reckless kindly old father, Harry Fielding" (p. 263).
Available in an Everyman edition and several others, including a 1916 Clarendon Press edition, edited by C. B. Wheeler. The 1885-91 Halle edition in six parts includes one of the earliest annotated Fielding bibliographies (mit bibliographischem Material, litterarischer Einleitung und sachlichen Anmerkungen . . .) by Ernst Regel.

1854 A BOOKS

1 FIELDING, HENRY. Tom Jones. Fortaelling. 2 vols. Copenhagen: Trykt hos S. B. Salomon, 674 (338 & 336) pp.
Danish translation; volume 2 was published in 1855.

1854 B SHORTER WRITINGS

1 LAWRENCE, FREDERICK. Henry Fielding - A Biography." Sharpe's London Magazine, n.s. 4 (Feb.-June), 73-79, 137-45, 203-11, 285-94, 337-47.
Later expanded and printed as The Life of Henry Fielding (1855.A1). Lawrence treats Fielding in the usual

way (as a solid realistic Englishman) and is upset by some of the moral looseness in Tom Jones.

2 SUARD, J. B. A. "Fielding, Henry," in Biographie Universelle. Paris: C. Desplace et Michaud, pp. 96-98.
Biography emphasizing Fielding's dissolute life. His dramas are dismissed as irregular; Joseph Andrews is thought to be his best novel; asserts that Tom Jones was criticized in England for its irregular hero but praised in France by de la Harpe; Fielding's strained relations with Richardson are mentioned. Appends a list of French and English editions of Fielding's works. The Biographie Universelle was first published in 1815. In French.

1855 A BOOKS

1 LAWRENCE, FREDERICK. The Life of Henry Fielding. London: Arthur Hall, Virtue, 384 pp.
Uses Fielding's works, "the newspapers and magazines of the period, . . . the works of contemporary memoir-writers" in order to set Fielding "in relation to his times and contemporaries, so that his works and character may be estimated by the standards of his age." Superseded by Cross (1918.A1). See 1855.B1 and 1858.B2.

1855 B SHORTER WRITINGS

1 [ELWIN, W.]. "Henry Fielding." Quarterly Review, 98 (Dec.), 100-148.
This long review of Lawrence's Life of Henry Fielding (1855.A1) is severe on Lawrence, objecting to his method of recounting the events surrounding Fielding. ("In order to get at the career of one man, we are compelled to read something about all the persons who flourished, and all the events which happened, in his age," p. 100) and the fanciful inaccuracies in the biography. Elwin then sets out the biographical "facts" about Fielding and briefly discusses his works. Love in Several Masques, which he sees as unsuccessfully modeled on Congreve, he calls "a cold, unreal, insipid world" (p. 104). He finally thinks that Fielding's wit is "far·racier and more abundant than that of his master" (p. 104), but that his strength was not in drama (where "to supply the deficiency of wit he seasoned his plays with the grossest indecorums," p. 106). He sets Joseph Andrews in its biographical context (models for the characters come from Fielding's life)

and in its literary context (as a parody of Pamela). Elwin thinks the Miscellanies prove that Fielding was no poet, that Jonathan Wild rises above particular political satire. He reverses Johnson's dictum and says "that there [is] more knowledge of the heart in particular chapters of Tom Jones than in all Sir Charles Grandison, Clarissa, and Pamela" (p. 142). Elwin sets out the best eighteenth- and nineteenth-century views of Fielding (Warton, Richardson, Grey, Johnson, Thackeray, Scott, and especially Murphy), defending Fielding ("There is no need to take him for a text, and deduce a moral from his life," p. 139) and commending him for the Englishness of his natural and unique characters (to be compared to Don Quixote and Falstaff), for his simple and masculine style, for his ability to build incidents around central characters like Adams, and for the wit of his narration. He thinks the weakening in Amelia the result of Fielding's physical breakdown. This city novel (unlike Fielding's earlier country novels) has a weak and "contemptible" hero who "will be duped by rogues and led astray by profligates to the close of his days" (p. 147).

Reprinted 1902.B2.

2 [PATMORE, C.]. "Fielding and Thackeray." North British Review, 24 (Nov.), 197-216.

This long review of Lawrence's (1855.A1) Life of Fielding and Thackeray's The Newcomes sets out the difference between the realism of the two, suggesting that Fielding's is a more accurate description of what chiefly consumes the "moral energies of almost all men during . . . the most dramatic years of their lives" (p. 200), and that nineteenth-century "refinement" is really very shallow. He calls Fielding's novels nearly flawless demonstrations of "what is gracious in human life" and feels "he comprehended and loved the source of that graciousness" (p. 203). Reviews Fielding's life, answering the charge of immorality by asserting that "no grossness is ever to be detected in the works of Fielding [including his plays], introduced simply for its own sake" (p. 205). He also praises Lawrence's treatment of Fielding.

3 P., P. T. "Woodfall's Ledger, 1734-1747." Notes and Queries, 1st. series, 11 (2 June), 418-20.

A brief extract from the printer Woodfall's ledger on the first printing of Joseph Andrews for Andrew Miller. 1500 were printed; three months later a "2nd edit." of 2000 was printed.

1856 A BOOKS

1 FIELDING, HENRY. The History of Amelia. Illustrations by George Cruikshank. New York: Harper & Brothers, 524 pp.
Reissue of 1837.A1.

1856 B SHORTER WRITINGS

1 B., A. "Facetious Writer." Notes and Queries, 2nd. series, 1 (31 May), 441.
Suggests that the allusion (1856.B2) is meant as a trap for the literal reader.

2 B., J. "Facetious Writer." Notes and Queries, 2nd. series, 1 (19 April), 313.
Asks to have an allusion to "the late facetious writer" in vol. 1 of Tom Jones explained. See 1856.B1.

1857 A BOOKS

1 FIELDING, HENRY. The Adventures of Joseph Andrews. Illustrations by "Phiz" [H. K. Browne]. London and New York: G. Routledge, 269 pp.
No indication of copy text.

2 _____. The History of Amelia. Illustrations by "Phiz" [H. K. Browne]. London and New York: G. Routledge, 406 pp.
No indication of copy text.

3 _____. The History of Tom Jones, A Foundling. Illustrations by "Phiz" [H. K. Browne], and an introduction by G. H. T[ownsend]. London and New York: G. Routledge, 640 pp.
Appears to reprint the "1750" edition followed by Murphy (1762.A10). Townsend relies on Murphy for his biographical "introduction."

*4 _____. The History of Tom Jones, a Foundling. Memoir by Thomas Roscoe. New York: Derby & Jackson.
Probably a reissue in one volume of 1836.A4. Issued without illustrations. See Roscoe (1840.A3).
Source: National Union Catalogue: Pre-1956 Imprints. Vol. 171, p. 685.

5 _____. The Miscellaneous Works of Henry Fielding. Memoir by Thomas Roscoe. 4 vols. New York: Derby & Jackson.

Vol. 1-2: Tom Jones. Vol. 3: Joseph Andrews and Jonathan Wild. Vol. 4: Amelia. See Roscoe (1831.A3).

1857 B SHORTER WRITINGS - NONE

1858 A BOOKS - NONE

1858 B SHORTER WRITINGS

1 JEAFFRESON, J. C. "Henry Fielding," in his Novels and Novelists, from Elizabeth to Victoria. Vol. 1. London: Hurst and Blackett, pp. 91-117.

A brief biography which passes on and embroiders the Fielding myth. Prefers Amelia to Tom Jones; thinks Fielding disgraced his respectability with his "Newgate calendar sketch," Jonathan Wild (p. 103); constantly confuses Fielding with his rake heroes.

2 KEIGHTLEY, THOMAS. "On the Life and Writings of Henry Fielding." Fraser's Magazine, 57, no. 337 (Jan.), 1-13.

Responding to Lawrence's (1855.A1) biography, Keightley sets out the facts of Fielding's life (as then known), carefully testing the authenticity of some of Murphy's anecdotes, but essentially accepting the legend of the dissipated youth. Keightley's first essay ends with the death of Fielding's first wife and says nothing about his works, merely providing factual information about his dramas.

Reprinted 1907.A9. See 1918.A1.

3 _____. "On the Life and Writings of Henry Fielding." Fraser's Magazine, 57, no. 338 (Feb.), 205-17.

This essay completes the account of Fielding's life and provides a brief criticism of Joseph Andrews, Jonathan Wild, Tom Jones, and Amelia. Keightley begins by simply asserting that "it is well known that he failed as a dramatist, and . . . that he had eminent success as a novelist" (p. 211). He discusses Joseph Andrews as a parody of Pamela (thinking that Fielding's novel "offends delicacy" in scene and language); he discusses the political satire in Jonathan Wild; he discusses the Tom and Blifil contrast in Tom Jones (like Edgar and Edmund in Lear), the careful plot and occasional anachronism, Tom's sexual irregularity (which he dismisses as a matter of cultural difference); he finds Amelia a serious falling off, offering as proof

Fielding's borrowing characters from his plays and several "improbabilities." Continuation of 1858.B2. Reprinted 1907.A9.

4 _____. "Postscript to Mr. Keightley's Articles on Henry Fielding." Fraser's Magazine, 57, no. 342 (June), 762-63.

Adds a few notes: on Fielding's attempted abduction of Miss Andrews; on Murphy's story of Fielding's country squire extravagance and Fielding's liveries; on the date of his second marriage; on the probability of Jonathan Wild being written in anger after the Licensing Act; on Fielding and Lyttleton climbing Mazzard Hill. Continuation of 1858.B2. Reprinted 1907.A9.

1859 A BOOKS

1 FIELDING, HENRY. The History of Amelia. Illustrations by George Cruikshank. New York: Derby & Jackson, 524 pp.

No indication of copy text.

*2 _____. The History of Tom Jones, a Foundling. London: C. Courtier, 380 pp. [1859?].

Source: National Union Catalogue: Pre-1956 Imprints. Vol. 171, p. 685.

*3 _____. The History of Tom Jones, a Foundling. Memoir by Thomas Roscoe and illustrations by George Cruikshank. New York: Derby & Jackson.

Reissue of 1857.A4.

Source: National Union Catalogue: Pre-1956 Imprints. Vol. 171, p. 685.

4 _____. The Works of Henry Fielding. Edited by Thomas Roscoe and illustrated by George Cruikshank. London: H. G. Bohn, 1144 pp.

Reissue of 1840.A3.

5 _____. Works of Henry Fielding. "Memoir of the Life . . . of the Author" by Sir Walter Scott and "Essay on His Life and Genius" by Arthur Murphy. Illustrations by Cruikshank. New York: G. A. Leavitt & Allen, 931 pp. [1859].

No indication of copy text but appears to be Murphy (1762.A10). Odd pagination: two "Memoirs" and Tom Jones paged continuously, 424 pp.; Joseph Andrews, Amelia, Jonathan Wild, and Journey From This World to the Next, 507 pp.

Even this is irregular (e.g., Joseph Andrews, pp. 9-142; Amelia, pp. 149-375; Jonathan Wild, pp. 381-456). Scott's "Essay" taken from 1821.A2.

1859 B SHORTER WRITINGS

1 K., T. "Cibber's Apology." Notes and Queries, 2nd. series, 8 (15 Oct.), 317.
Finds allusion for F. S. (1859.B6) and defends Cibber.

2 "LIBYA." "Cibber's Apology." Notes and Queries, 2nd. series, 8 (15 Oct.), 317.
The allusion F. S. (1859.B6) wants is in Joseph Andrews I, i. "Libya" also points out other allusions to Cibber in the novel.

3 MASSON, DAVID. "British Novelists of the Eighteenth Century," in his British Novelists and their Styles: Being a Critical Sketch of the History of British Prose Fiction. Cambridge and London: Macmillan, pp. 121-44.
Linking Fielding and Smollett, Masson constantly compares them to Richardson, repeating in a variety of ways the following observation: "It does seem to me that both Fielding and Smollett--broader as they are than Richardson, more rich, more various, more interesting--did work more according to the method of sheer superficial observation and the record of humours presented to their hand, and less according to the method of ideal development from within outwards" (pp. 135-36). Both are epic "after the comic fashion" (p. 132). As between Fielding and Smollett, Fielding is the more careful artist and the more joyous humorist.

4 MORLEY, HENRY. "Notes on Bartholomew Fair." Notes and Queries, 2nd. series, 7 (11 June), 472.
Agrees with Rimbault (1859.B5) that Fielding kept booths at fairs until 1736. See 1875.B2 for a refutation.

5 RIMBAULT, EDWARD F. "Gleanings for the History of Bartholomew Fair." Notes and Queries, 2nd. series, 7 (21 May), 411.
Says that Henry Fielding had booths at Bartholomew, Southwark, and Tottenham-Court Fairs before he went to the Middle Temple. See 1875.B2 for a refutation and 1966.B2 for a continuation.

6 S., F. "Cibber's 'Apology.'" Notes and Queries, 2nd. series, 8 (1 Oct.), 268.

Asks to have the allusion to Cibber in Tom Jones identified. See 1859.B1 and 1859.B2.

1860 A BOOKS

1 FIELDING, HENRY. The History of the Life of Jonathan Wild, the Great. Illustrations by "Phiz" [H. K. Browne]. London: Hodgson and Jones, 391 pp. [1860].
Reprint of 1840.A1.

1860 B SHORTER WRITINGS

1 [LEWES, G. H.]. "A Word about Tom Jones." Blackwood's Edinburgh Magazine, 87, no. 533 (March), 331-41.
Asks "whether the work deserves its reputation as a masterpiece of comic fiction" (p. 331). He thinks it does not, merely crediting Fielding with "a real talent for story-telling . . . an eye for characteristics in person, manner and speech, and a style easy, idiomatic and vigorous. . . . But these merits, exaggerate them as we may, do not suffice for a masterpiece" (p. 333). Applying as a touchstone, the aesthetic principle of economy and selection (each scene, each character, each word must be appropriate and incapable of being "cut out without rendering the story less intelligible," p. 333), Tom Jones is "very ill-constructed" (p. 335) and "an immense proportion . . . is episodical" (p. 336). He then illustrates digressions (Mrs. Fitzpatrick's) and irrelevant events (the puppet show at the inn and the gypsies). He thinks the secret of Tom's parentage is clumsily solved, and "excites no interest at all, after the first chapter." Lewes then attacks the accepted notion that Fielding had a "Shakespearean insight into character" (p. 337). He thinks morally pure and elevated characters like Allworthy are mawkish. "Fielding seems to have been a man of acute observation, of hearty kindliness, and generous impulse, but of a nature neither deep nor many-sided" (p. 337). With the exception of "Western," he considers Fielding's characters caricatures, and finds their actions often "stagy and inartistic" (p. 338). Though Fielding's burlesque style is adequate, his poetic style (the description of Sophia) is "maudlin." In short, Lewes thinks that Tom Jones is not well made; it has "liveliness, coarse fun, and irony, but not . . . fine humour" (p. 340), and it lacks both poetry and sentiment. A carefully argued attack.

1861

1861 A BOOKS

1 FIELDING, HENRY. The Adventures of Joseph Andrews. Illustrations by "Phiz" [H. K. Browne]. London: G. Routledge, 269 pp.

Reissue of 1857.A1.

2 _____. The Miscellaneous Works of Henry Fielding. Memoir by Thomas Roscoe. 4 vols. New York: Derby & Jackson.

Reissue of 1857.A5.

1861 B SHORTER WRITINGS - NONE

1862 A BOOKS

*1 FIELDING, HENRY. Tom Jones, of de totgevallen van een vondeling. Translated by Dr. M. P. Lindo. 3 vols. Haarlem: A. C. Kruseman.

The British Museum has lost its copy of this Dutch translation.

1862 B SHORTER WRITINGS

1 FOSS, EDWARD. "Henry Fielding: Sir Henry Gould." Notes and Queries, 3rd. series, 2 (23 Aug.), 146.

Attempts to work out Fielding's relationship to the Goulds. See 1862.B2 and 1862.B3, and 1918.A1.

2 KEIGHTLEY, THOMAS. "Henry Fielding: Sir Henry Gould." Notes and Queries, 3rd. series, 2 (6 Sept.), 199.

Offers the suggestion that Sir Henry Gould was Henry Fielding's cousin.

3 O., S. "Henry Fielding: Sir Henry Gould." Notes and Queries, 3rd. series, 2 (11 Oct.), 299.

Suggests that Middle Temple records be checked for the name of Henry's father.

1863 A BOOKS - NONE

1863 B SHORTER WRITINGS

1 KEIGHTLEY, THOMAS. "Tom Jones." Notes and Queries, 3rd. series, 3 (30 May), 424-25.

Notices three errors in Tom Jones. Although Books 5 through 8 contain about four weeks, from the "latter end of June" until presumably late July, Book 8, chapter 9 has Tom leaving Gloucester in "midwinter." The second error is Sophia's sending Jones all her money, then losing the money given her by her father in her fall from her horse, and yet never running short of money. The third error is topographical. The characters cross the River Avon where there was no bridge, and the way to London seems confused. Suggests that the first and third confusions were probably the results of Fielding having begun the book, set it aside, and begun it again, as well as of Fielding's desire, when he began it again, to set it during the 1745 uprising.

Answered by Dickson 1914.B10 and B11. Some of this had earlier been observed 1791.B1.

2 LANGDON, AUGUSTUS. "Joseph Andrews." Notes and Queries, 3rd. series, 3 (4 April), 279.

Answers L's (1863.B3) question about the Aristotle allusion.

3 L. "Notes and Queries on 'Joseph Andrews.'" Notes and Queries, 3rd. series, 3 (14 Feb.), 122-23.

Asks to have an allusion to Aristotle in Adams' conversation with an innkeeper cleared up. Offers the meaning of an obscure word (hagged); identifies a painter and an allusion to Aristotle in a passage from Book 3, chapter 6. See 1863.B2.

4 TAINE, H. A. "Fielding," in his Histoire de la Littérature Anglaise. Vol. 3. Paris: Librairie de L. Hachette, pp. 318-30.

Accepting the myth of the jovial, vital English rake, Taine sets Fielding in opposition to Richardson. He links his hearty laughter with Rabelais and Scarron and his exposure of vice and hypocrisy with Molière. He particularly praises Fielding for his Rubens-like quality, not quite fit for ladies, and his vital characters like Western (a wild and brutal Englishman). He also discusses the instinctive good-hearted virtue of Fielding's heroes (their John Bullish decency is Fielding's morality) and their unfortunate lack of poetic rapture and nervous sensibility. For an early response to this "essay," see 1874.B1.

1864

Translated by Henry Van Laun and published in The World's Great Classics. New York and London: The Colonial Press, 1900; also published London: Chatto & Windus, 1907.

1864 A BOOKS - NONE

1864 B SHORTER WRITINGS

1 MIDDLETON, A. B. "Passage in 'Tom Jones.'" Notes and Queries, 3rd. series, 5 (7 May), 385.
Identifies Dowdy as one of the Salisbury Sergeants at Mace.

2 S., J. "Passage in 'Tom Jones.'" Notes and Queries, 3rd. series, 5 (5 Mar.), 193.
Asks about allusion to Dowdy in Book 6, chapter 9. See 1864.B1.

1866 A BOOKS

1 FIELDING, HENRY. The History of Tom Jones A Foundling. World-Wide Library. 2 vols. London and New York: George Routledge & Sons, 353 (177 & 176) pp. [1866].
Appears to be a reprint of Fielding's revised 1749 "third" edition.

2 _____. The Novels of Henry Fielding. Illustrated by George Cruikshank. London: Bell and Daldy, 539 pp. [1866].
Includes Tom Jones, Joseph Andrews, and Amelia. No indication of copy text.

1866 B SHORTER WRITINGS - NONE

1867 A BOOKS

1 FIELDING, HENRY. The History of Tom Jones, A Foundling. Memoir by G. H. T[ownsend]. London and New York: George Routledge & Sons, 638 pp. [1867].
Reissue of 1857.A3 as part of "Routledge's Railway Library."

1867 B SHORTER WRITINGS - NONE

1868 A BOOKS

1 FIELDING, HENRY. The History of Tom Jones, A Foundling. World-Wide Library. 2 vols. London: George Routledge and Sons, 353 (177 & 176) pp. [1868].
Reissue of 1866.A1.

1868 B SHORTER WRITINGS - NONE

1869 A BOOKS

1 FIELDING, HENRY. The Complete Works of Henry Fielding. Edited by Thomas Roscoe and illustrated by George Cruikshank. London: Bell and Daldy, 1144 pp.
Reissue of 1840.A3. Novels illustrated by Cruikshank.

2 _____. Works of Henry Fielding. "Memoir of the Life . . . of the Author" by Sir Walter Scott and "Essay on His Life and Genius" by Arthur Murphy. New York: G. A. Leavitt & Allen, 931 pp. [1869].
Reissue of [1859].A5.

1869 B SHORTER WRITINGS - NONE

1870 A BOOKS

1 FIELDING, HENRY. The Complete Works of Henry Fielding. Edited by Thomas Roscoe and illustrated by George Cruikshank. London: Bell and Daldy, 1144 pp.
Reissue of 1840.A3. Novels illustrated by Cruikshank.

2 _____. Works of Henry Fielding. "Memoir of the Life . . . of the Author" by Sir Walter Scott and "Essay on His Life and Genius" by Arthur Murphy. New York: G. Routledge and Sons, 931 pp. [1870].
Reissue of [1859].A5.

1870 B SHORTER WRITINGS

1 ANON. "Henry Fielding," in Episodes of Fiction or Choice Stories from the Great Novelists. Edinburgh: William P. Nimmo, pp. 53-67.

1871

A brief life, in which he quotes Thackeray's disparagement with approval and yet commends Fielding as a creator of comic characters. Prints Adams' encounter with the hounds in Joseph Andrews.

1871 A BOOKS

*1 FIELDING, HENRY. The History of Tom Jones, a Foundling. Boston: Page, 512 pp.
Source: National Union Catalogue: Pre-1956 Imprints. Vol. 171, p. 685.

2 _____. The Miser, in Dicks' British Drama. Vol. 6. London: John Dicks, pp. 277-88.
No indication of copy text.

3 _____. The Mock Doctor; or The Dumb Lady Cur'd, in Dicks' British Drama. Vol. 9. London: John Dicks, pp. 153-60.
No indication of copy text.

4 _____. The Virgin Unmasked, in Dicks' British Drama. Vol. 8. London: John Dicks, pp. 122-28.
No indication of copy text; music not included.

5 _____. The Works of Henry Fielding. Edited by George Saintsbury and illustrated by George Cruikshank. 12 vols. London: Bickers & Son.
Vols. 1-6 Tom Jones; vols. 7-8 Joseph Andrews; vols. 9-11 Amelia; vol. 12 Jonathan Wild. No indication of copy text.

6 _____. The Works of Henry Fielding, Esq. With an Essay on His Life and Genius by Arthur Murphy. Edited by James P. Browne. 10 vols. London: Bickers and Son, H. Sotheran.
Reprints Chalmers' text (1806.A3). Browne's introduction describes Fielding as "characteristically straightforward" (p. ix), an attacker of vice and hypocrisy, and a creator of varied characters from life (justifying his occasional indecency). He argues for Fielding's high moral purpose, for the essential decency of Tom (he is passive in his sexual encounters), and for Fielding's natural male vigor. Browne specifically disagrees with Thackeray's assessment of Tom Jones, seeing the novel as a novel of education.

1871 B SHORTER WRITINGS

1 FORSYTH, WILLIAM. "Fielding. - Tom Jones, A Favourite of the Ladies. - Joseph Andrews. - Amelia," in his The Novels and Novelists of the Eighteenth Century, in Illustration of the Manners and Morals of the Age. London: John Murray, pp. 258-77.

Although Forsyth feels that leaving Richardson for Fielding is coming out of "the sick-room for the open common," he is almost unable to discuss Tom Jones for fear of "offending against the respect due to female delicacy now" (p. 258). He thinks his grandmothers might, and did, read the novel without harm, but he quotes Thackeray with approval ("the great humourist's moral sense was blunted by his life," p. 262). Merely quoting Lamb and Coleridge on Fielding, he offers several examples of the mock-heroic and some examples (from Western) of "wit and fun" (p. 267). He appreciates the character of Adams and thinks the adventures in Joseph Andrews low, offering the hog's blood fight and the mix-up in Fanny's bedroom as examples. In Amelia "there is much less coarseness, and also less licentiousness" (p. 274), but it "is not a comic novel" (p. 275). Forsyth quotes Richardson's evaluation of the novel with approval.

1872 A BOOKS

1 FIELDING, HENRY. Miscellanies and Poems. Edited by James P. Browne. London: Bickers and Son, H. Sotheran; Boston: Little, Brown, 226 pp.

Reprints "A Clear State of the Case of Elizabeth Canning . . .," "A True State of the Case of Bosavern Penlez . . .," the preface to the 1743 Miscellanies and the poems from the first volume. The preface defends Fielding as a magistrate and commends the "spirit of true philosophy" (p. xvii) in his poems. No indication of copy text.

2 _____. The Writings of Henry Fielding. With a memoir by David Herbert. Edinburgh: William P. Nimmo, 703 pp.

Includes a brief biographical sketch and modernized texts of Joseph Andrews, Tom Jones, and Amelia. Appears to follow the Murphy (1762.A10) edition.

1872

3 _____. Tom Jones čili Příbehové Nalezence. Translated by Primus Sobotka. 3 vols. Prague: Theodor Mourek.
Czech translation of Tom Jones.

1872 B SHORTER WRITINGS

1 CLARKE, CHARLES C. "Fielding, Smollett and Sterne," part 14 of his On The Comic Writers of England. Gentleman's Magazine, 232 (May), 556-80.
An enthusiastic appreciation of Fielding's characters, which "reveal to us the penetralia of the human heart, its secret and profound movements" (p. 557). He notices that Fielding is little concerned with narrative description of scene or character ("Fielding had very little external imagination") and that he is concerned "solely with human nature" (p. 558). He defends Tom's moral lapses by pointing to his "open, liberal, and humane" (p. 560) nature; he notices that for Fielding "the ne plus ultra of perfection in woman consists in implicit yielding" (citing Sophia, Amelia, and Mrs. Heartfree). Finally, he examines Fielding's ability to perceive ironically the niceties of character and human nature, particularly in Jonathan Wild.

1874 A BOOKS - NONE

1874 B SHORTER WRITINGS

1 SMITH, GEORGE B. "Our First Great Novelist." Macmillan's Magazine, 30, no. 175 (May), 1-18.
Smith considers Fielding "the Shakespeare of novelists" (p. 1) because of his wide and continuing appeal. He begins his defense of Fielding by setting aside the criticism of Samuel Johnson and Horace Walpole, by sympathetically relating the trying events of Fielding's life (although Smith relies on Murphy), and by asserting his superiority to Defoe in the mimetic creation of character and to Richardson in his ability to embody moral values. He commends Fielding for his Englishness and defends Tom Jones as one of the purest books "in its general tendency" (p. 10). Smith also defends Fielding against Taine's charge that he wants refinement (1863.B4) and points out his ability to create morally mixed characters. Throughout, Smith compares Fielding to Cervantes and emphasizes both the seriousness of his satiric intention and his humor (which is without "the slightest tinge of

bitterness," p. 13). He also briefly comments on his poetry and drama, commending Fielding's satiric plays like Pasquin. An effective early defense.
Reprinted 1875.B3.

1875 A BOOKS

1 FIELDING, HENRY. The History of Tom Jones a Foundling. Introduction by G. H. T[ownsend]. London and New York: George Routledge & Sons, 638 pp. [1875].
Reprint of 1857.A3.

2 _____. The Miser. French's Acting Edition of Plays. Vol. 103. London and New York: Samuel French, 36 pp. [1875].
Reprint of 1829.A1. Engraving by Cruikshank.

3 _____. Works of Henry Fielding. "Memoir of the Life . . . of the Author" by Sir Walter Scott and "Essay on His Life and Genius" by Arthur Murphy. New York: World Publishing House, 931 pp.
Reissue of [1859].A5 without Cruikshank illustrations but with the same irregular pagination.

1875 B SHORTER WRITINGS

1 JESSE, J. HENEAGE. "Henry Fielding," in his Memoirs of Celebrated Etonians. Vol. 1. London: Richard Bentley and Son, pp. 62-88.
The usual scandalous biography, based largely on Murphy (1762.A10) and Scott (1821.A2), but it includes an unpublished letter from Fielding to his half-brother John, written during Henry's final voyage to Lisbon. See 1918.B1.

2 LATREILLE, FREDERICK. "Henry Fielding and Timothy Fielding." Notes and Queries, 5th. series, 3 (26 June), 502-503.
An actor named Timothy Fielding began his career at about the same time as Henry Fielding, and they are often confused. It was Timothy who was mentioned in advertisements for the Haymarket in 1728 and later at Drury Lane. He also took booths at the fairs and the Buffalo Head Tavern in October of 1733. See 1859.B4, B5, and 1966.B2.

1875

3 SMITH, GEORGE B. "Henry Fielding," in his Poets and Novelists. A Series of Literary Studies. London: Smith, Elder, pp. 251-306.
Reprints 1874.B1.

1876 A BOOKS

1 FIELDING, HENRY. The History of the Adventures of Joseph Andrews, and His Friend Mr. Abraham Adams. Illustrations by George Cruikshank and biography by Thomas Roscoe. Bohn's Novelists' Library. London: George Bell and Sons, 433 pp.
Reissue of 1836.A2.

2 _____. The History of Tom Jones, A Foundling. Illustrations by George Cruikshank. Bohn's Novelists' Library. 2 vols. London: George Bell and Sons, 980 (498 & 482) pp.
Appears to reprint the 1749 "third" edition.

1876 B SHORTER WRITINGS

1 STEPHEN, LESLIE. "Fielding," in his History of English Thought in the Eighteenth Century. Vol. 2. London: Smith, Elder, pp. 376-80.
An early version of the standard defense of Fielding as a conveyor of ethical values ("the code by which men of sense generally govern their conduct, as distinguished from that by which they affected to be governed in language," p. 377). Stephen thinks that though Fielding lacked delicacy of perception, he was a great moral realist who defended homely virtues and who was "for a stringent enforcement of the moral laws, which actually keep society together," although he "has no patience with those who would attempt any radical reform, or draw the line higher than ordinary human nature can endure" (p. 378).
Reprinted often (three times by 1902).

1877 A BOOKS

1 FIELDING, HENRY. Amelia. Illustrations by George Cruikshank. Bohn's Novelists' Library. London: George Bell and Sons, 608 pp.
See 1884.A1.

2 _____. The Writings of Henry Fielding. Memoir by David Herbert. London and Edinburgh: William P. Nimmo, 703 pp.
Reissue of 1872.A2.

1877 B SHORTER WRITINGS

1 BOBERTAG, F. "Zur Characteristik Henry Fieldings." Englische Studien, 1:317-50.
Discusses the peculiarly English Protestant basis of Fielding's morality, and particularly his attack on hypocrisy. By outlining Fielding's critical theory of the comic and the tragic and by examining the "good" and "bad" characters in his novels, Bobertag argues that Fielding's aesthetic theories are so closely related to his general philosophy that it is impossible to speak of one independently of the other. In German. See 1959.A1.

2 STEPHEN, LESLIE. "Hours in a Library. Fielding's Novels." Cornhill Magazine, 35 (Feb.), 154-71.
Establishes Fielding as the head of the tradition that includes Thackeray and Scott and distinguishes him from his contemporaries Smollett and Richardson. Stephen sees Fielding's novels "as genuine studies in psychological analysis" (p. 179), but the analysis is quite different from Richardson's. Fielding's comes from a deep knowledge "drawn from observation rather than intuitive sympathy" (p. 181). Stephen goes on to discuss Fielding's "masculine" perception, his keen observation of "man in his domestic relations," and his unwillingness to dramatize "man as he appears in the presence of the infinite, and therefore with the deepest thoughts and loftiest imaginings of the great poets and philosophers" (p. 187). Stephen distinguishes his conception of Fielding's John Bullish "solid good sense" (p. 192) from Taine's (1863.B4) by discussing the conflict of ethics and morality in the novels and the way in which moral action and character are at one in his novels. Distinguishes between Scott, whom he thinks better as a social novelist, and Fielding, who absorbs us in the play of his characters' "passions and the conflict of their motives" (p. 206).

1878 A BOOKS

1 FIELDING, HENRY. The History of Tom Jones, A Foundling. 2 vols. London: Bickers and Son, 1159 (582 & 577) pp.

Appears to reproduce the "1750" edition followed by Murphy (1762.A10).

1878 B SHORTER WRITINGS - NONE

1879 A BOOKS

1 FIELDING, HENRY. Amelia. Illustrations by Cruikshank. New York: R. Worthington, 657 pp.
No indication of copy text.

2 _____. The History of Joseph Andrews. Illustrations by Cruikshank. New York: Gates, 394 pp.
Appears to be the same issue as 1880.A1.

3 _____. The History of Tom Jones, A Foundling. Illustrations by Cruikshank. 2 vols. New York: R. Worthington, 1084 (544 & 540) pp.
Called Fielding's Works on spine. Appears to reprint the first edition; reproduces Coleridge's notes in an appendix. Same edition as 1880.A1.

*4 _____. The History of Tom Jones, a Foundling. New York: Gates.
Source: National Union Catalogue: Pre-1956 Imprints. Vol. 171, p. 685.

1879 B SHORTER WRITINGS

1 BEDE, CUTHBERT. "Fielding the Novelist." Notes and Queries, 5th. series, 12 (26 July), 76.
Corrects I. P.'s (1879.B5) citation of the length of the Canning pamphlet.

2 HETTNER, HERMANN J. T. "Fielding," in his Die englische Literatur von 1669-1700. Vol. I of his Literaturgeschichte des achtzehnten Jahrhunderts. Braunschweig: Friedrich Vieweg, pp. 433-40.
Compares Richardson and Fielding, praising Richardson for bringing "realism" to the English novel and Fielding for creating realistic characters who are more than embodied ideas. Reviewing Fielding's biography, Hettner concludes that Fielding's hostility to the hypocritical Richardson turned him from journalism and his topical comedies to his great novels. Praises Fielding's novels

for their mimetic qualities, and for attacking the pretense of virtue, never virtue itself. Thinks Fielding both the founder of the English novel of manners and the comic novel (inspired by Cervantes). Joseph Andrews is Fielding's most humorous novel, Tom Jones his great novel of sensitive humanity, and Amelia shows his weakening powers and a didactic tendency. In German.

Reprinted 1894.

3 O. "Fielding the Novelist." Notes and Queries, 5th. series, 11 (28 June), 509-510.

Suggests that the Canning case was heard before John Fielding but that Henry did write the pamphlet. Response to 1879.B8. See 1879.B5, 1945.B1.

4 P., I. "Fielding the Novelist." Notes and Queries, 5th. series, 11 (28 June), 509.

The Canning case was not simple and is still not clear. Response to 1879.B8.

5 P., I. "Fielding the Novelist." Notes and Queries, 5th. series, 12 (12 July), 30.

Expands his earlier note (1879.B4). Henry Fielding was the magistrate; the case was very complicated and is still a classical legal puzzle.

6 SHAW, WILLIAM S. "Henry Fielding." Notes and Queries, 5th. series, 11 (15 March), 208.

Asks if Fielding wrote some of Tom Jones at Tiverton-on-Avon, as local legend has it.

7 STEPHEN, LESLIE. "Fielding's Novels," in his Hours in the Library. Vol. 2. London: Smith, Elder, pp. 177-207.

Reprints 1877.B2.

Reissued 1892, 1899, and 1907.

8 W., G. H. "Fielding the Novelist." Notes and Queries, 5th. series, 11 (21 June), 484-85.

Fielding was duped as a magistrate by Elizabeth Canning and even wrote a pamphlet in her defense. An article in Blackwood's Magazine on the Canning case (87, May 1860, 385-86) had earlier suggested that Fielding's casualness in handling the case amounted almost to improper conduct as a magistrate. See responses 1879.B1, 3, 4, 5.

9 W., G. H. "Fielding the Novelist." Notes and Queries, 5th. series, 12 (12 July), 30-31.

1880

Henry Fielding was the magistrate in the Canning case. See his earlier note (1879.B8).

1880 A BOOKS

1 FIELDING, HENRY. Fielding's Works. Illustrations by Cruikshank. 4 vols. Jersey City, N.J.: Frederick D. Linn.
Vols. 1-2 Tom Jones; vol. 3 Joseph Andrews; vol. 4 Amelia. No indication of copy text. The volumes of Tom Jones (544 & 540 pp.) and Amelia (657 pp.) appear to be the same as those issued by Worthington (1879.A1 and 1879.A3).

2 _____. The History of Tom Jones, A Foundling. Illustrations by George Cruikshank. Bohn's Novelists' Library. 2 vols. London: George Bell and Sons, 980 pp.
Reissue of 1876.A2.

3 _____. The History of Tom Jones, A Foundling. Illustrations by "Phiz" and an introduction by G. H. T[ownsend]. London and New York: G. Routledge & Sons, 640 pp. [1880].
Reissue of 1857.A3.

4 _____. Works of Henry Fielding. "Memoir of the Life . . . of the Author" by Sir Walter Scott and "Essay on His Life and Genius" by Arthur Murphy. New York: G. Routledge & Sons, 507 pp. [1880].
This double column book contains illustrations by "HEB" and five of Fielding's works (Tom Jones, Joseph Andrews, Amelia, Jonathan Wild, Journey from this World to the Next). No indication of copy text.

1880 B SHORTER WRITINGS - NONE

1881 A BOOKS - NONE

1881 B SHORTER WRITINGS

1 CHILD, THEODORE. "Tom Jones on the French Stage (6th S. iv. 221)." Notes and Queries, 6th. series, 4 (8 Oct.), 292.
A reponse to 1881.B2 that points out how common such adaptation of English literary work was in France. M. Desforges wrote a second adaptation of Tom Jones in 1787.

Also cites a one act vaudeville piece that takes place in Hogarth's studio, the characters in which are Hogarth, Garrick, Sophia, etc.

2 DOBSON, AUSTIN. "Tom Jones on the French Stage." Notes and Queries, 6th. series, 4 (17 Sept.), 221-22.
In 1782 Tom Jones was turned into a five act verse comedy by Desfarges. It had been made into an opera, Tom Jones, Comédie Lyrique en Trois Actes by M. Poinsinet, in 1764. The opera is briefly described. Joseph Reed's 1765 English opera of Tom Jones may have been partly based on this French opera.
Expanded by Child 1881.B1. See 1970.B28.

1882 A BOOKS

1 FIELDING, HENRY. The Adventures of Joseph Andrews. London and New York: George Routledge & Sons, 127 pp. [1882].
No indication of copy text; appears to be part of "Routledge's Railway Library."

2 _____. The History of Amelia. London and New York: George Routledge & Sons, 159 pp. [1882].
No indication of copy text; issued as part of the Routledge Railway Library.

3 _____. The History of the Adventures of Joseph Andrews, and His Friend Mr. Abraham Adams. Illustrations by George Cruikshank and biography by Thomas Roscoe. Bohn's Novelists' Library. London: George Bell and Sons, 433 pp.
Reissue of 1836.A2.

4 _____. The History of Tom Jones, A Foundling. Illustrations by W. Small. 2 vols. New York: White, Stokes, and Allen, 1084 (544 & 540) pp.
Reissue of 1879.A3 with new illustrations.

5 _____. The Writings of Henry Fielding. Memoir by David Herbert. Edinburgh: W. P. Nimmo, Hay and Mitchell, 703 pp.
Reissue of 1872.A2.

6 _____. The Works of Henry Fielding, Esq. Edited by Leslie Stephen. 10 vols. London: Smith, Elder.
Vols. 1 and 2 reprint Tom Jones; vol. 3 Amelia; vol. 4 Joseph Andrews and A Journey From This World to the Next; vol. 5 Jonathan Wild and Fielding's articles in The

Champion; vol. 6 Fielding's essays in The Covent Garden Journal, The True Patriot, The Jacobite's Journal, Miscellanies and the "cases" of Elizabeth Canning and Bosavern Penlez; vol. 7 A Voyage to Lisbon, a legal paper (i.e., "An Inquiry into the Causes of the Late Increase of Robbers") and the rest of the Miscellanies, including the poetry; vols. 8-10 reprint Fielding's plays. No indication of copy text, but Stephen appears to follow Murphy (1762.A10) in those works which both reprint. In his 104-page "biographical essay," Stephen vigorously attacks Murphy's priggish and inaccurate biographical and critical evaluation of Fielding. Stephen sets out to provide a more accurate account. He thinks Fielding's dramas lack polish because the English theater was in decline and asked nothing of him. This carelessness in craftsmanship shows itself in "the want of moral refinement" (p. xviii). Stephen does appreciate Fielding's dramatic burlesques and satires. He dismisses his poetry, but carefully reviews Fielding's political and social ideas as expressed in his journalism and occasional writing. In a long section on Fielding's novels, Stephen emphasizes Fielding's intentional and informing morality and his healthy manly power of enjoyment (in sharp contrast to Richardson), contrasts Fielding's and Shakespeare's artistic impartiality (Shakespeare's is "philosophic" and Fielding's pragmatic), and points out the strength and essential originality of Fielding's commonplace ideas. Finally Stephen distinguishes Fielding from modern "realism" or "naturalism." Stephen never quite escapes from Murphy's image of the reckless, hard-living but manly Fielding.

1882 B SHORTER WRITINGS

1 [HENLEY, W. E.]. "[Review of] The Works of Henry Fielding, Esq. With a Biographical Essay by Leslie Stephen . . ." Athenaeum, no. 2871 (4 Nov.), pp. 592-94.

Thinks the volumes too unwieldy, the illustrations wrong, and the editing inadequate (largely a reprint of Murphy), but Henley continues his high praise for Fielding, "one of the handsomest and noblest classics in the language," who "as an artist and as a thinker commands unending attention and lifelong friendship" (p. 592).

2 TUCKERMAN, BEYARD. "The Eighteenth Century . . . III. Richardson, Fielding, Smollett," in his A History of Prose Fiction from Sir Thomas Malory to George Eliot. New York: G. P. Putnam's Sons, pp. 203-11.

Fielding's novels generally praised for their historical realism, jovial tone, and dramatic nature.

1883 A BOOKS

1 DOBSON, AUSTIN. Fielding. English Men of Letters series. Edited by John Morley. London and New York: Macmillan, 205 pp.

In this brief critical biography, Dobson continues the argument for Fielding's personal and literary worth, which was begun by Lawrence (1855.A1) and Keightley (1858.B2). He elegantly answers those thought to be Fielding's defamers [Murphy (1762.A10), Thackeray (1853.B1), Horace Walpole], while discussing Fielding's plays, novels, journalism, miscellanies, and life. He speaks of Fielding's scholarship, interest in reform, and essential moral goodness. Dobson was one of the first to recognize that The Author's Farce, with its "direct censure of contemporary folly," was the field in which "his most brilliant theatrical success was won" (p. 17). Dobson speaks of the "inexhaustible good-humor . . . [the] large and liberal humanity" of Tom Jones; yet is chagrined that "the wisest and wittiest book ever written cannot, without hesitation, be now placed in the hands of women or very young people" (p. 133). Emphasizes biography rather than criticism. See 1918.A1. Reissued 1907. For an early French defense of Fielding, see 1832.B2.

2 FIELDING, HENRY. Amelia. New York: White, Stokes, and Allen, 657 pp.

No indication of copy text.

3 _____. The Complete Works of Henry Fielding. Edited by Thomas Roscoe and illustrated by George Cruikshank. London: George Bell and Sons, 1144 pp.

Reissue of 1840.A3.

4 _____. The History of Tom Jones, A Foundling. Illustrations by W. Small. 2 vols. New York: White, Stokes, and Allen, 1084 (544 & 540) pp.

Reissue of 1879.A3.

5 _____. The Miser, in Dicks' London Acting Edition of Standard English Plays and Comic Dramas. London: John Dicks, pp. 277-88. [1883?].

Reissue of 1871.A2.

6 _____. The Mock Doctor and The Miser, in Plays from Molière. Introduction by Henry Morley. London: George Routledge & Sons, pp. 180-260.

Vol. 61 of Lubbock's Hundred Book series. No indication of copy text.

7 _____. Tom Jones oder die Geschichte eines Findelkindes. Translated by J. J. Ch. Bode. Introduction by J. Schmidt. 3 vols. Stuttgart: W. Spemann. [1883].

German translation. Vols. 153-155 of Deutsche Hand-und Hausbibliothek. Englische Litteratur.

1883 B SHORTER WRITINGS

1 BENSLY, E. V. "Fielding's 'Amelia.'" Notes and Queries, 6th. series, 8 (6 Oct.), 266-67.

Commenting on a bit of Irish dialect in Amelia I, ii, asks for the meaning of the word "gra." See 1883.B13.

2 B., G. F. R. "A Fielding Relic." Notes and Queries, 6th. series, 7 (6 Jan.), 6.

Notes that the Somerset Archaeological Society has been given a table made for Fielding while he lived at East Stower.

3 DOBSON, AUSTIN. "Fielding and Sarah Andrew." Athenaeum, no. 2903 (2 June), pp. 700-701.

Biographical evidence to help Fielding's character. Fielding was a young man of 18 when he tried to take Sarah Andrew from her cynical and mercenary family and not a "dissipated" 21 or 22. Nor did he quickly marry his first wife Charlotte Cradock in disappointment. See 1931.B4.

4 _____. "Fieldingiana." Notes and Queries, 6th. series, 8 (1 Sept.), 161-62.

Cites evidence from the University of Leyden album for Fielding's residence there and reprints an anecdote about Fielding that first appeared in J. T. Smith's Nollekens and his Times (chapter 5, vol. 1, pp. 124-25). Fielding's character is defended; he had "dignified and gentlemanly manners." Fielding is also said to have claimed that he was "introducing the characters of all his friends" in Tom Jones. Dobson then finds a number of allusions to Fielding's friends.

5 _____. "Fielding's 'Tom Jones.'" Notes and Queries, 6th. series, 8 (20 Oct.), 314.

Says that there is no evidence for Prideaux's assertion (1883.B11).

6 _____. "Fielding Tracts." Notes and Queries, 6th. series, 7 (26 May), 406.
Asks help in finding various pamphlets relating to Fielding's works.

7 _____. "Henry Fielding." [?]: [?], 2 pp.
A poem written and printed for the occasion of the "unveiling by the United States Minister, the Hon. J. Russell Lowell, of the bust in the Shire Hall, Taunton." Copy in the British Museum.

8 [HENLEY, W. E.] "[Review of] English Men of Letters. Edited by John Morley. - Fielding. By Austin Dobson . . ." Athenaeum, no. 2896 (28 April), pp. 537-38.
An appreciative review that continues the restoration of Fielding's character, defending him against the people who "have chosen to believe the foolish fancies of Murphy" (p. 537). He defends Fielding as a scholar and as a rich and inventive artist. "He is an infinitely greater artist than Johnson, or than Walter Scott, or than Macaulay" (p. 537). Henley thinks Dobson's critical sense weak but that his biographical care is admirable ("He has cleared our minds of cant," p. 538).
Reprinted in a slightly revised version in 1890.B2 and 1892.B2.

9 MACLEAN, JOHN. "Fieldingiana." Notes and Queries, 6th. series, 8 (3 Nov.), 355.
Asks if there is anything to the local tradition that Fielding wrote Tom Jones in Tintern Parva in the Wye Valley.

10 PERRY, THOMAS S. "Fielding," in his English Literature in the Eighteenth Century. New York: Harper & Brothers, pp. 323-25, 345-51.
Briefly describes and quotes from Fielding's Tragedy of Tragedies. Describes Joseph Andrews as having the "full flavor of beer and tobacco" (p. 346), quotes some instances of horseplay and says that it only superficially resembles Don Quixote, because Fielding has "none of the poetical spirit which inspired Cervantes" (p. 351).

11 PRIDEAUX, W. F. "Fielding's 'Tom Jones.'" Notes and Queries, 6th. series, 8 (13 Oct.), 288.

1883

Corrects Austin Dobson, Fielding (1883.A1). Fielding was paid £100 a volume for Tom Jones by Andrew Miller before a line was written. See 1883.B5 and 1884.B1, 2, 3.

12 P., S. L. "A Barren Rascal." Notes and Queries, 6th. series, 7 (25 Aug.), 144.
Johnson admired Fielding despite his afterdinner outburst (cites his reading straight through Amelia).

13 WARD, C. A. "Fielding's 'Amelia.'" Notes and Queries, 6th. series, 8 (1 Dec.), 432.
Answers Bensly's query about Irish dialect (1883.B1).

1884 A BOOKS

1 FIELDING, HENRY. Amelia. Illustrated by George Cruikshank. London: George Bell and Sons, 608 pp.
Reprint of 1877.A1, now said to be "substantially a reprint of Roscoe's edition (1840.A3), carefully revised and corrected from the last edition published during the author's lifetime."

2 _____. Amelia. New York: White, Stokes, and Allen, 657 pp.
Reissue of 1883.A2.

3 _____. The History of Tom Jones, A Foundling. Illustrations by W. Small. 2 vols. New York: White, Stokes, and Allen, 1084 (544 & 540) pp.
Reissue of 1879.A3.

4 _____. The Miser. Dicks' Standard Plays. No. 146. London: John Dicks, 12 pp.
No indication of copy text, but reissue of 1871.A2.

5 _____. The Novels of Henry Fielding. Illustrations by H. K. Browne ["Phiz"]. 5 vols. London and New York: George Routledge & Sons.
Vol. 1 Joseph Andrews; vols. 2-3 Tom Jones; vol. 4 Jonathan Wild and A Journey from this World to the Next; vol. 5 Amelia. No indication of copy text. A brief anonymous introduction taken largely from Murphy (1762.A10). Browne's illustrations first appeared in 1840.A1 and in 1857.A1, 2, 3. The novels were also separately issued in 1884, 1886, 1890, and 1900.

1884 B SHORTER WRITINGS

1 DOBSON, AUSTIN. "Fielding's 'Tom Jones.'" Notes and Queries, 6th. series, 9 (26 Jan.), 77.

Rejects Prideaux's evidence (1884.B11) about the payment for Tom Jones. Identifies Rev. William Young as the model for Abraham Adams in Joseph Andrews and thinks "Dr. Brewster" in Tom Jones the name of a real surgeon.

2 PRIDEAUX, W. F. "Fielding's 'Tom Jones.'" Notes and Queries, 6th. series, 9 (19 Jan.), 54.

Cites his source for Miller's payment, a brief note in Athenaeum 26 July 1851, p. 806. See 1884.B1.

3 _____. "Fielding's 'Tom Jones.'" Notes and Queries, 6th. series, 9 (29 Mar.), 254.

Maintains that the Athenaeum passage is as good as Walpole's letter, quoted by Dobson (1883.B11, 1884.B1).

4 TRAILL, H. D. "Richardson and Fielding," in his The New Lucian. London: Chapman and Hall, pp. 200-215.

This dialogue between a priggish and spiteful Richardson and a hearty Fielding is largely a defense of the morality of Fielding's mimetically true novels with their morally mixed characters ("Are not good and evil mingled in life," p. 206); concludes that a few men still read Fielding and that women read neither of them. For another imaginary conversation, see 1785.B1.

1885 A BOOKS

1 FIELDING, HENRY. Amelia. New York: White, Stokes, and Allen, 657 pp.

Reissue of 1883.A2.

2 _____. The History of the Adventures of Joseph Andrews, and His Friend Mr. Abraham Adams. Illustrations by George Cruikshank and biography by Thomas Roscoe. Bohn's Novelists' Library. London: George Bell and Sons, 433 pp.

Reissue of 1836.A2.

3 _____. The Tragedy of Tragedies: or, The Life and Death of Tom Thumb the Great, in Burlesque Plays and Poems. Morley's Universal Library. London and New York: George Routledge & Sons, pp. 141-82.

Includes Fielding's preface and annotations. No indication of copy text.

1885

1885 B SHORTER WRITINGS

1 GRAY, GEORGE J. "Fielding's Covent Garden Journal." Book-lore, 2, no. 12 (Nov.), 180-81.
Describes the run of the journal (from 4 Jan. 1752 until 25 Nov. 1752); outlines its usual content; and reprints part of the preface to the first issue and the explanation for discontinuing it.

1886 A BOOKS

1 FIELDING, HENRY. Amelia. New York: White, Stokes, and Allen, 657 pp.
Reissue of 1883.A2.

2 _____. The Adventures of Joseph Andrews. Illustrations by "Phiz." London and New York: George Routledge & Sons, 349 pp.
Reissue of 1884.A5.

3 _____. The History of Amelia. Illustrations by "Phiz." London and New York: G. Routledge & Sons, 543 pp.
Reprint of 1884.A5.

4 _____. The History of Amelia. Illustrations by "Phiz." New York: G. Routledge & Sons, 406 pp.
Reprint of 1857.A1.

5 _____. The History of the Life of the Late Mr. Jonathan Wild the Great and A Journey from this World to the Next. London and New York: George Routledge & Sons, 325 pp.
Reissue of 1884.A5. Called "The Library Edition."

6 _____. The History of Tom Jones, A Foundling. Illustrations by W. Small. 2 vols. New York: White, Stokes, and Allen, 1084 (544 & 540) pp.
Reissue of 1882.A5.

7 _____. The History of Tom Jones, A Foundling. 2 vols. London, New York, etc.: George Routledge & Sons, 939 (485 & 454) pp.
Called "The Library Edition"; same as 1884.A5.

1886 B SHORTER WRITINGS

1 H., W. "Lord Rochester." Notes and Queries, 7th. series, 2 (13 Nov.), 387.
Asks to have allusion in Tom Jones Book 4, chapter 2 cleared up. See 1886.B3.

2 JESSERAND, JEAN ADRIEN A. J. Le roman anglais; origines et formation des grandes écoles de romanciers du XVIIIe siècle. Paris: E. Leroux, passim.
An anecdotal survey of the eighteenth-century English novel. Asserts that though the English came to the genre late, they eventually dominated it. Richardson created the cult of sensibility; Fielding brought "real life" to the novel and truly represented his race. In French.

3 M., C. B. "Lord Rochester in 'Tom Jones.'" Notes and Queries, 7th. series, 2 (4 Dec.), 458.
Answers W. H.'s inquiry (1886.B1).

4 NOBLE, JAMES A. "Fielding," in his Morality in English Fiction. Liverpool: W. & J. Arnold; London: Simpkin, Marshall, pp. 14-21.
Arguing that Fielding and Richardson have none of the subtle implied morality of nineteenth-century fiction, Noble maintains that Fielding "preaches by . . . portraiture which induces a foregone moral verdict," and although "there are light and shade, . . . they are not intermingled as in real life" (p. 15). This is essentially F. R. Leavis' position in The Great Tradition. Noble then goes on to compare Richardson and Fielding, whose works are respectively "the best . . . embodiments of the morality of Philistia and that of Bohemia" (p. 16). Fielding's strength is that he had the common sense and insight "to spurn a false, artificial, and altogether inadequate ideal; his weakness lay in a certain want of elevation, which expressed itself in an implied denial of any ideal whatsoever" (p. 19). See 1959.A1.

5 PRIDEAUX, W. F. "Fielding's Works." Notes and Queries, 7th. series, 2 (4 Sept.), 186.
Reminds Dobson that Joseph Andrews was printed a second time in three months rather than in six, as he suggests in Fielding (1883.A1). See 1855.B3.

6 RENDLE, WILLIAM. "Henry Fielding." Notes and Queries, 7th. series, 2 (11 Sept.), 215.

1886

Did he act at fair booths, or is he confused with Timothy Fielding? See 1875.B2.

7 URBAN. "Was Fielding Ever on the London Stage?" Notes and Queries, 7th. series, 2 (21 Aug.), 149.
Was Henry Fielding "Justice Quorum" in Charles Coffey's Phebe produced at Drury Lane 4 July 1729? See 1875.B2.

1887 A BOOKS

1 FIELDING, HENRY. A Voyage to Lisbon. Cassell's National Library. London, Paris, New York and Melbourne: Cassell, 192 pp.
Henry Morley adds a two page introduction to this printing. No indication of copy text.

2 _____. The History of Tom Jones, A Foundling. Illustrations by George Cruikshank. Bohn's Novelists' Library. 2 vols. London: George Bell and Sons, 980 pp.
Reissue of 1876.A2.

3 _____. The Mock Doctor and The Miser, in Plays from Molière. Introduction by Henry Morley. London: George Routledge & Sons, pp. 180-260.
Reissue of 1883.A6, called the "fifth" edition.

1887 B SHORTER WRITINGS

1 LOWELL, JAMES RUSSELL. "Fielding," in his Democracy and Other Addresses. London: Macmillan, pp. 65-88.
A speech in praise of Fielding's "genius." Lowell constantly qualifies his admiration for Fielding, saying that he was "absolutely sincere, if he had not always the tact to see where sincerity is out of place" (p. 72), and that he modeled from life, like Hogarth, and "we may regret that their model was too often no better than she should be" (p. 82). In defending Fielding's character, he admits "that the woof of his nature was coarse and animal" (p. 77), but that he lived in a coarse age and thus had more excuse for his behavior than the French realists. In short, Lowell completely confuses life and art.
Originally delivered in Taunton, Somerset, 4 Sept. 1883 at the unveiling of Fielding's bust in the shire hall.

2 MAURICE. "Fielding." Notes and Queries, 7th. series, 3 (30 April), 348.

Asks if any of Fielding's family are alive. See 1887.B3, 1888.B2.

3 WALFORD, E. "Fielding." Notes and Queries, 7th series, 3 (28 May), 432.
Answers Maurice (1887.B2) by suggesting that he look at Burke's Peerage under the Earl of Denbigh.

1888 A BOOKS

1 FIELDING, HENRY. The History of Tom Jones. Illustrations by D. H. Friston. People's Edition. Dicks' English Novels. 2 vols. London: John Dicks, 309 (155 & 154) pp.
Appears to reprint the third edition (12 April 1749).

1888 B SHORTER WRITINGS

1 D., F. W. "Fielding's 'Voyage to Lisbon.'" Notes and Queries, 7th. series, 5 (2 June), 428.
Asks about the authenticity of Fielding "besting" the captain of the ship on which he sailed to Lisbon.

2 PRIDEAUX, W. F. "Fielding's Daughter, Mrs. Montresor." Notes and Queries, 7th. series, 6 (21 July), 45.
Prints an uncomplimentary late eighteenth-century account of one of Fielding's daughters.

3 _____. "Henry Fielding." Notes and Queries, 7th. series, 6 (10 Nov.), 368.
Thinks that Fielding had a business interest in the Universal-Register office in the Strand because he "puffs" it in Amelia.

1889 A BOOKS

1 DOBSON, AUSTIN. Fielding. Edited by John Morley. English Men of Letters series. London and New York: Macmillan, 211 pp.
1883.A1, with brief appendix added.

2 FIELDING, HENRY. The Adventures of Joseph Andrews. Illustrations by "Phiz." London: George Routledge & Sons, 349 pp. [1889].
Reissue of 1884.A5.

1889

3 _____. The Adventures of Joseph Andrews. London, Glasgow, and New York: George Routledge & Sons, 269 pp. [1889].
Reissue of 1857.A1.

4 _____. The Adventures of Joseph Andrews. The Fielding Library. London: Michael Barstow, 357 pp.
No indication of copy text; a brief life by "M. M. B." precedes the text.

5 _____. The History of the Adventures of Joseph Andrews, and His Friend Mr. Abraham Adams. Illustrations by George Cruikshank and biography by Thomas Roscoe. Bohn's Novelists' Library. London: George Bell and Sons, 433 pp.
Reprint of 1836.A2.

6 _____. The History of Tom Jones, A Foundling. Illustrations by George Cruikshank. Bohn's Novelists' Library. 2 vols. London: George Bell and Sons, 980 pp.
Reissue of 1876.A2.

1889 B SHORTER WRITINGS

1 GOSSE, EDMUND. "Henry Fielding," in his A History of Eighteenth Century Literature (1660-1780). London: Macmillan, pp. 251-58.
A brief biographical sketch of the "greatest English novelist."
Reprinted many times.

2 LANG, ANDREW. "Fielding," in his Letters on Literature. London and New York: Longmans, Green, pp. 29-42.
Defends Fielding's morality against the attacks of Thackeray, Johnson, and Richardson (whom he thinks a jealous prig). Briefly mentions Fielding's satire (his reforming intention) and his realism, but coyly concentrates on Tom's sexual indiscretions. Ultimately thinks that "our only way of dealing with Fielding's morality is to take the best of it and leave the remainder alone" (pp. 34-35) and that there are some women "quite manly enough, to have good sense and good taste enough, to benefit by 'Amelia,' and by much of 'Tom Jones'" (p. 32).

3 PRIDEAUX, W. F. "Hogarth's Portrait of Fielding." Notes and Queries, 7th. series, 8 (12 Oct.), 289.
Wonders if the original is still in existence. See 1891.B1, 2, 3, 4, 5.

1890 A BOOKS

1 FIELDING, HENRY. Amelia. 2 vols. New York: American Publishers Corporation, 645 (320 & 325) pp. [189?].
No indication of copy text.

2 _____. The Adventures of Joseph Andrews. Illustrations by "Phiz." London: George Routledge & Sons, 349 pp.
Reissue of 1884.A5.

3 _____. The History of Amelia. Illustrations by "Phiz." London: G. Routledge & Sons, 543 pp.
Reissue of 1884.A5.

4 _____. The History of the Late Mr. Jonathan Wild the Great and A Journey From This World to the Next. London and New York: George Routledge & Sons, 325 pp.
Reissue of 1884.A5.

*5 _____. The History of Tom Jones, a Foundling. Boston: Estes and Lauriat. [1890?].
Source: National Union Catalogue: Pre-1956 Imprints. Vol. 171, p. 686.

6 _____. The History of Tom Jones, A Foundling. 2 vols. London and New York: George Routledge & Sons, 939 (485 & 454) pp.
Reissue of 1884.A5. Anonymous introduction and illustrations by Browne.

7 _____. The History of Tom Jones, A Foundling. 2 vols. New York: Frederick A. Stokes, 899 (456 & 443) pp.
Brief anonymous life, emphasizing early dissipation. Appears to reproduce the "1750" edition followed by Murphy (1762.A10).

8 _____. The History of Tom Jones, A Foundling. 2 vols. New York: Hovendon, 1160 (544 & 616) pp. [1890].
Appears to reproduce the first edition. Four volumes bound as two.

*9 PÉRONNE, JOHANNES. "Über englische Zustaende im XVIII. Jahrhundert nach den Romanen von Fielding and Smollett." Dissertation, Leipzig, 1890.
Source: McNamee, 1865-1964, p. 556. In German.

1890

1890 B SHORTER WRITINGS

1 AITKEN, G. A. "Henry Fielding." Athenaeum, n.s. 1 (1 Feb.), 149.

A few biographical facts added. Fielding's will in the Prerogative Court of Canterbury is printed. Various people, particularly Ralph Allen, who was to be executor, are identified. A letter from John Fielding about Henry's posthumous play The Fathers is printed; on 4 Dec. 1778 John Fielding says that there are no "Works left unpublished."

2 HENLEY, W. E. "Fielding," in Views and Reviews: Essays in Appreciation. London: David Nutt, pp. 229-35.

Incorporates the material from two earlier reviews, 1882.B1 and 1883.B8.

3 LOWELL, JAMES RUSSELL. "Inscription for a Memorial Bust of Fielding." Atlantic Monthly (Sept.), p. 322.

Lowell's poem describes Fielding as "Manly . . . generous and sincere; English in all" and asks "Did he good service? God must judge, not we."

4 STAPFER, PAUL. "Le grand classique du roman anglais: Henry Fielding." Revue des deux mondes (15 Sept.), pp. 412-54.

A biographical and critical appreciation based on 1879.B7, 1883.A1, 1855.A1. Praises Fielding for his attack on Pamela, which he saw with the eyes of a "modern" man, but thinks Joseph Andrews lacks unity, as Fielding shifts from parody to a study of Adams. Suggests French predecessors for Fielding's new way of writing. Objects to the narrative digressions in Tom Jones, but thinks it one of the great comic masterpieces (better than Don Quixote). Sees Fielding's major shortcoming as an indifference to the beauties of nature, only truly appreciated by nineteenth-century novelists. In French.

1891 A BOOKS - NONE

1891 B SHORTER WRITINGS

1 B., G. F. R. "Portrait of Fielding." Notes and Queries, 7th. series, 12 (22 Aug.), 154.

Reminds Bugbee (1891.B2) that only Hogarth's ink sketch is authentic.

2 BUGBEE, J. M. "Portrait of Fielding." Notes and Queries, 7th. series, 12 (18 July), 46-47.
Asks about the authenticity of the oil portrait of Fielding sold in 1870. See 1891.B1.

3 MANSERGH, J. F. "Portrait of Fielding." Notes and Queries, 7th. series, 12 (28 Nov.), 436-37.
The anecdote about Hogarth sketching Fielding after his death from a profile cut out by a lady.

4 PICKFORD, JOHN. "Portrait of Fielding." Notes and Queries, 7th. series, 12 (3 Oct.), 274.
Anecdote about Hogarth sketching Garrick dressed up as Fielding.

5 WARD, C. A. "Portrait of Fielding." Notes and Queries, 7th. series, 12 (28 Nov.), 437.
Rejects the anecdote passed on by Mansergh (1891.B3).

1892 A BOOKS

1 FIELDING, HENRY. Amelia. Illustrations by George Cruikshank. Bohn's Novelists' Library. London and New York: George Bell and Sons, 608 pp.
Reprint of 1877.A1.

2 _____. The Journal of a Voyage to Lisbon. Edited by Austin Dobson. London: Charles Wittingham, 298 pp.
Dobson sets out the vexed bibliographical history, arguing "that the longer version succeeded the shorter" (p. xi); reprints the 25 Feb. 1755 text edited by John Fielding and printed by Andrew Miller (including "A Fragment of a Comment on L. Bolingbroke's Essay"); supplies full notes which include variants from the unedited version. See 1917.B3, B7, B8, 1963.A6, 1971.B1.

3 _____. The History of Tom Jones, A Foundling. Illustrations by George Cruikshank. Bohn's Novelists' Library. 2 vols. London: George Bell and Sons, 980 pp.
Reissue of 1876.A2.

1892 B SHORTER WRITINGS

1 DOBSON, AUSTIN. "Fielding's 'Voyage to Lisbon.'" in his Eighteenth Century Vignettes. 1st series. London: Chatto & Windus, pp. 68-78.

1892

Briefly and sentimentally reconstructs Fielding's voyage to Lisbon.

2 HENLEY, W. E. "Fielding," in Views and Reviews: Essays in Appreciation. London: David Nutt, pp. 229-35.
Reprint of 1890.B2.

1893 A BOOKS

1 FIELDING, HENRY. A Voyage to Lisbon. Cassell's National Library. London, Paris, etc.: Cassell, 192 pp.
Reissue of 1887.A1.

*2 _____. Istorija Toma Dzonsa-naidenysa. 3 vols. Saint Petersburg: Suboria.
Russian translation.
Source: Hugh Amory's working bibliography.

3 _____. The Mock Doctor and The Miser, in Plays from Molière. Introduction by Henry Morley. London: George Routledge & Sons, pp. 180-260.
Reissue of 1883.A6.

4 _____. The Works of Henry Fielding. Edited by George Saintsbury and illustrated by Herbert Railton and E. J. Wheeler. 12 vols. London: J. M. Dent.
The texts and introductions are the same as those later printed as the Everyman Library editions (see 1909.A2, 1910.A6, 1930.A2, 1932.A1). The final two volumes are Miscellaneous Writings and contain Journey from This World to the Next, Voyage to Lisbon, The Author's Farce, The Tragedy of Tragedies, Pasquin, "Essay on Conversation," no. 13 of The True Patriot, no. 33 of The Covent-Garden Journal, and "Familiar Letters" from David Simple. All but the last three items are taken from Murphy (1762.A10). In his introduction, Saintsbury dismisses Fielding's drama and his party journalism, finding only the three plays he reprints "proper" enough to be reprinted. According to Saintsbury, only the Journal of a Voyage to Lisbon is of high enough quality to be interesting for its own sake.
Vols. 1-6 containing Joseph Andrews and Tom Jones were not issued until 1899.

1893 B SHORTER WRITINGS

1 HOOPER, JAMES. "Inscription to Fielding," Notes and Queries, 8th. series, 4 (26 Aug.), 164.
Proposed Latin inscription for Fielding's tomb indicates foreign interest in him. See 1893.B2.

2 PAGE, JOHN T. "Inscription to Fielding." Notes and Queries, 8th. series, 4 (14 Oct.), 314.
Reproduces the inscription actually on Fielding's tomb as printed in the Graphic, 8 Sept. 1883. Response to 1893.B1.

1894 A BOOKS

1 FIELDING, HENRY. The Adventures of Joseph Andrews. London, Manchester, and New York: George Routledge and Sons, 127 pp.
One of the "Caxton Novels" series. No indication of copy text.

1894 B SHORTER WRITINGS

1 [MORIARTY, G. P.] "The Political World of Fielding and Smollett." Macmillan's Magazine, 69, no. 411 (Jan.), 215-21.
Fielding and Smollett are used to illustrate the political history of "a period of Whig supremacy extending from the ascension of Walpole to the dismissal of Newcastle by George the Third" (p. 221). In defending George III and attacking the Whig oligarchy, this article points to the political cynicism that had crept into English life (illustrated by Booth's encounter with Mr. Bondum) and the provincialism that resulted from the lack of political information (Squire Western's old-fashioned Toryism). Despite Fielding's Hanoverian views (which the writer thinks widely held in his age), Fielding and Smollett "write as the bitter champions of a dissatisfied section, conscious of their ability, yet unable to show it for want of influence" (p. 220). See 1960.B4.

2 RALEIGH, WALTER. "Richardson and Fielding," in his The English Novel. London: John Murray, pp. 140-79.
Discusses Joseph Andrews, Jonathan Wild, Tom Jones, and Amelia after briefly outlining Fielding's dramatic career.

Touches on the preface to Joseph Andrews, the novel's movement beyond parody, Fielding's war against hypocrisy and sham, and the character of Adams. "The 'fundamental brain-work' necessary for a great work of fiction is not only present but apparent in all Fielding's novels; this can be stripped, as Shakespeare's plays cannot, of their picturesque expressions, and something at least of their purport stated in purely intellectual terms. But in Jonathan Wild above all Fielding indulges to the full his taste for clearness and unity of intellectual structure" (p. 167). He commends Jonathan Wild for its vivid characters, its driving force, and its moments of "play." In Tom Jones and Amelia, Raleigh feels that Fielding created characters "which transcend for reality and variety the work of all former English narrators, save perhaps Chaucer alone" (p. 170). Discusses Fielding as a "romantic" moralist (while Richardson is a "classic" moralist, one who conforms to the rules) who sets "warm-hearted humanity, and calculating prudence and rigid propriety" (p. 173) in opposition. He excuses Tom's lapse with Lady Bellaston as making the "intellectual framework all the clearer . . . he is not content to win the sympathy of the reader for Mr. Jones without giving that sympathy the severest obstacles to surmount in the shape of 'deeds done'" (pp. 174-75). For Fielding, cunning hypocrisy is the darkest sin. Raleigh thinks Amelia an exercise in practical rather than poetic justice, and praises Fielding for his characters, his narrative skill and his realism ("Fielding's acquaintance with life is fully as wide as Defoe's while his insight is keener and deeper," p. 178).

Reprinted by Scholarly Press (St. Clair Shores, Michigan), 1972.

3 SAINTSBURY, GEORGE, ed. "Henry Fielding," in English Prose Selections. Edited by Henry Craik. Vol. 4. London and New York: Macmillan, pp. 109-133.

Saintsbury provides a brief biography and an equally brief description of Fielding's evolving style, from his early carelessness with "relatives and demonstratives" to his later "crisp ironic phrase" (p. 112) and "power and range" (p. 115). He then prints selected passages from A Journey from This World to the Next, Joseph Andrews, Jonathan Wild, Tom Jones, Amelia, and A Voyage to Lisbon.

1895 A BOOKS

1 FIELDING, HENRY. The History of Amelia. Illustrations by "Phiz." London: G. Routledge & Sons, 406 pp.
Reprint of 1857.A2.

2 _____. The History of Tom Jones, A Foundling. Introduction by G. H. T[ownsend]. London: G. Routledge & Sons; New York: E. P. Dutton, 640 pp. [1895].
Reissue of 1857.A3.

3 LINDNER, FELIX. Henry Fieldings dramatische Werke. Litterarische Studie. Leipzig und Dresden: C. A. Koch, 185 pp.
Provides some theater history and an act by act plot summary of the 26 plays included in the 1783 edition of Fielding's works. Argues that Fielding learned his craft as novelist by writing for the stage; specifically examines Fielding's theories of comedy (which he had developed and tested in his plays) and his characters and situations (each play is an episode in a vast novel depicting social and class mores). Lindner thinks that Fielding's plays have been neglected because of their obscene language, their savage satire, and the careless hurry with which they were written. Briefly examines the sources for his drama, but thinks Fielding a unique observer of mankind. In German.

1895 B SHORTER WRITINGS

1 DOBSON, AUSTIN. "Two English Bookmen - (ii) Henry Fielding." Bibliographica, 1, part 2, 163-73.
Defends Fielding's learning against Thackeray's slur. Reviews his classical education at Eton and Leyden and the catalogue of the sale of Fielding's library in the British Museum. Notices that Fielding had no copies of his own works, little fiction and much drama, large collections of law and classical literature, and the standard works of biography, science, philosophy and theology. See 1973.B1.

1896 A BOOKS

1 FIELDING, HENRY. The History of the Adventures of Joseph Andrews, and His Friend Mr. Abraham Adams. Illustrations

by George Cruikshank and biography by Thomas Roscoe. Bohn's Novelists' Library. London: George Bell and Sons, 433 pp.

Reissue of 1836.A2.

2 _____. Tom Jones The History of A Foundling. Edited by J. E. M. Fielding. London: Swan Sonnenschein, 540 pp.

A bowdlerized version of the novel prepared by Fielding's great-granddaughter which abbreviates where possible and eliminates "grossnesses." No indication of copy text.

*3 WOOD, AUGUSTUS. "Einfluss Fieldings auf die deutsche Literatur." Dissertation, Heidelberg, 1896.

In German.

Source: McNamee, 1865-1964, p. 557. See review in English Studies, 25, no. 3 (Oct. 1898), 445-47. This dissertation may have been published at Yokohama.

1896 B SHORTER WRITINGS

1 DOBSON, AUSTIN. "Fielding's Library," in his Eighteenth Century Vignettes. 3rd. series. London: Chatto & Windus, pp. 164-78.

Reprints 1895.B1.

Reprinted by Oxford University Press in 1923.

1897 A BOOKS

1 CLARKE, CHARLES H. Fielding und der deutsche Sturm und Drang. Freiburg: C. A. Wagner, 100 pp.

This inaugural dissertation traces Fielding's influence on German works of the Sturm und Drang period (listed in a ten page appendix). Clarke argues that throughout the eighteenth century Fielding's reputation and influence were strong in Germany, where the Richardson-Fielding controversy raged. He was admired by Herder, Goethe, and Schiller for his humanity and love of the lower classes. After 1758, through the intermediary of Wieland, he influenced the German novel. The Sturm und Drang authors found inspiration in Fielding for their struggle against accepted rules and authority. Like Fielding, they attributed new importance to the individual and to feeling rather than reason.

Reviewed in Englische Studien, 25, no. 3 (Oct. 1898), 447-48.

2 FIELDING, HENRY. The History of Tom Jones A Foundling. London: Bliss, Sands, 512 pp.

"This edition is a verbatim reprint of the first edition, published in 1749."

1897 B SHORTER WRITINGS - NONE

1898 A BOOKS

1 FIELDING, HENRY. The Works of Henry Fielding. Introduction by Edmund Gosse. 12 vols. Westminster: Archibald Constable; New York: Charles Scribner's Sons.

Vols. 1-2 contain Joseph Andrews; vols. 3-6 Tom Jones; vols. 7-9 Amelia; vol. 10 Jonathan Wild; vols. 11-12 Miscellanies (including The Tragedy of Tragedies, A Journey from this World to the Next, Journal of a Voyage to Lisbon, "An Essay on the Knowledge of the Characters of Men," etc.). The texts appear to be taken from Murphy (1762.A10). In a brief biographical introduction, Gosse dismisses Fielding's dramas and contends that the first sign of Fielding's "genius" is to be found in A Journey from this World to the Next. Gosse finds the irony of Jonathan Wild "excessive and fatiguing" (p. xxi), commends the wholesome laughter of Joseph Andrews and the manliness and careful structure of Tom Jones; he sees Amelia as a falling off. For him, Fielding is an honest, vigorous and wholesome Englishman.

Issued over two years, 1898-99.

2 GOSSE, EDMUND. Henry Fielding. Westminster: Archibald Constable; New York: Charles Scribner's Sons, 32 pp.

A brief biography of Fielding that comments on the major novels. A publisher's advertisement for Gosse's edition of Fielding's Works put out in this year.

1898 B SHORTER WRITINGS

1 D. "'Tom Jones' in France." Notes and Queries, 9th. series, 1 (26 Feb.), 175.

Tom Jones was not suppressed in 1750 (see 1898.B3), but was translated by de la Place and illustrated by Gravelot in that year. See 1927.B5 and 1961.B8.

2 P. "Reputations Reconsidered: Henry Fielding." Academy, 29 Jan., pp. 127-28.

An excursion to the underworld where Fielding is a chief resident, admired by all other English novelists, but especially by Scott. Fielding is commended for his generous spirit, his narrative style, and his sweep; he is defended against the charges of lowness and immorality (on the grounds of his realism) and shallowness.

3 ROBERTS, W. "'Tom Jones' in France." Notes and Queries, 9th. series, 1 (19 Feb.), 147.
Asks if Tom Jones was suppressed in France as immoral in 1750, as the Monthly Review of March 1750 claims. Response 1898.B1. See 1927.B5 and 1961.B8.

4 WRIGLEY, G. W. "Fielding." Notes and Queries, 9th. series, 1 (26 Feb.), 168.
Asks if Fielding leased a house for his daughter in Canterbury and if one of his sons was vicar there.

5 Y., Y. "Names of Characters in Fielding's Novels." Notes and Queries, 9th. series, 2 (26 Nov.), 426.
A number of characters' names (Joseph Andrews, Abraham Adams, Henry Partridge, etc.) are to be found in the list of subscribers to Burnet's "History of his own Time" (1724-34).

1899 A BOOKS

*1 FIELDING, HENRY. Miscellanies. 2 vols. New York: Charles Scribner's Sons.
Source: National Union Catalogue: Pre-1956 Imprints. Vol. 171, p. 663.

2 _____. The History of Tom Jones A Foundling. London: Sands, 512 pp.
Reissue of 1897.A2.

*3 _____. The History of Tom Jones, a Foundling. New York: F. M. Lupton, 501 pp. [1899?].
An abridged edition.
Source: National Union Catalogue: Pre-1956 Imprints. Vol. 171, p. 686.

4 _____. The Tragedy of Tragedies or, The Life and Death of Tom Thumb the Great. Introduction by Felix Lindner. Englische Textbibliothek. 4. General editor Johannes Hoops. Berlin: Emil Felber, 111 pp.

Scholarly edition in English with a long German introduction providing a bibliography of works about Fielding, listing and discussing the plays Fielding parodied, setting out earlier uses of Tom Thumb, and describing the editions of the work.

5 _____. The Works of Henry Fielding. Edited by George Saintsbury and illustrated by Herbert Railton and E. J. Wheeler. 12 vols. London: J. M. Dent.
Reissue of 1893.A4.

1899 B SHORTER WRITINGS

1 CROSS, WILBUR L. "Fielding," in The Development of the English Novel. New York: Macmillan, pp. 42-57.
A brief but intelligent discussion of Fielding's parody of Pamela in Joseph Andrews and of Fielding's use of traditional forms (romance, epic, Greek drama). Cross credits Fielding with "the localization of scene" (p. 46), that is, with giving his novels a definite sense of place; he discusses Fielding's intrusions (introductory chapters and digressions) in light of French theory and Henry James, defending Fielding by asserting that these intrusions allowed for poetry; he argues that Fielding's novels repudiated the "prudential" morality of Addison and Richardson; he discusses Fielding's characters, which were essential types occasionally enlivened by careful psychology. "In Tom Jones character and incident are brought into equilibrium," and even in the burlesque scenes there is "conservation of character" (p. 51), but there are still psychological impossibilities in the novel (the discrepancy between Allworthy's goodness and his bad action). Cross sees Amelia as Fielding's "movement toward the specific in art and consequently toward realism" (p. 54), Fielding's satire as more carefully pointed in this novel, and only the artificial ending as differing from a "naturalistic" novel.
Reprinted New York and London: Macmillan, 1920, and New York: Greenwood Press, 1969.

2 CRULL, FRANZ. "Thomas Shadwells (John Ozells) und Henry Fieldings Comoedien 'The Miser' in ihrem Verhältnis unter einander und zu ihrer gemeinsamen Quellé." Dissertation, Rostock, 1899.
An act by act analysis of The Miser's deviation from L'Avare. Shadwell's earlier play did not influence Fielding. In German.

1899

3 THOMSON, CLARA. "A Note on Fielding's Amelia," Westminster Review, 152, no. 5 (Nov.), 579-88.
Suggests that Fielding was as important a creator of female characters as Richardson and that both led on to "Wordsworth's ideal of the 'perfect woman, nobly planned'" (p. 588). Sees Tom Jones as a balance between picaresque novel and character study and Amelia leaning to the latter. Thomson also sensibly discusses Booth, rejecting Saintsbury's idea that he is a fool, because that would lessen Amelia's worth; she sees Booth's weakness as bringing "into play that maternal element in [Amelia's] affection which is hardly ever absent from the love of good women" (p. 585). Thomson also points out the difference in sexual morality between Fielding's and her own age in order to justify Amelia's forgiving Booth. See 1907.B1.

*4 WILSON, F. Dickens in seinen Beziehungen zu den Humoristen Fielding und Smollett. Leipzig: [?].
Source: T. Humphrey, 233 and New Cambridge Bibliography of English Literature, 934 (1971.B5).

1900 A BOOKS

1 DOBSON, AUSTIN. Henry Fielding: A Memoir. New York: Dodd, Mead, 333 pp.
Slightly revised 1883.A1.

*2 FIELDING, HENRY. Amelia. 2 vols. New York: Bigelow. [19 ?].
Source: National Union Catalogue: Pre-1956 Imprints. Vol. 171, p. 666.

3 _____. Amelia. 2 vols. New York: John W. Lovell, 661 (320 & 341) pp. [1900?].
No indication of copy text; illustrations by several engravers (including Cruikshank and Small). Bound as "Fielding's Works Vols. 5-6."

*4 _____. Mr. Adams in a Political Light, in The Best of the World's Classics. Great Britain and Ireland: II. Volume 4. [?]: [?]. [1900?].
Source: National Union Catalogue: Pre-1956 Imprints. Vol. 172, p. 3.

5 _____. The Adventures of Joseph Andrews. Illustrations by "Phiz." London: George Routledge & Sons, 349 pp.
Reissue of 1884.A5.

6 _____. The Adventures of Joseph Andrews. London: Daily Telegraph, 357 pp. [1900?].

Brief life by "M. M. B." No indication of copy text.

*7 _____. The Adventures of Joseph Andrews. London: Blackfriars. [19 ?].

Source: National Union Catalogue: Pre-1956 Imprints. Vol. 171, p. 674.

*8 _____. The Adventures of Joseph Andrews. New York: Bigelow. [19 ?].

Source: National Union Catalogue: Pre-1956 Imprints. Vol. 171, p. 674.

9 _____. The History of Amelia. Illustrations by "Phiz." London: George Routledge & Sons, 408 pp. [1900].

Reprint of 1857.A2.

10 _____. The History of the Adventures of Joseph Andrews. Illustrated Library Edition. Boston and New York: Colonial Press, 394 pp. [19 ?].

Illustrations by various engravers. No indication of copy text.

*11 _____. The History of the Adventures of Joseph Andrews. New York: John W. Lovell. [1900?].

Bound as Fielding's Works.

Source: National Union Catalogue: Pre-1956 Imprints. Vol. 171, p. 674.

12 _____. The History of the Life of the Late Mr. Jonathan Wild the Great. Illustrations by W. Small. New York: John W. Lovell, 207 pp. [1900?].

No indication of copy text. Bound as "Fielding's Works. Vol. 7."

13 _____. The History of the Late Mr. Jonathan Wild the Great and A Journey From This World to the Next. London and New York: George Routledge & Sons, 325 pp.

Reissue of 1884.A5.

14 _____. The History of Tom Jones, a Foundling. Edited by A. W. Pollard. Macmillan's Library of English Classics. 2 vols. London, New York, Toronto: Macmillan, 1021 (532 & 489) pp.

Reprints "1750" edition of Tom Jones, the same text Murphy (1762.A10) reprints. In a bibliographical note

Pollard justifies reprinting the "1750" edition, which he calls the third.

15 _____. The History of Tom Jones, A Foundling. Library Edition. 3 vols. New York: Godfrey A. S. Wieners. [1900?].
Illustrations by several engravers, including Cruikshank. Called "Fielding's Works" on spine; appears to reprint the first edition of Tom Jones.

16 _____. The History of Tom Jones A Foundling. 3 vols. New York: John W. Lovell. [1900?].
Illustrations by Cruikshank and W. Small. Bound as "Fielding's Works. Vols. 1-3." Appears to reprint the first edition.

17 _____. The History of Tom Jones, A Foundling. 2 vols. London, New York, etc.: George Routledge & Sons, 939 pp.
Reissue of 1884.A5.

*18 _____. The History of Tom Jones, a Foundling. 2 vols. New York: American Publishers. [1900?].
Source: National Union Catalogue: Pre-1956 Imprints. Vol. 171, p. 686.

19 _____. The Works of Henry Fielding. Edited by George Saintsbury and illustrated by Herbert Railton and E. J. Wheeler. 12 vols. London: J. M. Dent.
Reissue of 1893.A4.

20 _____. The Works of Henry Fielding. Edited by George Saintsbury. 6 vols. New York: National Library. [1900].
Essentially a reprint of 1893.A4. Vol. 1 Joseph Andrews; vols. 2-3 Tom Jones; vols. 4-5 Amelia and Jonathan Wild; vol. 6 Miscellanies.

21 _____. The Works of Henry Fielding. Edition De Luxe. 6 vols. New York: Bigelow, Smith. [19 ?].
Reissue of [19 ?].A22 with colored plates.

22 _____. The Works of Henry Fielding. 6 vols. New York: Bigelow, Brown. [19 ?].
Reprinting of Saintsbury (1900.A20) edition, including plates by Wheeler and Saintsbury's introductions.

*23 HOMANN, WILHELM. "Henry Fielding als Humorist." Dissertation, Marburg, 1900.
In German.
Source: McNamee, 1865-1964, p. 557.

24 _____. Henry Fielding als Humorist. Marburg: N. G. Elwert, 92 pp.
After discussing the semantic development of the word "humorist," concludes that the humorist is never malicious and thus Fielding is one. Does not examine Fielding's plays; does illustrate (with quotation) his humorous character sketches, paraphrases, similes, addresses to the reader, and self-deprecation in Joseph Andrews. Also lists the perennial human weaknesses, those weaknesses particular to his time, and the professions and classes (e.g., lawyers, doctors, parsons, squires, etc.) from which Fielding creates his humor. Concludes surprisingly that Fielding's humor is naive and his formulation of the ridiculous too narrow in Joseph Andrews. The interfering narrator of Tom Jones (with whom Homann is not entirely happy) maintains the proper tension and balance of comedy. In German.

1900 B SHORTER WRITINGS

*1 OHNSORG, RICHARD. "John Lacys Dumb Lady, Mrs. Susanna Centlivres Love's Contrivance und Henry Fieldings Mock Doctor in ihrem Verhaeltnis zu einander und zu ihrer gemeinschaftlichen Quelle." Dissertation, Rostock, 1900.
In German.
Source: McNamee, 1865-1964, p. 557.

2 _____. John Lacys 'Dumb Lady,' Mrs. Susanna Centlivres 'Love's Contrivance' und Henry Fieldings 'Mock Doctor' in ihrem Verhältnis zu einander und zu ihrer gemeinschaftlichen Quelle. Hamburg: Bargsted und Ruhland, 60 pp.
Examines these three plays which derive from Molière's Le médicin malgré lui; the content of each is compared scene by scene with Molière. Fielding's is closest to Molière. Although Fielding has coarsened the language, added songs, enhanced the character of Dorcas, and given Gregory appealing traits, his play is essentially a translation and not an adaptation. In German.

1901 A BOOKS

1 FIELDING, HENRY. The History of Tom Jones, A Foundling. Illustrations by George Cruikshank. Bohn's Novelists' Library. 2 vols. London: George Bell and Sons, 980 pp.
Reissue of 1876.A2.

1901

1901 B SHORTER WRITINGS

1 DOBSON, AUSTIN. "The Covent-Garden Journal. Being a hitherto-unwritten Chapter in the Life of Henry Fielding." Living Age, 229 (29 June), 793-803.

Reviews the financial circumstances that brought Fielding's last journal into being (may have been motivated by a desire to promote his Register Office and to make use of the special news available to him as a criminal magistrate); describes the format of the journal and the paper war Fielding provoked (particularly his quarrel with Hill and Smollett and his defense of Amelia); and includes typical excerpts on crime, punishment, boxing, and sensational public events from the Journal.

Also printed in the National Review, 37 (May 1901).

2 FORMAN, BUXTON H. "Richardson, Fielding, and the Andrews Family." Fortnightly Review, n.s. 70, no. 420 (1 Dec.), 949-59.

Anticipates the reassessment of Fielding that followed Cross (1918.A1). Forman admires Richardson and begins by describing his apprenticeship as a novel writer, then describes Pamela, which caused a literary sensation for its realism ("a correspondence carried on by just such people as they were familiar with," p. 952). Describes Joseph Andrews, which began as parody but, because of Fielding's "strong manly sympathies" and his comedy ("in the largest and most human sense"), shifted through the creation of living characters to become "a perfect work" (p. 956). Although Forman thinks Pamela "a work of genius" (p. 958), he thinks that Fielding found the real moral defect in the novel, one so serious that even the shift in plan in the creation of Joseph Andrews makes Fielding's novel less flawed than Pamela.

3 M., F. "Fielding and Brillat-Savarin." Notes and Queries, 9th. series, 7 (30 March), 248-49.

Brillat-Savarin in Physiologie du Goût attributes a passage to Fielding that does not appear in Fielding's works.

4 WHITTUCK, CHARLES. "The 'Good Man' Human: The English Novel (Fielding). 'Parson Adams' in Joseph Andrews," in his The 'Good Man' of the XVIIIth Century: A Monograph on XVIIIth Century Didactic Literature. London: George Allen, pp. 69-92.

An interesting early assessment of Fielding's concept of a good man: "when the 'good man' is seen at his best, the inwardness of his disposition is unmistakably due to the influence of Christianity" (p. 91). "Nor is this same 'good man' either consciously or otherwise a Deist" (p. 92). Whittuck specifically considers Allworthy and Adams, and thinks Fielding's characters better than Richardson's because Richardson's aren't "human enough" (p. 71). He considers these two characters as a single type (sharing heroism and saintliness, tenderness for the weaknesses of human nature, and scorn for hypocrisy, etc.) created by Fielding to throw "light on the nature of men's moral ideals" (p. 89). He also distinguishes between them. Allworthy's character, he argues, was not vividly enough outlined to hold together the contrasting elements in it (i.e., a philosopher who toys with Deism, a Christian, a type of the amiable benevolent man, a spiritless country gentleman). Adams is completely successful because he is based on a truth Fielding recognized: "The sublime, if it exists at all in the world, must necessarily be ridiculous" (p. 80). He considers the pathos of Adams, the nature of his Christianity (not a Tillotsonian rationalist), and the strict orthodoxy of some of his views. He concludes that this good man is neither ancient, medieval nor modern.

This essay anticipates 1949.B6 and 1959.A1 without completely agreeing with either and without their careful scholarship.

1902 A BOOKS

1 DOBSON, AUSTIN. Fielding. English Men of Letters series. Edited by John Morley. New York and London: Harper, 205 pp.

Slightly revised 1883.A1.

2 FIELDING, HENRY. Miscellanies. Edited by George Saintsbury and illustrated by Herbert Railton and E. J. Wheeler. 2 vols. London: J. M. Dent.

Reissue of volumes 11 and 12 of 1893.A4.

3 _____. The Adventures of Joseph Andrews and His Friend Mr. Abraham Adams. Edited by George Saintsbury and illustrated by Herbert Railton and E. J. Wheeler. London: J. M. Dent, 387 pp.

See 1910.A6.

4 _____. The Complete Works of Henry Fielding, Esq., Comprising his Novels, Plays, Poems and Miscellaneous Writings

Complete and Unabridged. With an Essay on the Life, Genius, Achievement of the Author, by William Ernest Henley. 16 vols. New York: Croscup & Sterling; London: Heinemann (1903).

Reviewed in *Athenaeum*, no. 3993 (7 May 1904), 589.

These volumes remain the standard "works" until replaced by the "Wesleyan" Fielding (*see* 1967.A2, 1972.A3, 1974.A9, 1974.A7).

Vol. 1 contains *Joseph Andrews*; vol. 2 *Jonathan Wild*; vols. 3-5 *Tom Jones*; vols. 6-7 *Amelia*; vol. 8 *Love in Several Masques*, *The Temple Beau*, *The Author's Farce: The Pleasures of the Town*, *The Lottery*; vol. 9 *The Tragedy of Tragedies*, *The Coffee-House Politician*, *The Letter Writers*, *The Grub-Street Opera*, *The Debauchees*; vol. 10 *The Modern Husband*, *The Covent-Garden Tragedy*, *The Mock Doctor*, *The Miser*, *The Intriguing Chambermaid*, *An Old Man Taught Wisdom*; vol. 11 *Don Quixote in England*, *The Universal Gallant*, *Pasquin*, *The Historical Register for the Year 1736*, *Eurydice*, *Eurydice Hiss'd*; vol. 12 *Tumble-Down Dick*, *Miss Lucy in Town*, *The Wedding Day*, *The Fathers*, the preface to the 1743 *Miscellanies* and 38 poems; vol. 13 *An Inquiry into the Causes of the Late Increase of Robbers*, *A Proposal for Making an Effectual Provision for the Poor*, *A Charge to the Grand Jury*, *A Clear State of the Case of Elizabeth Canning*, *A True State of the Case of Bosavern Penlez*; vol. 14 *The True Patriot*, *The Jacobite's Journal*, *The Covent-Garden Journal*, "An Essay on Conversation," "An Essay on the Knowledge of the Characters of Men," "An Essay on Nothing," *The Opposition: A Vision*; vol. 15 *A Full Vindication of Her Grace the Duchess of Marlborough*, *The Vernoniad*, "Philosophical Transactions for the Year 1742-43," articles from *The Champion*, "A Proper Answer to a Scurrilous Libel," *Caelia: or, The Perjured Lover: 1733*; vol. 16 "Preface to *David Simple*," "Preface to *Familiar Letters*," Dedication and preface to *Plutus*, "The First Olynthiac of Demosthenes," "A Dialogue Between Jupiter, Juno, Apollo and Mercury," "Of the Remedy of Affliction for the Loss of Our Friends," *Examples of the Interposition of Providence*, *A Journal of a Voyage to Lisbon* with Austin Dobson's introduction and notes, "A Fragment of a Comment on Lord Bolingbroke's *Essay*."

Volume 16 also contains Henley's "Essay on the Life, Genius . . ." (credited to Fox-Davies in Henley's own edition), which reviews the real biographical evidence and partly corrects the legend of a hard-living, hard-drinking Fielding. "Henley" thinks Fielding's plays a series of dramatic clichés without the force of Wycherley's, Congreve's, or Farquhar's. Dismisses Fielding's essays and poetry as not intrinsically interesting and briefly discusses parody in Joseph Andrews. A. C. Fox-Davies provides a six page "Descent of Henry Fielding," which traces his family line from the fourteenth century. There is a sixteen page "Bibliographical List of the First Editions . . . ." A deluxe edition with engravings by Hoppner, Borel, Rowlandson, Gravelot, Rooker, Moreau, and Downman was also issued.

5 _____. The Complete Works of Henry Fielding. Preface and introductions by G. H. Maynadier. 12 vols. New York: P. F. Collier. [1902].

See 1903.A3.

6 _____. The History of the Adventures of Joseph Andrews and His Friend Mr. Abraham Adams. Illustrations by W. Small. The English Comedie Humaine. New York: Century, 320 pp.

No indication of copy text.

7 _____. The History of the Life of the Late Jonathan Wild the Great. Edited by George Saintsbury and illustrated by Herbert Railton and E. J. Wheeler. London: J. M. Dent, 227 pp.

Reissue of vol. 10 of 1893.A4.

8 _____. The Journal of a Voyage to Lisbon. Boston, New York, and Chicago: Houghton, Mifflin, 215 pp.

No indication of copy text; does not contain "A Fragment . . . ." Printed by the Riverside Press in Cambridge, Mass.

9 _____. The Novels of Henry Fielding, Esq. . . . complete and unabridged. Biographical essay by W. E. Henley. Sharpham edition. 7 vols. New York: Harper. [1902].

Reissue of part of 1902.A4. Vol. 1 includes "Henley's" biographical essay, Fox-Davies' Fielding lineage and Joseph Andrews; vol. 2 Jonathan Wild; vols. 3-5 Tom Jones; vols. 6-7 Amelia.

10 _____. The Temple Edition of the Works of Henry Fielding. Edited by George Saintsbury. 12 vols. London: J. M. Dent.

Reprint of the Works as first edited by Saintsbury in 1893 (see 1893.A4).

11 _____. The Works of Henry Fielding. Edited by George Saintsbury. 6 vols. New York and Philadelphia: The Nottingham Society. [1902-03].

Essentially a reprint of 1893.A4 following the order of [1900].A20.

12 _____. The Works of Henry Fielding. Edited by Maynadier. Edition deluxe. 12 vols. New York: Eighteenth Century Club. [1902].
See 1903.A3.

13 _____. The Works of Henry Fielding, Esq. With an Essay on His Life and Genius by Arthur Murphy, Esq. Edited by James P. Browne. 11 vols. London: Bickers and Son.
Reissue of 1871.A6 and 1872.A1. These volumes were issued over two years, 1902-1903.

14 _____. The Works of Henry Fielding. Introductions by G. H. Maynadier. 6 vols. Philadelphia: John D. Morris. [1902].
Vol. 1 contains Joseph Andrews; vols. 2-3 Tom Jones; vols. 4-5 Amelia and Jonathan Wild; vol. 6 Miscellanies. Maynadier provides a brief introduction to each "work." See 1903.A3.

15 _____. The Works of Henry Fielding. Preface and introductions by G. H. Maynadier. 12 vols. Boston: C. T. Brainard. [1902].
See 1903.A3.

16 _____. The Works of Henry Fielding. Preface and introductions by G. H. Maynadier. 12 vols. Boston: Old Corner Bookstore. [1902].
See 1903.A3.

17 _____. The Works of Henry Fielding. Preface and Introductions by G. H. Maynadier. 12 vols. New York: International. [1902].
See 1903.A3.

18 _____. The Works of Henry Fielding. Preface and introductions by G. H. Maynadier. 12 vols. New York: T. Y. Crowell. [1902].
See 1903.A3.

19 HÖHNE, FRIEDRICH. Komik und Humor in Henry Fieldings Roman Joseph Andrews. Greifswald: F. W. Knike, 62 pp.
Argues that Joseph Andrews has a two part structure. Book 1, chapters 1-10 and Book 4 are a parody of Pamela; the rest is a picaresque novel with Adams as protagonist. Höhne then applies Fielding's theory of the comic epic in prose to both parts of the novel. Fielding's theories of

the comic and the ridiculous are dramatized, but Höhne argues they do not account for much that is humorous in the novel. He then examines Fielding's satiric approach to character (coarse jokes, elaborate descriptions of meaningless events, ridiculous physical appearance, etc.). Fielding's satire, he argues, is based mainly on social and class differences and on the discrepancy between professed attitude and action. In German.

For another view of structure see 1966.B7.

20 MCSPADDEN, J. WALKER. Henry Fielding. Standard Authors' Booklets. No. 3. New York: Croscup & Sterling, 33 pp. [1902].

This pamphlet very briefly sets Fielding in his age, provides biography, and discusses his friends and enemies. Devotes a page to him as a playwright and a page each to Joseph Andrews, Jonathan Wild, Tom Jones, and Amelia. Largely an advertisement for the new Henley edition issued by Croscup & Sterling.

1902 B SHORTER WRITINGS

1 DOBSON, AUSTIN. "The Covent-Garden Journal. Being a hitherto-unwritten Chapter in the Life of Henry Fielding," in his Sidewalk Studies. London: Chatto & Windus, pp. 63-92.

Reprint of 1901.B1.

2 ELWIN, WARWICK. "Fielding," in his Some Eighteenth Century Men of Letters. Vol. 2. London: John Murray, pp. 83-152.

Reprint of 1855.B1.

3 OSCHINSKY, HUGO. Gesellschaftliche Zustände Englands während der ersten Hälfte des 18. Jahrhunderts im Spiegel Fieldingscher Komödien. Berlin: R. Gaertner, 19 pp.

Uses twenty-three of Fielding's comedies (which he thinks dramatically uninteresting) to examine the social conditions in England in the first half of the eighteenth century. Argues that Fielding is a moralist satirically attempting to correct French influence in England, which had led to hypocrisy, social pretension, cupidity, and social injustices. In German.

1903

1903 A BOOKS

1 FIELDING, HENRY. The History of the Adventures of Joseph Andrews and His Friend Mr. Abraham Adams. The English Comedie Humaine. New York: Century, 343 pp.
Reissue of 1902.A6.

2 _____. The Works of Henry Fielding. Edited by G. H. Maynadier. 12 vols. New York: Sully and Kleinteich. [1903].
Reissue of 1903.A3.

3 _____. The Works of Henry Fielding. Preface and introduction by G. H. Maynadier. 12 vols. Cambridge, Mass.: The University Press; New York: Sproul; London: Gay and Bird.
A modernized edition of (vols. 1-2) Joseph Andrews; (vols. 3-6) Tom Jones (the "1750" edition); (vols. 7-9) Amelia; (vol. 10) Jonathan Wild; (vols. 11-12) A Journey From This World to the Next, A Voyage to Lisbon, two acts of The Author's Farce, The Tragedy of Tragedies, Pasquin, "An Essay on Conversation," one number each of The True Patriot and The Covent-Garden Journal, and "Familiar Letters." No indication of copy text. Maynadier provides introductions to each work or group of works (the last two volumes are called Miscellanies and include the plays, etc.). For Joseph Andrews he briefly discusses parody, Fielding's sources (picaresque, romance and essay), the novel's realism, the structural weakness that results from the interpolated tales, and the vivid characters. In the introduction to Tom Jones he discusses its superiority to Joseph Andrews, the particular strength of the characters (although he finds Blifil and Allworthy weak), and Tom as an illustration of Fielding's normal hero--faulty but great-hearted. He sees Amelia as a continuation of Fielding's seriousness, displayed with less vigor, and compares it throughout with Tom Jones and Joseph Andrews. Jonathan Wild is discussed as a flawed satire (there is too much of the sentiment of the Heartfrees, and Wild is too "real"); the life of the real Wild is described.

1903 B SHORTER WRITINGS

1 BECKER, GUSTAV. "Die Bedeutung des Wortes 'romantic' bei Fielding und Smollett." Archiv fur das Studium der neueren Sprachen und Literaturen, 110 (10 n.s.), 56-66.

Briefly traces the English use of the word "romantic" from the middle of the seventeenth century (Pepys and Evelyn) through Steele. In all, it suggests either the fanciful, the unusual, the unreal, or the sublime. By examining Fielding's use of the word in Joseph Andrews, Tom Jones, and Amelia, as well as in six of his plays (including Love in Several Masks and The Author's Farce), Becker concludes that Fielding only occasionally uses the word to denote the unusual. More often in Fielding it loses its negative connotations and means instead noble or highminded. He also applies the adjective to other positive qualities, like generosity, honor, and the love of nature. Smollett uses the word in its more conventional sense of unusual or picturesque. In German.

2 WHEELER, ADRIAN. "Henry Fielding." Notes and Queries, 9th. series, 12 (25 July), 65.

Fielding's house in Uxbridge Road, Ealing, where he wrote Tom Jones and Amelia, is being demolished.

1904 A BOOKS

1 ANON. Henry Fielding. The Pickering Club Booklets. No. 1. London: William Heinemann, 34 pp. [1904].

Essentially an advertisement for the Henley edition of Fielding's Works, which briefly sets Fielding in his age and provides a paragraph or two on each of his novels.

2 FIELDING, HENRY. Fielding's Works. Illustrations by Sterling and biographical sketch by Alfred Trumble. 7 vols. Boston: Dana Estes.

Vols. 1-2 Amelia; vol. 3 The History of the Life of the Late Mr. Jonathan Wild, the Great and a sketch of Fielding's life by Alfred Trumble; vol. 4 The History of the Adventures of Joseph Andrews; vols. 5-7 The History of Tom Jones, A Foundling. No indication of copy text. Designated as Works on the binding but not on the title pages.

3 _____. The History of Joseph Andrews and his Friend Mr. Abraham Adams. Illustrations by George Cruikshank. Classic Novels. London: Hutchinson, 347 pp.

Reissue of 1832.A4.

1904

4 _____. The History of Joseph Andrews and his Friend Mr. Abraham Adams. Illustrations by George Cruikshank. Classic Novels. Philadelphia: G. W. Jacobs, 347 pp. [1904].
See 1832.A4.

5 _____. The History of the Adventures of Joseph Andrews and His Friend Mr. Abraham Adams. Illustrations by W. Small. The English Comedie Humaine. New York: Century, 343 pp.
Reissue of 1902.A6.

6 _____. The History of Tom Jones, A Foundling. Abridged by Burton E. Stevenson. Condensed Classics. New York: Henry Holt, 456 pp.
"The principal characters . . . and even most of the minor ones, remain full-length . . . no detail has been consciously omitted which assists the action of the story. . . . A re-arrangement of the chapters has, of course, been necessary, as well as the insertion, here and there, of a connecting word or phrase" (iii-iv).

7 _____. The History of Tom Jones, a Foundling. Edited by A. W. Pollard. Macmillan's Library of English Classics. 2 vols. London, New York, Toronto: Macmillan, 1021 (532 & 489) pp.
Reprint of 1900.A14.

8 _____. The History of Tom Jones a Foundling. Portrait and illustrations by George Cruikshank. Classic Novels. 2 vols. London: Hutchinson, 938 pp.
Reprint of 1831.A4.

9 _____. The History of Tom Jones a Foundling. Portrait and illustrations by George Cruikshank. Classic Novels. 2 vols. Philadelphia: G.W. Jacobs, 938 (476 & 462) pp. [1904].
See 1904.A8.

1904 B SHORTER WRITINGS

1 SCHACHT, HEINRICH R. Der gute Pfarrer in der englischen Literatur bis zu Goldsmiths Vicar of Wakefield. Berlin: Mayer and Müller, pp. 22-30.
In a study of the good parson from Wycliffe and Chaucer to Goldsmith, Fielding's Parson Adams, Dr. Harrison, and Vicar Supple are considered. Argues that ParsonAdams is a new kind of character, mixing the pathetic and the comic without satire. Adams, according to Schacht, has many of the traits of Richardson's Parson Williams (he is poor, he is a comforter, forgives his enemies, and has strained relations with his masters). Adams, unlike Williams, is also shown in relation to his family and community and gains experience on the highway. Dr. Harrison is another

new departure. A mixture of Adams and Richardson's Dr. Bartlett, he is the ideal parson, a gentleman and philosopher. In German.

1905 A BOOKS

1 FIELDING, HENRY. Amelia. Illustrated by George Cruikshank. Bohn's Novelists' Library. London: George Bell and Sons, 608 pp.
Reprint of 1877.A1.

*2 _____. Śaranagāta. Abridged and translated by M. R. Annaji Rav. Mysore: Karnataka granthamala, 127 pp.
Abridged Kannada translation of Tom Jones.
Source: Hugh Amory's working bibliography.

3 _____. The History of Amelia. Illustrations by George Cruikshank. Classic Novels. 2 vols. London: Hutchinson, 601 (302 & 299) pp.
No indication of copy text.

4 _____. The History of the Adventures of Joseph Andrews and His Friend Mr. Abraham Adams. Illustrations by W. Small. The English Comedie Humaine. New York: Century, 343 pp.
Reissue of 1902.A6.

5 _____. The History of the Life of the late Mr. Jonathan Wild the Great and A Journey from this World to the Next. Illustrations by "Phiz" [H. K. Browne]. Classic Novels. London: Hutchinson, 330 pp.
No indication of copy text.

6 _____. The History of Tom Jones a Foundling. The York Library. 2 vols. London: George Bell and Sons, 1011 (514 & 497) pp.
Appears to reprint the first edition.

7 _____. The Works of Henry Fielding. Preface and introductions by G. H. Maynadier. 12 vols. New York: The Jenson Society.
See 1903.A3.

8 _____. Tom Jones. The Works of Henry Fielding. Vol. 1. Edited by Sidney Lee. Methuen's Standard Library. London: Methuen, 744 pp.

1905

A brief headnote and a reprinting of the 1762 edition "corrected by the third edition of 1750" (p. vii). No more volumes seem to have appeared.

9 GEROULD, GORDON H., ed. Henry Fielding: Selected Essays. Boston, New York, Chicago and London: Ginn, 303 pp.

Of the thirty-three "essays" reprinted, only a few were separately printed by Fielding as essays in the Covent-Garden Journal and Miscellanies. Most are selections from his novels (Tom Jones, Joseph Andrews, Amelia, and Jonathan Wild), which Gerould titles (e.g., "On Liberty") or for which he uses chapter titles. Gerould's eighty-one page introduction includes a biographical sketch, based on Dobson (1883.A1) and Murphy (1762.A10), an analysis of Fielding's work (including a section on his poems and plays), and a brief review of his "philosophy of life and his prose style" (p. lxxiii). In this section Fielding is said to be cheerful, manly, tender, and brave, but not always careful of controlling the "taste of filth-loving readers" (p. lxxv). In his section on Fielding's essays, Gerould thinks Fielding one of the major English essayists (along with Dryden, Addison, Lamb, and Macaulay), and offers brief appreciations of several of the "essays" he reprints.

1905 B SHORTER WRITINGS - NONE

1906 A BOOKS

1 FIELDING, HENRY. Amelia. Illustrations by George Cruikshank. The York Library. London: George Bell and Sons, 608 pp.

Reprint of 1877.A1.

2 _____. The History of the Adventures of Joseph Andrews and His Friend Mr. Abraham Adams. Illustrations by W. Small. The English Comedie Humaine. New York: Century, 343 pp.

Reissue of 1902.A6.

3 _____. The History of the Adventures of Joseph Andrews and His Friend Mr. Abraham Adams. The York Library. London: George Bell and Sons, 369 pp.

"A reproduction of the fifth edition, which appeared in the year 1751" (p. v).

4 _____. The History of Tom Jones, A Foundling. Illustrations by W. Small. 2 vols. New York: Century, 871 (441 & 430) pp.

Reproduces sixteen illustrations prepared in 1881 and Coleridge's notes to Tom Jones. Appears to reprint the first edition.

5 _____. The History of Tom Jones, A Foundling. New York: A. L. Burt, 919 pp. [1906].
Appears to reproduce the 1749 first edition.

*6 WALDSCHMIDT, KARL. "Die Dramatisierungen von Fieldings Tom Jones." Dissertation, Rostock, 1906.
In German.
Source: McNamee, 1865-1964, p. 557.

1906 B SHORTER WRITINGS

1 BECKER, GUSTAV. "Der Einfluss des Don Quijote auf Henry Fielding," in Die Aufnahme des Don Quijote in die englische Literatur (1605-1700). Palaestra, no. 13. Berlin: Mayer and Müller, Introduction and pp. 122-57.
According to Becker, Fielding was one of the few English writers who openly expressed his admiration for Cervantes; he borrowed his notion of the comic character with noble traits from Don Quixote. Becker examines Don Quixote in England, concluding that Fielding emphasizes the serious traits of Quixote to create a moral ideal. Fielding follows the same pattern in Joseph Andrews, mixing the sublime and the ridiculous in Adams while emphasizing the sublime. Becker sees Tom as the perfect Quixote because both are ruled by passion that leads them into comic situations. He also briefly discusses other character parallels: Sancho and Joseph or Partridge, Maritornes and Betty. In German.

2 MACMICHAEL, J. HOLDEN. "Tom Thumb's First Appearance in London." Notes and Queries, 10th series, 6 (28 July), 76-77.
Notes that several women played Tom Thumb in the Tragedy of Tragedies. See 1916.B5.

3 PRIDEAUX, W. F. "Fielding's 'Journal of a Voyage to Lisbon,' 1755." Notes and Queries, 10th series, 6 (28 July), 61-62.
A bibliographical description of the two editions of the Journal of a Voyage issued in 1755. The shorter version is the earlier. This simply adds bibliographical data to Austin Dobson's 1892 reprint of the Journal of a Voyage. See also 1906.B6.

1906

4 "RANGER." "The Choice of Books: Henry Fielding." Bookman (London), 29, no. 173 (Feb.), 202-204.
Reviews adulatory response from Gibbon through Dobson, and including Thackeray and Coleridge, while briefly setting out Fielding's life and career.

5 S., H. K. ST. J. "Poem by Fielding." Notes and Queries, 10th. series, 5 (9 June), 446.
A brief poem said to be by Fielding, not printed in any editions. See 1916.B4.

6 ST. SWITHIN. "Fielding's 'Journal of a Voyage to Lisbon,' 1755." Notes and Queries, 10th. series, 6 (11 Aug.), 115.
A 1756 Dublin edition of Journal of a Voyage briefly described bibliographically.

7 SWAEN, A. E. H. "Fielding and Goldsmith in Leyden." Modern Language Review, 1, no. 4 (July), 327-28.
On the evidence of the student register, Fielding, aged 20, entered the University of Leyden on 16 Feb. 1728 where he studied classics. He might have stayed on until nearly January 1730.

8 T-E., W. "Fielding's First Marriage." Notes and Queries, 10th. series, 6 (21 July), 47.
Evidence from the parish of St. Mary Charlcombe that Fielding was married to Charlotte Cradock in this tiny rural church two miles from Bath. See 1907.B6.

1907 A BOOKS

1 DOLDER, ERNST. Henry Fielding's Don Quixote in England. Zürich: Buchdruckeri Gerb. Leemann, 58 pp.
This inaugural dissertation at Berne provides a bibliography of Fielding as a dramatist, sets Cervantes' novel in "universal literature," provides a chronology of English translations and imitations of Don Quixote, and describes Fielding's admiration for Cervantes and his relationship with Walpole. Dolder also provides a plot summary, describes the characters and their sources, and sets the play in Fielding's dramatic career. Because Dolder thinks Fielding a failure as a dramatist, this dissertation (with its emphasis on performance, editions, translations, and simple description) says little about the play except to set it superficially in the tradition of Fielding's political and social satires. In German.

2 FIELDING, HENRY. Jones Tamás, A Talált Gyerek. Translated by Szüry Dénes. 3 vols. Budapest: Franklin-Társulat.
Volume 2 of this Hungarian translation was printed in 1909 and volume 3 in 1910.

3 _____. The History of the Adventures of Joseph Andrews and His Friend Mr. Abraham Adams. Illustrated by W. Small. The English Comedie Humaine. New York: Century, 343 pp.
Reprint of 1902.A6.

4 _____. The History of Tom Jones, A Foundling. Illustrations by George Cruikshank. Bohn's Novelists' Library. 2 vols. London: George Bell and Sons, 980 pp.
Reissue of 1876.A2.

5 _____. The History of Tom Jones, A Foundling. Illustrations by W. Small. The English Comedie Humaine. 2 vols. New York: Century, 871 pp.
Reissue of 1906.A4.

6 _____. The Journal of a Voyage to Lisbon. Edited by Austin Dobson. World's Classics. London, New York and Toronto: Henry Frowde, Oxford University Press, 207 pp.
Reprint of 1892.A2.

7 _____. The Journal of a Voyage to Lisbon. Introduction by Hannaford Bennett. Carlton Classics. London: John Long, 155 pp.
A brief biographical sketch is added by Bennett. No indication of copy text.

8 _____. The Works of Henry Fielding. Preface and introductions by G. H. Maynadier. 12 vols. New York: The Jenson Society.
Reissue of 1903.A3.

9 KEIGHTLEY, THOMAS. The Life and Writings of Henry Fielding, Esq. Edited by F. S. Dickson. Cleveland: The Rowfant Club, 162 pp.
Dickson reprints Keightley's review essays of Frederick Lawrence's Life of Fielding, which had originally appeared in Fraser's Magazine (see 1858.B2, B3, B4), adds a brief preface describing Keightley, compiles a list of biographies of Fielding, and collates the first and second editions of Tom Jones.

1907

1907 B SHORTER WRITINGS

1 ANON. "Fielding Among the Immortals." Saturday Review (20 April), pp. 489-90.
Says that Fielding is seldom read but that his greatness and influence are still felt through nineteenth-century novelists like Scott and Thackeray. Discusses his reputation for being a bawdy novelist, which reduces the number of those who might read him, and concludes that Fielding's Tom Jones is innocent but that Richardson's Pamela has now become recognized as the "pornographic" novel it is.

2 _____. "How Fielding Measures up with Modern Novelists." Literary Digest, 34, no. 18 (4 May), 721-22.
Fielding is commended for his "modernness" in this digest of 1907.B7. His "greatness [is] that . . . he is still the one . . . to which we have swung round for our best ideals of what a good novel should be" (p. 721).

3 _____. "The Fielding Anniversary." Academy and Literature (London), 72-73 (20 April), 389-90.
Praises Fielding for his isolating Englishness, which makes him, unlike Richardson, unappreciated by the French. Also briefly discusses his career as dramatist and magistrate, his "radical nature," and his "thorough Saxon impatience of wrong-doing, unmodified by the slightest respect for convention" (p. 389).

4 _____. "The Fielding Bicentenary." Bookman (New York), 25 (April), 119-20.
An admiring outburst that sees Fielding as better than Richardson and almost up to Dickens' mark.

5 CHANDLER, FRANK W. "Fielding," in his The Literature of Roguery. Vol. 2. Boston and New York: Houghton, Mifflin, pp. 300-309.
In this survey of picaresque literature from the seventeenth century through to the nineteenth, Chandler briefly concludes that Joseph Andrews is not picaresque (despite the influence of Cervantes). He sees both Journey From This World to the Next and Jonathan Wild as more clearly in the tradition, but Jonathan Wild has few of the realistic elements of the genre, borrows few of the classic devices of roguery, and in its irony displays the "English instinct for morality" (p. 307). Tom Jones could not have come into being without picaresque predecessors, but it "transcends them all" (p. 308).

6 DOBSON, AUSTIN. "Fresh Facts About Fielding." Macmillan's Magazine, n.s. 2, no. 18 (April), 417-22.
Carefully sets out two facts about Fielding's life (both of which Murphy 1762.A10 got slightly wrong)--the exact period of his residence at Leyden (from 16 March 1728 to no later than 8 February 1730), and the precise date of Fielding's marriage to Charlotte Cradock (28 November 1734 at St. Mary's Church, Charlcombe). See 1906.B8.

7 GAINES, C. H. "The Bicentenary of Fielding, The Father of the English Novel, and His Art." Harper's Weekly (20 April), p. 578.
Enthusiastic praise for Fielding, the writer of "the first complete, full-grown, full-blooded English novel." Fielding is commended for his "modernity," his ability to "come nearer to the modern ideal of truth and vitality" than any novelist in "the past two centuries." His "nascent vigor" is commended, as is his "complete mastery of individual character" and his "manner half-way between raillery and earnest." His plays are said to be as witty as Sheridan's but "richer in their portrayal of life, more akin to the comedies of Shakespeare." For another view, see 1860.B1.

8 LOBBAN, J. H. "Henry Fielding." Blackwood's Magazine, 181, no. 1098 (April), 550-65.
"Among English men of genius Fielding has no superior in respect of virility and commonsense." He is commended for his "moderation and good humor" (p. 550). Lobban calls Journal of a Voyage to Lisbon "the most human of all his writings," and through it "we arrive at a new relation with its author" (p. 551). He then mixes biography with a little critical comment ("His plays are frankly negligible," pp. 551-52) as he reviews Fielding's career. He objects to the "text-book tradition" (p. 555) that Fielding abandoned the parody of Pamela after the opening, pointing to the conclusion of the novel. He comments on the interpolated tales in Joseph Andrews and sees "Fielding's ingenuity in plot construction . . . at its best in the closing chapters" where the history of Mr. Wilson, which looked like an interpolation, becomes "the pivot of his sharpest satire" (p. 555). He discusses Adams in light of Fielding's theory of the ridiculous and of Fielding's chief sin, "the sin of imposture" (p. 556), carefully indicating the nature of Adams' strength ("child-like simplicity") and the source of his comedy. He discusses the ethics and morality of Tom Jones, finding that "the moral deducible is a sane and healthy one. Fielding held that the sins

arising from a mean and treacherous heart are blacker than any intemperance" (p. 561). Lobban discusses the pathos and the humor of Amelia; however, he also accepts the old notion that Fielding is his own model for Booth. A surprisingly insightful early article.

9 MINCHIN, HARRY C. "Henry Fielding and His Writings." Fortnightly Review, n.s. 81, no. 484 (1 April), 620-34.

Fielding is celebrated as a realist who set down the events of "that noisy, robustious age" (p. 621). Minchin then discusses some of his favorite characters in Fielding's fiction, treating them as mimetically accurate and often based on biographical fact. Sophia and Amelia, for example, are both seen as Charlotte Cradock (Fielding's first wife) and are said to be nearly the only endurable female characters in Fielding's fiction; they are terribly mistreated by fathers, lovers and husbands.

10 SAINTSBURY, GEORGE. "Henry Fielding." Bookman (London), 32, no. 187 (April), 7-10.

Opens with a sharp reaction to the modern "internal" novel, briefly reviews favorable and unfavorable criticism of Fielding, and calls him the most English of English writers. Saintsbury compares him to Swift in his ability to attack "those two corruptions of the English character snobbishness and priggery" (p. 8); he discusses his "true mimesis," comparing him to Cervantes, Balzac, etc.; he discusses irony (in Jonathan Wild) and parody (in Joseph Andrews); and he briefly mentions Fielding's ability to unite incident and character.

Also includes several illustrations for the novels, several "portraits" of Fielding, and photographs of places important in Fielding's life (pp. 10-19).

11 SECCOMBE, THOMAS. "Henry Fielding: 1707-1754." Cornhill Magazine, 22, no. 570 (June), 789-801.

This bicentennial essay suggests that Fielding is the best-read author, although Tom Jones is inappropriate for the classroom and must be read by boys only "by stealth" (p. 789). Seccombe does not think him one of the founders of the novel (Defoe and Richardson are), but he thinks Fielding and Dickens among the great geniuses of it. He credits Fielding, like Shakespeare, with an Olympian pity and kindness to his characters. Seccombe's biography of Fielding passes on the most scandalous parts of the Fielding tradition, including his neglect of his wife. He at least grants Fielding the ability to do careful creative work in Tom Jones ("crowned with scholarship and lit up by a supreme and sleepless irony," p. 799) and the ability to sustain a Shakespearian joy and faith in man, despite his often portraying men as brutal and grotesque. See 1918.B1 and 1924.B1.

12 YARDLEY, E. "Fielding and Shakespeare." Notes and Queries, 10th series, 7 (8 June), 444-45.
Shows Fielding paraphrasing speeches from Hamlet, Othello, and Romeo and Juliet in Tom Jones.

1908 A BOOKS

1 BOSDORF, ERICH. Entstehungsgeschichte von Fieldings Joseph Andrews. Weimar: R. Wagner Sohn, 82 pp.
Inaugural dissertation for Berlin that sets out the publication history, the changes and additions in various editions, and relates the novel to the anti-Pamela controversy (rejecting the idea that Fielding wrote Shamela). Bosdorf then examines the second non-parody part of the novel (Joseph's road adventures), comparing them with "realistic" novels from Petronius' Satyricon through Gil Blas and Don Quixote. He traces the common motifs in Lesage's Gil Blas and Joseph Andrews as well as comparing Cervantes' and Fielding's ideas of character and mimesis. In German.

2 FIELDING, HENRY. Geschichte Jonathan Wilds des Grossen. Translated by Heinrich Stöhr. Kulturhistorische Liebhaberbibliothek. Series 4. Vol. 36. Leipzig: Friedrich Rothbarth, 327 pp. [1908].
In German.

3 _____. The History of the Adventures of Joseph Andrews, and His Friend Mr. Abraham Adams. Illustrations by George Cruikshank and biography by Thomas Roscoe. Bohn's Novelists' Library. London: George Bell and Sons, 433 pp.
Reissue of 1836.A2.

4 _____. The Novels of Henry Fielding, complete and unabridged. Biographical essay by W. E. Henley. Sharpham Edition. 7 vols. New York: Harper.
Reissue of [1902].A9.

1908 B SHORTER WRITINGS

1 ANON. "News for Bibliophiles." Nation (New York), 87, no. 2269 (24 Dec.), 624.

Distinguishes the "two distinct editions [of Tom Jones] in six volumes, from two separate settings of type," both of which appeared in 1749, one with a list of errata.

2 BENSLY, EDWARD. "Fielding's Grave." Notes and Queries, 10th. series, 9 (15 Feb.), 134.

L. A. W. (1908.B10) confused Austin Dobson's poem with the inscription on Fielding's tomb.

3 BERGER, T. W. Don Quixote in Deutschland und sein Einfluss auf den deutschen Roman, 1613-1800. Heidelberg: [?], pp. 25-31, 36-47.

Argues that novelists like Lessing, Schiller, Wieland, and Goethe were probably introduced to Don Quixote through Henry Fielding, whose novels in translation were extremely popular in eighteenth-century Germany. Looks at both Fielding's influence and importance and the probable understanding of Don Quixote that Fielding's works evoked. In German.

4 CHESTERTON, G. K. "Tom Jones and Morality," in his All Things Considered. New York: John Lane, pp. 256-66.

Attacks those who discuss Fielding's morality without having read him. Sees Tom Jones as Everyman, caught in a struggle between practical and theoretical morality, with all his aspects dramatized by Fielding. Such a man would be fragmented these days (Zola recording his bad moments, Kipling his brutality, etc.). Thus Tom Jones is the "terrible struggle of the human soul [which] is surely a very elementary part of the ethics of honesty" (p. 266).

Reprinted 1913; 1925, London: Methuen; 1956, New York: Sheed & Ward; 1969, Henley-on-Thames: Darwen Finlayson.

5 DOBSON, AUSTIN. "Fresh Facts about Fielding," in his De Libris: Prose & Verse. London: Macmillan, pp. 193-204.

Reprints 1907.B6.

6 HENLEY, W. E. "Fielding," in his Views and Reviews: Essays in Appreciation. Vol. 1. London: David Nutt, pp. 273-80.

Incorporates the general material from 1882.B1 and 1883.B8.

7 JACKSON, HOLBROOK. "Henry Fielding," in his Great English Novelists. London: Grant Richards, pp. 64-86.

Recounts Fielding's career; asserts that Fielding and Richardson "each fathered a type of novel which, with modifications and amplifications, has survived down to to-day" (p. 65); briefly discusses satire and burlesque (in his plays), irony (in Jonathan Wild), and Fielding's hatred of sham (in Joseph Andrews). About Tom Jones he says that "it marks at once the turning-point in the art of the novel, and its mastery" (p. 80); aligns Dickens and Meredith with this tradition. He quietly defends the morality of Tom (whom he thinks the least convincing character in the novel) because, as "the first English novelist to treat human nature as natural history" (p. 83), Fielding knew that thoughtless lapses did not make a villain. Ultimately, "one puts down Tom Jones with a feeling that on the whole life is a clean and decent thing, and one is almost convinced by the argument of Fielding's fine enthusiasm for life and his epic tolerance that virtue and instinct may be identical" (p. 85).

8 PAGE, JOHN T. "Fielding's Grave." Notes and Queries, 10th. series, 9 (4 April), 277.
Another response to L. A. W. (1908.B10).

*9 WICKLSIN, E. Das 'Ernsthafte' in dem englischen komischen Roman des xviii Jahrhunderts. Dresden: [?].
In German.
Source: New Cambridge Bibliography of English Literature: 1660-1800, II, 935; T. Humphrey, p. 233.

10 W., L. A. "Fielding's Grave." Notes and Queries, 10th. series, 9 (18 Jan.), 49.
Another query about the inscription on Fielding's tomb. See 1893.B1, B2. Responded to 1908.B2, B8.

1909 A BOOKS

1 BINGHAM, CHARLES W., ed. Wise Sayings and Favorite Passages From the Works of Henry Fielding. Cedar Rapids, Iowa: Torch Press, 132 pp.
Includes selected moral passages from Joseph Andrews, Tom Jones, Amelia, Jonathan Wild, Miscellanies, and all of an "Essay on Conversation."

2 FIELDING, HENRY. The History of Tom Jones, A Foundling. Introduction by George Saintsbury. Everyman's Library. 2 vols. London: J. M. Dent & Sons; New York: E. P. Dutton, 838 (425 & 413) pp.
Introduction comments on interpolated episodes and authorial intrusions (which Saintsbury thinks hors-d'oeuvres), on the weak characters (Allworthy and Blifil), and on the many strong characters, particularly Tom, whom

Saintsbury defends in the Lady Bellaston sexual episode by citing eighteenth-century mores. A modernized version of the "1750" edition is reproduced, the same text Murphy (1762.A10) reprinted.

3 GREEN, EMANUEL. Henry Fielding: His Work. An Independent Criticism. London: Harrison & Sons, 33 pp.

This pamphlet-length "critical biography" reviews Fielding's career and provides plot outlines of Shamela, Joseph Andrews, Tom Jones, Amelia, and Journal of a Voyage to Lisbon, with occasional "critical" judgments (the squire in Don Quixote in England is like Western, and Tom Jones is padded out with the Man of the Hill tale and Mrs. Fitzpatrick's story).

*4 KRIEG, HANS. "J. J. Chr. Bode als Übersetzer des Tom Jones von H. Fielding." Dissertation, Greifswald, 1909.

In German.

Source: McNamee, 1865-1964, p. 557.

5 SAINTSBURY, GEORGE, ed. Masters of Literature: Fielding. London: George Bell and Sons, 400 pp.

Large excerpts (with narrative bridges between passages added by Saintsbury) from Joseph Andrews, Tom Jones, and Amelia, as well as brief selections from Jonathan Wild (Book 4, chapter 15) and A Voyage to Lisbon. Saintsbury's introduction provides a biographical sketch, a brief survey of critical opinion, and an appreciation of Fielding's use of tradition, his careful artistry, and his irony. Headnotes to the excerpts also point out various aspects of each (e.g., the parody of Pamela in Joseph Andrews; the historical reality of Wild; plot, character contrast, and epic in Tom Jones). Selections taken from Roscoe (1840.A3).

1909 B SHORTER WRITINGS

1 BISPHAM, G. T. "Fielding's Jonathan Wild," in Eighteenth Century Literature: An Oxford Miscellany. Oxford: Clarendon Press, pp. 56-75.

Briefly traces the career of the real Wild and of his literary being (in The Beggar's Opera) and then examines this adventure novel "in that mock-heroic strain which exhibits Fielding's irony at its best" (p. 61). Bispham discusses Wild's human shortcomings, particularly his failure with women, commenting that "the force of Wild's personality at times masters us as we are mastered by Milton's

Satan" (p. 65) because Fielding "takes evident delight in portraying the ingenuity and boldness of his hero" (p. 64). He also discusses the Heartfrees as models of Fielding's ideal goodness, far weaker than Wild but not totally without life ("but the apologies that are continually made for Heartfree's goodness tend to weary us," p. 68). He thinks it a masterpiece of prose satire in style but not structure (the interruption of Mrs. Heartfree's adventure breaks the narrative), and finally compares it with Carlyle's Heroes and Hero Worship, thinking it a counterbalance.
Reprinted 1966, New York: Books for Libraries Press.

2 BLAKE, W. B. "Tom Jones in France." South Atlantic Quarterly, 8, no. 3 (July), 222-33.
This comparative study of Fielding's influence on French literature begins by listing the translations, imitations, and French "forgeries" fostered on Fielding; discusses the carelessness of the translations and the French inability to distinguish what was genuinely Fielding's; concludes by saying that the "hearty welcome" of Tom Jones in France was simply a result of Anglomania. Both the 'epic' story and the intrusive narrator "undeniably clash[ed] with Gallic notions of 'form'" (p. 233) and thus provoked no real imitators. See 1917.B4, 1922.B7, and 1962.B3.

3 BURTON, RICHARD. "Eighteenth Century Beginnings: Fielding," in his Masters of the English Novel. New York: Henry Holt, pp. 48-71.
Passes on the Fielding myth; chiefly compares Richardson and Fielding (thinking Fielding "more external and shallow," p. 52). Thinks Richardson the precursor of the modern novel; justifies Fielding's frankness as a reflection of his cruder society; finds Tom Jones and Joseph Andrews "unanalytic" and loosely constructed, strong chiefly in their characters. Amelia is uncharacteristic.

4 GODDEN, G. M. "Henry Fielding: Some Unpublished Letters and Records." Fortnightly Review, n.s. 86, no. 515 (1 Nov.), 821-32.
An early attempt to dispel the "vague cloud that for so long has hung over the name of [Henry Fielding]" (p. 822). He relates the events surrounding Fielding's late boyhood, as Lady Gould (Fielding's grandmother) succeeded in getting the Fielding children and their estate away from Colonel Fielding (Henry's father). His marriage and money affairs are described, to dispel the myth of an early impoverished life in a garret. Fielding's career is outlined through his time as a magistrate. Two letters are reproduced, one

to a bookseller and one to Lord Hardwick (which had accompanied the draft of a bill for the prevention of crime).

5 PRIDEAUX, W. F. "'Tom Jones' in French." Notes and Queries, 10th. series, 12 (20 Nov.), 407.
Asks which translation of Tom Jones, the 1751, 1804, 1833, or 1836, is best.

1910 A BOOKS

*1 DUEBER, RUDOLF. "Beitraege zu Henry Fieldings Romantechnik." Dissertation, Halle, 1910.
In German.
Source: McNamee, 1865-1964, p. 557.

2 FIELDING, HENRY. Amelia and Jonathan Wild. Introduction by G. H. Maynadier. Illustrations by J. W. Dunsmore. 2 vols. Boston and New York: C. T. Brainard, 1188 (580 & 608) pp. [1910?].
Reissue of volumes 7-10 of 1903.A3 Works. Still separately paged but bound as two volumes.

3 _____. Amelia. 2 vols. Boston and New York: Colonial Press, 661 (320 & 341) pp. [1910?].
Called the "Illustrated Library Edition"; illustrations by several engravers, including Cruikshank.

4 _____. Novels. Illustrations by Sterling and biographical sketch by Alfred Trumble. 7 vols. Boston: Dana Estes. [1910].
Reissue of 1904.A2, merely reversing the order of the volumes. Tom Jones is now first (vols. 1-3) and Amelia last (vols. 6-7).

5 _____. The History of the Adventures of Joseph Andrews and The History of the Life of the Late Mr. Jonathan Wild the Great. Boston and New York: C. T. Brainard, 606 pp. [1910?].
Each text separately paged and illustrated by several illustrators (including Cruikshank). Reissue in part of [1902].A15, without the introduction.

6 _____. The History of the Adventures of Joseph Andrews and his Friend Mr. Abraham Adams. Edited by George Saintsbury. Everyman's Library. London: J. M. Dent & Sons; New York: E. P. Dutton, 390 pp.

Reproduces the Murphy text (1762.A10). The introduction sums up Fielding's life (adjusting some of Murphy's anecdotes and presenting a balance between Fielding the rake and Fielding the man of regular habits) and comments on Fielding's achievement in the world of literature (briefly comparing him to Shakespeare, Milton, Swift, and the "Russian Nihilists"). Considering Joseph Andrews, Saintsbury says something about the parody of Pamela, Fielding's picaresque and romantic models (Scarron, Lesage, Cervantes, Marivaux, etc.), the novel's loose structure, and its characters ("the chief differentia of the novel," p. xxix).

7 _____. The History of Tom Jones, A Foundling. Illustrations by George Cruikshank. Bohn's Novelists' Library. 2 vols. London: George Bell and Sons, 980 pp.
Reissue of 1876.A2.

8 _____. The History of Tom Jones A Foundling. Introduction by George Saintsbury. Everyman's Library. 2 vols. London: J. M. Dent & Sons; New York: E. P. Dutton, 838 pp.
Reprint of 1909.A2.

9 GODDEN, G[ERTRUDE] M. Henry Fielding: A Memoir, Including Newly Discovered Letters and Records with Illustrations from Contemporary Prints. London: Sampson Low, Marston; Toronto: Musson Book Company, 339 pp.
Reviewed by N. Connell in English Review (London), 4 (1910), 754-60.
Godden avoids "literary criticism" and sets out a detailed account of Fielding's life, supplemented by the facts "disclosed by hitherto unpublished documents, or found hidden in the columns of contemporary newspapers, which add to our knowledge of Fielding's personality" (p. v). She does pause for appreciations of the "immortal" Parson Adams, who "reflects honour on his creator by the inflexible integrity of his goodness" (p. 129); she briefly defends Tom Jones by asserting that Tom finally "wholly purges himself from . . . sin" (p. 188) and "worships" (p. 190) innocence and virtue.
Superseded by Cross (1918.A1).

1910 B SHORTER WRITINGS

*1 FIELDING, HENRY. "Preface to Joseph Andrews," in Prefaces and Prologues to Famous Books, with Introductions, Notes and Illustrations. New York: P. F. Collier & Son. [1910].

1910

Source: National Union Catalogue: Pre-1956 Imprints. Vol. 172, p. 5.

*2 GESCHKE, EMIL. "Untersuchungen über die beiden Fassungen von Musäus Grandisonroman." Dissertation, Königsberg, 1910.
In German.
Source: T. Humphrey, p. 257.

3 ROBBINS, ALFRED F. "'Jonathan Wild the Great': Its Germ." Notes and Queries, 11th series, 2 (1 Oct.), 261-63.
Reprints two articles from Mist's Weekly Journal, written shortly after Wild's execution at Tyburn on 24 May 1725. He suggests that the young Henry Fielding wrote them and that they are an early "germ" of his later attack on Walpole through Wild. See 1916.B5.

4 SWAIN, CORINNE R. "Amelia Booth and Lucy Feverel," Nation (New York), 91, no. 2367 (10 Nov.), 440-41.
Compares Fielding's heroine to a "modern" heroine, Meredith's Lucy Feverel; both use food to placate their men and have robust constitutions. Feels that Fielding's style is stilted and that Meredith is excessive in his emphasis on the corrosive power of mental and spiritual distress.

1911 A BOOKS

1 FIELDING, HENRY. The Works of Henry Fielding. Preface and introductions by G. H. Maynadier. 12 vols. New York: The Jenson Society.
Reissue of 1903.A3.

1911 B SHORTER WRITINGS

1 ALDWORTH, A. E. "'Tom Jones': Dowdy." Notes and Queries, 11th series, 3 (15 April), 289.
Asks who "Dowdy" (Book 6, chapter 9) is. See 1864.B1.

2 DOBSON, AUSTIN. "A Fielding Find." National Review, 57 (Aug.), 983-92.
Reviews the reasons for the lack of Fielding manuscripts; reprints 12 July 1754 letter from Henry to John Fielding, written when Henry had reached the Isle of Wight in his voyage to Lisbon. Then prints two newly discovered letters to John Fielding (one written 22 July from Tor Bay and one from Lisbon); Dobson comments on both, particularly on the long second letter that appears to have been quickly

written and that continues the narration beyond the Journal of a Voyage, which ends when Fielding arrives in Lisbon. See 1971.B1.

3 HILL, N. W. "Henry Fielding and the Civil Power." Notes and Queries, 11th. series, 4 (30 Dec.), 534.

Agrees with Robbins (1911.B8) that Henry, rather than John, would have been referred to as "magistrate Fielding" before 1753.

4 METCALF, JOHN C. "Henry Fielding, Critic." Sewanee Review, 19, no. 2 (April), 138-54.

An early discussion of Fielding's dramas that begins with reference to dramatic rules, to which "Fielding was supremely indifferent" (p. 145). Metcalf believes that Fielding wrote for "no select audience" and was "essentially democratic" (p. 141) and that in his criticism he was largely responsible for bringing "English criticism back to nature and commonsense" (p. 153). He also discusses the objects of his satiric attack in various plays (particularly Restoration tragedy and its imitators), the botched Shakespeare of Cibber, and the theatrical opportunism of John Rich. See 1934.B3.

5 M., F. B. "Henry Fielding and the Civil Power." Notes and Queries, 11th. series, 4 (15 July), 58.

Corrects Robbins (1911.B8) and suggests that it was Sir John Fielding.

6 PRIDEAUX, W. F. "Henry Fielding and the Civil Power." Notes and Queries, 11th. series, 4 (18 Nov.), 419.

Adds precise information to the controversy (1911.B7, B5). John had come to help Henry as magistrate by 1751 and the Bow Street Runners (not a detective force) had been created.

7 ROBBINS, ALFRED F. "Henry Fielding and the Civil Power." Notes and Queries, 11th. series, 4 (30 Sept.), 277.

Sharply corrects F. B. M. (1911.B5) and reasserts that it was Henry.

8 _____. "Henry Fielding and the Civil Power." Notes and Queries, 11th. series, 3 (24 June), 486.

A note in the London Morning Penny Post 4-7 October 1751 reports that Justice Fielding, Robbins thinks Henry, committed a half-pay colonel to Bridewell. See 1911.B3, B5, B6, B7, B9.

1911

9 ST. SWITHIN. "Henry Fielding and the Civil Power." Notes and Queries, 11th. series, 4 (21 Oct.), 336.

Joins the quarrel with Robbins and F. B. M. (1911.B5, B8), and asks which Fielding was the great magistrate who created the Bow Street detectives.

10 WILLIAMS, HAROLD. "Henry Fielding (1707-54)," in his Two Centuries of the English Novel. London: Smith, Elder, pp. 53-77.

Thinks Tom Jones "the greatest novel ever written" (p. 53) and Fielding's morality, which embraces all of life with unshrinking realism, in no need of defense. Briefly reviews his life and his works, touching on what will become the accepted critical approaches (he discusses the preface to Joseph Andrews, the parody, Parson Adams, and the ethics of prudence and humanity). While he is charmed by the narrative intrusions in Tom Jones, he does not think it well plotted, only well and excitingly told. He also thinks Sophia "one of the first of the complete and convincing portraits of womanhood in fiction," who "belongs to the eighteenth century's conception of a woman's functions and deportment upon the stage of life" (p. 71). Although Amelia is an even greater character than Sophia, Williams thinks Amelia flawed by its open didacticism. Fielding's strength lies in his lack of prejudice and narrow convention, "the catholicity of his sympathy with life" (p. 76), and in the sense of "unspent forces lying beneath the surface of his work" (pp. 75-76).

1912 A BOOKS

1 FIELDING, HENRY. Amelia. Illustrations by George Cruikshank. Bohn's Novelists' Library. London: George Bell and Sons, 608 pp.

Reprint of 1877.A1.

2 _____. The History of Amelia. Illustrations by George Cruikshank. Classic Novels. 2 vols. Philadelphia: G. W. Jacobs, 601 pp. [1912].

Reprint of 1905.A3.

3 _____. The History of the Adventures of Joseph Andrews and His Friend Mr. Abraham Adams. Edited by George Saintsbury. Everyman's Library. London: J. M. Dent & Sons, 390 pp. [1912].

Reissue of 1910.A6.

4 _____. The History of the Life of the late Mr. Jonathan Wild the Great and A Journey from this World to the Next. Illustrations by "Phiz." Classic Novels. London: Hutchinson, 330 pp. [1912].
Reissue of 1905.A5.

5 _____. The History of Tom Jones A Foundling. Introduction by George Saintsbury. Everyman's Library. 2 vols. London: J. M. Dent & Sons; New York: E. P. Dutton, 838 pp.
Reprint of 1909.A2.

6 _____. The History of Tom Jones, A Foundling. New York: A. L. Burt, 919 pp. [1912].
Reissue of [1906].A5.

*7 JENSEN, GERARD E., ed. "The Covent-Garden Journal, by Sir Alexander Drawcansir, Knt. Censor of Great Britain, Henry Fielding." Dissertation, Yale, 1912.
Source: Stratman et al., Restoration and Eighteenth Century Theatre Research . . . (1971.B36), p. 291.
See 1915.A1.

1912 B SHORTER WRITINGS

1 DOBSON, AUSTIN. "A Fielding Find," in his At Prior Park and Other Papers. London: Chatto & Windus, pp. 128-49.
Reprints 1911.B2.
Collection reprinted by Oxford University Press 1923 and 1925.

2 _____. "A New Dialogue of the Dead." National Review, 60, no. 358 (Dec.), 609-17.
An imaginary dialogue between Henry Fielding and Arthur Murphy (1762.A10), in which Fielding points out Murphy's weaknesses as a biographer and corrects a number of his errors.

3 HOLLIDAY, CARL. "The Fiction of the Eighteenth Century . . . Henry Fielding," in his English Fiction from the Fifth to the Twentieth Century. New York: Century, pp. 228-39.
Passes on the Fielding myth and briefly outlines his career, praising him for his masculine reality as opposed to Richardson's feminine perception.

4 M., H. A. ST. J. "Fielding's Parson Thwackum." Notes and Queries, 11th.series, 6 (14 Dec.), 470.

1912

Identifies Sir Henry P. St. John Mildmay as Squire Western.

5 T., L. E. "Fielding's Parson Thwackum." Notes and Queries, 11th. series, 6 (2 Nov.), 348.
Identifies Richard Hele, Canon of Salisbury and Master of the Choir School, as Thwackum.

6 WELLS, JOHN E. "Fielding's Signatures in 'The Champion,' and the Date of His 'Of Good-Nature.'" Modern Language Review, 7, no. 1 (Jan.), 97-98.
Because the "C" signature quotes from Fielding's yet unpublished poem "Of Good-Nature," we can be fairly certain that the "C" and "L" signatures are essays by Fielding. It also appears that "Of Good-Nature" was in part written before 17 November 1739. See also 1913.B5, B8, B9, 1920.B11, 1953.B7, 1955.B8, B9, B10, 1963.B17.

7 _____. "Henry Fielding and The Crisis." Modern Language Notes, 27, no. 6 (June), 180-81.
Bibliographical evidence that Fielding wrote The Crisis, as well as a discussion of Fielding's various publishers (Watts, Roberts and Miller). See 1916.B14.

8 _____. "Henry Fielding and the History of Charles XII." The Journal of English and Germanic Philology, 11, no. 4 (Oct.), 603-13.
Attempts to discover whether Fielding translated Adlerfeld's History of Charles XII. "Beyond the receipt quoted in the first paragraph of this paper [from Fielding to John Nourse in payment for a translation] there is nothing directly to connect Fielding with the translation of a History of Charles XII. Beyond the evidence found in the facts of association with the publishers" (p. 606).

9 _____. "News for Bibliophiles." Nation (New York), 94, no. 2443 (25 April), 409.
Reviewing the preface to Fielding's Miscellanies (1743), Wells argues that Fielding had not written for The Champion for half a year before the winter of 1741-42. Both the winter of 1741-42 and 1742-43 were difficult times for Fielding, with his wife ill, his child dying, and his gout.

1913 A BOOKS

1 FIELDING, HENRY. Geschichte Tom Jones, eines Findlings. Translated by Wilhelm von Lüdemann. 2 vols. München: Albert Langen, 1183 (591 & 592) pp.
Illustrations by Gravelot and Moreau. In German.

2 _____. Journal of a Voyage to Lisbon. Edited by J. H. Lobban. English Literature for Schools. Cambridge: Cambridge University Press, 131 pp.
Lobban adds notes and a brief introduction in which he corrects the unjust portrait of Fielding created by the "free play" of Thackeray's imagination and by Johnson's unsympathetic comments. No indication of copy text.

3 _____. The History of the Adventures of Joseph Andrews, and His Friend Mr. Abraham Adams. Illustrations by George Cruikshank and biography by Thomas Roscoe. Bohn's Novelists' Library. London: George Bell and Sons, 433 pp.
Reprint of 1836.A2.

4 _____. The History of Tom Jones, a Foundling. Bohn's Popular Library. 2 vols. London: George Bell and Sons, 1011 pp.
Reissue of 1905.A6.

5 _____. The History of Tom Jones, A Foundling. New York: Hurst, 501 pp. [1913?].
An abridged edition, omitting the introductory chapters. May have been reissued in 1915.

6 KIRBY, JOHN, ed. The Fielding Calendar. London: Frank Palmer, 112 pp.
"A quotation from the works of Henry Fielding for every day of the year."

1913 B SHORTER WRITINGS

1 CHILD, HAROLD. "Fielding and Smollett," in The Age of Johnson. The Cambridge History of English Literature. Vol. 10. Edited by A. W. Ward and A. R. Waller. Cambridge: The University Press, pp. 22-51.
Rapidly surveys Fielding's life and works, beginning with his dramas, which Child thinks hurried because of financial need, emotionally shallow, and in a dying genre. He discusses the parody of Pamela in Joseph Andrews, the preface, and the character of Adams; he appreciates the irony of Jonathan Wild but thinks the poetry in the

Miscellanies slight. Discusses the interpolated tales in Tom Jones (thinking that the interpolations violate the structure), the morality (the "finer shades" of which were lost on Fielding because he was "without the golden dream of what life should be," p. 32), and the limits of Fielding's realism. In Amelia Child sees a lack of ebullience and strength, but greater "shadows and depths in character" (p. 35). Throughout, Child sees Fielding as a "humane, genial, sweet-tempered . . . philosopher and moralist" (p. 22).

Reissued 1921 and 1923.

2 CROSS, WILBUR L. "The New Fielding Collection." Yale Alumni Weekly, 21 February.

In a general way describes Frederick S. Dickson's Fielding collection, which he had just given to Yale and which was to be known as the Lounsbury collection.

3 DICKSON, FREDERICK S. "William Makepeace Thackeray and Henry Fielding." North American Review, no. 689 (April), pp. 522-37.

Dates Thackeray's shift from mediocre storyteller to good novelist from his careful reading of Fielding's works in 1840 in order to review them (1840.B1). Discusses Thackeray's ill-informed acceptance of the Fielding legend and the Lady Bellaston incident in light of the shoddier morality of the Newcomes and the less subtle moral characterization of Vanity Fair. Dickson illustrates the danger of "seeking autobiography in fiction" (p. 532); "you cannot make such a sturdy creature as Fielding out of the weaknesses of Captain Booth, alone, any more than you can create the big and generous Thackeray out of nothing but the selfishness of Pendennis" (p. 534). Finally, he points out the surprising parallels in their careers and their differences in personality. See 1947.B4, 1957.B12.

4 SAINTSBURY, GEORGE. "The Four Wheels of the Novel Wain," in his The English Novel. London: J. M. Dent & Sons, pp. 77-132.

In this essay on Richardson, Fielding, Smollett, and Sterne, Saintsbury discusses the parody (of Pamela) in Joseph Andrews and its vivid characters and dialogue (more mimetically satisfying than Richardson's). He has high praise for Jonathan Wild (a masterpiece for a partly corrupt world), which he compares to Swift's Tale of a Tub and Thackeray's Vanity Fair. Tom Jones is "the Way of the Novel" (p. 105) for Saintsbury, relying as it does on Cervantes, the epic, the Shakespearian tragicomedy. He shows little enthusiasm for the authorial intrusions or the digressions (only justified because Cervantes had them) and much for the life and human nature the novel displays. He finds Fielding's style a bit dated. He defends Amelia, saying it is dull only in comparison to Fielding's other novels. Finally, he thinks Fielding more important to the novel than Richardson (broadening its possibilities); "while Fielding had no inconsiderable command of the Book of Literature, he turned over by day and night the larger, more difficult, but still the greater Book of Life" (p. 114).

Reprinted by Scholarly Press (St. Clair Shores, Michigan), 1971.

5 WELLS, JOHN E. "Fieldings 'Champion' and Captain Hercules Vinegar." Modern Language Review, 8, no. 2 (April), 165-72.

The persona Fielding adopted for The Champion was actually "a well-known prize-ring champion who had formerly exhibited at Hockley in the Hole" (p. 169) and who was an object of farce. For a few issues at the beginning, Fielding plays satirically with this, but soon "the Captain is practically lost, the papers being written as a rule without regard to his individuality" (p. 167). See also 1912.B9, 1913.B8, B9, 1920.B11, 1953.B7, 1955.B8, B9, B10, 1963.B17.

6 _____. "Fielding's Political Purpose in Jonathan Wild." Publications of the Modern Language Association, 28, no. 1, 1-55.

An early article which sets out to prove the sensed political "under-significance" (p. 1) of Jonathan Wild. Wells asserts that the story of the gang "is largely political satire the chief butt of which is Robert Walpole" (p. 8). Wells attempts to demonstrate this from internal evidence and by citing Fielding's The Champion, his Vernoniad and some contemporary periodicals. See 1941.A2 and 1966.B5.

7 _____. "Some New Facts Concerning Fielding's Tumble-Down Dick and Pasquin." Modern Language Notes, 28, no. 5 (May), 137-42.

By using newspaper and magazine notices, Wells establishes the publication and the performance date of these two plays and outlines Fielding's quarrel with John Rich, manager of the Covent Garden Theatre.

1913

8 _____. "The 'Champion' and Some Unclaimed Essays by Henry Fielding." Englische Studien, 46, no. 3, 355-66.

Mostly on the strength of thematic echo, argues that unsigned essays in The Champion for Nov. 15, 17, 20 and 22 of 1739 are by Fielding, as are those of Feb. 28, March 25 (the second unsigned letter), May 6 and May 20. Wells also feels that Fielding may have written for The Champion after June 1740 and before June of 1741. See also 1912.B6, 1913.B5, B6, B9, 1920.B11, 1953.B7, 1955.B8, B9, B10, 1963.B17.

9 _____. "News for Bibliophiles." Nation (New York), 96, no. 2481 (16 Jan.), 53-54.

Describes a pamphlet of 1731, which links the names of Captain Vinegar and Jonathan Wild, and the pamphlet warfare of the period. Thinks the pamphlet a parody written by someone on the Ministerial side. See 1809.B1, 1912.B9, 1913.B5, B8, 1920.B11, 1953.B7, 1955.B8, B9, B10, 1963.B17.

1914 A BOOKS

1 FIELDING, HENRY. Amelia. Illustrations by George Cruikshank. Bohn's Popular Library. London: George Bell and Sons, 608 pp.

Reprint of 1877.A1.

2 _____. The History of Tom Jones A Foundling. Introduction by George Saintsbury. Everyman's Library. 2 vols. London: J. M. Dent & Sons; New York: E. P. Dutton, 838 pp.

Reprint of 1909.A2.

3 _____. Tom Thumb the Great, in Representative English Dramas from Dryden to Sheridan. Edited by Frederick Tupper and James W. Tupper. New York: Oxford University Press; London, Toronto, etc.: Humphrey Milford, pp. 291-317.

Headnote reviews Fielding's life, compares the play to Buckingham's Rehearsal and Sheridan's The Critic, and discusses the parody of heroic tragedy. Reprints the 1731 Tragedy of Tragedies; no indication of copy text.

*4 HILLHOUSE, JAMES T., ed. "The Tragedy of Tragedies: a Dramatic Burlesque, by Henry Fielding, Edited with Introduction and Notes." Dissertation, Yale, 1914.

Source: McNamee, 1865-1964, p. 557. See 1918.A4.

1914 B SHORTER WRITINGS

1 BENSLY, EDWARD. "Fielding Queries: Sack and 'the usual words.'" Notes and Queries, 11th. series, 10 (14 Nov.), 392.
Suggests that the passage in Tom Jones, Book 9, chapter 4, cited by Dickson (1914.B9) is really mock heroic and that by "sack" Fielding means beer. Offers a recipe for Sophia's sack-whey.

2 _____. "Fielding's 'Tom Jones': Its Geography." Notes and Queries, 11th. series, 10 (10 Oct.), 292-93.
Answers three of Dickson's queries (1914.B10). Cites a folk tale to explain Partridge's tale of the miller holding three horses while knee deep in blood and explains some of Squire Western's sister's strange language.

3 _____. "Fielding's 'Tom Jones': Its Geography." Notes and Queries, 11th. series, 10 (7 Nov.), 372.
Corrects Dickson (1914.B10). The Battle of Tannières is not the Battle of Ramillies but the Battle of Malplaquet.

4 DE CASTRO, J. PAUL. "A Cryptic Utterance of Fielding's." Notes and Queries, 11th series, 10 (1 Aug.), 85.
Explains Fielding's note to the opening sentence of Book 5, chapter 2 in Tom Jones. Fielding was upset by the devastation of the New Forest.

5 _____. "Fielding's Letters." Notes and Queries, 11th. series, 10 (12 Sept.), 214.
Responds to Digeon (1914.B12) by suggesting that the catalogue "letters" are Sarah Fielding's "Familiar Letters between the Principal Characters in 'David Simple'" and that most of Henry Fielding's letters and manuscripts were destroyed in the Gordon Riots.

6 _____. "Fielding Queries: Sack and the 'usual words.'" Notes and Queries, 11th. series, 10 (10 Oct.), 293.
Suggests a military toast but cannot help Dickson (1914.B9) with the composition of sack. Does describe "cyder-and," often mentioned in Joseph Andrews.

7 _____. "Fielding's 'Tom Jones': Its Geography." Notes and Queries, 11th. series, 10 (26 Sept.), 253.
Another precise reference to a place (Noyle) and a man (Justice Willoughby). An addition to Dickson (1914.B10).

1914

8 _____. "Fielding's 'Tom Jones.'" Notes and Queries, 11th. series, 9 (27 June), 507-508.

Asks whether Fielding disguised the location of Lawyer Dowling's residence so that a real mountebank lawyer could not sue Fielding for defamation. See 1914.B10.

9 DICKSON, FREDERICK S. "Fielding Queries: Sack and 'the usual words.'" Notes and Queries, 11th. series, 10 (12 Sept.), 209.

Inquires about the nature of sack and various toasts (one military). See 1914.B1, B6.

10 _____. "Fielding's 'Tom Jones': Its Geography." Notes and Queries, 11th. series, 10 (5 Sept.), 191-92.

Agrees with de Castro (1914.B8) that Fielding was concealing an attack on a real lawyer. He notes, however, that Fielding invented a number of place names and even a hill. He also notes an error in Voyage, but he cites an ingenious precision about the Battle of Ramillies, called in Tom Jones the Battle of Tannières. See 1914.B2, B3, 1915.B1, B3.

11 _____. "The Chronology of 'Tom Jones.'" Notes and Queries, 11th. series, 9 (30 May), 425-26.

Corrects Keightley's (1863.B1) errors. There was a bridge across the Avon. Sophia had plenty of time to get more money. Sophia's route to London is traceable and reasonable. Fielding makes up for the one large error in chronology by many small accuracies in time. See also 1917.B5.

12 DIGEON, AURÈLIEN. "Fielding's Letters." Notes and Queries, 11th. series, 10 (1 Aug.), 91.

Asks help in finding Fielding letters. He has found three catalogue references to three volumes of letters, but he cannot find the letters. See 1914.B5.

13 POPE, F. J. "Henry Fielding's Boyhood." British Archivist, 1, no. 11 (Jan.), 85-88.

Reconstructs a bit of Fielding's childhood from Court of Chancery documents: Dame Sarah Gould's bill "on behalf of her infant grandchildren, against their father, an answer to his bill, a bill filed by Colonel Fielding against Lady Gould, a dozen affidavits, and some orders of the Court" (p. 85). Pope is on Sarah Gould's side. See 1940.B14.

14 WELLS, JOHN E. "Fielding's First Poem to Walpole and His Garret in 1730." Modern Language Notes, 29, no. 1 (Jan.), 29-30.

Fielding reworked and improved his poem To the Right Honourable Sir Robert Walpole for his Miscellanies. Dodsley printed a corrupt version (probably an emasculated rather than an earlier one) in 1763, called A Letter to Sir Robert Walpole. The poem may incidentally help locate Fielding's "garret" on Piccadilly Road in relation to Walpole's house in Arlington Street. See 1949.B5.

1915 A BOOKS

1 [FIELDING, HENRY]. The Covent-Garden Journal, by Sir Alexander Drawcansir, Knt., Censor of Great Britain. Edited by Gerard E. Jensen. 2 vols. New Haven: Yale University Press; London: H. Milford, Oxford University Press, 668 pp.

Reprints "all of the leading articles irrespective of their authorship" (4 Jan. - 25 Nov. 1752), while omitting two reviews "obviously not" (p. vii) by Fielding. This essentially old spelling text (he substitutes the modern 'S' for the older forms and separates ligatures) fills in all of the "folio numbers missing in the British Museum" (p. vii). The introduction sets out the origin of the Journal, its general character (literary essays, moral essays, news from the Bow Street Court, etc.), its part in the newspaper war (describing the various opponents and supporters of Fielding), Fielding's typical word usage and signatures, and the texts and editions of The Covent-Garden Journal. Allusions and references in each number of the Journal are annotated. See 1916.B11. See dissertation 1912.A7.

2 _____. The History of Tom Jones, a Foundling. Edited by A. W. Pollard. Macmillan's Library of English Classics. 2 vols. London, New York, Toronto: Macmillan, 1021 pp.

Reissue of 1900.A14.

*3 LUECKER, HEINRICH. "Die Verwendung der Mundart im Englischen Roman des 18. Jahrhunderts. Fielding, Smollett." Dissertation, Giessen, 1915.

In German.

Source: McNamee, 1865-1964, p. 557. This may have been published in Darmstadt in 1915.

1915

*4 SCHÖNZELER, HEINRICH. "Fieldings Verhaeltnis zu Lesage und anderen Quellen." Dissertation, Meunster, 1915.
In German. See also 1915.A5.
Source: McNamee, 1865-1964, p. 557.

5 _____. Fieldings Verhältnis zu Lesage und zu anderen Quellen. Weimar: R. Wagner Sohn, 71 pp.
Rejects the idea that Lesage influenced Fielding, arguing that Cervantes and Marivaux are Fielding's inspirations. Sees Lesage as an unoriginal borrower and Fielding as an original creator who judges and invents. In German.
Response to 1908.A1.

1915 B SHORTER WRITINGS

1 BENSLY, EDWARD. "Fielding's 'Tom Jones': Its Geography." Notes and Queries, 11th. series, 11 (2 Jan.), 12.
Adds two more allusions to the battle of Malplaquet to his earlier note (1914.B3).

2 _____. "Henry Fielding." Notes and Queries, 11th. series, 12 (20 Nov.), 408.
Identifies the two contemporary portraits of Henry Fielding, one done by Hogarth after Fielding's death.

3 DE CASTRO, J. PAUL. "Fielding's 'Tom Jones': Its Geography." Notes and Queries, 11th. series, 11 (16 Jan.), 56.
Answers Bensly's inquiry (1915.B1) by demonstrating that it was unlikely that Fielding's father was at the Battle of Malplaquet.

4 _____. "Portrait of Miss Sarah Andrew as Sophia Western." Notes and Queries, 11th. series, 11 (17 April), 301.
Miss Andrew was not the original of Sophia Western as suggested by Dobson (1883.B3). Asks for portraits of Sarah Andrew, Fielding's first passion.

5 DOBSON, AUSTIN. "A New Dialogue of the Dead," in his Rosalba's Journal and Other Papers. London: Chatto & Windus, pp. 263-87.
Reprint of 1912.B2.

6 HOPKINS, ANNETTE B. and HELEN S. HUGHES. "The History of Tom Jones, A Foundling (1749," in their The English Novel Before the Nineteenth Century: Excerpts from Representative Types. Boston, New York, etc.: Ginn, pp. 303-95.

An excerpt from Tom Jones that breaks off in chapter 11 of Book 6.

1916 A BOOKS - NONE

1916 B SHORTER WRITINGS

1 DE CASTRO, J. PAUL. "Did Fielding Write 'Shamela'?" Notes and Queries, 12th. series, 1 (8 Jan.), 24-26.
Attempts to establish that Fielding wrote Shamela on the basis of contemporary references and stylistic evidence. An important early attempt to prove authorship. See 1916.B12, 1944.B3, 1946.B11, 1948.B6, 1950.B7, 1957.B.18, 1959.B5.

2 _____. "Fielding and the Collier Family." Notes and Queries, 12th. series, 2 (5 Aug.), 104.
Details Fielding's sustained and generous connection with the Collier family and one of the few cases he pleaded as a lawyer. Fielding had to abandon his journal, The True Patriot, because he lost Arthur Collier's case and became liable for his debt of £400.

3 _____. "Fielding at Boswell Court." Notes and Queries, 12th. series, 1 (1 April), 264-65.
From Rate Books, establishes Fielding's London residence in 1746-47 and answers a charge that Fielding had to be dunned for debt (1786.B1).

4 _____. "Fieldingiana." Notes and Queries, 12th. series, 1 (17 June), 483-85.
Notes that the discovered poem 1906.B5 is a part of Fielding's Miscellanies and that it may have been addressed to the future wife of Robert Henley, one of the leaders of the Western judicial circuit; identifies Partridge's allusion to the "merriest gentleman in England."

5 _____. "Fieldingiana." Notes and Queries, 12th. series, 2 (2 Dec.), 441-43.
Notes that Fielding read James Harris' unpublished work because he alluded to it in "Essay on Conversation"; dates Dr. Thomas Brewster's death (referred to in Tom Jones); corrects identification of actress who took the part of Tom Thumb (see 1906.B2). Also replies to Robbins's suggestion (1910.B3) that Fielding wrote the Mist's Weekly

Journal article, rejecting it on stylistic, political, intellectual and moral grounds.

6 _____. "Fielding's Parson Adams." Notes and Queries, 12th. series, 1 (18 Mar.), 224-25.
Discusses Fielding's use of his model for Parson Adams; Fielding's friend the Rev. William Young had some of Adams' characteristics and lacked others. Fielding morally improved on the model.

7 _____. "John Ranby: Henry Fielding." Notes and Queries, 12th. series, 2 (1 July), 11.
The surgeon John Ranby, to whom Fielding alludes in Tom Jones Book 8, chapter 13, rented Fielding the Ealing property that Fielding was forced to leave when he departed for Lisbon.

8 DICKSON, FREDERICK S. "Henry Fielding: Two Corrections." Notes and Queries, 12th. series, 2 (23 Dec.), 515.
As Dobson (1916.B11) suggests someone should, Dickson sets the dates in Journal of a Voyage to Lisbon straight (changing "Sunday, July 19, 1754" to "Sunday, July 14, 1754").

9 _____. "Tom Jones and His Sword." Notes and Queries, 12th. series, 1 (24 June), 506.
Dickson nicely demonstrates that Tom's essential goodness is shown by his fighting with fists or cudgel. Tom doesn't draw his sword until he is forced to by Fitzpatrick.

10 DOBSON, AUSTIN. "Fielding and Andrew Miller." Library, 3rd. series, 7, no. 27 (July), 177-90.
Reconstructs "Miller's financial relations with Fielding, to whom he paid a considerable sum, and to whose sons he left a substantial legacy" (p. 178). Describes "Fielding's deed of assignment of 'Joseph Andrews' to Andrew Miller" (p. 179) and the receipt and deed for Tom Jones; fills in a few biographical details of Fielding and Miller's later transactions (the payment for Amelia and its "puffing"); and concludes with Miller's will.

11 _____. "Henry Fielding: Two Corrections." Notes and Queries, 12th. series, 1 (8 April), 284.
Adjusts Fielding's landing date at Lisbon and suggests that other dates in the Journal of a Voyage to Lisbon need adjusting because of the new Fielding letters. Challenges

a bibliographical citation in the Gerard E. Jensen edition of The Covent-Garden Journal (1915.A1). See 1916.B8.

12 JENSEN, GERARD E. "An Apology for the Life of Mrs. Shamela Andrews, 1741." Modern Language Notes, 31, no. 4 (April), 310-11.

On the basis of verbal parallels with Fielding's other work and of the typical use of "hath" and "doth," Jensen argues that Fielding wrote Shamela. See 1916.B1 for another early attempt to establish Fielding's authorship.

13 _____. "Fashionable Society in Fielding's Time." Publications of the Modern Language Association, 31, no. 1, 79-89.

A general article describing Fielding as a seriously concerned satirist "more kindly than Swift" (p. 79), whose particular target was the fashionable world. Jensen discusses the attempts of Lady Booby to corrupt Joseph and of Lady Bellaston to corrupt Tom, as well as Mr. Wilson's corruption in the city. By looking at other novels of the period, Jensen concludes that "his pictures of contemporary society as we find them in his novels are reasonably faithful" (p. 83). He reviews some of Fielding's attempts in essay and pamphlet to improve "the general moral laxity of his time" (p. 83).

14 _____. "The Crisis: A Sermon." Modern Language Notes, 31, no. 7 (Nov.), 435-37.

Briefly describes the pamphlet bibliographically and describes its salient ideas. Offers external evidence (Nichol's Literary Anecdotes) and internal evidence (word usage, allusion, political purpose) for its being by Fielding; concludes, however, that "no one on reading the work for the first time would exclaim, 'Fielding!'" (p. 437). See 1912.B7.

15 PHELPS, WILLIAM L. "Fielding, Smollett, Sterne," in his The Advance of the English Novel. New York: Dodd, Mead; London: John Murray (1919), pp. 53-78.

After reviewing Fielding's continental reputation, argues that the introduction to Joseph Andrews and the introductory chapters in Tom Jones demonstrate the strong influence of the personal essay on Fielding and are both "tedious" and condescending; they illustrate Fielding's aesthetic "insincerity" and establish a "bad tradition in English fiction" of "caterers" (p. 58). Thinks Fielding less successfully didactic than Richardson. Fielding's strength lies in his humor (including satire and irony) and his creation of real men, "imperfectly tamed beasts." "Say what you will about the equality of the sexes, man is essentially a comic character; and woman, tragic" (p. 62).

16 SAINTSBURY, GEORGE. "Fielding," in his _The Peace of the Augustans: A Survey of Eighteenth Century Literature as a Place of Rest and Refreshment_. London: G. Bell and Sons, pp. 119-30.

Thinks Fielding's gift for story-telling almost overwhelms the parody in _Joseph Andrews_ (Adams is a pure Shakespearian creation), dislikes the intellectual pleasure of _Jonathan Wild_, deals in a general way (always defending Fielding) with Tom's immorality, the interpolated tales and the authorial intrusions (conveniently at the beginnings of the chapter so that they can be skipped if you don't like them). Saintsbury thinks _Amelia_ sentimental. Throughout he compares Fielding with Thackeray.

1917 A BOOKS

1 FIELDING, HENRY. _The History of the Adventures of Joseph Andrews and His Friend Mr. Abraham Adams_. Edited by George Saintsbury. Everyman's Library. London: J. M. Dent & Sons, 390 pp.

Reissue of 1910.A6.

2 _____. _The History of Tom Jones, A Foundling_. Introduction by Wm. A. Neilson. The Harvard Classics Shelf of Fiction. Selected by Charles W. Eliot. 2 vols. New York: P. F. Collier & Son, 1047 (509 & 538) pp. [1917].

"Introduction" by "S. P. C." briefly surveys "the novel in England" (emphasizing English realism and its rich detail); Neilson adds a biographical note and reprints selections from Thackeray, Leslie Stephen, Dobson, and Gerould. Appears to reproduce the "1750" edition followed by Murphy (1762.A10).

3 _____. _The Works of Henry Fielding_. Edited by George Saintsbury. 6 vols. New York: Hearst's International Library. [1917].

Texts (which follow 1762.A10) and introduction identical to those used for Saintsbury's Everyman's Library edition (e.g., 1910.A6, 1909.A2). Vol. 1 contains _Joseph Andrews_, vols. 2-3 _Tom Jones_, vols. 4-5 _Amelia_ and _Jonathan Wild_, vol. 6 _Miscellaneous Writings_.

4 _____. _The Works of Henry Fielding_. 6 vols. London: Jarrold & Sons.

The "Note to General Introduction" says that "this issue in the main follows that of the standard or first collected edition of 1762" (p. xxxviii). Vol. 1 contains Joseph Andrews; vols. 2-3 Tom Jones; vols. 4-5 Amelia and Jonathan Wild; vol. 6 A Journey from This World to the Next, The Journal of a Voyage to Lisbon, and Miscellaneous Writings (including three plays, two numbers of two journal essays, "An Essay on Conversation" and "Familiar Letters"). The anonymous general introduction and brief introductions to each work sum up criticism, deal with just and unjust objections to the novels (the immorality of Tom Jones is unjust and the criticism of the lifelessness of Blifil and Allworthy just; Amelia may have been criticized because it begins rather than ends with marriage), sketch out Fielding's strength as a creator of characters, and provide a brief critical biography. Fielding is constantly commended for his irony and his truthfulness.

1917 B SHORTER WRITINGS

1 DE CASTRO, J. PAUL. "Fieldingiana." Notes and Queries, 12th. series, 3 (10 Mar.), 181-83.

Notes that the benefit ticket for Pasquin may be a forgery; Fielding is probably not represented in Hogarth's painting "The Green-Room, Drury Lane"; an allusion in Amelia to the writer of "Three Letters" is discovered; an allusion to farmer Francis at Ryde in The Journal of a Voyage to Lisbon untangled.

2 _____. "Fieldingiana." Notes and Queries, 12th. series, 3 (Nov.), 465-68.

Notes on Edmund Fielding, Henry's father; on Strahan's printing of Joseph Andrews (1855.B3) and Amelia; on the models for Thwackum, Square, and Dowling; Charlotte Cradock was not illegitimate; the house in Salisbury where Fielding resided when on holiday from Eton identified; Fielding's birthplace noted.

3 _____. "Henry Fielding's Last Voyage." Library, 3rd. series, 8, no. 30 (April), 145-49.

Identifies Fielding's reference to 'a brother of mine' and briefly argues that Fielding carefully revised his own work rather than letting someone else like his brother John do it (see 1937.B5).

The article's real purpose is to set out the controversy between Dickson, Pollard, and Dobson (1917.B6, 1917.B7, 1892.A1) about the two substantially different versions of the Journal of a Voyage to Lisbon, both published in 1755, in order to discover which was Fielding's final intention. De Castro argues that Pollard in his bibliographical description confused the two texts. Ends by reprinting an eighteenth-century anecdote about Fielding's brief stay on the Isle of Wight during the voyage. See also 1906.B3.

4 DICKSON, FREDERICK S. "Fielding and Richardson on the Continent." Notes and Queries, 12th. series, 3 (6 Jan.), 7-8.
Despite the repeated assertion, which he traces to Anna L. Barbauld, that Richardson was more popular in translation than Fielding, it is not true. All of Fielding's novels were often translated (by the 1790s there were twenty continental editions of Joseph Andrews); it appears that he was more popular than Richardson in England and on the continent.

5 _____. "The Chronology of 'Tom Jones.'" Library, 3rd. series, 8, no. 31 (July), 218-24.
A significantly revised article (1914.B11) in which Dickson works out all of the possible chronologies in Tom Jones--ages of characters and dates of events--in order to point out the few discrepancies and the many careful accuracies which give the book its verisimilitude.

6 _____. "The Early Editions of Fielding's 'Voyage to Lisbon.'" Library, 3rd. series, 8, no. 29 (Jan.), 24-35.
A reconstruction of the events immediately before the voyage, the voyage, the early days in Lisbon, and the printing of The Journal by Andrew Miller. Dickson conjecturally describes John Fielding's butchering of the proofs of the first edition and Miller's saving "the original galley-proofs" and putting out "a second edition, in which all of John Fielding's alterations, and amendments were ignored" (p. 31). He offers internal evidence for this biographical reconstruction of the printing of the two editions. See 1917.B3, B7, B8.

7 POLLARD, A. W. "The Two 1755 Editions of Fielding's 'Journal of a Voyage to Lisbon.'" Library, 3rd. series, 8, no. 29 (Jan.), 75-77.
Disagrees with Dickson (1917.B6), using bibliographical evidence to prove that the unedited text was printed first and the "brother John version" (small-type edition) later. See 1917.B3, B6, and Pollard's retraction 1917.B8.

8 _____. "The Two 1755 Editions of Fielding's 'Journal of a Voyage to Lisbon.'" Library, 3rd. series, 8, no. 30 (April), 160-62.

Admits to having made an error (see 1917.B3, B7) and then sets out what is known about the two printings of Journal of a Voyage. Pollard now argues that, reversing the usual printing practice, the "small-type edition was printed before the handsomer one, . . . the handsomer one was printed in the same month, and . . . it was from a copy of the handsomer edition that a reviewer described the book in March, 1755" (p. 162).

1918 A BOOKS

1 CROSS, WILBUR L. The History of Henry Fielding. 3 vols. New Haven: Yale University Press; London: Humphrey Milford and Oxford University Press.

Reviewed by Raymond M. Allen, JEGP, 20 (1921), 110-18; J. Paul de Castro, MLR, 15 (1920), 181-88; F. S. Dickson, YR, 8 (1919), 415-22; Aurélien Digeon, RG, 13 (1922), 412-17; Helen S. Hughes, Dial, 66 (1919), 407-409; Chauncy B. Tinker, Bookman, 49 (1919), 697-700; N&Q, 12th. series, 8 (1921), 181-85.

Still the standard biography of Fielding; incorporates the best scholarship of its day. Vol. 1 traces his career through the publication of The Miscellanies; vol. 2, which devotes three chapters to Tom Jones (its publication, reception, and art), ends with the "Battle of the Wits" provoked by The Covent-Garden Journal; vol. 3 concludes his life, devotes a long section to his reputation, and includes a full bibliography of Fielding's works (including those erroneously attributed to him, those of doubtful authorship, dramas on Fielding or his works, and letters and manuscripts). In the third volume, Cross carefully discusses Fielding's reputation, defending him against the attacks of various defamers (including Samuel Johnson) and singling out Arthur Murphy (1762.A10) for careful comment. He is particularly upset by Murphy's selection from Fielding's works (no Champion essays, for example), which was slavishly followed by later editors and which limited Fielding's reputation; by Murphy's passing on the popular myth of the hard-living Fielding; by Murphy's disregard of Fielding's scholarship and learning; and by Murphy's assumption that Fielding was a careless writer. Cross deftly sets each work in its political and social milieu. He both illustrates elements of Fielding's personality from

1918

his work and indicates how events from his life found their way into his work. Carefully weighs popular anecdotes about Fielding against the facts available.

2 FIELDING, HENRY. Geschichte des Thomas Jones eines Findelkindes. Translated by J. J. Bode. 3 vols. München: Georg Müller.
German translation of Tom Jones.

3 _____. The History of Tom Jones A Foundling. Introduction by George Saintsbury. Everyman's Library. 2 vols. London: J. M. Dent & Sons; New York: E. P. Dutton, 838 pp.
Reissue of 1909.A2.

4 _____. The Tragedy of Tragedies; or, The Life and Death of Tom Thumb the Great; with the Annotations of H. Scriblerus Secundus. Edited by James T. Hillhouse. New Haven: Yale University Press; London: Humphrey Milford, Oxford University Press, 231 pp.
Reviewed by J. Paul de Castro, N&Q, 12th. series, 5 (1919), 54-56; H. S. Hughes, JEGP, 18 (1919), 464-67; T. P. C., MP, 17 (1919), 303.
This scholarly edition prints the text of Tom Thumb (1730) and Fielding's expanded and annotated version of this play, called The Tragedy of Tragedies (1731). In the introduction Hillhouse discusses the writing of both plays, their stage history, and the literary objects of Fielding's burlesque humor. Expands Fielding's annotations to the more than 42 plays burlesqued. See dissertation 1914.A4.-

*5 FROEHLICH, ARMIN. "Fieldings Humor in seinen Romanen." Dissertation, Leipzig, 1918.
In German.
Source: McNamee, 1865-1964, p. 557.

*6 NICHOLS, CHARLES W. "An Edition of Fielding's Satirical Plays of 1736 and 1737." Dissertation, Yale, 1918.
The first editions, with variant readings, of Pasquin, Eurydice, The Historical Register, as well as a study of the stage history, influences, criticism and their relation to the licensing Act.
Source: Dissertation Abstracts, 33, no. 2 (Aug. 1972), 731A.

1918 B SHORTER WRITINGS

1 CROSS, WILBUR. "The Legend of Henry Fielding." Yale Review, 8, no. 1 (Oct.), 107-27.

Sets out "the Fielding legend in its crudest and most vulgar form" (p. 109), that of the hard-living opportunist, and corrects it. Cross attributes the legend to Fielding's political enemies and corrects anecdotes as well as the general outline, particularly pointing out the absence of dissolute companions and his fair dealing with women. Cross also considers his capacity for hard creative work and his broad social (rather than narrow personal) satire. See 1907.B11 and 1924.B1.

2 _____. "The Secret of Tom Jones." Bookman (New York), 48 (Sept.), 20-29.

Reviews the novel's lasting reputation and then considers the nature of its mimetic quality. After speculating about the organic growth of its plot, Cross considers the way Fielding creates composite characters and scenes from the selected details of life. He emphasizes that Fielding's novel is not autobiographical, as some of Dickens' are. Cross then compares it to later successes and failures in the realistic novel (Eliot, Dickens, Hawthorne), emphasizing Fielding's ability to create morally mixed, "human" characters who are not patronizingly or sentimentally explained away.

3 DICKSON, FREDERICK S. "Errors and Omissions in Tom Jones." Library, 3rd. series, 9, no. 33 (Jan.), 18-26.

Notes fourteen errors: he records a misquotation from the Bible, and a time confusion (a shift from June to midwinter in a few weeks); in Book 6, chapter 12 Black George is sent to see Tom where Tom no longer is; the chambermaid in Book 7, chapter 15 appears to have two names; Dowling and a hackney attorney are confused; Mrs. Western is called both "Di" and "Bel" or "Bell"; the highwayman is called "Anderson" and "Henderson"; Mrs. Miller appears not to have been married long enough to account for her children; Mrs. Miller's knowledge of Tom is accounted for in two ways; oversights about which characters are in Allworthy's lodgings at the end of the novel suggest that there was an interruption between writing chapters 10 and 11 of the last book; Nightingale's cousin is called "Harriet" and "Harris"; Sundays are omitted from the day by day telling from Book 7 to the end.

He lists ten omissions: How did Sophia get money for her journey? Where is Molly Seagrim's child? Why didn't

Sophia pay Honour for accompanying her? What did Sophia wear in London? Why was the Gloucester guide's injury unrecorded? Didn't Sophia reward the beggar who found her purse? Dowling's relationship with Allworthy is unclear. When did Honour leave the play that Sophia left early? How does Blifil get news of Tom's imprisonment so quickly? What happened to Parson Adams' wife and children?

4 KURRELMEYER, W. "A German Version of Joseph Andrews." Modern Language Notes, 33, no. 8 (Dec.), 469-71.
Johann Heinrich Rüdigern's (1762) Fieldings Komischer Roman in vier Theilen is, in fact, not a spurious imitation but a German translation of a French translation of Joseph Andrews with the names of the characters changed and some incidents omitted. It was put out to catch the Fielding vogue.

5 WELLS, JOHN E. "Fielding's 'Miscellanies.'" Modern Language Review, 13, no. 4 (Oct.), 481-82.
The date of the first edition, according to newspaper advertisements, was 7 April 1743. The second edition is advertised the same month. Some copies of the second edition include the list of subscribers. Fielding's modernization of Juvenal's Sixth Satire was revised for the Miscellanies after the publication of Pamela. See 1962.B8.

6 WHITEFORD, ROBERT N. "Samuel Richardson, Henry Fielding, Sarah Fielding, and Tobias Smollett," in his Motives in English Fiction. New York and London: G. P. Putnam's Sons, pp. 86-118.
An appreciation of Fielding that touches on Fielding's "humors" characters in Joseph Andrews (a cross between those of Jonson and those of Congreve), the modern mechanism of plot in Tom Jones, the "sable land" (p. 106) of pathos in Amelia, and Fielding's narrative intrusions, which inspired Thackeray. Whiteford thinks Fielding altered the novel after Richardson to make "sentiment genuine" and characterization both substantial and localized.

1919 A BOOKS

1 FIELDING, HENRY. The History of Tom Jones, a Foundling. Bohn's Popular Library. 2 vols. London: George Bell and Sons, 1011 pp.
Reissue of 1905.A6.

2 HARPER, HENRY H., ed. The Genius of Henry Fielding. Boston: The Bibliophile Society, 208 pp.

Extracts from Tom Jones, Amelia, Jonathan Wild, Joseph Andrews, etc., organized by idea (Benevolence, Love, etc.), on which Harper comments. The introduction commends Fielding for his robust and right-thinking reflection of life and morality, but Harper is a bit upset by his wordy moral digressions.

1919 B SHORTER WRITINGS

1 BENSLY, EDWARD. "Tom Jones." Notes and Queries, 12th. series, 5 (Nov.), 303.

Answers query 1919.B8. Passage appears near the beginning of Gibbon's Memoirs.

2 DE CASTRO, J. PAUL. "Fielding as a Publicist." Notes and Queries, 12th. series, 5 (Nov.), 283-84.

Evidence that while Fielding was a justice of the peace and chairman of quarter sessions, he vigorously prosecuted two corrupt justices.

3 DUFF, L. "Tom Jones." Notes and Queries. 12th. series, 5 (Dec.), 327.

Answers query 1919.B8. Directs to Gibbon's Memoirs.

4 HARRISON, FREDERIC. "Bath-Somerset-Henry Fielding." Fortnightly Review, n.s. 104, no. 635 (1 Nov.), 734-44.

An after dinner speech given to the Bath Literary Club. Praises Fielding's works in a general way and then moves to his biography, particularly as it concerns Bath (Ralph Allen) and Somerset, his career as a magistrate, and his library. Relies heavily on Cross (1918.A1); throughout, Fielding is defended against charges of immorality.

5 JENSEN, GERARD E. "The Covent-Garden Journal Extraordinary." Modern Language Notes, 34, no. 1 (Jan.), 57-59.

A 1752 burlesque of Henry Fielding's periodical is described. Probably by Bonnell Thornton, but it may have been by Smollett. If it was, it is further evidence that Smollett joined the "paper war" against Fielding.

6 LOOMIS, ROGER S. "Tom Jones and Tom-mania." Sewanee Review, 27, no. 4 (Oct.), 478-95.

Though Loomis grants that Fielding showed "striking instances of sympathy and justice" (p. 485) and that he was a reformer, he insists that Fielding was a conservative reformer, attracting conservatives who prefer their reforms safely accomplished. Fielding's attitude toward women is "mediaeval"; he is a city man with no love of the country; his plots are far from perfect: hackneyed, ingenious and unsteady; his characters show none of the complex subtlety of Thackeray and Meredith; his morality is often the "school prize-book" stiffness of children. Loomis ultimately pays Tom Jones a high compliment (according to him), arguing that "it is a clear foreshadowing of the naturalistic novel. Amelia, to be sure, possesses far more clearly the earmarks of naturalistic method and philosophy; for its author knew the world far better than the younger author of Tom Jones" (p. 487). See 1966.A26.

7 NICHOLS, CHARLES W. "Fielding Notes." Modern Language Notes, 34, no. 4 (April), 220-24.
On the evidence of allusion to contemporary events, Pasquin may have been written between 27 Jan. 1736 and 1 March. Suggests, on internal evidence, that The Historical Register may have been first performed on 21 March 1737. On internal and external evidence, argues that a letter that appeared in Common Sense 21 May 1737 in defense of Pasquin and The Historical Register and signed "Pasquin" was by Fielding. See 1923.B3 and 1934.B1.

8 PAYEN-PAYNE, DE V. "Tom Jones." Notes and Queries, 12th. series, 5 (Oct.), 268.
Asks for the reference in Gibbon to Tom Jones's outliving the imperial eagle of Austria. Answered 1919.B1, B3.

9 WHITE, THOMAS. "Tom Jones." Notes and Queries, 12th.series, 5 (Nov.), 303.
In answer to 1919.B8, quotes passage from the opening of Gibbon's Autobiography.

1920 A BOOKS

1 ANON. Henry Fielding. The Pickering Club Booklets. No. 1. London: William Heinemann, 34 pp. [1920].
Reprint of [1904].A1.

*2 FIELDING, HENRY. The History of the Adventures of Joseph Andrews and his Friend Mr. Abraham Adams. New York: Lincoln MacVeagh, The Dial Press, 311 pp. [1920?].
Source: National Union Catalogue: Pre-1956 Imprints. Vol. 171, p. 676.

3 _____. The History of Tom Jones, A Foundling. Classic Novels. 2 vols. New York: Brentano, 953 (491 & 462) pp. [1920?].

Title page says "with a portrait and illustrations by George Cruikshank"; portrait is reproduced but illustrations are not. Brief anonymous "life" based on Murphy (1762.A10); appears to reprint the "1750" edition followed by Murphy.

*4 FRENCH, ROBERT D. "A Critical Edition of The True Patriot by Henry Fielding." Dissertation, Yale, 1920.

Presents the text, annotates it, sets it in its time, and argues for the importance of the journal in understanding Fielding's political philosophy.

Source: Dissertation Abstracts, 33, no. 3 (Sept. 1972), 1140A.

1920 B SHORTER WRITINGS

1 BIRON, H. C. "A Famous Magistrate." National Review, 74, no. 443 (Jan.), 669-78.

Reviews Fielding's legal and judicial career; cites several allusions to judges in two of his plays (Coffee-House Politician and The Debauchee) and in Amelia; discusses his work as a reformer (founder of the Bow Street Runners and writer of pamphlets about crime and poverty) and his penury.

2 _____. "Henry Fielding as an Eighteenth Century Magistrate." Living Age, no. 304 (7 Feb.), 344-52.

Reprint of 1920.B1.

3 DE CASTRO, J. PAUL. "Tom Jones." Notes and Queries, 12th. series, 6 (10 April), 118.

The Fielding family, even the best educated, signed their last name both "ie" and "ei." An answer to 1920. B10.

4 DIGEON, AURÉLIEN. "Autour de Fielding. I. Miss Fielding, son frère, et Richardson." Revue germanique, 11e année, no. 3 (July-Sept.), 209-210.

Seeing Sarah Fielding as the embodiment of the eighteenth-century reader's ambivalent feelings toward Richardson and Fielding, Digeon argues that there was no sharp split between them. Instead they observed and influenced each other; he points to Richardson's attempt at humor in Grandison and Fielding's virtuous woman in Amelia.

Actually suggests a more complex novel-by-novel reaction: Pamela begets Joseph Andrews; Clarissa, in response, improves the concept of virtue and in turn inspires Tom Jones. In French.

5 DIGEON, AURÉLIEN. "Autour de Fielding. II. Fielding, conseiller littéraire de sa soeur, est portraituré par elle en retour." Revue germanique, 11e année, no. 3 (July-Sept.), 353-62.

By examining style, Digeon attempts to determine the extent of Fielding's collaboration on David Simple. Fielding edited the second edition, changing or omitting words or phrases, streamlining occasional paragraphs, and occasionally expanding a favorite topic like friendship. His indirect influence was large: he probably served as a model for the character Le Vive and for Camille's younger brother. In French.

6 HAMILTON, GUY. "Fielding and the 'Motions.'" Times Literary Supplement (11 March), p. 172.

Points to the puppet show in Tom Jones (Book 12, chapter 5) as an example of Fielding's agreeing with the contemporary judgment that such entertainment was "low."

*7 HUFFMANN, CHARLES H. "The Eighteenth-Century Novel in Theory and Practice." Dissertation, Virginia, 1920.

Source: T. Humphrey, pp. 258-59.

8 POPE, F. J. "Fielding's Ancestors at Sharpham Park, Somerset." Notes and Queries, 12th. series, 6 (Feb.), 34.

Sharpham Park, Fielding's birthplace, came to his father through his mother Sarah Gould, who had inherited it from her London merchant father.

For a correct view see Cross 1918.A1 and Vincent 1940.B14.

9 SQUIRE, J. C. "Tom Thumb," in his Life and Letters. London: Hodder & Stoughton, pp. 104-10. [1920].

An appreciation of Fielding's ironic humor and the justice of his attack on bad theater; prompted by Hillhouse's edition (1918.A4).

10 TOTTENHAM, C. J. "Tom Jones." Notes and Queries, 12th. series, 6 (Jan.), 23.

If Fielding's family were high born, why did they sometimes transpose the "ie"? See 1920.B3.

11 WELLS, JOHN E. "Fielding's Champion - More Notes." Modern Language Notes, 35 (Jan.), 18-23.

Using notices from contemporary newspapers and magazines, Wells adds information about place and time of publication and identifies essays Fielding contributed to The Champion. He also briefly reviews the political struggle with Walpole. See his earlier articles (1912.B6, 1913.B5, B8, B9) and 1953.B7, 1955.B8, B9, B10, 1963.B17

1921 A BOOKS

1 FIELDING, HENRY. The History of the Adventures of Joseph Andrews and His Friend Mr. Abraham Adams. Edited by George Saintsbury. Everyman's Library. London: J. M. Dent & Sons; New York: E. P. Dutton, 390 pp. [1921].

Reissue of 1910.A6.

2 _____. The History of Tom Jones, a Foundling. Edited by A. W. Pollard. Macmillan's Library of English Classics. 2 vols. London: Macmillan, 1021 pp.

Reissue of 1900.A14.

3 _____. The History of Tom Jones, A Foundling. Introduction by G. H. T[ownsend]. London: G. Routledge & Sons; New York: E. P. Dutton, 640 pp. [1921].

Reissue of 1857.A3.

*4 _____. Tung ming chi. Translated by Lin Shu in collaboration with Ch'en Chia-lin. Shanghai: Commercial Press.

Classical Chinese translation of A Journey from This World to the Next.

Source: Hugh Amory's working bibliography (transliterated by Bonnie McDougall of the East Asian Institute).

1921 B SHORTER WRITINGS

1 DE CASTRO, J. PAUL. "Fielding's Pamphlet 'The Female Husband.'" Notes and Queries, 12th series, 8 (5 Mar.), 184-85.

Adds to Cross's (1918.A1) bibliographical entry and speculates about the circumstances of its composition. Thinks Fielding may have been in court to hear Mary Price's testimony. For another view, see 1959.B4.

1921

2 _____. "The Printing of Fielding's Works." Library (4th. series, 1), also called Transactions of the Bibliographical Society, 2nd. series, 1 (March), 257-70.
Provides details from printers' ledgers about Joseph Andrews; Miscellanies; Serious Address; History of the Rebellion; Dialogue Between Devil, Pope and Pretender; Tom Jones; Amelia; Proposal for the Poor; and Journal of a Voyage to Lisbon. See 1952.B13, 1963.B19.

3 GOSSE, EDMUND. "The Character of Fielding," in his Books on the Table. London: William Heinemann, pp. 259-64.
Reviews the nineteenth-century attack on Fielding's morality and the morality of his novels, Murphy's factual errors and the restoration of his character (by Dobson, de Castro, Cross and others). Gosse thinks this restoration may have gone too far, "putting up a spotless figure, all in sham Parian, in place of the bestained and besotted profligate of the Victorian legend" (p. 263).

4 HENLEY, WILLIAM E. "Henry Fielding," in his The Works of William Ernest Henley. Essays. London: Macmillan, pp. 1-46.
Reprints 1902.A4, "Essay on the Life, Genius . . . ." Actually written by Fox-Davies.

5 NICHOLS, CHARLES W. "The Date of Tumble-Down Dick." Modern Language Notes, 36, no. 5 (May), 312-13.
Unaware of Wells's earlier article (1913.B7), he repeats some of Wells's information.

1922 A BOOKS

*1 BLANCHARD, FREDERIC T. "Fielding's Reputation as a Novelist in English Literary History." Dissertation, Yale, 1922.
Source: McNamee, 1865-1964, p. 557. See 1926.A1 and 1922.B1.

2 FIELDING, HENRY. The History of Tom Jones, A Foundling. Illustrations by G. Spencer Pryse. London: Abbey Library, 770 pp. [1922].
Includes Coleridge's marginal notes in his copy (1773 edition) and twenty plates. Appears to reprint the first edition.

3 _____. The History of Tom Jones A Foundling. Introduction by George Saintsbury. Everyman's Library. 2 vols.

London: J. M. Dent & Sons; New York: E. P. Dutton, 838 pp. Reissue of 1909.A2.

1922 B SHORTER WRITINGS

1 BLANCHARD, FREDERIC T. "Coleridge's Estimate of Fielding." University of California Publications in Modern Philology (The Charles Mills Gayley Anniversary Papers), 11:155-63.
Carefully traces the evolution of Coleridge's attitude toward Fielding, setting it alongside those of Lamb and Hazlitt. Although Coleridge praised Amelia as the pattern of the perfect wife when he was twenty, he really preferred Richardson in the early part of his life. It was not until 1817 that Coleridge turned from Richardson to Fielding, and it was during the last ten years of his life that his "appreciation of Fielding rose to its culmination in his famous praise" (p. 159), written three weeks before his death. Even during the vogue for Scott in the 1820s, Coleridge's admiration for Fielding continued to increase.

2 DE CASTRO, J. PAUL. "Edmund Fielding." Notes and Queries, 12th.series, 11 (26 Aug.), 178.
It appears that Edmund Fielding, Henry's father, was married a fourth time.

3 DIBELIUS, WILHELM. "Chapter 3," in his Englische Romankunst: die Technik des englischen Romans im achtzehnten und zu Aufang des neunzehnten Jahrhunderts. Vol. 1. Berlin and Leipzig: Mayer und Müller, pp. 85-115.
A wide-ranging examination of Fielding's art as a novelist. Begins by establishing a sharp contrast to Richardson: Fielding represents merry old England and Richardson puritan morality; Fielding the picaresque novel and Richardson romance. Dibelius argues that Fielding extends the picaresque by using love as an integral part of plot and travel as a necessary part of character conflict and maturation. He also surveys Fielding's fictional techniques, didactic intentions, and the objects of his social satire. Finally compares Fielding's humor with that of Defoe and Richardson. In German.

4 HUGHES, HELEN S. "A Dialogue - Possibly by Henry Fielding." Philological Quarterly, 1, no. 1 (Jan.), 49-55.
Reproduces a song in dialogue form which appeared in Watts's Musical Miscellany, vol. 6 (1731) attributed to "Mr. Fielding." Reviews the career of the other possible candidate, the actor Timothy Fielding, and concludes that

it is more probably by Henry because Watts had published Henry Fielding's plays; Henry was better known; Watts referred to Henry elsewhere as Mr. Fielding; Timothy and Henry would not have been confused until 1732.

5 _____. "Fielding's Indebtedness to James Ralph." Modern Philology, 20, no. 1 (Aug.), 19-34.
Argues that James Ralph was "in part responsible for" (p. 19) Fielding's shift from artificial comedy (Love in Several Masques and The Temple Beau) to the literary burlesque of The Author's Farce and Tom Thumb. Reprints large sections of a book published by Ralph in 1728 which, among other things, discusses the dramatic possibilities of folk stories and popular entertainments. Hughes cites similar ideas and similar phrasing in Ralph's book and Fielding's two later plays. See 1943.B7.

6 NICHOLS, CHARLES W. "Fielding and the Cibbers." Philological Quarterly, 1, no. 4 (Oct.), 278-89.
By means of "the newspapers and periodicals of the time," Nichols shows that Pasquin and The Historical Register are all about "the social foibles of the year in London" (p. 278), particularly about theatrical affairs and the part the various Cibbers (Colley, Theophilus, and Mrs. Cibber) played in them. See also 1924.B4, 1931.B16.

7 ROBERTS, W. "Henry Fielding in French." National Review, 79, no. 473 (July), 723-28.
After briefly reviewing the literary interchange between France and England (illustrated by translations), Roberts discusses the translations and translators of Joseph Andrews, Tom Jones, and Amelia, concluding that Fielding's French reputation suffered at the beginning because he was badly translated ("Fielding was less fortunate than Richardson in his translators," p. 724). See 1909.B2, 1917.B4, and 1962.B3.

1923 A BOOKS

1 DIGEON, AURÉLIEN. Les Romans de Fielding. Paris: Hachette, 312 pp.
In French. Translated into English 1925. See 1925.A1.

2 _____. Le texte des romans de Fielding: Étude critique. Paris: Librairie Hachette, 104.
Reviewed by L. Cazamian, RAA (Dec. 1923).

Argues that as Fielding gained mastery of his craft, he made fewer and fewer corrections to successive editions. Thus, in the two editions of Jonathan Wild (1743 and 1754), Fielding makes many corrections in grammar and style, tightens the narrative, and, rather than specifically attacking Walpole, attacks politicians in general. In Amelia (1751 and 1752), the revisions are minimal and chiefly anecdotal. Digeon discusses the suppression of allusions to the "Universal Register Office," the clarification of the accident to Amelia's nose, and he prints chapter 2, Book 5, Concerning a brace of Doctors . . ., omitted in the 1762 Murphy edition. He had earlier reprinted chapter 12, Book 2 (Of Proverbs) and chapter 9, Book 4 (A Very Wonderful Chapter . . .) of Jonathan Wild; he sees no reason for Fielding's omitting either. His treatment of Joseph Andrews is cursory (see 1963.B3); he points out a few corrections in grammar and style and the more precise delineation of character, particularly Adams. His examination of Tom Jones centers on chapter 14, Book 8 (the Monmouth rebellion section). The fourth edition, Digeon argues, generally follows the corrections of the third edition, but in this passage it reverts to the text of the first and second editions. Digeon tentatively suggests that this might have been a printer's correction, advancing the hypothesis that the printer might have been a Papist or Jacobite (see 1974.A7). In an appendix, Digeon discusses Henry Fielding's correction of David Simple, his sister Sarah Fielding's novel.

3 FIELDING, HENRY. The Tragedy of Tragedies, or The Life and Death of Tom Thumb the Great, in Types of English Drama: 1660-1780. Edited by David H. Stevens. Boston, New York, Chicago, etc.: Ginn, pp. 565-93.

No indication of copy text.

4 _____. The Works of Henry Fielding. Preface and introductions by G. H. Maynadier. 12 vols. London: Gay and Bird. [1923].

Reissue of 1903.A3.

5 RICE-OXLEY, LEONARD, ed. Fielding: Selections. With Essays by Hazlitt, Scott and Thackeray. Oxford: The Clarendon Press, 192 pp.

Reprints part of Hazlitt's "Lectures on English Comic Writers," Scott's "Essay on Fielding" (1821.A2), Thackeray's "Lectures on the English Humorists of the Eighteenth Century" and selections from Joseph Andrews, Tom Jones, Amelia, A Journey from this World to the Next, Jonathan Wild, An Enquiry into the Causes of the Late

Increase of Robbers, and Journal of a Voyage to Lisbon, adding notes to each. Rice-Oxley's introduction is an appreciation of Fielding's genius as a novelist and a mild defense of Fielding the man.

1923 B SHORTER WRITINGS

1 HARRISON, FREDERIC. "Bath-Somerset - Henry Fielding," in his De Senectute. London: T. Fisher Unwin, pp. 134-51.
Reprint of 1919.B4.

2 MARR, GEORGE S. "Fielding," in his The Periodical Essayists of the Eighteenth Century, With Illustrative Extracts from the Rarer Periodicals. London: Clarke; New York: Appleton (1924), pp. 108-15.
Reviewed by Hamilton J. Smith, Sat. Rev., 1 (22 Nov. 1924), 324; Nation-Athen., 34 (19 Jan. 1924), 578.
Briefly discusses Fielding's Champion (1739), True Patriot (1745), Jacobite's Journal (1747), and Covent-Garden Journal (1752). Deplores the excessive political element in the middle two and thinks that even in The Champion politics "intrudes overmuch" (p. 111). After briefly describing some of the essays, suggests that periodical essays prepare for the "author stepping forward from behind the scenes" (p. 111) in his novels.

3 NICHOLS, CHARLES W. "A New Note on Fielding's Historical Register." Modern Language Notes, 38, no. 8 (Dec.), 507-508.
Items in St. James's Evening-Post and London Evening Post help date the first performance (see 1919.B7).

4 _____. "Fielding's Tumble-Down Dick." Modern Language Notes, 38, no. 7 (Nov.), 410-16.
Identifies the pantomime Fielding was parodying (Pritchard's The Fall of Phaeton) and suggests that Tumble-Down Dick was an integral part of Pasquin. The article carefully sets out Fielding's parody of The Fall of Phaeton.

5 VAN DOREN, CARL. "The Greatest English Man of Letters." Nation, 116, no. 3022 (6 June), 659-60.
A personal testimonial that Fielding was "the greatest man who has been a man of letters using the English tongue" (pp. 659-60). Van Doren prefers him for his vitality, energy, breadth and scholarship to Shakespeare, Milton, Spencer or Chaucer.

1924 A BOOKS

1 FIELDING, HENRY. The History of Tom Jones, a Foundling. Edited by A. W. Pollard. Macmillan's Library of English Classics. 2 vols. London: Macmillan, 1021 pp.
Reissue of 1900.A14.

2 _____. The History of Tom Jones, A Foundling. Introduction by Wilbur Cross. Borzoi Classics. 2 vols. New York: Alfred A. Knopf, 907 (465 & 442) pp.
Appears to reproduce the "1750" edition followed by Murphy (1762.A10). Cross's introduction briefly sets out Fielding's life, the history of the novel as a form, Fielding's use of a dramatic plot, his creation of characters from remembered people, and his faithful depiction of life.

1924 B SHORTER WRITINGS

1 BIRRELL, AUGUSTINE. "Henry Fielding and the Literary Tradition," in his More Obiter Dicta. London: William Heinemann, pp. 105-11.
Reviewed by Amy Loveman, Sat. Rev., 1 (6 Sept. 1924), 92; R. M. Lovett, New Rep., 40 (17 Sept. 1924), 76-77.
Suggests that the "Fielding tradition" attacked by Cross (1918.A1) has ceased to exist, if it ever really did. "Time mellows Tradition, and on the whole, and as things now stand, Fielding has no more reason than Richardson to quarrel with his tradition, and we feel sure he is content with it" (p. 110). See 1918.B1 and 1907.B11.

2 DE CASTRO, J. PAUL. "The Sale of Fielding's Farm." Times Literary Supplement (17 July), p. 449.
Adds information from the rate books to 1924.B3. John Ranby, George II's premier sergeant-surgeon, who is mentioned in Tom Jones (Book 8, chapter 13), paid the rates on the farm at Ealing after Fielding left it.

3 GEORGE, M. DOROTHY. "The Sale of Fielding's Farm." Times Literary Supplement (26 June), p. 404.
Reproduces an eighteenth-century newspaper advertisement for Fielding's farm and household goods at Ealing, sold six months after he left for Lisbon. See also 1924.B2.

4 NICHOLS, CHARLES W. "Social Satire in Fielding's Pasquin and The Historical Register." Philological Quarterly, 3, no. 4 (Oct.), 309-17.

These plays are not only political satires, they are "full of social, and theatrical and literary satire" (p. 309). Nichols proves this from newspaper and magazine items. See also 1922.B6, 1931.B16, and 1973.B26.

1925 A BOOKS

1 DIGEON, AURÉLIEN. The Novels of Fielding. London: George Routledge & Sons, 270 pp.

Reviewed by Frederic T. Blanchard, University of California Chronicles, 28 (Jan. 1926), 105-107; Wilbur L. Cross, Sat. Rev., 1 (18 July 1925), 905-906; Oswald Doughty, E. Studies, 7 (June 1925), 86-89; V. Larbaud, Revue de France, 1 (Feb. 1924), 631-41; S. B. Liljegren, Litteris, 3 (1926), 103-104; Roger P. McCutcheon, SAQ, 24 (1925), 447-48; George Saintsbury, Bookman, 68 (May 1925), 96-99; Mark Van Doren, Nation, 121 (14 Oct. 1925), 425; TLS, 23 Aug. 1923, p. 557; TLS, 4 June 1925, p. 381.

An important early critical work. In the first chapter, Digeon opposes the notion of Fielding as bohème; he bases his assumption on the best scholarship of the time and on his own research. He then devotes a chapter each to Joseph Andrews, Jonathan Wild, Tom Jones, and Amelia; his concluding chapter makes the argument of this organization explicit. Fielding developed like his century, moving from works of the intellect (Jonathan Wild) to those of sentiment (Amelia). To support this theory of development, Digeon argues (on internal evidence) that most of Jonathan Wild was written before Joseph Andrews. In his chapter on Jonathan Wild he also considers the nature of its irony, criminal biographies as genre and reality, allusions to Walpole, the opposition between Wild and Heartfree, and the essentially anarchical nature of such satire. In his chapter on Joseph Andrews he considers the parody of Richardson, Fielding's shift from this original intention, the dramatic construction of the novel (e.g., he sees the characterizing dialogue as dramatic), and the characters (particularly Adams). Digeon concludes that this is merry old John Bull England. His chapter on Tom Jones argues that the novel is a positive ideal rather than an attack, as were Fielding's first two, although he sees it as continuing the attack on Richardson (this time on Clarissa). It is also an explication of Fielding's moral idea of sentiment in action (not rigidly Christian, Digeon argues) and an English epic (considering characters and episodes that impede action and the piling up of good scenes, he thinks it carefully constructed but hardly mechanical).

With Amelia, Digeon argues that Fielding has begun something different, something well beyond the string of adventures. He discusses the perfection of the plot and Amelia's moral psychology (the love of a weak man), arguing that the center of interest is not the center of action and that Fielding has now accepted religion as the guiding principle of his moral doctrine. The strength of Digeon's book lies in his strong sense of literary history (e.g., the several stages of Jonathan Wild, Western as an old-fashioned squire, the attacks on Richardson), his sensitive analysis of character, and his easy ability to compare Fielding and his French "contemporaries" (Lesage, Marivaux, Molière, etc.). He does pass on some clichés: Fielding's plays are potboilers; Booth is modeled on Fielding's early life.

2 FIELDING, HENRY. Historien om Tom Jones, ett hittebarn. Translated by Richard Hejll. Världs Litteraturen De stora Mästerverken. 2 vols. Stockholm: Albert Bonniers Förlag, 1127 (574 & 553) pp. [1925].
Swedish translation.

3 _____. The History of the Adventures of Joseph Andrews and His Friend Mr. Abraham Adams. Harrap's Standard Fiction Library. London, Calcutta and Sydney: George G. Harrap, 311 pp.
No indication of copy text.

4 _____. The History of Tom Jones, a Foundling. Bohn's Popular Library. 2 vols. London: George Bell and Sons, 1011 pp.
Reissue of 1905.A6.

5 _____. The History of Tom Jones a Foundling. Illustrations by Rowland Wheelwright. London, Calcutta, Sydney: George G. Harrap, 728 pp.
Appears to reprint the first edition of Tom Jones. Also reprints Coleridge's notes in his copy of Tom Jones (the 1773 edition).

*6 _____. The History of Tom Jones, a Foundling. Illustrations by Rowland Wheelwright. New York: Brentano, 728 pp. [1925?].
See 1925.A5.
Source: National Union Catalogue: Pre-1956 Imprints. Vol. 171, p. 686.

1925

7 _____. The History of Tom Jones A Foundling. Introduction by George Saintsbury. Everyman's Library. 2 vols. London: J. M. Dent & Sons; New York: E. P. Dutton, 838 pp.
Reissue of 1909.A2.

8 _____. Tom Jones Die Geschichte Eines Findlings. Translated by Paul Baudisch. Afterword by Paul Ernst. Leipzig: Paul List Verlag, 1296 pp. [1925?].
Afterword provides biography and sets Fielding in the history of the novel from Cervantes to Dostoyevsky. In German.

1925 B SHORTER WRITINGS

1 ANON. "Books in the Sale Room. A rare anonymous Fielding turns up . . ." Bookman's Journal, n.s. 12, no. 47 (Aug.), 205.
Sale at Sotheby's of the first edition of Fielding's The Female Husband (anonymously issued).

2 _____. "Books in the Sale Room." Bookman's Journal, n.s. 12, no. 48 (Sept.), 245.
Another copy of the first edition of The Female Husband auctioned at Sotheby's. See 1925.B1.

3 BUCK, HOWARD S. A Study in Smollett: Chiefly "Peregrine Pickle." New Haven: Yale University Press; London: Humphrey Milford, Oxford University Press, passim.
Reviewed by Ernest A. Baker, RES, 2 (1926), 360-63; N&Q, 150 (1926), 323-24; TLS, 22 April 1926, p. 299.
Sets out the antagonism between Fielding and Smollett, and particularly Smollett's harsh attacks on Fielding in Peregrine Pickle and Habbakkuk Hilding.

*4 DEINHARDT, MARGRETH. "Beziehungen der Philosophie auf die Romane Fieldings," Beziehungen der Philosophie zu dem grossen englischen Roman des achtzehnten Jahrhunderts. Dissertation, Hamburg, 1925.
Source: Humphrey, p. 255 or 1952.A5.

5 JENSEN, GERARD E. "An Address to the Electors of Great Britain . . . Possibly a Fielding Tract." Modern

Language Notes, 40, no. 1 (Jan.), 57-58.
On the basis of linguistic and allusive evidence it seems to be Fielding's. But it does have odd spellings and clumsy style that argue against Fielding's authorship. See 1954.B7 and 1957.B1.

6 MACLAURIN, CHARLES. "Henry Fielding," in his Mere Mortals: Medico-Historical Essays. London: Jonathan Cape, pp. 121-27. [1925].
Recounts the harrowing end of Fielding's career (the Canning affair, his overwork as magistrate, etc.) and Fielding's attempt to dose himself with quack remedies. Concludes that Fielding was suffering from cancer, "spreading to the peritoneum" (p. 125), and that his 'gout' was the result of septic teeth. He believes Fielding misjudged the Canning case as a result and is amazed that his last works show so much good humor.

7 NICOLL, ALLARDYCE. A History of Early Eighteenth Century English Drama, 1700-1750. Cambridge: The University Press, passim.
Reviewed by Bonamy Dobrée, Nation-Athen., 36 (7 Feb. 1925), 650-51; Edith Morley, RES, 1 (1925), 364-66; George Saintsbury, Bookman, 67 (1925), 293-94; D. H. Stevens, MP, 23 (1925), 249-51; TLS, 12 March 1925, p. 169; N&Q, 148 (1925), 233; Bookman's Jour., 12 (1925), 103.
Provides a hand list (superseded by 1961.B13) of the performances of Fielding's plays and briefly discusses each of them under various headings: comedies of manners, comedies of intrigue, ballad opera, burlesque and rehearsals, etc. Nicoll feels that "unquestionably the finest plays of the later years of the period which show the influence of the manners style are those of Fielding, but Fielding was often too farcical to allow of the free expression of the spirit of the comedy of manners" (p. 158). It is as a writer of burlesques that "Fielding stands forward as the most important figure" (p. 263).
In the third edition of this work (issued 1952, 1955, 1961 and 1965), this discussion of Fielding will be found in vol. 2, Early Eighteenth Century Drama.

8 PRIESTLEY, J. B. "Parson Adams," in his The English Comic Characters. London: The Bodley Head; New York: Dodd, Mead, pp. 91-110.
Reviewed by Martin Armstrong, Bookman, 68 (June 1925), 145-46; Milton Waldman, Sat. Rev., 2 (27 Feb. 1926), 588; Leonard Woolf, Nation-Athen., 37, no. 6 (9 May 1925), 177; TLS, 30 April 1925, p. 297; Spectator (16 May 1925), 815;

Lond. Merc., 12 (Oct. 1925), 662-63.

"The real hero of Fielding's Joseph Andrews is Mr. Abraham Adams" (p. 91). Priestley briefly discusses the parody of Pamela, recounts the narrative, and then begins to look at the action. He first argues that Adams stands "outside" Fielding's notion of the true ridiculous and then that he was created to carry the weight of Fielding's romantic morality (his belief that there is a native impulse toward goodness). Adams constantly exposes those who merely conform to the prevailing code.

Reprinted several times, most recently 1963.

*9 PRINSEN, JACOB. De Roman in de 18e eeuw in West Europa. Groningen: J. B. Wolters U. M.

In Dutch.

Source: T. Humphrey, p. 232.

10 STONEHILL, CHARLES. "Fielding's The Miser." Times Literary Supplement (22 Oct.), p. 698.

Tentatively identifies a suppressed folio first edition (uncorrected) of this play, which was later published by J. Watts in 1733. See 1931.B14.

11 VAN DOREN, CARL. "Tom Jones and Philip Carey: Heroes of Two Centuries." Century Magazine, 110, no. 1 (May), 115-20.

Feels that each hero epitomizes his century. Thinks Tom "happily obtuse" (p. 119); "he was what beef and beer had made him, without any tincture of reflection. For him, nerves were nonsense" (p. 118). Maugham's Philip Carey is touched by the increase "of knowledge and of doubt since Tom's time" (p. 119). Admits that both the active and the reflective personality, each appropriate to its age, can also be found in either age. Each novelist used his character to achieve much the same thing, a revelation of what it was, and is, to be English.

1926 A BOOKS

1 BLANCHARD, FREDERIC T. Fielding the Novelist: A Study in Historical Criticism. New Haven: Yale University Press, 669 pp.

Reviewed by E. A. Baker, RES, 3 (1927), 227-32; F. Baldensperger, Litteris, 4 (1927), 222-25; Charles S. Baldwin, Dial, 81 (1926), 440-42; Wilbur Cross, YR, 16 (1927), 798-800; A. Digeon, RAA, 5 (1927), 57-59; Paul Dottin, RELV, 43 (1926), 450-55; Oswald Doughty, E. Studies, 9 (1927), 208-209; Oliver Elton, MLR, 22 (1927),

225-28; E. S. Noyes, Sat. Rev., 16 Oct. 1926, p. 198; P. F. B., SAQ, 26 (1927), 209-11; H. Schöffler, ESt, 62 (1927), 227-42; H. Schöffler, Beiblatt, 38 (1927), 65-68; Mark Van Doren, Nation, 123 (10 Nov. 1926), 483; RLC, 8 (1927), 395-96; TLS, 29 July 1926, p. 509.

An exhaustive study of Fielding's reputation as a man and as a novelist from 1742 to 1925. Blanchard begins by setting out the immediate responses, both positive and negative, to Joseph Andrews, Tom Jones, Amelia, and A Journal of a Voyage to Lisbon, and whenever possible examines motives and quality of the source. His sources are contemporary periodicals (particularly Gentleman's Magazine, London Magazine, and Monthly Review), pamphlets, and letters (Richardson, Lady Mary Wortley Montagu, etc.). He concludes that while Joseph Andrews was popular, it caused little significant literary stir. Fielding's serious contemporary reputation rested on Tom Jones, which was "considerably shaken by the public ridicule of Amelia. . . . He had not succeeded in dethroning Richardson, nor had he won that position as a writer we accord him today" (p. 103). A Journal did nothing to reverse this, and Fielding was left with a large popular audience and a reputation for wit. He had no support from men of letters and was vilified by Grub-Street. He thinks Murphy's "Essay" (1762.A10) a reflection "of accumulated contemporary enmity" (p. 157), and that it was condescending and harmful to his personal reputation. He then examines the damage done to Fielding's reputation by Samuel Johnson and Horace Walpole, balancing them against defenders like Beattie, Monboddo, Warton and Gibbon. By the end of the century, the Fielding-Richardson debate was still the central issue. Most nineteenth-century authors (Hazlitt, Coleridge, Byron, etc.) began to prefer Fielding to Richardson and to treat Fielding as the "Father of the English Novel" (p. 367). Scott and Thackeray, both influential, praised Fielding's art but worsened his personal reputation as "Artist-Prodigal" (p. 408). Blanchard then sketches in the remaking of Fielding's personal reputation through the historical-biographical work of Thomas Keightley, Austin Dobson, W. E. Henley, Edmund Gosse, and Wilbur L. Cross, who made us see Fielding as "a great and serious man of letters" (p. 579). See dissertation 1922.A1.

*2 BRANCH, MARY E. "Fielding's Attitude Toward the Chief Religious Groups of His Time." Dissertation, Chicago, 1926.
Source: T. Humphrey, p. 251.

1926

3 FIELDING, HENRY. An Apology for the Life of Mrs. Shamela Andrews. Edited by R. Brimley Johnson. Waltham St. Lawrence: Golden Cockerel Press, 91 pp.

Reviewed by A. Digeon, RAA, 4 (1926), 73; G[eorge] S[herburn], PQ, 6 (1927), 179-80.

"This reprinting is literally transcribed from the 'second issue,' with the original spelling, punctuation, capitals and abbreviations" (p. xi). Johnson's introduction briefly describes the objects of the satire (Pamela, Colley Cibber, and Conyers Middleton), the internal stylistic evidence for Fielding's authorship, and the external evidence (its being attributed to him); Johnson also briefly argues that the preface to Joseph Andrews was designed to distinguish it from the broad burlesque of Shamela. He provides a bibliographical description of three issues of the work. See 1946.B11.

4 _____. The History of the Life of the Late Mr. Jonathan Wild the Great. Introduction by John Macy. The Rogues' Bookshelf. New York: Greenberg, 307 pp.

Macy commends the appeal of this rogue book, its sustained irony, and Fielding's creation of character (seeing Wild as a prelude to his later fiction). No indication of copy text.

5 _____. The History of the Life of the Late Mr. Jonathan Wild the Great. Introduction by Wilson Follett. New York: Alfred A. Knopf, 345 pp.

This volume includes Daniel Defoe's The Life and Actions of Jonathan Wild. Follett superficially compares Fielding's and Defoe's accounts to the real life of Wild and then compares Fielding's ironic account with earlier ironic uses of Wild. No indication of copy text.

6 _____. The History of Tom Jones, a Foundling. Bohn's Popular Library. 2 vols. London: George Bell and Sons, 1011 pp.

Reissue of 1905.A6.

7 _____. The Novels of Henry Fielding. 5 vols. Boston and New York: Houghton Mifflin.

Reprint of the Shakespeare Head edition (1926.A8).

8 _____. The Shakespeare Head Edition of Fielding's Novels. 10 vols. Oxford: Basil Blackwell.

Vols. 1-3 reprint the Murphy (1762.A10) text of Amelia; vol. 4 the 1743 "second" edition of Jonathan Wild; vols. 5 and 6 "a careful comparison of the second and fourth editions, with an occasional reference to the fifth" edition of Joseph Andrews; vols. 7-10 are the "four volume edition, of April 1749, now generally called the third edition, and which is regarded by M. Digeon as the authentic text of Tom Jones." These are old spelling texts with brief notes and a textual note at the end of the final volume of each novel.

9 _____. The Works of Henry Fielding. Edited by George Saintsbury and illustrated by George Cruikshank. 12 vols. London: The Navarre Society.
Vols. 1-6 Tom Jones; vols. 7-8 Joseph Andrews; vols. 9-11 Amelia; vol. 12 Jonathan Wild. This is a photographic reproduction of the Bickers & Sons 1871 edition (1871.A5).

10 _____. Tom Thumb the Great. Edited by John Hampden. The Garrick Playbooks. London: Wells Gardner, Darton, 50 pp.
Hampden provides a primer on staging and acting; a brief life of Fielding; a note on the play's popularity; tips for producing Tom Thumb. He also substantially reprints the 1731 version of the play (called The Tragedy of Tragedies) and reproduces some of Fielding's notes and preface to this revised Tom Thumb. No indication of copy text.

*11 RADTKE, BRUNO. "Henry Fielding als Kritiker." Dissertation, Berlin-Humboldt, 1926.
In German.
Source: McNamee, 1865-1964, p. 557. See 1926.A12.

12 _____. Henry Fielding als Kritiker. Leipzig: Mayer & Müller, 118 pp.
Reviewed by F. B. K., PQ, 6 (1927), 180.
An exhaustive list of citations under various headings (invention, burlesque, etc.) that neither argues for the development of Fielding's critical ideas nor coherently organizes his aesthetic, as does Goldburg (1964.B6). In German.

1926 B SHORTER WRITINGS

1 BINZ-WINIGER, ELISABETH. Erziehungsfragen in den Romanen von Richardson, Fielding, Smollett, Goldsmith and Sterne. Thüringen: Thomas & Hubert, pp. 16-33.
Inaugural dissertation for the University of Zürich on the problem of education in these novelists. Sees characters as reflections of the author and discusses Fielding's depiction of children in Joseph Andrews, Tom Jones, and Amelia in three ways: as practical examples of the

1926

principles of education, as members of a family, as objects of psychological analysis. In German.

2 ERNLE, LORD. "Founders of the Modern Novel: II. Henry Fielding." Edinburgh Review, 243, no. 496 (April), 336-54.
Compares "the spiteful littleness of Richardson" (p. 336) with the generous Fielding. An essentially biographical survey of Fielding and his career which defends him against the slurs on his character, while continuing Murphy's critical attitudes and anecdotes (plays written on tobacco papers). Ernle calls the plays hurried and immature; likes the novels because they aren't pessimistic or misanthropic like Swift (he finds Jonathan Wild "unpleasant" in its "exposing [of] the undetected basenesses of men," p. 346). He rejects the idea that Fielding is the model for Booth, and praises Fielding's humor and ability to construct (particularly in Tom Jones). Concludes that if Fielding's women were not as good as Richardson's, his men were better.

3 [LILJEGREN, S. B.]. "Fielding's 'Charge to the Jury,' 1745." Times Literary Supplement (4 March), p. 168.
Describes the events leading up to the writing of this pamphlet (Walpole's illness and death), the evidence for its being by Fielding, and the location of other copies (in the British Museum under Earl of Orford). Cross (1918.A1) had not seen a copy. See 1946.B4.

4 WILLIAMS, ORLO. "Tom Jones," in his Some Great English Novels. London: Macmillan, pp. 1-25.
Opens with praise: "Stendhal's La Chartreuse de Parme, Dostoievsky's The Brothers Karamazov, and Tom Jones are by general consent great works of art by great writers" (p. 7). He appreciates Adams and Western as characters on the order of Don Quixote, Falstaff, Tartuffe, etc., who are "triumphs of the imagination" (p. 9), although he thinks Fielding came closer to an analysis of the human mind in Amelia. Williams impressionistically compares the irony in Jonathan Wild with Swift's The Tale of a Tub and describes the mellower comic irony of Tom Jones. He finds the quarrels of Thwackum and Square "psychologically trite and dramatically out of place" but serving Fielding's "strong, sensible and enlightened morality" (p. 18). Fielding often finds a "symbolic" (allegorical) form to express his psychological insights.

1927 A BOOKS

1 FIELDING, HENRY. Joseph Andrews in Seikkailut. Translated by Valfrid Hedman. [?]: Arvi A. Karisto Osakeyhtiö, 458 pp.
Finnish translation.

2 _____. The History of the Adventures of Joseph Andrews and His Friend Mr. Abraham Adams. Edited by George Saintsbury. Everyman's Library. London: J. M. Dent and Sons; New York: E. P. Dutton, 390 pp. [1927].
Reissue of 1910.A6.

3 _____. The History of the Adventures of Joseph Andrews, and His Friend Mr. Abraham Adams. Illustrations by George Cruikshank and biography by Thomas Roscoe. Bohn's Novelists' Library. London: George Bell and Sons, 433 pp.
Reissue of 1836.A2.

4 _____. The History of Tom Jones A Foundling. Introduction by George Saintsbury. Everyman's Library. 2 vols. London: J. M. Dent & Sons; New York: E. P. Dutton, 838 pp.
Reissue of 1909.A2.

*5 _____. Tom Jones. London: Methuen, 744 pp. [1927].
Source: National Union Catalogue: Pre-1956 Imprints. Vol. 171, p. 688.

1927 B SHORTER WRITINGS

1 BALDERSTON, KATHARINE C. "Goldsmith's Supposed Attack on Fielding." Modern Language Notes, 42, no. 3 (March), 165-68.
Goldsmith did not attack Fielding as a writer of romances in "Letter 83" of the Citizen of the World because he borrowed the letter from a translation of the French Description of the Empire of China and Chinese-Tartary.

2 BENNETT, JAMES O'DONNELL. "Fielding's 'Tom Jones,'" in his Much Loved Books. New York: Boni and Liveright; London: Hutchinson (1928), pp. 236-42.
Appreciates Tom Jones along with the Bible, Swiss Family Robinson, etc., claiming for it a supreme social realism and deep insight into human nature.

3 DE CASTRO, J. PAUL. "A Forgotten Salisbury Surgeon." Times Literary Supplement (13 Jan.), p. 28.

1927

Mr. Edward Goldwyre may have been the surgeon who repaired Mrs. Fielding's (Charlotte Cradock's) nose and thus may be the model for the surgeon who repairs Amelia's nose. See 1931.B3, B8.

4 ____. "Fielding's Invocation to Fame." Times Literary Supplement (10 Nov.), p. 818.
Asks why Fielding associated Milton with Hampstead or Highgate, as the invocation that opens Book 13 of Tom Jones seems to indicate.

5 DIGEON, AURÉLIEN. "La condemnation de Tom Jones à Paris." Revue Anglo-Américaine, 4 (1927), 529-31.
The Arrêt du Conseil (suppression order) does not mention or imply immorality as the reason for condemnation. See 1898.B1, 1898.B3, 1957.B13, and 1961.B8.

6 ____. "An Essay on Nothing," in Gems of the World's Best Classics. Edited by Llewellyn Jones and C. C. Gaul. Chicago: Geographical Publishing, pp. 412-20. [1927].
Brief headnote on Fielding and reprint of the essay (no indication of copy text).

7 HIBERNICUS. "Fielding's Invocation to Fame." Times Literary Supplement (24 Nov.), p. 888.
Answers 1927.B4. Lamartine too repeats the tradition of Milton's connection with Hampstead. Fielding's playful mythology in the invocation is also commented on.

8 MCCUTCHEON, ROGER P. "Amelia, or the Distressed Wife." Modern Language Notes, 42, no. 1 (Jan.), 32-33.
The pamphlet "secret history" of Amelia, which was published six months before Fielding's Amelia, is totally unlike Fielding's novel. Fielding borrowed nothing from it.

1928 A BOOKS

1 FIELDING, HENRY. Joseph Andrews. Introduction by C. A. Bodelsen and translated by Paul Boisen. [Denmark]: Gyldendalske Boghandel Nordisk Forlag, 278 pp. [1928-30].
Danish translation.

*2 ____. Ta-wei-jen Wei-li-t'e chuan. Translated by Wu Kuang-chien. Shanghai: Commercial Press. [1928?].
Chinese translation of Jonathan Wild.
Source: Hugh Amory's working bibliography (transliterated by Bonnie McDougall of the East Asian Institute).

3 _____. The History of Amelia. Illustrations by "Phiz." London: George Routledge & Sons, 543 pp. [1928].
Reprint of 1857.A2.

4 _____. The Tragedy of Tragedies, or Tom Thumb the Great, in Eighteenth Century Plays. Edited by John Hampden. Everyman's Library. London and Toronto: J. M. Dent & Sons; New York: E. P. Dutton, pp. 160-209.
"The text is printed from the third edition (1737) which differs from the first only in very trivial details."

*5 _____. Yueh-se An-t'e-lu chuan. Translated by Wu Kuang-chien. Shanghai: Commercial Press. [1928?].
Chinese translation of Joseph Andrews.
Source: Hugh Amory's working bibliography (transliterated by Bonnie McDougall of the East Asian Institute).

6 KÖHLER, FRIEDRICH. Fieldings Wochenschrift "The Champion" und das englische Leben der Zeit. Münster: Universität zu Münster, 62 pp.
Inaugural dissertation which examines The Champion as a moral and political journal, evaluating its relation to the life of the period and to public opinion. After studying its publication history, other contemporary periodicals, and its political affiliations (anti-Walpole), Köhler examines Fielding's position on marriage, education, pleasure and sports, law, the clergy, the merchant class, religion, philosophy, etc., suggesting that The Champion was an excellent sounding board for all aspects of public opinion. In German.

7 PARFITT, G. E. L'influence française dans les oeuvres de Fielding et dans le théâtre anglais contemporain de ses comédies. Paris: Les Presses Modernes, 158 pp.
Traces Fielding's knowledge of French literature and the effect of that literature on an original, creative British mind. After discussing the influence of a misunderstood Molière on Restoration comedy, Parfitt turns to Fielding and his contemporaries, considering Fielding's adaptations from the French (particularly Molière) and French influences on his other plays. She asserts that Fielding's literary theories were influenced by his classical studies and by French theorists like Le Bossu, La Motte-Hondart, Montaigne, etc. His novels were influenced by Scarron, Lesage, and particularly Marivaux. Two appendices list Fielding's French reading as quoted in his works and the French books in his library. In French.

1928

*8 THORNBURY, ETHEL MARGARET. "Henry Fielding's Theory of the Comic Prose Epic." Dissertation, Wisconsin, 1928.
Source: McNamee, 1865-1964, p. 557. See 1931.A9.

1928 B SHORTER WRITINGS

1 COBB, LILIAN. [Fielding], in her Pierre-Antoine de La Place: sa vie et son oeuvre, 1707-1793. Paris: Editions Boccard, pp. 86-111.
After establishing de la Place in the tradition of French translations of English literature (de la Place translated Fielding, Shakespeare, Ben Jonson, Addison, Aphra Ben, etc.), discusses his translation of Tom Jones , read in France for over half a century. De la Place openly admitted (in an "introductory" letter to Fielding) that he made major changes for French taste. He omitted all elements that did not further the plot, much dialogue, all theological and moral arguments, the narrator's comments, the descriptive passages, all conversations among the lower classes, the fist fight scenes, and the colorful language of the protagonists. In French.

2 ELTON, OLIVER. "Fielding and Smollett," in his A Survey of English Literature, 1730-1780. London: Edward Arnold, pp. 182-216.
Reviewed by R. S. Crane, New Rep., 60 (16 Oct. 1929), 248; P. Crowley, Commonweal, 10 (17 July 1929), 299; D. M. Stuart, Nation-Athen., 44 (Jan.), 586; TLS, 17 Jan. 1929, p. 41; Mercury, 19 (Mar. 1929), 551-52; Life and Letters, 2 (March 1929), 238-42.
Surveys Fielding's career and his reputation, sets him in his age, discusses the influence of "literary culture" and the law on his writings, and briefly discusses his plays, his journalism and his novels. Elton outlines the accepted approaches to each novel (e.g., Tom Jones: epic plan and mock epic elements, plotting and design, character contrasts, the immorality of the Lady Bellaston affair, Fielding's theory of human nature, etc.).

3 FORNELLI, G. H. "Fielding e la sua epoca." Annals of the Tuscan Universities, n.s. 12:80-124.
Sets Fielding's works in historical context. Discusses the early politically satiric plays and the social satire in Joseph Andrews and Jonathan Wild. Thinks that Fielding and Richardson together created the new social and psychological novel, discarding the picaresque form of Defoe and Smollett. In Tom Jones sees Fielding going beyond the

bourgeois Christianity of Richardson and anticipating Rousseau and the German Sturm und Drang. The novel reflects English duality which vacillates between moral rule and liberty. Thus Fielding is both a social satirist like Swift and a Christian political reformer like Pitt. In Italian.

4 HEIDLER, JOSEPH B. "The History of English Criticism of Prose Fiction from 1740 to 1760," in his The History, from 1700 to 1800, of English Criticism of Prose Fiction. University of Illinois Studies in Language and Literature, 13, no. 2 (May), 46-77.

Sets Fielding's critical theory in context (Addison, Dennis, Le Bossu, Du Bos, etc.). Compares Fielding's theoretical pronouncements in Joseph Andrews, Jonathan Wild, his preface to Sarah Fielding's David Simple, Tom Jones, and Amelia with those of Richardson and Smollett. Heidler also sets out selected comments on Fielding's novels to be found in the letters and journalism of his contemporaries. See 1930.B2, 1934.B3.

5 HILLHOUSE, JAMES T. "Fielding," in his The Grub-Street Journal. Durham, North Carolina: Duke University Press, pp. 173-85.

Reviewed by Walter Graham, MLN 44 (1929), 271-73; George Sherburn, MP, 26 (1929), 361-67; TLS, 23 May 1929, p. 416.

Sets out the attack begun in 1732 by The Grub-Street Journal (and responded to and sustained by other periodicals) charging that Fielding's plays were immoral and obscene (particularly The Covent Garden Tragedy and The Old Debauchee). Suggests that this attack began "the process by which Fielding acquired that false reputation for youthful immorality" (p. 185).

Reissued New York: Benjamin Blom, 1967.

6 MABBOTT, THOMAS O., ed. Selections from Richardson and Fielding. Evanston, Ill.: Northwestern University Press, pp. 13-25. [1928].

Provides a plot summary of Joseph Andrews and reprints the author's preface; Book 1, chapter 12; part of Book 2, chapter 13; and Book 2, chapters 14 and 15.

1929 A BOOKS

1 BANERJI, H. K. Henry Fielding: Playwright, Journalist and Master of the Art of Fiction, His Life and Works. Oxford: Blackwell, 349 pp.

1929

Reviewed by R. S. Crane, PQ, 10 (1931), 200-201; TLS, 3 April 1930, p. 293.

A biographical survey of Fielding's work. Banerji divides Fielding's work into eight groupings: the plays, early journalism (The Champion), Shamela and Joseph Andrews, Miscellanies (with special attention to Jonathan Wild), political journalism (True Patriot and Jacobite Journal), Tom Jones, Amelia, and the final phase (Covent-Garden Journal and Journal of a Voyage to Lisbon). Although he surveys the influences on Fielding ("realistic" fiction from Nash and Deloney through Smollett, and including Aphra Behn and the "romance" influence of Scarron, Lesage, and Marivaux on Joseph Andrews), his assumption throughout is that "his indebtedness to his literary predecessors is small compared to what he owed to the experience of his own life and to the world around him" (p. 12). He sees Fielding as the model for the hero in The Author's Farce and Fielding's father as a model for Booth in Amelia. Banerji is particularly interested in the reception of Fielding's work, and his critical judgments are confined to time-honored generalizations: Fielding's plays are indebted to Wycherley and Congreve; the strength of Joseph Andrews is its character sketches and its accurate portrayal of English life; Amelia is written in a "graver mood" (p. 233). He does set down the best opinions of the time about some things: Shamela is Fielding's; the "C" and "L" signatures in The Champion are Fielding's essays; Fielding pilloried Cibber, Walpole, lotteries, etc.

2 FIELDING, HENRY. The Adventures of Joseph Andrews. Edited by J. Paul de Castro. The Scholartis Eighteenth-Century Novels. London: The Scholartis Press, 409 pp.

Reviewed by A. Digeon, RAA, 7 (1930), 263; N&Q, 156 (1929), 342; TLS, 25 April 1929, p. 343.

"The text mainly followed here is that of the Second Edition of August, 1742. That Fielding made a few important additions and alterations to the Second Edition is incontestable, but the serious printers' errors it contains make it equally clear that he could have given it no careful revision" (p. 18). De Castro provides full notes; his introduction carefully sets out Fielding's parody of Pamela (in both Shamela and Joseph Andrews) and his attack on Cibber; briefly looks at Fielding's characters (pointing out parallels in his other fiction); defends Fielding's learning; and commends the novel as a social historical document. A bibliographical note records the publication information from Woodfall's and Strahan's ledgers for the first four editions; there is an index of characters, places, and events in the novel.

3 ____. The Adventures of Joseph Andrews. Introduction by Leonard Rice-Oxley. World Classics. London: H. Milford, Oxford University Press, 406 pp.
A modernized edition, apparently based on the 1742 (first and second) editions. The introduction briefly reviews Fielding's career to 1742, discusses the parody of Pamela, and outlines the development of the novel from Defoe and Richardson to Fielding.

4 ____. The History of the Adventures of Joseph Andrews and His Friend Mr. Abraham Adams. Edited by George Saintsbury. Everyman's Library. London and Toronto: J. M. Dent & Sons; New York: E. P. Dutton, 390 pp. [1929].
Reissue of 1910.A6.

5 ____. The History of the Adventures of Joseph Andrews and his Friend Mr. Abraham Adams. Introduction by J. B. Priestley and illustrations by Norman Tealby. London: John Lane, Bodley Head; New York: Dodd, Mead, 381 pp.
Priestley briefly compares Richardson and Fielding, commending Fielding's irony, and describes the humorous nature of Fielding's comic characters, particularly Adams. No indication of copy text.

6 ____. The History of Tom Jones A Foundling. Introduction by George Saintsbury. Everyman's Library. 2 vols. London: J. M. Dent & Sons; New York: E. P. Dutton, 838 pp.
Reissue of 1909.A2.

*7 ____. The Tragedy of Tragedies, in Eighteenth Century Comedy. Edited by William Duncan Taylor. London: H. Milford, Oxford University Press. [1929].
Source: National Union Catalogue: Pre-1956 Imprints. Vol. 172, p. 8.

1929 B SHORTER WRITINGS

1 BATESON, F. W. "Fielding," in his English Comic Drama: 1700-1750. Oxford: The Clarendon Press, pp. 115-43.
Reviewed by De Witt C. Croissant, MLN, 45 (1930), 406-407; Eduard Eckhardt, Deutsche Literaturzeitung, 50 (1929), cols. 1915-17; Paul Meissner, Beiblatt, 40 (1929), 306-309; Allardyce Nicoll, MLR, 24 (1929), 477-78; V. de Sola Pinto,

RES, 6 (1930), 366-68; N&Q, 156 (1929), 308; TLS, 11 April 1929, p. 291.

Thinks Fielding an "indifferent dramatist" (p. 115) whose "dramas are less mature and less profound than the novels" (p. 117) because they were written when he was younger (The Historical Register was produced when he was thirty). Bateson sensibly divides Fielding's plays into three groups (farces, comedies, and burlesques) and briefly but intelligently discusses the comedies and the burlesques. He examines their strengths, weaknesses, and sources (Restoration comedy for the comedies and The Rehearsal for the burlesques). By comparing passages that Fielding borrowed from Congreve, he demonstrates that Fielding did not have the Restoration comedy "style," and is best when he "plagiarized" from simpler, broader playwrights like Vanbrugh. He discusses the effectiveness of Fielding's "satirical extravaganzas" (p. 121), concluding that their strength is a result of "Fielding's concreteness" (p. 140). Bateson's brief conclusion on the aesthetics of comic drama (an impersonal ritual form) and Fielding's inability to generalize is particularly interesting.

Reprinted 1963 by Russell & Russell.

2 FAUSSET, HUGH I'A. "Fielding." Bookman (London), 76, no. 452 (May), 107-108.

Contrasts Richardson's "sentimental lie" (p. 107) with Fielding's "robust grasp of actuality" (p. 108) in Joseph Andrews, Jonathan Wild and Tom Jones. Thinks that Fielding's characters' vices and virtues come from life, that they are mixed (even Western shows moral worth), and that they never fall into caricature or melodrama. While he thinks that there is "no poetry about Fielding," he defends him as a novelist and a man.

3 PROPER, COENRAAD B. A. "Henry Fielding," in his Social Elements in English Prose Fiction Between 1700 and 1832. Amsterdam: H. J. Paris, pp. 49-62.

Sees Fielding extending the social range of the novel (begun by Defoe) but not defending middle class virtue. Thinks him a conservative, humane reformer who attacks political and legal corruption, prisons, "great" men, the exploitation of simple workers, and Whiggism. Thinks Amelia weakened because he tries to weave these reform ideas more closely into the fabric of the novel.

Reprinted New York: Haskell House, 1965.

4 SWANN, GEORGE R. "Philosophical Parallelism in Six English Novelists: The Conception of Good, Evil, and Human Nature."

Dissertation, Pennsylvania University, 1929.

Argues for the primary influence of Shaftesbury, as opposed to Hobbes and Mandeville, on Fielding's moral thought. Sees Fielding's contemporary, David Hume, as a kindred spirit who also reconstructed the philosophy of the school of Shaftesbury.

5 THOMAS, PAUL K. "Die literarische Verkörperung des philanthropischen Zuges in der englischen Aufklärung." Dissertation, Breslau, 1929.

In a section on philanthropy in the novel, Thomas discusses Adams, Heartfree, Dr. Harrison, and Mr. Allworthy. In German.

1930 A BOOKS

1 FIELDING, HENRY. A Journey from this World to the Next. Etchings by Denis Tegetmeir. Waltham Saint Lawrence: The Golden Cockerel Press, 175 pp.

"The text followed is that of the edition of 1743" (p. 175).

2 _____. Amelia. Introduction by George Saintsbury. Everyman's Library. 2 vols. London: J. M. Dent & Sons; New York: E. P. Dutton, 639 (319 & 320) pp.

Saintsbury suggests that Amelia is "weak" because its subject is less popular (life after marriage); also admits that its characters are less vivid (Amelia is nearly mawkish, and Dr. Harrison repeats the fickle weakness of Allworthy). Saintsbury finally thinks it an important part of Fielding's total achievement, with nuances and "mixed" characters (like Miss Matthews, Colonel Bath, and the Jameses) that Fielding seldom achieved in his earlier fiction. Reproduces Murphy's (1762.A10) text.

3 _____. An Apology for the Life of Mrs. Shamela Andrews. Introduction by Brian W. Downs. Cambridge: The Minority Press, 71 pp.

Briefly outlines the attack in Shamela on Richardson's Pamela, Colley Cibber, Conyers Middleton; discusses the similar parodic attack in Joseph Andrews. On the basis of internal evidence (phraseology, names used elsewhere by Fielding, similar parodic objects) and external evidence (letters by Dampier and Richardson), Downs concludes that it is Fielding's. No indication of copy text. See 1946.B11.

1930

4 _____. The Adventures of Joseph Andrews. Introduction by Bruce McCullough. The Modern Student's Library. New York, Chicago, Boston, etc.: Charles Scribner's Sons, 451 pp.

McCullough outlines the parody of Pamela (particularly attacking Richardson's "muddled ethics"), discusses Fielding's theory of comedy and his literary sources (from Homer and Virgil to Marivaux), and commends his healthy ironic vision of life, as illustrated by the characters he created. No indication of copy text.

*5 _____. The History of the Adventures of Joseph Andrews and his friend Mr. Abraham Adams. New York: [?], 311 pp. [1930?].

Source: National Union Catalogue: Pre-1956 Imprints. Vol. 171, p. 679.

6 _____. The History of the Adventures of Joseph Andrews and The History of the Life of the Late Mr. Jonathan Wild the Great. Boston and New York: C. T. Brainard, 606 pp. [1930].

Reissue in part of [1902].A15 without Maynadier's introduction and with plates by several illustrators, including Cruikshank. The spine of this "Edition de Luxe" calls it The Works of Fielding. Each work is separately paged.

7 _____. The History of Tom Jones, a Foundling. Illustrations by G. Spencer Pryse. London: John Lane, The Bodley Head; New York: Dodd, Mead, 770 pp.

Appears to reprint the first edition and reproduces Coleridge's notes in his 1773 copy of Tom Jones.

8 _____. The History of Tom Jones A Foundling. 3 vols. Boston and New York: Colonial Press. [1930?].

No indication of copy text; includes Coleridge's marginal notes.

9 _____. The History of Tom Jones: A Foundling. 3 vols. Boston and New York: C. T. Brainard. [1930].

Reissue in part of [1902].A15 without Maynadier's introduction and with plates by several illustrators, including Cruikshank. The spine of this "Edition de Luxe" calls them The Works of Fielding.

10 _____. Tom Jones The History of a Foundling. 2 vols. London: Odhams Press, 944 (476 & 468) pp. [1930].

No indication of copy text; a two-page introduction, condescending to Fielding.

1930 B SHORTER WRITINGS

1 BAKER, ERNEST A. "Fielding: Early Life, and Joseph Andrews" etc., in his The History of the English Novel. Intellectual Realism: From Richardson to Sterne. Vol. 4. London: H. F. & G. Witherby, pp. 77-196.

Reviewed by R. F. Russell, Mercury, 23 (1931), 293-95; H. Williams, RES, 6 (1930), 360-61; TLS, 17 July 1930, pp. 581-82.

Reviews Fielding's life and career, passing on accepted opinions of the day (e.g., discusses Joseph Andrews as a parody of Pamela and as comedy rather than burlesque, Adams as a character and Christian idealist, the parallels with Don Quixote, the real life model for Adams, and Fielding's debt to Lesage and Marivaux). Baker provides outlines for the "stories" of Fielding's novels, as well as several plays and minor works, and discusses major characters and themes. He also suggests that the characters draw themselves "in the dialogue" (p. 97); that Fielding specialized in double allegories (satires like Jonathan Wild with both general and particular subjects); that an "ironical attitude is of the very essence of his art" (p. 141); that Amelia differs from Tom Jones in epic plan, tone (sentimental), and in its more overtly Christian outlook; that we must not see Fielding in his characters. Baker emphasizes and discusses influences on Fielding (Molière, Lucian, Shakespeare, Swift, Lesage, etc.) and Fielding's reputation, asserting that he not only established the genre but that "his novels contain the germs of every kind of fiction that has come to maturity since" (p. 190).

Reissued New York: Barnes & Noble, 1957.

2 BOSKER, AISSO. "Henry Fielding. Laurence Sterne," in his Literary Criticism in the Age of Johnson. Groningen and Den Haag: J. B. Wolters' Uitgevers-Maatschappij; New York: Stechert, pp. 107-13.

Reviewed by H. Jenkins, MLR, 26 (1931), 357-58; W. van Doorn, ESt, 13 (1931), 30-32.

Gleaning Fielding's critical opinions from his journalism, prefaces, and dedications, Bosker contends that Fielding believed that a critic should be thoroughly grounded in classical literature but that he was no slave to the "classical" rules of his age (e.g., he rejected the rule of unity in time and place). Fielding believed that all had to be tested by truth and nature; thus, the author had to stay with the reasonable and probable. According to Bosker, Fielding also rejected popular approval as true judgment; the critic was a man of taste.

Reprinted Groningen: Wolters', 1954. See 1928.B4, 1934.B3. For a similar survey, see 1970.A20.

3 GRAHAM, WALTER. English Literary Periodicals. New York: Thomas Nelson & Son, passim.

Reviewed by E. A. B., MLR, 26 (1931), 499; O. Burdett, Spectator, 146 (21 Feb. 1931), 278; M. V. Schappes, Nation, 133 (15 July 1931), 72; E. N. S. Thompson, PQ, 10 (1931), 410-11; N. I. White, SAQ, 30 (1931), 332-33; D. Willoughby, Sat. Rev., 151 (28 Feb. 1931), 316; TLS, 4 June 1931, p. 442.

In this survey of periodicals, The Covent-Garden Journal, The Champion, and The Jacobite's Journal (but particularly the latter two) are briefly set in their tradition.

4 HABEL, URSULA. "Smollett und Fielding," in her Die Nachwirkung des picaresken Romans in England (von Nash bis Fielding und Smollett. Sprache und Kultur der germanischen und romanischen Völker. A. Anglistische Reihe. Vol. 4. Breslau: Priebatsch, pp. 37-72.

Argues that Smollett and Fielding changed the picaresque novel and prepared the way for the modern English novel. Both use the picaresque form for satire and humor, Fielding's with a moral, reforming purpose. Habel considers their picaresque sources (Fielding's are more diverse) and their technical borrowings (travel, adventure, incident, tricks and fights, morals, realism, satire, and composition). Fielding is more innovative in all ways than Smollett and more loosely connected to the tradition. He is most clearly distinguished by his seriousness of purpose and his unified plot. In German.

*5 HORN, ROBERT D. "The Farce Technique in the Dramatic Work of Henry Fielding and Samuel Foote and its Influence on the Maerchensatiren of Ludwig Tieck." Dissertation, Michigan, 1930.

Source: McNamee, 1865-1964, p. 557.

6 R., E. "An Advertisement of Henry Fielding's." Notes and Queries, 159 (1 Nov.), 315.

Fielding's note in the Daily Journal, asserting that he has not seen a new act added to his tragedy of Tom Thumb, implicitly denies authorship of "Battle of the Poets."

7 THOMSEN, EJNAR. Studier I: Fieldings Romaner. Studier Fra Sprog-og Oldtidsforskning. No. 157. Copenhagen and Oslo: Jespersen og Pios Forlag, 88 pp.

In Danish.

1931 A BOOKS

*1 BISSEL, FREDERICK D. "Fielding's Theory of the Novel." Dissertation, Cornell, 1931.
Source: McNamee, 1865-1964, pp. 557-58. See 1933.A1.

*2 FIELDING, HENRY. Istorija Toma Džonsa, naidenyša. Moscow and Leningrad: Molodaaja gvardija, 349 pp.
Abridged Russian translation of Tom Jones.
Source: Hugh Amory's working bibliography.

3 _____. The Adventures of Joseph Andrews. Introduction by Henry H. Harper. Illustrations by Haydon Jones. 2 vols. Boston: The Bibliophile Society, 599 (329 & 270) pp.
No indication of copy text. Harper appreciates the characters in the book, particularly Adams. Thinks the Wilson episode is Fielding's self-portrait of his wild youth. Commends Fielding as a careful observer who includes violence and immorality to instruct and to entertain. The introduction was separately issued in 1931 as a pamphlet called "About Books in General and Henry Fielding in Particular."

4 _____. The History of the Adventures of Joseph Andrews and His Friend Mr. Abraham Adams. Edited by George Saintsbury. Everyman's Library. London and Toronto: J. M. Dent & Sons; New York: E. P. Dutton, 316 pp. [1931].
Reprint of 1910.A6.

5 _____. The History of Tom Jones, a Foundling. New York: The Modern Library, 884 pp. [1931].
Text appears to follow Murphy (1762.A10).

6 _____. The Mock Doctor. Edited by John H[ampden]. The Nelson Playbooks. London and Edinburgh: Thomas Nelson & Sons, 54 pp. [1931].
No indication of copy text. Stage business added to prepare it for performance by amateur groups under the auspices of "The Village Drama Society." Brief introduction calls Fielding's plays "youthful pot-boilers" that are simply "good theatre."

7 _____. Tom Jones: The History of a Foundling. Introduction by J. B. Priestley and illustrations by Alexander King. New York: The Limited Editions Club, 870 pp.
Appears to reprint the "1750" edition followed by Murphy (1762.A10). In his brief appreciation, Priestley mentions

Fielding's ability to create character (despite their conventional "high-falutin' talk") and his dramatic irony.

*8 GLENN, SIDNEY E. "Some French Influences on Henry Fielding." Dissertation, Illinois, 1931.

Source: T. Humphrey, p. 257. See Abstracts of Theses. Urbana: University of Illinois, 1932, p. 21.

9 THORNBURY, ETHEL MARGARET. Henry Fielding's Theory of the Comic Prose Epic. University of Wisconsin Studies in Language and Literature, no. 30. Madison: University of Wisconsin Press, 202 pp.

Reviewed by O. Burdett, Lond. Merc., 26 (June 1932), 181; G. Kitchin, MLR, 28 (1933), 110-11; A. E. Secord, JEGP, 32 (1933), 417-18; J. R. Sutherland, RES, 9 (1933), 342-43; H. N. Taylor, MP, 30 (Nov. 1932), 239-40; F. P. van der Voorde, ESt, 15 (1933), 154-55.

By studying the books in Fielding's library, Thornbury concludes that Fielding "knew a great deal about . . . the epic and epic theories, as conceived by various Renaissance critics, and by the critics and poets of antiquity" (p. 18). Thornbury examines these two traditions, concentrating on the didactic purpose of the epic, the distinction between epic and historic romance, and on the national epic. She goes on to consider French epics and epic theories through the seventeenth century (with special attention to theorists like Le Bossu and Boileau and with an aside on the balancing comic spirit of Molière) and epic theory in England from Dryden to Fielding (with special attention to the "Ancients and Moderns" controversy that had been an important part of the discussion of the epic since the Renaissance). Among English writers of epic and epic theory she discusses Milton, Davenant, Dryden, Blackmore, Dennis, Addison, and Pope. She devotes a chapter to the ways in which Fielding adapted the epic structure to contemporary material in Joseph Andrews, as well as discussing his definition of the comic epic in prose. She then discusses the large epic structure in Tom Jones, as well as "the same working out of epic formulae in small details" (p. 128), and Fielding's adaptation of the epic formula in his creation of realistic characters. Finally she sets out Fielding's comic theory and practice in his two Odysseys (Joseph Andrews and Tom Jones). The appendix is a "verbatim copy of the pamphlet in the British Museum which gives a list of Fielding's library" (p. 168). See 1958.B16, 1974.B16, and dissertation 1928.A8.

10 VOORDE, FRANS PIETER VAN DER. Henry Fielding: Critic and Satirist. Gravenhage: Westerbaau, 233 pp.

An analysis of Fielding as a satirist; while not as vitriolic as Swift's, "far from being casual, the satire is direct and determinate: the satiric spirit is prevalent from first to last" (p. 9). Van der Voorde briefly reviews the social and political conditions of the age and Fielding's life and career. Then he divides Fielding's satiric attacks into three categories: literary comment, political comment, and social comment. By examining the novels, plays and journalism, he first establishes "what positive rules he has laid down for the art of writing" (p. 45) and then describes Fielding's satiric attacks on literary types (the romance in Joseph Andrews and Tom Jones and heroic drama in The Tragedy of Tragedies), on the theater (managers, critics, etc.), and on particular people (Cibber). In the section on political satire he examines Fielding's anti-Jacobite Whig attitudes and his attacks on Walpole. In the final section he sets out Fielding's attacks on law and its administration (prisons, lawyers, etc.), medicine, the church (particularly popery), and social class and money (the basis for the "appearance" theme). He concludes by saying that "love of country is the ground of Fielding's satire" (p. 185).

1931 B SHORTER WRITINGS

*1 BOLLES, EDWIN C. "Sea Travelling from Fielding to Today." Dissertation, Pennsylvania University, 1931.

Source: McNamee, 1865-1964, p. 558.

*2 BRASS, HERTA. "Der Wandel in der Auffassung des Menschen im englischen Roman vom 18 zum 20 Jahrhundert." Dissertation, Tübingen, 1931.

Source: National Union Catalogue: Pre-1956 Imprints. Vol. 172, p. 697.

3 DE CASTRO, J. PAUL. "A Forgotten Salisbury Surgeon." Times Literary Supplement (26 March), p. 252.

Corrects 1931.B8. Dr. Baker was a physician and not a surgeon; according to the dates of his training, he could not have repaired Charlotte Cradock's nose.

4 _____. "Fielding and Lyme Regis." Times Literary Supplement (4 June), p. 447.

Reproduces several documents from the town archives that illustrate Fielding's trouble in his unsuccessful wooing of

Sarah Andrews (Fielding was set upon and beaten; he then called John and Andrew Tucker cowards). Fielding was living at Upton Grey in Hampshire and not in Salisbury as had been thought. See 1883.B3.

5 _____. "Fielding's 'Jonathan Wild.'" Notes and Queries, 160 (16 May), 351.
Asks to have the nature of the lottery in Book 3, chapter 7 explained. See 1931.B6.

6 _____. "Fielding's 'Jonathan Wild.'" Times Literary Supplement (6 Aug.), p. 609.
Asks about the "chair" in the lottery in chapter 7, Book 3 of Jonathan Wild. See 1931.B5.

7 DIGEON, AURÉLIEN. "Fielding a-t-il écrit le dernier chapitre de 'A Journey From This World into the Next.'" Revue Anglo-Américaine, 8, no. 5 (June), 428-30.
Reviewing the Golden Cockerel Press edition (1930.A1), Digeon attributes the Anna Boleyn chapter to Sarah Fielding because its tone is different from the rest of the work and similar to David Simple. In French.

8 DU BOIS, ARTHUR E. "A Forgotten Salisbury Surgeon." Times Literary Supplement (19 March), p. 234.
Suggests that Dr. John Baker might be Amelia's nose surgeon. See 1927.B3 and 1931.B3.

*9 GRAY, ERNEST W. "The Fielding-Smollett Tradition in the English Novel from 1750 to 1835." Dissertation, Harvard, 1931.
Source: T. Humphrey, p. 258. See Summaries of Theses . . . 1931. Cambridge: Harvard University Press, [1932], pp. 229-232.

10 HUXLEY, ALDOUS. "Tragedy and the Whole Truth," in his Music at Night and Other Essays. New York and London: Harper & Row, pp. 3-16.
Huxley calls Tom Jones "one of the very few Odyssean books written in Europe between the time of Aeschylus and the present age; Odyssean because never tragical" (p. 7). Such "Wholly-Truthful" books are not tragical because they don't shirk "the irrelevancies which, in actual life, always temper . . . situations and characters" (p. 8). Huxley cites Sophia's tumble from her horse as an example that we know to be true both to our physical and spiritual experience.

Reprinted Freeport, New York: Books for Libraries Press, 1970.

11 KNIGHT, GRANT C. "Henry Fielding," in his The Novel in English. New York: Richard R. Smith, pp. 42-53.
An old-fashioned review of Fielding's career, emphasizing his high living, his parody of Richardson, his less than Swiftian irony in Jonathan Wild, his technical advances in dramatic action, speech, and the use of the omniscient narrator, and his "naturalism, or loyalty to truth, agreeable or disagreeable" (p. 51). Knight is offended by the morality of Tom Jones: "what good purpose can be served in the end by Tom Jones, in which the hero, warm-hearted enough, is none the less a scoundrel without too sensitive an honor, in spite of which he triumphs and wins Sophia?" (p. 50).

12 MCKILLOP, ALAN D. "The Personal Relations Between Fielding and Richardson." Modern Philology, 28, no. 4 (May), 423-33.
Sets out the facts of their personal relations, beginning with the hostility between the Gazetteer (supporting Walpole and printed by Richardson) and The Champion, the antagonism created by Shamela and Joseph Andrews, Richardson's first hostile comment in 1749, Fielding's open admiration of Clarissa, Richardson's jealous response to Tom Jones, Richardson and his admirers' dismissal of Amelia, and ending with an anecdote about Richardson aiding Fielding. McKillop concludes "that there was no diametrical opposition between them except in the minds of a very few extreme partisans" (p. 433). See 1948.B5 and 1971.A2.

13 NICHOLS, C. W. "Fielding's Satire on Pantomime." Publications of the Modern Language Association, 46, no. 4 (Dec.), 1107-112.
Examines allusions to the popular pantomimes in The Grub-Street Journal and Aaron Hill's Prompter, briefly illustrating the way in which Fielding attacked these entertainments in Pasquin and Tumble-Down Dick.

14 READ, STANLEY E. "Fielding's Miser." Huntington Library Bulletin, 1, no. 1 (May), 211-13.
On bibliographical evidence, the folio printing of Fielding's adaptation of Molière's Miser was "a somewhat careless reprint from the octavo" (p. 211). It is impossible to date the printing of the play.
Answers 1925.B10. See also 1964.B16.

1931

15 SEYMOUR, MABEL. "Correspondence: Henry Fielding." London Mercury, 24, no. 140 (June), 160.

Says that Fielding's Compleat and Authentick History of the Rise, Progress, and Extinction of the Late Rebellion . . . was published as A Succinct History of the Rebellion in Dodsley's Museum (on 29 March, 12 and 26 April, and 13 Sept., 1746) and in the fourth edition of Defoe's A Tour (1748). See 1945.B3 for another, more considered, view.

16 TAYLOR, HOUGHTON W. "Fielding upon Cibber." Modern Philology, 29, no. 1 (Aug.), 73-90.

Argues that Fielding began to satirize Cibber in an impersonal way, "but as his experience with Cibber ripened, he turned this method to the use of a definite and fundamental criticism of Cibber's character--a satire personal in a quite proper sense" (p. 73). Fielding's satire began in 1730 with The Author's Farce and continued until his death (Journal of a Voyage to Lisbon); for the first ten years, Fielding's jibes were directed against Cibber as actor, manager, and writer. Taylor examines the early cordial relations when Love in Several Masques was performed at Drury Lane; Fielding's career at the Little Haymarket, where The Author's Farce with its attack on Cibber was performed; and the subsequent attacks on Cibber in Fielding's plays (Tom Thumb through The Historical Register), his journalism (Champion), and his fiction (Joseph Andrews). Fielding's "bitter, more unmistakably sneering" attacks in Joseph Andrews are "the true climax of Fielding's attacks on Cibber" (p. 90). See 1922.B6.

1932 A BOOKS

1 FIELDING, HENRY. Jonathan Wild and The Journal of a Voyage to Lisbon. Introduction by George Saintsbury. Everyman's Library. London: J. M. Dent & Sons; New York: E. P. Dutton, 304 pp.

Saintsbury reprints the Murphy (1762.A10) text. Thinks Jonathan Wild comparable to Swift's Tale of a Tub but greater than Swift's work because it more carefully mixes "reality" with its irony.

2 _____. Jonathan Wild Den Store. Translated by Hans Krag. Oslo: Forlagt Av H. Aschehoug, 226 pp.

Norwegian translation of Jonathan Wild.

3 _____. The Adventures of Joseph Andrews. Introduction by L. Rice-Oxley. World Classics. London: H. Milford, Oxford University Press, 406 pp.
Reprint of 1929.A3.

4 _____. The History of Tom Jones, a Foundling. Edited by A. W. Pollard. 2 vols. Macmillan's Library of English Classics. London: Macmillan, 1021 pp.
Reissue of 1900.A14.

5 _____. The History of the Life of the Late Mr. Jonathan Wild the Great. Introduction by Ben Ray Redman. The Comparison Classics. New York: Walter J. Black, 320 pp. [1932].
Introduction briefly discusses the novel's irony and sets the novel in Fielding's career. No indication of copy text.

6 _____. The History of Tom Jones, A Foundling. Introduction by George Saintsbury. Everyman's Library. 2 vols. London: J. M. Dent & Sons; New York: E. P. Dutton, 838 pp.
Reissue of 1909.A2.

7 _____. The Life of Jonathan Wild. World Classics. London: H. Milford, Oxford University Press, 289 pp.
"The text of the present reprint is that of 1743 with the variants of 1754 in an appendix" (p. 1).

8 _____. The Life of Mr. Jonathan Wild the Great. Etchings by Denis Tegetmeir. Waltham Saint Lawrence: The Golden Cockerel Press, 279 pp.
"The text is taken from the edition of 1743" (p. 279).

*9 _____. The Tragedy of Tragedies; or, The Life and Death of Tom Thumb the Great. Narberth, Pa.: Robert L. Dothard, 78 pp.
Issued 1938; includes Fielding's annotations.
Source: National Union Catalogue: Pre-1956 Imprints. Vol. 172, p. 9.

*10 _____. Tom Jones; die Geschichte eines Findlings. Translated into German by Paul Baudisch and afterword by Paul Ernst. Berlin: Deutsche Buch-Gemeinschaft, 1295 pp. [1932].
Reprint of [1925?].A8.
Source: National Union Catalogue: Pre-1956 Imprints. Vol. 171, p. 691.

11 JOESTEN, MARIE. Die Philosophie Fieldings. Kölner Anglistische Arbeiten. Vol. 15. Leipzig: Tauchnitz, 107 pp.

Reviewed by E. A. Baker, MLR, 28 (1933), 533-36; G. K. Bauer, GRM, 21 (1933), 156; J. Buck, LGRP, 59 (1938), 253-55; W. Kalthoff, NS, 42 (1934), 420; J. Kohlund, Ang. Bbl, 45 (1934), 57-58.

Studies Fielding's debt to Socrates, the Stoics, and Locke. In German. See 1952.A5.

*12 MATHESIUS, V. Henry Fielding a jeho dílo. Příběh malezenců. Prague: [?].

Henry Fielding and his work. Appendix to a new Czech translation of Tom Jones.

Source: T. Humphrey, p. 231 and MHRA, 13 (1932), 149.

1932 B SHORTER WRITINGS

1 COLLINS, NORMAN. "Henry Fielding," in his The Facts of Fiction. London: Victor Gollancz, pp. 38-55.

Reviewed by E. Boyd, Nation, 136 (7 June 1933), 646; G. Greene, Spectator, 148 (23 Jan. 1932), 117; TLS (28 Jan. 1932), p. 57.

Largely biographical essay which attempts to defend Fielding against his critics. The best he can say is that Tom Jones "bears almost every mark of evidence that we should expect in a production of painstaking intelligence and conscientious application of intellect" (p. 38). Thinks that Fielding has a "huge and heroic conviviality" (p. 40) that is essentially vulgar, and that his novels are saved from offensively distorted realism only because we detect the "hopeless romantic" (p. 45) behind the high spirits.

2 GRAHAM, WALTER. "The Date of the Champion." Notes and Queries, 163 (27 Aug.), 150-51.

Reprints 1932.B3.

3 _____. "The Date of the 'Champion.'" Times Literary Supplement (4 Feb.), p. 76.

Considers the dates various scholars (Cross 1918.A1, etc.) give for the termination of The Champion. Graham then shows that it ran longer than imagined, and on the evidence of an excerpt in the Gentleman's Magazine suggests that the last issue was as late as 3 April 1744.

4 LOVETT, ROBERT M. and HELEN S. HUGHES. "Richardson and Fielding," in their The History of the Novel in England. Boston, New York, etc.: Houghton Mifflin, pp. 63-75.

Briefly discusses Joseph Andrews and Jonathan Wild as literary satires; Tom Jones as a comic epic with a careful plot and as the story of "a young man's life, the same story which Thackeray dared not tell to Victorian readers in Pendennis" (p. 70); and Amelia as an attack on crime and moral laxity. Fielding, according to Lovett and Hughes, contributed careful plotting and realistic (although shallow) character portrayal.

Reprinted 1971 St. Clair Shores, Mich.: Scholarly Press.

1933 A BOOKS

1 BISSELL, FREDERICK O. Fielding's Theory of the Novel. Ithaca, New York: Cornell University Press; London: Humphrey Milford, Oxford University Press, 93 pp.

Reviewed by V. de S. Pinto, RES, 11 (1935), 101-103; A. E. Secord, JEGP, 33 (1934), 57-58; N&Q, 165 (19 Aug. 1933), 126; TLS, 3 Aug. 1933, p. 526; YR, 75 (28 June 1933), 189.

Asserts that the major shaping forces on Fielding's theory were the character sketches of the seventeenth century, the essays of Addison and Steele, the dialogue, satire and structure of Restoration comedy, the picaresque novel (both English and continental), and the burlesque romance. The latter two, as they combined in Scarron, Furetière and Lesage, are the major influences, although "Fielding's most considerable debt for Joseph Andrews is to Marivaux's . . . Le Paysan Parvenu (1735-1736)" (p. 5). Bissell sets out, in a general way, Fielding's theory of the novel as it develops in the preface to Joseph Andrews and the introductory chapters of Tom Jones, and then briefly discusses its application in the two novels, concentrating on realism, satire, and burlesque. See dissertation 1931.A1.

2 FIELDING, HENRY. La Historia de Tomás Jones, El Expósito. Translated by G. Sans Huelin. 4 vols. Madrid: Talleres Espasa-Calpe.

Spanish translation.

3 _____. The History of Tom Jones. Introduction by George Saintsbury. Dent's Double Volumes. London: J. M. Dent & Sons, 838 pp.

A single volume reissue of 1909.A2.

1933

*4 FISCHER, HILDEGARD. "Das subjektive Element in den Romanen Fieldings." Dissertation, Breslau, 1933.
In German.
Source: McNamee, 1865-1964, p. 558.

5 JONES, B. M. Henry Fielding: Novelist and Magistrate. London: George Allen & Unwin, 256 pp.
Reviewed by M. D. G., History, 19 (1935), 376; P. Meissner, Ang.Bbl., 45 (Feb. 1934), 54-57; V. de S. Pinto, RES, 11 (1935), 101-103; R. E. Roberts, Obs, 13 Aug. 1933; J. R. Sutherland, MLR, 29 (1934), 198; G. S. T., EHR, 49 (Oct. 1934), 745-46; Holb.Rev., 157 (Oct. 1933), 554; J. Paul de Castro, TLS, 10 Aug. 1933, p. 537.
This biography of Fielding's legal career is divided into three sections: his early life (which includes his time as a dramatist and concludes with the Licensing Act of 1737); his time as a law student and young lawyer; and his career as a magistrate. The first section discusses Fielding's early life, emphasizing his connection with Sir Henry Gould (his grandfather), who was Judge of the King's Bench, and Lady Gould's successful attempt to get custody of the Fielding children on the death of her daughter. It examines the "nearly five hundred legal allusions and references" (p. 30) in Fielding's plays, as well as Fielding's connection with the Licensing Act. The second section discusses Fielding as a law student and journalist and as a young barrister and novelist, examining the legal characters and questions in Joseph Andrews, Jonathan Wild, and Tom Jones. The final section examines Fielding's considerable public career as a magistrate, with its practical accomplishments (Bow Street Runners, his suggested reforms of the criminal law, etc.) and its literary results (his Charge to the Grand Jury, his proposals for the poor, and his pamphlet on the Elizabeth Canning case). Amelia is particularly discussed in the chapter on prison reform.

1933 B SHORTER WRITINGS

1 EDGAR, PELHAM. "Henry Fielding and Tom Jones," in his The Art of the Novel. New York: Macmillan, pp. 52-67.
Dismisses the myth and tries to find the man of exuberance who was Fielding. Thinks Fielding's art strong because of its mimetic quality (he poured "the full tide of life through his pages" and created "the most diverse world of credible human beings," p. 57). Then briefly analyzes Tom Jones under several headings: theme and author's

intention, conditions of composition, general method, organization, time element, handling of incident, description, author's comment, and analysis. Asserts that the "book lives by its narrative vigor, its author's witty comment, and its rich and racy humanity" (pp. 66-67).

2 LESLIE-MELVILLE, A. R. "Henry Fielding." Times Literary Supplement (27 July), p. 512.

Summarizes nine letters by "Philanthropos" that appeared in the London Daily Advertiser and the Gentleman's Magazine between 16 March 1751 and 12 May 1753 and suggests they were written by Fielding or by a close friend of his. He also notes Fielding's visit to Glastonbury spa in 1751 and the part he played in removing the leading justice of Middlesex, Henry Broadhead, from office.

3 NAGASAWA, YOSHIJIRO. "Studies in the Language of Fielding." Studies in English Literature (Tokyo), 13, no. 4 (Oct.), 566-75.

Examines "the difference between the languages then and now" (p. 566) by considering selected plural nouns, pronouns, adjectives of comparison, articles, verbs (including perfect tenses, preterite participles, archaic conjunctions, etc.), adverbs, prepositions, conjunctions, and methods of indicating quotation in narration. Jespersen's Philosophy of Grammar is Nagasawa's grammatical source.

1934 A BOOKS

1 FIELDING, HENRY. The Adventures of Joseph Andrews. Three Sirens Classics. 2 vols. New York: Three Sirens Press, 539 (262 & 277) pp. [1934].

No indication of copy text.

2 _____. The History of the Present Rebellion in Scotland. Introduction by Ifan Kyrle Fletcher. Newport, Monmouthshire: I. Kyrle Fletcher, 55 pp.

Reprints ("line-for-line and page-by-page") the M. Cooper 1745 edition of this work. The introduction briefly sets out Fielding's career, the rebellion of 1745, and the bibliographical information about this pamphlet.

3 _____. The History of Tom Jones: a Foundling. Illustrations by W. R. S. Scott. 2 vols. London: Hutchinson, 991 (507 & 484) pp.

Includes a brief anonymous biography and appears to reprint the "1750" edition followed by Murphy (1762.A10).

4 _____. The History of Tom Jones. Three Sirens Classics. 4 vols. New York: Three Sirens Press. [1934].

Appears to reproduce the "1750" edition followed by Murphy (1762.A10).

*5 _____. T'o-mu Tsung-ssu. Selected and translated by Wu Kuang-chien. Shanghai: Commercial Press.

Selections from Tom Jones in both English and Chinese.

Source: Hugh Amory's working bibliography (transliterated by Bonnie McDougall of the East Asian Institute).

*6 HUBBARD, LESTER A. "Fielding's Ethics Viewed in Relation to Shaftesbury's Characteristics." Dissertation, California-Berkeley, 1934.

Source: McNamee, 1865-1964, p. 558.

*7 ROUSSEV, RUAL. Henry Fielding. Godishnik. No. 31. Sophia: Universitet Istoriko-filologiecheski fakultet, 26 pp.

Bulgarian critical work.

Source: New York Public Library Reference Department: Slavonic Collection, Vol. 7, p. 5494.

1934 B SHORTER WRITINGS

1 AVERY, EMMETT L. "An Early Performance of Fielding's Historical Register." Modern Language Notes, 49, no. 6 (June), 407.

Adds to Nichols' evidence (1919.B7) for a first performance on 21 March.

2 BAUM, RICHARD M. "Hogarth and Fielding as Social Critics." The Art Bulletin, 16, no. 1 (March), 30-41.

Sets out their similar backgrounds and then shows both satirizing a French quack (Dr. Misaubin), the parsimonious, republicans, Jacobites, the French, dissenting Protestants, and the excesses of the poor. Finally Baum suggests that the success of both was due to their "direct observation of nature" (p. 39). See 1948.B7.

3 BEATTY, RICHMOND C. "Criticism in Fielding's Narratives and His Estimate of Critics." Publications of the Modern Language Association, 49, no. 4 (Dec.), 1087-1100.

A mixed article that contains a general discussion of Fielding as a positive critic (setting up dicta about character, digressions, chapter divisions, the nature of fiction, etc.) and as a negative critic (attacking rules, critics). A brief section on Fielding's regard for "books of travel" (p. 1094) precedes a section setting down some critical attacks on Fielding's works. See 1911.B4, 1928. B4, 1930.B2.

1935 A BOOKS

*1 EWALD, EUGEN. "Abbild und Wünschbild der Gesellschaft bei Richardson und Fielding." Dissertation, Cologne, 1935.
In German.
Source: McNamee, 1865-1964, p. 558.

3 _____. Abbild und Wünschbild der Gesellschaft bei Richardson und Fielding. Cologne: Wuppertaler Drucksera, 106 pp.
Inaugural dissertation. In German.
Source: National Union Catalogue: Pre-1956 Imprints. Vol. 164, p. 348.

3 FIELDING, HENRY. The Adventures of Joseph Andrews. Introduction by L. Rice-Oxley. The World Classics. London: H. Milford, Oxford University Press, 406 pp.
Reissue of 1929.A3.

4 _____. The History of the Adventures of Joseph Andrews and His Friend Mr. Abraham Adams. Edited by George Saintsbury. Everyman's Library. London: J. M. Dent & Sons; New York: E. P. Dutton, 316 pp. [1935].
Reprint of 1910.A6.

5 RONTE, HEINZ. Richardson und Fielding: Geschichte ihres Ruhms. Literarsociologischer Versuch. Kölner anglistische Arbeiten. Vol. 25. Leipzig: Tauchnitz, 217 pp.
A naive socio-literary evaluation of Richardson and Fielding that maintains that Richardson's roots are in the Bible (with Collier and Defoe as predecessors) and Fielding's in pagan myth (with Shakespeare and his modern predecessors). Richardson's characters are tied to a Christian value system and Fielding's to a humane; thus Fielding's writings have an everlasting quality. Ronte also outlines the shift in their fortunes: Richardson was more popular among his contemporaries and the Victorians; Fielding among late eighteenth-century readers, the Romantics, and modern readers (when "scientific" research gave the world a true picture of the writer). In German.

*6 WOODS, CHARLES B. "Studies in the Dramatic Works of Henry Fielding." Dissertation, Harvard, 1935.

1935

Source: T. Humphrey, p. 270. See Summaries of Theses . . . 1937. Cambridge, Mass.: Harvard University Press [1937], pp. 292-94.

1935 B SHORTER WRITINGS

1 AVERY, EMMETT L. "Some Notes on Fielding's Plays." Research Studies of the State College of Washington, 3, No. 2 (Dec.), 48-50.

Adds dates of opening performances and other performances to the known lists for The Historical Register, Don Quixote in England, Covent-Garden Tragedy, Eurydice Hiss'd, The Lottery, The Miser, The Mock Doctor, and Pasquin.

2 EVANS, W. "Dickens and Fielding." Notes and Queries, 168 (22 June), 443.

Asks where to find Dickens's allusion to Fielding in chapter 8 of Pickwick.

3 GREEN, F. C. "Wise Virgins," in his Minuet: A Critical Survey of French and English Literary Ideas in the Eighteenth Century. London: J. M. Dent & Sons, pp. 392-98.

Briefly and precisely compares Joseph Andrews (and Tom Jones) with Marivaux's Le Paysan parvenu (in theme, moral point of view, humor, dramatic use of character), concluding that there is no warrant for the assumption that Fielding imitated Marivaux.

For another view see 1969.A13 and 1910.A6.

4 JENSEN, GERARD E. "A Fielding Discovery." Yale University Library Gazette, 10, no. 2 (Oct.), 23-32.

Argues that the anonymous pamphlet, An Attempt towards a Natural History of the Hanover Rat (1744), was by Henry Fielding, on the following grounds: the phrase 'Hanover Rat' is used twice in Tom Jones; the pamphlet was printed by M. Cooper, who was printing Fielding's political tracts in 1745; it has Fielding's characteristic "hath, doth, durst, etc."; it attacks two of Fielding's usual targets (science and corruption in government). Jensen thinks that the pamphlet is simultaneously a burlesque of Henry Baker's Natural History of the Polype and the government's use of mercenary troops from Hanover. In 1743 Fielding had made a similar complex attack in Some Papers Proper to be Read before the Royal Society . . . .

5 MUNDY, P. D. "Fielding's 'Tom Jones.'" Notes and Queries, 169 (28 Dec.), 456.

Prints a letter from Joseph Spence, who claims to have read Tom Jones in manuscript and who discusses the publication history of the book.

6 OBLOMIEWSKY, D. "Fil'ding," from his Early Bourgeois Realism. Moscow: [?], pp. 187-241.
Offprint in Russian in the British Museum.

7 SEYMOUR, MABEL. "Fielding's History of the Forty-Five." Philological Quarterly, 14, no. 2 (April), 105-25.
Examines Fielding's use of the London Gazette's reports of the Battle of Prestonpans in his timely pamphlet, The History of the Present Rebellion; Fielding padded out these accounts with dramatic detail and Whig propaganda. Goes on to describe Fielding's Succinct History in Dodsley's Museum, calling it a complete history of the Jacobite rising. Jarvis (1945.B3-5) says this is not by Fielding, nor is the Compleat and Authentick History, which Seymour also attributes to Fielding.

1936 A BOOKS

*1 HESSLER, MABEL D. "Literary Opposition to Sir Robert Walpole, 1721-1742: Fielding's Attacks on Walpole." Dissertation, Chicago, 1936.
Source: T. Humphrey, p. 258.

2 FIELDING, HENRY. The Works of Henry Fielding. Edited by George Saintsbury and illustrated by George Cruikshank. 12 vols. London: The Navarre Society.
Reissue of 1871.A5.

1936 B SHORTER WRITINGS

1 COOLIDGE, ARCHIBALD. "A Fielding Pamphlet?" Times Literary Supplement (9 May), p. 400.
Argues that Stultus versus Sapientem was not written by Fielding but instead by an obscure Irish writer, William Chaigneau. See 1953.B1.

2 GARNETT, DAVID. "Richardson, Fielding and Smollett," in The English Novelists: A Survey of the Novel by Twenty Contemporary Novelists. Edited by Derek Verschoyle. London: Chatto & Windus, pp. 69-79.
Despite Fielding's enormous influence, most of which Garnett sees as bad (i.e., inspiring the boring lectures

on morality and the author-centered novel), Richardson is the greater writer. According to Garnett, Fielding lacked imagination, carried a load of common sense, lacked idealism (only believing in self-interest), and had a crude sense of humor.

3 GILL, W. W. "Early Fielding Documents." Notes and Queries, 171 (3 Oct.), 242.
Reprints an amusing note written by the young Fielding after the Sarah Andrew affair. Reported earlier by de Castro, 1931.B4.

*4 HAAGE, RICHARD. "Charakterzeichnung und Komposition in Fieldings Tom Jones in ihrer Beziehung zum Drama." Britannica, 13, 119-170.
In German.
Source: T. Humphrey, p. 230 and 1971.B5 (New Cambridge Bibliography of English Literature).

5 LIND, LEVI R. "Lucian and Fielding." Classical Weekly, 29, no. 11 (20 Jan.), 84-86.
Examines the parallels (in episode and theme) between Fielding's Journey from This World to the Next, "A Dialogue Between Alexander the Great . . .," "An Interlude between Jupiter . . ." and Lucian's Dialogues.

6 MACLEAN, KENNETH. John Locke and English Literature of the Eighteenth Century. New Haven: Yale University Press; London: Humphrey Milford, Oxford University Press, passim.
Reviewed by I. L. Bredvold in JEGP, 36 (1937), 588-90; R. S. C., PQ, 16 (1937), 180-81; TLS, 13 Mar. 1937, p. 186.
Studies Locke's influence on Fielding (among many other writers), particularly Fielding's use of Locke's concept of the blind man who imagined scarlet, the effect of size on the imagination, and Locke's concept of the abuse of words.

7 MCKILLOP, ALAN D. Samuel Richardson: Printer and Novelist. Chapel Hill: University of North Carolina Press, passim.
Reviewed by J. W. Beach, JEGP, 36 (1937), 438-42; L. Kronenberger, NYTBR, 27 Dec. 1936, p. 5; F. T. Wood, E St., 72 (1937), 115-17; Sat. Rev., 15 (26 Dec. 1936), 16: TLS, 10 April 1937, p. 270.
Considers Richardson's attitude toward Fielding ("Richardson's personal spite had no profound effect on literary history, though it has proved most disastrous for his own reputation," p. 177), Fielding's admiration for Clarissa, and the attacks on Fielding by Richardson's circle, particularly after the publication of Tom Jones.

Concludes that Richardson was provoked less by the parodies of Pamela (Shamela and Joseph Andrews) than by the success of Tom Jones. See 1971.B12.

8 RAUSHENBUSH, ESTHER M. "Charles Macklin's Lost Play About Henry Fielding." Modern Language Notes, 51, no. 8 (Dec.), 505-14.

The play is to be found in the Larpent Collection at the Huntington Library. Called The Covent-Garden Theatre, or Pasquin Turn'd Drawcansir, it is a "thoroughly sympathetic portrait of Fielding in the rôle of public censor" (p. 505). This article describes Fielding's "paper war" with Dr. John Hill in 1751-52 and the Macklin play, which was a part of the "paper war."

9 SHEPPERSON, ARCHIBALD B. "Richardson and Fielding: Shamela and Shamelia," in his The Novel in Motley: A History of the Burlesque Novel in English. Cambridge: Harvard University Press, pp. 9-38.

Reviewed by J. W. Beach, JEGP, 36 (1937), 438-42; G. Buck, AngBbl, 48 (1937), 370-74; C. Grabo, MP, 35 (1937), 107-108; W. L. Myers, VQR, 13 (1937), 296-99; G. B. Needham, Sat. Rev., 15 (23 Jan. 1937), 10; M. Van Doren, Nation, 144 (30 Jan. 1937), 136.

Reviews Fielding's Shamela and the beginning and end of Joseph Andrews as among the Pamela burlesques. Then briefly describes the attacks on Fielding inspired by Tom Jones and particularly Amelia (including the new chapter for Amelia added by The Drury Lane Journal).

Reprinted New York: Octagon Books, 1967.

10 SHERBURN, GEORGE. "Fielding's Amelia: An Interpretation." Journal of English Literary History, 3, no. 1 (March), 1-14.

Argues that in Amelia Fielding constructed "a history that yet should, in its structure, its organizing themes, and in its pictures of domesticity, recall at least remotely the masterpiece of Virgil [the Aeneid]" (p. 3). Fielding's chosen theme, the struggle against distress and foolish conduct, is fought and won domestically with the moral and psychological rescue of Booth, finally symbolized by his conversion to Christianity in which Stoic (pagan) ethics and Christian principles are reconciled. Although Fielding sets out "the corruption of the aristocracy and their failure to distinguish and reward merit [which] is as public a theme as the fall of Troy" (p. 10), he does not resolve it, content to let his happy couple retire to the safe countryside.

Reprinted 1962.A12, 1972.A8, and in Studies in the Literature of the Augustan Age: Essays Collected in Honor of Arthur Ellicott Case. Edited by Richard Boys. Ann Arbor, Mich.: George Wahr, for the Augustan Reprint Society, 1952. See 1956.B11 and 1977.B9.

11 SMITH, DANE F. "The Rise and Fall of Henry, Grand Mogul of Satirical Farce," in his Plays About the Theatre in England from The Rehearsal in 1671 to the Licensing Act in 1737 or, The Self-Conscious Stage and its Burlesque and Satirical Reflections in the Age of Criticism. London and New York: Oxford University Press, pp. 205-37 and passim.

Reviewed by F. E. Budd, MLR, 32 (1937), 613-14; R. Kirk, MLN, 52 (1937), 611-13; P. Legouis, EA, 1 (1937), 536-37; N&Q, 172 (1937), 396; TLS, 10 July 1937, p. 513.

Sets Fielding's plays, particularly Pasquin, Tumble-Down Dick, Eurydice, Eurydice Hiss'd and The Historical Register, in their satiric and theatrical (rehearsal play) tradition. Discusses Fielding's effrontery in his theatrical and political satires (surprisingly calling The Historical Register the best ever dramatic political satire), the audience he portrayed (changed very little between 1671 and 1737), and the weakness of his dramas (no structure, no dramatic objectivity and little characterization). Fielding's plays, Smith concludes, are "hardly more than journalistic offerings on the stage" (p. 231).

12 STREETER, HAROLD W. The Eighteenth Century English Novel in French Translation: A Bibliographical Study. New York: The Institute of French Studies, pp. 76-91.

Reviews French reaction (Fielding was immediately condemned for his vulgarity and progressively praised for moral earnestness and naturalness). Streeter thinks Fielding was less successful than the sentimental Richardson in France and that the dramatizations of Tom Jones hurt his reputation among the literary élite. Argues that the French did not understand English realism but that by mid-century (despite bad translations) the English novel was extremely popular in France.

13 STUDT, ANNELISE. "Fieldings Charakterromane." Britannica, 13:101-118.

Argues that Fielding believed men to be hypocrites ruled by their passions (as Mandeville suggests) but capable of redeeming love. To illustrate this Fielding turned the novel of adventure into the novel of character, and in his three great novels tested his theory on a variety of characters. In German.

1937 A BOOKS

*1 BROWN, JACK R. "Four Plays by Henry Fielding." Dissertation, Northwestern, 1937.
Source: T. Humphrey, p. 252. See Summaries of Doctoral Dissertations, Northwestern University, 5 (1937), 5-9.

2 FIELDING, HENRY. Miscellaneous Writings. 2 vols. New York: Literary Guild of America, 641 (359 & 282) pp.
Reprinted from Maynadier's Works of Henry Fielding (1903.A3).

3 _____. The Adventures of Joseph Andrews. Introduction by L. Rice-Oxley. World Classics. London: H. Milford, Oxford University Press, 406 pp.
Reissue of 1929.A3.

4 _____. The Adventures of Joseph Andrews. Parts I and II. Introduction by G. H. Maynadier. New York: Literary Guild of America, 308 pp.
Reprinted from Maynadier's Works of Henry Fielding, 1903.A3.

5 _____. The History of the Life of the Late Mr. Jonathan Wild the Great. Introduction by G. H. Maynadier. New York: Literary Guild of America, 314 pp.
Reprinted from Maynadier's Works of Henry Fielding, 1903.A3.

6 _____. The History of Tom Jones, a Foundling. London: Modern Library, 884 pp.
Reissue of [1931].A5.

7 _____. The History of Tom Jones, A Foundling. New York and Chicago: A. L. Burt, 919 pp. [1937].
Reissue of [1906].A5.

1937 B SHORTER WRITINGS

1 CHANDLER, KNOX. "Two 'Fielding' Pamphlets." Philological Quarterly, 16, no. 4 (Oct.), 410-12.
Two pamphlets in the 1742 "dunces" attack on Pope, sometimes said to be by Fielding, are not by Fielding. Durgen (The Cudgel) is by Edward Ward. The other, Blast upon Blast, had been written and printed earlier by Edward Roome.

1937

2 ESDAILE, K. A. "Fielding's Danish Translator: Simon Charles Stanley The Sculptor." Times Literary Supplement (3 April), p. 252.

A brief biography of Stanley, who probably knew Fielding through Hogarth and who translated Joseph Andrews into Danish (it appeared anonymously in 1749, perhaps because Stanley was "doubtful of the reaction of the Danish public to Fielding's boisterous masterpiece").

3 FOX, RALPH. "The Novel as Epic," in his The Novel and the People. London: Lawrence and Wishart, pp. 47-58.

Reviewed by K. Arns, ESt, 72 (1938), 420-21; H. Levin, Nation, 144 (5 June 1937), 651.

This Marxist analysis praises Fielding for his social criticism, for telling "the truth about life as he saw it" (p. 52) in a brutal "world of conquering capitalism" (p. 53). Fox objects to both Fielding's narrative intrusions and his failure to plumb the "intimate depths of the human heart" (p. 53).

4 GREENE, GRAHAM. "Fielding and Sterne," in From Anne to Victoria: Essays by Various Hands. Edited by Bonamy Dobrée. Originally published by Cassell. Reprinted Freeport, New York: Books for Libraries Press, pp. 279-89.

Greene thinks the age empty of poetry with the death of Dryden, and "it was left to Fielding, who had not himself the poetic mind . . . to construct a fictional form which could attract the poetic imagination" (p. 282). In fact, Sterne, for all his formal madness, is the poet of the novel, according to Greene. He has a "musical style" and a genius of self-portraiture. Fielding had a sense of careful architecture, moral seriousness, and continuity. Greene thinks novelists are in Fielding's debt because "he had gathered up in his novels the two divided strands of Restoration fiction: he had combined on his own lower level the flippant prose fictions of the dramatists and the heroic drama of the poets" (p. 287).

Reprinted 1951.B2 and 1969.

5 JENSEN, GERARD E. "Proposals for a Definitive Edition of Fielding's Tom Jones." Library (4th.series, 18), also called Transactions of the Bibliographical Society, 2nd. series, 18 (Dec.), 314-30.

There were only four editions of Tom Jones in Fielding's lifetime, all published in one year (1749-50). Jensen isolates the date of publication and describes each edition. He concludes that edition three is closest to Fielding's corrected intention and that someone else, probably the Rev. William Young, corrected the fourth edition. Jensen reprints a part of the extensively rewritten Man of the Hill episode (rewritten for the third edition), which the fourth edition rejects (perhaps on the whim of a compositor) in favor of the first edition version, and concludes that the "third edition of the novel reveals the hand of its author" (p. 330). See 1923.A2, 1973.A15, 1974.A7 and 1977.B1.

6 UTTER, ROBERT P. and GWENDOLYN B. NEEDHAM. Pamela's Daughters. London: Lovat Dickson, passim.

Reviewed by K. John, New Statesman, 20 Mar. 1937, p. 484; W. L. Myers, VQR, 13 (1937), 296-99; J. J. R., CW, 146 (1937), 119-20; M. Stack, Commonweal, 25 (15 Jan. 1937), 337-38; L. Wann, Personalist, 18 (1937), 440-42.

Breezy survey of woman's role in literature and life from the eighteenth through the nineteenth centuries, briefly discussing Fielding's more substantial and non-Richardsonian heroines (Fanny, Sophia, and Amelia), Fielding's attitude toward sex, emotion and marriage, and Fielding's males (excessively emotional and less controlled than Richardson's).

7 WOODS, CHARLES B. "Notes on Three of Fielding's Plays." Publications of the Modern Language Association, 52, no. 2 (June), 359-73.

Historical article briefly describing the contemporary situations behind three of Fielding's plays. The Letter Writers "was inspired by the contemporary attempts at extortion" (p. 361). The Modern Husband is an attack on the divorce laws, which encouraged collusion in damage suits for "criminal conversation." Eurydice Hiss'd was, among other things, an attack on Walpole's unpopular "excise" on wine and tobacco.

1938 A BOOKS

1 FIELDING, HENRY. The History of the Life of the Late Mr. Jonathan Wild the Great. Introduction by G. H. Maynadier. New York: Book League of America, 314 pp.

Reissue of 1903.A3.

2 _____. The History of Tom Jones, A Foundling. Introduction by George Saintsbury. Everyman's Library. 2 vols. London: J. M. Dent & Sons; New York: E. P. Dutton, 838 pp.

Reissue of 1909.A2.

3 _____. The Tragedy of Tragedies; or, The Life and Death of Tom Thumb the Great, in Representative English Plays From the Miracle Plays to Pinero. Edited by J. S. P. Tatlock and R. G. Martin. 2nd. ed. New York: Appleton-Century-Crofts, pp. 613-35.

A brief introduction discusses Fielding's burlesque attacks on scholarship, on heroic plays (said to be pragmatic theater and not serious protest), and on pretentious language. No indication of copy text, but the general introduction says "in no case have careless and popular modern editions been followed."

1938 B SHORTER WRITINGS

1 AVERY, EMMETT L. "Fielding's Universal Gallant." Research Studies of the State College of Washington, 6, no. 1 (March), 46.

On the strength of a notice in the Daily Advertiser, Avery asserts that this play was "in the process of writing if not completed by December of 1733," although it was not produced until February of 1735.

2 BLANCHARD, F. T. "The Art of the Novel." Journal of the Royal Society of Arts, 87, no. 4492 (16 Dec.), 165-79.

Traces the history of the novel, calling Fielding the "great pivotal figure" (p. 171).

3 COLLINS, RALPH L. "Moore's The Foundling - An Intermediary." Philological Quarterly, 17, no. 2 (April), 139-43.

Moore borrowed an incident from Clarissa for his play The Foundling, and ended the story happily, as Fielding and others wanted Clarissa to end. Moore's rake, Belmont, is a mixture of good and bad, not a Lovelace. Fielding praised Moore's play, gave Tom Jones the subtitle "a foundling," and created a character (Tom) like Belmont. Collins concludes that Fielding, while praising the first two volumes of Clarissa, did not like all, or even a substantial part, of Richardson's novel.

4 CREAN, P. J. "The Stage Licensing Act of 1737." Modern Philology, 35, no. 3 (Feb.), 239-55.

Reviewing "the march of events in the early decades of the eighteenth century" (p. 239) that made the Licensing Act inevitable (an increase in the number of theaters and of dramatic satires), Crean describes Fielding's opening of the Little Theatre in the Haymarket and his two most successful satires, Pasquin and The Historical Register.

He feels that these plays, as well as Fielding's promise of more, and The Golden Rump affair, forced the government's hand. By attacking religion, law, and medicine in Pasquin, Fielding alienated critical opinion, providing his political enemies with a pretext for restraining the stage, and "did the theatre a grave disservice" (p. 250).

5 DRAPER, JOHN W. "The Theory of the Comic in Eighteenth-Century England." Journal of English and Germanic Philology, 37, no. 2 (April), 207-223.

Surveys the development of comic theory in the eighteenth century. Briefly includes Fielding's discussion of comedy (from the preface to Joseph Andrews and from Tom Jones): points out the limits of his theory and the discrepancy between the theory of affectation and the comic character Adams. Concludes that neo-classical theory (satire or burlesque depiction of human affectation by means of incongruity of style or character) "accords well" with the practice of Congreve, Pope, Fielding, Addison and Farquhar. See 1964.B6.

6 MC C[USHER], H. "First Editions of Fielding." More Books: Bulletin of the Boston Public Library, 13:114.

Announces the acquisition of first editions of Amelia and both the longer and shorter (edited by John Fielding) versions of Journal of a Voyage to Lisbon. Sets out selected contemporary opinions--including Samuel Johnson's and Richardson's.

7 ______. "The Life of Jonathan Wild the Great." More Books: Bulletin of the Boston Public Library, 13:72-73.

Briefly describes some of the pieces in the first edition of Fielding's Miscellanies, just purchased by the Boston library, concentrating on his political satire of Walpole in Jonathan Wild.

8 MCKILLOP, ALAN D. "An Iconographic Poem on Tom Jones." Philological Quarterly, 17, no. 4 (Oct.), 403-406.

The Fan (1749) is a long "advice to a painter" poem suggesting that scenes from Tom Jones be painted on fans. McKillop reprints the part of Canto I which deals with "scenes" from Tom Jones.

9 SLAGLE, KENNETH C. "The English Country Squire as Depicted in English Prose Fiction from 1740 to 1800." Dissertation, University of Pennsylvania, 1938.

Briefly discusses Fielding's squires.

1939

1939 A BOOKS

1 FIELDING, HENRY. The History of the Adventures of Joseph Andrews and His Friend Mr. Abraham Adams. Introduction by Howard Mumford Jones. Modern Library. New York: Random House, 460 pp. [1939].

Introduction briefly reviews the novel as a literary form, Fielding's life and work (calling him a "theatrical carpenter" and demonstrating his trick, learned in the theater, of immediately presenting his characters in his novels), the satiric butts of Joseph Andrews (Cibber and Richardson), the influence of Don Quixote, and finally the structuring device of the comic epic in prose. Jones warns readers about bringing modern aesthetic and social expectations to the novel, particularly Marxian ones. No indication of copy text.

2 _____. The History of Tom Jones, A Foundling. Introduction by George Saintsbury. Everyman's Library. 2 vols. London: J. M. Dent & Sons; New York: E. P. Dutton, 838 pp.

Reissue of 1909.A2.

3 _____. Tom Thumb (The Tragedy of Tragedies; or, The Life and Death of Tom Thumb the Great), in British Drama From Dryden to Sheridan. Edited by George H. Nettleton and A. E. Case. Boston: Houghton Mifflin, pp. 575-98.

No indication of copy text but appears to reprint the 1731 Tragedy of Tragedies collated against the 1751 (fourth) edition.

*4 FOWLER, A. MURRY. "A Comparative Study of Humours Characters in Ben Jonson and Henry Fielding." University of Oregon Thesis Series. No. 15. Eugene, Oregon, 22 pp.

Argues that "humours" comedy is at its best in satire; "when the appeal is entirely intellectual, as in Volpone or Jonathan Wild, it is supreme in its kind" (p. 22).

Source: T. Humphrey, p. 191.

*5 PARKER, ALICE. "Views of Crime and Punishment in Fielding and Smollett." Dissertation, Yale, 1939.

Source: McNamee, 1865-1964, p. 558.

1939 B SHORTER WRITINGS

1 "ALAIN" [EMILE CHARTIER]. "En lisant Fielding." Nouvelle Revue Française, 52 (March), 484-91.

A lighthearted appreciation of Tom Jones, which contrasts the early innocent "Prologue campagnard" (where men Homerically fight with fists) with the end of the novel (where city men fight with swords). Also discusses the male dominated world of the novel, where the good benevolent tyrant is ruled by his beloved. "Alain" also discusses the intrusive narrator, comparing him to Stendhal's. In French.

2 AVERY, EMMETT L. "Fielding's Last Season with the Haymarket Theatre." Modern Philology, 36, no. 3 (Feb.), 283-92.

By examining "material appearing in the columns of the Daily Advertiser" (p. 283), Avery reconstructs the theatrical event at the Haymarket in 1737, the final year before the Licensing Act and the last year during which Fielding produced his plays at the New Theatre in the Haymarket. He conjectures about Fielding's and Ralph's roles in an adaptation of Polly and The King and Titi, both stopped by the Act, and describes the lively season of topical satire.

3 BARKER, RICHARD H. "Fielding," in his Mr. Cibber of Drury Lane. Columbia University Studies in English and Comparative Literature. No. 143. New York: Columbia University Press, pp. 221-32.

Reviewed by F. E. Budd, MLR, 35 (1940), 395-97; J. Butt, RES, 16 (1940), 229-30; B. H., QJS, 26 (1940), 474; W. H. Irving, SAQ, 39 (1940), 271-72; H. Spencer, MLN, 55 (1940), 641-42; TAM, 24 (1940), 151-52.

Details Fielding's shifting relations with the Cibbers (Colley and Theophilus), from his compliment to Colley in Love in Several Masques to his attack on him in Joseph Andrews. For a brief time in 1732, Fielding complimented the Cibbers (he was writing for their theater), and they him. When Fielding opened a rival company, both began trading insults: Fielding attacking Cibber in The Historical Register (1736); Cibber responding in Apology (1740); and Fielding parodying the Apology in Joseph Andrews. Fielding attacked Cibber as manager, as laureate and adapter of Shakespeare, as prose writer, and as apologist-biographer.

Reissued 1966 by AMS Press (New York).

4 BROWN, JACK R. "From Aaron Hill to Henry Fielding?" Philological Quarterly, 18, no. 1 (Jan.), 85-88.

If a letter from Hill is addressed to Fielding and if it can be seen as New Style rather than Old Style (Feb. 1736/37), then Fielding wrote A Rehearsal of Kings, which was never published but was clearly an attack "on the English government" (p. 88).

5 IYENGAR, K. R. S. "Fielding's Tom Jones." Journal of the University of Bombay, 8, no. 2, 29-44.
A graceful summary of the best contemporary opinions, beginning with the objections to the novel: agrees that the introductory chapters break the organic integrity but thinks them the result of "the novel . . . fumbling to reach its potential" (p. 31); justifies the Man of the Hill episode as a typical epic intrusion and relevant to the central theme; sees the immorality as "realism" and necessary to Tom's development. After discussing Fielding's "dull uniformity of laughter" (p. 37) that refuses to take human emotions seriously, Iyengar discusses the weak allegorical characters (Allworthy, Sophia, and Blifil) and the strong mixed characters. Finally considers whether it is a realistic, dramatic, or character novel.

6 MARION, DENIS. "Lectures inactuelles: Tom Jones." Europe, no. 50 (Aug.), 665-69.
Sees Tom Jones as a means of explaining a quarrel between Sartre and Mauriac. According to Sartre's dicta, Fielding's characters should be "dead," because Fielding violates all Sartre's rules (he is an interfering, privileged narrator; strong plot events direct characters). Marion argues that they are alive because they are found in an English (romanesque) rather than a French (dramatic) novel. The romanesque novel pits man against external forces; the dramatic allows characters to test their conception of life. In French.

7 S., E. "Fielding as a Dramatist." More Books: Bulletin of the Boston Public Library, 14:260.
Brief description of Pasquin, a first edition of which the library had just acquired.

8 TOBIN, JAMES E. "Fielding," in his Eighteenth Century English Literature and its Cultural Background: A Bibliography. New York: Fordham University Press, pp. 105-107.
Includes a selected bibliography of modern editions and criticism of Fielding's works.
Reissued New York: Biblo and Tannen, 1967.

9 V., E. H. "A Curious Double Parallel between Milton and Fielding." Notes and Queries, 176 (15 April), 260.

A possible allusion to Milton's "Of Education" in Tom Jones.

1940 A BOOKS

*1 BRUHN, ERNST. "Fieldings Gesellschafts- und Staatsauffasung." Dissertation, Hamburg, 1940.
In German.
Source: McNamee, 1865-1964, p. 558.

*2 BRYANT, VIRGINIA M. "The Literary and Philosophical Background of Tom Jones." Dissertation, Cincinnati, 1940.
Source: McNamee, 1865-1964, p. 558.

3 FIELDING, HENRY. The History of Tom Jones, a Foundling. New York: Modern Library, 884 pp. [1940].
Reissue of [1931].A5.

1940 B SHORTER WRITINGS

1 BAYLEY, A. R. "A Portrait of Fielding." Notes and Queries, 178 (17 Feb.), 124.
In response to 1940.B2, reprints DNB assertion about Fielding's portrait.

2 C., D. "A Portrait of Fielding." Notes and Queries, 178 (27 Jan.), 63-64.
Asks again if Hogarth's drawing was inspired by Garrick's impersonation of Fielding.
Response 1940.B1. See also 1889.B3.

3 DE CASTRO, J. PAUL. "A Presentation Inscription by Fielding." Notes and Queries, 178 (11 May), 337-39.
In response to 1940.B12, prints and annotates a long letter by Jane Collier to Mrs. Baker. Fielding had signed and dated a gift book to the young, clever Miss Collier before leaving for Lisbon.

4 _____. "Fielding Manuscripts." Times Literary Supplement (1 June), p. 267.
Doubts the story that there were significant works of Fielding's destroyed in the Gordon Riots. If Fielding's commonplace book were found (and it had little chance of surviving), it would be likely to be "almost unintelligible to a third person" (p. 267). Response to 1940.B15.

5 _____. "Queries from Fielding's 'Voyage to Lisbon.'" Notes and Queries, 179 (28 Dec.), 461.
The eighteenth-century London drink called "wind" (made largely of cheap port and turnip juice) is described in answer to 1940.B10.

6 _____. "Revivals of Fielding's Plays." Notes and Queries, 179 (28 Dec.), 461.
Answers 1940.B11. The Letter Writers and The Lottery were staged in 1928.

7 _____. "Source Wanted." Notes and Queries, 179 (28 Sept.), 225.
Asks to have an allusion in Tom Jones, Book 8, chapter 1 explained.

8 _____. "Ursula Fielding and 'Tom Jones.'" Notes and Queries, 178 (9 Mar.), 164-67.
A letter from Fielding's second sister, Ursula, is printed. The letter mentions Tom Jones and an address in Brownlow Street (hitherto unknown) where the final books of Tom Jones were written.

9 MARKS, ARTHUR W. "The Chapel Attached to Doctors' Commons." Notes and Queries, 179 (13 July), 28.
Asks about the chapel in which Tom marries Sophia.

10 N., A. E. "Queries from Fielding's 'Voyage to Lisbon.'" Notes and Queries, 179 (7 Dec.), 407.
A number of questions asked, about the definition of dishabille, a sailor's superstition, a drink called "wind," etc.
Replies 1940.B5, 1941.B6, B12.

11 _____. "Revival of Fielding's Plays." Notes and Queries, 179 (14 Dec.), 423.
Asks when any Fielding play was last performed. See 1940.B6, 1941.B1, B5, B10, B17.

12 OLYBRUIS. "A Presentation Inscription by Fielding." Notes and Queries, 178 (27 April), 298.
Prints the inscription in a book that Fielding gave to Jane Collier. See 1940.B3.

13 ROGERS, WINFIELD H. "The Significance of Fielding's Temple Beau." Publications of the Modern Language Association, 55, no. 4 (June), 440-44.

Argues that in Fielding's plays he is beginning to enunciate the ethical principles of his more mature work. By examining Fielding's use of Addison's idea of pedantry (Spectator 105), around which Fielding created "the central family of The Temple Beau" (p. 441), Rogers briefly argues that Fielding began to find "his ideal of the balanced individual" (p. 444).

14 VINCENT, HOWARD P. "The Childhood of Henry Fielding." Review of English Studies, 16, no. 64 (Oct.), 438-44.

Reproduces and comments on court depositions in the case between Edmund Fielding and Lady Gould, Henry's grandmother, for the care of Edmund's six children by Anne Gould Fielding. These vivid depositions by servants tell about food, religious training, and discipline. Vincent concludes that Mrs. Cottington, the aunt placed in the house by Lady Gould on the death of her daughter, was "harsh and spiteful" and "an agent provocateur" (p. 443), although she is often quoted as a reliable source. See 1909.B4, 1914.B13.

15 WALLACE, ROBERT M. "Fielding Manuscripts." Times Literary Supplement (May 18), p. 243.

While several unpublished works of Fielding's were destroyed, his commonplace book may still survive (argued on the evidence of Fielding's law manuscripts in the Harvard Library). See reply 1940.B4.

16 WORCESTER, DAVID. The Art of Satire. Cambridge: Harvard University Press; London: Oxford University Press, pp. 81-88, passim.

Reviewed by Louis I. Bredvold, JEGP, 40 (1941), 434-35; O. J. Campbell, MLN, 56 (1941), 318-19; A. Guérard, NYTBR, 15 Sept. 1940, p. 21; M. C. Randolph, PQ, 20 (1941), 93-95; B. Willey, RES, 17 (1941), 105-106.

Describing both the development of satire in western literature and some of its main elements (invective, burlesque, irony), Worcester discusses Fielding's ironic inversion in the mock encomium of Jonathan Wild, comparing it to others of the type (Beggar's Opera, Barry Lyndon, etc.). He also discusses Fielding's use of the "great man" tradition and his irony of understatement (litotes). Elsewhere he suggests that Fielding turned to satire because he was overburdened by the "unfelt oppressions of this earth" (p. 33).

1941

1941 A BOOKS

1 HAMMOND, GERALDINE E. Evidences of the Dramatic Technique in Henry Fielding's Novels. Bulletin of the University of Wichita, 16, no. 10, 27 pp.

Briefly studies the epic influence (the division into books, subplots and digressions, poetic diction) and the picaresque influences on his novels, before turning to the dramatic influences. After cataloguing direct references to the "stage" in Joseph Andrews, Hammond briefly illustrates a number of dramatic techniques to be found in the novel: the heavy use of direct and indirect discourse, the convention of two characters talking in a scene, the parenthetical use of stage directions, Slipslop's malapropisms, descriptions of life in fashionable London, humorous names, speeded-up dialogue omitting the verb "saying," stage directions about gesture, and the lack of direct description. She finds the same weight of direct references to the "stage" in Tom Jones, and the plot of the later novel more dramatic and less epic than Joseph Andrews. In both novels she finds Fielding's creation of character "by action and dialogue almost entirely" (p. 27) to be the best proof of the dramatist's technique.

2 IRWIN, WILLIAM R. The Making of Jonathan Wild: A Study in the Literary Method of Henry Fielding. Columbia University Studies in English and Comparative Literature. No. 153. New York: Columbia University Press, 164 pp.

Reviewed by Ernest Bernbaum, MLN, 59 (1944), 137-39; Arthur W. Secord, JEGP, 43 (1944), 254-55; D. F. Smith, NMQ, 13 (1943), 106-109; James A. Work, MLQ, 3 (1942), 482-84.

A study of the literary background of Jonathan Wild. Irwin very briefly relates the facts about Wild and then examines the Wild myth as created in poems, pamphlets, essays, and plays (some famous like The Beggar's Opera and some obscure like The Prison Breaker) written before Fielding's Jonathan Wild. He then examines Fielding's use of this material, concluding that Fielding used few factual details, and those only from the end of Wild's life, but that Fielding did make extensive use of the political innuendo that had accumulated around this myth. Irwin then sets out the contemporary use of the term "great" and "good" because "Fielding did not invent the terms 'greatness' and 'goodness' or the meanings which he attached to them" (p. 44); he discusses the ethical questions raised by the use of these terms in popular morality and in "learned speculation of time" (p. 59). Fielding's writings before Jonathan Wild are examined to illustrate that the ethical and political problems set out in this book were not new to Fielding. Irwin also argues that his attack in Jonathan Wild is not narrowly satiric (aimed entirely at Walpole) but broadly so. Finally, the work is set in its generic tradition. Irwin sees it as somewhere between the criminal biography (popular in the seventeenth and early eighteenth centuries) and the "comic epic poem in prose" (Fielding's new form, which he thinks is derived in part from Cervantes and Scarron). See dissertation 1941.A3, also 1966.B5 and 1972.A9.

*3 IRWIN, WILLIAM R. "The Making of Jonathan Wild, a Study in the Literary Method of Henry Fielding." Dissertation, Columbia, 1941.
Source: McNamee, 1865-1964, p. 558.

1941 B SHORTER WRITINGS

1 BAYLEY, A. R. "Revivals of Fielding's Plays." Notes and Queries, 180 (4 Jan.), 15.
Answers 1940.B11. The Tragedy of Tragedies was recently revived.

2 BUCK, GERHARD. "Written in imitation of the manner of Cervantes." Germanisch-romanische Monatschrift, 29: 53-61.
Attempts to discover why Fielding subtitled Joseph Andrews "written in the manner of Cervantes" by reviewing various critical explanations (emphasizing Bosdorf's 1908.A1 argument about realism). After comparing Don Quixote and Joseph Andrews, Buck concludes that the critical confusion has arisen because Fielding was not very skillful: he was inexperienced as a novel writer, confused the definitions of "comic romance" and "comic epic in prose," and was unable to work out his comic theories in the action of the novel. In German.

3 DE CASTRO, J. PAUL. "Durham." Notes and Queries, 180 (15 Feb.), 123.
Response to 1941.B13. "Durham" was the Rev. William Derham, author of Physico-Theology (1713), a strange theological work which Fielding must have read.

4 _____. "Gravelot." Notes and Queries, 180 (1 Feb.), 87.
"Gravelot," the French illustrator of Tom Jones, was H. F. Bourguignon, an article on whose prints appeared in Fielding's Champion in 1740. Answer to 1941.B8.

1941

5 _____. "Revivals of Fielding's Plays." Notes and Queries, 180 (11 Jan.), 35.
Tom Thumb was revived in 1932. Answer to 1940.B11.

6 DODDS, M. H. "Queries from Fielding's 'Voyage to Lisbon.'" Notes and Queries, 180 (18 Jan.), 50.
Answer to 1940.B10. Eighteenth-century feminine "dishabille" is carefully described.

7 ELISTRATOVA, A. "Realizm Fil'dinga," in Iz Istorŭ anglŭskogo realizma. Edited by I. I. Anisimov. Moscow: Akademii nauk SSSR, pp. 57-132.
"The Realism of Fielding," in On the History of English Realism. In Russian.

8 F., C. "Gravelot." Notes and Queries, 180 (11 Jan.), 29.
Asks to have "Gravelot," the French illustrator of Tom Jones, identified. See 1941.B4.

9 IRWIN, WILLIAM R. "An Attack on John Fielding." Modern Language Notes, 56, no. 7 (Nov.), 523-25.
Briefly describes a pamphlet entitled Jonathan Wild's Advice to his Successors . . . (1758), in which Henry's brother, John Fielding, Justice of the Peace for Westminster and Middlesex, is seen as "the natural heir of the notorious thief and thief-taker Jonathan Wild" (p. 524). The pamphlet capitalizes on Henry Fielding's Jonathan Wild, which had recently been reissued.

10 JAGGARD, WILLIAM. "Revivals of Fielding's Plays." Notes and Queries, 180 (4 Jan.), 15.
The Joseph Reed adaptation of Tom Jones was revived in 1907. The Kane O'Hara burletta of Tom Thumb has been frequently performed. Answer to 1940.B11.

11 MEAD, HERMAN R. "Fielding, Henry (1707-1754)." The Papers of the Bibliographical Society of America, 35 (first quarter), 69.
A brief bibliographical description of three copies of The Coffee-House Politician, all published in 1730.

12 M., E. F. "Queries from Fielding's 'Voyage to Lisbon.'" Notes and Queries, 180 (12 April), 269.
Offers a possible answer to the query about "Cornaro's case" (1940.B10).

13 N., A. E. "Derham." Notes and Queries, 180 (18 Jan.), 46.
Asks the identity of a "Derham" whom Fielding quotes in Journal of a Voyage to Lisbon on human moral composition. See 1941.B3.

14 PRIESTLEY, J. B. "A Preface to The History of Tom Jones," in A Book of Prefaces. New York: Limited Editions Club, pp. 48-53.
Reprints the preface from 1931.A7.

15 PRITCHETT, V. S. "Books in General." New Statesman and Nation, 22, no. 565 (20 Dec.), 510.
Says that Fielding's unpopularity in the 1930s was the result of the age's interest in sex and psychology (better supplied by Richardson) and ungarnished realism (better done by Defoe). Pritchett particularly thinks that modern readers are put off by Fielding's polished Augustan prose. Argues that we ought not to think Fielding a complacent member of the establishment (reminds us of Jonathan Wild and Fielding's social concerns). Thinks the English novel did not develop from Defoe's reporting but from Fielding's dramatic ordering of his "slice of life." Argues that it is only in Tom Jones that Fielding makes the most of his dramatic training, treating "episodes as subjects and not as simple slices of life." Pritchett discusses the novel's tight economy of structure (with its quickly set scenes, which illustrate action, followed by brief commentary), the moral development of its characters, and its subtle dramatization of good and evil. Amelia, a less successful novel, returns to the earlier episodic slice of life technique and yet looks forward (in the subtle influence of Miss Matthews on the book) to the psychological novel.
For another view of the development of the novel see 1957.B17.

16 RICE-OXLEY, LEONARD. "Henry Fielding (1707-1754)," in The Cambridge Bibliography of English Literature. Edited by F. W. Bateson. Vol. 2. Cambridge: The University Press; New York: Macmillan, 517-20.
Superseded by 1971.B5.

17 ROLLESTON, J. D. "Revivals of Fielding's Plays." Notes and Queries, 180 (25 Jan.), 70.
Asks about a stage version of Tom Jones in the 1880s called Sophia.

18 VINCENT, HOWARD P. "Henry Fielding in Prison." Modern Language Review, 36, no. 4 (Oct.), 499-500.

1942

Reprints part of an obscure pamphlet in which it is alleged that Fielding was imprisoned for debt, perhaps before 1728, and generously released by Sir Robert Walpole, whom Fielding then libeled.

For another "debt" anecdote, see 1786.B1. For a refutation, see 1916.B3.

1942 A BOOKS

*1 CLARK, CHARLES M. "The Life of Mr. Jonathan Wild the Great by Henry Fielding. Edited with Introduction and Notes." Dissertation, Cornell, 1942.

Source: T. Humphrey, p. 253. See Cornell University Abstracts of Theses, 1942 (1943), pp. 19-22.

2 FIELDING, HENRY. The Adventures of Joseph Andrews. Introduction by L. Rice-Oxley. World Classics. London, New York, Toronto: H. Milford, Oxford University Press, 406 pp.

Reprint of 1929.A3.

3 _____. The History of Tom Jones, A Foundling. Introduction by George Saintsbury. Everyman's Library. 2 vols. London: J. M. Dent & Sons; New York: E. P. Dutton, 838 pp.

Reissue of 1909.A2.

1942 B SHORTER WRITINGS

1 AVERY, EMMETT L. "Proposals for a New London Theatre in 1737." Notes and Queries, 182 (23 May), 286-87.

Describes Fielding's 1737 proposal to build a new theater and his renovation of the New Theatre in the Haymarket in that year.

Reponse 1942.B2, B7.

2 DE CASTRO, J. PAUL. "Proposals for a New Theatre in 1737." Notes and Queries, 182 (20 June), 346.

Explains the letter (1942.B1) from the lease-holder in light of the Licensing Act and describes the theater's subsequent history.

3 GEROULD, GORDON H. "The Dominance of the Novel," in his The Patterns of English and American Fiction. Boston: Little, Brown, pp. 81-92.

Reviews Fielding's career as a novelist and superficially sets him in the history of the novel; particularly commends Tom Jones for its pace, though not its plot, and

Fielding for his tolerant sympathetic curiosity and his comic detachment. Gerould thinks Allworthy and Blifil the only two Fielding characters that fail.

4 HEILMAN, ROBERT B. "Fielding and 'The First Gothic Revival.'" Modern Language Notes, 57, no. 8 (Dec.), 671-73.

In the 1740s (in Journey from This World to the Next and Tom Jones) Fielding seemed to approve of Gothic architecture and thus participate in the Gothic revival. By 1754 (Voyage) he had changed his mind and condemned the medieval, Manueline, and Renaissance architecture of Lisbon.

5 HUMPHREYS, A. R. "Fielding's Irony: Its Method and Effect." Review of English Studies, 18, no. 70 (April), 183-96.

Argues that Fielding uses "irony of integration rather than disintegration," which, unlike Swift's "radically disturbing" irony, "is, in intention, corrective and orthodox; it undermines deviations from a healthy, sensible, social morality" (p. 183). Humphreys then analyzes how such orthodox irony can still be effective; he describes Fielding's rapid shifts in tone (unlike Swift's), his use of innuendo or double-entendre, his proof of the obvious, his use of the mock heroic, and his ironic style. All of these ironic techniques impose a formal patterning on the spontaneous actions of the novel. The balancing of complex contradictory behavior and form Humphreys sees as a kind of psychological analysis deeply satisfying in a work of literature. Special emphasis on Jonathan Wild. See 1958.B6.

Reprinted 1962.A12 and 1972.A8.

6 PONS, EMILE. "Fielding, Swift et Cervantes." Studia neophilologica, 16 (1942-43), 305-333.

Pons argues that Fielding is principally indebted to Cervantes for the inspiration that created the modern novel (Parson Adams is imbued with Quixote's ideals). One passage in his play Don Quixote in England, however, Pons finds Swiftian (the end of scene 1, act 2). This spirit will guide him in Jonathan Wild. In French.

7 POTTER, JOHN. "Proposals for a New Theatre in 1737." Notes and Queries, 182 (20 June), 346.

Challenges Avery (1942.B1). Fielding had neither money nor lease to build or renovate theaters; prints a letter from the lease-holder of the New Theatre.

1942

8 PRICE, LAWRENCE M. "The Works of Fielding on the German Stage, 1762-1801." Journal of English and Germanic Philology, 41, no. 3 (July), 257-78.

"The history of Fielding's works on the German stage is chiefly an account of the dramatizations of Tom Jones. Several of Fielding's dramas were translated, but only one, The Wedding Day, established itself even precariously in Germany" (p. 257). The article includes a history of the translations, from Eurydice in 1759 to Pasquin in 1789, a brief discussion of the translators and translations, and some stage history. Price discusses the dramatizations of Tom Jones (including the translation of Coleman's Jealous Wife, the translation of Poinsinet's French operetta, and a German dramatization by Heinrich Beck) and offers information on the production of Fielding's dramatized works by the chief theatrical companies in the major German cities. After briefly looking at the dramatization of other English novels, he concludes "that Pamela was the only English novel which rivalled or perhaps exceeded Tom Jones in popularity on the German stage" (p. 278). See 1974.B22.

9 RANDALL, D.A. and J. T. WINTERICH. "One Hundred Good Novels. Fielding, Henry: The History of Tom Jones." Publishers' Weekly, 141 (21 March), 1200-1202.

A short history of early editions and translations; also a collation of the six volumes of the first edition and a brief note on the second edition "same year, six volumes, . . . reset throughout."

1943 A BOOKS

1 FIELDING, HENRY. Jonathan Wild. Translated by Carlo Izzo. [Milano]: Bompiani, 321 pp. [1943].

Italian translation.

2 _____. The History of the Life of the Late Mr. Jonathan Wild the Great. Introduction by Louis Kronenberger and illustrations by T. M. Cleland. New York: Limited Editions Club, 249 pp.

Kronenberger briefly discusses Fielding as a worldly moralist, the real Wild, and this work as sustained irony (he thinks the sympathetic handling of the Heartfrees a damaging violation of tone). No indication of copy text.

3 _____. The History of Tom Jones, a Foundling. Illustrated by Warren Chappell. New York: A. S. Barnes, 909 pp.
Called an "Illustrated Modern Library" edition. See 1943.A4.

4 _____. The History of Tom Jones, a Foundling. Illustrated by Warren Chappell. New York: Modern Library, 884 pp.
Appears to follow Murphy (1762.A10), as did the earlier Modern Library edition ([1931].A5).

1943 B SHORTER WRITINGS

1 ANON. "Jonathan Wild." Times Literary Supplement (14 Aug.), p. 396.
Argues from internal evidence that A Journey From this World to the Next was written before Joseph Andrews and probably around 1730, despite Fielding's mentioning Parson Adams in Journey. On the evidence of style, suggests that Jonathan Wild is also an early and immature work written "before [Fielding] had shaken off the burlesque tradition of the state" (p. 396). See 1943.B3.

2 BOYCE, BENJAMIN. "News from Hell: Satiric Communications with the Nether World in English Writing of the Seventeenth and Eighteenth Centuries." Publications of the Modern Language Association, 58, no. 2 (June), 402-437.
In his survey of this literary type, Boyce briefly describes the infernal puppet show in The Author's Farce (1730), and the infernal elements in Eurydice, A Farce (1737), Champion (24 May 1740), and Journey from this World to the Next. In the latter, Boyce sees Fielding in debt to his favorite Lucian, to Tom Brown, and to Quevedo. In fact, "in spite of its genuine Fielding quality it might almost be a recapitulation of the whole tradition" (p. 425).

3 DOWNS, BRIAN W. "Jonathan Wild." Times Literary Supplement (11 Sept.), p. 444.
Briefly refutes 1943.B1. On the basis of its political allusions and the delay in the publication of the Miscellanies, Jonathan Wild was written in the spring of 1742 and after Joseph Andrews.

4 HILL, ROWLAND M. "Setting in the Novels of Henry Fielding." Bulletin of the Citadel, 7: 26-52.
Attempts to account for Fielding's "opportune evasion" (p. 27) of setting and locale-painting by suggesting that

it was partly the result of his experience as a playwright ("putting out on a bare 'stage' just enough properties to provide the illusion of 'somewhere,'" p. 30) and partly that he was too busy solving the "dynamic interrelationships" (p. 29) between incident and character to bother with setting. Hill then examines his descriptive settings, his mock-heroic settings (used to provide contrast with the action), his interior settings (which reflect character), and his exterior settings. Hill concludes that Fielding "omitted much of the localization which adds so greatly in making the reader feel the semblance of reality" (p. 42) and that he only used setting "to advance characterization or incident" (p. 52).

5 MACAULAY, ROSE. "Lines on Fielding." Times Literary Supplement (9 Oct.), p. 487.
Asks to have the author of some lines of poetry written in praise of Fielding identified.

6 ROGERS, WINFIELD H. "Fielding's Early Aesthetic and Technique." Studies in Philology, 40, no. 4 (Oct.), 529-51.
By examining the works of Fielding's "apprentice years from 1729 to about 1740" (p. 529), particularly his plays, Rogers sets out to demonstrate Fielding's development of farce as a satiric medium, his adaptation of the humours as serious psychology, his development of certain words like "good" and "great" as symbols, and his creation of a complex "three directional satire or symbolism" which allows him "to comment at once on literature and life" (p. 547).
Reprinted 1962.A12.

7 VINCENT, HOWARD P. "Early Poems by Henry Fielding." Notes and Queries, 184 (13 March), 159-60.
Two poems not included in the Miscellanies (1743) are printed: "An Original Song" and "A Dialogue between a Beau's Head and his Heels." See 1922.B4.

8 WAGENKNECHT, EDWARD. "Fielding and the Prose Epic," in his Cavalcade of the English Novel. New York: Henry Holt, pp. 58-68.
Reviewed by Robert B. Heelman, KR, 5 (1943), 624-28; J. F. Matthews, JA, 2, no. 8 (1943), 94-95; Robert Shafer, MLN, 59 (1944), 287-90.
Calls Fielding the first "unashamed novelist in England" (p. 59), the creator of the omniscient narrator and of the verisimilitude of art. Briefly discusses his comedy of affectation, the political satire in Jonathan Wild, Adams

as more than a character from Cervantes, the comic use of the conventional plot in Joseph Andrews, the motif of uncertain identity in Tom Jones, and the "study of economic distress" (p. 66) in Amelia. Finally he discusses his morality, emphasizing, and not quite comfortable with, the sexual looseness of Fielding's heroes. He feels that only in Amelia does Fielding insist "on Christian dogma and Christian ethics"; before this "he falls in grave danger of Rousseauism" (p. 68).

1944 A BOOKS

1 FIELDING, HENRY. The History of Tom Jones, a Foundling. Illustrated by Warren Chappell. New York: A. S. Barnes, 909 pp.
Reissue of 1943.A3.

1944 B SHORTER WRITINGS

1 C., T. C. "Fielding and Bentley." Notes and Queries, 186 (20 May), 245-46.
An allusion in Amelia (Book 10, chapter 1) to an annotation of Horace by Bentley proves the extent of Fielding's classical learning and the demands Fielding makes on his reader's general knowledge.

*2 EAVES, T. C. DUNCAN. "Graphic Illustration of the Principal English Novels of the Eighteenth Century." Dissertation, Harvard, 1944.
Source: T. Humphrey, p. 256. See Summaries of Theses . . . 1943-1945. Cambridge: Harvard University Press, 1947, pp. 469-71. See 1946.B1.

3 GREENE, CHARLES R. "A Note on the Authorship of Shamela." Modern Language Notes, 59 (Dec.), 571.
More stylistic evidence offered, a parallel passage in The Mock Doctor and Shamela. See 1916.B1.

*4 LØSKE, OLAV. "Henry Fielding og det Komiske." Edda. Nordisk tidsskrift for litteraturforskning, 44:34-43.
"Henry Fielding and the comic." Danish article.
Source: T. Humphrey, p. 231.

*5 _____. "Henry Fielding og Robert Walpole." Edda. Nordisk tidsskrift for litteraturforskning, 44:153-70.

1944

"Henry Fielding and Robert Walpole." Danish article. Source: T. Humphrey, p. 231.

6 SWAEN, A. E. H. "Fielding's The Intriguing Chambermaid." Neophilologus, 29:117-20.

Examines the parallels in plot, scene, and character between Plautus' Mostellaria, Regnard's Le Retour imprévu, and Fielding's Intriguing Chambermaid, concluding that Fielding thoroughly "englished" his French model and that he also added details directly borrowed from Plautus' play, which Regnard had earlier adapted "to French conditions, manners and tastes" (p. 119).

7 VAN DOREN, MARK, ed. "Henry Fielding, Tom Jones," in his The New Invitation to Learning. New York: New Home Library, pp. 192-205.

Reviewed by C. J. Gallagher, Thought, 18 (1943), 154-55; E. C. Knowlton, SAQ, 42 (1943), 301-302.

In this CBS radio conversation Katherine Anne Porter, Allen Tate and Mark Van Doren vaguely discuss the Richardsonian as opposed to the picaresque tradition, Fielding's lack of subtlety, the classic Tom and Partridge pair, Fielding's common sense and worldly wisdom, high comedy vs. tragedy, etc.

1945 A BOOKS

1 FIELDING, HENRY. The Adventures of Joseph Andrews. Introduction by L. Rice-Oxley. World Classics. London, New York, Toronto: G. Cumberlege, Oxford University Press, 406 pp.

Reprint of 1929.A3.

2 _____. The History of Tom Jones, a Foundling. Illustrated by Warren Chappell. New York: Modern Library, 909 pp. [1945].

Reissue of 1943.A3.

3 _____. Tom Jones Geschichte eines Findlings. Translated by J. J. C. Bode and revised by Fritz Guttinger. Illustrations by Stichen von Moreau. Zürich: Manesse-Verlag and Conzett & Huber, 886 pp.

4 _____. Tom Jones (Sokakta bulunmuş bir Cocuğun Hikâyesi). Translated by Mina Urgan. 4 vols. Istanbul: Tan Basımevi.

Turkish translation bound as three volumes (vols. 1 and 2 as one). Vols. 3 and 4 were issued in Istanbul by Millî eğitim basımevi in 1946.

*5 SHERWOOD, IRMA Z. "The Influence of Digressive Didacticism on the Structure of the Novels of Richardson and Fielding." Dissertation, Yale, 1945.
Source: Dissertation Abstracts, 30 (1970), 3436A. See 1949.B3.

*6 WALLACE, ROBERT M. "Henry Fielding's Narrative Method: Its Historical and Biographical Origins." Dissertation, North Carolina, 1945.
Source: T. Humphrey, p. 267. See University of North Carolina Record, no. 429 (1946), 147-48.

1945 B SHORTER WRITINGS

1 DE LA TORRE, LILLIAN [LILLIAN B. MCCUE]. Elizabeth is Missing or, Truth Triumphant: An Eighteenth Century Mystery. New York: Alfred Knopf; London: Michael Joseph (1947), 279 pp.
Dramatic reconstruction of the Canning case from contemporary documents (including Fielding's A Clear State of the Case of Elizabeth Canning), which sets out Fielding's involvement in the case. See 1879.B3.

2 HUGHES, LEO. "The Influence of Fielding's Milieu upon His Humor," in Studies in English, The University of Texas, 1944. Austin: University of Texas Press, pp. 269-97.
"Selects from [Fielding's] background some of the more obvious items which could have influenced his comic practice" (p. 269). Hughes discusses the classical requirement to educate as well as entertain, as well as literary and political factionalism. Fielding's creative life is divided into three periods. In the first, his theatrical career, Hughes sees Fielding succeeding at farce and burlesque, while learning to write more sophisticated comedy. In the middle period, through Tom Jones, Hughes sees moral purpose developing and farce diminishing. In the last period, Amelia is seen to be as serious as a Richardson novel, relieved only by "ridiculous portraits" (p. 295). In the last two periods Hughes discusses only the first of the three elements that influenced Fielding. He does not find Fielding's comic theory very interesting.

3 JARVIS, R. C. "Fielding, Dodsley, Marchant, and Ray. Some Fugitive Histories of the '45." Notes and Queries, 189 (8 Sept.), 90-92.

Four accounts of the 1745 Jacobite rising. Fielding's Whig propaganda work is described (History of the Present Rebellion, 1745) and Cross's (1918.A1) and Seymour's (1935.B7, B15) assertions that Fielding wrote the Compleat and Authentick History (1747) are challenged. Jarvis also rejects the idea that Fielding contributed to Dodsley's Museum in 1746, when A Succinct History of the Rebellion was running.

4 _____. "Fielding, Dodsley, Marchant, and Ray. Some Fugitive Histories of the '45." Notes and Queries, 189 (22 Sept.), 117-20.

Continues 1945.B3.

5 _____. "Fielding, Dodsley, Marchant, and Ray. Some Fugitive Histories of the '45." Notes and Queries, 189 (6 Oct.), 138-41.

Continues 1945.B3 and 4.

1946 A BOOKS

1 FIELDING, HENRY. Les Aventures de Joseph Andrews. Translated by P. F. G. Desfontaines and revised by Gilbert Sigaux. Introduction by André Maurois. Paris: Nouvelles Editions Latines, 452 pp.

The brief introduction outlines the parody of Pamela, Fielding's form, and his elegant simplicity. French translation.

2 _____. The History of the Adventures of Joseph Andrews and His Friend Mr. Abraham Adams. Edited by George Saintsbury. Everyman's Library. London: J. M. Dent & Sons; New York: E. P. Dutton, 316 pp. [1946].

Reprint of 1910.A6.

*3 LOCKE, MIRIAM A. "An Edition of The True Patriot by Henry Fielding, with an Introduction and Critical Notes." Dissertation, Northwestern, 1946.

Source: McNamee, 1865-1964, p. 558. See 1964.A17.

1946 B SHORTER WRITINGS

1 EAVES, T. C. DUNCAN. "The Publication of the First Translations of Fielding's Tom Jones." Library, 4th. series, 26,

nos. 2 and 3, also called Transactions of the Bibliographical Society (Sept. and Dec.), 189-90.

On the evidence of the title pages and the engravings, it is clear that the French translation by de la Place came before Le Clercq's Dutch translation in 1750. See dissertation 1944.B2.

2 GRAHAM, W. H. "Fielding's Tom Jones." Contemporary Review, 169 (March), 164-68.

After quoting Gibbon and Hazlitt and asserting that "coarse and vulgar as we may find it Tom Jones faithfully records the life of the eighteenth century" (p. 165), Graham provides a set of character sketches. He calls Western "an unmitigated barbarian" (p. 166), wonders how Allworthy can be so easily deceived, thinks there is a Shakespearian echo about Black George, and sees Sophia as a physical and moral beauty.

3 IRWIN, W. R. "Satire and Comedy in the Works of Henry Fielding." Journal of English Literary History, 13, no. 3 (Sept.), 168-88.

By examining Fielding's dramatic satire, Irwin hopes to illustrate how "satiric principles and devices . . . became a flexible theory of comedy operating in the novels" (p. 169). He examines Fielding's attack on literary affectations as it develops in his satires (particularly as it is aimed at illiterate and pretentious critics and playwrights) and his attack on literary affectation in Shamela and Joseph Andrews. Irwin appears to conclude that Fielding learned little about character making as he shifted "from fantasy [in the satires] to reality in representing human action" (p. 183), although the novels continue to include burlesque characterization and action typical of the satires. Less a study of Fielding's technique than of his comic theory.

See 1952.B4, and particularly 1943.B6.

4 JARVIS, R. C. "The Death of Walpole: Henry Fielding and a Forgotten Cause Célèbre." Modern Language Review, 41, no. 2 (April), 113-30.

A "paper war" about the part the medical profession played in Sir Robert Walpole's death occurred in 1742. In this historical-biographical article Jarvis argues that Fielding joined the war with The Charge to the Grand Jury. After setting out the "literary" events sparked by the death, Jarvis describes the printing of The Charge and the pamphlet itself, which he concludes is typical of Fielding in both content and style ("hath-doth" trait). He also suggests that several other small pamphlets bound up with The Charge may be by Fielding. The Charge had formerly been called one of the items of "uncertain or doubtful authorship" by Cross (1918.A1). See review by W. R. Irwin, PQ, 26 (1947), 120-21. See also 1926.B3 and 1960.B4.

5 MCCULLOUGH, BRUCE. "The Novel of Manners. Henry Fielding: Tom Jones," in his Representative English Novelists: Defoe to Conrad. New York and London: Harper and Brothers, pp. 42-57.

Begins by briefly comparing Fielding to Defoe and Richardson in theme (Richardson the novel of sensibility, Defoe of personality, and Fielding of manners) and point of view (Fielding's omniscience vs. the involved narrator). Argues that Fielding "reveals the tendency of his age to think in terms of abstractions." The novel for him was not "a study of individual lives" (p. 46) but a representative picture of manners. McCullough describes the types of the various characters (e.g., Tom Jones is "eager and impulsive youth," p. 47) and the way in which Fielding follows "the structural principles of the epic" merely to "hold the characters in place" (p. 50). After setting out the organization of the books, McCullough suggests that the end of the novel is like a well made play (clearly manipulated rather than inevitable), in that the characters, even the minor ones, illustrate the humor of human foibles and the value of social experience.

6 PRITCHETT, V. S. "The Ancestor," in his The Living Novel. London: Chatto & Windus, pp. 1-8.

Reviewed by Maxwell Geismar, SRL, 30 (11 Oct. 1947), 20; M. Wade, Commonweal, 47 (1947), 236-37; Alan Walbank, LL, 52 (1947), 72-73; Margaret Willy, English, 6 (1947), 204-205; TLS, 16 Nov. 1946, p. 564.

Thinks Fielding the shallow ancestor of a deep tradition (Dickens, Thackeray, Meredith, Kipling, Galsworthy and Wodehouse) in which middle-class sociability attempts reform. Thinks Fielding combined the picaresque tradition and the theater to make the new novel, succeeding where Defoe's reporting failed. Amelia's weakness is a result of both the weakening force of Fielding's comic dramatic strain and the middle-class brooding of the Victorian novel.

Published in New York by Reynal and Hitchcock in 1947, and as The Living Novel and Later Appreciations by Random House, also in 1947.

7 RENWICK, W. L. "Comic Epic in Prose," in Essays and Studies by Members of the English Association. Vol. 32. Edited by Basil Willey. Oxford: Clarendon Press, pp. 40-43.
Defines what the terms "comic" and "epic" would have meant for Fielding and how "comic epic in prose" would have triangulated his new genre. See 1931.A9, 1964.B6.

*8 SAKMANN, PAUL. "Die Denker und Kämpfer der englischen Aufklärung." Dissertation, Stuttgart, 1946.
In German.
Source: Wolfgang Iser, Weltanschauung Henry Fieldings (1952.A5), p. 318.

9 TILLETT, NETTIE S. "Is Coleridge Indebted to Fielding?" Studies in Philology, 43, no. 4 (Oct.), 675-81.
Coleridge borrowed his famous dicta about the willing suspension of disbelief and other passages in the Biographia Literaria from the introduction ("A Wonderful Long Chapter concerning the Marvellous . . .") to Book 8 of Tom Jones. See 1958.B4.

10 WARD, J. A. "Dining with the Novelists." Personalist, 45, no. 3 (Summer), 399-411.
In an essay on "some uses of dining" (p. 399) from Tom Jones to Joyce's Ulysses and including Emma, Vanity Fair, and Great Expectations, Ward suggests that the "bill-of-fare" in the narrative opening of Tom Jones perfectly defines the "prevailing moral norm" (p. 399) of naturalness in his novels. The actual meals that are eaten in Fielding's novels are hearty activities, a "zestful indulgence in the commonplace activities of life" (p. 401).

11 WOODS, CHARLES B. "Fielding and the Authorship of Shamela." Philological Quarterly, 25, no. 3 (July), 248-72.
Provides a useful bibliography of the controversy (begun in 1900 by Clara L. Thomas in her book Samuel Richardson) about authorship, much of it published in books and articles on Richardson. Woods goes on to show that Fielding's particular enemies are pilloried in Shamela, that there are parallel passages in other Fielding works, that it contains Fielding's typical religious and ethical concerns, and briefly that it is a stage in the development of Joseph Andrews. See 1916.B1.

1947

1947 A BOOKS

1 FIELDING, HENRY. La vie de Jonathan Wild le Grand. Translated by Jules Castier. Editions Stock. Paris: Delamain et Bontelleau, 286 pp. [1947].
French translation with a brief critical introduction.

2 _____. The Adventures of Joseph Andrews. Introduction by L. Rice-Oxley. World Classics. London, New York, Toronto: G. Cumberlege, Oxford University Press, 406 pp.
Reprint of 1929.A3.

3 _____. The History of the Adventures of Joseph Andrews and His Friend Mr. Abraham Adams. Edited by George Saintsbury. Everyman's Library. London: J. M. Dent & Sons; New York: E. P. Dutton, 316 pp.
Reprint of 1910.A6.

4 _____. The History of the Adventures of Joseph Andrews and his Friend Mr. Abraham Adams. The Novel Library. London: Hamish Hamilton, 395 pp.
A brief introduction by "A. H." sketches in Fielding's ability as a creator of characters (particularly satiric characters), the picaresque precursors of the novel, the parody, a few of the details of publication, and Fielding's "realism" (his borrowing from life). No indication of copy text.

5 _____. The History of the Life of the Late Mr. Jonathan Wild the Great. The Novel Library. London: Hamish Hamilton, 228 pp.
A brief note by "A. H." sets out Fielding's career and identifies this novel as a work of sustained irony. No indication of copy text.

6 JENKINS, ELIZABETH. Henry Fielding. English Novelists Series. London: Home and Van Thal; Denver: Alan Swallow (1948), 101 pp.
Reviewed by John Farrelly, New Repub., 3 Jan. 1949, p. 27; N&Q, 193 (1948), 65-66; TLS, 24 Jan. 1948, p. 50.
This book, based largely on Dobson (1883.A1), Murphy (1762.A10), Godden (1910.A9), and Jones (1933.A5), recounts biographical and historical facts about Fielding's friendships and enmities, his marriages, his financial affairs and about the eighteenth century in general. Brief comments on his works are interspersed; the stories of his major novels are retold, and the events and characters are treated mimetically. His friendship with Hogarth allows

Jenkins to observe that his characters are Hogarthian, and she sides with Fielding on the old charges of immorality.

7 WEIDE, ERWIN. Henry Fieldings Komödien und die Restaurations-Komödie. Hamburg: Hansischer Gildenverlag, 140 pp.

Reviewed by V. de S. Pinto, MLR, 44 (1949), 111-12.

A detailed study of the influence of the "Restoration" comedy of manners, from Etherege to Farquhar (and including Cibber and Steele), on Fielding's comedies. After examining Fielding and the Restoration playwrights' attitudes toward love, friendship, family, honor, etc., Weide argues that Fielding's comedies are suffused with the spirit of humane sentiment (as opposed to the hard intellectualism of the Restoration playwright) that will lead to the sentimentalism of the late eighteenth century. In German.

8 WILLCOCKS, M[ARY] P. A True-Born Englishman: Being a Life of Henry Fielding. London: George Allen & Unwin; New York: Macmillan (1948), 288 pp.

Reviewed by Carlos Baker, NYTBR, 7 March 1948, p. 6; Howard Mumford Jones, Sat. Rev., 31 (3 April 1948), 29-30; V. S. Pritchett, NSN, 34 (13 Dec. 1947), 472; C. R. T., QQ, 55 (1949), 517-18; Philip Trower, Spectator, 179 (5 Dec. 1947), 720; TLS, 24 Jan. 1948, p. 50.

A popular biography relying on the standard lives of Fielding, Murphy (1762.A10), Dobson (1883.A1), Cross (1918.A1), etc. Rather uncritically dramatizes the events of Fielding's life (e.g., accepts the Gould side in the custody dispute with Fielding's father; see 1940.B14), and shows a certain fastidiousness about works like Shamela and Jonathan Wild ("of those who have intelligence enough to understand it, few have enjoyed it," p. 178).

1947 B SHORTER WRITINGS

1 COOKE, ARTHUR L. "Henry Fielding and the Writers of Heroic Romance." Publications of the Modern Language Association, 62, no. 4, part 1 (Dec.), 984-94.

In Joseph Andrews Fielding specifically eschews romances, yet "the heroic romance constituted the most detailed theory of prose fiction prior to his own day, [and it is also] in many instances strikingly similar to the theories which Fielding himself advanced" (p. 984). After examining the parallels between the theories, Cooke concludes that both created their theories from the classical epic, not that Fielding borrowed from the writers of romance. What

1947

is surprising is that with similar theories their fiction should be so different. See 1968.B34.

2 MACK, EDWARD C. "Pamela's Stepdaughters: The Heroine of Smollett and Fielding." College English, 8, no. 6 (March), 293-301.

Argues that Richardson created an ideal of womanhood in Pamela (virtuous; a prophet of love, pity, and benevolence, who promised a married life of pastoral domestic bliss and cultivated simplicity). Smollett followed this ideal in all "his leading ladies" (p. 295), but perverted it. Fielding, despite his temperamental difference from Richardson, believed in many of these ideals and so, while all his women follow the pattern, he could "re-create the ideal in terms of his own personality" (p. 299). After describing Fielding's several recreations of the ideal, Mack concludes that Fielding's heroines are weaker than Richardson's because Fielding "never understood the female heart in the intimate way that Richardson did" (p. 300).

Reprinted 1972.A8.

3 MAUGHAM, SOMERSET. "The Ten Best Novels: Tom Jones." Atlantic Monthly, 180, no. 6 (Dec.), 120-26.

Essentially biographical essay in which Maugham also briefly discusses how Fielding benefitted from being a playwright (economy in action, character, and dialogue). Maugham asserts that the style of Tom Jones is easier and more natural than Jane Austen's and that the prefaces and digressions, while interesting, could have been omitted. He considers this novel a biography: asserting that Fielding "was very like his own Tom Jones" (p. 123), and that in Sophia he "was remembering his own beloved (and I am afraid, long-suffering) wife" (p. 126). Dickson rejects such old-fashioned biographical readings.

Reprinted 1954.B10 and as "Henry Fielding and Tom Jones," in Great Novelists and Their Novels: Essays on the Ten Greatest Novels of the World and the Men and Women Who Wrote Them. Philadelphia, Toronto: John C. Winston, 1948.

4 TONSTER, EVA B. "The Literary Relationship of Thackeray and Fielding." Journal of English and Germanic Philology, 46, no. 4 (Oct.), 383-94.

A study of Thackeray's views of Fielding in "theory and practice" to see "whether his practice of the novel is in accord with his judgment of Fielding's art" (p. 383). Begins by examining Thackeray's pronouncements on Fielding (the rake) and his art (which he admired). Tonster points

points out that early in their careers both Fielding and Thackeray wrote burlesque and parody ("Thackeray in his chief parodies was following Fielding's example," p. 389); Barry Lyndon is Thackeray's Jonathan Wild. The article then briefly sums up the less direct later influence when there was "no evidence of imitation" (p. 391), seeing it in "epical structure . . .; Quixotic humor; intellectual realism . . .; and (in The Virginians) the depiction of a genuinely eighteenth century atmosphere" (p. 391). See 1913.B3 and 1957.B12.

5 WALLACE, ROBERT M. "Fielding's Knowledge of History and Biography." Studies in Philology, 44, no. 1 (Jan.), 89-107.

Tries to alter the impression that Fielding's learning was largely confined to the classics. By examining his library (1895.B1) and allusions in The Champion and The Covent-Garden Journal, he demonstrates that Fielding read widely in history and biography and was interested in historiography. He suggests that history and biography had as much influence on Fielding's novels as the epic did. See 1964.B14 and 1977.B3.

6 WARNER, GILMORE. "Fielding's Voyage to Lisbon." Colby Library Quarterly, series 11, no. 3 (Aug.), 39-42.

Briefly reviews the reputation of the work and describes the circumstances that created two editions in 1755. Colby had just purchased a second edition (which is the unrevised first printing).

1948 A BOOKS

*1 DAVIES, E. O. "A Critical Edition of Pasquin and the Historical Register by Henry Fielding." Dissertation, Oxford-Jesus, 1948.

Source: Stratman, et al., Restoration and Eighteenth Century Theatre Research . . . (1971.B35), p. 286.

*2 FIELDING, HENRY. The Adventures of Joseph Andrews. Translated by Natsuo Shumuta. 2 vols. Tokyo: Shin-getsu-sha, 490 (264 & 226) pp.

Japanese translation based on the 1915 Macmillan edition.

Source: Hugh Amory's working bibliography.

3 _____. The History of the Adventures of Joseph Andrews and of His Friend Mr. Abraham Adams. Edited by Maynard Mack. New York: Holt, Rinehart and Winston, 368 pp. [1948].
Essentially modernizes and reprints the 1742 edition. The introduction describes the nature of Fielding's parody of Pamela (using Coleridge's image of a sick room and a breezy day to compare Richardson and Fielding), discusses the characters and the structure of the novel as outgrowths of Fielding's dramatic training and the influence of Cervantes, briefly distinguishes between tragic and comic plot and character.
Preface reprinted 1962.A12 and 1972.A8. By 1960 this edition had been reprinted thirteen times.

4 _____. The History of Tom Jones A Foundling. Edited by W. Somerset Maugham and illustrated by Harry Diamond. Philadelphia and Toronto: John C. Winston, 400 pp.
Maugham, relying heavily on Murphy (1762.A10), reviews Fielding's career, confusing Fielding with the character Tom Jones. He prints an abridged version of the novel, principally omitting the introductory chapters to each book.

5 _____. The History of Tom Jones A Foundling. Great Books of the Western World. No. 37. Chicago, London, Toronto: Encyclopedia Britannica/Wm. Benton, 420 pp.
Appears to reprint the 1750 edition followed by Murphy (1762.A10).
According to the National Union Catalogue Authors List, 1942-62, this edition was reissued in 1952 and 1955.

6 _____. The History of Tom Jones, A Foundling. Illustrated by Harry Diamond. Garden City, New York: Literary Guild of America, 374 pp.
An abridged version (prefaces omitted). No indication of copy text.

1948 B SHORTER WRITINGS

1 CORDASCO, FRANCESCO. Henry Fielding: A List of Critical Studies Published from 1895 to 1946. Eighteenth-Century Bibliographical Pamphlets, 5. Brooklyn: Long Island University Press, 17 pp.
Reviewed PQ, 39 (1950), 273-75.
An incomplete and selectively annotated list organized alphabetically under eleven headings, including

bibliography, biography, criticism, individual novels, periodical writings, plays, and miscellaneous.

2 DODDS, M. H. "Phrase's Sources Wanted." Notes and Queries, 193 (7 Feb.), 64.

A phrase from Amelia that has become part of common usage.

*3 HELSZTYNSKI, S. "U źródefo powiesii angielskiej." Nowiny Literackie, 58: 1-2. ("At the source the English Stories.") Polish article.

Source: T. Humphrey, p. 231 and MHRA, 28 (1948), 143.

4 HOOKER, EDWARD N. "Humour in the Age of Pope." Huntington Library Quarterly, 11, no. 4 (Aug.), 361-85.

Sees Tom Jones and Tristram Shandy as illustrating the two attitudes toward humour in this period. Sterne's characters are not subject to disapproval; they reveal "the quirks and oddities of humour" (p. 381) that demonstrate the richness of human individuality. Fielding also creates strong, untamed individuals, but, particularly in his humorous character Tom, he "perceived a norm in social wisdom" (p. 384). Tom learns to control his passions with humane wisdom "as Fielding acknowledged a higher value than the unrestrained play of oddity or genius" (p. 384). Thus Fielding continues, but modifies, the tradition of Pope and Swift; Sterne looks forward to Romanticism.

5 MCADAM, E. L. "A New Letter from Fielding." Yale Review, 38, no. 2 (Dec.), 300-310.

Describes the discovery of a letter from Fielding to Richardson, sets the letter in the context of Fielding's praise for Richardson's Clarissa (in the Jacobite's Journal), provides a resumé of Clarissa, and reproduces the letter. McAdam speculates on the possibility that there was further correspondence between the two and on the motives and responses of each, concluding that it shows Richardson, in his later response, "as spiteful and small-minded." The letter shows Fielding to have been "overflowing with warmth and friendliness for his rival, witty and tender at the same time" (p. 310). See 1931.B12 and 1971.A2, B12.

6 MAXWELL, J. C. "Fielding and 'Shamela.'" Notes and Queries, 193 (21 Aug.), 364-65.

Adds to Greene's evidence (1944.B3) for Fielding's authorship by citing parallel passages in Shamela, Amelia, and The Mock Doctor. See also 1916.B1.

7 MOORE, ROBERT E. "Hogarth and Fielding Invade the Theatre" and "Hogarth's Role in Fielding's Novels," in his Hogarth's Literary Relationships. Minneapolis: University of Minnesota Press; London: Geoffrey Cumberlege, Oxford University Press, pp. 77-161 and passim.

Reviewed by Delancey Ferguson, NYTBR, 12 June 1949, p. 8; Robert Halsband, SRL, 14 May 1949, p. 21; H. L. Seaver, WMQ, 6 (1949), 525-26; C. R. T., QQ, 56 (1949), 309.

The first chapter outlines the satiric portrait of the contemporary theater that each created, discussing Hogarth's satire from Masquerades and Operas through his more sophisticated satire of opera in A Rake's Progress and Marriage à la Mode, and Fielding's from Author's Farce through Pasquin. Moore discusses specific parallels between The Lottery and The Covent-Garden Tragedy and A Harlot's Progress, and between Pasquin and Hogarth's A Just View of the British Stage. He believes that both artists evolved towards a more serious and grimmer satire but that Fielding always pandered to his audience more openly than Hogarth, descending at times to "smut." In his chapter on the novels, Moore argues that Hogarth gave Fielding, as Fielding acknowledges in Joseph Andrews, his notion of tight didactic plotting and especially character (helping him distinguish between character and caricature). Sees Hogarth as the creator of "realistic" character and suggests that Fielding borrowed a number of specific scenes and characters from Hogarth (the lady who stares at the naked Joseph from behind the sticks of her fan is taken from the lady who ogles a naked Bedlamite in Rake's Progress, Bridget Allworthy from Four Times of the Day, etc.). Moore then compares their theories of comedy, concluding that Fielding was able to attack affectation and Hogarth was not, because Fielding's medium allowed him to unmask it before other characters; at the real heart of the comedy of both is the recognition that incongruity causes laughter. He then briefly considers the way both artists use real people and events to create their comic illusion of reality. Sees the difference between Tom Jones and Joseph Andrews (which he calls Hogarthian in their comic conception) and Amelia (which has no Hogarthian spirit) as evidence of Fielding's shift to his announced intention to unmask affectation.

8 RADZINOWICZ, LEON. A History of English Criminal Law and Its Administration from 1750. 3 vols. London: Stevens & Sons, passim.

Fielding's careers as lawyer, journalist, and magistrate are extensively discussed in vols. 1 and 3 (vols. 2 and 3 were published in 1956). Sees Fielding's Inquiry into the Causes of the Late Increase in Robbers as "a mixture of bold and creative anticipation and narrow, regressive tendencies imprinted upon his mind by the age in which he lived" (I, 415) and concludes that the Committee of 1750, while agreeing with Fielding in many things, was "much more enlightened" (I, 420) than Fielding. Credits Fielding with creating a "police" force and raising the status of metropolitan magistrates. See 1966.A26, 1967.B35, and 1971.B2.

9 SHERBURN, GEORGE. "The Restoration and Eighteenth Century (1660-1789)," in A Literary History of England. Edited by A. C. Baugh. New York and London: Appleton-Century-Crofts, pp. 881, 889-91, 955-61.

Fielding is mentioned as a "lesser essayist" in the section on the periodical essay; briefly discussed as a dramatist in "The Drama, 1700-1740"; more fully discussed as a novelist in the section called "The Mid-Century Novel." Donald Bond added a bibliographical supplement to the second edition of this work (1967).

10 STEPHENS, JOHN C. "The Verge of the Court and Arrest for Debt in Fielding's Amelia." Modern Language Notes, 63, no. 2 (Feb.), 104-109.

In this darker novel Fielding attacked "the complicated and oppressive laws concerning arrest and detention for debt" (p. 104). The article explains the "verge of the court" and the process of "arrest for debt."

1949 A BOOKS

1 FIELDING, HENRY. Istoriiâ prikliûchenu Dzhozefa Endrusa i ego druga Abraama Adamsa napisano v podrazhanie manere Servantesa, avtora Don-Kikhota. Moscow: Gosudarstvennoe Khodozhest-vennoĭ Literatury, 395 pp.

"History of the Adventures of Joseph Andrews and his friend Abraham Adams. Written in imitation of the manner of Cervantes, author of Don Quixote."

Loose Russian translation under the editorship of M. F. Por'e.

1949

2 _____. The Adventures of Joseph Andrews. Introduction by L. Rice-Oxley. World Classics. London, New York, Toronto: G. Cumberlege, Oxford University Press, 406 pp.
Reprint of 1929.A3.

1949 B SHORTER WRITINGS

1 GLÄTTLI, WALTER E. Die Behandlung des Affects der Furcht im englischen Roman des 18. Jahrhunderts. Zürich: Juris-Verlag, pp. 9-16 and 70-83.
This study of the literary use of terror in the eighteenth century uses Freud's distinction between fear (which lies in the individual) and terror (which springs from external circumstances and dangers). Glättli compares Richardson and Fielding: in Richardson terror is integral, often provoking fear; in Fielding it is largely external and comic. Examines both Fielding's ghosts and imaginary dangers, and his real dangers (Adams attacked by the pack of dogs) in Joseph Andrews and Tom Jones. Fielding normally treats terror in a summary fashion, wildly exaggerating it. He usually uses it to provoke responses of love or friendship, or (as narrator) to indulge human weakness or superstition. He is always satisfied with a simple description of the facts and occasionally adds external description of reaction to help characterization. In German.

2 MOORE, ROBERT E. "William Hogarth: The Golden Mean," in The Age of Johnson: Essays Presented to Chauncey Brewster Tinker. New Haven: Yale University Press; London: Geoffrey Cumberlege; Oxford: Oxford University Press, pp. 385-94.
Argues that Fielding rightly commended Hogarth for creating character rather than caricature; both artists attained a balance between pity for suffering and unsentimental judgment. Moore argues that Hogarth is superior to Fielding because Fielding "refuses to be serious. Flippancy is Fielding's most characteristic attitude" (p. 391); this accounts for the failure of Amelia.
Reprinted 1964.

3 SHERWOOD, IRMA Z. "The Novelists as Commentators," in The Age of Johnson: Essays Presented to Chauncey Brewster Tinker. New Haven: Yale University Press; London: Geoffrey Cumberlege; Oxford: Oxford University Press, pp. 113-25.
Argues that the narrative intrusion in novels by such different novelists as Richardson, Fielding, Smollett, Goldsmith, and Burney share a "similarity of sentiment and expression" (p. 114). Sherwood asserts that such

digressions are a result of "the whole bias of the century in favor of a moral purpose in art" (p. 114) and of this new genre's growing out of didactic conduct books, essays, and polite letters. She also includes the speeches of "wise" mentor characters like Allworthy and Dr. Harrison. See dissertation 1945.A5.

Reprinted 1964 and 1972.A8.

*4 WALLACE, ROBERT M. "Henry Fielding's Narrative Method: Its Historical and Biographical Origins." University of North Carolina Record, no. 429, 147-48.

Source: MHRA, 29 (1949), 155.

4a WATT, IAN P. "The Naming of Characters in Defoe, Richardson, and Fielding." Review of English Studies, 25, no. 100 (Oct.), 322-38.

Argues that, unlike either Richardson's or Defoe's (whose names came respectively from romance and from real life), Fielding's "characters, especially his secondary ones but also his first two heroes, tend to have the traditional 'characteristic names' of comedy, reflecting Fielding's preoccupation with 'not men but manners'" (p. 335). Watt goes on to suggest that Fielding began to use a more "realistic" random selection of names in his later novels, where there are a decreasing "proportion of characters whose names alone were enough to show that they were seen entirely from a comic or satiric point of view" (p. 335). He discusses Tom Jones and Amelia as names common to Fielding's age, concluding that, while they are more realistic, Fielding still selected them because he wanted to avoid "suggesting, even in their names, that his characters are unique human beings." Richardson's names, on the other hand, "suggest the unique individuality of his main characters" (p. 338).

Reprinted 1972.A8.

5 WOODS, CHARLES B. "Fielding's Epilogue for Theobald." Philological Quarterly, 28, no. 3 (July), 419-24.

Identifies a hitherto unidentified epilogue that Fielding wrote for Lewis Theobald's Orestes. In 1731 Fielding was probably a friend of Theobald and was probably thought of as on "the outskirts" (p. 423) of Walpole's camp. Fielding a short time later attacked Theobald as a critic and as a playwright (in The Tragedy of Tragedies, Shamela, The Champion, etc.). See 1960.B4, 1966.B4, 1967.B2, 1972.B7 and 1977.B15.

1949

6 WORK, JAMES A. "Henry Fielding, Christian Censor," in The Age of Johnson: Essays Presented to Chauncey Brewster Tinker. New Haven: Yale University Press; London: Geoffrey Cumberlege; Oxford: Oxford University Press, pp. 139-48.

This important essay argues that "Christian beliefs and feelings" (p. 140) were the driving force behind Fielding's work. States that Fielding was not a Deist; and that, instead, "by the time of The Champion, when he first spoke out in his own voice, Fielding was in all significant points an orthodox believer in the rational supernaturalism of such low-church divines as Tillotson, Clarke, and Barrow, and that he experienced no important changes in belief throughout the remainder of his life" (p. 141). Work then briefly considers Fielding's attitudes toward God, reward, and punishment; Fielding's reading; his Christianity of action; and his Christian social and political analysis. See 1959.A1 for the full elucidation of this position. See also 1901.B4.

1950 A BOOKS

*1 BAKER, SHERIDAN W. "Setting, Character, and Situation in the Plays and Novels of Henry Fielding." Dissertation, California-Berkeley, 1950.

Source: McNamee, 1865-1964, p. 558. See 1967.B4.

*2 FIELDING, HENRY. A história de Tom Jones. Translated by Otávio Mendes Cajado. Porto Alegre: Globo, 261 pp. [1950].

Illustrated Portuguese edition; reissued in São Paulo 1970.

Source: Hugh Amory's working bibliography.

*3 _____. Josip Andrews. Translated by Josip Horvat. Zagreb: Matica Hrvatska, 314 pp.

Croatian translation.

Source: National Union Catalogue: Pre-1956 Imprints. Vol. 171, p. 681.

4 _____. The History of the Adventures of Joseph Andrews and His Friend Mr. Abraham Adams. Introduction by Howard Mumford Jones. Modern Library. New York: Random House, 460 pp. [1950].

Reissue of [1939].A1.

*4a _____. The History of the Adventures of Joseph Andrews and his Friend Mr. Abraham Adams. A Doubleday Dolphin Book. Garden City, N.Y.: Doubleday, 350 pp. [1950?].

Source: National Union Catalogue: Pre-1956 Imprints. Vol. 171, p. 674.

5 _____. The History of Tom Jones A Foundling. Introduction by George Sherburn. Modern Library. New York: Random House, 924 pp.

Appears to reproduce "1750" edition followed by Murphy (1762.A10). The introduction briefly reviews his life, the action of the novels (a fusion of formula, like the lost parent, and observation), the characters (mimetically true and united to the action), and the serious moral intention of the work. A brief bibliography of critical studies is included.

6 _____. The History of Tom Jones A Foundling. Introduction by George Sherburn. Vintage Books. New York: Random House, 924 pp.

Another issue of 1950.A5.

*7 _____. Tom Jones. Translated by Olli Nuorto. Porvoo-Helsinki: Werner Söderström, 548 pp.

An abridged Finnish edition; reissued 1959.
Source: Hugh Amory's working bibliography.

*8 _____. Tom Jones. Translated by Viktor Julow. 2 vols. Budapest: Franklin.

Hungarian translation reissued 1957, 1961, 1970.
Source: Hugh Amory's working bibliography.

*9 GOGGIN, LEO P. "The Development of Fielding's Technique as a Writer of Comedies." Dissertation, Chicago, 1950.

Source: McNamee, 1865-1964, p. 558. See 1952.B4 and B5.

10 HADFIELD, JOHN, ed. Henry Fielding: Scenes and Characters. London: Falcon Press, 96 pp.

Includes a brief biography and an introduction in which Hadfield discusses irony in the novels, the technical skill of Tom Jones, Fielding's reputation, and his place in the development of the novel. Reprints excerpts from Joseph Andrews, Jonathan Wild, Tom Jones, and Amelia.

*11 HOLLOWAY, JEAN M. "Law and Literature in the Age of Enlightenment: Blackstone and Fielding." Dissertation, Texas, 1950.

Source: McNamee, 1865-1964, p. 558.

1950

1950 B SHORTER WRITINGS

1 ANON. "Our Immortal Fielding." Times Literary Supplement (24 Jan.), p. 50.

Reviews 1947.A6 and 1947.A8 and gives a general appreciation of Fielding and his works. He is praised for his craftsmanship, his smiling irony, his robust morality (as opposed to Richardson's "namby-pamby sentimentality"), and his candid wisdom.

2 CRANE, R. S. "The Plot of Tom Jones." Journal of General Education, 4 (Jan.), 112-30.

One of the classic Chicago neo-Aristotelian essays. Defines the nature of mimesis (the imitation of reality) in literary art and argues that plot is the synthesis of action, character, and thought. Crane carefully demonstrates that the comic unity of Tom Jones is embodied in its plot and that the reader's comic pleasure is the result of the working out of the plot. He sees interpolations (Man of the Hill episode, Mrs. Fitzpatrick's narrative, etc.) as flaws, and character, narrative technique, etc. as inventions in the "service of his comic form" (p. 128).

Reprinted 1968.A2, 1972.A8, and 1973.A15. Slightly expanded and reprinted in Critics and Criticism: Ancient and Modern. Edited by R. S. Crane: Chicago: University of Chicago Press, 1952, and in Essays on the Eighteenth-Century Novel. Edited by Robert Spector. Bloomington: Indiana University Press, 1965.

For a reaction to Crane see 1969.B7, 1972.B13, and 1973.B2.

3 ELWES, WINEFRIDE. The Feilding Album. London: Geoffrey Bles, p. 29.

Traces the history of the family to which Fielding is related. Henry is dealt with in a paragraph.

4 HALSBAND, ROBERT. "Fielding: the Hogarth of Fiction." Saturday Review of Literature, 33, no. 39 (30 Sept.), 20-21.

Fielding is praised for his sanity, his readability, his sympathetic humanness, his comic realism (so much better than the "scientific novelists who give you slices of life as unfeelingly as a scientist," p. 21), and his vital "large canvas" fiction.

5 JACKSON, T. A. "Pamela and Tom Jones," in his Old Friends to Keep. London: Lawrence and Wishhart, pp. 39-43.

Compares the middle-class sexual ethics of Pamela with the aristocratic parody of such ethics in Joseph Andrews. Thinks Tom Jones and Amelia reflect this same easy aristocratic morality.

6 KERMODE, FRANK. "Richardson and Fielding." Cambridge Journal, 4:106-14.

Begins by comparing Fielding's reputation with Richardson's, claiming that until Coleridge, Fielding's reputation suffered from the "English custom of naturalizing the desirable but plainly immoral by secreting it in the very act of condemning it" (p. 66). Coleridge asserted Fielding's "moral superiority in a contest where his technical superiority had already been conceded" (p. 68). Kermode then briefly compares the way in which "Fielding the moralist completely evades the only genuinely crucial test that confronts his hero [Tom] as a moral being" and Richardson penetrates "to the level of archetypal integration of character and motive" (pp. 70-71) with Lovelace. For him, Richardson has a unity of method quite different from the simple, allegorical duality (found in the dissociation of conduct and character) in Fielding. Kermode thus challenges the old notion of Fielding's technical superiority and thinks that the earliest critics who associated Richardson with Shakespeare were right.

Reprinted 1965.B18, 1972.A8. For a different view see 1894.B2, 1966.B1, 1967.B27.

7 MAXWELL, J. C. "Fielding and 'Shamela.'" Notes and Queries, 195 (1 April), 152.

Adds bibliography on the Fielding-Shamela debate to his earlier note (1948.B6).

8 PETERSON, WILLIAM. "Satire in Fielding's An Interlude Between Jupiter, Juno, Apollo, and Mercury." Modern Language Notes, 65, no. 3 (March), 200-202.

Suggests various political parallels (particularly Queen Caroline and Walpole) to the events in this burlesque of Greek mythology.

9 PRITCHETT, V. S. "Our First Comic Novelist." Listener, 43, no. 1097 (2 Feb.), 203-204.

After briefly setting out the usual case for rejecting Fielding because of his downright simplicity, Pritchett discusses the reforming zeal of eighteenth-century novelists and particularly Fielding's intelligent attack on moral hypocrisy. He sees Fielding as "always falling into percipience and charity" (p. 204) rather than cynicism, despite his wide knowledge of the world. Pritchett calls Amelia a restful novel after a life of brilliant intellectual satire, a novel in which Fielding creates one of the first studies in domestic and psychological realism in English.

*10 SHOUP, LOUISE. "The Use of the Social Gathering as a Structural Device in the Novels of Richardson, Fielding, Smollett, and Sterne." Dissertation, Stanford, 1950.
Source: T. Humphrey, p. 267. See Stanford University Abstracts of Dissertations, 25. Stanford: Stanford University Press, 1950, pp. 139-41.

11 WILLY, MARGARET. "Portrait of a Man: Henry Fielding," in her Life Was Their Cry. London: Evans Brothers, pp. 98-152.
Reviewed TLS, 5 May 1950, p. 274.
A popular and old-fashioned critical biography that relies heavily on Arthur Murphy (1762.A10) corrected by Dobson (1883.A1). Her critical opinions appear to come from Dobson and Lowell (1887.B1). Chiefly contrasts Fielding with Richardson, preferring Fielding's "burlier masculinity" (p. 139) and commending him for his mimetic qualities (putting life into the novel).

1951 A BOOKS

1 FIELDING, HENRY. The Adventures of Joseph Andrews. World Classics. London, New York, Toronto: G. Cumberlege, Oxford University Press, 406 pp.
Reprint of 1929.A3.

*2 _____. Tom Jones. Translated by Natsuo Shumuta. 4 vols. Tokyo: Iwanami shoten.
Vols. 1-2 of this annotated Japanese translation were issued in 1951, vol. 3 in 1952, vol. 4 in 1955. It had gone through a third printing by 1975.
Source: Hugh Amory's working bibliography.

3 ROTHSCHILD, NATHANIEL M. V. The History of Tom Jones, A Changeling. Cambridge: Privately printed for Lord Rothschild, 160 pp.
The report of a lawsuit brought by Lord Rothschild against G. Wells and O. D. Young, arising from the sale of a copy of the first edition of Tom Jones.

1951 B SHORTER WRITINGS

1 DAVIS, JOE LEE. "Criticism and Parody." Thought: Fordham University Quarterly, 26: 180-204.

In a study of parody as "creative and cognitive criticism" (p. 181) that ranges from parodies of Richardson to parodies of Hemingway, Fielding's Shamela is briefly described, and Joseph Andrews is mentioned.

2 GREENE, GRAHAM. "Fielding and Sterne," in his The Lost Childhood and Other Essays. London: Eyre & Spottiswoode, pp. 58-65.

Reprint of 1937.B4. Later reprinted in his Collected Essays. New York: Viking, 1969.

3 KETTLE, ARNOLD. "Richardson, Fielding, Sterne," in his An Introduction to the Novel. Hutchinson University Library. Edited by Basil Willey. Vol. 1. London: Hutchinson, pp. 45-51, 71-81, passim.

Reviewed by S. Monod, EA, 5 (1952), 271; NCF, 7 (1952), 231-32; TLS, 16 May 1952, p. 330.

Discusses Joseph Andrews (and Shamela), Tom Jones, and Jonathan Wild. Thinks Joseph Andrews an anti-romance with a journey motif, raised above the level of parody because of Parson Adams (the defender of the impracticable ideal). He briefly discusses Fielding's attack on hypocrisy (often linked with class) and the thematic justification for the interpolated tales. Discusses Fielding's skeptical optimism and the limitations of Tom Jones (too much plot, too many flat characters), as well as its mimetic strength ("a panoramic commentary on England in 1745," p. 78) and its thematic unity (the symbolic struggle of the naturally good man Tom for a happy union of the heart). Calls Jonathan Wild a moral fable (not a picaresque novel) that in its antithesis between goodness and greatness satirizes "almost every aspect of bourgeois society" (p. 48). Its weakness is the passive nature of the good figure. "Heartfree is not vital because Fielding castrates him as a moral agent and yet at the same time makes him bear the positive values of the fable on his shoulders" (p. 49). While Kettle sees in Fielding common sense, decency, and a strong moral concern, he thinks Fielding shallow, taking a comic survey of life with a "simple confidence in the value of the heart" (p. 80) and without any of Richardson's intensity.

Often reprinted. Reprinted in part 1970.A4 and 1972.A8.

1951

4 MOORE, R. E. "Dr. Johnson on Fielding and Richardson." Publications of the Modern Language Association, 66, no. 2 (March), 162-81.

Sets out to illustrate "that Fielding's opinions on literature are constantly and consistently reflected in Johnson, and that Fielding's novels are in large measure splendid illustrations of many of Johnson's most deeply felt principles, better illustrations by far than the novels of Richardson" (pp. 163-64). Moore describes Johnson's "perceptive" approval of Richardson and illustrates the similarities between Fielding and Richardson, which invalidate Johnson's criticism of Fielding. Moore then mentions qualities Johnson should have admired in Fielding (his forthrightness, his distinctions in sexual morality, his use of the epic, his learning) and analyzes Rambler 4 (Johnson's essay on the novel), comparing it to the introduction to Book 9 of Tom Jones. He concludes that Johnson may have missed Fielding's serious moral purpose because of Fielding's "flip, irreverent irony" (p. 180). See 1971.B18 and 1976.B7.

5 NEILL, S. DIANA. "The Broad Highway," in her A Short History of the English Novel. London, New York, Melbourne, etc.: Jarrolds, pp. 57-65.

Retells the stories of Joseph Andrews, Tom Jones, and Amelia, contrasting Fielding's comic characters and broad cross-sections of society with Richardson's psychological realism. Thinks that in Amelia Fielding, too, looked "at life through the tears of one who feels" (p. 64).

6 NEWTON, WILLIAM. The Poetics of the Rogue-Ruined. Bulletin of the Oklahoma State University of Agriculture and Applied Science. Monographs in the Humanities, Social and Biological Sciences. Humanities Series. No. 1. Stillwater, Oklahoma: Oklahoma A & M College Press, 15 pp.

By examining Jonathan Wild, Thackeray's Barry Lyndon, and Ring Lardner's "Haircut", Newton defines a new genre which "represents an action of mounting seriousness in which the protagonist, an unsympathetic and morally bad man, is taken from undeserved good fortune to deserved misfortune, the mild indignation aroused by the complication being allayed by the satisfaction produced by the resolution" (p. 7). He also examines the narrator's role (controlled irony) in such fiction as well as the limits of plot and character (what the protagonist may do and be; he may not, for instance, be too clever a villain).

7 SHEPPERSON, ARCHIBALD B. "Fielding on Liberty and Democracy." English Studies in Honor of James Southall Wilson. University of Virginia Studies, 5:265-75.

Studies Fielding's works (especially legal and sociological pamphlets like the Charge Delivered to the Grand Jury) to ascertain his attitude toward liberty and democracy. Concludes that he believed in constitutional monarchy, political evolution, and reform (over which he had fought with Walpole). He believed in rule by those of talent and ability of whatever class, rather than republicanism, which he took to mean leveling. His political doctrine grew out of his Christianity, which saw men as morally mixed but equal before God. Despite his conservatism, Fielding is seen by Shepperson as in essential agreement with much in the American Declaration of Independence. For another view, see 1966.A26.

8 SHIPLEY, JOHN B. "Fielding and 'The Plain Truth' (1740)." Notes and Queries, 196 (22 Dec.), 561-62.

This pamphlet is redated and ascribed to Fielding.

1952 A BOOKS

1 DUDDEN, F. HOMES. Henry Fielding: His Life, Works, and Times. 2 vols. Oxford: Clarendon Press, 1192 pp.

Reviewed by James L. Clifford, NYTBR, Jan. 1953, p. 4; Cyril Connolly, Sunday Times (London), 23 Nov. 1952, p. 5; Aurélien Digeon, EA, 7 (1954), 402-404; Delancey Ferguson, NYHTB, 18 Jan. 1954, p. 4; Robert Halsband, Sat Rev., 7 March 1953, p. 23; George Sherburn, SR, 61 (1953), 316-21; J. M. S. Tompkins, RES, 5 (1954), 302-305; R. W., TC, 156 (1954), 382-83; Can. F., 33 (1953), 42; Listener, 49 (1954); TLS, 23 Jan. 1953, p. 56.

Volume 1 is an account of Fielding's life and works through his second marriage and The Jacobite's Journal, including three chapters on Joseph Andrews and two on Jonathan Wild. Volume 2, which includes five chapters on Tom Jones and three on Amelia, concludes the account of his life and works, as well as briefly looking at "the fortunes of Fielding's family." An appendix sums up his historical reputation and provides a chronological bibliography of Fielding's works and a select bibliography of criticism and background studies. In a chapter on "Henry Fielding: The Man and The Artist," Dudden sums up Fielding's aesthetic achievement under nine headings: his realism, his reflection of contemporary manners, his lively characters, his careful construction, his method of "direct narration," his humor, his pathos, his didacticism, and his careful but easy style. Although Dudden aims to write "a fresh [biographical] study, in the light of the evidence at present available" (I, v), he often adds little to Cross (1918.A1) and on occasion slights the evidence available. For instance, he ignores Work's essay (1949.B6) on Fielding's latitudinarian Christianity, and argues that Shaftesbury was the major influence on his ethical doctrine.

The book is easy to use because of Dudden's method of systematically listing and categorizing.

*2 FIELDING, HENRY. The History of Tom Jones, a Foundling. Illustrations by T. M. Cleland and introduction by Louis Kronenberger. 2 vols. New York: Limited Editions Club.

Reissue of 1952.A3.

Source: National Union Catalogue: Pre-1956 Imprints. Vol. 171, p. 689.

3 _____. The History of Tom Jones, A Foundling. Introduction by Louis Kronenberger and illustrations by T. M. Cleland. New York: Heritage Press, 798 pp.

A brief bibliographical note by A. W. Pollard describes the various states of the text and indicates that this edition follows the "1750" printing, also followed by Murphy (1762.A10). Kronenberger's brief note commends its mimetic qualities, its male lustiness, its simplicity; he avoids assessing it critically. However, he doesn't think Fielding a Tolstoy and is sorry that the Tom-Blifil contrast has become a cliché of English fiction.

*4 FREY, BERNHARD. "Shaftesbury und Henry Fielding: Shaftesburys Ethik und Humorgedanke in Henry Fieldings komischem Epos." Dissertation, Bern, 1952.

In German.

Source: T. Humphrey, p. 257.

*5 ISER, WOLFGANG. "Die Weltanschauung Henry Fieldings." Dissertation, Heidelberg, 1952.

In German. See 1952.A6.

Source: McNamee, 1865-1964, p. 558.

6 _____. Die Weltanschauung Henry Fieldings. Buchreihe der Anglia, Zeitschrift für englische Philologie. Vol. 3. Tübingen: Max Neimeyer, 320 pp.

Reviewed by E. A. J. Honigmann, MLR, 49 (1954), 114; Siegfried Korminger, Anglin, 73 (1955), 532-33; Henri A.

Talon, EA, 15 (1962), 189-90; J. M. S. Tompkins, RES, n.s. 5 (1954), 302-305.

Provides a survey of current and historical critical opinion about Fielding and then attempts to discern Fielding's philosophy of life (Weltanschauung). Considers events in Fielding's life and Enlightenment attitudes (an "anthropocentric" period concerned with the average man) that determine his balanced virtue (a combination of spirituality and sensuality). Iser then surveys the development of Fielding's philosophy, beginning with his plays and early prose works (including Jonathan Wild and The Champion), through its full expression in Joseph Andrews and Tom Jones, to the waning of his comic spirit in Amelia. Opposes Joesten's (1932.A11) view of Fielding's moral position. In German. See 1959.A1.

*7 SHEA, BERNARD D. "Classical Learning in the Novels of Henry Fielding." Dissertation, Harvard, 1952.

Source: McNamee, 1865-1964, pp. 558-59.

1952 B SHORTER WRITINGS

1 ANTAL, F. "The Moral Purpose of Hogarth's Art." Journal of the Warburg and Courtauld Institutes, 15, nos. 3 and 4: 169-97.

Studies the relationship between Hogarth and Fielding, and in particular Fielding's social and literary ideas "for the light they throw upon those of the artist" (p. 169). Antal begins with an analysis of the evolution of the serious moral intention in both artists, from the "serious moral kernel" (p. 178) in Fielding's plays and Hogarth's early paintings to "the last phase when their collaboration was closest and Hogarth was contributing to the vigorous efforts of Fielding, the magistrate, to reduce criminality by social and penal reforms" (p. 185). He also examines parallels in their political and religious views and in their technique for disseminating these views (finding Hogarth's engravings like Fielding's inexpensive pamphlets).

2 BOOTH, WAYNE C. "The Self-Conscious Narrator in Comic Fiction before Tristram Shandy." Publications of the Modern Language Association, 67, no. 2 (March), 163-85.

Argues that Fielding's narrator, who "indulges in 'rhetorical' commentary on the characters or events of his story, in order to induce appropriate attitudes in the reader" (p. 164), is "far beyond anything to be found in Cervantes" (p. 175), although very like Marivaux, and close

to Sterne's self-conscious narrator. He then discusses several kinds of Fielding intrusions (those that characterize the reader, those that insure comic response, those that discuss fictional procedure) and compares them to Sterne's. See 1963.B5, 1967.B18, 1974.B28.
Reprinted 1972.A8.

3 BROGAN, HOWARD O. "Fiction and Philosophy in the Education of Tom Jones, Tristram Shandy, and Richard Feverel." College English, 14, no. 3 (Dec.), 144-49.
Studies the "continuing tradition of educational theory" (p. 144) in these three novels. He sees both Fielding and Sterne dramatizing Locke's theory of education but less certain than Locke that this will "solve the problems of growing up" (p. 146). He argues that Fielding adds chance and will to the educational process; "the seeds of virtue can be planted by education but they must grow up by themselves, running such natural hazards as fall to their lot" (p. 146). For both Fielding and Sterne, the reasonable life is a mixture of thought and feeling, which is learned by human association. Meredith follows the educational theory of Spencer. All of the novelists take sex into account, as neither educational theorist does. See 1968.B17 and 1974.B11.

4 GOGGIN, L. P. "Development of Techniques in Fielding's Comedies." Publications of the Modern Language Association, 67, no. 5 (Sept.), 769-81.
An examination of Fielding's eight comic plays (the farces and satires are dismissed as irrelevant) in order to demonstrate that in them Fielding developed techniques that served him as a writer of fiction. Goggin examines his development of the arts of "indirect representation," "characterization," and "dialogue" (p. 773), concluding that Fielding steadily learned to write with greater "verisimilitude, integration, and vividness" (p. 781).
For a different view of the importance of Fielding's farces, see 1943.B6 and 1946.B3. See dissertation 1950.A9.

5 _____. "Fielding and the Select Comedies of Mr. de Molière." Philological Quarterly, 31, no. 3 (July), 344-50.
Compares Fielding's adaptations from Molière (The Mock Doctor and The Miser) with a translation of Molière's Select Comedies and concludes that Fielding adapted The Mock Doctor from the French and recommended the Select Comedies (probably by Henry Baker and James Miller) because his publisher John Watts asked him to. For The Miser, he probably worked with both the French play by Molière

(Le Médecin malgré lui) and the translation in the Select Comedies. See dissertation 1950.A9.

6 KNAPP, LEWIS M. "Fielding's Dinners with Dodington, 1750-1752." Notes and Queries, 197 (20 Dec.), 565-66.
Records Fielding's intimacy with George Babb Dodington, whose Diary records that Fielding dined with him ten times between 1750 and 1752.

7 LONGHURST, JOHN E. "Fielding and Swift in Mexico." Modern Language Journal, 36, no. 4 (April), 186-87.
Reprints a report on Tom Jones prepared for the Mexican inquisition in 1803. The friar who examined it found nothing sexually explicit enough to object to, but he had several theological objections, one about the nature of providence.

8 LYND, ROBERT. "Henry Fielding," in his Books and Writers. London: J. M. Dent & Sons, pp. 67-71.
Worries about the coarse touches in Fielding and the partly legitimate Victorian objections to Tom Jones. Concludes that "only a man of a twisted mind could regard Fielding as a corrupter of human nature . . . he was . . . a preacher of the more pedestrian and attainable virtues" (p. 71).

9 MASENGILL, JEANNE A. "Variant Forms of Fielding's Coffee-House Politican." Studies in Bibliography, 5:178-83.
An exact bibliographical description of the three issues (the last in two states) of the London 1730 edition. Masengill then speculates about which gatherings were printed in the spring (23 June) and used for the reissue of the play in December, and which gatherings were reprinted from altered standing type.

10 PRAZ, MARIO. "Hogarth e Fielding." Saggi di Letteratura e d'Arte. Milano: La Casa della Fama, pp. 206-211.
Reviewed TLS, 5 Sept. 1952, p. 582.
Compares Hogarth and Fielding as founders of traditions, reformers, and innovators. Also suggests that they shared a deep humanistic sense. In Italian.

11 ROBERTSON, OLIVIA. "Fielding as Satirist." Contemporary Review, 181, no. 1034 (Feb.), 120-24.
Describes Fielding's A Journey from this World to the Next and isolates several of "Julian's narrations of his various metempsychoses" (p. 122) for discussion. Robertson thinks that his portrait of Anna Boleyn "shows an understanding of a woman's mind not found in his other

works"; she is complex enough to "remind one of a Russian heroine" (p. 123). Generally the work has "virtuosity and cynicism worthy of Voltaire," although Fielding never loses the "good nature of Tom Jones" (p. 122).

*12 SHUMUDA, NATSUO. "Fielding's Daughter." Rising Generation, 98:157-59.
Source: 1976.B15 (p. 206).

13 TODD, WILLIAM B. "Press Figures." Library, 5th. series, 7, also called Transactions of the Bibliographical Society, 3rd. series, 7 (Dec.), 283.
Comments on Andrew Miller's "puff" of Amelia (claiming that four presses had to be used to satisfy the demand). Using press figures, Todd attempts to reconstruct the printing. See 1921.B2 and 1963.B19.

1953 A BOOKS

1 FIELDING, HENRY. An Apology for the Life of Mrs. Shamela Andrews. Edited by Sheridan W. Baker. Berkeley and Los Angeles: University of California Press; London: Cambridge University Press, 1954, 122 pp.
Reviewed by F. Wölcken, Archiv, 191 (1954), 230; Charles B. Woods, PQ, 33 (1954), 272-74; TLS, 17 Sept. 1954, p. 592.
The introduction briefly reviews the evidence for Fielding's authorship, the multiple targets of the satire (the Methodists, Colley Cibber, Conyers Middleton, and Robert Walpole), and Fielding's serious moral parodic criticism of Richardson. The text is a transcription of the first edition (4 April 1741), corrected from the second (which may have been set from a marked copy of the first edition corrected by Fielding).

*2 _____. Przygody Józefa Andrewsa. Translated by Maria Kornilowicz. Warsaw: Panstwowy Instytut Wydawniczy. [1953].
Polish translation.
Source: National Union Catalogue: Pre-1956 Imprints. Vol. 171, p. 681.

3 _____. The History of the Adventures of Joseph Andrews and his Friend Mr. Abraham Adams. Wood engravings by Derrick Harris. Westminster: The Folio Society, 322 pp.
A brief foreword by "C. D. W." on Fielding's career and on the parody in Joseph Andrews. No indication of copy text.

4 _____. The History of Tom Jones, A Foundling. Introduction by Malcolm Elwin. Macdonald Illustrated Classics. London: Macdonald, 848 pp.
"Apart from the correction of certain inconsistencies, this Edition reproduces the Text of the Second Edition of 1749." In his "biographical and bibliographical note" Elwin briefly reviews Fielding's career, as well as answering Johnson's criticism and the charge of immorality leveled at the book.

*5 MILLER, HENRY K. "Fielding's Miscellanies: A Study of Volumes I and II of Miscellanies, by Henry Fielding Esq.; in Three Volumes, 1743." Dissertation, Princeton, 1953.
See 1961.A13 and 1972.A3.
Source: McNamee, 1865-1964, p. 559.

*6 TOWERS, AUGUSTUS R. "An Introduction and Annotations for a Critical Edition of Amelia." Dissertation, Princeton, 1953.
"Attempts to provide the scholarly material for a critical edition of Amelia" by setting the novel in Fielding's life and in its age (intellectual, social, and literary), by providing the contemporary reaction and a bibliographical description of the various editions.
Source: Dissertation Abstracts, 14, no. 2 (1954), 351-52.

1953 B SHORTER WRITINGS

1 BAKER, SHERIDAN W. "Fielding and 'Stultus versus Sapientem.'" Notes and Queries, 198 (Aug.), 343-44.
Demonstrates that Stultus versus Sapientem is not by Fielding and, incidentally, describes Fielding's attitude toward the Irish. See 1936.B1.

2 BOAS, FREDERICK S. "Henry Fielding," in his An Introduction to Eighteenth-Century Drama: 1700-1780. Oxford: Clarendon Press, pp. 220-38.
Reviewed by William W. Appleton, Sat. Rev., 20 June 1953, p. 23; J. Hamard, EA, 6 (1954), 361-62; Allardyce Nicoll, MLR, 49 (1954), 70-71; A. H. Scouten, MLN, 69 (1954), 524-26; Listener, 49 (1954), 733; N&Q, 198 (1954), 456; TLS, 20 March 1953, p. 188.
Reviews Fielding's dramatic career, briefly outlining the basic situation in fourteen of his plays. Asserts that Fielding's strength lies in burlesque; discusses his topical satire (literary and especially political); and

compares several characters in his plays to characters in his novels.

Reprinted by Clarendon Press in 1965.

*3 CROCKETT, HAROLD K. "The Picaresque Tradition in English Fiction to 1770: A Study of Popular Backgrounds, with Particular Attention to Fielding and Smollett." Dissertation, Illinois, 1953.

Illustrates the connection between popular realism, the native jest-books, criminal biographies, the anti-hero, etc. and the eighteenth-century picaresque, particularly in Fielding and Smollett.

Source: Dissertation Abstracts, 14, no. 2 (1954), 355-56.

4 MALONE, KEMP. "Fielding's Tom Jones," in Literary Masterpieces of the Western World. Edited by Francis H. Horn. Baltimore: Johns Hopkins Press, pp. 242-55.

Reviews the evolution of the novel from the medieval exemplum and briefly sets Tom Jones in this "romance" tradition (with its fairy tale plots, characterizing names, and idealized characters). He also considers the novel as a reflection of the concerns of Fielding's day (in architecture and landscape, in medicine, etc.) and as an expression of Fielding's satiric reforming nature.

5 PICKLE, PEREGRINE. "Some Pickwick Queries." Notes and Queries, 198 (April), 181.

Asks about a proverb said to come from Fielding.

6 PRICE, LAWRENCE MARSDEN. "Fielding and the Realistic Novel," in his English Literature in Germany. University of California Publications in Modern Philology. Vol. 37. Berkeley and Los Angeles: University of California Press, pp. 180-92.

Reviewed by Hermann Heuer, Archiv 192 (1956), 73-74; K. W. Maurer, MLR, 50 (1956), 76; Wolfgang Paulsen, JEGP, 54 (1955), 140-41; Heinrich Schneider, MLN, 70 (1955), 144-47; L. L. Schücking, GRM, 36 (1956), 179-82; H. Sparnaay, Neophilologus, 38 (1954), 235-36; T. C. van Stockum, E. Studies, 35 (1954), 132-34; J. Weisgerber, RBPH, 32 (1954), 2-3; R. F. Wilkie, MLQ, 15 (1954), 86-87.

Studies Fielding's influence in Germany. According to Price, until about 1764 German critics failed to grasp the fundamental difference between Fielding and Richardson (which he identifies as the difference between the developing and the perfect character). Even then, Lessing appeared quite insensitive to Fielding's style. Argues that the "Richardson-Fielding contest was reenacted in Wieland's person" (p. 183), and through Wieland, Fielding's style and method of character development came to be increasingly important, ultimately influencing Goethe.

7 SHIPLEY, J. B. "Essays from Fielding's Champion." Notes and Queries, 198 (Nov.), 468-69.

Locates seven essays from The Champion, none by Fielding. See also 1912.B6, B9, 1913.B5, B8, B9, 1920. B11, 1955.B8-10, 1963.B17.

8 _____. "On the Date of the 'Champion.'" Notes and Queries, 198 (Oct.), 441.

A brief bibliographical history of The Champion, noting Fielding's connection with it. See 1953.B7 and 1962.B6.

9 SMITH, DANE F. The Critics in the Audience of the London Theatre from Buckingham to Sheridan: A Study of Neoclassicism in the Playhouse, 1671-1779. University of New Mexico Publications in Language and Literature, no. 12. Albuquerque: University of New Mexico Press, passim.

Reviewed by George Winchester Stone, MLN, 69 (1954), 375-76.

Briefly discusses critics and audience in nine of Fielding's burlesque and satiric plays, suggesting that Fielding is "pre-eminently representative of the authors of his age" (p. 65) and that he "was the most conspicuous figure in theatrical London" (p. 70).

10 SPILKA, MARK. "Comic Resolution in Fielding's Joseph Andrews." College English, 15, no. 1 (Oct.), 11-19.

Argues that "the night adventures at Booby Hall" (p. 11) act as an emotional purgation for the tension created by the incest theme and for the novel as a whole. Spilka contends that Joseph, Fanny, and Adams are "touchstones" of virtue and goodness whereby we are able to judge the vanity and hypocrisy of the other characters. Fielding involves these three at Booby Hall in an adventure built on the central moral problem of the book, the parody of the preservation of chastity. For Spilka, Adams is the most comically complex character; thus he turns his attention to him, describing Adams' adventures in bed. Spilka sees him as an archetypal symbol of naked virtue whom Fielding sends from bed to bed to "put a kind of comic blessing upon the novel; he has resolved the major themes

and passions through benevolent humor" (p. 19). See 1969.B27.
Reprinted 1962.A12, 1965.B18, 1972.A2 and A8.

11 TODD, WILLIAM B. "Three Notes on Fielding." Papers of the Bibliographical Society of America, 47 (first quarter), 70-75.
Describes the two carelessly printed editions of An Apology for the Life of Mr. T[heophilus] C[ibber] (1740), indicating errors and revisions. Offers bibliographical evidence that A Dialogue between a Gentleman of London . . . and an Honest Alderman of the Country Party (1747) was rushed through the press. Challenges the time-honored notion that Amelia was given two "editions" in December 1751. Press figures suggest that the second edition "is a venerable ghost" (p. 74), and the entry in Strahan's (the printer's) ledger suggests only the abortive beginning of a "second" edition.

12 VAN GHENT, DOROTHY. "On Tom Jones," in her The English Novel: Form and Function. New York: Holt, Rinehart and Winston, pp. 65-81.
Reviewed Nation, 177 (1953), 335.
Argues that while Tom Jones is a complex book, "its complexities are within the immediate view of reason" and that it is characterized "by a systematic organization of contrasts" (p. 65) in idea, character, scene, language and even in form (between the creator and his creation). This wide-ranging discussion touches on, among other things, "human nature," as defined in Tom Jones, on fortune, on the character of Allworthy, and on the architecture of the novel. The discussion is confined to Tom Jones.
Reprinted New York: Harper, 1961, and 1970.A4 and 1972.A8.

1954 A BOOKS

1 BUTT, JOHN. Fielding. Writers and Their Work, No. 57. Toronto: Longmans, Green, pp. 36.
Reviewed by J. Hamard, LM, 49 (1955), 179; TLS, 27 May 1955, p. 290.
Briefly describes the traditions (ancient and contemporary) from which the novel grew; Fielding's early life and theatrical and journalistic preparation for writing his novels; the conflict between "being" and "seeming" and the parody of Pamela in Joseph Andrews; the structure and

morality of Tom Jones; Amelia as a modified and Christianized epic and as a study of marriage; and Fielding's social service (as satirist and magistrate) and his final work (Journal of a Voyage to Lisbon). Includes a select bibliography of works by and about Fielding.

*2 COLEY, WILLIAM B. "Fielding's Comic: A Study of the Relation between Wit and Seriousness in a Comic Augustan." Dissertation, Yale, 1954.
Source: McNamee, 1865-1964, p. 559. See Dissertation Abstracts, 30 (1970), 4403.A. See also 1959. B8.

*3 DEBRUYN, JOHN R. "Tom Jones: A Genealogical Approach, Fielding's Use of Type Characters in Tom Jones." Dissertation, New York, 1954.
Describes the conventional elements in Tom, Partridge, Blifil, Sophia, Squire Western, Mrs. Western, and Lady Bellaston. Fielding had used most of these types before.
Source: Dissertation Abstracts, 15, no. 6 (1955), 1070.

*4 ELISTRATOVA, ANNA A. Fil'ding, Kritiko-biografičheskij Očherk. Moscow: Gos. Izd-vo khudozh, Lit-ry, 97 pp.
In Russian. "Fielding: a critical-biographical essay."
Source: T. Humphrey, p. 230.

*5 FIELDING, HENRY. Chung-kuo hsien-tai ch 'u-pan shih liao. Edited by Ching-lu Chang. 4 vols. Peking: [?]. (1954-59)
Chinese translation of Tom Jones.
Source: Hugh Amory's working bibliography (transliterated by Bonnie McDougall of the East Asian Institute).

6 _____. Komedii. Vstup. stat'ia i obshchaia red. Moscow: Gos. izd-vo "Iskusstvo," 410 pp.
Introduction by M. P. Alekseev and translated by P. V. Melkova. Russian translations of The Temple Beau, The Coffee-House Politician, Don Quixote in England, Pasquin, and The Historical Register.

7 _____. The History of the Adventures of Joseph Andrews and His Friend Mr. Abraham Adams. Introduction by P. N. Furbank. Harmondsworth, Middlesex: Penguin Books, 352 pp.
Brief introduction discusses the myth of Fielding; the Richardson-Fielding antagonism in Pamela, Shamela, Joseph Andrews; Fielding as a satirist attacking hard-heartedness; and the kind ridicule directed at Adams. No indication of copy text.

1954

8 _____. Toma Dzhonsa naĭdenysha. 2 vols. Moscow: Khudozhestvennoĭ Literatury, 1613 (786 & 827) pp.
Russian Tom Jones, translated by "selected educators."

*9 _____. Tom Jones. Translated by Decio Pettoello. 2 vols. Torino: Unione tipog. editr. torinese.
Italian translation.
Source: Hugh Amory's working bibliography.

*10 _____. Tom Jones. Translated by Mário Domingues. Lisbon: Romano Torres, 498 pp. [1954].
Portuguese translation.
Source: Hugh Amory's working bibliography.

11 GOLOVNI͡A, IRINA V. Velikĭ prosvetitel' i gumanist: Genri Fil'ding. Vsesoi͡uznoe obshestvo no rasprostraneni͡iu politicheskikh i nauchnykh znaniĭ. Series 6, no. 21. Moscow, Znanie, 32 pp.
In Russian. "The great representative of the Enlightenment and humanist, Henry Fielding." A brief review of Fielding's career.

*12 GOYNE, ARLIE V. "Defoe and Fielding: A Study of the Development of English Novel Technique." Dissertation, Texas, 1954.
Source: McNamee, 1865-1964, p. 559.

*13 GREASON, A. LEROY. "The Political Journals of Henry Fielding." Dissertation, Harvard, 1954.
See 1954.B7 and 1958.B8.
Source: McNamee, 1865-1964, p. 559.

*14 LEVIDOVA, I. M. Genri Fil-ding: bio-bibliograficheskŭ ukazatel'. Moscow: Vsesoi͡uznai͡a gosudarstvennai͡a biblioteka inostrannoĭ literatury, 28 pp.
"Henry Fielding: Biobibliographical Index."
Part of a Russian series on "progressive writers of capitalist countries."
Source: MHRA, 31 (1953-54), 246.

1954 B SHORTER WRITINGS

1 ALLEN, WALTER. "Fielding," in his The English Novel: A Short Critical History. London: J. M. Dent & Sons, pp. 50-63, passim.
Reviewed by Roger Becket, NYHTB, 7 Aug. 1955, p. 3; Henry T. Moore, NYTBR, 7 Aug. 1955, p. 4; W. R., Obs., 16

Jan. 1955, p. 9; H. C. Webster, Sat. Rev., 10 Sept. 1955, pp. 39-40; NY, 20 Aug. 1955, p. 96.

In this history of prose fiction from the Satyricon (but especially from the Elizabethans) to Joyce and Lawrence, Allen asserts that "the main tradition of the English novel as it was commonly written until well into the second half of the nineteenth century, derives from Henry Fielding" (p. 50). He calls Fielding's "the most powerful artistic expression of the social conscience of the age" (p. 51). Discusses irony, the vitality of his characters, his moral accuracy and honesty, his technical innovations, and his borrowings in Joseph Andrews, Tom Jones, Jonathan Wild, and Amelia.

Often reprinted (11 editions by 1975).

2 ANON. "Henry Fielding." Times Literary Supplement (8 Oct.), p. 641.

A commemoration of his death. Fielding is described as squandering "not only his health but his talents." His irony is said to be only "one layer deep" and his burlesque habit to be unfortunate. Only Tom Jones is praised as "pointed to the road--the road of moral exploration, against an accepted social background, of actions and their consequences--that the major English novelists were to follow."

3 BLOOM, EDWARD A. "The Paradox of Samuel Boyse." Notes and Queries, 199 (April), 163-65.

Fielding praises Boyse's poem "The Deity" (1740) in The Champion and quotes it in Tom Jones.

4 DAIX, PIERRE. "Une Angleterre que Voltaire n'a pas connue: de L'opéra de quat' sous, par John Gay (1728), à Amelia, roman par Henry Fielding (1751)." Lettres françaises, no. 536 (30 Sept. - 7 Oct.), pp. 1-4.

Compares the England of Gay and Fielding with the France of Montesquieu, Voltaire, and Diderot. England was less repressive, but not as perfect as Voltaire makes it seem (Voltaire does not mention political plays like Fielding's Coffee-House Politician). The low life depicted in English literature (Defoe and Fielding) and ignored by Voltaire was not dramatized in France until the nineteenth century. Finally asserts that Fielding's optimism is that of a militant political fighter. In French.

This issue is a special number for "le 200e anniversaire de la mort de Henry Fielding."

1954

5 ELISTRATOVA, ANNA. "Henry Fielding." Soviet Literature, 10 (Oct.), 161-66.

Reviews Russian interest in Fielding's work, beginning in the 1770s. Describes Fielding's "broad canvases" and "unaffected sympathy for the common people" which spurred on "the fight for a democratic national culture" (p. 163) in the nineteenth century. Attacks "bourgeois literary criticism [that] has tried hard to push Fielding back into the past" (p. 164) and praises the progressive English writers (Fox, Jackson, and Kettle) who keep Fielding alive. Fielding is particularly praised for keeping "Man, common earthy Man with his earthy interests, needs and passions," at the center of his "working philosophy" (p. 166). See 1966.A26.

6 ENGLAND, DENZIL. "Henry Fielding." Contemporary Review, 186, no. 1066 (Oct.), 218-23.

Briefly reviews Fielding's career as a dramatist and novelist. Thinks Fielding's dramas innovative and that his novels (the efforts of a "Micawberish" "big tavern-haunting scholar and wit," p. 221) lack poetry but have a great deal of carefully observed life (Fielding is a "robust" moralist). A very old-fashioned essay that appears to rely heavily on Murphy (1762.A10) and Taine (1863.B4).

7 GREASON, A. LEROY. "Fielding's An Address to the Electors of Great Britain." Philological Quarterly, 33, no. 3 (July), 347-52.

Argues that An Address first appeared in The Champion (a new publication date is assigned to the pamphlet) and that (on the strength of style and content) it is probably by Fielding, although he did not sign it with a "C" or "L." See 1925.B5, 1957.B1, and dissertation 1954.A13.

*8 KAGARLIȂSKIĬ, IȂ. "Fil'ding-dramaturg: K 200-letiiu co Inia smerti pisateliia." Teatr, no. 10, pp. 144-50.

"Fielding-dramatist: on the 200th anniversary of the death of the writer." Russian article.

Source: T. Humphrey, p. 231 and MHRA, 31 (1953-54), 276.

9 _____. "Genri Fil'ding: K 200-letiiu so dnia smerti." Ogonek, no. 40, pp. 29-30.

"Henry Fielding: on the 200th anniversary of his death." Article in a popular Russian magazine.

10 MAUGHAM, WILLIAM SOMERSET. "Henry Fielding and Tom Jones," in his Ten Novels and Their Authors. London, Toronto, Melbourne: William Heinemann, pp. 21-43.

A slight reworking of 1947.B3.

Reprinted by John C. Winston (Philadelphia and Toronto) as Great Novelists and Their Novels in 1948, and by Doubleday as The Art of Fiction in 1955.

11 MERLE, ROBERT. "Le Premier roman d'Henry Fielding: Joseph Andrews." Lettres françaises, no. 536 (30 Sept. - 7 Oct.), pp. 1-4.

Argues that Fielding moves from parody of Pamela to picaresque novel when Joseph rejects Lady Booby's advances. Adams (the prototype of a long line of English eccentrics) becomes the true hero and Fanny a desirable female (whose distresses reflect Fielding's healthy sensuality). Finally asserts that Fielding's satire is as fierce as Swift's, except that it doesn't attack the state. In French.

Special issue for "le 200e anniversaire de la mort de Henry Fielding."

12 MILLER, HENRY K. "Benjamin Stillingfleet's Essay on Conversation, 1737, and Henry Fielding." Philological Quarterly, 33, no. 4 (Oct.), 427-28.

Stillingfleet's poem was published in 1737; Fielding's Essay on Conversation was published in 1743. There is no connection between the two, but they are often confused.

Incorporated in 1961.A13.

13 PRIESTLEY, J. B. "Henry Fielding: Then and Now." Listener, 52, no. 1337 (14 Oct.), 609-10.

After lightly running through Fielding's life, passing on several unsubstantiated anecdotes, Priestley contends that Fielding "arrived at the novel almost by accident" in response to Richardson's "hot-house, tea-party twaddle" (p. 609). He calls him the father of the novel, commends his "horse-play and high spirits," and thinks that Tom Jones, while necessary and enjoyable reading, could be cut because "the narrative is held up too often" (p. 610).

14 PRITCHETT, V. S. "The Tough School." Listener, 51, no. 1316 (20 May), 861-63.

This essay on "the poetic nature of the comic gift," which Pritchett intends to set against the naturalist tradition that enlarges our sensibilities by argument and analysis, includes a discussion of Fielding and Smollett. Pritchett thinks both in the same "masculine" (high animal spirits) tradition of the novel. He briefly discusses Parson Adams as a character in the picaresque tradition and Western as a full comic creation like Caliban; also Fielding's intelligent and ironic tolerance of mixed humanity, and his ability to vary, elaborate, and frame situations. Pritchett is particularly taken with the mixture of the stylized and artificial and the real and natural in Fielding.

15 SHEPPERSON, ARCHIBALD B. "Additions and Corrections to Facts About Fielding." Modern Philology, 51, no. 4 (May), 217-24.

Clearly sets out the evidence for Fielding's having been justice of the peace for Westminster "five weeks before he has hitherto been thought to have begun his duties" (p. 217). He speculates about the delay "between his appointment and his beginning active duty" (p. 218), suggesting that he waited until he had finished Tom Jones or until he had done some political writing for the Pelham administration (see 1965.B4). He identifies another Fielding residence, prints several "cases" from the newspaper that Fielding may have written or dictated, and gives more exact or more complete publication dates for five of Fielding's later works (Wedding Day, A True State of the Case of Bosavern . . ., An Enquiry Into the Causes of the Late Increase of Robbers, Amelia, Charge to the Grand Jury).

16 SHIPLEY, JOHN B. "General Edmund Fielding." Notes and Queries, 199 (June), 253-54.

Prints and briefly comments on two letters written by Henry Fielding's father, requesting the sinecure post of lieutenant governor of the Island of Jersey from Lord Harrington. The second letter mentions his four daughters.

17 STANZEL, FRANZ. "Tom Jones und Tristram Shandy: ein Vergleich als Vorstudie zu einer Typologie des Romans." English Miscellany (Rome), 5:107-148.

Rejecting the conventional division of the novel into two categories based on content (adventure and psychological), Stanzel attempts a preliminary structural topology of the novel. Studies Fielding and Sterne under four headings: manner of narration, medium (author as narrator, character as narrator, etc.), narrative distance (both spatial and temporal between narrator and narrative), and time structure (chronology and causality vs. Sterne's irregularity). In German.

Reprinted 1972.A8.

*18 STERN, GUY. "Fielding, Wieland, and Goethe: A Study in the Development of the Novel." Dissertation, Columbia, 1954.

Source: Dissertation Abstracts, 14 (1954), 1731-32.

See 1956.B1 and 1958.B14.

19 TOWERS, A. R. "Amelia and the State of Matrimony." Review of English Studies, n.s. 5, no. 18, 144-57.
Briefly examines the "contemporary . . . literary programme designed to glorify the pleasures of conjugal love" (p. 145) to be found in conduct books, in the Tatler and Spectator, and in Fielding's earlier work. Towers argues that Fielding illustrates certain ideas about married conduct in Amelia: marriage should be for love, not convenience; a wife should obey and support her husband in all lawful things (suggests that a wife should be submissive but not subservient); a mother should lavishly love but not spoil her children; a marriage needs confidence and mutual trust; the sexual double standard continues after marriage. Towers also briefly points out the other contrasting marriages in the novel. See 1965.B16.

*20 TURAEV, S. "Genri Fil'ding: K 200-letiu͡i so dni͡a smerti." Literatura v Shkole, no. 5, pp. 85-87.
"Henry Fielding: on the 200th anniversary of his death." Russian article.
Source: T. Humphrey, p. 233 and MHRA, 31 (1953-54), 276.

*21 VERT͡SMAN, I. "Genri Fil'ding, velikiĭ prosvetitel' i gumanist: K 200-letiu͡i so dni͡a smerti." Novyĭ Mir, no. 10, pp. 245-53.
"Henry Fielding, great representative of the Enlightenment and humanist: on the 200th anniversary of his death." Russian article.
Source: T. Humphrey, p. 233 and MHRA, 31 (1953-54), 277.

22 VILLELAUR, ANNE. "La Vie de Fielding." Lettres françaises, no. 536 (30 Sept. - 7 Oct.), pp. 1-2.
A biographical article emphasizing his theatrical, journalistic, and legal careers. Underlines his political activity (opposition to Walpole) and his humane approach to social problems. Includes an aside on Joseph Andrews, which was translated in 1743 by Desfontaines under the title Une Dame anglaise and found its way into Marie Antoinette's library. In French.

1955 A BOOKS

1 FIELDING, HENRY. Dzieje Wielkiego Jonatana Wilda. Translated by Jan Rusiecki and introduction by Grzegorz Sinko. Warsaw: Czytelnik, 306 pp.
Polish translation of Jonathan Wild, with Hogarth prints.

2 _____. Historia Życia Toma Jonesa, czyli dzieje podrzutka. Translated by Anna Bidwell, with afterword by Wlodzimierz Lewik. 2 vols. Warsaw: Panstwowy Instytut Wydawniczy, 1218 (607 & 611) pp.

Polish translation of Tom Jones.

*3 _____. Pamestinuko Tomo Džonso istorija. Translated by E. Kuosaite. 2 vols. Vil'njus: Goslitizdat. [1955].

Lithuanian translation of Tom Jones.

Source: Hugh Amory's working bibliography.

*4 _____. Stāsts par Tomu Dzonsu Atradeni. Translated by Ilga Melnbarde. Riga: Latgosizdat, 787 pp. [1955].

Illustrated Latvian translation of Tom Jones.

Source: Hugh Amory's working bibliography.

5 _____. The History of Tom Jones A Foundling. Introduction by Alan Pryce-Jones. Collins Classics. General editor G. F. Maine. London and Glasgow: Collins, 798 pp.

Includes a brief biographical note and an introduction, which emphasizes Fielding's moral purpose, his well-drawn characters and the naturalness and realism of the novel. The list of Fielding's works is taken from Chalmers (1806. A3); it appears that the "third" edition of Tom Jones has been modernized and reproduced.

6 _____. The History of Tom Jones, A Foundling. Introduction by George Saintsbury. Everyman's Library. 2 vols. London: J. M. Dent & Sons; New York: E. P. Dutton, 864 pp.

Reprint of 1909.A2.

*7 MEREDITH, ROBERT C. "Henry Fielding and the Idea of Benevolence: A Study of the Structure of Tom Jones." Dissertation, Wisconsin, 1955.

Source: T. Humphrey, p. 262. See Summaries of Doctoral Dissertations, University of Wisconsin, 16 (1956), 548-49.

*8 SOLON, JOHN J. "Fielding in the Twentieth Century." Dissertation, Wisconsin, 1955.

Source: T. Humphrey, p. 267. See Summaries of Doctoral Dissertations, University of Wisconsin, 16 (1956), 558-60.

1955 B SHORTER WRITINGS

1 ALLEN, WALTER. "Henry Fielding," in his Six Great Novelists. London: Hamish Hamilton, pp. 38-63.

A survey of Fielding's life (passing on unauthenticated anecdotes) and work. Touches on Fielding's ethics of "good nature," his imitation of Cervantes in Joseph Andrews, and the sustained irony of Jonathan Wild.

2 BROWN, JACK R. "Henry Fielding's Grub-Street Opera." Modern Language Quarterly, 16, no. 1 (March), 32-41.
Sets out the stage history (only played in its earlier version, The Welsh Opera, and probably later suppressed as too political), the printing of the three versions (Welsh Opera, Genuine Grub-Street Opera, and Grub-Street Opera), and the changes between them ("Fielding is softening the printed version of the play in order to make it appear as non-partisan as possible," p. 40). See 1973.A11.

3 KRONENBERGER, LOUIS. "Fielding: Tom Jones" and "Fielding: Jonathan Wild," in his The Republic of Letters. New York: Alfred A. Knopf, pp. 74-88.
Essentially a reprint of the introductions to 1943.A2 and 1952.A2.

4 LEDERER, JOSEPH H. "Fielding." New York Times Book Review (22 May), p. 27.
Sharply critical of "Maugham's heartless emasculation of Tom Jones" (1948.A4).

*5 NEDIC, BORIVOJE. "Henry Fielding." Savremenik I (Belgrade), pp. 71-80.
Serbian article.
Source: T. Humphrey, p. 232 and MHRA, 32 (1955-56), 328.

6 PRACHT, ERWIN. "Henry Fielding zu Fragen der Romantheorie." Zeitschrift für Anglistik und Amerikanistik, 3:152-74.
Asserts that the novel (a new character-centered art form) arose from the diverse and contradictory conditions of bourgeois society. Realistic eighteenth-century fiction depicts the new man and woman caught in the struggle between a fast-rising bourgeoisie and a disintegrating feudalism. Argues that Fielding in particular depicts the events which shape social life. His positive middle-class hero both illustrates a cultural process and reflects the emerging literature of a bourgeois society. In German. See 1966.A26 and 1974.A16.

7 PRINGLE, PATRICK. "Mr. Fielding's People" and "An Inquiry and a Plan," in his Hue and Cry: The Birth of the British Police. London: Museum Press, pp. 77-113 and passim.
Reviewed by Roger Becket, NYHTB, 15 Jan. 1956, p. 2; Jacob Korg, Nation, 182 (1956), 224-25.

1955

Chapters 5 and 6 describe Fielding's part in controlling crime in eighteenth-century London and in the creation of an effective police force. Pringle briefly discusses Fielding's satiric plays (the works of "a cynic and an idealist," p. 78), his honesty (he was a trading justice who would not "trade"), and his three-pronged attack on crime (to arouse public opinion, create a strong police force and remove the causes of crime). He describes Fielding's rise to prominence as a London magistrate, the lawless state of London (particularly a riot in the summer of 1749), and Fielding's An Enquiry into the Causes . . ., as well as the secret plan he drafted for the Duke of Newcastle. Sees the tone of Fielding's Preface to An Enquiry . . . as "revolutionary" (p. 91) and his sympathy for the poor as profound; in his attitude toward English constitutional liberty and a preventative police force "he was eighty years ahead of the country as a whole" (p. 113).

For a different view see 1966.A26.

8 SHIPLEY, JOHN B. "Fielding's Champion and a Publishers' Quarrel." Notes and Queries, 200 (Jan.), 25-28.

Reprints two pieces, probably by Ralph, in which The Champion joins a quarrel between two booksellers. See 1912.B6, 1913.B5, B8, B9, 1920.B11, 1953.B7, 1963.B17.

9 _____. "The 'M' in Fielding's Champion." Notes and Queries, 200 (June), 240-45.

Tries to distinguish between Fielding's and Ralph's contributions to The Champion. Some of the debated material is reprinted; Shipley concludes by correcting W. L. Cross's (1918.A1) and J. E. Wells's (1912.B6, 1913.B5, 1920.B11) attributions of Champion material and by deciding that much of the material signed 'M' is by Fielding.

Continued 1955.B10.

10 _____. "The 'M' in Fielding's Champion." Notes and Queries, 200 (Aug.), 345-51.

Continuation of 1955.B9.

11 STANZEL, FRANZ. Die typischen Erzählsituationen im Roman. Vienna: W. Braumüller, Universität-Verlagsbuchhandlung, 184 pp.

Reviewed by Joseph Warren Beach, AL, 28 (1956), 250-52.

Translated 1971.B34.

12 TOWERS, A. R. "Fielding and Dr. Samuel Clarke." Modern Language Notes, 70, no. 4 (April), 257-60.

Illustrates "how closely the novelist followed one of his favorite latitudinarian divines, Dr. Samuel Clarke, in dealing with a central religious issue in Amelia" (p. 258). That issue is the deism, or atheism (according to Fielding), of "the materialistic determinist" (p. 260) Robinson, whom Booth encounters in prison. See 1956.B12.

1956 A BOOKS

1 BUTT, JOHN. Fielding. Writers and Their Work, no. 57. London: Longmans, Green, for The British Council and The National Book League, 36 pp.

Reprint of 1954.A1.

2 [FIELDING, HENRY]. An Apology for the Life of Mrs. Shamela Andrews (1741). Introduction by Ian Watt. Augustan Reprint Society, no. 57. Los Angeles: William Andrews Clark Memorial Library and the University of California, 82 pp.

Reproduces the "second" edition of the text (which might in fact be a corrected first edition; see the T. C. Duncan Eaves and Ben D. Kimpel edition of Pamela. Boston: Houghton Mifflin, 1971, p. xviii, n. 2). The introduction briefly sums up the evidence for Fielding's authorship and then turns to his satiric targets (Colley Cibber, Conyers Middleton, Walpole, and the clergy, not necessarily Methodist, who preached faith rather than works). Fielding's narrative strategy (the dual framework of moral and literary criticism worked out in parallel actions) and his attack on Richardson's moral and psychological ambiguities are outlined.

Introduction reprinted 1962.A12 in a slightly revised form. Reissued 1967 as a Kraus Reprint. See 1946.B11 and 1968.B31.

*3 _____. Ta-wei-jen Chiang-nai-sheng Wei-erh-te chuan. Translated by Hsiao Ch'ien. Peking: Tso-chia press.

Chinese translation of Jonathan Wild.

Source: Hugh Amory's working bibliography (transliterated by Bonnie McDougall of the East Asian Institute).

*4 _____. Tom Jones. Povestea Unui Copil Găsit. Translated by Al. Iacobescu and Ion Pas. Bucharest: E.S.P.L.A., 1194 pp. [1956].

Romanian translation; four editions by 1968. Reissued 1969.A11.

Source: Hugh Amory's working bibliography.

*5 _____. Tom Jones. Translated by Siegfried Lang. Zürich: Büchergilde Gutenberg, 678 pp.
German translation; reissued 1963, 1965, 1967.
Source: Hugh Amory's working bibliography.

*6 _____. Tom Jones ühe leidiku lugu. Translated by Valda Raud. Tallin: Estgosizdat, 782 pp.
Estonian translation.
Source: Hugh Amory's working bibliography.

*7 KREUTZ, IRVING. "A Study of Henry Fielding's Plays." Dissertation, Wisconsin, 1956.
Studies twenty-four of Fielding's twenty-eight plays in their dramatic tradition, in the Fielding canon, and as examples of dramatic types.
Source: Dissertation Abstracts, 16, no. 11 (1956), 2165-66.

*8 SACKETT, SAMUEL. "The Place of Literary Theory in Henry Fielding's Art." Dissertation, UCLA, 1956.
Source: McNamee, 1865-1964, p. 559.

*9 SHUMUDA, NATSUO. Henry Fielding. Tokyo: Kerkyusha, 204 pp.
Source: MHRA, 32 (1955-56), 328.

*10 SMITH, LE ROY WALTER. "The Doctrine of the Passions as it Appears in the Works of Henry Fielding, Particularly in Amelia." Dissertation, Duke, 1956.
Source: McNamee, 1865-1964, p. 559. See 1961.B15 and 1962.B18.

*11 WENDT, ALLEN E. "Richardson and Fielding: A Study in the Eighteenth-Century Compromise." Dissertation, Indiana, 1956.
Source: Dissertation Abstracts, 17 (1957), 859. See 1957.B18 and 1960.B23.

1956 B SHORTER WRITINGS

*1 ANON. "Satira Fil'dinga." Uchenye zapiski Leningradskogo Universiteta, no. 212. Seriía filologicheskikh nauk, 28: 24-52.
"The satire of Fielding." In Russian.
Source: T. Humphrey, p. 233 and MHRA, 32 (1955-56), 327.

2 CAUTHEN, I. B. "Fielding's Digressions in Joseph Andrews." College English, 17, no. 7 (April), 379-82.

Justifies the three interpolated tales (Leonora's story, Mr. Wilson's history, and the story of Paul and Leonard) on the grounds that "they are closely related to Fielding's aesthetic of the novel, the exposure of affectation that arises from vanity and hypocrisy." These digressions at regular intervals act as "the exemplum, a story told with moral intent" (p. 382), explaining three phases of life (courtship, marriage, and the beginning of a career) that the novel cannot include. See 1973.B34.

*3 D'I͡AKONOVA, N. I͡A. "K. voprosu o Fil'dinge kak satirike i prosvetitele." Vestnik Leningradskogo Universiteta, no. 2, 95-104.
"Satirical and educational questions on Fielding." In Russian.
Source: MHRA, 32 (1955-56), 327.

4 IMBERT, HENRY-FRANCOIS. "Stendhal et Tom Jones." Revue de Littérature Comparée, 30, no. 3 (July-Sept.), 351-70.
Argues that Stendhal, particularly in Lucien Leuwen and La Chartreuse de Parme, was influenced in theme and technique by Tom Jones, which he had read in translation in 1803 and in the original by 1810. Stendhal's Marginalia confirms this influence. Imbert points out the similarities in character: like Stendhal's more sophisticated heroes, Fabrice and Lucien, Tom undergoes many adventures in his search for true identity. Both novelists are aware of various kinds of love, depict the social climate of their time, have sharp psychological insights, and consider hypocrisy the worst threat to society. Fielding's influence is also clear in Stendhal's handling of time, dialogue, and narrative intrusion. In French.

5 JARVIS, RUPERT C. "Fielding and the Forty-Five." Notes and Queries, 201 (Sept.), 391-94.
A bibliographical and biographical article that describes Fielding's shifting political allegiance between the Licensing Act and the 1745 rebellion, once thought to be a period of silence. Jarvis sorts out which Fielding pamphlets from that period, once unknown or thought to be lost, are now available (Charge to the Jury, 1745; History of the Present Rebellion, 1745; Ovid's Art of Love Paraphrased, 1747) and which pamphlets once attributed to him are now known not to be his (A Compleat and Authentick History of the . . . Rebellion, 1747; A Calm Address to All Parties, 1745). Continued 1956.B6 and 1957.B9. See his earlier article, 1945.B3. See also 1926.B3.

1956

6 _____. "Fielding and the Forty-Five." Notes and Queries, 201 (Nov.), 479-82.

Continuation of 1956.B5.

7 LYNCH, JAMES J. "Evil Communications." Notes and Queries, 201 (Nov.), 477.

Both Milton and Fielding misattribute the maxim about evil communications corrupting good manners. It is from Menander, but Fielding attributes it to Solomon in Tom Jones (Book 5, chapter 2) and to Diodorus Siculus in A Voyage to Lisbon.

8 MCKILLOP, ALAN D. "Henry Fielding," in his The Early Masters of English Fiction. Lawrence: University of Kansas Press, pp. 98-146.

Reviewed by Douglas Grant, MLR, 52 (1957), 420-21; Frederick W. Hilles, PQ, 37 (1957), 328-30; Martin Price, YR, 46 (1957), 303-304; Arthur Sherbo, JEGP, 56 (1957), 284-86; Ian Watt, MP, 55 (1957), 132-34; Charles B. Woods, MLN, 72 (1957), 622-24.

After briefly discussing Fielding's class background (aristocratic) and the influence of drama and the works of Cervantes, Scarron, and Marivaux on Fielding, McKillop turns to an analysis of Joseph Andrews, Jonathan Wild, Tom Jones, and Amelia. He discusses Fielding's comic aesthetic in Joseph Andrews (comparing it to his age's changing attitude toward humor and to Cervantes), the narrator, and the burlesque and mock heroic method of the action. He also argues that Fielding's comedy teaches more profoundly than Richardson's moral earnestness. He then briefly argues that Jonathan Wild is an attack on the root evils of human nature and not merely on Walpole. McKillop discusses the way Tom Jones embodies Fielding's moral purpose in its plot (which he thinks limits the presentation of Tom), character, and style. He sees Amelia as motivated by Fielding's "increasing preoccupation with the morals of contemporary society" (p. 136) and the central characters as limited by Fielding's moral doctrine that society corrupts the natural goodness in man.

Reprinted 1968.

9 MURRY, JOHN MIDDLETON. "In Defence of Fielding," in his Unprofessional Essays. London: Jonathan Cape, pp. 11-52.

Reviewed by Cyril Connolly, Sunday Times, 1 April 1956, p. 5; Kathleen Nott, Obs., 25 March 1956, p. 17; The Times, 21 May 1956, p. 13; New York Times, 8 Sept. 1956, p. 156.

In defending Fielding against F. R. Leavis' charge that he is too simple to deserve careful attention, Murry defines a positive sexual ethic in Fielding. After examining the relationships of desire (Lady Booby and Joseph; Lady Bellaston, Mrs. Waters, Molly and Tom; Miss Matthews and Booth), which have often troubled commentators, and those of love (Joseph and Fanny; Tom and Sophia; Booth and Amelia), Murry maintains that Fielding has illustrated an ethic of love. In this ethic, sexual desire and good-nature, that "classless generosity of soul" which is so rarely found, unite to "exhibit a system of moral values which we . . . recognize to be sound" (p. 49).

Reprinted in shortened form 1962.A12 and 1970.A4.

10 PARKER, A. A. "Fielding and the Structure of Don Quixote." Bulletin of Hispanic Studies, 33, no. 1, 1-16.

Studies the technical dissimilarity between Fielding's and Cervantes' "two different approaches to the problem of constructing a novel" (p. 1). Largely by examining the structure of Don Quixote, Parker argues that Fielding misunderstood the episodic nature of Cervantes' novel; "he failed to understand the technique that exemplifies it--a technique which does not link episodes in a chain of cause and effect, but which progressively varies the pattern of episodes in order to communicate through this changing pattern the expanding ramifications of the theme [Don Quixote's delusion]" (p. 14). Fielding adds causality to Tom Jones but at the expense of Tom's necessary moral development. "Tom's fall from favour would have happened just the same if he had been a wholly virtuous young man, and his restoration to favour would have happened just the same if he had remained a scapegrace" (p. 15).

11 POWERS, LYALL H. "The Influence of the Aeneid on Fielding's Amelia." Modern Language Notes, 71, no. 4 (April), 330-36.

Fielding not only models his novel on the twelve-part division of the Aeneid, he also borrows situations, pace, and general structure from the Aeneid for the first quarter of Amelia. It continues to be his general model for the rest of the novel. Powers outlines the parallels and identifies the various character models. Fielding has created a domestic and Christian Aeneid with both the pagan Stoic ethic and Christian principles. See 1936.B10, 1961.A11, and 1977.B9.

12 RADER, RALPH W. "Ralph Cudworth and Fielding's Amelia." Modern Language Notes, 71, no. 4 (April), 336-38.

Fielding may also have relied on Ralph Cudworth's True Intellectual System for the Robinson/Booth religious "doubt." See Tower's 1955.B12 article.

13 RAMONDT, MARIE. "Between Laughter and Humor in the Eighteenth Century." Neophilologus, 40:128-38.

Considers Fielding's comic theory and practice along with Molière's, Lessing's (in Laokoon), and Marivaux's. Argues that Marivaux was the creator of the tragedy of common life and of humor in which tragedy meets laughter. Ramondt rather poetically asserts that Fielding banished the primitive comic figures of puppets and defined the comic psychologically, sociologically, and historically (all summed up in the image of the fool or jester). She then asserts that, despite Fielding's apparently precise and rather Aristotelian definition of the humor of affectation, "Romantic humor, the humor in which the tragic note is heard, casts its shadow before it upon [Parson] Adams as upon Marivaux's Dubois" (p. 138).

14 SHERBURN, GEORGE. "Fielding's Social Outlook." Philological Quarterly, 35, no. 1 (Jan.), 1-23.

Argues that "Fielding was fundamentally a moralist" (p. 251). Sherburn begins by extracting Fielding's social philosophy from his works, asserting that he believed in a stratified society but also believed strongly in the need for charity and social reform. Sherburn then considers Fielding's moral position (his belief in benevolence, good nature, and good works), his attitude towards the passions (seeing Amelia as a dialectic between the Stoic and Christian attitude toward the passions), and the way in which the digressions and authorial intrusions support Fielding's ethical position. Finally he briefly compares him to "his master," Cervantes, whose wit is less self-conscious than Fielding's. Fielding "does not lack sympathy, though his typical attitude towards life is likely to be ironic" (p. 23). See 1949.B6, 1966.A26, and review by Allan Wendt, PQ, 36 (1957), 364-66.

Reprinted 1959.B23 and 1972.A8.

15 STERN, GUY. "Fielding and the Sub-Literary Novel: A Study of Opitz' Wilhelm von Hohenberg." Monatshefte, 48, no. 6 (Nov.), 295-307.

This comparative study of Fielding and Christian Opitz demonstrates how pervasive Fielding's influence was in eighteenth-century Germany and what, at the most popular level, his novels were thought to have contributed to the form. Stern discusses Opitz' borrowing of plot and incident (the plot of Wilhelm is from Amelia, but he borrows incidents and the contrasting brothers from Tom Jones), his use of Fielding's narrative techniques (including direct address to the reader and the narrator spanning gaps in time), his use of the structural device of books and chapters, his realism (of description and language), and his borrowed characters. Opitz also made use of Fielding's irony, but it had none of Fielding's resonance because it had neither erudition nor satiric intent behind it. See dissertation 1954.B18.

1957 A BOOKS

1 FIELDING, HENRY. Jonathan Wild and The Journal of a Voyage to Lisbon. Introduction by George Saintsbury. Everyman's Library. London: J. M. Dent & Sons; New York: E. P. Dutton, 286 pp.
Reprint of 1932.A1.

2 _____. The Adventures of Joseph Andrews. Introduction by George Saintsbury. Everyman's Library. London: J. M. Dent & Sons; New York: E. P. Dutton, 314 pp.
Reprint of 1910.A6.

3 _____. The Adventures of Joseph Andrews. Introduction by L. Rice-Oxley. World Classics. London, New York, Toronto: Oxford University Press, 406 pp.
Reprint of 1929.A3.

4 _____. The History of Tom Jones A Foundling. Edited by W. Somerset Maugham and illustrated by Harry Diamond. New York: Fawcett World Library, 384 pp.
Reissue of 1948.A4.

*5 HUTCHENS, ELEANOR N. "Verbal Irony in Tom Jones." Dissertation, Pennsylvania University, 1957.
Source: McNamee, 1865-1964, p. 559. See 1965.A15.

6 LEVIDOVA, ANNA M. Genri Fil'ding. Moscow: Vsesoi͡uznoĭ Knizhnoĭ Palaty, 28 pp.
"Henry Fielding."
A brief appreciation and a biography of Fielding, as well as a selected bibliography of works by and about Fielding in Russian and English.

*7 PRACHT, ERWIN. "Die Gnoseologischen Grundlagen der Romantheorie Henry Fieldings." Dissertation, Berlin-Humboldt, 1957.
Source: McNamee, 1865-1964, p. 559. See 1955.B6.

*8 RYAN, MARJORIE. "The Tom Jones Hero in Plays and Novels, 1750-1800: A Study of Fielding's Influence." Dissertation, Minnesota, 1957.

Studies the influence of the Tom Jones hero on 135 plays and 300 novels between 1750 and 1800, also considers the influence of Fielding's form (digressions, introductory chapters, similar episodes).

Source: Dissertation Abstracts, 19, no. 4 (Oct. 1958), 815-16.

1957 B SHORTER WRITINGS

1 COLEY, WILLIAM B. "The Authorship of An Address to the Electors of Great Britain." Philological Quarterly, 36, no. 4 (Oct.), 488-95.

Challenges bibliographical, stylistic, and shared content evidence that Greason (1954.B7) had used to prove Fielding's authorship. On the basis of style and the references to Sidney, An Address is at least as likely to be by Ralph, but it is not certainly by either Ralph or Fielding. See 1925.B5.

2 DYSON, A. E. "Satiric and Comic Theory in Relation to Fielding." Modern Language Quarterly, 18, no. 3 (Sept.), 225-37.

Distinguishes between satire, comedy, and "ridicule as a test of truth" (set out by Shaftesbury and Hutchinson). Although all three terms assume that "clear cut social and religious convictions . . . were shared ever where" (p. 225), satire is a dangerous mode that includes vicious attacks and impossible ideals; comedy "inflames" as well as "sublimates." Dyson considers Fielding of the third type: "primarily a comic writer [whose] . . . ridicule as a rule points toward not an ideal but a norm" (p. 230). Oddly, Dyson finds Lady Booby "too disquieting to be wholly funny" (p. 231) and three of Fielding's novels (Shamela, Joseph Andrews, and Jonathan Wild) too acerbic for comedy. However, by arguing that "the broad outline [of Tom Jones] is fully comic" (p. 233), he concludes that Fielding's norm is sentimental: "one which prefers 'good nature' to prudential calculation, 'Feeling' to 'Reason,' warmly benevolent good will to coolly accepted sense of duty" (p. 237). Throughout he relies upon conventional character analysis. Largely ignores Amelia.

3 ERZGRÄBER, WILLI. "Das Menschenbild in Henry Fieldings Roman Amelia." Die neueren Sprachen, 6:101-116.

Attempts to discover Fielding's concept of human nature as it is expressed in Amelia. Thinks the novel opens with a scene reminiscent of Dante's or Virgil's progress through hell, but the punishment is not commensurate with the crime and the world seems ruled by biological determinism. In this Hardy-like world, the Mandevillian idea of passion and self-love (represented by Booth and agreed to by Fielding) struggles with the Christian notion of free will and good example (represented by Dr. Harrison and dramatized by Amelia). Suggests that Fielding was unaware of the essential contradiction between the enlightened humanistic image of man and the Christian view, and settled for a simple notion of the good man which is common to both. The contradiction drives Fielding towards sentimentality. In German.

Reprinted 1972.A8. For another view, see 1955.B12.

4 GOGGIN, L. P. "Fielding's The Masquerade." Philological Quarterly, 36, no. 4 (Oct.), 475-87.

Studies "Fielding's first printed work" (p. 475) by examining its object (a satire on the immorality of masked balls), material, and techniques. Goggin looks at other contemporary criticism of masquerades (the Spectator and Hogarth's prints) and at references to masquerades in Fielding's later works (he continued to be critical of them). He also suggests that the poem and the play Love in Several Masques may indicate that Fielding was in London in 1726 and 1727, and that he probably spent his time "reading well-known works of wit" (p. 486).

5 HARDER, KELSIE B. "The Preacher's Seat." Tennessee Folk Lore Society Bulletin, 23: 38-39.

A practical joke in Joseph Andrews (Adams' dunking in a tub of water in Book 3, chapter 7) is identical to one called "the preacher's seat" still in use in Tennessee in the 1930s.

6 HIBBETT, HOWARD S. "Saikaku and Burlesque Fiction." Harvard Journal of Asiatic Studies, 20, nos. 1 and 2 (June), 53-73.

Compares Ihara Saikaku, a writer of the Tokugawa period, with Fielding and Defoe. Though Saikaku and Fielding are both "novelists" who use "burlesque to point up the satirical comedy of manners" (p. 60), Saikaku has no particular parodic targets, nor does he attempt to create sympathetic characters. Saikaku is apparently a creator of more disjointed satiric novels than Fielding, but Hibbett asserts that Fielding "is read chiefly for his witty, ironic manner of satirizing the foibles of human nature, rather than for the celebrated vitality of any of his characters." If this is true, both Fielding and Saikaku are "primarily wits, rather than novelists of an illusionistic realism" (p. 63).

7 HUMPHREYS, A. R. "Fielding and Smollett," in From Dryden to Johnson. The Pelican Guide to English Literature. Edited by Boris Ford. Vol. 4. Harmondsworth, Baltimore, Toronto, Mitcham (Australia): Penguin Books, pp. 313-32.

Feels that both writers "exact from the reader a degree . . . of labour" (Fielding because of a formal style which disciplines "his abundant vigour of idea," p. 313), but both offer vigorous and abundant landscapes of their time. Argues that Fielding's balanced emotion and morality is a product of his life experience, and briefly discusses Fielding's novels: the character of Adams and parody in Joseph Andrews, the epic and comic conventions in Tom Jones (as well as the digressions, interpolations, and the mock-heroic style), and the developing social conscience implied in Amelia.

8 HUNTING, ROBERT S. "Fielding's Revisions of David Simple." Boston University Studies in English, 3, no. 2 (Summer), 117-21.

Argues that despite personal hardships Fielding undertook extensive revision of the second edition of Sarah Fielding's David Simple. Hunting sees six categories of changes in style, diction, and content (including the addition of irony); he appears to think that all changes between the first and second editions were made by Fielding.

9 JARVIS, RUPERT C. "Fielding and the 'Forty-five.'" Notes and Queries, 202 (Jan.), 19-24.

Continuation of 1956.B5.

10 JONES, CLAUDE E. "Fielding's 'True Patriot' and the Henderson Murder." Modern Language Review, 52, no. 4 (Oct.), 498-503.

Reprints Fielding's True Patriot essay (13 May 1746) on the young Scottish footman, Matthew Henderson, who had killed his lady; also reprints the Gentleman's Magazine's more factual account.

*11 PUHALO, DUŠAN. "Henri Filding u svom i našem vremenu." Ogledi (Belgrade), 3, 31-51.

Serbian article.

Source: T. Humphrey, p. 232 and MHRA, 33 (1957-58), 330.

12 RADER, RALPH W. "Thackeray's Injustice to Fielding." Journal of English and Germanic Philology, 56, no. 2 (April), 203-12.

Attempts to account for Thackeray's "drastically revised . . . opinion of Fielding and his work" between 1840 and 1851. After 1851 Tom Jones was "an immoral rogue, Captain Booth a wretched sinner, and Fielding himself a much less excusable profligate" (p. 205) because Thackeray, who had always connected his life and work with Fielding, went through a period of "personal guilt . . . after his wife's attempted suicide" (p. 208); he became upset at the sexual infidelity of Tom and Booth, the gambling of Booth, and Fielding's supposed excessive drinking. "In purging his own sins Thackeray did great damage to Fielding and his novels" (p. 212).

For a different view see 1913.B3, 1947.B4, and 1962.B13.

13 SHAW, E. P. "A Note on the Temporary Suppression of Tom Jones in France." Modern Language Notes, 72, no. 1 (Jan.), 41.

Tom Jones was suppressed to punish the Parisian bookseller, Jacques Rollin, who did not first get permission from the official censor. See 1927.B5 and 1961.B8.

14 SHEA, BERNARD. "Machiavelli and Fielding's Jonathan Wild." Publications of the Modern Language Association, 72, no. 1 (March), 55-73.

This "source" article sets out in detail the verbal "echoes of passages," the "parallels in content, structure and diction," the adaptation of biographical method, and the burlesquing of Machiavelli's historical method in Jonathan Wild, which "is at once an imitation, a parody, and a criticism of Machiavelli" (p. 55). Although, according to Shea, Fielding borrowed from a number of political writings by Machiavelli, the Life of Castruccio in particular was "a model for the biographical portions of his narrative" (p. 73). See response by R. S. Crane in PQ, 37, no. 3 (July), 328-33.

15 SHERBO, ARTHUR. "Fielding and Dr. South: A Post Mortem." Notes and Queries, 202 (Sept.), 378-79.

Disagrees with Allan Wendt's (1957.B18) conclusion that Fielding became increasingly morally serious by pointing out Fielding's high-spirited references to Dr. South's Sermons in The Covent-Garden Journal and his joking about sacred things as late as 1752.

1957

16 TAYLOR, DICK. "Joseph as Hero in Joseph Andrews." Tulane Studies in English, edited by Aline Taylor. Vol. 7. New Orleans: Tulane University, pp. 91-109.

Argues that Joseph is as important as Adams and that he undergoes a "considerable increase in dignity and stature in the progress of the novel" (p. 91). According to Taylor, the turning point for Joseph comes in Book 2, chapter 12, when Adams and Fanny listen to the unknown singer (Joseph) sing a bawdy song from Dryden's Marriage à la Mode. This song "sets the pattern for the amorous behavior between Joseph and Fanny in the rest of the novel" (p. 95). By examining the scene and its relation to the novel, Taylor argues that by Book 2, chapter 12, the burlesque of Pamela has ended (replaced by a healthy sexuality) and that Joseph is given "his share of the serious burden of the novel as well as the jocular, and in some instances Joseph is [Fielding's] spokesman as well as a counterbalance to Parson Adams" (p. 109).

Reprinted 1972.A2.

17 WATT, IAN. "Fielding and the Epic Theory of the Novel" and "Fielding as Novelist: Tom Jones," in his The Rise of the Novel: Studies in Defoe, Richardson, and Fielding. London: Chatto & Windus, pp. 239-59, 260-89, passim.

Reviewed by Benjamin Boyce, PQ, 37 (1958), 304-306; Curtis C. Davis, WMQ, 3rd s., 17 (1960), 425-26; A. J. Farmer, EA, 11 (1958), 57-58; Daniel F. Howard, KR, 21 (1959), 309-20; Irving Howe, PR, 25 (1958), 145-50; Alan D. McKillop, MP, 55 (1958), 208-10; J. R. Moore, MLQ, 21 (1960), 373-75; B. Evan Owen, CR, 191 (1957), 315; V. S. Pritchett, NSN, 53 (1957), 355-56; Mark Roberts, EIC, 8 (1958), 428-38; F. K. Stanzel, Anglia, 76 (1958), 334-36; Robert Weimann, ZAA, 8 (1960), 315-17; F. Wölcken, Archiv, 196 (1959), 214-15; Charles B. Woods, MLN, 72 (1957), 622-24; TLS, 15 Feb. 1957, p. 98; YR, 46 (1957), xviii-xxiv.

Argues that this new genre is distinguished from earlier narratives because it grew out of a new philosophical realism (Descartes and Locke) which assumed that truth could be discovered by the individual through his senses. The formal realism of the novel, according to Watt, is based on the premise "that the novel is a full and authentic report of human experience, and is therefore under an obligation to satisfy its readers with such details of the story as the individuality of the actors concerned, the particulars of the times and places of their actions, details which are presented through a more largely referential use of language than is common in other literary forms" (p. 32). Defoe and Richardson fulfilled the requirements of the new genre; Fielding did not because of his more traditional and external view of reality (expressed in his characterization and style). In chapters on "Fielding and the Epic Theory of the Novel" and "Fielding as Novelist: Tom Jones," Watt continues his analogy of external vs. internal reality (first suggested by Samuel Richardson and repeated by Samuel Johnson). Watt feels that Fielding brought the epic analogy to the discussion of this new form to impress his literary peers (something that neither Defoe or Richardson, who were not classically educated, could do), that the epic analogy is in fact not impressive, and that Fielding implicitly admitted the opposition between verisimilitude (the imitation of nature) and the epic model. According to Watt, the epic was fruitful only in Amelia, where it became no more than a narrative metaphor. In Fielding's novels his comic aim kept him from rendering characters through speech and action (or scene) in all its physical and psychological detail. Instead, plot dominated, and Fielding's plots were static and archetypal. Fielding's major contribution was his attempt to bring a "wise assessment of life" (p. 288) to this new form. His distancing style and narration helped do this, but he did it at the expense of "formal realism."

This important critical book has often been reprinted and is now a Penguin Book. See Watt's later reflections on this work (1968.B38). Reprinted in part 1968.A2 and 1970.A4. For another view of the development of the novel see 1941.B15.

18 WENDT, ALLAN. "Fielding and South's 'Luscious Morsel': A Last Word." Notes and Queries, 202 (June), 256-57.

Provides a bibliography of recent articles on Fielding's frequent use of the phrase 'luscious morsel' (1916.B1, 1944.B3, 1946.B11, 1948.B6) and suggests that it is further proof of his authorship of Shamela. Wendt also speculates that Fielding's references to the Sermons of Dr. South change as Fielding's moral attitudes change.

For another view see 1957.B15. See dissertation 1956.A11.

19 _____. "The Moral Allegory of Jonathan Wild." Journal of English Literary History, 24, no. 4 (Dec.), 306-20.

Studies "the character of Heartfree in the light of eighteenth-century ethical thought" (p. 306). Comparing Heartfree's and Wild's behavior to the ethics of Tillotson, South, Barrow, Bishop Hoadly, and Shaftesbury, Wendt concludes that "not only Wild, but Heartfree as well, may . . . be taken as a portrait of unsatisfactory temperament" (p. 307). "As an ethical allegory, Jonathan Wild primarily criticizes immoderate 'greatness,' as embodied in its 'here'; but as a secondary purpose, the allegory also presents the limitations of passive goodness" (pp. 319-20). Heartfree has too little intelligent self-interest and too little courage and energy to be an ideal. See dissertation 1956.A11.

1958 A BOOKS

*1 ASHMORE, CHARLES D. "Henry Fielding's 'Art of life': A Study in the Ethics of the Novel." Dissertation, Emory, 1958.
Relates Fielding's ethical philosophy to that of his age and discusses the importance of the moral purpose (the head-heart dichotomy) in his work.
Source: Dissertation Abstracts, 19, no. 10 (April 1959), 2610.

*2 BATTESTIN, MARTIN C. "Henry Fielding's Joseph Andrews, Studies Towards a Critical and Textual Edition." Dissertation, Princeton, 1958.
Source: McNamee, 1865-1964, p. 559. See 1959.A1 and 1967.A2.

3 FIELDING, HENRY. The History of the Adventures of Joseph Andrews and His Friend Mr. Abraham Adams. Introduction by Mary Ellen Chase. Norton Library. New York: W. W. Norton, 347 pp.
Chase briefly reviews the parody of Pamela, the influences on Fielding (Cervantes, Homer, the drama, etc.), Fielding's theory of humor, and the characters in this "companionable" (p. vi) novel. No indication of copy text.

4 _____. The Voyages of Mr. Job Vinegar from The Champion (1740). Edited by S. J. Sackett. The Augustan Reprint Society, no. 67. Los Angeles: William Andrews Clark Memorial Library and the University of California, 43 pp.
Reprints this work ("a good deal like Gulliver's Travels with the narrative left out"), "which appeared serially in Fielding's periodical, the Champion, in 1740" (p. ii). The introduction reviews scholarly opinion about which of the thirteen essays are by Fielding (one may be by Ralph or Lyttelton), discusses Fielding's familiar satiric targets (in particular good breeding), and connects it to other eighteenth-century works (Gulliver's Travels, Robinson Crusoe, and Hogarth's Marriage-à-la-Mode). A glossary of

"Ptfghsiumgsk" words is provided. The text (of The Champion 55, 98, 106, 108, 112, 114, 116, 119, 120, 123, 127, 131, and 139) is an exact copy of the original papers, including printers' errors.
Reissued as a Kraus Reprint 1967.

*5 _____. Tom Džons, istorija jednog nahoda. Translated by Borivoje Nedić. Rijeka: Otokar Kersovani, 1188 pp. [1958].
Serbo-Croatian translation of Tom Jones.
Source: Hugh Amory's working bibliography.

6 _____. Tom Jones Příběh nalezence. Translated by František Marek. 2 vols. Prague: Státní nakladetelství krásné literatury, hudby a umění, 905 (457 & 448) pp.
Czech translation with notes. Reproduces sixteen Hogarth engravings; Jaroslav Hornát provides brief biographies of Fielding and Hogarth.

*7 _____. Tom Jones. Zgodba najdenčka. Translated by Mira Miheličeva. Ljubljana: Državna založba Slovenije. [1958].
Slovenian translation; reprinted 1970 and 1971.
Source: Hugh Amory's working bibliography.

*8 LAVIN, REV. HENRY ST. CLAIR. "The Ethical Structure of Tom Jones." Dissertation, Fordham, 1958.
Source: McNamee, 1865-1964, p. 559. See 1965.B9.

*9 RADER, RALPH W. "Idea and Structure in Fielding's Novels." Dissertation, Indiana, 1958.
Studies the thematic conflict between the good-natured Christian hero and an evil society ("falling away from a normative . . . harmonious mutuality") in Joseph Andrews, Tom Jones, and Amelia.
Source: Dissertation Abstracts, 19, no. 6 (Dec. 1958), 1367.

*10 WILSON, ROBIN S. "Henry Fielding and the Passionate Man." Dissertation, Illinois, 1959.
Attempts to review Fielding's ethical ideas systematically, concluding that he saw men as good, evil, and mixed and controlled by religion, social stricture, and law.
Source: Dissertation Abstracts, 20, no. 8 (Feb. 1960), 3285-86.

1958

1958 B SHORTER WRITINGS

1 BARROW, BERNARD E. "Macklin's Costume & Property Notes for the Character of Lovegold: Some Traditional Elements in Eighteenth-Century Low-Comedy Acting." Theatre Notebook, 13, no. 2 (Winter 1958/59), 66-67.
On the evidence of contemporary reports and Macklin's notes, Macklin clearly borrowed two bits of stage business for the part of Lovegold in Fielding's adaptation of L'Avare from the creator of the part, Ben Griffin. He probably borrowed his idea for Lovegold's costume from Thomas Doggett's creation of Moneytrap in Farquhar's The Confederacy.

2 BELL, INGLIS F. and DONALD BAIRD. The English Novel 1578-1956: A Checklist of Twentieth-Century Criticism. Denver: Alan Swallow, pp. 45-59.
Lists selected criticism of Amelia, Jonathan Wild, Joseph Andrews, Shamela, Tom Jones.

3 CARVER, WAYNE. "The Worlds of Tom and Tristram." Western Humanities Review, 12, no. 1 (Winter), 67-74.
Compares Fielding's "unshakable world of the lunch bucket and the city hall and all the naive assumptions of enduring values" (p. 70) in Tom Jones with Sterne's Tristram Shandy, where "every line quivers with the threat of annihilation" (p. 69). Sees the comic element in Tom Jones as "the froth" in an essentially serious and mundane work; Tristram Shandy is "comic at the core - and therefore, pathetic too" (p. 71). In this rather metaphoric response to these two novels, Tristram Shandy is seen as making the reader "teeter . . . with the precariousness of all humans" and Tom Jones as keeping us aloof from the pleasure and pain that "momentarily threaten the solid world of fixed relationships" (p. 74).

4 DILWORTH, E. N. "Fielding and Coleridge: 'Poetic Faith'." Notes and Queries, 203 (Jan.), 35-37.
A response to 1946.B9. Coleridge has borrowed Fielding's ironically witty phrase "poetic faith" and made it a critical shibboleth.

5 DOOLEY, D. J. "Some Uses and Mutations of the Picaresque." Dalhousie Review, 37, no. 4 (Winter), 363-77.
Traces the picaresque from Lazarillo de Tormes (1554) to Amis' Lucky Jim. Fielding made his hero honest and gullible (not a rogue), changed the master-servant relationship, made folly and not knavery the subject matter,

added strong plotting and a unified action (in Tom Jones), and readopted Cervantes' irony.

6 EMPSON, WILLIAM. "Tom Jones." Kenyon Review, 20 (Spring), 217-49.

Feeling that critics have not taken Tom Jones seriously enough as a moral document, Empson devises an interesting definition of double irony in order to analyze the way Fielding's style expresses serious ethical concerns. Empson spends little time with style, instead he demonstrates from the text that Tom moves from being a "noble savage" to being a "gospel" Christian by being subjected to a wide variety of human experiences. He particularly answers the charges of immorality or class antagonism often leveled at Tom (and through him, at Fielding), suggesting that we must understand Fielding's "double irony" to understand the paradoxes of the novel.

A slightly simpler version of this essay appeared as "Great Writers Rediscovered. The Grandeur of Fielding's Tom Jones," in the Sunday Times (London), 30 March 1958, p. 13. See 1942.B5, 1959.A1, and C. J. Rawson's response 1959.B19. Reprinted 1962.A12, 1968.A2, 1970.A4, 1972.A8 and 1973.A15.

7 ERÄMETSÄ, ERIK. "Über den englischen Einfluss auf den deutschen Wortvorrat des 18. Jahrhunderts." Neuphilologische Mitteilungen, 59.

An alphabetical list of words that entered the German language through the works of a number of English writers, among them Fielding, Richardson, and Sterne. In German.

8 GREASON, A. LEROY. "Fielding's The History of the Present Rebellion in Scotland." Philological Quarterly, 37, no. 1 (Jan.), 119-23.

A bibliographical article briefly describing the two printings of the London "first" edition, a Dublin edition, and a Boston edition (with two printings) of "the most popular of his writings directed against the Stuart uprising" (p. 123). See dissertation 1954.A13.

9 LANGE, VICTOR. "Erzählformen im Roman des achtzehnten Jahrhunderts." Anglia, 76:129-44.

Discusses the narrator as mediator who must define himself, then differentiate himself, and finally, through irony, reduce himself to a mere organizing agent. Illustrates the narrator's role in and the cross-influences between Defoe, Richardson, Fielding, Sterne, and Wieland. Concludes that the reader largely identifies himself with

Fielding's narrator; thus Fielding lacks Sterne's tension. In German.

For another view see 1974.B26. Reprinted 1972.A8.

10 MILLER, HENRY K. "Fielding and Lady Mary Wortley Montagu: A Parallel." Notes and Queries, 203 (Oct.), 442-43.

Fielding and Lady Mary share a couplet, but it isn't clear who borrowed from whom. They did have an interest in each other's work.

Incorporated in 1961.A13.

11 NATHAN, SABINE. "The Anticipation of Nineteenth-Century Ideological Trends in Fielding's Amelia." Zeitschrift für Anglistik und Amerikanistik, 6, no. 4, 382-409.

This Marxian analysis concludes that in Amelia Fielding had forsaken his earlier optimism for deeper insight "into the system of government in England" (p. 409). Argues that Fielding's social criticism is directed at corruption that is not just incidental and individual but something "trained up in people from the influence of their environment" (p. 386); thus Fielding shifts from an aristocratic to a bourgeois ideal and anticipates the remedies of the nineteenth century (religion, the "homely" ideal of Amelia, the educated heart). Argues for the limitation of these ideals even within the novel, and although Fielding "clings to it as the gods cling to Shen-te's goodness in a wicked world in Der gute Mensch von Sezuan" (p. 407), he may have been aware of some of the shortcomings of the emerging bourgeois ideal.

See 1951.B7, 1959.B17, 1966.A26. For another Marxian analysis see 1937.B3.

12 PRACHT, ERWIN. "Probleme der Entstehung des Romans." Zeitschrift für Anglistik und Amerikanistik, 6:283-96.

Argues that before the rise of the bourgeoisie, private and public life coincided; the novel developed out of the conflict that emerged as these separated. In Fielding's novels, the private world is in conflict with the public world: the future is set against the past, progress against reaction, everyday life against people of fashion, democratic culture against aristocratic values, etc. Fielding's strength is that he is the sympathetic historian of the private life and created living characters from this welter of contradiction. In German. See 1966.A26 and 1974.A16.

13 SHERBO, ARTHUR. "Fielding and Chaucer - and Smart." Notes and Queries, 203 (Oct.), 441-42.

"A Pleasant Balade, or Advice to the Fayre Maydens," which appeared in The Covent-Garden Journal and is sometimes attributed to Fielding, is very likely by Christopher Smart.

14 STERN, GUY. "A German Imitation of Fielding: Musäus Grandison der Zweite." Comparative Literature, 10, no. 4 (Fall), 335-43.

Musäus, in his parody of Richardson's Sir Charles Grandison, both imitates and uses Fielding's technique. Musäus' novel does not transcend literary parody, as Fielding's Joseph Andrews does, but he models his social satire (directed at clergymen, "great" men, lawyers, etc.) on Fielding's. He is most like Fielding in his use of irony; Stern compares Musäus' and Fielding's use of overt and covert (or subtle) irony. See dissertation 1954.B18.

15 SUTHERLAND, JAMES. "The Novel," in English Satire. Cambridge: The University Press, pp. 108-16.

Reviewed by A. Demedre, EA, 13 (1960), 70-71; Irvin Ehrenpreis, MLR, 54 (1959), 247-48; Norman Knox, SAQ, 58 (1959), 138-39; Helmut Papajewski, Anglia, 77 (1959), 78-79; T. Wood, E. Studies, 41 (1960), 112-13.

In his chapter on "the novel," Sutherland discusses parody and Fielding's outraged sense of truth in Joseph Andrews. He particularly discusses the beating and stripping of Joseph by the robbers and Adams' reaction to the supposed drowning of his son, Jacky, as Fielding's means of attacking the "professions" we cannot live by. About Jonathan Wild he merely says that it "is a brilliant and sustained performance, but I must add the damaging reservation that no one ever wished it longer" (p. 115).

Reissued 1962.

16 TILLYARD, E. M. W. "Tom Jones," in his The Epic Strain in the English Novel. London: Chatto & Windus, pp. 51-58.

Reviewed by A. J. Farmer, EA, 12 (1959), 82; Mark Schorer, MLN, 74 (1959), 643-44.

Seeing the epic as one of the strains in the novel along with the satiric, the idyllic, and the picaresque, Tillyard briefly argues that Tom Jones "lacks sustained intensity; it does not make the heroic impression; and on that account it fails of the epic effect." He sees it as "reflecting the manners rather than the soul of a generation" (p. 58) and as in the "tradition of the medieval and Renaissance romance of chivalry" (p. 52). See 1931.A9, 1969.B33, and 1974.B11.

1958

17 WEST, REBECCA (CICILY I. ANDREWS). "The Great Optimist," in her The Court and the Castle: A Study of the Interactions of Political and Religious Ideas in Imaginative Literature. New Haven: Yale University Press, 1957; London: Macmillan, pp. 73-89.

Reviewed by R. M. Adams, VQR, 34 (1958), 130-33; Newton Arvin, NYTBR, 3 Nov. 1957, p. 28; Marjorie Bremner, Twentieth Cent., 164 (1958), 409-10; Jacob Korg, Nat., 186 (1958), 15-16; Joseph Wood Krutch, Sat. Rev., 26 Oct. 1957, pp. 21-22; John Pick, Books Abroad, 32 (1958), 138; Dachine Rainer, NR, 137 (25 Nov. 1957), 18-19; John Wain, London Mag., 5 (Dec. 1957), 62-65; TLS, 8 Aug. 1958, p. 443.

Calling Fielding "in the largeness of his creation . . . most like Shakespeare" (p. 77), West comments on the realistic portrait of the "hideousness" of some eighteenth-century class attitudes in Amelia (to dueling and debt), Fielding's appeals for good government, his preoccupation with crime, his belief in the redemptory power of women, his belief in intelligent good nature, and his defense of his new form in Tom Jones.

1959 A BOOKS

1 BATTESTIN, MARTIN C. The Moral Basis of Fielding's Art: A Study of Joseph Andrews. Middleton, Conn.: Wesleyan University Press, 207 pp.

Reviewed by L. C. B., EA, 14 (1961), 366-67; Jessie R. Chambers, MLN, 76 (1961), 464-67; William W. Combs, SAQ, 59 (1960), 299-300; A. R. Humphreys, RES, n.s. 12 (1961), 211-12; C. J. Rawson, N&Q, 205 (1960), 154-56; H. Winston Rhodes, AUMLA, 13 (1960), 81-82; Albrecht B. Strauss, BA, 35 (1961), 388-89; Ian Watt, PQ, 39 (1960), 325-26; Aubrey Williams, YR, 49 (1960), 454-57; TLS, 25 Dec. 1960, p. 756.

An important book in which Battestin argues that Fielding did not believe in either the Stoic ethic or deism. "The modified Pelagian doctrine of such latitudinarian churchmen as Isaac Barrow, John Tillotson, Samuel Clarke, and Benjamin Hoadly--all of whom Fielding read with sympathy and admiration--is the essential background for a right interpretation of his ethics in general and the meaning of Joseph Andrews in particular" (p. 14). Joseph Andrews is not merely another parody of Pamela but "structurally as well as thematically" (p. 26) the work of a Christian moralist who argues for the good man as moral exemplar. Battestin briefly examines the Christian, romance, and epic backgrounds of the novel and illustrates Fielding's ethics in poems, essays, and other novels. He then sets out the Christian debate in the novel: Joseph and Adams ("as moral exemplars") versus the theme of vanity, "the chief vice subsuming all others" (p. 53). Battestin's discussion of "structure" merely extends his argument about theme. He sees the "broad allegory of the novel represent[ing] the pilgrimage of Joseph Andrews and Abraham Adams--like their scriptural namesakes . . . from the vanity of the town to the relative naturalness and simplicity of the country" (p. 129). According to Battestin, the Wilson episode is not a digression but, allegorically, "very near the heart of Joseph Andrews" (p. 44). Battestin also argues that Joseph Andrews is part of the eighteenth-century debate about the nature of the clergy.

See 1901.B4, 1949.B7. For another view, see 1969.B29 and 1975.A6. See dissertation 1958.A2.

2 BUTT, JOHN. Fielding. Writers and Their Work, no. 57. London: Longmans, Green, for The British Council and The National Book League, 36 pp.

Revision of 1954.A1.

*3 CALIUMI, GRAZIA. Il Romanzo di Henry Fielding. University Commerciale "Lugi Bocconi" Collana: Lingue e lettere straniere, no. 4. Milano: Instituto Editoriale Cisalpino.

Reviewed by Guido Fink, Convivium, 29 (1961), 751-52.

Source: T. Humphrey, p. 229.

4 FIELDING, HENRY. Amelia. Introduction by George Saintsbury. Everyman's Library. 2 vols. London: J. M. Dent & Sons; New York: E. P. Dutton, 639 pp.

Reprint of 1930.A2.

*5 _____. Amelie. Translated by František Marek. Prague: Státní nakladetelství krásné literatury, hudby a umění, 622 pp.

Czech translation.

Source: National Union Catalogue Author Lists, 1942-1962. Vol. 47, p. 474.

6 _____. Josef Andrewsin Seikkailut. Translated by Valfrid Hedman. [?]: Arvi A. Karisto Osakeyhtiö, 403 pp.

In Finnish.

Reprint of 1927.A1.

7 _____. The Adventures of Joseph Andrews. Introduction by L. Rice-Oxley. World Classics. London, New York, Toronto: Oxford University Press, 406 pp.

Reprint of 1929.A3.

1959

8 _____. The History of Tom Jones. Engravings by Derrick Harris. Bungay, Suffolk: The Folio Society, 655 pp.
A brief appreciative introduction by Kenneth Hopkins. Appears to reprint the "1750" edition followed by Murphy (1762.A10).

9 _____. Tom Jones. Suomentanut Olli Nuorto. Porvoo and Helsinki: Werner Söderström, 547 pp.
A slightly abridged Finnish translation.

1959 B SHORTER WRITINGS

1 ALLOTT, MIRIAM. Novelists on the Novel. London: Routledge and Kegan Paul, passim.
Reviewed by A. O. J. Cockshut, EC 10 (1960), 473-75; G. A. Craig, Victorian Stud., 4 (1960), 173-75; K. J. Fielding, Dickensian, 56 (1960), 160-64; Margaret Lane, London Mag., 7 (Feb. 1960), 81-85.
Selected quotations from novelists (including Fielding) organized under various headings: the novel and the marvelous, the novel as a portrait of life, the ethics of the novel, the novelist's approach and equipment, germination, the novelist at work, etc. In a final section Allott discusses "the craft of fiction," including structural problems, narrative technique, and style. Fielding is quoted on realism, moral example, the novelist's skills, inspiration, epic regularity, structural unity, beginnings and endings, time, the epistolary method, characterization, style, and allusion. He is also discussed in the prefaces to most of the sections.

2 BAKER, SHERIDAN. "Fielding's 'Female Husband': A Correction." Notes and Queries, 204 (Nov.), 404.
A correction of the date on which Mary Hamilton was arrested. See 1959.B4.

3 _____. "Henry Fielding and the Cliché." Criticism, 1, no. 4 (Fall), 354-61.
Examines Fielding's use of several borrowed and even cliché phrases or figures of speech (i.e., "voracious pike," the gifts of Nature and Fortune, the "bill of fare," "solid comfort," and especially the love chase as hunt), concluding "that Fielding is using his clichés deliberately, using the common expectations as a base for variations of phrase and meaning" (p. 358). These clichés give his style a colloquial ring and give us "pleasure at finding

them suddenly fitting the new context with all the old pertinence" (p. 360).

4 ______. "Henry Fielding's The Female Husband: Fact and Fiction." Publications of the Modern Language Association, 74, no. 2 (June), 213-24.

Argues that this "nearly pornographic" (p. 213) piece of journalism is by Henry Fielding and describes the ways in which Fielding worked on the newspaper accounts and court records in order to make them more sensational. Only a small part of the pamphlet is based on authoritative accounts. Baker identifies the parallels between The Female Husband and Fielding's other fiction and speculates about the reason for its composition (Fielding needed money) and about Fielding's eye for a sensational story. Baker also notes the location of the four known copies of the pamphlet.

For another view see 1921.B1.

5 BERNARD, F. V. "Shamela and Amelia: An Unnoticed Parallel." Notes and Queries, 204 (Feb.), 78.

Another parallel pointed out. See 1916.B1.

6 CARROLL, JOHN J. "Henry Fielding and the 'Trunk-Maker.'" Notes and Queries, 204 (June), 213.

The "famous Trunk-maker in the Playhouse" referred to in Tom Jones is identified as the audience of the upper gallery, who vigorously expressed approval and disapproval.

7 COLEY, WILLIAM B. "Gide and Fielding." Comparative Literature, 11, no. 1 (Winter), 1-15.

Argues that eighteenth-century literature, and particularly the art of Fielding, was important to Gide's developing aesthetic. He saw in it "the 'raw meat' of life (as opposed to the enervating and irrelevant forms of artifice," p. 2) and a proper mixture of laughter and seriousness. Gide felt that in the novel of action, "with its motives, its consequences" (p. 5), "a relatively 'pure' art form" (p. 4) had been achieved. Fielding's intervening narrator in Tom Jones also excited Gide, and his reading of Richardson and Fielding provoked him to define "realism." Finally, this essay sums up Gide's arguments about "Fielding's reservations concerning formal religion" (p. 12) and his rhetorical analysis of the complex self-parody of Tom Jones, which "by confusing the reader as to what is reality and what is the distortion of artifice . . . seek[s] to arouse his curiosity to examine the claims of each in a new light" (p. 14).

1959

8 _____. "The Background of Fielding's Laughter." Journal of English Literary History, 26, no. 2 (June), 229-52.

Tries to right the imbalance caused by modern studies which emphasize Fielding as moralist; there was a tradition of wit that did not demand Fielding be either exclusively serious or comic. Coley uses the "example of South, the aesthetic of Shaftesbury and the practice of Swift" (p. 252), as well as statements by Fielding in The Champion and Covent-Garden Journal (particularly no. 18) to indicate why Fielding did not believe in the "dissociation of gravity from wit" (p. 233). Like South and Shaftesbury, who discuss mixing humor with religious subjects, Fielding devised a mixed mode "neither dull gravity . . . nor witty levity" (p. 232) to deal with morally contradictory characters like Adams or Wild. Finally, by examining the difference between Fielding's treatment of earlier parsons and of Dr. Harrison, Coley illustrates the "three modal changes that occur when Fielding deserts laughter for solemnity" (p. 249) in Amelia. See dissertation 1954.A2.

Reprinted 1972.A8.

*9 HORŇÁT, JAROSLAV. "Pamela, Shamela a Josef Andrews." Časopis pro moderni filologii (Prague), 41: 1-22.

Czech article.

Source: T. Humphrey, p. 231 and MHRA, 34 (1959), 184.

10 JOHNSON, MAURICE. "The Device of Sophia's Muff in Tom Jones." Modern Language Notes, 74, no. 8 (Dec.), 685-90.

Argues that Fielding used the muff to symbolize the unconscious sexual attraction between Tom and Sophia, thus giving them a subjective dimension. It also neatly symbolizes the trials of physical attraction. Later incorporated in chapter 8 of 1961.A11.

*11 KISHLER, THOMAS C. "The Satiric Moral Fable, A Study of an Augustan Genre with Particular Reference to Fielding." Dissertation, Wisconsin, 1959.

Attempting to develop a coherent aesthetic of nonrealistic eighteenth-century works of satiric fiction, Kishler examines Fielding's essays in The Champion, Jonathan Wild, and Shamela.

Source: Dissertation Abstracts, 20, no. 4 (Oct. 1959), 1352-53.

12 LOFTIS, JOHN. Comedy and Society from Congreve to Fielding. Stanford Studies in Language and Literature. Vol. 19. Stanford: Stanford University Press, pp. 114-21 and passim.

Reviewed by Emmett L. Avery, PQ, 39 (1960), 299-301; Allan R. Bevan, DR, 42 (1962), 248-53; Benjamin Boyce, SAQ, 59 (1960), 458-59; Arthur Eastman, Crit Q, 3 (1961), 88-89; George Falle, UTQ, 30 (1960), 95-100; John C. Hodges, MP, 58 (1960), 134-35; Claude E. Jones, MLQ, 21 (1960), 270-71; Clifford Leech, MLR, 56 (1961), 104-105; William R. McGraw, QJS, 46 (1960), 221-22; Sybil Rosenfield, TN, 14 (1960), 135-36; Edward Rosenheim, JMH, 32 (1960), 160-61; Arthur Sherbo, JEGP, 59 (1960), 578-81; John C. Stephens, EUQ, 16 (1960), 121; G. L. Vincitorio, Cath HR, 46 (1960), 113; Aubrey Williams, YR, 49 (1960), 454-57; W. K. Wimsatt, ES, 43 (1962), 454-56; Calhoun Winton, CE, 22 (1960), 56.

In a book designed to study "the interaction of dramatic formalism and social forces" (p. vii) and specifically to illustrate the changing attitudes to class and politics in dramatic comedies, Loftis argues that after about 1710 the better dramatists "openly espous[ed] the claims of the merchants" (p. 3). Only the obscure dramatists accepted the Restoration comic notion of the justice of an aristocratic society based on land. As one of the better dramatists, Fielding was aggressively critical of social and political conditions (along with Gay, Robert Dodsley, James Miller). Loftis sees "Fielding's comedies, farces, burlesques, and ballad operas, in their forms and in their themes, [as] an epitome of the dramatic activity from 1728 to 1737" (p. 114), a time of vigor and experiment. Loftis briefly discusses Fielding's attitude toward the contemporary preoccupation with money, his contemporary allusiveness, his political plays, and his attacks on contemporary theater. Loftis finds some of Fielding's attitudes "curiously ambivalent" (p. 115): though he is conservative about social and literary change, his chief fools are old aristocrats; though he attacks fashionable London, he also attacks London low life; he attacks contemporary money grubbing while defending the merchant class. Loftis sees the central antithesis of Fielding's plays and novels as that between city and country rather than the older antithesis between merchant and gentleman. Finally he thinks "Fielding's writings reveal a certain conservatism, notably in their rather strict observation of the traditional relationship between classes" (p. 120). Some of the plays anticipate his novels: The Modern Husband, corrupted by money, anticipates the psychological realism of Amelia.

13 LYNCH, JAMES J. "Structural Techniques in Tom Jones," in Stil- und Formprobleme in der Literatur. Vorträge des 7. Kongresses der internationalen vereinigung für moderne

Sprachen und Literaturen in Heidelberg. Edited by Paul Böckmann. Heidelberg: Carl Winter, pp. 238-243.
Reprints 1959.B14.

14 _____. "Structural Techniques in Tom Jones." Zeitschrift für Anglistik und Amerikanistik, 7, no. 1, 5-16.
Examines two kinds of structural devices. "The first type control large segments of the plot and run continuously throughout the narrative"; they are plot diversion, spatial and temporal verisimilitude, and parallelism. "The second type are used to manage the small details and appear sporadically" (p. 6); they are planned reappearances, undisclosed motive, blurred consequences, minute cause, and alternate interpretation. Lynch examines each of these in some detail, distinguishing, for instance, between the parallelism of character, the parallelism (polarity) of country and city, and paired incidents. He concludes that all of these devices establish "tight causal relationships among a considerable quantity of incident and character" (p. 16). See 1969.B7.

15 MCBURNEY, WILLIAM H. "Mrs. Mary Davys: Forerunner of Fielding." Publication of the Modern Language Association, 74, no. 4 (Sept.), 348-55.
Sees this female novelist of the 1720s as in the "cheerful, sunshiny, breezy" Fielding strain rather than in the "close, hot, day-dreaming" Richardson line, but he argues for no direct influence.

16 MCKILLOP, ALAN D. "Some Recent Views of Tom Jones." College English, 21, no. 1 (Oct.), 17-22.
Surveys, summarizes, and compares the views of some critics--Booth (1952.B2), Crane (1950.B2), Sherburn (1956.B14), Van Ghent (1953.B12), Watt (1957.B17)--on such things as Fielding's use of plot, his concept of human nature, comedy, and character psychology.

17 PRACHT, ERWIN. "Bittere Enttäuschung und erschütterter Optimismus in Fielding's Spätwerk?" Zeitschrift für Anglistik und Amerikanistik, 7:288-93.
Disagrees with Nathan's view (1958.B11) that in Amelia Fielding optimistically turned to the bourgeoisie for a social solution to English problems. Argues instead that Fielding did not belong to the bourgeoisie that benefited from the 1688 compromise, but to the revolutionary bourgeoisie that had not subjugated society. Fielding saw exploiter and exploited and fought on two fronts: against the relics of feudalism and against developing capitalism. By

the time he wrote Amelia he had lost his "enlightened" optimism and developed more complex class attitudes and a more complex world view. In German. See 1966.A26.

18 _____. "Literatur und Wahrheit." Zeitschrift für Anglistik und Amerikanistik, 7:17-34.
Marxist article examining truth in literature; focuses on Fielding because he was a realist and because he felt it his duty to unmask hypocrisy. Although Pracht concludes that realism is not the only way to convey truth (the specific form of social consciousness), realism does have a firm grasp on reality and truth. Fielding was aided by his conviction (apparent in his novels, plays, and journalism) that literature and truth are inseparable.

19 RAWSON, C. J. "Professor Empson's 'Tom Jones.'" Notes and Queries, 204 (Nov.), 400-404.
A response to 1958.B6. Rawson thinks Empson's classic reappraisal is wrong in one important matter, Tom's sexual morals. Empson suggests that Fielding's treatment of chastity is ambiguous. Rawson argues that Fielding's opinion is explicit and clear: "Tom's minor unchastities are to be seen as manifestations of the same 'benevolent disposition' of which his love for Sophia is the full flowering" (p. 404).
Reprinted 1970.A4.

20 SACKETT, S. J. "Fielding and Pope." Notes and Queries, 204 (June), 200-204.
Sorts out Fielding's printed response to Pope. Sackett reproduces allusions from four periods: before Fielding met Pope, after he met him, from Pope's death to the publication of Amelia, and Fielding's final years. Although the responses are almost all respectful, after Pope's death Fielding appears willing to criticize "some of Pope's works that he had praised during Pope's lifetime" (p. 204). See 1972.B7.

21 _____. "To Write Like an Angel." Western Folklore, no. 18: 250-51.
Fielding may be the first "literary source for this proverb" (p. 250), although it may have been a common phrase by his day.

22 SCHMIDT-HEIDDING, WOLFGANG. "Henry Fielding," in his Sieben Meister des literarischen Humors in England und Amerika. Heidelberg: Quelle und Meyer, pp. 61-77.

Extracts Fielding's theory of the comic from the "preface" to Joseph Andrews and the "Essay on the Knowledge of the Character of Men." Then examines the comedy created by the contradiction between word or intention and deed (often the difference between reason and passion). Also examines Fielding's use of stylistic devices for humor (e.g., inflated diction, mock-poetic diction, mock-heroic style, etc.). Thinks that Fielding's satire mellows between plays and novels; in the latter his humor is benevolent and often self-deprecating. In German.

23 SHERBURN, GEORGE. "Fielding's Social Outlook," in Eighteenth-Century English Literature: Modern Essays in Criticism. Edited by James L. Clifford. New York: Oxford University Press, pp. 251-73.
Reprint of 1956.B14.

24 SMITH, ROBERT A. "The 'Great Man' Motif in Jonathan Wild and The Beggar's Opera." College Language Association Journal, 2:183-84.
Compares Gay's and Fielding's use of the motif, finding the opera "milder, yet the more subtle" (p. 184). The chief difference seems to be in Fielding's use of clear symbolic contrasts.

1960 A BOOKS

*1 CHAMBERS, JESSIE R. "The Allegorical Journey in Joseph Andrews and Tom Jones." Dissertation, Johns Hopkins, 1960.
Source: McNamee, 1865-1964, p. 560.

*2 DERSTINE, VIRGINIA. "Fielding's Shift in Instructional Method as Reflected in His Early Prose Fiction." Dissertation, Washington-Seattle, 1960.
Argues that Fielding shifts from a moral emphasis on "carefully to avoid" to "eagerly to imitate" as he moves from the comic satire of Shamela through Joseph Andrews, Tom Jones, and finally to Amelia.
Source: Dissertation Abstracts, 21, no. 12 (June 1961), 3780.

3 FIELDING, HENRY. Istorii͡a Toma Dzhonsa, naĭdenta. Translated by A. Frankovskogo. 2 vols. Moscow: "Izvestii͡a," 1042 (539 & 503) pp.
Russian translation of Tom Jones.

4 _____. Jonathan Wild and The Journal of a Voyage to Lisbon. Introduction by George Saintsbury. Everyman's Library. London: J. M. Dent & Sons; New York: E. P. Dutton, 304 pp.
Reissue of 1932.A1.

*5 _____. La storia di Tom Jones. Translated by Anna Maria Speckel. Milano: Mursia e C.-A.P.E. Corticelli, 256 pp. [1960].
Italian translation.
Source: Hugh Amory's working bibliography.

6 _____. The Female Husband and other Writings. Edited by Claude E. Jones. English Reprints Series, no. 17, edited by Kenneth Muir. Liverpool: Liverpool University Press, 65 pp.
Reviewed by John Graham, JEGP, 61 (1962), 189-90; C. J. Rawson, N&Q, 207 (1962), 158-59; Rachel Trichett, RES, n.s. 14 (1963), 438; Charles B. Woods, PQ 41 (1961), 587-88.
Reprints The Female Husband (M. Cooper 1746), the epilogues Fielding wrote for Theobald's Orestes (1731), Bodens' Modish Couple (1732), Lillo's Fatal Curiosity (1737) and The True Patriot (1746), as well as the poem "The Masquerade" (J. Roberts "1728"). See 1921.B1 and 1959.B4.

7 _____. The History of the Adventures of Joseph Andrews and His Friend Mr. Abraham Adams. Afterword by Irvin Ehrenpreis. Signet Classic. New York and Toronto: New American Library; London: New English Library, 319 pp.
Modernized edition "based on the 1762 edition. In removing errors and inconsistencies found there, the 1742 edition, with which this has been compared word for word, has occasionally been relied on" (p. 319). Ehrenpreis discusses the "ironies, unmaskings, conflicts, and reversals [that] stand behind the full pattern of the book" (p. 300); the precedents for some of these techniques (Marivaux, Cervantes), as well as for the ancient device of concealed parentage (Sophocles); the connection between these techniques and Fielding's "teaching us to trust in Providence" (p. 308); and theatrical conventions rather than Pamela as a model for the techniques of the novel.

8 NO ENTRY

9 _____. The History of the Adventures of Joseph Andrews and of his friend Mr. Abraham Adams. Introduction and notes by Maynard Mack. New York: Holt, Rinehart and Winston, 378 pp.
Reprint of 1948.A3; called the thirteenth printing.

10 _____. The History of the Adventures of Joseph Andrews and of His Friend Mr. Abraham Adams. Introduction by Carlos Baker. Bantam Classic. New York: Bantam Books, 320 pp.
Brief bibliography and notes. Introduction outlines the development of the novel form, Fielding's concept of the comic epic in prose, the parody of Pamela, Fielding's concept of Christian charity, and his mimetic and comic spirit. No indication of copy text.

*11 _____. Tom Jones, storia d'un trovatello. Translated by Ada Prospero. Milano: A. Garzanti, 888 pp.
Italian translation.
Source: Hugh Amory's working bibliography.

*12 _____. Tom Jones. Translated by Giuseppina Limentani Pugliese. Milano: Editr. AMZ, 199 pp. [1960].
Abridged Italian translation.
Source: Hugh Amory's working bibliography.

*13 ROBERTS, EDGAR V. "The Ballad Opera of Henry Fielding, 1730-1732, A Critical Edition. (The Author's Farce, The Grub-Street Opera, The Lottery, The Mock Doctor.)" Dissertation, Minnesota, 1960.
Source: McNamee, 1865-1964, p. 560. See 1962.B16, 1963.B14, 1966.B19, 1968.A7.

*14 SACKS, SHELDON. "From Artistic Judgment to Ethical Statement, The Shape of Belief in Fielding's Novels." Dissertation, Chicago, 1960.
Source: McNamee, 1865-1964, p. 560. See 1964.A24.

*15 WRIGHT, KENNETH D. "Henry Fielding and the London Stage, 1730-1737." Dissertation, Ohio State, 1960.
Source: Dissertation Abstracts, 21, no. 5 (Nov. 1960), 1293-1294. See 1964.B17.

1960 B SHORTER WRITINGS

1 [ANON.]. "Adventurer in Politicks. On Henry Fielding's political burlesques," in Essays on the Theatre from Eighteenth-Century Periodicals. Selected by John Loftis. The Augustan Reprint Society, no. 85-86. Los Angeles: William Andrews Clark Memorial Library and the University of California, pp. 54-57.
Reprints an article from 7 May 1737 Daily Gazeteer discussing Fielding's growing political impudence (from Pasquin to The Historical Register to Eurydice Hiss'd),

which threatens "to unloose the fundamental Pillars of Society, and shake it from its Basis." Attacks poetic license that undermines English liberty and threatens to make restraint necessary.

2 AVERY, EMMETT L., ed. The London Stage 1660-1800: A Calendar of Plays, Entertainments and Afterpieces Together with Casts, Box-Receipts and Contemporary Comment. Compiled from the Playbills, Newspapers and Theatrical Diaries of the Period. Part 2: 1700-1729. 2 vols. Carbondale: Southern Illinois University Press.

Reviewed by Eugene K. Bristow, QJS, 47 (1961), 81-82; J. G. M[cManaway], SQ, 13 (1962), 241-43; Edgar V. Roberts, Drama S, 1 (1962), 366-68; Arthur Sherbo, JEGP, 60 (1961), 299-305; Charles B. Woods, PQ, 40 (1961), 356-57.

The London Stage replaces Nicoll's (1925.B7) calendar of performances. In vol. 1 of this part Avery describes the playhouses (finances, managements, facilities, etc.), the companies (repertory, acting, music, etc.), and the audience and criticism prevailing when Fielding's career began. Vol. 2 records all of the performances of Love in Several Masques in the period. See 1961.B13 for Part 3 and the rest of Fielding's dramatic career.

3 BAKER, SHERIDAN. "Henry Fielding's Comic Romances." Papers of the Michigan Academy of Science, Arts, and Letters, 45: 411-19.

Correcting Fielding's designation of Joseph Andrews as a comic epic in prose and Tom Jones as a history, Baker sees the novels as comic romances. Sorts out parallels with Tom Brown's translation of Scarron's Comical Romance and Fielding's serious use of romantic patterns mocked by Cervantes. Briefly reviews the "blend of the romantic attitude with the burlesque of romance" (p. 417) in Fielding's work (the novels and The Author's Farce) and in his life.

Reprinted 1972.A2.

4 BATTESTIN, MARTIN C. "Fielding's Changing Politics and Joseph Andrews." Philological Quarterly, 39, no. 1 (Jan.), 39-55.

This historical article sets out the case for Fielding's changing politics (a shift from strong opposition to Walpole as late as 1739 to support in the satirical poem The Opposition in 1741). Recounts the pamphlet war against the faltering Walpole and Fielding's financial difficulty, suggesting that he may have sought financial aid from Walpole. Both The Opposition and the original version of

Joseph Andrews indicate a disillusionment with the Patriots (Walpole's opposition). Battestin concludes that Fielding was not "a paragon of political integrity" (p. 53) and that during the composition of Joseph Andrews he "may well have been driven for a time to accept Walpole's patronage" (p. 55). See 1894.B1, 1949.B6, 1966.B4, 1967.B2, 1973.B9, 1974.B5, and 1977.B10.

5 COLEY, WILLIAM B. "Fielding's Journalism." Notes and Queries, 205 (Oct.), 396.

Asks help in locating two pieces of Fielding's journalism (no. 45 of The Jacobite's Journal and no. 33 of The True Patriot).

6 COOLIDGE, JOHN S. "Fielding and 'Conservation of Character.'" Modern Philology, 57, no. 4 (May), 245-59.

Although the absence of the creating author makes immediately clear the difference between the controlled creation of Fielding's earlier novels and the method of Amelia, it can best be seen in a new emerging character. Fielding's first conception of character (conservation of character) comes from Horace and implies a stable character. Once set going, Fielding mixes fortune, a character's basic "nature," and ironic omniscience to create his full comic characters. In Amelia his intention changed; he took up the moral and psychological dilemmas implicit in Tom's character after the "comic romance" was over. Coolidge argues that, while Fielding abandoned fortune, subdued his irony, and introduced characters by means of impression rather than a full character sketch, he was not able fully to free Booth, or the novel, from the demands of his old form. Only in Mrs. Atkinson does Fielding seem capable of a "less controlled process of imagination," and this more organic character, who demonstrates the "art of life," Fielding "neither desired at the outset nor welcomed when it came" (p. 258).

For the originator of the term 'conservation of character,' see Cross, 1899.B1.

Reprinted 1962.A12 and 1972.A8.

7 EHRENPREIS, IRVIN. "Fielding's Use of Fiction: The Autonomy of Joseph Andrews," in Twelve Original Essays on Great English Novels. Edited by Charles Shapiro. Detroit: Wayne State University Press, pp. 23-41.

Begins by examining the "small oscillations of emotion which gather, as the large design, into massive waves of reversal" (p. 23). Describes the geographical countermovement, the scenes interrupted ("advancing by retreats,"

p. 26), the formula use of Fanny as a provoker of male lust who must constantly be rescued, and the negative analogues of the interpolated tales as the "ironies, unmaskings, conflicts, and reversals [which] stand behind the full pattern of the book" (p. 25). Ehrenpreis also discusses the biographical reason for Fielding's use of the Freudian "family romance" and incest motifs, his use of conventions borrowed from Cervantes, Marivaux, and others, the "fatherly reassurance" (p. 37) of his interventions, the foreshadowings in his dramas of some of the situations in Joseph Andrews, the scenic rather than the narrative quality of some events, and the symbolic comedy achieved by moving characters into and out of Adams' world.

Reprinted 1972.A8.

8 FEIL, J. P. "Fielding's Character of Mrs. Whitefield." Philological Quarterly, 39, no. 4 (Oct.), 508-10.

Compares Fielding's portrait of Mrs. Whitefield of the Bell in Gloucester with a contemporary account of her contained in a letter by a half-pay captain named Lewis Thomas.

9 FIELDING, HENRY. "Author's Preface to Joseph Andrews," in The Comic in Theory and Practice. Edited by John J. Enck, Elizabeth T. Forter and Alvin Whitley. New York: Appleton-Century-Crofts, pp. 7-9.

Selection from the preface.

10 FLEISSNER, ROBERT F. "'Kubla Khan' and 'Tom Jones': An Unnoticed Parallel." Notes and Queries, 205 (March), 103-105.

Argues for a surprising parallel between Fielding's description of Allworthy's house in Tom Jones and the "sunny pleasure-dome" in Coleridge's Kubla Khan. See 1974.B19.

11 HUTCHENS, ELEANOR N. "'Prudence' in Tom Jones: A Study of Connotative Irony." Philological Quarterly, 39, no. 4 (Oct.), 496-507.

Defines connotative irony (the literal meaning intact and the connotations stripped away) and illustrates how Fielding is able in Tom Jones to teach the desirable qualities of the word (idea) "prudence" directly and its "dangers and limitations . . . obliquely through connotative irony"(p. 506).

Incorporated in 1965.A15. For another discussion of "prudence," see 1967.B23.

1960

12 JOHNSTON, ARTHUR. "Fielding, Hearne and Merry-Andrews." Notes and Queries, 205 (Aug.), 295-97.

Fielding makes a satiric jibe at the scholar Thomas Hearne when he constructs a mock biography at the beginning of Joseph Andrews and borrows details from Hearne's discussion of the merry-andrews.

13 JORDAN, ROBERT M. "The Limits of Illusion: Faulkner, Fielding, and Chaucer." Criticism, 2, no. 3 (Summer), 278-305.

Begins by examining modern critical theory and asserting that "the comparative lack of critical interest in such fiction [Chaucer's and Fielding's] is attributable, I believe, to the incapacity of organicism, or the paradoxical disposition, to deal fruitfully with" (pp. 281-82) fiction in which form and content are distinguishable. Jordan, in the third section of this essay, argues that in Joseph Andrews Fielding "distinguishes clearly between theme and form, between content and container" (p. 292). He discusses the reader's relation with the narrator rather than the tale, the obtuseness of the pseudo-Fielding (the narrator), the rhetoric of shifting style, and his use of character (particularly Wilson) to teach us discernment. Throughout the novel "madness is embodied in the narrator, the apparent viewpoint of the novel; reason is activated in the mind of the reader who corrects the narrator's vision" (p. 297).

14 KREISSMAN, BERNARD. "Fielding," in Pamela-Shamela: A Study of the Criticisms, Burlesques, Parodies and Adaptations of Richardson's "Pamela." University of Nebraska Studies, N.S. no. 22. Lincoln: University of Nebraska Press, pp. 10-22 and passim.

Reviewed by Ronald Paulson, JEGP, 61 (1962), 410-13.

Outlines the parody of Pamela in Shamela and Joseph Andrews but does not explore the complexity of the parody in either. Thinks that "Fielding sounded most of the notes which were to be amplified by later critics of Pamela" (p. 22) and showed up Richardson's meretricious attitude that insisted on "the conventional trappings symbolic of virtue" (p. 46). See 1956.A2 and 1968.B31.

15 LUTWACK, LEONARD. "Mixed and Uniform Prose Styles in the Novel." Journal of Aesthetics and Art Criticism, 18 (March), 350-57.

Distinguishes between novels written in a single uniform style (Pamela and The Ambassadors) and novels written in a mixed style (Tom Jones and Ulysses); the latter, according to Lutwack, do not properly belong to the novel. He argues that Tom Jones embodies styles from three genres (narrative, essay, and drama). In addition it has three narrative styles (the plain, the Homeric, and the formal periodic). These mixed styles cause the novel to be loosely structured and reflect Fielding's ambiguous attitude toward the material of his novel.

Reprinted in The Novel: Modern Essays in Criticism, ed. Robert Murray Davis. Englewood Cliffs, N.J.: Prentice-Hall, 1969.

16 MANDELKOW, KARL R. "Der deutsche Briefroman. Zum Problem der Polyperspektive im Epischen." Neophilologus, 44, no. 3 (July), 200-208.

Argues that the modern novel with its self-effaced author is the direct descendant of Richardson's epistolary novels and not, as Stanzel (1955.B11) maintains, an outgrowth of Fielding's "classical" directed novel. For Mandelkow the epistolary novel grew into the novel of dialogue and then into the stream of consciousness. Goethe's Werther is moving in this direction, towards the modern poly-perspective; his Wilhelm Meister reverts to the "classical" novel. Mandelkow also quotes at length from Christian Friedrich von Blankenburg's essay Versuch über den Roman (1774), which kept the Richardson-Fielding opposition alive and defended Fielding's story-telling and the poly-perspective of his dialogue. In German.

17 MILLER, HENRY K. "Henry Fielding's Satire on the Royal Society." Studies in Philology, 57, no. 1 (Jan.), 72-86.

Shows that Fielding's Some Papers Proper to be Read before the R-L Society is a detailed parody of 28 January 1742/3 Philosophical Transactions of the Royal Society, which had printed a paper by the Genevan naturalist, Abraham Trembley. This satiric attack was in the tradition of the eighteenth-century humanists, like Swift, and consistent with Fielding's position in other works. Miller then suggests that Fielding broadened this parody to make it comment "upon the vices and follies of humanity at large" (p. 84).

18 SHERBO, ARTHUR. "The Time-Scheme in Amelia." Boston University Studies in English, 4, no. 4 (Winter), 223-28.

Argues that Amelia was written to a strictly kept time-scheme which Sherbo sets out in detail ("he observes a time-scheme that outdoes the one in Tom Jones for exactness," p. 224). Because Booth can only walk out without being arrested for debt on Sunday, Sherbo argues that

Fielding needed to pay special attention to the calendar and thus set the novel very close to the time in which it was written. It was published in December 1751; Sherbo's time-scheme for the novel runs from 1 April 1750 to 20 or 21 June 1750. Sherbo sees this as indicating that Fielding probably wrote the whole novel before the Enquiry into the Increase of Robbers.

For a very different view of the time-scheme in Amelia see Aleš Tichý, 1960.B21; Tichý follows Dudden in dating the novel in 1733.

19 TAUBE, MYRON. "Tom Jones with French Words and Music." Southern Speech Journal, 26:109-17.

Theater history article describes the dominance of the romanesque and the comic opera in eighteenth-century French theater. After an "uncertain beginning" the "musical comedy" Tom Jones became a hit in France. Taube describes the action of the play by Poinsinet (lyrics) and Danican (music), taken from the de la Place translation of the novel, and compares it briefly with its English original. Among the changes were the dropping of such characters as Square, Mrs. Waters, and Lady Bellaston, and Tom being changed from a "red-blooded young man" to a "somewhat pathetic" (p. 116) character. See 1881.B2; 1970.B28, B30.

20 TAVE, STUART M. The Amiable Humorist: A Study in the Comic Theory and Criticism of the Eighteenth and Early Nineteenth Centuries. Chicago and London: University of Chicago Press; Toronto: University of Toronto Press, passim.

Reviewed by A. O. Aldridge, MLN, 76 (1961), 164-65; John Carroll, UTQ, 32 (1961), 98-101; W. M. C[rittenden], Person, 42 (1961), 117-18; Arthur M. Eastman, SQ, 13 (1961), 250; George Goodin, JEGP, 60 (1961), 179-81; W. R. Irwin, PQ, 40 (1961), 362-63; D. W. Jefferson, MLR, 56 (1961), 409-410; C. J. Rawson, N&Q, 207 (1962), 37-38.

Tracing the development of a new more kindly aesthetic of comedy (in contrast to Renaissance and Hobbesian theories), Tave sees Fielding as one of the central figures in its development, particularly with his creation of Adams ("a comic character not designed for contempt," p. 142) and his "new concept of Don Quixote" as a "noble symbol" (p. 155).

Reprinted 1967.

21 TICHY, ALEŠ. "Remarks on the Flow of Time in the Novels of Henry Fielding." Brno Studies in English, 2:55-75.

Sharply disagrees with Dickson's (1917.B5) analysis of Fielding's use of time. After carefully setting out the time-schemes of Joseph Andrews and Amelia, Tichý concludes that there are not only occasional contradictions between the characters' statements about time and the time-scheme established in the narration, but that the scheme is essentially a simple day-night sequence that "does not reflect any definite historical succession of days characterized by means of outstanding events and dates" (p. 61). Fielding even disregards the normal division of weeks by Sundays, with their changed routine (he only uses Sunday to remind us of Booth's debt). Tichý then considers the influence of the tight dramatic time-schemes of Fielding's early plays on his novels, concluding that it is negligible. Finally he examines the strong influence of Cervantes' Don Quixote on the time-scheme of Joseph Andrews; Fielding's theory of dramatic unity and his complex practice in his dramatic satires (where in the "play-within-a-play" he abandoned tight time sequence) influences the time-scheme of Tom Jones.

For a different view see 1960.B18.

22 ULANOV, BARRY. "Sterne and Fielding: the Allegory of Irony," in his Sources and Resources: The Literary Traditions of Christian Humanism. Westminster, Maryland: Newman Press, pp. 206-27.

Contrasts Fielding's warm "even sentimental" attachment to his characters (Squire Western, Parson Adams, etc.) with Sterne's "imperial" attitude. Only in Jonathan Wild does Fielding effect such distance. Ulanov then appreciates the ironic consistency of Wild's character in this work, which is "to be read with the same sort of coolness and detachment that A Sentimental Journey invites" (p. 227).

23 WENDT, ALLAN. "The Naked Virtue of Amelia." Journal of English Literary History, 27, no. 2 (June), 131-48.

Argues that "Amelia is tested as real woman and as symbol." "As symbol of naked human virtue . . . she is tested doubly: for the genuine human need men have of her, and for her own ability to stand alone and unaided in an imperfect society." She fails this second test, illustrating "Fielding's final moral position: the naked beauty of virtue is a necessary but not a sufficient motive to ethically satisfactory actions" (p. 134). Wendt sees the parallel with the book of Job as stronger than that with the Aeneid, and argues that fortune becomes an agent of Amelia's trial, like Satan in Job. Booth is like Job's faithless friends. This essay on Fielding's moral doctrine concludes that Fielding did not give up his "benevolist doctrines" (p. 146) in Amelia; he merely tested them and found that with the addition of Christian orthodoxy they could be reaffirmed. See dissertation 1956.A11.

1961 A BOOKS

*1 DIRCKS, RICHARD J. "Henry Fielding's A Proposal for Making an Effectual Provision for the Poor." Dissertation, Fordham, 1961.

Source: Dissertation Abstracts, 23 (1962), 223. See 1962.B7 and 1966.B5.

2 FIELDING, HENRY. Hry Paleček, Kavárensky Politik, Don Quijote v Anglii, Historický Kalendář na Rok 1736, Jonathan Wild. Translated by Jaroslav Hornát, Dagmar Steinová, and Jarmila Fastrová. Prague: Knihovna Klasiků, 535 pp.

Czech translations of Pasquin, Coffee-House Politician, Don Quixote in England, Historical Register, and Jonathan Wild.

3 _____. Joseph Andrews and Shamela. Edited by Martin C. Battestin. Riverside Edition. Boston: Houghton Mifflin, 414 pp.

Reviewed by David Lodge, MLR, 26 (1967), 317-18; Terence Wright, N&Q, 211 (1966), 231; TLS, 6 Jan. 1966, p. 5.

The text of Joseph Andrews "is based largely on that of the fourth edition, published 29 October 1748" with a few "readings from previous editions and from the fifth edition . . . admitted" (p. 341). The text of Shamela "is based largely on that of the second edition" (p. 367). In both, the "accidentals" (spelling, capitalization, punctuation, and italics) have been modernized. Brief explanatory notes to both texts are provided, as well as a select bibliography. The introduction discusses Fielding's early career (particularly as a political satirist), the parody of Richardson's Pamela and other satiric objects, the distinction between comedy and burlesque in this "comic-epic in prose," and Fielding as a latitudinarian moral censor (with special attention to the character of Adams and the architecture of the novel).

4 _____. Joseph Andrews. Edited by Martin C. Battestin. Riverside Edition. Boston: Houghton Mifflin, 367 pp.

Same introduction, text, and notes as 1961.A3, omitting Shamela.

5 _____. The Adventures of Joseph Andrews. Introduction by L. Rice-Oxley. World Classics. London, New York, Toronto: Oxford University Press, 406 pp.
Reprint of 1929.A3.

6 _____. The History of Tom Jones A Foundling. Introduction by George Sherburn. Vintage Books. New York: Random House, 901 pp. [1961].
Reprint of 1950.A5.

*7 _____. The Life of Jonathan Wild. World Classics. London: Oxford University Press, 289 pp. [1961].
Source: National Union Catalogue Author Lists, 1963-1967. Vol. 17, p. 320.

8 _____. The Lover's Assistant, or, New Art of Love (1760). Edited by Claude E. Jones. The Augustan Reprint Society, no. 89. Los Angeles: William Andrews Clark Memorial Library and the University of California, 39 pp.
Reviewed by William B. Coley, PQ, 41 (1961), 58-88.
Briefly reviews the publication history of The Lover's Assistant (originally called Ovid's Art of Love Paraphrased) and prints the 1760 edition, collated with the 1759 issue (the 1747 first edition no longer being available).

*9 GOLDBERG, HOMER B. "Joseph Andrews and the Continental Comic Romances." Dissertation, Chicago, 1961.
Source: McNamee, 1865-1964, p. 560. See 1969.A13.

*10 HARRIS, KATHLEEN. "Beitraege zur Wirkung Fieldings in Deutschland, 1742-1792." Dissertation, Goettingen, 1961.
In German.
Source: McNamee, 1865-1964, p. 560. Reviewed by Wayne Wonderly, Monatshefte für deutschen Unterricht, 56 (1964), 117-18.

11 JOHNSON, MAURICE. Fielding's Art of Fiction: Eleven Essays on Shamela, Joseph Andrews, Tom Jones, and Amelia. Philadelphia: University of Pennsylvania Press; Oxford: Oxford University Press (1962), 182 pp.
Reviewed by Martin C. Battestin, PQ, 41 (1962), 588-90; William W. Combs, SAQ, 61 (1962), 422-23; Andrew Wright, MLR, 58 (1963), 464; TLS, 3 Aug. 1962, p. 555.
In "a series of separate explications, interpreting structural effects or analyzing specific passages," Johnson "illustrates the growth and refinement of Fielding's art" (p. 11), as it developed from parody to

noble allusion. Some essays, no. 8 for example, are more precisely formalistic than others. One essay on Shamela traces the verbal parallels to Pamela. The first of the three essays on Joseph Andrews demonstrates the shift from parody in Shamela to comic romance in Joseph Andrews, where caricatured figures gradually turn into "heartfelt persons drawn from human nature" (p. 53). Johnson argues that at Book 2, chapter 12 the novel alters mood, turning from burlesque into love story. The second essay on Joseph Andrews best illustrates Johnson's technique, as he isolates a related but contrasting pair of chapters to demonstrate the way in which "fiction and life are juxtaposed for a purpose" (p. 62). The third essay is on the testing of Adams' Christian resignation with the supposed death of Jacky. The first of the four essays on Tom Jones discusses the self-conscious artfulness of the "prefaces," which describe the qualifications for a novelist, elucidate the craft of fiction, and describe the art of reading fiction. The second essay compares Tom and Hamlet in order to describe Fielding's characterization, the poetic functioning of the plot, and the nature of comic fiction. The third essay demonstrates how Sophia's "character is shaped . . . by . . . ironical commentary" (p. 107). The fourth examines the literal and symbolic function of objects and images and "the play of language in action" (p. 115). (Expansion of 1959.B10). The first of the three essays on Amelia demonstrates how its twelve books are based on Virgil's Aeneid; the whole dramatizes the establishing of a marriage, not a nation. The second essay is devoted to an analysis of the ambiguous use of Dr. Harrison's sermon on adultery when it is read at a masquerade. The third essay on Amelia, and the final one in the collection, argues for Fielding's move toward becoming an overt Christian censor.

Reprinted 1969.A15.

*12 LEVINE, GEORGE R. "The Techniques of Irony in the Major Early Works of Henry Fielding." Dissertation, Columbia, 1961.

Source: McNamee, 1865-1964, p. 560. See 1967.A12.

13 MILLER, HENRY K. Essays on Fielding's Miscellanies: A Commentary on Volume One. Princeton: Princeton University Press, 489 pp.

Reviewed by John Carroll, UTQ, 32 (1962), 98-101; Donald D. Eddy, MP, 60 (1961), 290-93; Bernhard Fabian, Archiv., 201 (1965), 461-65; L. P. Goggin, PQ, 41 (1961), 590-91; Ronald Paulson, JEGP, 61 (1962), 413-16; C. J.

Rawson, RES, n.s. 14 (1963), 88-90; Andrew Wright, MLR, 57 (1962), 422.

Studies "the literary and intellectual traditions upon which" (p. viii) Fielding drew in his Miscellanies, which "is almost a microcosm of Henry Fielding's intellectual world" (p. vii). An opening chapter provides all of the available information about the "circumstances of publication" (from printers' ledgers to the political nature of the subscribers). The book is then divided into five major sections: poetry, essays, satires, translations, and Lucianic sketches. Each section opens with a brief general discussion: Fielding's poetic style, prose style, rhetorical and parodic techniques, the state of translation and Fielding's knowledge of Greek, and the similarities in tone and style between Lucian and Fielding. The brief sections on poetry and prose are particularly interesting because of Miller's careful use of terms from classical rhetorical analysis. The general openings are then followed by sections on individual works, setting each in its time and in the context of Fielding's thought. A number of important ideas for Fielding and his age are discussed (e.g., "true greatness," "liberty," marriage and women, "good breeding"). In conclusion Miller finds Fielding a latitudinarian Christian whose comedy embraces the "sadder truths with full comprehension and yet remains a yea-saying acceptance of life" (p. 423) and whose complexity is not in his "few and relatively uncomplicated" ideas but in his "ironic vision and his concern to give equal weight to many antipodal values" (p. 421). He also argues for "a gradual and natural progression in the direction of greater conservatism" (p. 94). See dissertation 1953.A5.

*14 ROLLE, DIETRICH. "Fielding und Sterne: Untersuchungen ueber die Funktion des Erzaehlers." Dissertation, Muenster, 1961.

In German.

Source: McNamee, 1865-1964, p. 560. See 1963.A8.

1961 B SHORTER WRITINGS

1 ALLOTT, MIRIAM. "A Note on Fielding's Mr. Square." Modern Language Review, 56, no. 1 (Jan.), 69-72.

Square, in Tom Jones, has often been identified (1918.A1 and 1952.A1) as a specific man (Thomas Chubb). Allott argues that "Square is an abstraction. He is half of an antithesis representing two doctrinaire and opposed ethical attitudes: his fellow-tutor, Thwackum, represents authority while he represents non-Christian deism" (p. 71). Through him Fielding is able to satirize the arid end of the deist controversy epitomized by men like Samuel Clarke.

*2 BASSEIN, BETH ANN (CROSKEY). "Crime and Punishment in the Novels of Defoe, Fielding, and Godwin." Dissertation, Missouri, 1961.

Studies the calls by these three novelists for reformation, in particular Fielding's Amelia, written "solely for the purpose of revealing social evils connected with crime and punishment."

Source: Dissertation Abstracts, 22, no. 8 (Feb. 1962), 2783.

3 BLAND, D. S. "Endangering the Reader's Neck: Background Description in the Novel." Criticism, 3, no. 2 (Spring), 121-39.

Considers the use of description from Fielding to Hardy, concluding that description was first used to localize characters and to evoke mood and only in the nineteenth century as symbol. By comparing a passage of description from Joseph Andrews with one from Tom Jones, Bland shows how Fielding used the first to underline the romantic mood and the second (the description of Allworthy's estate) to place "Allworthy on the social map and display his character" (p. 126).

4 BOOTH, WAYNE C. "'Fielding' in Tom Jones," in his The Rhetoric of Fiction. Chicago: University of Chicago Press, pp. 215-21, passim.

Reviewed by Francis Connolly, Thought, 38 (1963), 134-35; Paul Goetsche, NS, 11 (1962), 268-72; David Lodge, MLR, 57 (1962), 580-81; Frederick P. McDowell, PQ, 41 (1962), 547-48; B. R. McElderry, Person, 44 (1963), 263-64; Alan D. McKillop, MP, 60 (1963), 295-98; Martin Price, YR, 51 (1961), 469-73; Donald H. Reiman, SAQ, 61 (1962), 427; Mark Roberts, EIC, 12 (1962), 322-34; Earl Rovit, BA, 37 (1963), 73; Peter Swiggart, SR, 71 (1963), 142-59; Andrew Wright, KR, 24 (1962), 566-70; MFS, 7 (1961), 373-74. See also John Killham, "The 'Second Self' in Novel Criticism," BJA, 6 (1966), 272-90; Wayne C. Booth, "The Rhetoric of Fiction and the Poetics of Fiction," Novel, 1 (1968), 105-17; John Killham, "My Quarrel with Booth," Novel, 1 (1968), 267-72.

Booth uses Fielding as a constant source of examples throughout this important theoretical work. For instance, Joseph Andrews offers a perfect example (the robbing and stripping of Joseph) of a dramatic situation which is narrated in what we do not "normally think of as a dramatic manner" (p. 161). In Tom Jones, Fielding, as one of "the great narrators," illustrates one of the ways irony can be used to make narrative summary interesting. Fielding is again used as the chief example for Booth's notion that every novelist, as a rhetorician, must reinforce beliefs we have or mold new ones. But it is in the illustration of Booth's concept of the author's "second self" and the reader's relationship with this "second self" that Fielding is most important. Rejecting the dictum that authors should be objective, Booth constructs a rhetoric of fiction in which an ideal author ("no single version of Fielding emerges" (p. 72) from reading Fielding's fiction) creates a self that is both generously humane and "strictly in keeping with the special effects [of] the work as a whole" (p. 73). This author creates a special bond with the reader ("if we read straight through all of the seemingly gratuitous appearances of the narrator, leaving out the story of Tom, we discover a running account of a growing intimacy between the narrator and the reader," p. 216) and with the characters ("It is from the narrator's norms that Tom departs when he gets himself into trouble, yet Tom is always in harmony with his most important norms," p. 217).

Often reprinted in full (ten impressions by 1973) and in part (1968.A2 and 1973.A15). For a reaction to Booth see 1973.B2.

5 COLEY, WILLIAM B. "Henry Fielding's 'Lost' Law Book." Modern Language Notes, 76, no. 5 (May), 408-13.

On the basis of advertisements issued by Andrew Miller, Fielding was preparing several folios on crown law in 1745. Coley conjectures that they were probably in part based on notes of his maternal grandfather, Sir Henry Gould, who had had a reputation on King's Bench. It is unclear why Fielding never finished them, but this activity with the law around the time of his first wife's death partly dispels the notion of his overwhelming grief keeping him from creative work. See 1968.B1.

6 FRIEDMAN, WILLIAM A. "Joseph Andrews: Clothing and the Concretization of Character." Discourse, 4, no. 4 (Autumn), 304-310.

Argues that, because in Fielding's aesthetic doctrine example is more effective than precept, clothing becomes the "principal means of character revelation" (p. 306) and demonstrates "the disparity between appearance and reality" (p. 308). Briefly examines Joseph and Adams to show

Fielding both approving of the idea that "clothes make the man" (p. 304) and inverting it. See 1967.B13.

7 JOHNSON, E. D. H. "Vanity Fair and Amelia: Thackeray in the Perspective of the Eighteenth Century." Modern Philology, 59, no. 2 (Nov.), 100-113.

Argues that for biographical and literary reasons Thackeray used Amelia as a model for Vanity Fair. "Thackeray accepted the tradition that through the Booths, Fielding had presented a version of his own marital life, in which the later novelist might have seen many parallels with his own domestic situation" (p. 101). In addition "the graver and more reflective mood of Amelia would be congenial to the moral elevation at which he was aiming in Vanity Fair" (p. 100). Johnson finds parallels in character (Amelia Booth and Amelia Osborne), setting (upper-middle-class London), and theme (conflict of moral values). Thackeray, however, was not able to embody the redeeming Christian values of Amelia Booth in Amelia Osborne; "she exists between two worlds . . . one that of Vanity Fair . . . the other that of transcendant values inhabited by Fielding's Amelia" (p. 111). See 1977.B12.

8 JONES, B. P. "Was There a Temporary Suppression of Tom Jones in France?" Modern Language Notes, 76, no. 6 (June), 495-98.

If Tom Jones was suppressed in Paris to punish a bookseller for printing without the permission of the official censor, little was made of the suppression. It is likely that it was only threatened. See 1898.B1, 1898.B3, 1927.B5, and 1957.B13.

9 JONES, CLAUDE. "Henry Fielding as Translator," in Langue et Littérature: Actes du VIII Congrès de la Fédération Internationale des Langues et Littératures Modernes. Paris: Société d'Edition (Les Belles Lettres), pp. 212-13.

Resumé of a paper which discusses Fielding's translations and adaptations from French, Greek, and Latin, with special attention to his paraphrase imitation (a mixture of Dryden's two types) from Latin called Ovid's Art of Love. Claims that Fielding translated Alderfeld's History of Charles XII from the French and may have assisted in preparing Hedrick's Greek lexicon (1755). See 1912.B8.

10 LANE, WILLIAM G. "Relationships Between Some of Fielding's Major and Minor Works." Boston University Studies in English, 5, no. 4 (Winter), 219-31.

Illustrates how certain elements in his major works are "illuminated and enlarged by a reading of various representative minor pieces" (p. 231). Lane compares Fielding's method of moral instruction, his humorous satire, his varied use of similar material, his interest in and use of language in The True Patriot, The Covent-Garden Journal, A Journey from This World to the Next, and The Journal of a Voyage to Lisbon with his use of these in Tom Jones and and Joseph Andrews. He also suggests that a similar comparative study could be made of several typical Fielding "characters" (i.e., the country squire and the country gentlewoman).

11 MURRAY, PETER B. "Summer, Winter, Spring, and Autumn in Tom Jones." Modern Language Notes, 76, no. 4 (April), 324-26.
Characters in Tom Jones through name, metaphors, and imagery are associated with the seasons. "Tom's father is summer, . . . Tom's mother is associated with winter, Tom and Sophia with spring, and Lady Bellaston with autumn" (p. 324).

12 ROBERTS, EDGAR V. "Eighteenth-Century Ballad Opera: The Contribution of Henry Fielding." Drama Survey, 1, no. 1 (May), 77-85.
After generally describing the ballad opera tradition which led to German Singspiel and Gilbert and Sullivan, Roberts examines Fielding's two types of ballad opera: burlesque and farce/intrigue. Fielding used both for satiric purposes, but he is never misanthropic. Roberts also briefly examines Fielding's use of music and his skill as a lyricist.

13 SCOUTEN, A. H., ed. The London Stage 1660-1800: A Calendar of Plays, Entertainments and Afterpieces Together with Casts, Box-Receipts and Contemporary Comment. Compiled from the Playbills, Newspapers and Theatrical Diaries of the Period. Part 3: 1729-1747. 2 vols. Carbondale: Southern Illinois University Press.
Reviewed by Eugene K. Bristow, QJS, 49 (1963), 89; David P. French, BA, 37 (1963), 77-78; Arthur Sherbo, JEGP, 61 (1962), 926-31; Charles B. Woods, PQ, 41 (1962), 556-58; TLS, 25 May 1962, p. 368.
In volume 1 Scouten, like Avery (1960.B2), reviews the theatrical scene. Because Fielding now plays a significant role in it, Scouten discusses his bold and innovative management at the New Haymarket, his dramas, and his role in the Licensing Act. The calendar of performances provides a stage history of all of Fielding's plays performed

1961

in the period and thus of nearly all of Fielding's plays. For the stage history of Fielding's plays for the rest of the eighteenth century, as well as the stage history of his posthumous The Fathers, see the continuation of The London Stage by G. W. Stone (1747-1776) in 1962 and C. B. Hogan (1776-1880) in 1968.

*14 SEN, S. C. "Richardson and Fielding: Moral Sense and Moral Vision." Bulletin of the Department of English, University of Calcutta, 2: 38-40.
Source: T. Humphrey, p. 215.

15 SMITH, LE ROY W. "Fielding and Mandeville: The 'War Against Virtue.'" Criticism, 3, no. 1 (Winter), 7-15.
Establishes Fielding's indebtedness to the skeptics, antirationalists, or self-love psychologists "headed by Hobbes, Bayle, and Mandeville" (p. 7). Smith particularly examines the allusions and parallels to Mandeville in Fielding's work, arguing that "their analyses of society are closely akin" (p. 11), but Fielding refused to accept the inevitability of a society dominated by passions and self-love. Fielding's heroes embody those qualities that Mandeville thinks beyond men (benevolence, love, friendship) and that Fielding thinks beyond many men. See dissertation 1956.A10.

16 TANNENBAUM, EARL. "A Note on Tom Jones and the Man of the Hill." College Language Association Journal, 4:215-17.
Argues that Fielding uses the old man to form a moral contrast with Tom. Neatly sets out similarities (both born in Somerset, rejected by mistress and friend, full of animal spirits, etc.) and the significant difference (Tom does not believe mankind to be totally evil and corrupt). If it weren't for this difference "Tom too might become a veritable 'Man of the Hill'" (p. 216). See 1968.B32 and 1969.B12.

1962 A BOOKS

1 BANERJI, H. K. Henry Fielding: Playwright, Journalist and Master of the Art of Fiction, His Life and Works. New York: Russell & Russell, 349 pp.
Reissue of 1929.A1.

*2 COMBS, WILLIAM W. "Man and Society in Fielding's Works." Dissertation, Harvard, 1962.
Source: McNamee, 1865-1964, p. 560.

3 FIELDING, HENRY. Amelia. Dolphin Books. Garden City, New York: Doubleday, 559 pp.
No indication of copy text.

4 _____. Amelia. Introduction by A. R. Humphreys. Everyman's Library. 2 vols. London: J. M. Dent & Sons; New York: E. P. Dutton, 638 (318 & 320) pp.
Reprint of 1930.A2. Introduction touches on its reception, the characters (particularly Amelia, Booth and Dr. Harrison), and the moral struggle between passion and Christianity embodied in the central action of the novel. Biographical note and select bibliography included.

5 _____. Joseph Andrews. Introduction by A. R. Humphreys. Everyman's Library. London: J. M. Dent & Sons; New York: E. P. Dutton, 304 pp.
Text reprints 1910.A6, based on the "second" edition of August 1742. The introduction touches on the parody, the symbolic journey, the thematic purpose of the interpolated tales, and the skill with which Fielding embodies his morality in the characters, plot, and style. Biographical note and select bibliography included.

6 _____. The History of Tom Jones a Foundling. Edited and abridged by W. Somerset Maugham. Introduction by Bergan Evans. Premier World Classic. Greenwich, Conn.: Fawcett Publications, 392 pp.
Reissue of 1957.A4 without illustrations. By 1964 this edition was in its fourth printing. Introduction touches on the irony, the city-country motif, Tom's not preying on women, etc. Sees Fielding as arguing that "self-interest is man's chief motivation" (p. vii).

7 _____. The History of Tom Jones. Introduction by A. R. Humphreys. Everyman's Library. 2 vols. London: J. M. Dent & Sons; New York: E. P. Dutton, 711 (355 & 356) pp.
Text reprints 1909.A2. The introduction touches on Fielding's serious moral purpose, the intellectual nature of his comedy, the plotting, characterization and style, and on the sexual morality implied in the novel. Select bibliography and biographical note included.

8 _____. The Life of Mr. Jonathan Wild the Great. Foreword by J. H. Plumb. Signet Classic. New York and Scarborough, Ontario: New American Library, 222 pp.
Plumb reviews Fielding's career (particularly his political attacks on Walpole), his political journalism, and

his knowledge of the underworld. Reprints the second edition of 1754.

*9 _____. Tom Jones. Translated by Paul Baudisch. Leipzig: München List, 1441 pp.
German translation; reissued in 1963 and 1971.
Source: Hugh Amory's working bibliography.

*10 KAISER, JOHN L. "A Study of the Plays of Henry Fielding as a Commentary on the Early Eighteenth-Century Theatre." Dissertation, St. John's-Brooklyn, 1962.
Source: McNamee, 1865-1964, p. 560.

11 MCKILLOP, ALAN D., ed. An Essay on the New Species of Writing Founded by Mr. Fielding (1751). The Augustan Reprint Society, no. 95. Los Angeles: William Andrews Clark Memorial Library and the University of California, 57 pp.
Reprints the pamphlet with a few notes. McKillop's introduction describes the ways in which the anonymous author borrows Fielding's ideas in order to praise him, the author's unimaginative use of the developing critical concept of a "new species," and his complaint about inferior imitators of Fielding like Smollett.

12 PAULSON, RONALD, ed. Fielding: A Collection of Critical Essays. Twentieth-Century Views. Edited by Maynard Mack. Englewood Cliffs, N.J.: Prentice-Hall, 192 pp.
Reprints essays and parts of chapters by A. R. Humphreys, "Fielding's Irony: Its Method and Effect" (1942.B5); Winfield H. Rogers, "Fielding's Early Aesthetic and Technique" (1943.B6); Ian Watt, "Shamela" (1956.A2); Maynard Mack, "Joseph Andrews and Pamela" (1948.A3); Mark Spilka, "Comic Resolution in Fielding's Joseph Andrews" (1953.B10); Aurélien Digeon, "Jonathan Wild" (1925.A1); André Gide, "Notes For a Preface to Fielding's Tom Jones"; Arnold Kettle, "Tom Jones"(1951.B3); J. Middleton Murry, "Fielding's 'Sexual Ethic' in Tom Jones" (1956.B9); Ian Watt, "Tom Jones and Clarissa" (1957.B17); William Empson, "Tom Jones" (1958.B6); George Sherburn, "Fielding's Amelia: An Interpretation" (1936.B10), and John S. Coolidge, "Fielding and 'Conservation of Character'" (1960.B6). The introduction argues for the modernity of Fielding, describing his irony, ambiguity and complexity, his moral richness and stability, and his superiority to Richardson. Selected bibliography, organized by work (Tom Jones) and theme (Fielding's "Intense Moral Preoccupation"), and a chronological table of important dates included.

*13 ZIRKER, MALVIN R. "Henry Fielding's Social Attitudes: A Study of An Enquiry into the Causes of the Late Increase of Robbers, and A Proposal for Making Effectual Provision for the Poor." Dissertation, California-Berkeley, 1962.
Source: McNamee, 1865-1964, p. 560. See 1966.A26 and 1967.B35.

1962 B SHORTER WRITINGS

1 BAKER, SHERIDAN. "Fielding's Amelia and the Materials of Romance." Philological Quarterly, 41, no. 2 (April), 437-49.
Argues that "however domesticated, several incidents and the general plot of Amelia . . . follow the unfactual and inquotidian tradition of romance" (p. 438). Baker briefly looks at the mixing of romance and fact in Fielding's other work (particularly his dramas) and then sets out the way he has "embraced the noble, passionate, generous life of romance" (p. 440) in Amelia. Fielding uses the ancient disguise-motif, the unnamed foster brother with overtones of incest, the long-lost inheritance, and a man at arms serving a lady above him. Baker argues that with the comic controls removed, "the realism turns Fielding's habitual romance techniques sentimental, and lures him into the further temptations and pious self-deceptions of sentimentalism" (p. 449).
Reprinted 1972.A8.

2 _____. "Political Allusions in Fielding's Author's Farce, Mock Doctor, and Tumble-Down Dick." Publications of the Modern Language Association, 77, no. 3 (June), 221-31.
This ingenious study of political innuendo examines the two versions of the Author's Farce (1730 and 1734) and concludes that "though the actual scenes concerning the Cibbers take more of a literary than a political turn in 1734, Fielding's revision . . . is not without some direct heightening of anti-Walpole satire" (p. 226). Baker also suggests that there are anti-Walpole jibes in the apparently innocent Mock Doctor (1732). Tumble-Down Dick (1736), although its announced target is John Rich, is full of Fielding's "characteristic double satire" (p. 228); its object is again Walpole. See 1970.B12.

3 BUNDY, JEAN. "Fréron and the English Novel." Revue de Littérature Comparée, 36, no. 2, 258-65.
Sets out Fréron's developing appreciation of Fielding's novels. In his first review of de la Place's translation of

Tom Jones, Fréron thought the novel too long, too didactic, and psychologically inconsistent. As he later (in the 1760s) began to appreciate the real difference in national taste, Fréron praised both Amelia and Jonathan Wild, despite passages of questionable taste. Finally he came to see in Tom Jones and Joseph Andrews a greater realism than he found in the French novel, and he considered both to be important works in the genre. See 1909.B2, 1917.B4 and 1922.B7.

4 CARSWELL, JOHN. "Kubla Khan." Times Literary Supplement (16 March), p. 185.

Fielding's description of Paradise Hall in Tom Jones (Book 1, chapter 4) is echoed in "Kubla Khan."

5 COLEY, WILLIAM B. "Fielding and the Two 'Covent-Garden Journals.'" Modern Language Review, 57, no. 3 (July), 386-87.

Although Fielding had nothing to do with the 1749 Covent-Garden Journal, the opposition (particularly in the periodical Old England) accused him of writing it. Fielding probably borrowed the title and the pseudonym (Drawcansir) for his Covent-Garden Journal from Old England, turning their irony back on them.

6 _____. "The 'Remarkable Queries' in the Champion." Philological Quarterly, 41, no. 2 (April), 426-36.

Traces the vexed history of the "Remarkable Queries" (signed B. T.), which were reprinted in the 1741, 1743, and 1766 collected editions of The Champion under the date 14 June 1740, even though they did not appear in 1740. Coley discusses the political reasons for this piece appearing in the collected editions and not in the original (the essay it replaces might be thought more inflammatory, but the Queries were clearly more tendentious); he follows the controversy it stirred. He also discusses the authorship, concluding that this piece, like so much in The Champion, is not clearly by either Ralph or Fielding. See 1953.B8.

7 DIRCKS, RICHARD J. "Some Notes on Fielding's 'Proposal for the Poor.'" Notes and Queries, 207 (Dec.), 457-59.

More circumstantial evidence that Thomas Gibson may have drawn up Fielding's plan for a building for the poor; the plan Fielding presented to Pelham may have been in the form of a bill to be debated in the 1752 sessions of parliament. Both the Gosse (1898.A1) and the Henley

(1902/67.A4) editions of this work are inaccurate. See 1966.A26 and 1971.B2. See dissertation 1961.A1.

8 EDDY, DONALD D. "The Printing of Fielding's Miscellanies (1743)." Studies in Bibliography, 15: 247-56.

A complete bibliographical description (including press figures and speculation about imposition) of "two" editions of the Miscellanies (April 1743), which "indicates not only that they are in truth one edition, but also that they are merely varying states of the same impression" (p. 249). See 1918.B5.

9 GREENBERG, BERNARD L. "Fielding's 'Humane Surgeon.'" Notes and Queries, 207 (Dec.), 456-57.

The model for the Man of the Hill's 'humane surgeon' may be William III's sergeant-surgeon, Etienne Roujat.

10 HORN, ANDRÁS. "Social Morality: Fielding," in his Byron's "Don Juan" and the Eighteenth-Century English Novel. Swiss Studies in English. No. 51. Bern: A. Francke, pp. 9-27.

Reviewed by A. H. Elliott, RES, 15 (1964), 118-19; Kaspar Spinner, E. Studies, 45 (1964), 326-27.

Horn's study of the influence of Fielding, Sterne, and Smollett on Byron links Fielding's and Byron's tolerance, their satiric exposure of hypocrisy, and their humanitarianism (though Fielding's tolerance of human frailty decreases as he ages). Horn briefly examines the philanthropy and the political liberalism of both and concludes that "the novels of Fielding and Don Juan are built upon a self-consistent moral attitude, comprising eroticism and social conscience in a positive whole" (p. 27).

11 HUTCHENS, ELEANOR N. "Verbal Irony in Tom Jones." Publications of the Modern Language Association, 77, no. 1 (March), 46-50.

Verbal irony makes Tom Jones a masterpiece, and only in that novel did Fielding "achieve the triumphant mastery" (p. 46) of it. According to Hutchens, the "forms of verbal irony are the ways in which the suggestion [at odds with its context or with a view shared by author and reader] may be made: by the denotation, connotation, tone, or implied reference of the words or of their arrangement" (p. 46). Her article illustrates four kinds of irony, avoiding problems with the often elusive term "tone" by discussing what she calls the "irony of reference" (p. 49). At the end of the article she briefly distinguishes between substantial and verbal irony.

Incorporated in 1965.A15. For another discussion of irony in Tom Jones see 1958.B6.

12 MAYO, ROBERT D. The English Novel in the Magazines 1740-1815: with a Catalogue of 1375 Magazine Novels and Novelettes. Evanston: Northwestern University Press; London: Oxford University Press, passim.

Reviewed by Richard D. Altick, LQ, 34 (1964), 131-32; Geoffrey Carnall, MLR, 59 (1964), 278; M. Levy, EA, 17 (1964), 77-78; J. M. S. Tompkins, RES, 15 (1964), 208-10.

Comments on Fielding's apparent lack of interest in prose fiction in his periodicals. The Champion "published nothing except short essay-type narratives" (p. 76). Fielding's one attempt at prose fiction, the "Voyages of Mr. Job Vinegar, . . . studiously seems to avoid a narrative structure" (p. 76). Mayo also comments on Samuel Johnson's analysis of Fielding's theory of the novel in The Rambler, on the reaction of various periodicals to Joseph Andrews, Tom Jones, and Amelia, and on Fielding's response to various criticisms.

13 PANTUČKOVÁ, LIDMILA. "The Relationship of W. M. Thackeray to Henry Fielding." Bruenn Universita. Filosoficka Fakulta. Sborník Prací, Rada Literarnevedna. No. 9:99-114.

Traces "Thackeray's critical opinions of Fielding" (p. 99) from the time Thackeray was ten through the 1860s. Argues that in the 1830s and '40s, Thackeray "continues to assess highly the strength and sharpness of Fielding's satire" (p. 103), and in the 1850s and 1860s (in lectures and statements), Thackeray shifts and "admires above all the qualities of mercifulness, pity, kindness and benevolence" (p. 105). His "protest against the moral laxity of Tom Jones . . . shows more than convincingly how far his identification with the hypocritical Victorian bourgeois society has gone" (p. 106). Asserts that Thackeray's changed attitude to Fielding is motivated by a "growing fear of any revolutionary changes in the society in which he had at last secured for himself . . . the place which belonged to him by . . . birth and education" (p. 108). See 1957.B12.

14 POWERS, LYALL H. "Tom Jones and Jacob de la Vallée." Papers of the Michigan Academy of Science, Arts, and Letters, 47: 659-67.

Argues "that Fielding apparently saw in Marivaux's Le Paysan parvenu a reasonable and useful basic pattern for the instructive story of a young man's learning wisdom or prudence. . . . The main lines of Tom Jones' career follow rather closely those of Jacob de la Vallée" (p. 667). After briefly setting out the initial similarity in the two novelists' general humanistic attitude to good and evil, Powers discusses the nature of sexual fidelity in each novel, suggesting that Tom gains wisdom and Jacob only a sort of sentimental education. Reprinted 1973.A15.

15 ROBERTS, EDGAR V. "Henry Fielding's Lost Play Deborah, or A Wife for You All (1733): Consisting Partly of Facts and Partly of Observations upon Them." Bulletin of the New York Public Library, 66, no. 9 (Nov.), 576-88.

Using the only three available sources of information about the play (two brief newspaper advertisements and Genest's English Stage) "combined with a study of (a) Fielding's treatment of similar characters and scenes elsewhere in his works, and (b) the type of roles commonly taken by the actors who performed in Deborah," Roberts argues that there are "fairly obvious conclusions about the plot and tone of the play" and that "many of the play's significant details are virtually knowable" (p. 577). Roberts examines the probability of its having music, its political and artistic allusions (to the Handel-Humphreys oratorio Deborah), the outline of a typical Fielding trial scene, comic and farcical character types, and the songs he might have used from The Grub-Street Opera. See dissertation 1960.A13.

16 _____. "Possible Additions to Airs 6 and 7 of Henry Fielding's Ballad Opera 'The Lottery.'" Notes and Queries, 207 (Dec.), 455-56.

Extra stanzas were added to two songs from The Lottery when they were later published in eighteenth-century song books. It is impossible to know whether Fielding wrote them. See dissertation 1960.A13.

17 SACKETT, S. J. English Literary Criticism: 1726-1750. Fort Hays Studies, n.s. Literature Series, no. 1 (June), pp. 25-26, 89-93, 105-110, 117, 145-55.

Reprints the preface to The Tragedy of Tragedies, The Champion (13 Dec. 1739), the preface to Joseph Andrews, part of chapter 8 of A Journey from This World to the Next, the preface to David Simple, and the opening chapters to Books 5, 8, 9, 14 of Tom Jones. Introduction discusses Fielding's theory of comedy, of the novel, and of witty ridicule.

1962

18 SMITH, LEROY W. "Fielding and 'Mr. Bayle's' Dictionary." Texas Studies in Literature and Language, 4, no. 1 (Spring), 16-20.

Suggests that Fielding may have borrowed some of his skeptical antirationalist ideas from Bayle's Critical and Historical Dictionary (1697). Smith particularly examines the similarity in their concept of love and fortune; he also sees them as sharing a tolerant pessimism and turning to the Christian system for relief. See dissertation 1956.A10.

19 WATSON, GEORGE. "The Augustans: Fielding," in his The Literary Critics: A Study of English Descriptive Criticism. Baltimore: Penguin Books, pp. 72-80; New York: Barnes & Noble; London: Chatto & Windus, 1964, pp. 66-74.

Reviewed by R. L. Brett, RES, 14 (1963), 429-30; D. J. Enright, N. St., 63 (1962), 761-62; Philip Hobsbaum, Listener, 68 (1962), 111; E. R. Marks, Criticism, 5 (1963), 293-95; J. C. Maxwell, MLR, 58 (1963), 115-16; Allan Rodway, DUJ, 24 (1963), 158-59.

Suggests that, although Fielding began the criticism of the novel, it "was a false start" because "he failed to create a tradition, and had no disciples" (p. 68). Thinks that the two weaknesses in Fielding's theories result from his training as a dramatist (which conflicted with epic seriousness) and from the contemporary incoherence of comic theory. Watson principally examines the incoherence in the "preface" to Joseph Andrews and the weakness in Fielding's parodic practice.

20 WOODS, CHARLES B. "The 'Miss Lucy' Plays of Fielding and Garrick." Philological Quarterly, 41, no. 1 (Jan.), 294-310.

In "its earliest versions [David Garrick's Lethe] contains episodes which form a sequel to The Virgin Unmask'd" (p. 296), thus demonstrating Fielding's influence. Fielding may have met Garrick before 1740 and aided Garrick's theatrical career. Woods suggests that they collaborated in writing the sequel to The Virgin Unmask'd, Miss Lucy in Town (1742). He also sorts out various historical and biographical errors surrounding Miss Lucy made by Cross (1918.A1) and Lawrence (1855.A1).

1963 A BOOKS

*1 CHAUDARY, AWADHESH. "Henry Fielding, His Attitude Towards the Contemporary Stage." Dissertation, Michigan, 1963.

Examines Fielding's plays, journalism, and novels to describe his sense of the declining theatrical taste of his age and his desire for reform.

Source: Dissertation Abstracts, 26, no. 3 (Sept. 1965), 1642-43.

2 CROSS, WILBUR L. The History of Henry Fielding. 3 vols. New York: Russell & Russell.

Reissue of 1918.A1.

3 FIELDING, HENRY. Joseph Andrews. Introduction by Irvin Ehrenpreis. New York: Washington Square Press, 368 pp.

Ehrenpreis provides a brief, interesting biography and discusses Fielding's human sympathy, morality, and social criticism in Joseph Andrews. Includes a brief bibliography. No indication of copy text.

4 _____. The History of Tom Jones, A Foundling. Introduction by Ralph Singleton. New York: Washington Square Press, 862 pp.

Introduction reviews Fielding's career, defends Tom's morality ("In each of his sexual amours, indeed, the woman, rather than Tom, is the aggressor," p. xxv), praises the plot and characters (naively calls Tom "a picture of Fielding himself as a young man," p. xxviii). No indication of copy text but appears to reproduce the "1750" edition followed by Murphy (1762.A10).

Edition had gone through six printings by 1969.

5 _____. The History of Tom Jones. Introduction by A. R. Humphreys. Everyman's Library. 2 vols. London: J. M. Dent & Sons; New York: E. P. Dutton, 711 pp.

Reprint of 1962.A7.

6 _____. The Journal of a Voyage to Lisbon. Edited by Harold E. Pagliaro. New York: Nardon Press, 159 pp.

Reviewed by William B. Coley, CE, 25 (1964), 640; C. J. Rawson, N&Q, 209 (1964), 159; Charles B. Woods, PQ, 43 (1964), 360-61; Andrew Wright, MLR, 69 (1964), 460.

Briefly explains the textual history of the two 1755 editions of The Journal, reprinting "the original (Francis) text" (p. 18) rather than the Humphreys version edited by John Fielding. Sets the book in the eighteenth-century tradition of travel literature: "a work showing so much disrespect for voyage literature that it all but disqualifies itself from the tradition" (p. 8). Defends Fielding against the charge of irascibility by discussing his attacks on Cibber, Walpole, and Richardson. Includes full explanatory notes and selective bibliography. See 1892.A2.

*7 _____. Tom Jones. Translated by Ursula Bruns. Gütersloh: Bertelsmann Lesering, 895 pp.
German translation.
Source: Hugh Amory's working bibliography.

8 ROLLE, DIETRICH. Fielding und Sterne: Untersuchungen über die Funktion des Erzählers. Neue Beiträge zur englischen Philologie, 2. Münster: Aschendorff, 203 pp.
Reviewed by Paul Goetsche, NS (1964), 254-55; H. Van Gorp, Leuv Bijdr, 53, no. 2 (1964), 54-56; Gunter Welch, ZAA, 15 (1967), 201-204; F. Wölcken, MP, 65 (1967), 78-79; George J. Worth, JEGP, 64 (1965), 176-77.
Extending the theories of Kate Hamburger, Roman Ingarden, and particularly Wayne Booth, Rolle argues that Fielding essentially created the self-conscious narrator of the "authorial novel" (as opposed to the "I" novel) and that Sterne continued this tradition. Both are distinct from Richardson, Defoe, and Smollett. This careful and precise rhetorical analysis examines the similarities and the important and subtle differences between Fielding and Sterne in chapters on "Telling," "Teller," and "Teller and Reader." In German. See dissertation 1961.A14.

*9 STEVICK, PHILIP T. "Fielding, The Novelist as Philosopher of History." Dissertation, Ohio State, 1963.
Source: McNamee, 1865-1964, p. 560. See 1964.B14.

*10 STUART, WALTER H. "The Role of the Narrator in the Novels of Fielding." Dissertation, Wisconsin, 1963.
Studies the relationship between the narrator and the attack on middle-class values in Joseph Andrews, Tom Jones, and Amelia, also sums up the recent critical revaluation of Fielding.
Source: Dissertation Abstracts, 24, no. 6 (Dec. 1963), 2489-90.

*11 WILLIAMS, MURIEL BRITTAIN. "Henry Fielding's Attitude Toward Marriage." Dissertation, Alabama, 1963.
Source: McNamee, 1865-1964, p. 560. See 1973.A20.

1963 B SHORTER WRITINGS

1 [ANON.] "Henry Fielding's Famous Novel 'Tom Jones' as a Film," Illustrated London News, 242 (23 March), 436-37.
A photo "essay" on the film.

2 BAKER, SHERIDAN. "The Idea of Romance in the Eighteenth-Century Novel." Studies in English Literature (Tokyo). English Number, pp. 49-61.
Arguing that the novel "was not altogether new . . . [but] drew . . . deeply from preceding narrative fiction," Baker cites examples of romance action in Amelia and the romantic plot of dispossession in Joseph Andrews and Tom Jones. Fielding "dispels yet teases our romantic illusions" (p. 60).

3 BATTESTIN, MARTIN C. "Fielding's Revisions of Joseph Andrews." Studies in Bibliography, 16:81-117.
A complete history of the publication of Joseph Andrews in Fielding's lifetime. Battestin argues that "Fielding's own hand was at work in much, though certainly not in all, of the 'revising and correcting' of the third and fourth, as well as of the second, editions" (p. 83) and that he made significant revision in character and theme (rewriting to "correct weaknesses in his story," to improve style, and to "achieve a certain symmetry in the architecture of the novel," p. 88). As well as illustrating this general thesis, the article provides a sample "of the more than six hundred substantive variants that occur among the editions" (p. 95). See 1967.A2.

4 _____. "Lord Hervey's Role in Joseph Andrews." Philological Quarterly, 42, no. 2 (April), 226-41.
Suggests that Hervey is the model for Beau Didapper and examines the novel in light of Hervey's character and career (including Conyers Middleton's dedication of The Life of Cicero to Hervey). Battestin suggests that Pope and Fielding may have met at Ralph Allen's Prior Park in the fall of 1741, and that Fielding in his portrait of Didapper then borrowed from and alluded to "Pope's [unpublished] ironic account of Fannius in A Letter to a Noble Lord" (p. 234). Battestin also suggests that Didapper illustrates how "the local, the topical, the private, are shaped into the timeless and symbolic" (p. 240) by Fielding. See 1963.B18 and 1964.B8.

5 BLISS, MICHAEL. "Fielding's Bill of Fare in Tom Jones." Journal of English Literary History, 30, no. 3 (Sept.), 236-43.

Argues that "there is an important relationship between the introductory chapters and the novel as a whole . . . [they] provide a value universe with which the reader comes to identify more and more closely, and this very identification 'proves' the philosophical theme of the novel, which is located in and around mutuality" (p. 238). A good deal is made of the cookery/innkeeper metaphor as a means of establishing an ethical and aesthetic relationship with the reader; followed by brief discussions of narrator/reader distance, judgment, and prudence. Bliss concludes that the narrative carried the ethical "thematic strain" and the aesthetic strain, the "'subplot' of the introductory chapters" (p. 242), and that the two become one because "creation and criticism are complementary perceptual activities" (p. 243). See 1952.B2 and 1967.B18.

6 COLEY, WILLIAM B. "Fielding, Hogarth, and Three Italian Masters." Modern Language Quarterly, 24, no. 4 (Dec.), 386-91.

Untangles an allusion in Book 3, chapter 6 of Joseph Andrews to Hogarth, "Ammyconni" (Jacopo Amigoni), "Paul Varnish" (Paolo Veronese), and "Hannibal Scratchi" (Annibale Carracci). Fielding compliments Hogarth as the only English painter who "could breach the foreign monopoly in the arts" (p. 388). The distortion of the names may be significant: "The distortion of Amigoni's name by Joseph translates roughly and colloquially into something like the Dupes Delight" (p. 389) (Hogarth had competed with Amigoni). Hogarth satirically objected to darkening with varnish, thus "Paul Varnish" is "a perfect terminus, for the mingled ideas of the sublime tradition, false connoisseurship, and the need for a painter of 'modern moral subjects'" (p. 391). See 1968.B33, 1969.B5, and 1969.B31.

*7 DEMAREST, DAVID P. "Legal Language and Situation in the Eighteenth-Century Novel: Readings in Defoe, Richardson, Fielding, and Austen." Dissertation, Wisconsin, 1963.

Studies the patterns of legal language and situation in order to identify "their ideological positions, allow for comparison and contrast between authors, and provide a new approach to . . . individual works."

Source: Dissertation Abstracts, 24, no. 7 (Jan. 1964), 2907.

8 DENT, ALAN. "Faithful and Freakish." Illustrated London News, 242 (20 July), 106.

Praises John Osborne and Tony Richardson for their film adaptation which, while it misses "the deep irony of Fielding's wit," catches the "gusto and bawdry of the book" as well as its story-telling and characterization. Dent thinks that Osborne's additions show that he "has been impregnated with the style of his model."

9 DREW, ELIZABETH. "Henry Fielding (1707-1754): Tom Jones," in her The Novel: A Modern Guide to Fifteen English Masterpieces. New York: A Laurel Edition, Dell, pp. 59-74.

Briefly sets out the Fielding-Richardson quarrel among critics and readers, discusses plot ("which really forbids any psychological revelation," p. 62), the intrusive author, the weakness of the burlesque and farce, irony ("which is his hallmark," p. 65), Tom's sexual lapses, the standard of sexual honor represented by Sophia, and the contrast between the generous and benevolent characters (Allworthy and Tom) and the "self-interest, greed, hypocrisy and snobbery" (p. 72) that rule most of the rest. Finally she sees the novel as not so much an attempt to discover who Tom is as "what Tom is" (p. 73).

10 JONES, CLAUDE E. "Satire and Certain English Satirists of the Enlightenment." Studies on Voltaire and the Eighteenth Century, 25:885-97.

Outlines some of the objects of attack in Fielding's and Hogarth's satires (fashion, lack of aesthetic or critical taste, political and legal corruption, quackery, the Dutch, French and Scots). Related to Fielding's social satire are Examples of the Interposition of Providence . . . and An Enquiry into the Causes of the Late Increase of Robbers . . ., moral pamphlets Fielding arranged to have cheaply printed and widely distributed.

11 LOFTIS, JOHN. "Fielding and the Stage Licensing Act of 1737," in his The Politics of Drama in Augustan England. Oxford: Clarendon Press, pp. 128-53 and passim.

Reviewed by Matthew Grace, EUQ, 20 (1964), 63-64; Chester Kirby, AHR, 69 (1964), 1124; C. J. Rawson, MLR, 69 (1964), 458-59; A. H. Scouten, PQ, 43 (1964), 327-28; George W. Stone, MLQ, 25 (1964), 371-72.

Briefly discusses the political implications of thirteen of Fielding's plays. Traces the evolution of political satire in Fielding's plays from the "mild excursions" (p. 130) of 1730 to the "intensely partisan plays . . . Pasquin and The Historical Register" (p. 137), which compelled Walpole to give dramatic satire his attention. Also briefly discusses the possibility that Fielding wrote The Golden Rump, the pretext for the Licensing Act.

12 PLUMB, J. H. "Henry Fielding and Jonathan Wild," in his Men and Places. London: Cresset Press, pp. 281-87.

Reviewed by John Brooks, Listener, 69 (1963), 386-89; Betty Kemp, NSN, 65 (1963), 681-82; TLS, 29 March 1963, p. 214.

Reviews Fielding's career at the edge of poverty in the "rip-roaring" (p. 282) London of his day with its corruption and scandal. Then briefly discusses the vigor of Jonathan Wild and the good but "pasteboard" (p. 286) Heartfrees.

13 QUIGLY, ISABEL. "Confused Alarums." Spectator, no. 7045 (5 July), 13-15.

Reviews the John Osborne/Tony Richardson film Tom Jones. While praising the film for its gusto and general excellence, thinks that it lacks the book's serious moral preoccupation, "its variety, richness, satire or heart" (p. 13).

14 ROBERTS, EDGAR V. "Fielding's Ballad Opera The Lottery (1732) and the English State Lottery of 1731." Huntington Library Quarterly, 27, no. 1 (Nov.), 39-52.

Carefully describes the state lottery of 1731 (including a "Table Showing the Distribution of Prizes") in order to supply the "body of experience, knowledge, and attitudes" (p. 52) shared by Fielding and his audience. See dissertation 1960.A13.

15 SEYMOUR, WILLIAM K. "Henry Fielding: Son of Somerset." Contemporary Review, 203 (Jan.), 31-34.

Not using the best or latest biographical evidence, Seymour reviews Fielding's life from his birth to the Licensing Act in 1737, when Fielding was 30. See 1963.B16 for continuation.

16 _____. "Henry Fielding: The Years of Achievement." Contemporary Review, 203 (March), 154-59.

This survey of his work as lawyer, magistrate, novelist, and journalist completes 1963.B15.

17 SHIPLEY, JOHN B. "A New Fielding Essay from the Champion." Philological Quarterly, 42, no. 3 (July), 417-22.

Reprints an essay from the Dublin Evening Post (30 Dec. 1740) which may be "the only one of Fielding's missing leaders for the Champion [those from 15 Nov. 1740 and June 1741 are missing] to have survived" (p. 417). Shipley's attribution of this to The Champion and to Fielding is based on internal evidence (stylistic similarities and similarities in content). See also 1912.B6, 1913.B5, B8, B9, 1920.B11, 1953.B7, 1955.B8-10.

18 STEAD, P. J. "The Trial of Mary Blandy." Police College Magazine, 7:433-44.
Report on the re-creation of the murder trial of Mary Blandy, whose fiancé William Cranstoun is said to be the model for Beau Didapper.

19 THOMAS, D. S. "The Publication of Henry Fielding's Amelia." Library (5th. series, 18), also called Transactions of the Bibliographical Society, 3rd. series, 18 (Dec.), 303.
Discusses the slow sale of Amelia and the several stories about Fielding's publisher (Andrew Miller) trying to stimulate sales. He concludes that the entry in William Strahan's ledger (printer for Miller) is not good evidence for a second edition of Amelia. See 1921.B2 and 1952.B13.

20 WRIGHT, ANDREW. "Work in Progress III: Joseph Andrews, Mask and Feast." Essays in Criticism, 13, no. 3 (July), 209-21.
Brief opening section of 1965.A20.

1964 A BOOKS

*1 AMORY, HUGH. "Law and the Structure of Fielding's Novels." Dissertation, Columbia, 1964.
Source: Dissertation Abstracts, 27 (1966/67), 451A-52A. See 1968.B1, 1971.B1, 1971.B2, and 1972.B1.

2 BATTESTIN, MARTIN C. The Moral Basis of Fielding's Art: A Study of Joseph Andrews. Middletown, Conn.: Wesleyan University Press, 207 pp.
Reprint of 1959.A1.

*3 DEPPE, WOLFGANG G. "History versus Romance: ein Beitrag zur Entwicklungsgeschichte und zum Verständnis der Literaturtheorie Henry Fieldings." Dissertation, Münster, 1964.
In German.
Source: McNamee, 1964-1968, p. 222. See 1965.A3.

1964

*4 DEVINE, MARY E. "Fielding on Walpole: A Study of Henry Fielding's Major Political Satires." Dissertation, Loyola-Chicago, 1964.

Source: McNamee, 1964-1968, p. 222.

5 EHRENPREIS, IRVIN. Fielding: Tom Jones. Studies in English Literature, 23. London: Edward Arnold, 77 pp.

A rhetorical study of Tom Jones that sums up much of the best recent criticism. Ehrenpreis opens with an analysis of the intrusive author and Fielding's moral and social position. He sees the novel balancing formal unity with historical and psychological reality, as Fielding strives for "symmetry and clarity" (p. 16) in form and style. In chapters on "story," "doctrine," and "meaning and form," he analyzes Fielding's willingness to dramatize the pleasure-pain psychology of his age, which "dwells on the paradoxical darkness of human motivation" (p. 39), and his radical and yet socially constructive morality. He argues that the narrator and many events are there merely to teach the characters and us; the real events in the novel are the "moments of sudden understanding" (p. 23). A final chapter on comedy describes our attitude toward the "ironic balancing of the novelist" (p. 59), as Fielding keeps us off balance with shifts of tone, comic anticlimaxes, surprises, and comic characters. Constant comparisons are drawn with Sterne, Defoe, and Richardson, but attention is on the events in Tom Jones.

*6 FIELDING, HENRY. Die Geschichte eines Findelkindes. Translated by Horst Hockendorf. 2 vols. Berlin (Weimar): Aufbau-Verlag.

German translation of Tom Jones.

Source: Hugh Amory's working bibliography.

7 _____. Histoire de Tom Jones, Enfant Trouvé. Translated by Francis Ledoux. 2 vols. Paris: Gallimard, 996 (503 & 493) pp.

French translation.

Reprint of Tom Jones, without apparatus, from Romans (1964.A9).

8 _____. Jonathan Wild and The Journal of a Voyage to Lisbon. Introduction by A. R. Humphreys. Everyman's Library. London: J. M. Dent & Sons; New York: E. P. Dutton, 306 pp.

Reprint of 1932.A1, with a new introduction, touches on the dating of Jonathan Wild, the history of the actual man, other attacks on Walpole, and Fielding's mock-heroic style.

The touching biographical background to The Journal of a Voyage to Lisbon is provided, as well as a biographical note and a select bibliography.

9 _____. Romans. Les aventures de Joseph Andrews et son ami M. Abraham Adams; Vie de feu M. Jonathan Wild le Grand; Histoire de Tom Jones, enfant trouvé. Translated by Francis Ledoux. Paris: Gallimard, 1633 pp.

Translation of the three novels with full notes, as well as bibliography, chronology of his life, and brief introduction reviewing his life, his reputation, the publication history of his major works, and giving an appreciation of each novel. Introduction relies heavily on Scott (1821.A2).

*10 _____. Storia di Tom Jones trovatello. Translated by Laura Marchiori. Milano: Rizzoli. [1964].

Italian translation of Tom Jones.

Source: National Union Catalogue Author Lists, 1968-1972. Vol. 29, p. 438.

*11 _____. T'ang mu ch'iung szǔ. Translated by Sun Chu Min. Taipei: Wu Chou pub. service. [1964].

Abridged Chinese Tom Jones.

Source: Hugh Amory's working bibliography (transliterated by Bonnie McDougall of the East Asian Institute).

12 _____. The Adventures of Joseph Andrews. Introduction by L. Rice-Oxley. World Classics. London, New York, Toronto: Oxford University Press, 406 pp.

Reprint of 1929.A3.

13 [_____]. The Covent-Garden Journal, by Sir Alexander Drawcansir, Knt. Censor of Great Britain. Edited by Gerard E. Jensen. 2 vols. New York: Russell & Russell, 668 pp.

Reprint of 1915.A1.

14 _____. The History of Tom Jones, A Foundling. Afterword by Frank Kermode. Signet Classic. New York: New American Library of World Literature, 864 pp.

Modernized edition, "based on the third of 1749," with an appendix of "some passages from the first edition of 1749" (p. 863). Includes a very selected bibliography. Kermode calls this the "second great novel" (Clarissa is the first). He discusses its "planning," specifically its careful structure and plot, paying particular attention to the inn at Upton sequence. Thinks the novel does not

1964

"give one the full sense of actual life" (p. 859) because of its careful plotting and because the characters are types taken from drama. Briefly reviews Fielding's "warm ethical Christianity" (p. 862).

By 1971 this edition was in its seventh printing.

15 _____. The History of Tom Jones a Foundling. Illustrated by L. B. Smith. New York: Random House, 744 pp.

Appears to reprint the "1750" edition followed by Murphy (1762.A10).

16 _____. The Tragedy of Tragedies, or Tom Thumb the Great, in Eighteenth Century Plays. Edited by John Hampden. Everyman's Library. London: J. M. Dent & Sons; New York: E. P. Dutton, pp. 160-209.

Reissue of 1928.A4.

17 _____. The True Patriot: and The History of Our Own Times. Edited by Miriam A. Locke. Alabama: University of Alabama Press; London: Macdonald, 1965, 272 pp.

Reviewed by Richmond Bond, ELN, 2 (1965), 307-308; W. B. Coley, PQ, 44 (1965), 347-48; Frank Kermode, NYRB, 28 Oct. 1965, pp. 5-6; TLS, 27 Jan. 1965, p. 67.

Locke prints a reduced facsimile of all but the final issue of this periodical, with annotations after each. Her introduction sets out the European prelude to the '45, the political milieu in England in 1745, Fielding as a patriot (he may have been encouraged by the government to return to journalism), his attitude toward the Hanoverians, and his attitude toward the rebels (she speculates that he cannot have approved of the butchery after Culloden). She also sets out the publication history, the authorship, the contents of leading articles, letters, and apocrypha, and evidence of Fielding's wide reading. See dissertation 1946.A3.

Reprinted 1975.A5.

18 _____. Tom Jones. Abridged by M. L. Howe. A Laurel Edition. New York: Dell, 349 pp.

Omits the prefaces and all other "digressions" by the narrator.

*19 _____. Tom Jones. Translated by Gun and Nils Bengtsson. 2 vols. Stockholm: Natur och kultur. [1964].

Swedish translation.

Source: Hugh Amory's working bibliography.

*20 _____. Tom Jones. Translated by Ramón Moix. Barcelona: Mateu, 307 pp.
Spanish translation.
Source: Hugh Amory's working bibliography.

*21 HATFIELD, GLENN W. "Fielding's Irony and the Corruption of Language." Dissertation, Ohio State, 1964.
Source: McNamee, 1964-1968, p. 222. See 1968.A9.

*22 LE PAGE, PETER V. "Fielding's Immanent Symbology." Dissertation, Bowling Green, 1964.
Source: Dissertation Abstracts, 25, no. 9 (March 1965), 5282. See 1967.B26.

*23 NEUENDORF, MARY M. S. "The 'Great Man' in the Works of Henry Fielding." Dissertation, Rice, 1964.
Surveys Fielding's treatment of the great man theme from his poem "Of True Greatness" (in the Miscellanies) through Jonathan Wild, Joseph Andrews, Tom Jones, and Amelia.
Source: Dissertation Abstracts, 25, no. 4 (Oct. 1964), 2498.

24 SACKS, SHELDON. Fiction and the Shape of Belief: A Study of Henry Fielding with Glances at Swift, Johnson, and Richardson. Berkeley and Los Angeles: University of California Press, 281 pp.
Reviewed by Martin C. Battestin, CE, 27 (1966), 654; Benjamin Boyce, SAQ, 64 (1965), 567-68; Frank Brady, JGE, 17 (1966), 332-35; George A. Cevasco, LJ, 90 (1965), 249-50; William B. Coley, YR, 55 (1965), 126-30; George P. Elliott, Hud R., 18 (1965), 433-41; Ronald Paulson, JEGP, 65 (1966), 602-604; C. T. P., ABC, Jan. 1966, p. 5.
In this study of literary genre, Sacks begins by defining three major fictional types (satire, apologues, and "represented actions"). He asserts, as a genre critic must, that "if we interpret part of a work organized by another principle as if it were part of a satire, we cannot discuss the artistic choices which have, in fact, made the work effective" (p. 13). Within the category of represented actions, he establishes three subcategories--comedy, tragedy, and melodrama. While he discusses the "demands" of [generic limitations of] satire and apologues, the book is primarily concerned with those fictions "organized as [representative] actions" (p. 61). Sets out specifically the signals that Fielding gives the reader that allow him to make clear ethical judgments. Sacks' assumption is "that novelists' ethical beliefs, opinions,

and prejudices are expressed as the formal signals which control our responses to the characters, acts, and thoughts represented in their novels" (p. 231). His middle chapters set out these various signals, ranging from the "split commentator" (the narrator in Joseph Andrews who can be either serious or ironic) to the fallible paragons (flawed ideal characters like Allworthy). Along with several interesting subdivisions of "signals," like Fielding's various uses of "situation character" (good for only one situation or for closely similar situations), Sacks introduces several which seem unnecessarily clever or obscure (Joseph's being robbed and beaten is described as "The Unconscious Protagonist Adrift in a Sea of Situation Characters," p. 96). He ultimately discusses narration, major characters, type characters, the digressions (both those told by "strayed lambs" like the Man of the Hill and by "demireps" like Mrs. Fitzpatrick). In his final chapter he considers whether he has strayed into the intentional fallacy, whether "the legitimacy of those inferences [about Fielding's beliefs] must remain suspect since they may have been postulated upon rhetorical signals dictated by purely aesthetic considerations" (p. 230). He concludes that belief does not determine genre, but genre does determine "the shape which a writer gives to his beliefs" (p. 263).

Reprinted 1966.A22.

1964 B SHORTER WRITINGS

1 ALTER, ROBERT. "The Picaroon Domesticated," in his Rogue's Progress: Studies in the Picaresque Novel. Harvard Studies in Comparative Literature, no. 26. Cambridge: Harvard University Press, pp. 80-105.

Reviewed by Homer Goldberg, MLQ, 27 (1966), 353-56; C. J. H. O'Brien, AUMLA, no. 26 (1966), 318-20; TLS, 4 June 1964, p. 495.

Generic study comparing Tom Jones to the conventional picaresque novel, and Tom to other picaresque heroes (Gil Blas, Roderick Random). By examining narrative technique (omniscient narrator rather than first person), the logical progress, the habit of narrative generalization, the diction, the implied social attitude, and the nature of the hero, Alter distinguishes Tom Jones from the picaresque tradition. The picaresque "is a literary form characteristic of a period of disintegration, both social disintegration and the disintegration of belief" (p. 84). Fielding uses his naturally moral hero as the picaresque hero is used to unmask social corruption, but Fielding's irony has a positive moral purpose because his moral stand is clear, unlike the narrating picaro, whose "irony need not have any positive moral purpose; it is critical without necessarily assuming a clear standard of behavior" (p. 102). Alter concludes that Fielding took "important elements from the picaresque novel . . . to reshape them for new uses in new surroundings" (p. 105).

2 BROICH, ULRICH. "Fieldings Shamela und Pamela or, the Fair Imposter: zwei Parodien von Richardsons Pamela." Anglia, 82, no. 2, 172-90.

Arguing that parodies appear in periods of transition when earlier literary forms no longer correspond to taste and when new ones have not evolved (e.g., Boileau's Le Lutrin, Pope's Rape of the Lock, and Cervantes' Don Quixote), Broich sees these two parodies of Richardson's Pamela as an indication that the years after 1740 were a transition period in narrative fiction. Neither is a true parody (which changes the content and retains the form); Fielding changes content, form, and language, achieving tension by opposing truth and pretense rather than form and content. Fielding's fiction evolves until it ultimately approaches Richardson's "new species of writing" rather than the classical genre he first upheld. In German.

3 CAZENAVE, MAURICE. "A propos de Tom Jones." Nouvelle revue française (Nov.), pp. 891-94.

Although Cazenave thinks the novel utterly clear and created before us, he does discuss the subtle interplay between character analysis, story-telling, culture, and benevolent irony. The story-telling in particular is ambiguous, done with innocent guile; Fielding's insistence on telling the whole truth is often the best way to confuse the reader. In French.

Reprinted 1972.A8.

4 CHANDLER, S. B. "A Shakespeare Quotation in Fielding and Manzoni." Italica, 41: 323-25.

Although Manzoni could have relied on the de la Place translation of Tom Jones for a quotation from Julius Caesar, he more likely relied on Le Tourneur's translation of Shakespeare's play.

5 FERGUSON, OLIVER W. "Partridge's Vile Encomium: Fielding and Honest Billy Mills." Philological Quarterly, 43, no. 1 (Jan.), 73-78.

1964

"Mills [an actor who often supported Garrick] was clearly the Claudius at Drury Lane during the period in question, and on this evidence alone a fairly tenable case could be made for identifying him as the Claudius satirized by Fielding" (p. 74) when Tom and Partridge went to see Hamlet. Fielding also satirically alluded to this weak actor in Joseph Andrews and The Jacobite's Journal.

6 GOLDBERG, HOMER. "Comic Prose Epic or Comic Romance: The Argument of the Preface to Joseph Andrews." Philological Quarterly, 43, no. 2 (April), 193-215.
Sets out the critical debate that has gone on over the meaning and nature of Fielding's comic epic in prose, retraces the logic of the preface (deciding that the term comic is the real differentia), and distinguishes between the comic and the burlesque (arguing that the ridiculous is "Fielding's name for the distinctive emotional quality or literary effect specific to the kind of writing he is attempting to define," p. 205). Goldberg then examines the preface to The Adventures of David Simple, arguing for "a considerable continuity of thought between" (p. 212) the two prefaces and seeing them as Fielding's Poetics (intelligently modeled on Aristotle). Fielding is never "the legatee of some body of literary doctrine or convention" (p. 214).

7 KISHLER, THOMAS C. "Heartfree's Function in Jonathan Wild." Satire Newsletter, 1, no. 2 (Spring), 32-34.
Although Kishler concludes that, "with or without Heartfree as a counter symbol, Jonathan Wild implies everywhere a scheme of values" (p. 34), and further that Heartfree is not an effective character (nor, in an Augustan satire manipulated by a persona, is he supposed to be), he nevertheless maintains that Heartfree does "make more concrete the other half of the central dichotomy between greatness and goodness" (p. 32). Heartfree is not an ideal but only part of an ethical dialectic.

8 MCCULLEN, J. T. "Fielding's Beau Didapper." English Language Notes, 2, no. 2 (Dec.), 98-100.
Notices the appropriateness of his name. According to Three Books of Occult Philosophy by Henry Cornelius Agrippa, a "didapper" is a ludicrous asexual lunary production; according to McCullen, Fielding uses him in just this way.

9 MAXWELL, J. C. "Hazlitt and Fielding." Notes and Queries, 209 (Jan.), 25.

Hazlitt paraphrases a sentence from Joseph Andrews in his essay on Godwin. See 1964.B15.

10 PLUMB, J. H. "Henry Fielding: The Journey Through Gin Lane." Horizon, 6, no. 1 (Winter), 75-83.

This popular article, with illustrations from Hogarth and Rowlandson, combines sensational biography ("In the late 1720s a tall, saturnine, hawk-nosed man with a lean, lined face might be seen staggering from the stews of Covent Garden in the early dawn, sometimes alone, sometimes with a pretty girl of easy virtue on his arm," p. 75), history of the novel, and literary generalization ("One of the great subtleties of his character studies is the way he depicts his characters being molded by their social circumstances as well as by their innate desires," p. 82).

11 PRICE, MARTIN. "Fielding: The Comedy of Forms," in his To the Palace of Wisdom: Studies in Order and Energy from Dryden to Blake. Garden City, N.J.: Doubleday, pp. 286-312, passim.

Reviewed by Reuben A. Brower, PR, 31 (1964), 654-57; Jeffrey Hart, KR, 26 (1964), 405-411; Curt A. Zimansky, PQ, 44 (1965), 325-26.

Argues that Fielding emphasizes artifice. "Unlike Defoe and Richardson, Fielding shows no desire to achieve minute realism. He does not provide the illusion of actuality that allows the reader to participate immediately in the lives of his characters" (p. 286). Instead, this quintessential Augustan writer (in comparison with Swift and Sterne) balances "the flow of soul--of selfless generosity--and the structures--screens, defences, moats of indifference--that people build around themselves" (p. 287). Price discusses Fielding's "problematic" morality (including the duality of love and sex), his subversion and testing of form (particularly through irony), the conceptual nature of his novels (Fielding's limiting of both reader and character), the comic ("the weight of folly and triviality that impedes the best and worst intentions," p. 304) rather than the tragic morality of his novels, and, finally, the radical Christian innocence developing from Adams to Amelia, which is superior to ridicule.

Available in several editions, including the 1970 Arcturus Books edition, Carbondale and Edwardville: Southern Illinois University Press; London and Amsterdam: Feffer & Simons.

12 RAWSON, C. J. "The Phrase 'Legal Prostitution' in Fielding, Defoe and Others." Notes and Queries, 209 (Aug.), 298.
This "cant phrase" is briefly traced in the eighteenth century.

13 ROBERTS, EDGAR V. "Henry Fielding and Richard Leveridge: Authorship of 'The Roast Beef of Old England.'" Huntington Library Quarterly, 27, no. 2 (Feb.), 175-81.
Works out the problem of authorship of this song. "Fielding's first version was prior to Leveridge's by at least three, and probably four, years and . . . his second version anticipated Leveridge's by perhaps as much as a year. The disputed authorship must therefore be awarded to Fielding" (p. 176). "Thus the extent of Leveridge's claim . . . must be limited to the third line of the second stanza, the last five stanzas, and the music ascribed to him" (p. 181).

14 STEVICK, PHILIP. "Fielding and the Meaning of History." Publications of the Modern Language Association, 79, no. 5 (Dec.), 561-68.
Fielding was aware of the several possible theories of history in the eighteenth century, and with "tough-minded, ironic amusement" (p. 561), he freed himself from the "historical certainties of the philosophers of history" (p. 562). By looking at Fielding's comments on history and on his age in his poems, pamphlets, essays, and novels, Stevick concludes that his skepticism allowed him "a pleasure in the contemplation of his own time" (p. 565). He compares Fielding's uniqueness to the fictions of some primitivists (Goldsmith) and some antiprogressivists and concludes that Fielding created his mixed mode (comedy, romance, satire, romance burlesqued) because of a theory of "history of development" (p. 568), different from any historical theory of his age. See 1947.B5 and 1977.B3. See dissertation 1963.A9.

15 SWAMINATHAN, S. R. "Hazlitt, Lamb and Fielding." Notes and Queries, 209 (May), 180.
Hazlitt uses a paraphrased sentence from Joseph Andrews in his "The South-Sea House." See 1964.9 for another use of the same sentence.

16 WOODS, CHARLES B. "The Folio Text of Fielding's The Miser." Huntington Library Quarterly, 28, no. 1 (Nov.), 59-61.
Dates The Miser (see 1931.B14) and explains why it had no author or cast list. It was "published between May 11 and July 16, 1734" (p. 59) in Cote's Weekly Journal. "Cote

expunged from his text every direct indication that the supplement to his journal was an unauthorized reprint of a current theatrical success" (p. 61).

17 WRIGHT, KENNETH. "Henry Fielding and the Theatres Act of 1737." Quarterly Journal of Speech, 50:252-58.

Using contemporary periodicals as well as Coxe's Memoirs . . . of Sir Robert Walpole, Corbett's Parliamentary History, and Smollett's History of England, Wright sets out the events leading up to and the passage of the Licensing Act. He attempts to assess Fielding's role in its passage by recording judgments from Cibber to Genest, concluding that "Fielding's participation in the events leading to the passage of the Act was certainly important" (p. 258). See dissertation 1960.A15.

1965 A BOOKS

*1 BORTHWICK, SISTER MARY C. "Henry Fielding as Critical Realist: An Examination of the East German Estimate of Fielding." Dissertation, Fordham, 1965.

Examines "German Marxist criticism of Henry Fielding as a possible means of revealing relationships between Marxist and non-Marxist concepts of realism."

Source: Dissertation Abstracts, 26, no. 7 (Jan. 1966), 3945-46.

2 BUTT, JOHN. Fielding. Writers and Their Work, no. 57. London: Longmans, Green, for The British Council and The National Book League, 36 pp.

Reprint of 1959.A2 with additions to the bibliography.

3 DEPPE, WOLFGANG G. History versus Romance; ein Beitrag zur Entwicklungsgeschichte und zum Verständnis der Literaturtheorie Henry Fieldings. Neue Beiträge zur englischen Philologie. No. 3. Münster: Verlag Aschendorf, 178 pp.

Arguing that the narrator and Fielding's characters are often his spokesmen, Deppe examines a number of Fielding's social and artistic theories (345 of them). Deppe does not think Fielding a literary traditionalist; he does find him contradictory (neither a classicist nor a revolutionary). He sees a similar contradiction in his politics (Fielding is ethically a democrat and politically a conservative). Deppe also defines the nature of Fielding's fictional histories (he creates an external world only to embody inner truths). In German.

1965

4 FIELDING, HENRY. Harpatka'ot G'ozef Andruz. Translated by Esther Kaspi. Tel Aviv: Am Oved, 318 pp.
Modern Hebrew translation of Joseph Andrews.

*5 _____. Historien om Tom Jones, ett hittebarn. Translated by Nils Holmberg. Stockholm: Folket i bild, 373 pp.
Swedish translation.
Source: Hugh Amory's working bibliography.

6 _____. Joseph Andrews and Shamela. Edited by Martin C. Battestin. London: Methuen, 414 pp.
Reissue of 1961.A3.

7 _____. Joseph Andrews és barátja, Mr. Abraham Adams kalandjai. Translated by Peter Balabán and illustrated by Ádám Würtz. Budapest: Magyar Helikon, 477 pp.
Hungarian translation based on the Everyman edition (1962.A5) of the novel.

8 _____. Joseph Andrews. Introduction by A. R. Humphreys. Everyman's Library. London: J. M. Dent & Sons; New York: E. P. Dutton, 304 pp.
Reissue of 1962.A5.

9 _____. The Adventures of Joseph Andrews. Introduction by L. Rice-Oxley. World Classics. London, New York, Toronto: Oxford University Press, 406 pp.
Reissue of 1929.A3.

*10 _____. The History of Tom Jones, a foundling. 2 vols. New York: Century. [1965].
Source: National Union Catalogue Author Lists, 1968-1972. Vol. 29, p. 438.

*11 _____. Tom Jones. Translated by Helge Åkerhielm. Stockholm: B. Wahlström, 253 pp. [1965].
Swedish translation.
Reissued in 1969.
Source: Hugh Amory's working bibliography.

12 _____. Tom Jones. Translated by Julow Viktor. Budapest: Europa Konyvkiado, 521 pp.
Hungarian translation.

*13 _____. Tom Jones. Translated by Marise Ferro. Milano: C. Del Duca (Carim), 248 pp.
Italian translation (abridged).
Source: Hugh Amory's working bibliography.

*14 GRACE, MATTHEW S. "Fielding in the Eighteenth Century." Dissertation, Wisconsin, 1965.

Examines "Fielding's career, his philosophical views, his critical reception during his lifetime, and his influence on some eighteenth-century novelists."

Source: Dissertation Abstracts, 25, no. 11 (May 1965), 6624.

15 HUTCHENS, ELEANOR N. Irony in Tom Jones. University of Alabama: University of Alabama Press, 190 pp.

Sets out to demonstrate "a certain kind of verbal irony --introduced by Fielding into the English novel--which accounts for some of his most characteristic effects of style," the device "of making the literal meaning fit the context while the connotative significance clashes with it" (p. 9). After briefly defining irony, Hutchens discusses Fielding's dialectic irony (borrowed from Lucian), his practical irony ("making facts add up to the unexpected," p. 30), and his rhetorical (verbal) irony which depends on the intrusiveness of a narrator. The first two kinds are discussed in a chapter called "Substance," the latter in three chapters called "Denotation, Tone, and Reference," "Connotation," and "Prudence: A Case Study." Having decided that Fielding's verbal irony is perfect only in Tom Jones (it is "not in control" in Joseph Andrews, and in Amelia "it is mired in the emotionalism which renders the text boggy," p. 37), she examines the irony of substance in the novel: irony of plot, irony of unexpected response (ours and the characters), and irony of theme (the good seeming bad). She then examines irony of tone, reference, denotation, and connotation in the text of Tom Jones, as well as tracing the ironic play on a single word "prudence." A final chapter considers verbal irony as it develops in the novels of Austen, Thackeray, Dickens, and Joyce. This study has inexact metaphoric writing ("Connotative irony may take the form of a shift aside from, rather than upward or downward from, the straightforward word," p. 129). See 1967.A12, 1971.B25, and dissertation 1957.A5.

16 JOHNSON, MAURICE. Fielding's Art of Fiction: Eleven Essays on Shamela, Joseph Andrews, Tom Jones, and Amelia. Philadelphia: University of Pennsylvania Press; London: Oxford University Press, 182 pp.

Reprint of 1961.A11.

*17 PENNER, ALLEN R. "Fielding and Cervantes: The Contribution of Don Quixote to Joseph Andrews and Tom Jones." Dissertation, Colorado, 1965.

Source: McNamee, 1964-1968, p. 222. See also Dissertation Abstracts, 26 (1966), 6720-21, and 1967.B28.

*18 RINEHART, HOLLIS. "Fielding's Jonathan Wild: Form and Intention." Dissertation, Chicago, 1965.
Source: McNamee, 1964-1968, p. 222. See 1969.B19.

*19 WINTEROWD, WALTER R. "The Poles of Discourse: A Study of Eighteenth-Century Rhetoric in Amelia and Clarissa." Dissertation, Utah, 1965.
Source: Dissertation Abstracts, 26, no. 1 (July 1965), 360-61. See 1968.B39.

20 WRIGHT, ANDREW. Henry Fielding: Mask and Feast. Berkeley and Los Angeles: University of California Press; London: Chatto & Windus, 214 pp.
Reviewed by Sheridan Baker, ELN, 4 (1966), 142-44; Martin C. Battestin, JEGP, 65 (1966), 196-98; William B. Coley, YR, 55 (1965), 126-30; George P. Elliott, Hud. R, 18 (1965), 433-41; William J. Farrell, MP, 64 (1966), 81-82; Frank Kermode, NYRB, 28 Oct. 1965, pp. 5-6; W. H. McBurney, SAQ, 64 (1965), 568-69; R. E. Moore, CE, 27 (1966), 515; John Preston, MLR, 61 (1966), 499-501; V. S. Pritchett, NSN, 69 (1965), 324; Timothy Rogers, English, 15 (1965), 193-95; Michael G. Tosh, RES, n.s. 17 (1966), 326-27; Stephen Wall, Listener, 74 (1965), 352-53; Choice, 2 (1965), 230-31; TLS, 11 Feb. 1965, p. 108.
Wright devises a series of metaphors, some derived from Fielding (fiction as "feast" and narrator as "masked" persona) and some not ("character as bas relief," language as play, and scene as tableau), which he attempts to apply to Joseph Andrews, Tom Jones, and Amelia. His thesis is that as a civilized artist (one who gave aesthetic rather than moral pleasure), Fielding "aimed at neither the excoriation nor the amendment of mankind." Fielding's aesthetic simply demanded comically "disengaged" novels. He was able to keep to this plan in Joseph Andrews and Tom Jones, but "life became so clamorous that his last novel, Amelia, failed to be the masterpiece he had hoped it would be" (p. 17). In fact, it "is a failure not in detail but in whole conception" (p. 142). The first section of this book discusses the narrator, often confusing him with the biographical Fielding whose "bodily illness had begun to take its painful toll" (p. 44), and his manipulation of the reader which fails, or darkens, as Fielding's moral view shifts. The second section is a discussion of "structure" in the three novels. This term, as Wright uses it, sometimes means actual division of the novel, but more often it

means the patterned, or contrasting, arrangements of tone which create mood. In the final sections he briefly discusses the "artifice" of scene, character, and language, which "makes for a festive atmosphere" (p. 122). The section on language illustrates a number of devices (mock epic, panegyric, jargon, etc.) in "the kaleidoscope of Fielding's styles" (p. 172) but analyzes none carefully. Wright again sees Fielding able to reverse the "moral pressure [that] threatens to destroy the light and festive tone" (p. 190) of Tom Jones and failing to do this in Amelia.

See 1963.B20, where the opening section appears, and 1968.A2, where parts of this book are reprinted. See also 1969.B25 for a response.

1965 B SHORTER WRITINGS

1 ASHLEY, LEONARD R. N. Colley Cibber. Twayne's English Authors Series. New York: Twayne, pp. 136-39.

Briefly reviews the cordial relations between Cibber and Fielding, and Fielding's subsequent attacks in his plays, journal (The Champion), and Joseph Andrews, as well as Cibber's retaliation in his Apology. Thinks "that Fielding could not resist ignoring friendship for fashion" and that he "finally goaded the generally good-natured Cibber into retaliation for a decade of insults" (pp. 136-37).

For a more detailed analysis of this relationship, see 1939.B3.

2 BORT, BARRY D. "Incest theme in Tom Jones." American Notes and Queries, 3:83-84.

Suggests that the implicit allusions to Oedipus are Fielding's mock-heroic way of "saying that Tom will not be fitted into a tragic mold" (p. 84).

3 BUTT, JOHN. "Henry Fielding," in British Writers and Their Work. No. 6. Lincoln: University of Nebraska Press, pp. 43-76.

Reprint of 1959.A2.

4 COLEY, WILLIAM B. "Fielding's Two Appointments to the Magistracy." Modern Philology, 63, no. 2 (Nov.), 144-49.

Attempts to sort out the vexed biographical problem of Fielding's appointment to the bench; "his transition from a life of political journalism and apparently unsuccessful lawyering to a career on the inferior bench" (p. 144). New evidence by Shepperson (1954.B15) makes it clear that

Fielding was working as a magistrate a month earlier than Godden (1910.A9) or Cross (1918.A1) suggest. Coley carefully describes the various documents having to do with Fielding's appointment (the appointment fiat, oaths, etc.) and concludes that Fielding probably had trouble making arrangements about the property qualification. He corrects Shepperson's confusion about Fielding's two appointments (Middlesex, 20 June 1747, and Westminster actively in November 1748) and suggests that more work needs to be done before we can speculate about who helped Fielding to his appointment, or about his delaying his appointment to write for the Pelham administration or to finish Tom Jones.

5 HASLINGER, ADOLF. "Die Funktion des Stadt-Land-Themas in Henry Fieldings Tom Jones und Joseph Andrews." Die neueren Sprachen, 14 (March), 101-109.

Argues that Fielding uses the country-highway-city movement (with both Tom and Joseph ultimately returning to the country) as an artistic device. The city-country conflict delineates character and illustrates theme (natural goodness); Fielding relies on irony to avoid the simplification to which this might lead. Fielding thus embodies ideas about natural goodness (shared by philosophers like Shaftesbury and Rousseau) in his art. In German. See 1968.B15.

6 HERMAN, GEORGE. "Fielding Defends Allworthy." Iowa English Yearbook, no. 10, pp. 64-70.

Argues that Fielding attempts to keep us from judging Allworthy as having defects either of character or intelligence by keeping him in the background. Herman examines instances in which Allworthy's discernment, judgment, and benevolence are concerned (his treatment of Jenny; his conduct over Bridget's marriage; his judgment of Partridge; his preference of Blifil to Tom; his banishment of Tom). In most instances Allworthy's response is both reasonable and benevolent. In only two instances (the rejection of Tom, and Bridget's psychologically complex relation to Tom) did the demands of plot force Fielding to be "fast and shifty" (p. 69). Fielding's intention was to make him "the ideal country squire" (p. 70).

For another view, see 1965.B13.

7 JENKINS, OWEN. "Richardson's Pamela and Fielding's 'Vile Forgeries.'" Philological Quarterly, 44, no. 2 (April), 200-201.

Considers "Richardson's supposed offenses against truth and morality in the original Pamela, Fielding's criticism, and Richardson's reply" (p. 201) in Pamela II. Because Richardson specifically answers Parson Oliver's first four charges, as well as being ponderously "witty" at Fielding's expense, Jenkins thinks of Pamela II as Richardson's "dramatized defense of himself against the charges made in Shamela" (p. 206). According to Jenkins, it was enough for Richardson to have answered the moral charges, because Shamela has little value "as a criticism of [Richardson's] art" (p. 205).

See 1968.B22 and 1971.B3; also review by Frederick W. Hilles, SEL, 6 (1966), 610.

*8 JENNINGS, EDWARD M. "Reader-Narrative Relationships in Tom Jones, Tristram Shandy, and Humphry Clinker." Dissertation, Wisconsin, 1965.

Studies "the reader's distance from and his involvement with the narrative," contending that "distant" novels like Tom Jones and Tristram Shandy are "significantly different in their effect on the reader from those [like Humphry Clinker that] demand reader involvement."

Source: Dissertation Abstracts, 26, no. 6 (Dec. 1965), 3303-304.

9 LAVIN, REV. HENRY ST. C. "Rhetoric and Realism in Tom Jones." University Review--Kansas City, 32:19-25.

Argues that Fielding's ethical purpose in Tom Jones led him to "sacrifice certain elements of realism" (p. 19). Lavin examines the diction and rhetoric in the set speeches of Allworthy, Tom, and Sophia, finding them "largely unrealistic" (p. 24). He notes the homiletic structure of Allworthy's speeches and Tom's balanced doublets, recondite mythological references, apostrophe, inversion, and climactic periods, concluding that all three characters are "formal and flowery" (p. 24), except when with low characters, and that their rhetoric is only occasionally undercut by ironic action. Fielding's "major characters [are] in places spokesmen for his own views" (p. 25). See 1974.B28 and dissertation 1958.A8.

10 LEVINE, GEORGE R. "Henry Fielding's 'Defense' of the Stage Licensing Act." English Language Notes, 2, no. 3 (March), 193-96.

Describes the persona Fielding created for The Champion 10 Dec. 1739-40. Instead of his usual characterization of an individual, this persona represents the two groups most responsible for the Licensing Act. For the first part of the essay Fielding assumes the guise of "the self-righteous bourgeois" (p. 194), the London merchant; for the second half he becomes "a self-appointed guardian of public morality" (p. 195) of the Walpole administration. In this attack Fielding follows the lead of the parliamentary opposition.

For another view of his use of persona, see 1967.B27.

11 MAZZA, ANTONIA. "Coincidenze." Vita e Pensiero, 48 (Jan.), 6-13.

Draws a parallel between Fielding's Tom Jones and Alessandro Massini's The Betrothed. Both were precursors of the "modern" novel; both dramatized their cutting morality in picaresque novels; both had a tolerant world view, a broad understanding of man's psychological complexity, and a deep love of life. Specifically compares Tom and Sophia with Renzo and Lucia: both pairs are victims of absurd and unjust social situations which frustrate the triumph of feeling and love. Mazza also thinks that both novelists create better female than male characters. In Italian.

12 PIERCE, ROBERT B. "Moral Education in the Novel of the 1750s." Philological Quarterly, 44, no. 1 (Jan.), 73-87.

Studies Fielding's influence, particularly the influence of Tom Jones; this influence ranges from the simple borrowing of incident and character to the "adoption of a moral psychology like Fielding's; that is, characters who are to become truly moral must begin with innate good nature and then learn by experience the prudential values of their society" (p. 76). Pierce uses Tom's moral development as a model against which he sets heroes and heroines from novels by Mrs. Lennox, Mrs. Haywood, John Cleland, and also Fielding's Captain Booth. Only in William Chaigneau's The History of Jack Connor, and of course in Amelia, is there anything like Tom's moral development.

13 ROSCOE, ADRIAN A. "Fielding and the Problem of Allworthy." Texas Studies in Literature and Language, 7, no. 2 (Summer), 168-72.

Argues that in the creation of Allworthy Fielding is caught between his compliment to Ralph Allan and his intention not to make superhuman characters. Sees Fielding carefully "paring the good squire down to human proportions" (p. 169) through his mistakes in judgment (i.e., Partridge). Ultimately Allworthy is used to expose social corruption; "even a thoroughly good man like Allworthy can make disastrous mistakes in such a system" (p. 172). For another view, see 1965.B6.

14 SCHILLING, BERNARD N. "Fielding's 'Preface' and Joseph Andrews," in his The Comic Spirit: Boccaccio to Thomas Mann. Detroit: Wayne State University Press, pp. 43-70.

Reviewed by P. T. Nolan, Satire NL, 4 (1966), 44-45; S. M. Tave, MP, 64 (1967), 379-80; J. L. Thorson, CE, 28 (1967), 335.

Although Schilling is aware that there are "funny things" in Joseph Andrews unconnected with his theory of affectation, he sets out to examine only those elements that have to do with this vice, asserting that we must keep in mind the balance in Fielding between intellect and compassion. He begins by examining the parody of Pamela, suggesting that Fielding wickedly plays with the image of the bed and that Joseph is pure for the wrong, largely intellectual, reasons. After examining Fielding's "thrusts" at the professions and practical jokers, Schilling turns to the contrast between the compassion of Betty (which Fielding approves) and the hard materialism of Mrs. Tow-wouse, and between the Christian charity of Adams and the pretended piety of the rest of the clergy in Joseph Andrews. The essay becomes largely an appreciation of the Quixotic compassionate Adams.

15 _____. "Slipslop, Lady Booby, and the Ladder of Dependence," in his The Comic Spirit: Boccaccio to Thomas Mann. Detroit: Wayne State University Press, pp. 71-97.

This discussion of Fielding's special scorn for the vanity of high-born and low-born (which he often expresses with the metaphor of ladders, gradations, connections, or chains) centers on Slipslop and Lady Booby. Beginning with the absurdity of Mrs. Slipslop's social vanity, Schilling goes on to discuss female affectations and the clear-sighted cynical realism that female rivalry brings to the females in the novel. The essay largely becomes a discussion of the way Fielding uses Slipslop and Lady Booby to "illustrate vanity and hypocrisy by example" (p. 80), as the desire of each is foiled by her own vanity.

16 SMITH, J. OATES. "Masquerade and Marriage: Fielding's Comedies of Identity." Ball State University Forum, 6, no. 3, 10-21.

This article promises to trace "the antipodal symbols of masquerade and marriage . . . [the] central metaphor--one might even say central myth" (p. 10) as it develops in Fielding's works. The article best illustrates an allegorical "struggle of the morally virtuous in a hypocritical world" (p. 21) that is psychologically less well realized than Bunyan's The Life and Death of Mr. Badman. It ranges briefly over Fielding's plays: from Love in Several Masques and Temple Beau, where innocence is not tried in the conflict between appearance and reality, to The Modern Husband, where it is. The latter play, with its celebration of marriage that can endure trial, and of love beyond the game of love, anticipates the novels. Smith argues that characters in Joseph Andrews and Tom Jones move to discover their identity and then to marriage through a series of implied and literal masquerades. Although masquerade is important in Amelia, the novel failed because Fielding could not relate the accidents of circumstances "to inner or psychological necessity" (p. 16) and because he could not imaginatively conceive the Richardson-like dream quality of the endless pursuits of Amelia (which Smith carefully sets out) and Booth's mischances. See 1954.B19 and 1967.B26.

17 SMITH, RAYMOND. "The Ironic Structure of Fielding's Jonathan Wild." Ball State University Forum, 6, no. 3, 3-9.

Sees the novel, like Joseph Andrews and Tom Jones, as a working out of the "classical device of the eiron, the character who appears to be inferior to his antagonist, the alazon, but in the course of the struggle, or agon, is proven to be really superior" (p. 4). Smith sets out the events of the novel in terms of this struggle, which he sees as a struggle not just between two individuals but between two social groups (extended families) and their social concepts (Heartfree, the eiron, is the benevolent man, and Wild, the alazon, the self-interested man). See 1972.A9.

18 SPECTOR, ROBERT D., ed. Essays on the Eighteenth-Century Novel. Bloomington and London: Indiana University Press, 216 pp.

Reprints essays by Frank Kermode, "Richardson and Fielding" (1950.B6); Mark Spilka, "Comic Resolution in Fielding's Joseph Andrews" (1953.B10); R. S. Crane, "The Plot of Tom Jones" (1950.B2).

19 STEEVES, HARRISON R. "A Manly Man (Henry Fielding)," in his Before Jane Austen: The Shaping of the English Novel in the Eighteenth Century. London: George Allen & Unwin; New York: Holt, Rinehart and Winston, pp. 103-30, passim.

Reviewed by W. J. Harvey, Listener, 76 (1966), 781; J. L. Mahoney, Thought, 41 (1966), 602-604.

Old-fashioned essay on Fielding that briefly discusses all of his novels (including Shamela and Jonathan Wild). Sums up the story of Joseph Andrews and devotes a paragraph each to the "comic epic poem in prose," the modeling of the novel on Don Quixote, and Parson Adams as a vital character. The action of Tom Jones is summarized, the plot and characters discussed (ignoring shift in tone, Steeves sees the description of Sophia as "flat" and "bloodless"). Steeves thinks Fielding's characters develop, but that "none of his characters . . . stands up to an exacting test of lifelikeness" (p. 119). Fielding's plots, like his characters, are mechanical, and Fielding's intrusive narrator offensive to some and "not typically a characteristic of the novel" (p. 121). He thinks Amelia a realistic novel "supported by realistic expedients" (p. 125) and "lovable" for readers "who have seen more of life than their teens" (p. 127). Steeves' judgment is illustrated by his preference for Robert Bage's humor, morality, and characters over Fielding's.

20 STEVICK, PHILIP. "The Augustan Nose." University of Toronto Quarterly, 34, no. 2 (Jan.), 110-17.

Briefly describes how Fielding inadvertently drew on "the subterranean sexual folklore of the period" when he gave Amelia a broken nose, and how he deliberately used smell for satiric purposes when Beau Didapper sniffs out Mrs. Slipslop. The use of the images of smelling and noses for satiric and polemical purposes was shared by many of the important writers of the period (Sterne, Swift, Smollett, Pope).

21 THOMAS, D. S. "Fortune and the Passions in Fielding's Amelia." Modern Language Review, 60, no. 2 (April), 176-87.

Throughout Fielding's works his view of fortune (by which he sometimes means the fickle Roman goddess and sometimes chance) is ambivalent. This ambivalence "is reflected in the sermons of Barrow, Tillotson, Clarke and South . . ." (p. 179). Amelia in particular begins, and never completes, a number of discussions of chance and determinism, many of them having to do with "the psychology of the passions" (p. 184).

22 WOODS, CHARLES B. "Cibber in Fielding's Author's Farce: Three Notes." Philological Quarterly, 44, no. 2 (April), 145-51.

First, Woods demonstrates from contemporary newspapers and magazines how common the appellation Mr. Keyber for Colley Cibber was. Fielding uses it in The Author's Farce. Second, allusions to Cibber in the second act (as Murphy) are identified. Third, in act three Cibber becomes Sir Farcical Comick.

1965

23 _____. "Theobald and Fielding's Don Tragedio." English Language Notes, 2, no. 4 (June), 266-71.

Identifies the models for the puppet characters in The Pleasures of the Town (the puppet show in the last act of The Author's Farce). On the evidence of Fielding's parody of Theobald's plays in The Tragedy of Tragedies, Woods identifies Theobald as Don Tragedio.

1966 A BOOKS

*1 BAKER, MYRA M. "Satiric Characterizations in the Novels of Henry Fielding." Dissertation, Alabama, 1966.

Argues that in his novels Fielding uses the rhetorical techniques of satire (particularly in characterization) developed in his essays, plays, and pamphlets.

Source: Dissertation Abstracts, 27, no. 9 (March 1967), 3033A-3034A.

2 BLANCHARD, FREDERIC T. Fielding the Novelist: A Study in Historical Criticism. New York: Russell & Russell, 669 pp.

Reissue of 1926.A1.

3 DUDDEN, F. HOLMES. Henry Fielding: His Life, Works, and Times. 2 vols. Hamden, Conn.: Archon Books, 1192 pp.

Reprint of 1952.A1.

*4 FIELDING, HENRY. Storia di Tom Jones, un trovatello. Translated by Pina Sergi. 2 vols. Firenze: Sansoni. [1966].

Italian translation.

Source: Hugh Amory's working bibliography.

5 _____. The Author's Farce (Original Version). Edited by Charles B. Woods. Regents Restoration Drama Series, edited by John Loftis. Lincoln: University of Nebraska Press; London: Edward Arnold, 1967, 171 pp.

Reviewed by Joseph A. Byrnes, SCN, 25 (1967), 34-35; Dean L. Morgan, Personalist, 48 (1967), 430.

A modernized edition of the 1730 edition of the play (three editions were printed in 1730; all were collated), which is distinct from the completely revised "third" edition (1750), prepared when the play was revived in 1734. The introduction describes Fielding's part in the "explosion in the theatrical life of London" (p. xii), describes Fielding's revision of the play for the 1734 season, discusses its importance for Fielding ("it is in this kind of irregular drama that Fielding's excellence as a playwright lies," p. xv), and provides a stage history for the play.

The text has running explanatory notes. Appendix A includes the revisions for the 1734 production. Appendix B carefully describes the chief targets (Cibber, etc.). Appendix C includes all of the tunes but two (from sources published in Fielding's time). Appendix D is a chronology of political and literary events in Fielding's life.

6 _____. The History of the Adventures of Joseph Andrews, And of his Friend Mr. Abraham Adams. Afterword by Ian Watt. A Perennial Classic. New York: Harper & Row, 320 pp.
Select bibliography and a biographical note. Watt discusses Fielding's comedy (distance, external presentation, its base in affectation) and his narrative (the repetitive structure and narrative distance), both of which insist on the artfulness of the creation. "The text of this edition is substantially that of the fourth edition, published in 1748."

7 _____. The History of Tom Jones, A Foundling. Introduction by Louis Kronenberger and illustrations by T. M. Cleland. New York: Heritage Press, 798 pp. [1966].
Reissue of 1952.A2.

8 _____. The History of Tom Jones. Edited by R. P. C. Mutter. Penguin English Library. Harmondsworth, Baltimore, Victoria (Australia): Penguin Books, 911 pp.
Includes introduction, notes, glossary and brief bibliography. Text is a "slightly modernized" reprinting of the "third" (the four volume April 1749) edition. Introduction discusses the sexual morality of the book, the theme of hypocrisy (appearance and reality), Fielding's use of irony, Fielding's conservative social conscience, his combination of realism and comedy, the country and city structure of the book, and the nature of Fielding's "broad, sane, extroverted humor" (p. 27).

9 _____. The History of Tom Jones. Introduction by A. H. Humphreys. Everyman's Library. 2 vols. London: J. M. Dent & Sons; New York: E. P. Dutton, 711 pp.
Reprint of 1962.A7. Also issued by Heron Books (London) as part of the Literary Heritage Collection.

10 _____. The Life of Mr. Jonathan Wild The Great. Wood engravings by Frank Martin. London: The Folio Society, 187 pp.
Includes a brief note on the real Wild and on Fielding's life by "R. M." No indication of copy text.

1966

*11 _____. Tom Jones. Translated by Carlos Castresana. Barcelona: Bruguera, 888 pp.
Spanish translation. Five editions by 1972.
Source: Hugh Amory's working bibliography.

*12 _____. Tom Jones. Translated by Gianni Rebaudengo. Torino: Ed. dell 'albero, 308 pp.
Abridged Italian translation.
Source: Hugh Amory's working bibliography.

*13 _____. Tom Jones. Translated by Javier Tomeo. Barcelona: Circulo de lectores, 729 pp.
Spanish translation.
Source: Hugh Amory's working bibliography.

*14 _____. Tom Jones. Translated by Maria Casamar. Barcelona: Ramon Sopena, 798 pp.
Spanish translation.
Source: Hugh Amory's working bibliography.

*15 _____. Tom Jones. Translated by María Franco and João Cabral do Nascimento. Lisbon: Portugália, 373 pp.
Portuguese translation.
Source: Hugh Amory's working bibliography.

16 GOLDEN, MORRIS. Fielding's Moral Psychology. Amherst: University of Massachusetts Press, 177 pp.
Reviewed by Martin C. Battestin, MLQ, 28 (1967), 368-77; John A. Dussinger, JEGP, 66 (1967), 591-94; W. R. Irwin, PQ, 46 (1967), 345; Maxmillian E. Novak, Novel, 1 (1968), 286-88; Ronald H. Paulson, SEL, 7 (1967), 549-50; Raymond Smith, Literature and Psychology, 17 (1967), 141-43; Andrew Wright, MLR, 63 (1968), 945-46; JNL, 27 (March 1967), 11.
By examining the ideas in Fielding's essays, tracts, poems, plays, and novels, Golden establishes Fielding's position in the eighteenth-century epistemological debate about self and the nature of reality. He concludes that Fielding wanted his readers to believe in the reality of the outer world so that they could "interact humanely with it" (p. 123) and that for "Fielding, man's basic duty was the need to understand and sympathize with others, and his basic problem was psychological isolation" (what Golden calls the enclosed self) (p. 147). For the individual, this good desire to break out of isolation is complicated "by the whole cast of his disposition--whether indrawn or outgoing" (p. 148), by his environment with its "formal social order or the rules of good breeding [which] may

become poisonous" (p. 149), and by his secret desires and lusts. In two chapters on the novels, one on the enclosed self and the other on the environment, he sees a developing complexity from Joseph Andrews, through Tom Jones, to Amelia. "In Joseph Andrews, knowledge of the outside world is almost totally limited to reflections of the character's own experiences modified by various degrees of vanity and affectation" (p. 73). "In Amelia, Fielding is more subtly concerned to show the distortions which the mind and its passions themselves create" (p. 74). He concludes that by the time of Tom Jones the "world has become both darker and more complex psychologically," and "in Amelia Fielding's system seems less adequate in the face of complicated and determined reality" (p. 97). Thus, although Fielding "provides us with gloriously triumphant fantasies [of human perception and interaction] he frequently forces us to abandon them, or at least subordinate them to sane awareness of surrounding actuality" (p. 124). He finally links Fielding with Swift and Pope's "vision of a disintegrating world under the sway of chaos and old night" (p. 146), which Golden thinks "inevitable when happiness is seen as residing only within the mind" (p. 124). He also strangely includes Richardson and Smollett in this group. In Fielding's moral psychology, society never achieves its ideals, and so it cannot be, as in classical comedy, "a positive counter to the oddity of the comic figures" (p. 146).

*17 HUSSEIN, M. A. "The Eighteenth-Century Concept of the Good Man in Relation to the Novels of Fielding." Dissertation, Leicester, 1966.

Source: McNamee, 1964-1968, p. 222.

18 IRWIN, WILLIAM R. The Making of Jonathan Wild: A Study in the Literary Method of Henry Fielding. Hamden, Conn.: Archon Books, 159 pp.

Reprint of 1941.A3.

*19 JACOBSON, WILLIAM S. "The Rhetorical Structure of Fielding's Epic Joseph Andrews." Dissertation, Stanford, 1966.

A detailed rhetorical analysis of Joseph Andrews reveals the model for Tom Jones and Amelia.

Source: Dissertation Abstracts, 27, no. 4 (Oct. 1966), 1057A-1058A.

20 JENKINS, ELIZABETH. Henry Fielding. London: Arthur Baker, 101 pp.

Reprint of 1947.A6.

*21 PALMER, EUSTACE J. "The Relationship of the Morality of Henry Fielding's Novels to their Art." Dissertation, Edinburgh, 1966.

Source: McNamee, 1964-1968, p. 222.

22 SACKS, SHELDON. Fiction and the Shape of Belief: A Study of Henry Fielding with Glances at Swift, Johnson, and Richardson. Berkeley and Los Angeles: University of California Press, 281 pp.

Reprint of 1964.A24.

*23 STEWART, MAAJA A. "The Artifice of Comedy: Fielding and Meredith." Dissertation, Michigan, 1966.

Studies the striking similarities in comic attitude and technique in these two writers. Both move away from ridicule to the comedy of self-examination; both use the self-conscious ironic narrator, parody, and shifts of focus.

Source: Dissertation Abstracts, 27, no. 7 (Jan. 1967), 2163A.

24 TAYLOR, DUNCAN. Fielding's England. Living in England Series. London: Dennis Dobson, 256 pp.

A popular account of English life, customs, and manners that uses Fielding's works (and still photographs from the movie "Tom Jones") to illustrate conditions in eighteenth-century England.

25 VOORDE, FRANS PIETER VAN DER. Henry Fielding: Critic and Satirist. New York: Haskell House, 233 pp.

Reprint of 1931.A10.

26 ZIRKER, MALVIN R. Fielding's Social Pamphlets: A Study of "An Enquiry into the Causes of the Late Increase of Robbers" and "A Proposal for Making an Effectual Provision for the Poor." University of California English Studies, no. 31. Berkeley and Los Angeles: University of California Press, 174 pp.

Reviewed by Martin C. Battestin, MLQ, 28 (1967), 368-77; Ronald Paulson, JEGP, 67 (1968), 161-65, and SEL, 7 (1967), 550.

By carefully setting these pamphlets in their social and journalistic contexts, Zirker invalidates the claim that Fielding was a radical social reformer. Zirker sees Fielding as a conservative accepting "unquestioningly a hierarchical, static society nearly feudal in some of its outlines" (p. 136). Fielding was "able to maintain the serenity and ideality of the classical-Christian virtues" (p. 139) only in his fiction, where his characters escape from the real world. Zirker sets out the eighteenth-century English attitude toward the poor and the laws pertaining to them; then he sets Fielding's pamphlets in their context (concluding that Fielding expressed only the conventional "wisdom" of his time, and had little effect on the legal reform movement of the 1750s). Zirker examines metaphors, epithets for the poor, and parallel passages in other contemporary pamphlets, and concludes "[Fielding's] language in general will be nearly anonymous in its conventionality" (p. 117). Fielding shared the contemporary conservative belief in the "luxury" of the poor (considered under several subcategories: amusements, gin-drinking, gambling). He thinks that Fielding's attitude toward beggars is a striking illustration of how "one's preconceptions [shared with most of his contemporaries] can control his perception of fact" (p. 96). He examines Fielding's economics ("conventional mercantile doctrine," p. 101) and Fielding's proposal for a large workhouse for the able-bodied poor (a scheme he may have borrowed from writers like Mathew Hale, Josiah Child, John Cary, and William Hay).

<u>See</u> 1958.B12, 1962.B7, 1967.B35, 1971.B2, 1974.A16 and dissertation 1962.A13.

<u>1966 B SHORTER WRITINGS</u>

1 ALTER, ROBERT. "On the Critical Dismissal of Fielding: Post-Puritanism in Literary Criticism." <u>Salmagundi</u>, 1, no. 2 (Winter), 11-28.

Reviews the critical attitude, still held by some, that sees Fielding as simple and hearty. Thinks that it is Fielding's attitude toward sex, "as skylarking, not skirting the abyss" (p. 15), that offended Dr. Johnson and many modern critics, who still hold the Puritan notion "that sex is something portentous, involving man's ultimate moral responsibilities" (p. 16). Carefully analyzes the arguments of Samuel Johnson and particularly Kermode (1950.B6) as they apply to <u>Tom Jones</u>, and concludes that the lingering Puritan attitude toward sex blinds critics like Kermode to the strikingly complex and modern quality of Fielding's novels, which "were written to be ideally read in the way we have been reading the so-called art-novel since the time of Conrad and James. Each book is a reflexive system of significations" (p. 27). Fielding has simply suffered for Tom's exuberant non-Puritan sexuality and for writing less visceral (mythopoeic) novels than Richardson.

1966

2 BATTESTIN, MARTIN C. "Fielding and 'Master Punch' in Panton Street." Philological Quarterly, 45, no. 1 (Jan.), 191-208.

This biographical article demonstrates that Fielding set up a "puppet theatre in Panton Street under the name of 'Madame de la Nash'" (p. 192). He may have taken his hint for a satiric puppet theater from Beau Nash, thus the name. In this satiric form he carried on a war with Samuel Foote in the spring of 1748.

For another version, see 1875.B2.

3 _____. "Osborne's Tom Jones: Adapting a Classic." Virginia Quarterly Review, 42, no. 3 (Summer), 378-93.

Begins by seeing the rapport between modern writers and "the master novelist of an age which found satiric laughter the most congenial antidote to the perversion of order and the corruption of the Establishment" (p. 379), and then strongly objects to the film's unwillingness to deal with Fielding's "moral seriousness," with his "celebration of that rational design which gives meaning to vitality" (p. 381). Battestin then examines some of the ways in which the film "brilliantly recreated [the novel's] essential spirit and manner" (p. 383), citing analogous rhetorical techniques that created the proper comic detachment, the well adapted scene in Molly Seagrim's bedroom and the eating scene at Upton; and also the addition of scenes (the stag hunt) and symbolic contrasts (introducing Jones in the woods and Blifil in the formal garden) that emphasized thematic and structural oppositions in the novel.

Reprinted 1967.B6 and 1970.A4.

4 COLEY, WILLIAM B. "Henry Fielding and the Two Walpoles." Philological Quarterly, 45, no. 1 (Jan.), 157-78.

This biographical article throws some light on the "'family tradition' of hostility between Fielding and the two Walpoles" (p. 177), Robert and his son Horace. Coley concludes that Fielding "changed his politics, to be sure, but he changed with his party, so to speak, or with a considerable segment of it" (p. 178), and he did not take "pay from the Great Man" (p. 177). See 1949.B5, 1960.B4, 1967.B2, and 1977.B10.

5 DIRCKS, RICHARD J. "The Perils of Heartfree: A Sociological Review of Fielding's Adaptation of Dramatic Convention." Texas Studies in Literature and Language, 8, no. 1 (Spring), 5-13.

Asserts that Fielding's Jonathan Wild is not primarily a political attack on Walpole but Fielding's "focusing the attention of the readers of his novel on the problems of the poor" (p. 5). Fielding accomplished this, according to Dircks, with the Heartfree episode. After first reviewing Fielding's analysis of those social problems common to The Champion and Jonathan Wild, he looks at the techniques from the drama of sensibility that Fielding adapts to his task. These include a burlesque of the sentimental romance, a study of the theme of repentance and conscience, and typical characters (the villain, the loyal wife, the ideal merchant). See 1913.B6, 1941.A2, 1966.A26, B11.

6 DOBLIER, MAURICE, GEORGE D. CROTHERS, and GLENWAY WESCOTT. "Henry Fielding: Tom Jones," in Invitation to Learning: English and American Novels. Edited by G. D. Crothers. New York and London: Basic Books, pp. 36-43.

Radio conversation between M. Doblier, G. D. Crothers, and G. Wescott in which they discuss the movie version, the plot of the novel, and the puppetmaster narrator. Wescott attacks Fielding for his moral ambivalence (saying that he played on reader salaciousness), his exhibitionism, his hypocrisy, his rhetorical excesses, and his failure to make Tom and Sophia sound colloquial and real. He also thinks that Tom is Fielding's self-portrait.

7 DONOVAN, ROBERT A. "Joseph Andrews as Parody," in his The Shaping Vision: Imagination in the English Novel from Defoe to Dickens. Ithaca, New York: Cornell University Press; London: Oxford University Press, pp. 68-88.

Reviewed by T. J. Cribb, RES, 18 (1967), 468-69; TLS, 18 Aug. 1966, p. 738.

Argues that Joseph Andrews, like Shamela, is a parody of Pamela, although of "a different, less pointed, but more comprehensive, kind" (p. 86). Sees Joseph Andrews as "an extraordinarily subtle and far-reaching commentary on Richardson's ethical assumptions" (p. 70). For Donovan the explicit parody of the opening chapters is altered when Joseph becomes a romantic lead and Adams takes over the parody role, becoming "the principal instrument of Fielding's reductio ad absurdum of the moral view exemplified by Pamela" (p. 74). Distinguishes between Pamela, whose formulas work, and Adams, whose formulas do not; between the wider world of Fielding's novel and the narrower of Richardson's; and between Adams' honesty and Pamela's hypocrisy. Finally argues that even the double discovery of the end is a parody of the moral assumptions of Pamela.

For another view, see 1960.B7 and 1970.B37.

1966

8 DYSON, A. E. "Fielding: Satiric and Comic Irony," in his The Crazy Fabric: Essays in Irony. London, Melbourne, Toronto: Macmillan; New York: St. Martin's Press, pp. 14-32.

Reviewed by G. D. Josipovici, RES, 17 (1966), 106-108; R. C. Stephens, MLR, 61 (1966), 126-27; Juliet Sutton, DR, 46 (1966), 391-93; Marshall Waingrow, YR, 56 (1966), 138-41.

Sees Fielding mingling the satiric and comic elements in his work, temperamentally incapable of Swift's "misanthropy." Dyson briefly examines this balance in Shamela, Joseph Andrews, and Jonathan Wild, suggesting that in Jonathan Wild Fielding lacks conviction and that his ordinary "comic tolerance and poise" (p. 21) undermines the satiric vigor of this work. Finally briefly examines the moral basis of Tom Jones to illustrate that it is an instance of "a major ironic talent achieving its true relation to temperament, after a somewhat uncertain and fluctuating start," where "satiric irony is restricted only to certain local episodes" and "the main irony is wholly assimilated to the comic purpose" (p. 32).

For a very different view of Jonathan Wild see 1972.A9. For a precise discussion of irony in Tom Jones, see 1971. B25.

9 FARRELL, WILLIAM J. "The Mock-Heroic Form of Jonathan Wild." Modern Philology, 63, no. 3 (Feb.), 216-26.

Argues that Fielding adopted the high-flown techniques of "the traditional biography of the illustrious man" to "satirize his hero" and "to link him with other greats whose lives are presented in a similar fashion" (p. 216). Rejecting the idea that Jonathan Wild is generically a rogue biography, Farrell examines the topics ("the traditional loci of rhetoricians," p. 218) of the biographies of the great, comparing Wild to Middleton's serious biography of Cicero and to The Life of Alexander, and concluding that "the rhetorical loci (especially those in Book I) become an important vehicle for the author's ethical and political thought, underlining his dual role as pseudo-biographer and pseudo-panegyrist" (p. 226).

10 GOLDBERG, HOMER. "The Interpolated Stories in Joseph Andrews or 'The History of the World in General' Satirically Revised." Modern Philology, 63, no. 4 (May), 295-310.

Argues that with the history of Leonora and the story of Paul and Leonard, Fielding is playing "upon the tradition he espoused" (p. 295). "Most of the interpolations of Cervantes, Lesage, and Scarron are 'straight' melodramatic or pathetic love stories" (p. 296); Fielding makes his "detached stories comic" (p. 298). Goldberg suggests prototypes in Cervantes for Fielding's two stories and analyzes Fielding's comic play with the convention. He also suggests that the Wilson tale has a parallel in Don Quixote and that Fielding uses it to comment ironically on the artist in his own age. See 1956.B2, 1968.B9, and 1968.B14.

11 HOPKINS, ROBERT H. "Language and Comic Play in Fielding's Jonathan Wild." Criticism, 8, no. 3 (Summer), 213-28.

Begins "by redefining the genre of Jonathan Wild not as a novel but as an anatomy or satire written in the form of criminal biography describing the life of a confidence man in a mock-heroic fashion" (p. 214). Hopkins sees the narrator, "who parodies continually the flatulent language of the confidence men" (p. 216), as exposing the two dupes of the novel (Heartfree, the naif, who is taken in by Wild's rhetoric, and Wild, who verbally reduces life to the bestial). Hopkins first examines the verbal "lock-and-key pattern of inclusion and exclusion" (p. 217) in this satire and then the covert language of bestial sexual appetite. The Heartfrees too are caught in this bestial language; "Fielding strikes here at the very heart of an absurd prudery in which virtue and sexual enjoyment are incompatible" (p. 228). Hopkins concludes that "the world of Jonathan Wild offers either raw bestiality and obscenity or a fastidious asceticism and prudery" (p. 228), the extremes of comic satire. For another view, see 1966.B5.

12 KOLJEVIĆ, SVETOZAR. "Fildingv Tom Džons i ljubavna etika evropskog romana." Izraz, 10, no. 12 (Dec.), 533-49.

"Fielding's Tom Jones and the love ethic of the European novel." Slovene article published in Sarajevo, Yugoslavia.

13 MILBURN, D. JUDSON. "The Psychology of Wit in Henry Fielding's Tom Jones and in Laurence Sterne's Tristram Shandy," in his The Age of Wit: 1650-1750. New York: Macmillan; London: Collier-Macmillan, pp. 106-19.

Reviewed by Frederic V. Bogel, SCN, 25 (1967), 15-16; R. I. Cook, MLQ, 28 (1967), 111-13; B. A. Robie, LJ, 91 (1966), 1425.

Argues that Fielding essentially agreed with Hobbes' analysis of psychology. Fielding sees the creative process as a balance of genius (wit) and invention (fancy), but "Fielding felt judgment to be the primary faculty in the creative process" (p. 107).

14 MILLER, HENRY K. "Some Functions of Rhetoric in Tom Jones." Philological Quarterly, 45, no. 1 (Jan.), 209-35.

Argues that although rhetoric is not the only source of Fielding's literary art, it is an important one. "It is my conviction that the use of a rhetorical vocabulary is one profitable approach to Henry Fielding's habits of composition, even down to the smallest particles" (p. 212). He begins by demonstrating Fielding's "consciousness of rhetoric" (p. 213) in the orations of Tom Jones and goes on to argue that "Fielding found not only the techniques of rhetoric to be of fundamental service to him, but the values associated with the discussion of [it] as well" (p. 218). Miller then discusses the rhetorical reader/author relationship and Fielding's style, concluding that Fielding was interested in making the reader aware of "the play between a universal order and a contingent [rhetorical] order" (p. 235). Precise terms from classical rhetoric are used throughout the essay. See 1967.B18.

15 PARK, WILLIAM. "Fielding and Richardson." Publications of the Modern Language Association, 81, no. 5 (Oct.), 381-88.

This historical genre study surveys the "common ground which they share with each other and with other novelists of the 1740s and 50s" (p. 381). They shared the same theory of the novel (satisfying the demands of nature and morality); both believed in neoclassical general histories; used stock figures. They borrowed from novels with picaresque heroes (which often had interpolated tales of the persecution of a virgin), and from romantic novels (which overtly emphasized courtship while covertly implying that rape is essential to courtship). Richardson and Fielding differ from their contemporaries in transforming this stock material through pathos and wit; they also, according to Park, share a belief in a "radical individualism" (p. 385). All of the novelists of the period believed in the family, the purity of the countryside, the conservative reality of culture and society, and the static nature of history. All of this is the common ground against which they played "the individuality, feeling, detail, complexity, irony, and motion which make up the so-called 'realism' of the novels" (p. 388).

See 1951.B4, and for a contrary view see 1957.B17.

16 PRESTON, JOHN. "The Ironic Mode: A Comparison of Jonathan Wild and The Beggar's Opera." Essays in Criticism, 16, no. 3 (July), 268-80.

Both these works are about the same man, and "Gay's theme is in fact very similar to Fielding's. . . . There are, however, marked differences in the handling of the irony" (p. 269). Fielding uses it as "a stylistic device, a means of clarification, even of simplification. Gay, on the other hand, uses it as a means of articulating and organizing his knowledge of life" (p. 269). Both begin with a political intention; both follow some of Pope's ironic rules in Peri Bathous. Preston argues that Gay is subtler and Fielding more conventional. Fielding, by varying tone (from irony to anger), can create powerful local effects, but his ironic effect "is created not by action but by vocabulary" (p. 274). Gay's irony, on the other hand, "forms part of a dramatic argument" (p. 275). He concludes that Gay's criticism goes deeper: "The basis of Fielding's humor is that his characters act as though they believed in their roles . . . [Gay] makes us see the reason why his characters should believe in their roles, and then shows the whole moral premise to be amusing" (p. 280).

17 _____. "Tom Jones and the Pursuit of True Judgment." Journal of English Literary History, 30, no. 3 (Sept.), 315-26.
Asserts that we do not find the "moral sense in Tom Jones . . . in the action. . . . In fact Fielding's plot is amoral, for it centres on Fortune" (p. 315). Thus in relation to epic theory of his time, Fielding has written a flawed work, but the book is moral. It is "about judgment, and the understanding necessary for good judgment. This is where the moral sense is located, in the analysis and evaluation of diverse judgments" (p. 316). Preston then sets out the various ways in which Fielding makes us conscious readers and involved judges (like Bishop Butler, whom Tom resembles, rather than Shaftesbury, whom Allworthy resembles). Tom's judgment from compassionate knowledge is ultimately better than "the hollowness of Allworthy's rectitude" (p. 324). See 1965.B21.
Reprinted 1970.B24.

18 RAWSON, C. J. "Source Wanted: Fielding on Louis XIV." Notes and Queries, 211 (Aug.), 305.
For a passage in "Essay on Conversation" about a discourtesy Louis XIV offered an Englishman.

19 ROBERTS, EDGAR V. "Mr. Seedo's London Career and His Work with Henry Fielding." Philological Quarterly, 45, no. 1 (Jan.), 179-90.
Describes the London career of this theater music director who worked at the New Haymarket and then at Drury Lane during the period when Fielding was connected with

these theaters. Roberts argues that "Seedo's most significant work in London was done in collaboration with Henry Fielding" (p. 183). Seedo composed an overture and conducted the music for The Author's Farce and may have composed tunes for The Intriguing Chambermaid and Don Quixote in England. He may also have collaborated with Fielding on The Grub-Street Opera (suppressed) and The Lottery (1731). See 1971.B22 and dissertation 1960.A13.

20 SEAMON, ROGER G. "The Rhetorical Pattern of Mock-Heroic Satire." Humanities Association Bulletin, 17, no. 2 (Autumn), 37-41.
Uses Jonathan Wild along with The Dunciad, Joyce's Ulysses, and other works to help define the rhetorical pattern of mock-heroic. See dissertation 1966.B21.

*21 _____. "The Rhetorical Patterns of Neoclassical Mock-Heroic Satire." Dissertation, Claremont, 1966.
Source: Dissertation Abstracts, 28, no. 3 (Sept. 1967), 1058A.
See 1966.B20.

22 SPEARMAN, DIANA. "Fielding," in her The Novel and Society. London: Routledge & Kegan Paul; New York: Barnes & Noble, pp. 199-213 and 214-24.
Reviewed by Robert E. Kelley, PQ, 47 (1968), 346; TLS, 11 May 1967, p. 400.
Argues that we ought not to treat novels as perfectly accurate social documents (precise and literal reflections of their societies) but rather as both passive reflection and active and peculiar choice by the novelist. Very briefly, and with little historical support, considers a number of ways in which elements in Fielding's novels accurately reflect his time. Considers his Christianity, his Whig political theories, and his description of social problems. Briefly argues that the comic political exaggeration of Squire Western seems authentic because of Fielding's "ability to reproduce the idiom" (p. 201), that Amelia is a strikingly accurate description of London social and legal problems ("Colonel Bath is so rooted in social reality as to be practically incomprehensible to modern readers," p. 208), and that Fielding's distance from his characters (different from Richardson's) makes his novels better reflections of contemporary social relations.

1967 A BOOKS

*1 BROOKS, DOUGLAS. "Henry Fielding's Joseph Andrews: A Critical Study." Dissertation, Liverpool, 1967.

Source: McNamee, 1964-1968, p. 222. See 1968.B7, B9, 1970.A8 and B5.

2 FIELDING, HENRY. Joseph Andrews. Edited by Martin C. Battestin. The Wesleyan Edition of the Works of Henry Fielding. Middletown, Conn.: Wesleyan University Press; Oxford: Clarendon Press, 436 pp.

Reviewed by Sheridan Baker, MQR, 6 (1967), 298; Douglas Brooks, MLR, 64 (1969), 146-47; H. W. Drescher, Anglia, 87 (1969), 101-103; J. D. Fleeman, RES, n.s. 19 (1968), 208-209; F. W. Hilles, YR, 57 (1967-68), 278-82; Arthur Sherbo, JEGP, 67 (1968), 520-22; Niels Jørgen Skydsgaard, ES, 50 (1969), 409-10; Ian Watt, PQ, 47 (1968), 379; Choice, 4 (1967), 824; TLS, 20 April 1967, p. 334; VQR, 44 (1968), xxvi.

This definitive edition of "a critical unmodernized text of Joseph Andrews" (p. xxxix) includes a textual introduction by Fredson Bowers describing Battestin's procedure. The first edition was used as a copy text (in order to come "as close as documentary evidence permits to the desirable reproduction of authorial characteristics in spelling, pointing, and the like," p. xli), and later authorial corrections and revision were inserted. Appendix I lists the "substantive emendations," Appendix II "accidental emendations," Appendix III "end-of-the-line hyphenation." Appendix IV offers an "historical collation," Appendix V a bibliographical description of the first five editions, and Appendix VI a description of the "Murphy editions" of Joseph Andrews. There are running explanatory notes to the text. The general introduction provides biographical background (politics and patrons), briefly discusses the parody of Pamela and other allusions, and provides a careful publication history of the novel during Fielding's lifetime. See dissertation 1958.A2.

*3 _____. Korot Tom G'ones. Translated by Ester Caspi. Introduction by A. A. Mendilow. 2 vols. Jerusalem: Mosad Bialik. [1967].

Modern Hebrew translation of Tom Jones.

Source: National Union Catalogue Authors Lists, 1968-1972. Vol. 29, p. 438.

4 _____. The Complete Works of Henry Fielding, Esq. With an Essay on the Life, Genius and Achievement of the Author by William Henley. 16 vols. New York: Barnes & Noble; London: Cassell.

Reprint of 1902.A4.

1967

5 _____. The Historical Register for the Year 1736 and Eurydice Hissed. Edited by William W. Appleton. Regents Restoration Drama Series, edited by John Loftis. Lincoln: University of Nebraska Press; London: Edward Arnold, 1968, 101 pp.

Conservatively modernized edition of these two plays based on the 48 page edition (which Cross designates the "second") of 12 May 1737. There are running explanatory notes to both texts and an appendix that parallels Fielding's career with "political and literary events" of his time. The introduction describes some of the central allusions in "this patchwork entertainment, with its glancing allusions to politics, society, and the theatre" (p. x) and the sharp political reaction to such dramatic satires.

6 _____. The History of the Adventures of Joseph Andrews and his Friend Mr. Abraham Adams. London: The Folio Society, 319 pp.

Reprint of 1953.A3.

7 _____. The History of Tom Jones, A Foundling. Introduction by Arthur Sherbo. Great Illustrated Classics. Titan editions. New York: Dodd, Mead, 734 pp.

Reproduces selected illustrations, from Borel in 1788 to still photographs from the 1963 Tony Richardson film. Appears to reprint the "1750" edition followed by Murphy (1762.A10). The introduction very briefly discusses the plot, characters, style, point of view, and "scope" of Tom Jones.

*8 _____. Tom Jones. Preface by Gilbert Sigaux. Translated by M. Desfauconpret. Paris: Club français du livre, 1207 pp.

French translation.

Source: National Union Catalogue Author Lists, 1968-1972. Vol. 29, p. 439.

9 IRWIN, MICHAEL. Henry Fielding The Tentative Realist. Oxford: Clarendon Press, 155 pp.

Reviewed by F. W. Hilles, YR, 57 (1968), 278-82; Juliet McMaster, DR, 48 (1968), 266-68; Ronald Paulson, Novel, 2 (1968), 79-80; C. J. Rawson, N&Q, 213 (1968), 474-77; Timothy Rogers, English, 17 (1968), 61-62; J. A. Wightman, So RA, 3 (1968), 95-97; JNL, 27 (Dec. 1967), 13; TLS, 19 Oct. 1967, p. 985. See also correspondence between Andrew Bean and reviewer in TLS, 7 Dec. 1967, p. 1197 and Michael Irwin and reviewer in TLS, 18 Jan. 1968, p. 69.

Attempts to illustrate "that Fielding was a didactic writer, a moralist, from the very beginning of his literary career" by examining "the regularity with which he returns . . . to a number of specific social and ethical issues" (p. vii). Irwin merely sets out these issues as they appear in his journalism, plays, and minor narrative works (Jonathan Wild and A Journey from this World to the Next) before examining their use in Joseph Andrews, Tom Jones, and Amelia. Among the "issues" Irwin considers are Fielding's attitude toward virtue and charity (which he thinks not entirely latitudinarian) as they affect his sexual ethic; and his attitude toward ambition, egotism, and visible social evils as they are reflected in manners and amusements as well as in politics and the professions. In these early writings, Irwin argues, "Fielding was manipulating . . . existing form[s] in the interest of his didactic intention. When he came to write his first novel . . . he was free to design a new form expressly to embody his moral ideas" (p. 50). After briefly examining the influence of the drama and the continental romance on Fielding's novels, Irwin discusses Joseph Andrews as a reconciliation of his moral aim (to expose vanity and hypocrisy) with the picaresque form, arguing that it is "inappropriate" to judge "it, like any other novel, in terms of character and plot" (p. 66). Irwin sees the characters as "semi-allegorical" and the episodes as an arbitrary stylization of life. In Tom Jones, Irwin sees an increasing sophistication of technique, although there is still much undigested picaresque and didactic material. Among the didactic and narrative excellencies in Tom Jones which "are not only independent of, but almost inconsistent with, one another" (p. 111), Irwin identifies a conflict between plot and character depth (or the realism of perception). He argues that in Amelia Fielding gave up theoretical narrative schemes (romantic interest and picaresque variety) as a means of embodying his themes: the ideal wife and mother, the rescue of Booth from a wicked philosophy, and the exposure of social evils. In Amelia Fielding tried "a century too soon, to write a realistic, socially-reformative novel" (p. 134); it is only weakened by a few remaining narrative artifices (the Aeneid parallel). Irwin's belief is that "many of Fielding's chosen narrative techniques were incompatible" (p. 135) with his moral purposes. See 1956.B11, 1959.A1, and 1964.B1.

*10 KINDER, MARSHA. "Henry Fielding's Dramatic Experimentation: A Preface to His Fiction." Dissertation, University of California at Los Angeles, 1967.

Studies the technical and thematic relation of Fielding's dramatic burlesque satires to his novels.

Source: Dissertation Abstracts, 28, no. 2 (Aug. 1967), 633A-34A.

*11 KURTZ, ERIC W. "Fielding's Thoughtful Laughter." Dissertation, Yale, 1967.

Argues that in Joseph Andrews, Tom Jones, and Amelia Fielding's comedy and his moral judgment enhance each other.

Source: Dissertation Abstracts, 28, no. 1 (July 1967), 234A.

12 LEVINE, GEORGE R. Henry Fielding and the Dry Mock: A Study of the Techniques of Irony in His Early Works. Studies in English Literature, no. 30. The Hague and Paris: Mouton, 160 pp.

Reviewed by Ronald Paulson, SEL, 7 (1967), 549; P. H. van Huizen, LT (1970), 56-58; Malvin R. Zirker, PQ, 47 (1968), 382-83; JNL, 27 (March 1967), 11-12.

A careful examination of the ironic techniques in the early works of Fielding (in the plays, The Champion, Joseph Andrews, and Jonathan Wild). Levine first briefly sets out the eighteenth-century attitude toward irony (a tool for an intellectual elite), the ironic techniques favored by the century ("rhetorical irony . . . was . . . the only type of irony the eighteenth century was conscious of using," p. 126), and Fielding's conventional use of these techniques. He then carefully discusses the "ironic mask" (the persona), distinguishing four kinds used by Fielding (editor, public defender, two politicians, and traveler) and comparing Fielding's and Swift's use of persona The third chapter is devoted to a study of the seven "basic techniques of verbal [rhetorical] irony" (p. 65): denotative irony, connotative irony, understatement, reversal of statement, irony of implication, ironic undercut, ironic defense. Chapter four shows "how the techniques of verbal irony function collectively in a single work [Joseph Andrews]" (p. 8). Chapter five distinguishes between rhetorical and dramatic irony ("the ambiguity inherent in what a character . . . says or does," p. 126) and examines his development of this ironic technique from mere double-edged language (in his plays) to situational ambiguity for characterization (in Joseph Andrews). See 1965.A15, 1971.B25, and dissertation 1961.A12.

13 MACALLISTER, HAMILTON. Fielding. Literature in Perspective, edited by K. H. Grose. London: Evans Brothers, 140 pp.

Briefly reviews Fielding's reputation (from Samuel Johnson through F. R. Leavis), Fielding's early life (emphasizing the satire in his early plays and journalism), and his later career as a novelist. Also discusses the novel as a new literary form and Augustan ideas (Locke, Shaftesbury, deism, latitudinarianism, etc.). Macallister occasionally confuses Fielding with his characters: "Fielding had often behaved like Captain Booth" (p. 45). He then has two chapters each on Joseph Andrews and Tom Jones (discussing sources, structure, character, and themes). For example, he discusses Richardson's Pamela, Don Quixote, Fielding's classical scholarship, the Bible, Hogarth, and the French romances as "sources" for Joseph Andrews, seeing their influence in the journey motif and the shifting intention. He also discusses the satire and humor of Joseph Andrews, as well as its interpolated tales. Each of the major characters (e.g., Adams, Western, Tom, Blifil) is separately discussed. In a brief final chapter he discusses Jonathan Wild, Amelia, and Journal of a Voyage to Lisbon. Macallister sees the purposefulness of every event and character in Fielding as a limitation; he thinks Tom Jones weakened by the unrealized character of Allworthy; and he finds a basic pessimism in all of Fielding's humor.

*14 RIZVI, SYED M. "Political Satire in the Plays of Henry Fielding." Dissertation, Edinburgh, 1967.

Source: McNamee, 1964-1968, p. 222.

1967 B SHORTER WRITINGS

1 ALTER, ROBERT. "Fielding and the Uses of Style." Novel, 1 (Fall), 53-63.

Discusses Fielding's manipulation of the reader into comprehending his many levels of irony by looking at what he says and at his word order. This occasionally ingenious essay argues for the extreme artificiality of Fielding's style; Alter compares the balance and antithesis of Fielding's sentences to Pope's couplets. Some excellent precise analysis of style and reader expectation.

Incorporated in 1968.A1. Reprinted 1968.A2.

2 AMORY, HUGH. "Henry Fielding's Epistle to Walpole: A Reexamination." Philological Quarterly, 46, no. 2 (April), 236-47.

This biographical and historical article, examining events in Walpole's and Fielding's careers, argues that the "First Epistle appeared in 1738, and the implications of its satire are typical of Opposition satire at that time; the changes of the later version mirror Fielding's political attitude in 1743; the additions are all designed to create a 1730 'climate' for the poem, and the subtitle read together with the note on Arlington Street is a specific device to contrast Walpole at the height of his power with Walpole fallen" (p. 245). Amory is persuaded by all this to see the First Epistle as written in 1738, in revenge for the Licensing Act, then revised in 1742, though still essentially critical of Walpole. See 1949.B5, 1960.B4, and 1966.B4.

3 ______. "Two Lost Fielding Manuscripts." Notes and Queries, 212 (May), 183-84.

Attempts to reconstruct two Fielding mss. (a letter and a bond) from sales catalogues.

4 BAKER, SHERIDAN. "Bridget Allworthy: The Creative Pressures of Fielding's Plot." Papers of the Michigan Academy of Science, Arts, and Letters, 52:345-56.

Attempting to redefine plot after R. S. Crane's broadening of the concept (1950.B2), Baker distinguishes between plot (everything that happens) and plotting (the limited evidence) and says that character is a creation of the two. By looking at Bridget Allworthy, Baker illustrates the "supreme example of how plot generates character, as the nearly fabulous story strains against the necessities of plotting a realistic mystery and a moral education" (p. 346). The tensions in her character (plot demanding a passionate and lonely woman and plotting a comic old maid) help Fielding conceal Tom's parentage and deepen Bridget's character. Baker finally argues that Bridget has "a strangely authentic streak of sadism against the boy [Tom] she cannot let alone, a sly pleasure in punishing her beloved love-child for the psychic strain he has caused her" (p. 356). See dissertation 1950.A1.

Reprinted 1973.A15.

5 BARTLETT, LYNN C. and WILLIAM R. SHERWOOD, eds. "Henry Fielding: Tom Jones 1749," in their The English Novel: Background Readings. Philadelphia and New York: J. B. Lippincott, pp. 1-35.

This book selects representative criticism of the eighteenth and nineteenth centuries about ten novels (including Clarissa Harlowe, Bleak House, and Jude the Obscure).

There are eleven critical responses to Tom Jones, ranging from Thomas Cawthorn's poem (printed in the Gentleman's Magazine in 1749) to Thackeray's "The English Humorists . . ." (1853), and including Coleridge, Samuel Johnson, and Scott.

6 BATTESTIN, MARTIN C. "Osborne's Tom Jones: Adapting a Classic," in Man and the Movies. Edited by W. R. Robinson. Baton Rouge: Louisiana State University Press, pp. 31-45.

Reprint of 1966.B3.

7 _____. "Pope's 'Magus' in Fielding's Vernoniad: The Satire of Walpole." Philological Quarterly, 46, no. 1 (Jan.), 137-41.

Pope's Magus (IV, l. 516) in The Dunciad and Fielding's magician in the Vernoniad are both to be seen as Walpole. Both Pope and Fielding use as the "presiding deity of disorder" in their poems the "crassness and materialism" (p. 141) of Whiggism. For this Pope may not have relied on Fielding, but he antedates Fielding in this symbolic portrait.

8 _____. "Tom Jones and 'His Egyptian Majesty': Fielding's Parable of Government." Publications of the Modern Language Association, 83, no. 1 (March), 68-77.

Battestin points out that in its historical context the "utopia of rogues" (p. 68), gypsy society, may not be ideal. By examining a number of contemporary sources (among them Carew's and Rollin's accounts of gypsies and their Egyptian heritage) but particularly a sermon by Bishop Hoadly, he argues that the gypsies are like the Houyhnhnms; they expose the inefficiency of constitutional government in crisis (1745), but they are an untenable alternative. They are used by Fielding to make "the Tory (Jacobite) dream of utopia . . . appear foolish" (p. 73). See 1967.B9, B19 and 1974.B5.

9 BLOCH, TUVIA. "Bampfylde-Moore Carew and Fielding's King of the Gypsies." Notes and Queries, 212 (May), 182-83.

Fielding did not model his King of the Gypsies on Carew; but Tom Jones had an effect on Carew, because he revised his Life and Adventures (1745), calling it an Apology for the Life (1750) and inserting his uncomplimentary references to Fielding as well as borrowed events from Tom Jones. See 1967.B8, B19.

10 _____. "Smollett's Quest for Form." Modern Philology, 65, no. 1 (Aug.), 103-13.

Argues that "in the course of his career Smollett attempted to emulate Fielding" (p. 103) and that even the novel which abandons this attempt (Humphry Clinker) is heavily influenced by Fielding. Bloch examines Smollett's attempts to use theoretical prefaces, characters linking unconnected episodes, chapter headings, structural unity of a few simple plots with a central love story, the narrative tone of soft ridicule, and characters who reveal themselves through their language. Smollett used several of these techniques in his epistolary masterpiece Humphry Clinker.

11 BOYCE, BENJAMIN. The Benevolent Man: A Life of Ralph Allan of Bath. Cambridge: Harvard University Press, passim.

Reviewed by Richard W. Bailey, MQR, 8 (1969), 144-45; Martin C. Battestin, MLQ, 28 (1967), 368-77; William B. Coley, MP, 66 (1969), 278-80; K. L. Ellis, History, 53 (1968), 121-22; Robert E. Kelley, PQ, 47 (1968), 298; Alison G. Olson, AHR, 73 (1967), 135-36; Henry Pettit, ELN, 5 (1967), 63; Charles Pullen, QQ, 74 (1967), 533-34; C. J. Rawson, MLR, 64 (1969), 148-49; A. L. Rowse, HT, 17 (1967), 719-20; Michael F. Shugrue, JEGP, 66 (1967), 589-91; TLS, 7 March 1968, p. 230.

Discusses Allen's patronage of Fielding and its political implications, Allen as a model for Allworthy, Fielding's dedication of Amelia to Allen, etc. Good social background for a study of Fielding.

*12 BRAUDY, LEO R. "The Narrative Stance: Problems of History and Methods of Fiction in David Hume, Henry Fielding, and Edward Gibbon." Dissertation, Yale, 1967.

Source: Dissertation Abstracts, 28, no. 10 (April 1968), 4118A. See 1970.B4.

13 BROOKS, DOUGLAS. "Richardson's Pamela and Fielding's Joseph Andrews." Essays in Criticism, 17, no. 2 (April), 158-68.

With extensive citation from the texts, Brooks sets out the parallels between Pamela I and II and Joseph Andrews (he thinks Joseph Andrews a continuation of Fielding's battle with Richardson, whose "method and technique he disagreed with," p. 162). The parallels range from the name of Parson Adams ("which he could well have got . . . from Parson Adams in II Pamela," p. 166) to Fielding's substituting mock-epic similes for the "dream symbol passages in Pamela" (p. 162) and including clothes imagery, emotional conflict ("Lady Booby's psychomachy . . . originates in the ludicrous indecisiveness of Mr. B. over Pamela," p. 160), and parallel scene. Finally Joseph reminds us of both the chaste Pamela and the lusty Booby, whose "clothes fit him exactly" (p. 159).

See responses and rejoinders 1968.B8, B22, 1969.B3. For another discussion of clothing in Joseph Andrews, see 1961.B6.

Reprinted 1972.A2.

14 CARRIÈRE, MARTINE. "Fielding dramaturge se veut-il moraliste?" Caliban (Toulouse), 3 fac. 2 (March), 21-28.

Briefly describes the ways in which Fielding makes dramatic use of the social institutions, the economic circumstances, the morality, the pleasures, and the frivolities of the epoch of the Georges. Particularly discusses the theme of appearance and reality and Fielding's satirizing of justice, medicine, and politics. Arguing that Fielding is clearly a reforming moralist, Carrière attempts to find a consistent moral theory in his plays and fails, concluding that, although his morality is apparent in all his dramas, it is impossible to raise it to the level of a system. In French.

*15 CLEMENTS, FRANCES M. "Social Criticism in the English Novel: 1740-1754." Dissertation, Ohio State, 1967.

Studies Richardson's, Fielding's, Smollett's, and others' approach to social problems in light of the "liberal thinkers of their day."

Source: Dissertation Abstracts, 28, no. 12 (June 1968), 5011A.

16 COLEY, WILLIAM B. "Hogarth, Fielding, and the Dating of the March to Finchley." Journal of the Warburg and Courtauld Institutes, 30:317-26.

Coley redates Hogarth's painting The March to Finchley on the basis of a number of anachronisms, among them the news vendor selling Fielding's Jacobite's Journal, which did not appear until 5 Dec. 1747. He concludes that it was more or less completed by February of 1749 (but perhaps not until March 1750); he bases this on a redating of Jean-André Rouquet's Description Du Tableau de Mr. Hogarth. Coley also thinks that the frontispiece for Fielding's Jacobite's Journal, thought to be from a sketch by Hogarth, is not by Hogarth because of the use Hogarth makes of the Jacobite's Journal in March.

17 EVANS, DAVID L. "The Theme of Liberty in Jonathan Wild." Papers on Language and Literature, 3, no. 4 (Fall), 302-13.

Argues that the opposition between moral imprisonment and moral freedom "actually informs and controls the book"

(p. 303). This theme of liberty makes certain incidents (Mrs. Heartfree's misfortunes) appear relevant rather than irrelevant digressions. Evans sets out what Fielding has said of liberty elsewhere and the antithesis between "moral anarchy (Wild's 'insatiability') and moral order (Heartfree's 'moderation' and acceptance of the law); the book's ironic method is dissolved when Wild, who is apparently free and unrestrained, is imprisoned, and Heartfree, who spends most of his time in physical confinement, is released and is free" (p. 305). He also illustrates how "the theme of true and false liberty is manifested in . . . the sexual passions in the book, in Wild's abuse of language, in the political satire, and in the scenes or physical settings of the action" (p. 308).

18 FARRELL, WILLIAM J. "Fielding's Familiar Style." Journal of English Literary History, 34, no. 1 (March), 65-77.
Examines the style of eighteenth-century biographies and histories as well as eighteenth-century judgments about the style appropriate for biography and history, concluding that the source for Fielding's intimate intrusive narrator, with his easy, natural, and familiar style, is probably popular history and biography of the eighteenth century, with which Fielding associated his novels. This article is not so much about style as it is about "the narrator's ethos" (p. 76). See 1952.B2, 1963.B5 and 1966.B14.

19 FRASER, ANGUS M. "Bampfylde-Moore Carew and Fielding's King of the Gypsies." Notes and Queries, 212 (Nov.), 424.
Fielding knew more about gypsies than Carew, distinguishing them socially from simple "maunders" and characterizing them linguistically, not by borrowed "cant." See 1967.B8, B9.

20 HASSALL, ANTHONY J. "The Authorial Dimension in the Plays of Henry Fielding." Komos, 1, no. 1 (March), 4-18.
Sees Fielding's ten plays in which an "author" (this includes editor and commentator) makes an appearance as precursors of his use of the author in his novels. Hassall divides these plays into two groups: the first five, up to and including Don Quixote in England (1734), he calls experimental and the second five, beginning with Fielding's return to the little Haymarket theater and Pasquin (1736) to Eurydice Hiss'd (1737), rehearsal plays. In the first group he discusses the juxtaposition of life and work (Author's Farce) and the ironic editor persona (Tragedy of Tragedies). Argues that Pasquin and Eurydice Hiss'd in the last group are "rhetorically complex and

indirect" and force the reader to be "alert in order to ascertain the true directions of Fielding's thought" (p. 17), much as do the narrators in Tom Jones and Joseph Andrews.

21 HATFIELD, GLENN W. "Puffs and Pollitricks: Jonathan Wild and the Political Corruption of Language." Philological Quarterly, 46, no. 2 (April), 248-67.
Hatfield argues that Fielding's political concern often takes the form of representing the "political rhetoric of persuasion and equivocation as a corruptive perversion of language" (p. 249). He demonstrates this by examining Fielding's direct and indirect (ironic) attacks (in plays, essays, and particularly Jonathan Wild) on the language used and misused by political hack writers and politicians.
For an expanded version of this essay see 1968.A9.

22 _____. "Quacks, Pettyfoggers, and Parsons: Fielding's Case against the Learned Professions." Texas Studies in Literature and Language, 9, no. 1 (Spring), 69-83.
Asserts that Fielding was a "responsible" satirist who "turned his fire against the pedantic doctors, dishonest lawyers, and canting clergymen" because he had "a clear conception of the ideal standard of these professions, and respect for them" (pp. 69-70). Hatfield examines Fielding's attacks on these professions (which should have been public guardians of property and wealth) in his plays, journalism, and novels. He particularly examines their use of cant and jargon by means of which they cultivated obscurity and mystery, which Fielding felt corrupted both language and society.
Incorporated in 1968.A9.

23 _____. "'The Serpent and the Dove': Fielding's Irony and the Prudence Theme in Tom Jones." Modern Philology, 65, no. 1 (Aug.), 17-32.
Argues that Fielding, who was always concerned with the purity and precision of language in his journalism and essays, used irony to purge words and "dramatic exemplification" (p. 19) to define them in his dramatic and narrative works. Hatfield then illustrates (from earlier sources) the corruption of the moral term "prudence" and Fielding's attempt in Tom Jones to return it to its original purity. He concludes that "if Joseph Andrews is Fielding's attempt to rescue 'virtue' as a moral term from its degradation in Richardson's . . . novel, Tom Jones may be regarded as a similar attempt to reclaim the 'proper and

original' moral sense of 'prudence'" (p. 32).
Incorporated in 1968.A9. For other discussions of "prudence," see 1960.B11 and 1968.B3.

24 ITKINA, N. L. "Fil'ding i Stern." Moskovskii gosudarstvennvi pedagogicheskii institut imeni Lenina (Moscow): 280, 140-54.
"Fielding and Sterne"; Russian article.

25 JASON, PHILIP K. "Samuel Jackson Pratt's Unpublished Comedy of 'Joseph Andrews.'" Notes and Queries, 212 (Nov.), 416-18.
Describes this newly discovered afterpiece performed once in 1778. It follows Fielding's characterization, taking many of Mrs. Slipslop's "speeches directly from the novel" (p. 417) and cunningly sees Didapper as moonstruck (see 1964.B8). The action is limited to incidents from the first and fourth books and is set at Booby Hall.

26 LE PAGE, PETER V. "The Prison and the Dark Beauty of Amelia." Criticism, 9, no. 4 (Fall), 337-54.
Argues that Amelia is Fielding's "most carefully constructed work" (p. 337) by discussing the coherent symbolism of imprisonment in the novel and the recurring unity of the plot. He sets out the various symbols of confinement in the novel: the prison, where "Booth spends his entire dramatic life" (p. 338), small locked rooms, a locked casket, a wine hamper. ["The prison and its analogues connote the tyranny of the social will and the injustice of that will," p. 342.] "Love in a physical sense in Amelia is [also] an imprisoner; very few can escape" (p. 344). Rather than being a Bildungsroman, with a single plot like Tom Jones and Joseph Andrews, Amelia puts its beautiful young people through a series of dramatic plots (he sees eight) in which purpose, passion, and perception follow each other again and again. Even the interpolated tales (Matthews, Booth, Bennet) symbolize the recurring attempts to escape this moral confinement: "Each of the confessions in itself is also an analogue of the dramatic action of the novel" (p. 352). The narration too changes as Fielding "attempts to share in the struggles of his actors through asides that do not judge but provide personal observation and amplification" (p. 354). See dissertation 1964.A22.

27 PAULSON, RONALD. "Fielding the Satirist," "Fielding the Anti-Romanticist," and "Fielding the Novelist," in his Satire and the Novel in Eighteenth Century England. New Haven

and London: Yale University Press, pp. 52-99, 100-131, 132-64.

Reviewed by Wayne C. Booth, PQ, 47 (1968), 340-42; Frank Brady, SEL, 8 (1968), 551-72; Morris Golden, St N, 2 (1970), 222-28; Glenn W. Hatfield, Novel, 2 (1969), 284-86; Derek Hudson, English, 17 (1968), 59-60; A. B. Kernan, JEGP, 68 (1969), 182-86; A. E. McGuinness, SNL, 5 (1968), 171-75; Juliet McMaster, DR, 48 (1968), 266-68; John L. Mahoney, Thought, 23 (1968), 617-18; John Preston, RES, n.s. 20 (1969), 232-35; Eric Rothstein, MLQ, 29 (1968), 222-29; Michael F. Shugrue, SCN, 26 (1968), 75-76.

Paulson discusses Fielding in three chapters in this book, which examines the evolution of "a series of distinctive types of novel as they grew out of contact with satiric forms" and culminated "in Pride and Prejudice" (p. 309). In the first of these chapters, Paulson distinguishes between the "Tory" satirists (Pope, Swift, and Gay) and the honnête homme ethic of the "Whig" satirists (Addison and Steele), putting Fielding at the beginning of his career in the "Tory" camp, because Fielding used devices and motifs used by them and because he rejected the concept of humor "as an amiable, individualizing foible" (p. 71). Paulson goes on to compare and contrast Fielding's typical villain with those of Gay, Pope, and Swift, arguing that he shares some assumptions (that they ought to be based on live models, for example) and diverges from others (his is a more optimistic view of human nature than Swift's). Paulson considers the main action of Fielding's satiric plays (the farce in the middle is a metaphor for contemporary life) and his use of the persona commentator, which, unlike Swift's persona, is there to fix meaning rather than convey reality. Finally, Paulson briefly examines Fielding's use of the judicial metaphor, which moves from satirist as judge to reader as judge.

The second chapter sets out the Fielding/Richardson debate that led to Shamela, arguing that Fielding was particularly upset by the detected romance beneath the apparent psychological and social realism of Pamela. Fielding posited instead a middle area of the ridiculous, "where there were neither paragons nor Satanic villains" (p. 118), inhabited by Adams and Don Quixote. Paulson finally argues that Fielding developed a satiric "touchstone" structure (in which profession was followed by action exposing the profession) largely by patterning Joseph Andrews on Pamela.

The final chapter examines Fielding's use of the Lucianic commentator-narrator in Tom Jones, whose job it is to keep the reader in sympathy with the morally mixed character Tom while still judging him. Contrasting

Fielding's use of the satiric "touchstone" scenic structure in Joseph Andrews with his use of it in Tom Jones, Paulson argues that in Tom Jones Fielding has moved beyond the relatively simple classical tradition into a "shadowy Richardsonian realm" (p. 150) in which the whole being rather than the individual action must be judged. Under the pressure of Lucianic and Shaftesburyian satire, Fielding has moved "away from castigation and . . . circumscribed symbolic action" (p. 156). After briefly discussing the parallels between the eighteenth-century attitude toward an analytical history and toward satire, Paulson illustrates how in Amelia the "two kinds of writing exist side by side" (p. 159). Amelia is both "Juvenalian" (with entrenched evil and inept goodness) and "novelistic" (with the "Christian individual overcoming adversity . . . by rising above" it, p. 163). In Tom Jones his satiric technique still essentially remained a tool of analysis; Amelia fails because of the discontinuity between its public (Juvenalian) and its private (novelistic) aims.

Reprinted in part 1970.A4. See 1962.B1, 1965.B10, 1968.B40, 1970.B4 and 1972.A9.

28 PENNER, ALLEN R. "Fielding's Adaptation of Cervantes' Knight and Squire." Revue de Littérature Comparée, 41, no. 4, 508-14.

Studies the parallels between Joseph and Adams and Cervantes' knight and squire. Joseph, like Sancho, plays the practical realist to Adams' idealist; he is also loyally devoted to Adams, as is Sancho. Penner also examines the parallel between Don Quixote and Joseph in their defense of their chastity, in their use of literary models for their exemplary behavior, and in their excessive posturing. He concludes that Fielding "reproduces the essential qualities of Don Quixote and Sancho Panza . . . without closely imitating either of Cervantes' characters." Fielding also changes Cervantes' mocking of courtly love conventions into a "serious concern for the fate of Joseph and Fanny" (p. 513). See dissertation 1965.A17.

29 PRICE, JOHN V. "Sex and the Foundling Boy: The Problem of 'Tom Jones.'" Review of English Literature, 8, no. 4 (Oct.), 42-52.

Studies the ironic and the historical context of Tom's three sexual encounters (with Molly, Mrs. Waters, and Lady Bellaston). In light of both Locke's and Hume's theories of the passions (based on pleasure and pain) and "Fielding's choice of language for making moral observations" (p. 43), "sexual weakness turns out to be the least reprehensible of moral 'crimes'" (p. 51). Price observes (conventionally) that Tom is passive, that only Sophia and Blifil remain chaste, that this may be Fielding's answer to the punishment for sexuality in Clarissa, and that "the novel shows the futility of making judgments where the evidence is scanty or incomplete" (p. 51).

30 RAWSON, C. J. "Gentlemen and Dancing-Masters: Thoughts on Fielding, Chesterfield, and the Genteel." Eighteenth-Century Studies, 1, no. 2 (Dec.), 127-58.

Looks at good breeding, and particularly at the breeding learned from dancing masters, "to help to define certain social attitudes of Fielding" (p. 127). By examining Fielding's and Chesterfield's attitudes toward this "ambiguous figure, who nagged the imaginations of many men of letters and the lives of young or would-be gentlemen" where "the sublime and the ridiculous sometimes seem to meet" (p. 158), Rawson concludes that both firmly believed in a gentility that included dancing lessons. But Chesterfield and Fielding "lived in very different moral worlds"; while "they seem logically in agreement, the difference in the quality of the feeling is radical. . . . For Fielding, not only is the moral basis of manners always kept in close view, but there is often a note of disturbed oscillation, of passionate self-doubt" (p. 143). Fielding's essays and novels (especially Amelia) are examined, and Chesterfield's and Fielding's balancing of hauteur and "loyalty towards dancing-masters" (p. 158) discussed.

Incorporated in 1972.A9.

31 _____. "'Tom Jones' and 'Michael': a Parallel." Notes and Queries, 212 (Jan.), 13.

Parallel passages: Michael 11.448-50 and Tom Jones VII. ii.

32 REID, B. L. "Utmost Merriment, Strictest Decency: Joseph Andrews." Sewanee Review, 75:559-84.

Argues that Joseph Andrews is an archetypal journey ("The quest grows spiritual while remaining both dramatic and comic," p. 561). Reid traces several patterns of trope (mode of transport, clothing, and speech as metaphor, and Biblical and classical analogy) through the novel to illustrate that "with great good humor, Fielding is assembling a comprehensive moral system, or more accurately a moral vision, on Christian principles" (p. 562). In the working

out of this moral vision, Joseph and Parson Adams, for instance, "stay as close to the earth as they can. Their instinct is locomotive, to move their own bodies by an act of their own will" (pp. 567-68), and the journey from London to Somerset "becomes a comic Tao, the way" (p. 576).
Reprinted 1969.B18.

33 REXROTH, KENNETH. "Tom Jones." Saturday Review (1 July), p. 13.
Opens with a discussion of the mimetic quality of the novel (as a panorama of eighteenth-century England), character stereotypes, Tom as archetypal hero (the foundling prince), and the good-natured man. This article includes one of the best discussions of the "Brechtian alienation" of a narrator who knows better, and tells the readers they should know better than to believe (as Richardson, James, and Proust naively do) that he has revealed life. Finally he asserts that the eighteenth century created two kinds of men. Out of Descartes and Rousseau came the inward turning man, the "Continental radical, intellectual." Out of Locke and Fielding "came the active, pragmatic man of whom Jefferson is probably the best exemplar."
A version of this essay was originally printed in Classics Revisited. Chicago: Quadrangle Books, 1965, pp. 212-17. Reprinted 1973.A15.

34 SCHNEIDER, DANIEL J. "Sources of Comic Pleasure in Tom Jones." Connecticut Review, 1:51-65.
Using the work in comic theory done by Northrop Frye, Suzanne Langer, and Albert Cook, Schneider discusses comedy in Tom Jones under four headings. First, he considers the frustration of the impulse to freedom by the life-denying power of property (chiefly represented by the two families but also by a host of minor characters like the pious Quaker and the landlords). Second, he considers the comic punishment of the life-deniers (including Square, Thwackum, and Western), some of whom (Bellaston and Blifil) are punished by sympathetic comic characters. Third, he considers the genial, expansive exuberance of spirit of the narrator (who is a life-affirmer), as well as his fertility of wit and learning. Finally, he considers the pure sense of joy (represented by the copulating, eating, and drinking) as it opposes the nightmare forces of property and propriety and a whimsical universe. The lovers escape because of the "propensity of the comic world towards chaos and irrationality" (p. 63).

35 ZIRKER, MALVIN R., JR. "Fielding and Reform in the 1750s." Studies in English Literature: 1500-1900, 7, no. 3 (Summer), 453-65.

Reviews the social situation which provoked pamphlets on the poor in the 1750s, among them Fielding's An Enquiry Into the Causes of the Late Increase of Robbers and A Proposal for Making an Effectual Provision for the Poor. After reviewing the evidence for Fielding being a government agent who had "a dominant role in the reform movement of the fifties" (p. 463), Zirker concludes that he may have been asked to express his opinion to the parliamentary committee on disorder and the poor, but "he did not direct the Committee of 1750, nor did he affect later legislation except, in some cases, indirectly" (p. 464). Nor were Fielding's ideas on reform either particularly enlightened or advanced ("Fielding's pamphlet expresses views which, taken individually, were commonplaces of the time," p. 462).

An attack on the view of Fielding in 1918.A1 and 1926.A1. See also 1966.A26 and 1971.B2 from which this essay is drawn.

1968 A BOOKS

1 ALTER, ROBERT. Fielding and the Nature of the Novel. Cambridge: Harvard University Press, 221 pp.

Reviewed by Martin C. Battestin, Ga. R., 23 (1968), 100-103; Richard Dircks, Novel, 3 (1970), 276-78; John A. Dussinger, JEGP, 68 (1969), 529-35; Michael Irwin, RES, n.s. 22 (1971), 89-93; Juliet McMaster, DR, 49 (1968), 268-70; Thomas E. Maresca, Genre, 3 (1970), 289-91; Henry K. Miller, SEL, 9 (1969), 559-60; John Preston, EIC, 21 (1971), 91-100; Martin Price, PQ, 48 (1969), 354; Arthur Sherbo, ECS, 3 (1970), 560-66; Philip Stevick, Criticism, 12 (1970), 76-78; Clarence Tracy, QQ, 77 (1970), 293-94; Andrew Wright, StN, 2 (1970), 239-45.

Begins by analyzing some of the critical objections to Fielding: that he is shallow, that he fails to treat sex with Puritan portentousness, that he is wedded to the rational and not the mythic world, and especially that he dissociates character from conduct. Alter shows through style, design of character, and architecture that Fielding is not the shallow novelist he is often considered. His rhetoric makes him one of the "great intellectual novelists . . . [alongside] Flaubert, Joyce, James, Gide" (p. 30) who theorizes, keeps us aware of the literary artifice, fuses content and context, and through irony keeps us withdrawn and yet deeply involved in the discerning of truth in words. Alter discusses Fielding's integration of character through "the multiple strategies he adopts to relate individual characters to one another and to a large, coherent moral vision" (p. 65). Among these strategies (which are replaced by character analysis in other novelists) are Fielding's reticence in detail, which invites "us to reconstruct character by inference" (p. 67), the narrator's linking of individual action to the larger scheme of the novel or the moral universe, Fielding's use of ironic and satiric portraiture (with its implied authorial certainty), his use of artifice, antithesis, and balance. Alter argues that "in the structure of the narrative, the texture of the narration, the juxtaposition and repetition of narrated events, the deployment of thematic materials" (p. 102), Fielding constantly exploits the art he is creating. To illustrate this, Alter discusses interrelated moral themes, interpolated tales, parallelism, as well as the literal story mechanism of Joseph Andrews and Tom Jones. In a chapter on Amelia (which he calls Fielding's "problem novel," like Shakespeare's problem plays), Alter discusses the strengths and weaknesses in the use of the Virgilian analogy, Fielding's inability to observe "a subtle interplay of social forces in fictional relationships" (p. 144), his integration of narrative and thematic material which looks forward to Middlemarch, his nearly mythic use of masking, and the indications in narration and plot that Fielding is moving toward "the cult of sensibility" (p. 168). Alter thinks the novel uneven (not in any single mode). In a final chapter, Alter argues that Fielding still offers certain possibilities for the genre in his dialectic balancing between consciousness and objects and in his ironic intelligence that can hold good and evil in balance in a character without blame.

Incorporates 1967.B1. Reprinted in part 1970.A4.

2 BATTESTIN, MARTIN C., ed. Twentieth Century Interpretations of Tom Jones. Twentieth Century Interpretations, edited by Maynard Mack. Englewood Cliffs, N.J.: Prentice-Hall, 120 pp.

Reprints essays and parts of chapters by F. R. Leavis, "Tom Jones and 'The Great Tradition': A Negative View"; Ian Watt, "Fielding as Novelist: Tom Jones" (1957.B17); William Empson, "Tom Jones" (1958.B6); Andrew Wright, "Tom Jones: Life as Art" (1965.A20); R. S. Crane, "The Plot of Tom Jones" (1950.B2); Wayne C. Booth, "'Fielding' in Tom Jones" (1961.B4); and Robert Alter, "Fielding and the Uses of Style" (1967.B1). Introduction offers biographical information and a very brief summary of critical attitudes from Fielding's day to the present. Also includes selected bibliography and chronology of important dates from Fielding's life and works.

3 BUTT, JOHN. Fielding. Writers and Their Work, no. 57. London: Longmans, Green, for The British Council and The National Book League, 36 pp.
Reissue of 1965.A2.

4 DOBSON, AUSTIN. Henry Fielding: A Memoir. New York: AMS Press, 333 pp.
Reprint of 1900.A1.

5 FIELDING, HENRY. Amelia. Introduction by A. R. Humphreys. Everyman's Library. 2 vols. London: J. M. Dent & Sons; New York: E. P. Dutton, 638 pp.
Reprint of 1962.A4.

6 _____. Jonathan Wild and The Journal of a Voyage to Lisbon. Introduction by A. R. Humphreys. Everyman's Library. London: J. M. Dent & Sons; New York: E. P. Dutton, 306 pp.
Reprint of 1964.A8.

7 _____. The Grub-Street Opera. Edited by Edgar V. Roberts. Regents Restoration Drama Series, edited by John Loftis. Lincoln: University of Nebraska Press; London: Edward Arnold (1969), 189 pp.
Reviewed by Richard H. Dammers, SCN, 29 (1971), 72-73; Jacques Michon, EA, 24 (1971), 166-70.
Introduction discusses complicated circumstances surrounding the performance and publication of the play, as well as its strength as a political satire and as a ballad opera (he calls it the best of Fielding's nine ballad operas). Reprints a modernized edition of the "1731" edition of the play. Appendix A briefly discusses the play's revision from Welsh Opera to Grub-Street Opera; Appendix B offers modern scores for the tunes in the opera based on contemporary ballad tunes. See 1973.A11 and dissertation 1960.A13.

8 _____. The History of Tom Jones. Edited by R. P. C. Mutter. Penguin English Library. Harmondsworth, Baltimore, Victoria (Australia): Penguin Books, 911 pp.
Reissue of 1966.A8.

9 HATFIELD, GLENN W. Henry Fielding and the Language of Irony. Chicago and London: University of Chicago Press, 235 pp.

Reviewed by Martin C. Battestin, MLQ, 30 (1969), 149-51; John A. Dussinger, JEGP, 68 (1969), 529-35; Michael Irwin, RES, n.s. 20 (1969), 507-508; Charles Ledbetter, QJS, 55 (1969), 86; Henry K. Miller, SEL, 9 (1969), 560-61 and St N, 2 (1970), 230-38; Martin Price, PQ, 48 (1968), 356; G. S. Rousseau, Novel, 3 (1970), 279-81; Arthur Sherbo, ECS, 3 (1970), 560-66; Philip Stevick, Criticism, 12 (1970), 76-78; JNL, 28 (1968), 7; TLS, 2 Jan. 1969, p. 8.

Argues that Fielding was acutely aware of language, sensitive "to the linguistic prostitutions of his age" (p. 5), and concerned, along "with the whole seventeenth- and eighteenth-century movement of language reform," that truth be communicated "in plain, unequivocal words" (p. 152). By examining Fielding's plays, novels, and non-ironic essays, Hatfield proves that "Fielding's concern with language and its corruptions was an earnest and a longstanding one and that it had a serious philosophical basis in the linguistic theory of John Locke" (p. 27). He then argues that Fielding was "more pessimistic than Locke about the condition of the language" (p. 52) and closer to Augustan satirists like Swift and Pope. In a long chapter called "Language and Society," Hatfield examines Fielding's attacks "on those elements of society he held most responsible for the corruption of words" (p. 53): writers, critics and hacks, politics and politicians, polite society, the professions. Fielding's plays illustrate the debasement of various words (gentleman, newspaper, patriot). In the last section of the book, Hatfield argues that in his novels both Fielding's irony and his dramatic techniques "are conscious and deliberate attempts to approximate . . . the conditions of truth in a hypocritical and nominalistic world" (p. 197) where men are known by their actions and not by their words. Fielding constantly attempts to keep "the reader aware of language . . . alert to the meanings of words" (p. 158); his irony and his action "attempt to distinguish the 'true' (or 'original') meaning from the 'false' (or 'corrupt') meaning" (p. 159). Hatfield discusses Fielding's testing of major ideas (and words) such as honor, love, and prudence. In a final chapter he argues that the intrusive narrator in Tom Jones is "a triumph of Fielding's art" (p. 199) because it dramatizes "the author, struggling with his materials" against the linguistic forces of corruption. In "Amelia he demands nothing less than the right he has earned in his earlier writings to use language directly and literally" (p. 220).

Incorporates 1967.B21, B22 and B23. See dissertation 1964.A21.

*10 LONGMIRE, SAMUEL E. "The Narrative Structure of Fielding's Amelia." Dissertation, Indiana, 1968.
Argues that the narrative structure of Amelia (a hybrid of romance, novel, and anatomy) prepares the reader for a happy ending.
Source: Dissertation Abstracts, 29, no. 9 (March 1969), 3103A-104A. See 1972.B15.

*11 ODEN, RICHARD L. "Fielding's Drama in Relation to Restoration Comedy and to Tom Jones." Dissertation, Tulane, 1968.
Argues that Fielding's knowledge of Restoration comedy aided his work in the theater and equipped him for his prose fiction, where he adapted stock characters to suit his fictional purpose.
Source: Dissertation Abstracts, 29, no. 9 (March 1969), 3106A-107A.

*12 PERSKY, CHARLES. "The Comic Alternative: A Study of Henry Fielding and his Novels from Shamela to Tom Jones." Dissertation, Harvard, 1968.
Source: McNamee, 1964-1968, p. 222.

13 RAWSON, C. J. Henry Fielding. Profiles in Literature Series, edited by B. C. Southern. London: Routledge & Kegan Paul; New York: Humanities Press, 176 pp.
Reviewed TLS, 23 May 1968, p. 529.
After a brief chronological table and a brief critical biography (which concentrates on Joseph Andrews, Tom Jones, and Amelia, with an aside on Fielding's narrative style), Rawson selects a series of passages from Fielding's works and arranges them in an order which "moves broadly from matters of style and technique to moral and social attitudes and doctrines" (p. 12). The groupings include "comic epic and the true ridiculous," "mock-heroic: three treatments of heroines," "mock-heroic: public executions," "mock-heroic: comic softening and self-conscious similes," "ironic climaxes," "Irony," "Dialogue," "Character: two sketches from real life," "further character sketches," "professions and codes," "the value of 'the world,'" "snobbery and class," "benevolence and good-nature," "benevolence and love." Each section is introduced by a headnote briefly explaining a particular Fielding technique and the purpose of Rawson's grouping. Selective bibliography included.

*14 ROBINSON, R. D. "Henry Fielding: Social Themes and the Novel Form." Dissertation, Cambridge University, 1968.
Source: McNamee, 1964-1968, p. 223.

*15 ROSENBLOOD, BYRAN N. "Some Aspects of Henry Fielding's Heroes." Dissertation, Pittsburgh, 1968.

A study of Fielding's changing concept of the hero, emphasizing the effect of the city on the hero's career.

Source: Dissertation Abstracts, 30, no. 2 (Aug. 1969), 695A.

*16 SKINNER, MARY L. "The Interpolated Story in Selected Novels of Fielding and Smollett." Dissertation, Tennessee, 1968.

Studies the ways in which Smollett and Fielding used and modified the complex "conventions" of interpolation.

Source: Dissertation Abstracts, 29, no. 11 (May 1969), 4020A-21A.

*17 STITZEL, JUDITH C. "Comedy and the Serious Moralist: The Concept of Good-Nature in the Novels of Henry Fielding." Dissertation, Minnesota, 1968.

Source: McNamee, 1964-1968, pp. 222-23.

See 1970.B36.

1968 B SHORTER WRITINGS

1 AMORY, HUGH. "A Preliminary Census of Henry Fielding's Legal Manuscripts." Papers of the Bibliographical Society of America, 62, no. 4 (Oct.-Dec.), 587-601.

Reviews several theories for the paucity of Fielding manuscripts and conjectures that some of Fielding's legal manuscripts are "still in the possession of the heirs of W. F. Fielding or of J. Scott, who received a volume of these manuscripts from W. H. Fielding in 1820" (p. 588). Amory then provides a careful and detailed census of autograph legal manuscripts taken from sales records (at Sotheby's, etc.), commenting on the items. He convincingly concludes that nearly "all the known pieces of Fielding's legal manuscripts can be traced to W. H. Fielding" (p. 597) and that the two volume work on crown law that Murphy (1762.A10) claims to have seen fits the "surviving fragments of Fielding's legal manuscripts" (pp. 600-601). See 1961.B5 and dissertation 1964.A1.

2 BAKER, SHERIDAN. "Fielding and the Irony of Form." Eighteenth-Century Studies, 2, no. 2 (Winter), 138-54.

Argues "that the structure of Joseph Andrews derives principally from the repetitive structural impulse of simple narrative fiction whereas the structure of Tom Jones derives from the formal outline of dramatic comedy, . . . in Joseph Andrews structure emphasizes . . . in Tom Jones it insulates, . . . in Joseph Andrews structure is more supportive than ironic . . . in Tom Jones structure is much more ironic" (pp. 138-39). The repetitive impulse in Joseph Andrews is represented by the parodic "bedroom scenes" which "hold the Cervantic ramble together at beginning and end" (p. 138). Tom Jones' three part structure (country, road, and city) is like a three act play, but its emotional patterning is like a five act play. In this highly metaphoric article ("structural bastions," "central peaks of perplexity"), we are asked, among other things, to see Joseph Andrews as road ("linear, repetitive structure") and Tom Jones as bridge ("arched irony"), and then this bridge as the "detaching force of structure" (p. 151), "a balancing and ordering irony" (p. 152).

3 BATTESTIN, MARTIN C. "Fielding's Definition of Wisdom: Some Functions of Ambiguity and Emblem in Tom Jones." Journal of English Literary History, 35, no. 2 (June), 188-217.

Explores "the substance and the form of the novel's most important theme, the definition of Wisdom" (p. 188), by examining verbal ambiguity and emblem in Tom Jones. Battestin studies the shifting meaning of "Prudence" in Fielding's work and in history (particularly in the works of English Christian humanists), illustrating both its positive and its pejorative meanings. He concludes that Fielding uses this ambiguous word for worldly or moral wisdom in order to force us to assess our sense of values as Tom must his. In the second half of the essay Battestin argues that Fielding, with his usual "iconomatic impulse" (he points to the pictorial or iconographic tableau scenes Fielding often creates), "shares with the allegorist the desire to render the abstractions of his theme" (p. 205). Sophia is the virtue that it is prudent to pursue. She is Plato's essential spiritual beauty (idea) made manifest. Tom goes on a journey, midway through which is "the emblematic projection of Fielding's theme" on Mazard Hill (p. 217), toward "marriage with Wisdom herself" (p. 204).

Reprinted 1973.A15. See also 1960.B11, 1967.B23, 1971.B33, and 1974.B2.

2 _____. "On the Contemporary Reputations of 'Pamela,' 'Joseph Andrews,' and 'Roderick Random': Remarks by an 'Oxford Scholar,' 1748." Notes and Queries, 213 (Dec.), 450-52.

A pamphlet published in 1748 evaluates these three novels. Both Richardson and Smollett are found wanting; Fielding's Joseph Andrews is highly praised. See 1926.A1.

5 BLOCH, TUVIA. "Accidentally on Purpose." Notes and Queries, 213 (Dec.), 463-64.

This phrase, said by Partridge's Dictionary of Slang to be a twentieth-century addition, was used by Fielding in The Covent-Garden Journal in 1752 and called a "usual phrase."

6 BOYCE, BENJAMIN. "The Comical Romance and the English Novel," from his "Introduction" to Paul Scarron, The Comical Romance. Translated by Tom Brown, et al. New York and London: Benjamin Blom, pp. xvii-xxii.

Compares Scarron's and Fielding's temperaments and then points to similarities between Joseph Andrews and The Comical Romance (partly a result of borrowing and partly of temperament). Specifically considers the similar events, narrative tone, farcical scenes, the handling of the action, and the interpolated tales (particularly "the Unfortunate Jilt"). Earlier Boyce suggests that Fielding's definition of his new form was borrowed from Scarron (p. xiv).

7 BROOKS, DOUGLAS. "Abraham Adams and Parson Trulliber: The Meaning of Joseph Andrews, Book II, Chapter 14." Modern Language Review, 63, no. 4 (Oct.), 794-801.

Argues that the Trulliber episode is not just a mimetic copy of the actions of a real parson whom Fielding knew but that Book 2, chapter 14 is a "conflation of Odyssey Books X and XIV, and carries their allegorical weight accordingly" (p. 794). Book 14 is the Eumaeus episode, which epitomized charity, and Book 10 is the Circe Episode; thus "Fielding is measuring the protestations of eighteenth-century humanity by the centuries-old absolute standards of (a) charity and (b) wisdom and temperance against brutishness" (p. 798). To further support his contention, Brooks examines the Latin and dialect roots of the name Trulliber. See dissertation 1967.A1.

8 _____. "Pamela and Joseph Andrews." Essays in Criticism, 18, no. 3 (July), 348-49.

A point-by-point response to Kearney (1968.B22) in defense of 1967.B13.

9 _____. "The Interpolated Tales in Joseph Andrews Again." Modern Philology, 65, no. 3 (Feb.), 208-13.

Works out the parallels between the main narrative and "The Unfortunate Jilt" (Fanny and Leonora are nearly the same age; the Horatio/Bellarmine duel is parodied in the hog's blood quarrel in the inn, etc.) and "The History of

Two Friends" (the wife fits into the "marriage spectrum" [p. 210] of the book; Joseph and Adams finish the tale). Brooks asserts that "an awareness of the thematic functions of [the two tales as they comment on the narrative and the narrative comments on them] is a heightened appreciation of Fielding's architectonic skill" (p. 213). For discussions of the interpolated tales, see 1956.B2 and 1966.B10.

For a response to this article, see 1968.B22 and Brooks' replies 1968.B8 and 1969.B3. See dissertation 1967.A1.

10 BURTON, A. P. "Cervantes the Man Seen Through English Eyes in the Seventeenth and Eighteenth Centuries." Bulletin of Hispanic Studies, 45, no. 1, 1-15.

In this article, which traces the changing attitudes toward Don Quixote and Cervantes, Burton suggests, without proof, that Fielding created a "second self," about whom we wish to know nothing more than is revealed, because Fielding would have "known little more of Cervantes than was to be learnt from the pages of Don Quixote" (p. 15); and that Sterne's more confusing "second self" is the result of his knowing something of Cervantes' biography.

*11 COHEN, MURRY A. "Forms of True Judgment in the Eighteenth-Century English Novel." Dissertation, Johns Hopkins, 1968.

Studies the meaning of social experience in Fielding, Smollett, and Sterne.

Source: Dissertation Abstracts, 29, no. 5 (Nov. 1968), 1533A-34A.

12 COMBS, WILLIAM W. "The Return to Paradise Hall: An Essay on Tom Jones." South Atlantic Quarterly, 67, no. 3 (Summer), 419-36.

Argues that Fielding held conflicting moral attitudes about the nature of evil. He believed that as a social being man was "capable of much goodness" (p. 419), but he also knew the reality of evil. Like Pope, he had to reconcile these views. Combs argues that he embodied the struggle "in Bridget Allworthy's two sons" (p. 420) and in the abstract conflict between fortune and nature in the novel. Combs describes Tom's primal innocence, the misfortune of his birth, and his general struggle against fortune, arguing that Fielding combined classical attitudes about fortune with the concept of "the fortunate fall" as Tom moved from passive innocence to prudential wisdom. Because of his use of the paradoxical "fortunate fall," Fielding's world is more "open" than Pope's.

1968

13 CONTI, PAOLA C. "Nature e Civilità in Henry Fielding." English Miscellany, 19: 105-32.

Argues that the Wilson episode (which had its origin in The Champion 26/2/1740) is Fielding's spiritual autobiography, designed to teach the reader both Providence's generosity to the reformed sinner and the human values of working on the land. The episode grows out of contemporary religious writings that idealized contentment as the opposite to "vanity." Fielding often sets the evil urban world of vanity in opposition to an ideal "golden age" rural life. Wilson, who represents the virtues of the simple life, harks back to the classical era and anticipates Voltaire and Rousseau. In Italian. See 1968.B15 and 1974.B10.

14 DRISKELL, LEON V. "Interpolated Tales in Joseph Andrews and Don Quixote: The Dramatic Method as Instruction." South Atlantic Bulletin, 33 (May), 5-8.

Sums up several recent views on the interpolated tales, then carefully demonstrates that "none of Fielding's three major interpolated tales is heard in its entirety by everyone who should hear it, and, further, even when heard from the beginning to end, the tales are imperfectly comprehended and fail of their instructive potential" (p. 5). If the characters fail to learn, Driskell suggests that the reader is to learn. First the tales function as tests of narrative reliability and then, as in Don Quixote, they relieve the "bleak and fatalistic world view" (p. 7), embodied in Joseph's theory of education, by offering romantic idealism and dramatized moral truths. See 1966.B10 and 1973.B34.

15 DUNCAN, JEFFREY L. "The Rural Ideal in Eighteenth-Century Fiction." Studies in English Literature, 1500-1900, 8, no. 3 (Summer), 517-35.

Argues that Fielding (along with Smollett, Goldsmith, and Sterne) uses the pastoral and georgic rural ideal as a "symbol of values opposed to the new realism of Defoe and Richardson" (p. 517). Duncan pays special attention to the Wilson episode in Joseph Andrews. See 1965.B5 and 1968. B13.

16 EAVES, T. C. DUNCAN and BEN D. KIMPEL. "Henry Fielding's Son by His First Wife." Notes and Queries, 213 (June), 212.

Fielding seems to have had a son, Henry, who died in 1750 when he was eight years old, the same age as Billy Booth.

17 EDWARDS, P. D. "Education and Nature in 'Tom Jones' and 'The Ordeal of Richard Feverel.'" Modern Language Review, 63, no. 1 (Jan.), 23-32.

Compares Tom Jones ("the comedy of nature triumphant over education") and Richard Feverel ("the tragedy of education triumphant over nature," p. 24), to examine what they have in common and why they reach such different conclusions. Argues, by examining the education of Tom and Richard, that Fielding and Meredith share an "affection for the 'natural' man, the man of warm feelings and uninhibited instincts, and their dislike of theorists and system-mongers who suppose that human nature conforms, or can be made to conform, to rules" (pp. 30-31). Edwards contends that their conclusions are different because of a different moral climate. Neither prudence nor reason can impose sexual guilt on Tom; Richard feels an excess of such guilt fostered by the scientific humanism of the time. See 1952.B3 and 1974.B11.

*18 GOLDKNOPF, IRMA. "Crime and Prison-Experience in the Early English Novel: Defoe, Fielding, Smollett." Dissertation, Syracuse, 1968.

Discusses Jonathan Wild and Amelia and argues for Fielding's concern for legal and moral justice.

Source: Dissertation Abstracts, 29, no. 4 (Oct. 1968), 1207A.

*19 GUTHRIE, WILLIAM B. "The Comic Celebrant of Life." Dissertation, Vanderbilt, 1968.

Studies the artistic embodiments of the Dionysian life force from Aristophanes to Fielding.

Source: Dissertation Abstracts, 29, no. 9 (March 1969), 3098A.

*20 HARTELIUS, KIRSTEN. "Satire i Henry Fieldings Romaner." Extracta, 1:104-11.

An abstract ("Satire in Henry Fielding's Novels") in a Spanish journal.

Source: T. Humphrey, p. 230.

21 HILLES, FREDERICK W. "Art and Artifice in Tom Jones," in Imagined Worlds: Essays on Some English Novels and Novelists in Honour of John Butt. Edited by Maynard Mack and Ian Gregor. London: Methuen, pp. 91-110.

An attempt to reexamine some of the "frankly artificial elements" in Tom Jones. Compares a diagram of the plot of Tom Jones to John Woods' original design for Ralph Allan's Prior Park, suggesting that while such contrivance is certainly not like life, it would once have been thought the legitimate contrivance of art. Hilles thinks Fielding's verbal innovativeness (mock heroic, self-parody, etc.) Joycean, and that his ability to construct, particularly in Book 5, is like Dante's. He then briefly compares Fielding's narrator with the aloof narrator of the epic who "is forcing us to read the book the way the author wishes it read" and keeping "detached so that we can see clearly" (p. 108).

Reprinted 1973.A15. See 1970.B1.

22 KEARNEY, A. M. "Pamela & Joseph Andrews." Essays in Criticism, 18, no. 1 (Jan.), 105-107.

Rejects some of the parallels Brooks (1967.B13) sees between the two novels: Joseph is not like Mr. B; Slipslop is not modeled on Mrs. Jewkes; the climactic bedroom scene has the wrong number of characters to be a parallel scene. He particularly rejects Brooks' thesis that Fielding was showing Richardson how to write. Kearney thinks Fielding so misunderstood Richardson that it "ultimately makes Fielding's parodies irrelevant" (p. 107). Jenkins (1965.B7) supports this position. See 1968.B8, B9, 1969.B3.

23 MACANDREW, M. ELIZABETH. "Fielding's Use of Names in Joseph Andrews." Names, 16, no. 4 (Dec.), 362-70.

Carefully argues that Fielding names his characters according to "their particular significance and their function in his work" (p. 370). MacAndrew considers the "romance" names of the interpolated tales, the "theatrical tradition of type-naming" (p. 369) of most of the ordinary characters in the novel (including Fanny Goodwill), and the naming of the two heroes, Joseph and Abraham. By carefully examining the biblical sources for the names Joseph, Abraham, and Barnabas, MacAndrews establishes the heroes' "Christian names as a key to Fielding's Christian message, while the last names . . . establish the parody" (p. 362). With the use of Barnabas and Trulliber, Fielding was able to signal his conviction that "Pamela represented a shallow and worldly view of morality which was responsible for and encouraged by . . . those members of the clergy, who . . . were shielding themselves behind . . . Methodism" (p. 368).

24 MACEY, SAMUEL L. "Fielding's Tom Thumb as the Heir to Buckingham's Rehearsal." Texas Studies in Literature and Language, 10, no. 3 (Fall), 405-14.

Describes some of the elements in Tom Thumb that show Fielding "to be the true successor to Buckingham, attacking precisely that element of heroics, bombast, and rant . . . which had outlived continuing revivals of The Rehearsal" (p. 408). Notices that most of Fielding's targets come from the Restoration, but not from the best Restoration tragedies which continued to be acted. Considers Fielding's attack on unmotivated character action in weak tragedy, his mock rhetoric, and his attack on critics and scholars. Sees the play as an important "theatrical satire."

25 MCNAMEE, LAWRENCE F. Dissertations in English and American Literature: Theses Accepted by American, British and German Universities, 1865-1964. New York and London: R. R. Bowker, pp. 556-60.

Computer list.

*26 MELLEN, JOAN. "Morality in the Novel: A Study of Five English Novelists, Henry Fielding, Jane Austen, George Eliot, Joseph Conrad, and D. H. Lawrence." Dissertation, City University of New York, 1968.

Studies two moral traditions in the novel: one represented by Fielding and Austen, and another by Conrad and Lawrence. The first accepts the morality of its age; the second rejects it.

Source: Dissertation Abstracts, 29, no. 5 (Nov. 1968), 1543.A.

27 MURPHY, ARTHUR. The Lives of Henry Fielding and Samuel Johnson Together with Essays from the Gray's-Inn Journal. Facsimile Reproductions, with an introduction by Matthew Grace. Gainesville, Florida: Scholars' Facsimiles and Reprints, pp. 227-73.

Reproduces "An Essay on the Life and Genius of Henry Fielding, Esq." from The Works of Henry Fielding (1762. A10). Introduction includes a brief biography of Murphy and an analysis of Murphy's "Essay on the Life . . .," suggesting that Murphy was essentially hostile to Fielding and damaged Fielding's reputation and that even Murphy's best insights illustrate the critical limits of his time.

*28 ODA, MINORU. "Joseph Andrews as a Literary Experiment." Memoirs of Osaka Kyoiku University, 17, no. 1, 69-80.

Source: T. Humphrey, p. 119.

29 PRESTON, JOHN. "Plot as Irony: The Reader's Role in Tom Jones." Journal of English Literary History, 35, no. 3 (Sept.), 365-80.

Assuming that "it is quite clear that [Fielding] has been deliberately unserious about the plot" (p. 366), which is artificial and "subdues character to the demands of comic action" (p. 367), Preston sets out to prove that the plot demands a "dual response which secures [its] ironic structure" (p. 368). If we read the book in the past tense, as history, "we may well find in it a degree of order that Fielding hardly intended. If, on the other hand, Fielding is trying in many ways to undermine our sense of objectivity and privilege, we must find ourselves drawn into the confusion and hazard of the action" (p. 376). By examining the unreliable narrator, fortune, and the irrational in character behavior, Preston attempts to persuade us that "the book begins to escape from the narrow designs imposed on it, from the conscious intention of the narrator" (p. 380).

Reprinted 1970.A4 and 1973.A15.

For another view of the plot, see 1950.B2.

30 REGAN, CHARLES L. "Fielding's Stage Career: Repetition of an Error." American Notes and Queries, 6, no. 7 (March), 99-100.

Points out the nineteenth-century scholarly confusion between Henry Fielding and the actor Timothy Fielding (at Drury Lane from 1728 to 1733, with one season--1729-30--at the Haymarket). See 1875.B2.

31 ROTHSTEIN, ERIC. "The Framework of Shamela." Journal of English Literary History, 35, no. 3 (Sept.), 381-402.

Examines the framework technique of the book (a dedication by Keyber, two letters to the editor, and "a pair of letters between Parson Tickltest and Oliver," p. 381) and its effect upon the burlesque. Rothstein untangles the sexual and historical allusions to conclude that the dedication is aimed at Hervey, Middleton, and Cibber because of their politics (their support of Walpole) and because they represented "the three cultural forms by which eighteenth-century society defined itself and its achievements: the state, the church, and the arts" (p. 387). The Methodists are attacked in Tickletext's letter. And all (Methodists, Shamela, Cibber, Hervey, and Middleton) are united in a tangle of bad English, sexual innuendo, and greed. In fact, "the burlesque appears as the translation into action of principles set forth by Keyber and Tickletext" (p. 395). Rothstein further argues that the contradictions of the introductory material reflect the "trust in mechanical principles" throughout Shamela "which entrusts set forms with the wrong content" (p. 400). This "trust in mechanism" is a further attack on both the morality and the formula plot of Pamela.

An expansion of Watt, 1956.A2. See 1971.B3.

32 SCHONHORN, MANUAL. "Fielding's Digressive-Parodic Artistry: Tom Jones and The Man of the Hill." Texas Studies in Literature and Language, 10, no. 1 (Summer), 207-14.

Argues for the structural necessity of this digression on three grounds: "(1) that there is a superficial though antithetical resemblance between the Man of the Hill and his digressive counterpart in Joseph Andrews, Mr. Wilson [The Man of the Hill is a parodic reversal of Wilson]; (2) that the Man of the Hill's autobiographical account, while similar to the presented facts of Tom Jones' career, nevertheless reveals to us its obvious divergence from the subsequent maturation of Fielding's good-natured hero [illustrated metaphorically and topographically as Jones runs down to rescue Jenny Waters]; (3) that the confrontation between the old Man of the Hill and young Tom at this midpoint in the novel parallels, though in parodic form, a father-son sequence at the pivotal centre of another journey, Virgil's Aeneid" (pp. 207-208).

For some recent views of digressions and interpolations in Fielding's novels, see 1959.A1, 1961.B16, 1969.B30, B35, 1970.B37, 1973.B34.

33 SHIPLEY, JOHN B. "Ralph, Ellys, Hogarth, and Fielding: The Cabal Against Jacopo Amigoni." Eighteenth-Century Studies, 1, no. 4 (June), 313-31.

Contends that "Fielding had firsthand knowledge of the 'friction between Hogarth and Amigoni'" (p. 314) and thus his satiric allusion in Joseph Andrews Book 3, chapter 6 (see 1963.B6). Fielding was part of a circle that included James Ralph, the painter John Ellys, and Hogarth in 1729-30, when Amigoni came to London. Amigoni, in competition with James Thornhill, the mentor of both Ellys and Hogarth, was attacked by Ellys, Ralph, and others in print, while The Grub-Street Journal defended him. Fielding was then probably only a close and sympathetic observer in this fight for a national art. Fielding later paid Hogarth a backhanded compliment by including his name in the list of painters in Joseph Andrews and making it Italianate ("Hogarthi"). In 1742, "Hogarth would have kicked a real-life Joseph downstairs for a 'compliment' like this" (p. 331). See 1963.B6, 1969.B5, B9 and B31.

1968

34 SIMON, IRÈNE. "Early Theories of Prose Fiction: Congreve and Fielding," in Imagined Worlds: Essays on Some English Novels and Novelists in Honour of John Butt. Edited by Maynard Mack and Ian Gregor. London: Methuen, pp. 19-35.

"Fielding . . . applied the theory of the prose epic to the matter of the roman comique, and thereby created a new species of writing" (p. 19). Simon sets Fielding against the background of seventeenth-century epic theory and roman comique in order to explain Fielding's formulation of the "comic epic in prose." Concludes that Fielding's "theory of affectation" is the moral paradigm that gives Joseph Andrews the epic unity of design that the roman comique lacked. In this new mixed genre even the old digressions and interpolations "are thematically linked with the main design" (p. 29). See 1947.B1.

35 SPACKS, PATRICIA M. "Some Reflections on Satire." Genre, 1:22-30.

In an article on satire, Spacks argues that Joseph Andrews is "gentle satire, close to the line of comedy" that "involves Joseph and Parson Adams and finally the reader" (p. 485). Specifically examines the famous coach scene, Lady Booby's seduction of Joseph, and the dichotomy between tone and substance in dialogue and narration, in order to illustrate the ways Fielding plays with the "human tendency to be sure of oneself in exactly the situations where one should doubt" (p. 484). Reprinted in 1972.A2.

36 STEWART, KEITH. "History, Poetry, and the Terms of Fiction in the Eighteenth Century." Modern Philology, 66, no. 1 (Aug.), 110-20.

Theoretical essay, examining the "terminology" of both fiction and history, arguing that as attitudes towards (and definitions of) epic poetry, romance, tragedy, comedy, and history changed it became possible for Fielding to call himself an historian. Distinctions "of a conventional kind between history and fiction [only] appear to have persisted until about the middle of the century" (p. 111). Examining the statements about both by novelists, rhetoricians, and critics, Stewart argues that in the last half of the century the novel came to be seen as having "the historical function of recording the way things were" (p. 120).

37 TURNER, PAUL. "Novels, Ancient and Modern." Novel, 2, no. 1 (Fall), 15-24.

Using Ian Watt's headings (1957.B17), Turner shows how many "agreed characteristics of the modern novel" (p. 15) the ancient Greek novel Daphnis and Chloe contains. He compares Daphnis and Chloe to Tom Jones in its mimetic plot and in its use of specific time and place (in which Longus is more careful than Fielding). He then shows how many elements of the ancient novel survive into the eighteenth century. Specifically he examines parallels in Joseph Andrews, Jonathan Wild, Tom Jones, and Amelia to the Ephesiaca pattern (lovers separated for most of the novel, adventuring, and then reunited at the end) and the parallels in Joseph Andrews and Tom Jones to Daphnis and Chloe. He suggests that Fielding was consciously using materials from the Ancient Greek novel.

38 WATT, IAN. "Serious Reflections on The Rise of the Novel." Novel, 1, no. 3 (Spring), 205-18.
Reasserts the importance of Fielding's "realism of assessment" which "got beyond 'the tedious asseveration of literal authenticity' which characterized 'the formal realism of Defoe and Richardson,' in order to bring the novel 'into contact with the whole tradition of civilized values'" (p. 213). "Fielding's words and phrases intentionally invoke not only the actual narrative event, but the whole literary, historical, and philosophical perspective in which character or action should be placed by the reader" (p. 214). Watt also admits to a much less homogeneous view of the Augustan sensibility than that taken in Rise of the Novel. See 1957.B17.

39 WINTEROWD, W. R. "Rhetoric in a Novel," in his Rhetoric a Synthesis. New York, Chicago, etc.: Holt, Rinehart and Winston, pp. 196-212.
Carefully argues that "the author, as a character functioning in the book, applied a rhetoric of persuasion; the fable itself, and the characters who acted it out, supplied a rhetoric of transport through sublimity. And it is in the discrepancy between these two types of rhetoric that one of the failures of Amelia lies" (p. 212). Winterowd examines the pathetic, moving talk and the nature of narrative persuasion (the style, the argument taken from Cicero's five parts of oration, the dialectic method, the businesslike tone). The narrator as psychologist, explicator, and moralist distances the tale with his Aristotelian rhetoric of reason. According to Winterowd, by largely avoiding the Ciceronian manner Fielding weakened Amelia, demonstrating the failure of mid-eighteenth-century rhetoric. See dissertation 1965.A19.

1968

40 WOLFF, CYNTHIA G. "Fielding's Amelia: Private Virtue and Public Good." Texas Studies in Literature and Language, 10, no. 1 (Spring), 37-55.

Begins by examining the character of Amelia (passive innocence) and her inability to understand or affect a corrupt world. Wolff sees this novel as Fielding's attempt to reconcile his careers as novelist and as man of law; "the problem of morality within a society involves two separate questions: how may those inclined to moral behavior . . . be brought to act morally; and how may those inclined to criminality . . . be restrained?" (p. 45). After examining innocence and the law in the novel, Wolff concludes that the novel fails because Fielding cannot reconcile his official view of man's nature with his unofficial assumptions about characterization. Although the law has evolved to restrain and protect man, the good characters either recoil from the use of power or unwittingly undermine the law. Thus Fielding discovers no way in which to protect "the good and innocent man in a corrupt society" (p. 54), and he fails in the task he set himself (reconciling public and private morality).

1969 A BOOKS

*1 BENNETT, ROBERT C. "Fielding and the Satiric Dance." Dissertation, Pennsylvania University, 1969.

Studies the influence of Fielding's satiric plays on Joseph Andrews. Source: Dissertation Abstracts, 30, no. 10 (April 1970), 4397A.

*2 BEVANS, C. H. K. "Henry Fielding: The Relationship of the Plays and the Novels." Dissertation, Nottingham, 1969.

Source: McNamee, 1969-1973, p. 320.

3 BISSELL, FREDERICK O. Fielding's Theory of the Novel. New York: Cooper Square, 93 pp.

Reprint of 1933.A1.

*4 COBURN, LEON. "In Imitation of the Manner of Cervantes: Don Quixote and Joseph Andrews." Dissertation, California - Davis, 1969.

A comparative study of narrative and structural techniques.

Source: Dissertation Abstracts, 31, no. 6 (Dec. 1970), 2870A.

*5 COOPER, FRANK B. "The Structure of the Novels of Henry Fielding." Dissertation, Claremont, 1969.

Discusses the "concrete devices" of unity and the relationship between unity and structure in Fielding's novels.
Source: Dissertation Abstracts, 30, no. 12 (June 1970), 5404A.

*6 DOLAND, VIRGINIA M. "Versions of Pastoral in Henry Fielding's Prose Fiction." Dissertation, Southern California, 1969.
Applies Empson's definition of the "pastoral" to Fielding's fiction.
Source: Dissertation Abstracts, 31, no. 3 (Sept. 1970), 1222A.

7 FIELDING, HENRY. Amelia Booth. Translated by D. R. A. D. Q. Biblioteca Breve de Bolsillo. Barcelona: Editorial Seix Barral, 541 pp.
Reissue of the 1795-96 Spanish translation in five volumes; now continuously paged as one volume.

8 _____. An Apology for the Life of Mrs. Shamela Andrews. Edited by Brian W. Downs. Folcroft, Pa.: Folcroft Press, 71 pp.
Reprint of 1930.A3.

9 _____. The Adventures of Joseph Andrews. Introduction by L. Rice-Oxley. World Classics. London, New York, Toronto: Oxford University Press, 406 pp.
Reprint of 1929.A3.

10 _____. The Tragedy of Tragedies; or, The Life and Death of Tom Thumb the Great, in British Drama From Dryden to Sheridan. Edited by G. H. Nettleton, A. E. Case and George Winchester Stone. Second edition. Boston, New York, etc.: Houghton Mifflin, pp. 571-98.
Brief introduction added to 1939.A3.

11 _____. Tom Jones: Povestea Unui Copil Gasit Roman. Translated by Al. Iacobescu with a preface by Petre Solomon. 4 vols. Bucharest: Editura Pentru Literatua.
Romanian translation of Tom Jones; reissue of 1956.A4.

*12 _____. Tom Jones. Translated by Vittoria Comucci. Milano: Fabbri, 305 pp.
Italian translation.
Source: Hugh Amory's working bibliography.

13 GOLDBERG, HOMER. The Art of Joseph Andrews. Chicago and London: University of Chicago Press, 304 pp.

Reviewed by Jacob H. Adler, StN, 2 (1970), 371-73; Howard Anderson, PQ, 49 (1970), 349-50; Sheridan Baker, CE, 32 (1971), 817-22; John A. Dussinger, JEGP, 69 (1970), 315-18; Michael Irwin, RES, n.s. 22 (1971), 89-93; Arthur Sherbo, ECS, 3 (1970), 560-66; John Preston, EIC, 21 (1971), 91-100; Marshall Waingrow, SEL, 10 (1970), 628-29; Andrew Wright, SAQ, 69 (1970), 293-94; JNL, 30 (1970), 12.

An attempt to write a "literary history 'founded on the principle of artistic synthesis' . . . in which the constructional aspects of literary works are considered from the standpoint of the 'problems faced by writers in the process of making . . . narratives'" (p. ix). Throughout, Goldberg argues that "Fielding's tendency [is] to define compositional problems in terms of intended emotional effects" (p. 17). "In contrast to Richardson's jerry-built rhetorical structure, he offered another kind of evolving narrative, whose seemingly casual shifts and changes were part of a planned system of actions with its own internal probabilities and ethical and emotional coherence" (p. 286). Goldberg begins by carefully examining the tradition (prototypes) from which Joseph Andrews grew (Cervantes' Don Quixote, Scarron's Roman Comique, Lesage's Gil Blas, Marivaux's La Vie de Marianne) in order to determine what rhetorical material he could have borrowed from each. He concludes that he borrowed from Cervantes the series of actions leading to a necessary end and growing from the hero's obsession; physical action, interwoven plots, parody, and allusion to create reality from Scarron; comic exposure from Lesage; and comic narrative perspective from Marivaux. He then "reconstructs" Fielding's reasons for altering this borrowed material (the nature of the character obsession, for example) and illustrates the four part division of the novel (each with its change of tone, interest, and direction). All of this underlines Fielding's conscious and clear "artistic strategy." Fielding's characters, he contends, get their psychological reality from the "dramatic dialogue of innocence and affectation" (p. 151). Continuing to compare Fielding to his prototypes, he discusses character psychology ("the dialogue of affectation," p. 176), interpolations, Fielding's characteristic scene making or incident development, and his narrative technique ("narrator as comedian and satirist," p. 227). Throughout this sometimes difficult study, Goldberg argues that Fielding consciously shaped his borrowed material to manipulate tone, pace, mood, and moral contention. See dissertation 1961.A9.

*14 JOHNSON, JEFFREY L. L. "The Good-Natured Young Man and Virtuous Young Women in the Comedies of Henry Fielding." Dissertation, Florida State-Tallahassee, 1969.

Demonstrates that Fielding's heroes (Jones and Booth) and heroines (Sophia and Amelia) developed from the traditional types with which he worked as a dramatist. Fielding had specifically developed examples of natural goodness who revealed the moral failings of other characters.

Source: Dissertation Abstracts, 30, no. 12 (June 1970), 5411A-5412A.

15 JOHNSON, MAURICE. Fielding's Art of Fiction: Eleven Essays on Shamela, Joseph Andrews, Tom Jones, and Amelia. Philadelphia: University of Pennsylvania Press, 182 pp.

Reprint of 1961.A11.

*16 JORDAN, BURT A. "The Moral Code in Fielding's Novels: Jonathan Wild, Joseph Andrews, Tom Jones, and Amelia." Dissertation, South Carolina, 1969.

Argues that Fielding is interested in the lives and acts of men who grow toward the moral action and social consciousness of benevolent Christians.

Source: Dissertation Abstracts, 31, no. 1 (July 1970), 360A-61A.

*17 KRAUSE, LOTHAR P. "The Conflict between Social Communities and Individuals in the Novels of Henry Fielding." Dissertation, Pittsburgh, 1969.

Jones, Andrews, and Booth are all compassionate characters who clash with people obsessed with self-interest. In Amelia Fielding attempts to write a tragic novel combining "humor" characterization, and characterization through social interaction.

Source: Dissertation Abstracts, 30, no. 11 (May 1970), 4991A.

18 PAULSON, RONALD and THOMAS LOCKWOOD, eds. Henry Fielding: The Critical Heritage. Critical Heritage Series, edited by B. C. Southam. London: Routledge & Kegan Paul; New York: Barnes & Noble, 473 pp.

Reviewed by Douglas Brooks, YES, 1 (1971), 274-75; TLS, 29 Jan. 1970, p. 103.

A comprehensive anthology of commentary on Fielding's plays and novels made between 1730 and 1787, although the "effective cut-off date is 1762, when the first collected edition of Fielding's work was published" (p. xxi). This book provides us with the material from letters, poems, magazine articles and reviews, prefaces, etc. to make an informed judgment about Fielding's contemporary English and French reputation. In a brief introduction this reputation is summed up. Arthur Murphy is seen as summing "up Fielding's reputation in his lifetime" (p. 17) and as developing "a critical view of Fielding . . . very close to the one we have followed" (p. 18). Thus Wilbur Cross' view (1918.A1) of Murphy is modified, as is Blanchard's (1926.A1) of the opposition between the defenders of Richardson and those of Fielding.

*19 RUDUS, RAYMOND J. "The History of Tom Jones in Adaptation." Dissertation, Nebraska, 1969.
Source: Dissertation Abstracts, 30, no. 4 (Oct. 1969), 1535A. See 1974.B22.

*20 WOOD, DAVID C. "The Dramatic Tradition of Henry Fielding's Regular Comedies." Dissertation, Bowling Green, 1969.
Reexamines Fielding's regular five-act comedies and places them in the sentimental tradition of Cibber, Steele, and Goldsmith.
Source: Dissertation Abstracts, 30, no. 10 (April 1970), 4428A.

1969 B SHORTER WRITINGS

1 BLOCH, TUVIA. "Antedatings from Fielding." Notes and Queries, 214 (May), 188-89.
A list of words (including Balragger, catchpenny, harl, pin down, trumped-up, etc.) that Fielding used at an earlier date than is recorded in the Oxford English Dictionary.

2 _____. "The Prosecution of the Maidservant in Amelia." English Language Notes, 6, no. 4 (June), 269-71.
Argues that while Fielding may have intended Booth's prosecution of the servant Betty for stealing Amelia's shifts (Book 2, chapters 5-7) to illustrate Booth's strong-tempered defense of Amelia, "he would not have regarded Booth's behavior as either cruel or lacking in verisimilitude" (p. 269). Proves her argument by showing that Booth's justification for the prosecution is very much like the position taken by Fielding in Enquiry into the Causes of the Late Increase of Robbers and "Essay on the Knowledge of the Characters of Men" and by Allworthy in his final attitude to Black George in Tom Jones.

3 BROOKS, DOUGLAS. "Joseph Andrews and Pamela." Essays in Criticism, 19, no. 3 (July), 348-51.

A further response to 1968.B22. Insists on the clothes symbolism in Joseph Andrews, on parallel bedroom scenes in Joseph Andrews and Pamela, and on a subtle Fielding allusion to Pope's Dunciad and the chaos of Pamela.

*4 CARTER, CHARLOTTE A. "Personae and Characters in the Essays of Addison, Steele, Fielding, Johnson, Goldsmith." Dissertation, Denver, 1969.

The essay form helped create the expansive, good-natured persona and the circumscribed and selfish "character" open to satiric scrutiny.

Source: Dissertation Abstracts, 30, no. 11 (May 1970), 4938A.

5 COLEY, WILLIAM B. "Forum: Fielding and the 'Cabal' Against Amigoni: A Rebuttal." Eighteenth-Century Studies, 2, no. 3 (Spring), 303-307.

Thinks Shipley's evidence (1968.B33) for a "cabal" including Hogarth, Ellys, Ralph, and Fielding "highly circumstantial" (p. 304). There is little evidence that Fielding and Ralph were friends much before the "early 1730s" (p. 305), and Coley feels that James Ralph has been made the "common denominator" (p. 306) in events he may have had nothing to do with.

6 FERNANDEZ-ALVAREZ, J. "Un probable eco de Henry Fielding en La Fe de Armando Palacio Valdés." Filología moderna (Madrid), nos. 33-34: 101-108.

A probable echo in La Fe of the confrontation between Parson Trulliber and Parson Adams. In Spanish.

7 GOLDKNOPF, DAVID. "The Failure of Plot in Tom Jones." Criticism, 11, no. 3 (Summer), 262-74.

Argues, with careful attention to the text, that "the novel's inner structure--that is to say, its plot [is inadequate] to its sense-supporting task" (p. 262). Goldknopf first examines and briefly dismisses some of Fielding's self-justification for the irregularities of his new form (to be found in Joseph Andrews and Tom Jones); he then examines the often discussed three part "architecture" of the novel, maintaining that the second section (on the road) heavily outweighs the other two (country and city) and that each section has its own organizing method. Goldknopf carefully examines the socio-political structuring of the first part (demonstrating the particular limits Fielding set for it), the symbolism of the second section (dominated by the inn symbol), and the plot of the third section (the farce complication of events). He sees the third section as poorly (less intelligently) organized and as an evocative failure (it isn't really the city, just an enclave of "country" and "road" characters). Finally, he challenges the idea that Tom Jones is the perfectly plotted novel, saying instead that "the author compensates for the disengagement of our interest in the narrative by setting up a comradery between himself and us" (p. 272) and that it does not even sustain Fielding's rather limited vision of life.

Shortened reprint, 1972.B5. For other views, see 1950.B2, 1970.B1, and 1972.B13.

8 GRUNDY, ISOBEL. "Some Unpublished Early Verse of Henry Fielding." New Rambler, 7, Ser. C (June), 2-18.

This find in the Earl of Harrowby's library is fully set out in 1972.B7.

9 LA FRANCE, MARSTON. "Fielding's Use of the 'Humor' Tradition." Bucknell Review, 17, no. 3 (Dec.), 53-63.

Argues that in his novels Fielding united epic form and "humors" characters (derived from the tradition of Jonson and Congreve). La France sees Fielding's characters as of two kinds: central characters (Joseph, Fanny, Adams, Tom, etc.) who are round, morally balanced, and capable of development, and "humors" characters who are flat, self-betraying, and morally unbalanced (Mrs. Slipslop, Mrs. Fitzpatrick, Partridge, etc.). By examining Fielding's concept of character in theory and practice, La France indicates how this simplifies Fielding's job in his many-peopled scenes and suggests how it serves his satiric purpose. Such a concept of character is traditionalist and "depends upon a world where norms are taken seriously and departures suffer according to the extent of the deviation" (p. 62).

10 LEVI, ELDA. "'Novel': L'Affermarsi di un Genere Letterario." English Miscellany, 20 (1969), 101-40.

Argues that neither the practice nor the theory of the novel originated with Richardson or Fielding. Writers like John Davies, William Congreve, Mrs. Manly, and Defoe are distinguishing the novel from romance and setting out its serious moral purpose between 1653 and 1760. In Italian.

11 MCNAMEE, LAWRENCE F. Dissertations in English and American Literature: Theses Accepted by American, British, British

Commonwealth and German Universities, 1964-1968. New York and London: R. R. Bowker, pp. 221-23.
Continuation of 1968.B25.

12 MANDEL, JEROME. "The Man of the Hill and Mrs. Fitzpatrick: Character and Narrative Technique in Tom Jones." Papers on Language and Literature, 5, no. 1 (Winter), 26-38.
Begins by examining the thematic similarity of the two tales and "the relevance of [both] to the structure of the novel as a whole" (p. 27), arguing for parallels in both theme and structure (city vs. country pattern). Mandel then examines the different narrative technique of each (a monologue and a dialogue) as they reveal the character of the speaker and as parodies of Fielding's own narrative techniques. The Man of the Hill's narrative illustrates an unbalanced version of Fielding's own narrative logic (following a narrative sequence and not a chronological one), inefficiently punctuated by narrative digressions and dialogue to break the logic of narrative. Mrs. Fitzpatrick illustrates a narrative dominated by a narrator who abandons logic to generalize, interrupt, show social concern, and call on the reader's imagination. Mandel analyzes two passages to illustrate the technique and character of each. Mrs. Fitzpatrick is self-justificatory and a blamer of society, and the Man of the Hill accepts responsibility and is a believer in the individual. Through them Fielding parodies his own style by "allowing Mrs. Fitzpatrick to emphasize digression to the exclusion of logic and the Man of the Hill to emphasize logic to the exclusion of digression" (p. 38). See 1961.B16 and 1968.B32.

13 MILES, KATHLEEN. "Richardson's Response to Fielding's Felon." Studies in the Novel, 1, no. 3 (Fall), 373-74.
Argues that in vol. 1, letter 36, Richardson deliberately has Clarissa refute Jonathan Wild when she says, "Goodness, I thought, was greatness."

14 OLSEN, FLEMMING. "Notes on the Structure of Joseph Andrews." English Studies, 50, no. 4, 340-51.
Discusses "structure" under three headings: theme, character handling, and "compositional build-up" (p. 340). Olsen sees three themes--Joseph's chastity (Joseph is always pure and passive, even with Fanny), Adams and the journey, and a sociology of Fielding's England. Under character, Olsen discusses the several identities of the first person narrator and the various techniques used for the creation of third person characters ("the book's

gallery of characters," p. 342), particularly their dramatization and description. Olsen sees most of the characters as flat, acting in stereotyped situations, and incapable of inner awareness or judgment. The composition of the novel is organized to make Fielding's empirical aim work; "he gives concrete examples . . . in order to expose hypocrisy" (p. 345). Olsen discusses contrast, the inset stories, and dramatized essays (Leonora/Horatio, Mr. Wilson, poet and player) that illustrate Fielding's sociological purpose. He finally briefly discusses time (events happen in the present, now, before us), the paucity of description, the lack of causality, the unity of action of individual chapters, the use of dramatic and argumentative chapters to control pace.

15 OLSHIN, TOBY A. "Form and Theme in Novels about Non-Human Characters, a Neglected Sub-Genre." Genre, 2, no. 1 (March), 43-56.

Considers Fielding's A Journey from This World to the Next, along with Coventry's The History of Pompey the Little: or, the Life and Adventures of a Lap Dog (1751), and four other eighteenth-century novels in this sub-genre. Argues that all have an "underlying religious theme for each dramatizes the same moral message: know how fallible a thing is a human being." Fielding illustrates this "both rhetorically and dramatically" (p. 45) with the disembodied and transmigrating soul of Julian the Apostate.

16 PAYNE, LADELL. "The Trilogy: Faulkner's Comic Epic in Prose." Studies in the Novel, 1, no. 1 (Spring), 27-37.

Argues that Faulkner's trilogy adapts to twentieth-century artistic practice an attitude toward fiction begun by Fielding. Specifically, Payne compares Fielding's use of epic devices like the flashback, in medias res, and an elevated style in Joseph Andrews to Faulkner's telling of the myths of Yoknapatawpha. Payne distinguishes between Fielding's comic burlesque and Faulkner's absurd humor; he also briefly compares Faulkner's and Fielding's styles.

17 RADNOTI, SÁNDOR. "Walpole-ok és Jonathan Wild-ok. Jegyzet a XVIII századi angol irodalom egy tipikus motívumáról." Filológiai Közlöny, 15:19-23.

"Walpole's and Jonathan Wild's notes on a typical motif of eighteenth-century English literature."

Hungarian article.

18 REID, B. L. "Utmost Merriment, Strictest Decency: Joseph Andrews," in his The Long Boy and Others. Athens: University of Georgia Press, pp. 52-77.
Reviewed by H. K. Russell, GaR, 24 (1970), 241-44; Marshall Waingrow, SEL, 10 (1970), 625-26.
Reprint of 1967.B32.

19 RINEHART, HOLLIS. "Jonathan Wild and the Cant Dictionary." Philological Quarterly, 48, no. 2 (April), 220-25.
Identifies the two sources for the cant terms in Jonathan Wild (A New Dictionary of the Terms Ancient and Modern of the Canting Crew and its revision, called A New Canting Dictionary) and briefly compares Fielding's use of cant terms with Defoe's. They are used to characterize a person in the story, rather than the narrator as in Defoe; they are often metaphorically appropriate to the situation and not just colorful; they reinforce the basic ironic strategy of the book (the cant term often passes a judgment on an action). See dissertation 1965.A18.

20 RUBINSTEIN, ANNETTE T. "Henry Fielding," in her The Great Tradition in English Literature from Shakespeare to Shaw. Vol. 1. New York and London: Modern Reader Paperbacks, pp. 287-315.
Reviews Fielding's career, emphasizing his social criticism and setting him against his contemporaries, Defoe and Richardson, and against the developing "bourgeois" life of his age.

21 SACKS, SHELDON. "Golden Birds and Dying Generations." Comparative Literature Studies, 6, no. 3 (Sept.), 274-91.
Asserts that Fielding and Austen each uniquely used "the special resources of narrative to create morally serious comedies" (p. 282) and then demonstrates how in Tom Jones "he pushed the bounds of comedy far beyond those which limited the effects realized in Joseph Andrews" (pp. 282-83). Fielding includes serious, even tragic, events in Tom Jones and then with narrative reassurances disarms them (i.e., Tom's pattern of escapes, contemptible villainous agents, etc.). But Fielding never completely disarms the potential evil, thus keeping us aware that only an "artificer's hand" saves Tom and that undefeated evil still remains. See 1950.B2 and 1970.B1.

*22 SHARP, RUTH M. M. "Rational Vision and the Comic Resolution: A Study in the Novels of Richardson, Fielding, and Jane Austen." Dissertation, Wisconsin, 1969.

Studies the ways in which these novelists transform "reality into the ideal and the ideal into a convincing illusion of reality."

Source: Dissertation Abstracts, 31, no. 1 (July 1970), 369A.

23 SHERBO, ARTHUR. "Character Description in the Novel," in his Studies in the Eighteenth Century Novel. East Lansing: Michigan State University Press, pp. 177-207.

Reviewed by Morris Golden, HSL, 4 (1972), 87-94; A. J. Hassall, AUMLA, 35 (1971), 99-100; John Traugott, PQ, 50 (1971), 398-99; Marshall Waingrow, SEL, 10 (1970), 626-28; TLS, 14 Aug. 1970, p. 896.

Fielding shares with the major and minor writers of his century (Defoe, Richardson, Smollett, Cleland, Radcliffe, Austen, etc.) a habit of generalized physical description of characters. Sherbo points out the striking similarity in the descriptions of Joseph, Fanny, and Sophia. Fielding saved physical description for his grotesque caricatures, often referring to Hogarth or quoting others to confirm beauty (Amelia by citing Milton, Waller, and Suckling). This latter habit he shares with Smollett.

24 _____. "'Characters of Manners': Notes Toward the History of a Critical Term." Criticism, 11, no. 4 (Fall), 343-57.

Sets Samuel Johnson's distinction between Richardson's and Fielding's characters (characters of nature as opposed to characters of manners) in the context of Johnson's own criticism and the criticism of the period (beginning with Dryden and Dennis). In passing, Sherbo shows that Fielding and Johnson shared an interest in "manners" characters and that Johnson was confusing comic and tragic characters in his distinction. See 1951.B4.

25 _____. "Fielding's Amelia a Reinterpretation," in his Studies in the Eighteenth Century Novel. East Lansing: Michigan State University Press, pp. 85-103.

In this extended response to Andrew Wright (1965.A20), Sherbo argues, with extensive citation, that "Amelia contains virtually all of the playful . . . uses of language that Professor Wright finds in Tom Jones and Joseph Andrews" (p. 89). Sherbo compares the history of Mr. Trent and other episodes to similar episodes in the earlier novels and discovers the same use of simple irony, extended comic metaphor, high-flown bombastic language, understatement, playful tentativeness, and "satire" (against doctors, layers, etc.). He only concedes that there are fewer comically conceived characters in Amelia. He does not find its tone tragic, its structure weak, or its narrator infirm.

26 _____. "'Inside' and 'Outside' Readers in Fielding's Novels," in his Studies in the Eighteenth Century Novel. East Lansing: Michigan State University Press, pp. 35-57.

Sherbo postulates "a real audience--the 'outside' reader--and an 'implied,' or 'assumed,' or 'postulated' audience--the 'inside' readers within the same novel" (p. 37). He begins by discussing Wayne Booth's (1952.B2, 1961.B4) analysis of the postulated reader, Ehrenpreis' analysis of the narrator (1964.A5), and Paulson's projected reader (1967.B27); he finds them all either confused or inaccurate descriptions of the reader, or limited because they did not carefully describe the readers implied by Fielding's narrator. Sherbo defines the 'inside' reader as "male, of the upper class, either city-bred or sometimes resident of London, married . . . acquainted with the passion of love, good-natured, likely to be forgetful, naïf, curious, and not up to the narrator's own level of culture, sophistication, and understanding" (p. 48). He also describes the female reader occasionally addressed by Fielding. Sherbo then briefly argues that the narrator is still witty in the same way and at the expense of the same "inside" reader in Amelia. The "inside" reader has been created to "further contribute to the delight of the 'outside' reader" (p. 51). See 1974.B28.

27 _____. "'Naked' Innocence in Joseph Andrews," in his Studies in the Eighteenth Century Novel. East Lansing: Michigan State University Press, pp. 120-27.

Responds to Spilka's article (1953.B10) on symbolic naked innocence in Joseph Andrews by illustrating from the novel that only when Joseph is stripped and beaten does a character in the novel appear totally without clothes and that "naked" did not mean without clothes in the eighteenth century. By examining other sources, Sherbo also indicates that nakedness was not linked with innocence but with extreme poverty by eighteenth-century writers.

28 _____. "Some Aspects of Fielding's Style," in his Studies in the Eighteenth Century Novel. East Lansing: Michigan State University Press, pp. 58-84.

Examines the "mannerisms, techniques, tricks of style . . . that appear in Fielding's novels, not only binding them together as the work of the same stylist but also . . . complementing one another to help produce the unique tone of those novels" (p. 58). Sherbo identifies and describes, by citing evidence from the novels, the "economical statement" (excuses for omissions), the heavy-handed but courteous reminders for the obtuse reader, the parenthetical expression (often indicating causality or creating a deprecatory stance and usually an effective ironic device), the shift from inflated to workaday prose, the "tentative phrase" ("I believe," "I think"), and variations on the "that is" phrase and the ampersand. Sherbo sees that "all of these devices of style are amenable to ironic manipulation; and they are so manipulated" (p. 79). After briefly comparing Smollett's use of the economical statement, he finds the texture of Smollett's prose "closer, more formidable" (p. 81).

29 _____. "The 'Moral Basis' of Joseph Andrews," in his Studies in the Eighteenth Century Novel. East Lansing: Michigan State University Press, pp. 104-19.

Argues that Joseph Andrews has none of the thematic architectonic sophistication that Battestin (1959.A1) finds in it; "as far as the 'philosophical core' of the novel is concerned, I do not think there is one" (p. 104). Nor does he think that Fielding's novel can withstand the rigorous examination of modern criticism of the novel. Although this is primarily an extended critique of Battestin's argument and method, Sherbo also argues that Fielding was "slapdash" with his characters and had a comic and not serious intention.

30 _____. "The Narrator in Fielding's Novels," in his Studies in the Eighteenth Century Novel. East Lansing: Michigan State University Press, pp. 1-34.

Reviews the criticism of the narrator in Fielding's fiction and then precisely establishes the kind of narrator Fielding creates in Joseph Andrews, Tom Jones, Jonathan Wild, and Amelia. After setting out the complicated and sometimes contradictory view of Fielding's narrators articulated by Booth, Crane, McKillop, Ehrenpreis, Sacks, Price, and others, Sherbo asserts, and sets out to prove by extensive citation from the texts, that "there is very little difference between Henry Fielding, the real author, and the narrator he creates for his novels" (p. 13). The narrator in all of Fielding's novels is acquainted with the country but his habitat is the city; he knows the theater intimately; he has traveled in England and abroad; he is a man of rank and good schooling; he admires the classics (particularly Horace) as well as Shakespeare, Pope, and

Milton; he has a wide range of emotion (most tender and compassionate); he is concerned for his reader.

31 SHIPLEY, JOHN B. "Forum: Fielding and the 'Cabal' Against Amigoni: Reply to W. R. Coley." Eighteenth-Century Studies, 2, no. 3 (Spring), 307-11.
Contends that Coley's articles (1963.B6 and 1969.B5) examine "the passage in Joseph Andrews from the point of view of a mid-twentieth-century reader possessing information about events and meaning of words (e.g., Varnish) that even Fielding himself may not have known. My purpose, in part, was to establish the sequence of events" (p. 307). Proves that Ralph wrote articles against Amigoni and reviews his evidence for friendship and "cabal." See 1968.B33.

32 SOLOMON, STANLEY J. "Fielding's Presentational Mode in Tom Jones." College English Association (Philadelphia) Critic, 31 (Jan.), 12-13.
Argues that Fielding does not merely present external comic characters, as Ian Watt suggests, but that, with Tom, Fielding "invents a double mode of external, indirect characterization" (p. 13). Tom is half reflective, full of "fine sentiments about love, morality, religion, and loyalty," and half "active" (p. 13). Fielding presents these two halves externally and without comment, letting the reader see that the two halves must be united for Tom to become a member of his class. "With this approach, Fielding was able to capture the vitality of Tom's inner life from the external disparity between what the hero says and what he does" (p. 13). See 1972.B9.

33 SPILKA, MARK. "Fielding and the Epic Impulse." Criticism, 11, no. 1 (Winter), 68-77.
In this theoretical essay, Spilka first sets out the ways in which Fielding reduces the heroic scale of the epic (the fate of nations not in the balance, not concerned with the shapers of human destiny, the gods no longer intervene) and then argues that "Fielding and all novelists after him are actually working on a larger scale than traditional epic narrative affords, that they connect with epic narrative through their extension of epic scale and variety to . . . what was left--the social, personal and domestic life and the traditional and changing norms that apply to it" (p. 71). Spilka considers the novel's move into "the unexplored immensity of social, personal and domestic life" (p. 72), the omniscient narrator as bringer

of order, and the novel's concern with "the importance of social life to self-realization" (p. 75). See 1931.A9, 1958.B16, 1974.B16.
Reprinted 1972.A8.

34 STEWART, MARY M. "Notes on Henry Fielding as Magistrate." Notes and Queries, 214 (Sept.), 348-50.
By using contemporary newspapers, Stewart establishes various facts about Fielding's career as magistrate: who his predecessor was, when he was chairman of Westminster Sessions, that he was chairman of Middlesex County Sessions, when he began sitting as a Middlesex justice. See 1973.B32.

35 SUERBAUM, ULRICH. "Das Gasthaus zu Upton: zur Structur von Fieldings Tom Jones," in Festschrift für Edgar Mertner. Edited by Bernhard Fabian and Ulrich Suerbaum. Munich: Fink, pp. 213-30.
Rejects the idea of careful ordered symmetry in Tom Jones; Fielding offers order in vanity. The Upton episode, rather than being integrated in the overall structure of the novel, is an independent episode which is a mirror and a parody of the plot of Tom Jones; the whole novel is contained and repeated in this central episode. Argues that this diverse and hectic episode at Upton is a metaphor for the world, and the protagonists in it represent human nature in all its variety. The episode, a static repetition and variation on previous themes, presents the world as it is, while the novel as a whole strives to present the world as a harmonious whole. In German. See 1968.B32.

1970 A BOOKS

*1 BAILEY, VERN D. "Fielding's Politics." Dissertation, California-Berkeley, 1970.
Studies the nature of Fielding's beliefs and offers "a rationale for his political activities."
Source: Dissertation Abstracts, 31, no. 12 (June 1971), 6588A-89A.

*2 CAPERS, CONNIE. "From Drama to Novel: A Study of Fielding's Development." Dissertation, New Mexico, 1970.
Studies the influence of his drama on narrator, fable, language, burlesque form, and on marriage as a satiric object.
Source: Dissertation Abstracts, 31, no. 10 (April 1971), 5353A.

*3 CLEARY, THOMAS R. "Henry Fielding as a Periodical Essayist." Dissertation, Princeton, 1970.

Source: Dissertation Abstracts, 31, no. 12 (June 1971), 6544A.

See 1973.B7a and 1975.B36.

4 COMPTON, NEIL, ed. Henry Fielding: Tom Jones: A Casebook. Casebook Series, edited by A. E. Dyson. London: Macmillan, 272 pp.

A brief introduction reviews the history of the English novel (from Defoe), Fielding's parodies of Pamela, the Palladian structure and the narrator in Tom Jones, and Fielding's critical reputation. The first section reprints snippets before 1920 (including Lady Mary Wortley Montagu, Samuel Johnson, Coleridge, and Chesterton). The next section includes essays and extracts by Arnold Kettle, "Tom Jones" (1951.B3); Dorothy Van Ghent, "On Tom Jones" (1953. B12); J. Middleton Murry, "In Defence of Fielding" (1956. B9); Ian Watt, "Tom Jones and Clarissa" (1957.B17); William Empson, "Tom Jones" (1958.B6); C. J. Rawson, "Professor Empson's Tom Jones" (1959.B19); A. E. Dyson, "Satire and Comic Irony in Tom Jones" (1966.B8); M. C. Battestin, "Osborne's Tom Jones: Adapting a Classic" (1966.B3); Ronald Paulson, "Lucianic Satire in Tom Jones" (1967.B27); Robert Alter, "On the Critical Dismissal of Fielding" (1968.A1); and John Preston, "Plot as Irony: The Reader's Role in Tom Jones" (1968.B29).

Select bibliography included.

*5 DAVIS, CHARLES G. "Satire on the Reader in the Novels of Henry Fielding." Dissertation, North Carolina, 1970.

Studies the "reflective" satire (that which makes the reader reflect) in Fielding's novels.

Source: Dissertation Abstracts, 31, no. 11 (May 1971), 6006A-7A.

6 FIELDING, HENRY. An Apology for the Life of Mrs. Shamela Andrews. Edited by R. Brimley Johnson. Folcroft, Pa.: Folcroft Press, 91 pp.

Reprint of 1926.A3.

7 _____. Romans. Les aventures de Joseph Andrews et de son ami M. Abraham Adams; Vie de feu M. Jonathan Wild le Grand; Histoire de Tom Jones, enfant trouvé. Translated by Francis Ledoux. Paris: Gallimard, 1633 pp.

Reissue of 1964.A9.

8 _____. The History of the Adventures of Joseph Andrews and of His Friend Mr. Abraham Adams and An Apology for The Life of Mrs. Shamela Andrews. Edited by Douglas Brooks. Oxford English Novels, edited by James Kinsley. London, New York, Toronto: Oxford University Press, 422 pp.

Follows the "Wesleyan" (1967.A2) text for Joseph Andrews; for Shamela, a first edition (4 April 1741) is collated with a second (3 November 1741) and those emendations which seem to be by Fielding are accepted. The textual notes include a few of the variant readings of the two texts; brief explanatory notes are provided, as well as a select bibliography. The introduction outlines the publishing history of the two works, the reason for two parodies of Pamela (Shamela is "random shafts loosed at disparate topical targets," p. ix, and Joseph Andrews is a positive alternative to Richardsonian "virtue"). Sees biblical allusions and allusions to Hercules, the Odyssey, and Don Quixote brought together in a balanced moral architecture in Joseph Andrews. Includes Conyer Middleton's "Dedication" from his History of . . . Cicero, one of the objects of Fielding's attack, in an appendix.

9 _____. The History of the Adventures of Joseph Andrews and of his friend Mr. Abraham Adams and An Apology for the Life of Mrs. Shamela Andrews. London: Fraser Press, 401 pp.

The text of Joseph Andrews is "based upon a comparison of the second and fourth editions"; the copy text of Shamela is not indicated. Both are old spelling texts (unmodernized); no bibliographical apparatus is provided.

10 _____. The Tragedy of Tragedies; or, The Life and Death of Tom Thumb the Great; with the Annotations of H. Scriblerus Secundus. Edited by James T. Hillhouse. St. Clair Shores, Mich.: Scholarly Press, 231 pp.

Reprint of 1918.A4.

11 _____. Tom Thumb and The Tragedy of Tragedies. Edited by L. J. Morrissey. Fountainwell Drama Series, edited by John Horden. Edinburgh: Oliver and Boyd; Berkeley and Los Angeles: University of California Press, 128 pp.

This old spelling text (neither punctuation nor spelling modernized) of the two plays expands Hillhouse's (1918.A4) annotations and provides a complete discussion of the bibliographical problems. The introduction briefly sets the play in Fielding's dramatic career and provides its stage history.

*12 GLOCK, WALDO S. "The Plot of Tom Jones: Its Significance and Effect." Dissertation, Minnesota, 1970.
Argues that the logically connected plot of Tom Jones projects an "intellectual view of the world" which illuminates Fielding's themes.
Source: Dissertation Abstracts, 31, no. 7 (Jan. 1971), 3546A.

*13 HILLOCKS, GEORGE. "The Synthesis of Art and Ethic in Tom Jones." Dissertation, Western Reserve, 1970.
Argues that an amalgam of latitudinarian and Aristotelian ethics underlie the novel.
Source: Dissertation Abstracts, 32, no. 1 (July 1971), 434A.

*14 JOBE, ALICE J. C. "Fielding Criticism: A Twentieth-Century Selective Enumeration with Commentary." Dissertation, Texas, 1970.
Source: McNamee, 1969-1973, p. 321. See 1970.B15.

*15 MACANDREW, MARY E. "The Debate Between Richardson and Fielding." Dissertation, Columbia, 1970.
Sets out the aesthetic and moral debate between Pamela I and II and Shamela and Joseph Andrews.
Source: Dissertation Abstracts, 34, no. 1 (July 1973), 280A.

*16 PASTALOSKY, ROSA. Henry Fielding y la tradición picaresca. Buenos Aires: Solar.
In Spanish.
Source: T. Humphrey, p. 232.

*17 SELLS, LARRY F. "Fielding's Central Triad: Repetition and Variation in the Novels." Dissertation, Pennsylvania State, 1970.
Studies Fielding's repetition and variations on the erring hero, the virtuous heroine, and the spiritual father as archetypal patterns.
Source: Dissertation Abstracts, 32, no. 2 (Aug. 1971), 932A.

*18 SHESGREEN, SEAN N. "The Literary Portraits in the Novels of Henry Fielding." Dissertation, Northwestern, 1970.
Source: McNamee, 1969-1973, p. 320. See 1970.B34 and 1972.A11.

19 STASIO, CLOTILDE DE. Henry Fielding e Il Giornalismo. Biblioteca di Studi Inglesi. No. 20. Bari: Adriatica, 249 pp.

Study of Fielding's social satire, with special emphasis on his theater and his journalism. There are chapters on "the theater of journalism," The Champion, The True Patriot, The Jacobite's Journal, The Covent-Garden Journal, the anti-Jacobitism in Tom Jones, and the introductory chapters of Tom Jones. Specifically, Stasio discusses Fielding's remaking of the comedy of manners and his new theatrical language, both of which create his acerbic dramatic journalism. Fielding's Swift-like journalistic masks (personae) are discussed, as are his attacks on Walpole, the judicial system, the power of money in a mercantile society, on social customs, and on Jacobitism. Maintains that Fielding gave his journalism literary form with his persona and his rhetoric and that his wit is not cerebral like Swift's. In Italian.

20 WILLIAMS, IOAN, ed. The Criticism of Henry Fielding. London: Routledge & Kegan Paul; New York: Barnes & Noble, 404 pp.
Reviewed by John Preston, EIC, 21 (1971), 91-100; TLS, 9 July 1970, p. 746.
Reprints seventy-two selections "from the whole range of Fielding's work" that "represent with the minimum of repetition, every aspect of his social and literary criticism" (p. ix). Each of the nine sections (the theater, Colley Cibber, the art of criticism, Grub Street, laws of good writing, wit and humor, approbations, The Jacobite's Journal, the "new province" of writing) is organized chronologically, and each selection is introduced by a brief bibliographical or historical headnote. The introduction sets out Fielding's major moral and critical ideas. See 1928.B4, 1934.B3, 1951.B4. For a briefer survey, see 1930.B2.

1970 B SHORTER WRITINGS

1 BATTESTIN, MARTIN C. "Tom Jones: The Argument of Design," in The Augustan Milieu: Essays Presented to Louis A. Landa. Edited by Henry K. Miller, Eric Rothstein, and G. S. Rousseau. Oxford: Clarendon Press, pp. 289-319.
Argues for the philosophical sophistication of the design of Tom Jones, "the consummate literary achievement of England's Augustan Age" (p. 289). "Tom Jones is the celebration of the rational values of Art, of the controlling intelligence which creates Order out of Chaos and which alone gives meaning to vitality"; sees "Providence and Prudence [as the] defin[ing] . . . ethos of Tom Jones" (p. 291). In this article, Battestin discusses Providence

(the macrocosmic form of these two related themes). Battestin first sets Fielding's moral aesthetic ("the paradigm in art of cosmic Justice and Order," p. 292) in its Christian humanist context, arguing that none of the rhetorical manipulation is accidental ("Design is . . . the primary . . . determinative factor in the structure of the book," p. 303). He then argues that all of "the fortunate contingencies and surprising turns are . . . the expression of Fielding's Christian vision of life" (p. 306) in which there is an ordering creator and fortunate, or providential, coincidence leading to a "comic apocalypse" in which "the innocent [are] redeemed, an unerring justice meted out" (p. 316). He briefly illustrates this in the events immediately after Upton.

For a contrary view, see 1969.B7 and 1971.B37. Included in 1974.B2. See also 1968.B21.

2 BELL, MICHAEL. "A Note on Drama and the Novel: Fielding's Contribution." Novel, 3, no. 2 (Winter), 119-28.

Compares the episode in which Tom is sent by Squire Western to Sophia to plead Blifil's cause with the scene in which Sophia finally accepts Tom, arguing that in the latter the situation is artificial but the language expresses "the relationship between Sophia and her situation as opposed to simply treating her as an aspect of that situation" (p. 121). Bell sees Sophia's witty manipulation of language and Tom's broken syntax as a demonstration of Sophia's "self-conscious manipulation of the conventions" (p. 123) of marriage proposals. This mixing of real psychology and the artificiality of comic ritual, he sees as a combination of the aesthetic of the novel and the aesthetic of the theater (citing Molière, Restoration comedy, and opera) which will ultimately lead to Jane Austen's "complete fusion of two aesthetic modes" (p. 127).

3 BEVAN, C. H. K. "The Unity of Fielding's Amelia." Renaissance and Modern Studies, 14 (Oct.), 90-110.

Argues that Amelia is anti-Mandevillian; that it is "a fruitful union of moral vision and representational techniques" (p. 90); that it is an effective dramatization of the conflict between the individual and social mores and institutions; and that it is a partial failure because of inconsistencies in technique and intention. Bevan sees the Booth household as Fielding's effective narrative demonstration of a benevolent anti-Mandevillian morality and Dr. Harrison as its ineffective "mouthpiece" (p. 94). Fielding tests this morality in "situational" (p. 96) conflict (Booth's adultery with Miss Matthews). Amelia establishes even more firmly than Tom Jones that the individual's surrender to unsocial passions leads to personal isolation, and that "mixed" characters are capable of causing real suffering. The novel is weakened because Fielding does not rely completely enough on the narrative conflict he has established; both his and Dr. Harrison's narrative intrusions simplify and confuse the novel's morality. Bevan believes the overly long Miss Matthews' story demonstrates Fielding's tendency for baroque elaboration.

4 BRAUDY, LEO. "Fielding," in his Narrative Form in History and Fiction. Princeton: Princeton University Press, pp. 91-212.

Reviewed by M. C. Battestin, MLQ, 31 (1970), 508-11; Benjamin Boyce, SAQ, 69 (1970), 547-48; John A. Dussinger, JEGP, 70 (1971), 676-79; Susan Gubar, ELN, 8 (1971), 331-34; Michael Morrisroe, EE, 1 (1970), 70-71; George H. Nadel, AHR, 77 (1972), 730-31; Irène Simon, E Studies, 54 (1973), 395-98; Grant L. Voth, ECS, 5 (1971), 172-74; JNL, 30 (Mar. 1970), 10-11; YR, 60 (1971), xviii-xxiv.

Argues that "Fielding's ideas for the possibilities of his 'new species of writing' arise . . . from a background of past historiographical practice." Along with Hume, Montesquieu, and Voltaire, he was "one of the first to believe that the role of the historian necessitated a commitment to the chronicling of customs and classes" (p. 93), but Fielding also believed that his novels were to be "exercises in the reinvigoration of perceptions that have been dulled by the overheated fantasies of romance writers and 'romancing historians'" (pp. 94-95). Braudy sees Joseph Andrews and Jonathan Wild as "epistemological and aesthetic manifestoes, in which Fielding, faced by the problems of an embryonic literary mode, explores in minute detail its claims to approximate reality"; in Tom Jones and Amelia "he has begun to formulate his own categories" (p. 94). Braudy discusses Joseph Andrews as "an experiment in writing about life without a deductive pattern, an experiment in using facts properly to convey a plausible world" (p. 96), and as an illustration of the discrepancy between theoretical statement and actual experience. In Jonathan Wild Braudy sees the characters' attempts "to manipulate abstractions in order to understand the multiplicity and confusion of their lives" as parallel to the narrator's "various techniques of history" (p. 134); through these techniques Fielding explores "the public, the structured, the institutionalized" (pp. 121-22). Thus, "almost every character in Jonathan Wild is caught in a web of self-imposed pattern . . . like Adams, they do not have the sense of other possibilities that is necessary to live in the world" (p. 142). In Tom Jones Fielding implies that "only by admitting that his general pattern is arbitrary can the historian be free to demonstrate what he believes to be specifically true. Pattern by its nature falsifies" (p. 145). Braudy then examines the several artifices of the novel (the narrator's imposition of arbitrary order, the human habit of generalization from incomplete evidence, and causality). Braudy, arguing for a developing sense of the possibilities in history, sees Amelia as closer to the real world than the "laboratory world" (p. 180) of Tom Jones. He thinks Amelia "more real and more uncertain" but "still a created world, embodied in a work of literature" (p. 181). Specifically, Braudy discusses the reaction of various characters to experience (some of whom misinterpret and some manipulate it), "the revitalizing of public institutions through individual reflection and action" (p. 196), and the causal justification of institutions. Braudy concludes that "the process of Fielding's fiction attempts to free the reader from the false forms imposed by other literary structurings of actuality" (p. 211).

For another view of Fielding's use of history, see 1968.B36. See dissertation 1967.B12.

5 BROOKS, DOUGLAS. "Symbolic Numbers in Fielding's Joseph Andrews," in Silent Poetry: Essays in Numerological Analysis. Edited by Alastair Fowler. London: Routledge & Kegan Paul, pp. 234-60.

For a slightly fuller treatment, see his later essay (1973.B6).

6 CORDASCO, FRANCESCO. Eighteenth-Century Bibliographies: Handlists of Critical Studies Relating to Smollett, Richardson, Sterne, Fielding, Dibdin, Eighteenth-Century Medicine, Eighteenth-Century Novel, Goodwin, Gibbon, Young, and Burke. To Which is Added John P. Anderson's Bibliography of Smollett. Metuchen, N.J.: Scarecrow Press, pp. 98-118.

Reprint of 1948.B1 without additions or corrections.

7 DIRCKS, RICHARD J. "Cumberland, Richardson, and Fielding: Changing Patterns in the Eighteenth Century Novel." Research Studies Washington State University, 38, no. 4 (Dec.), 291-99.

Argues that "Cumberland found the source of the sentimentalism of his second novel, Henry, in the work of Fielding" (p. 295). Briefly compares Henry and Tom Jones to illustrate that although Cumberland's benevolence is broader-based, it still relies for its dramatization on "techniques" borrowed from Fielding.

8 DONALDSON, IAN. "High and Low Life: Fielding and the Uses of Inversion," in his The World Upside-Down: Comedy from Jonson to Fielding. Oxford: Clarendon Press, pp. 183-206.

Reviewed by Brian Corman, MP, 70 (1972), 68-70; Harold E. Pagliaro, GaR, 25 (1971), 376-78; Roger Warren, N&Q, n.s. 19 (1972), 396-99; TLS, 9 April 1971, p. 415.

In this study of the tropes of an upside-down world, Donaldson argues that Fielding borrows the apocalyptic myth and the notion that high and low are merging from the Scriblerians (Pope, Swift, Gay, etc.), but that Fielding gradually "converts the Tory satirists' despondent myth of a civilization falling to ruins to more optimistic comic ends" (p. 189). Donaldson briefly examines the evolution from Tom Thumb, through The Author's Farce ("a good-natured romp," p. 194), Jonathan Wild (which displays "Fielding's cheerful trust in the basic worthiness of low life," p. 198), to his other novels with their last minute reprieves and egalitarian comedy. Fielding masters a comedy in which social distinction seems artificial "in face of human passion and incompetence" (p. 7).

9 _____. "The Clockwork Novel: Three Notes on an Eighteenth-Century Analogy." Review of English Studies, n.s. 21, no. 81, 14-22.

Examines the characteristic eighteenth-century clockwork analogy to establish its philosophical background and then examines the presentation of time in Tom Jones and Tristram Shandy. Donaldson establishes that Fielding is aware of the analogy, probably as used by Locke and Hobbes, and then briefly shows him rejecting the dramatic unities of "the racing clock" in Tom Jones.

10 DULCK, JEAN. "Henry Fielding, Joseph Andrews," in Samuel Richardson, Pamela par Christian Pons . . . Henry Fielding, Joseph Andrews par Jean Dulck . . . Paris: A. Colin, pp. 169-265.

Dulck begins with a biographical summary of Fielding's life and career and then offers a naive and old-fashioned psychological portrait of Fielding as a roast beef eating Englishman (see 1836.B4) who expresses his emotions with restraint and understatement. Thinks Joseph Andrews a Sartrian anti-novel (in opposition to the romanticism of Pamela); considers its predecessors (Cervantes, Lesage, and Marivaux); thinks Pamela and Joseph Andrews embody complementary attitudes to psychological questions, social relations, and moral principles. Dulck then repeats a number of conventional ideas about the book: it is structurally weak, expands the picaresque by instructing, adapts old genres like the epic to a new form, uses comedy to attack vanity and hypocrisy. Also suggests that Fielding managed the "durée" of the novel (in adjusting its rhythm to the important events) but had some lapses of style. In French.

11 EVANS, JAMES E. "Fiction Rather than Fact: A New Look at The King of the Beggars." University of Pennsylvania Library Chronicle, 36:110-114.

Argues that The King . . . is not fact but an "interesting case in the emergence of the new genre, the novel" (p. 113), sharing with Fielding affinities in style (the mock heroic) and narrative technique (self-conscious narrator). See 1967.B9.

12 GOLDGAR, BERTRAND A. "The Politics of Fielding's Coffee-House Politician." Philological Quarterly, 49, no. 3 (July), 424-29.

This historical article argues that Rape Upon Rape (The Coffee-House Politician) is the first serious attack on the Walpole administration and that behind the play lies the case of Francis Charteris, a "runner" for Walpole, who was found guilty of raping his maidservant. Justice Squeezum may be a caricature of Walpole.

See 1962.B2 and 1972.B18. A shortened version appears in 1976.B6.

*13 GRAVES, WILLIAM T. "National Characters in the Novels of Henry Fielding, Samuel Richardson, and Tobias Smollett." Dissertation, New York, 1970.

Studies the ways in which these three novelists used the contemporary concept of a national character for political, social, and artistic effect.

Source: Dissertation Abstracts, 31, no. 12 (June 1971), 6549A-50A.

14 HOWSON, GERALD. Thief-Taker General: The Rise and Fall of Jonathan Wild. London: Hutchinson, passim.

Reviewed by M. Richardson, New Statesman, 19 (June 1970), 888; Economist (London), 13 (June 1970), 71; Scriblerian, 3 (1971), 71; TLS, 7 Aug. 1970, p. 870.

A careful account of the career of Jonathan Wild and crime in general during the period. Fielding is briefly mentioned, for the Bow Street Runners (modeled on Wild's gang) and for his naive portrait of the criminal world in the novel.

15 JOBE, ALICE J. C. "Fielding's Novels: Selected Criticism (1940-1969)." Studies in the Novel, 2, no. 2 (Summer), 246-59.

Selected criticism on Amelia, Jonathan Wild, Joseph Andrews, Shamela, Tom Jones, and two or more works, as well as occasional critical biographies and dissertations after 1964. See dissertation 1970.A14.

16 KAUL, A. N. "The Adjudication of Fielding's Comedy," in his The Action of English Comedy: Studies in the Encounter of Abstraction and Experience from Shakespeare to Shaw. New Haven and London: Yale University Press, pp. 151-92.

Reviewed by M. S. Barranger, ETJ, 23 (1971), 358-59; Ralph Berry, Mosaic, 4, no. 4 (1971), 107-10; James R. Kincaid, JEGP, 70 (1971), 299-301; Richard Nickson, Independent Shavian, 9 (1970-71), 28-29.

Argues that Fielding's solution to the new sentimental love convention is not a return to the Restoration libertine convention. "He is a judge over both; and . . . both sentimentalism and libertinism stand convicted for . . . partial and misleading theories of love" (pp. 152-53). Kaul discusses Fielding's concept of love in Amelia, Joseph Andrews, Shamela, and especially Tom Jones; Fielding's comic confrontation between romance (the interpolated tales) and reality; and the moral dialectic of the novels (e.g., between Adams and the examples of depravity, hypocrisy, and cupidity). Kaul particularly sees Tom as moving slowly through the shoals of both sentimentalism and libertinism. He does not see Amelia as sentimental but as a continuation of the adjudication, with a symbolic "threat of negation at the novel's core, the sense of both external stress and crisis and inner weakness, guilt, loss --and yet somehow ultimate resilience" (p. 192).

17 LEDLIE, J. M. A. "Hard At It." Notes and Queries, 215 (March), 93-94.

Fielding used this slang phrase 120 years before the first instance recorded in Partridge's Dictionary of Slang.

18 MILLER, HENRY K. "The Voices of Henry Fielding: Style in Tom Jones," in The Augustan Milieu: Essays presented to Louis A. Landa. Edited by Henry K. Miller, Eric Rothstein, and G. S. Rousseau. Oxford: Clarendon Press, pp. 262-88.

First argues that Henry Fielding wants the reader to respond to him ("a successful comic dramatist, a political pamphleteer, a well-known wit, and (at the last) an important magistrate," p. 265) as "the 'actual' hero (the mind in which we are interested) in Tom Jones" (p. 267). Then argues that Fielding, slightly out of step with his own age, created the voices he would use in speaking to us from Renaissance rhetoric and the concept of "decorum" of style. Miller illustrates "the art of prosopopoeia, of reproducing or 'counterfeiting' modes of speech" (p. 267), in the novel which forces the reader to apprehend "at a level of complexity . . . the fictive event or predication, as such, and the implications surrounding it because of the cognitive-emotive envelope in which it is presented by the narrator" (p. 263). Specifically, he shows the ways in which Fielding modulates between high, middle ("the norm"), and low styles, as well as discussing epic allusion and echo and his use of several kinds of jargon, in order to create "the felt distinction between the narrator's point of view and the point of view implicit in the style of one or another mimetic voice" (p. 283). Finally, he briefly considers sentimentalism and skepticism in the novel, concluding that "there is no narrative voice of sentimentalism, as there is . . . of skepticism" (p. 287).

19 NASSAR, EUGENE P. "Complex Irony in Tom Jones," in his The Rape of Cinderella: Essays in Literary Continuity. Bloomington and London: Indiana University Press, pp. 71-84.

Reviewed by Jan Pinkerton, CE (33), 602-604.

Using Empson's (1958.B6) definition of double irony, which turns on both the sentimental and the sophisticated reader in order to dramatize "deep and large ambiguities of life in Tom Jones" (p. 84), Nassar argues that Fielding is irresolute himself, alternately sentimental and skeptical. He sees this dialectic revealed in style, in situation, and in character. He thinks him "an opportunist with Bridget and with all his characters" (p. 79), alternately "caring very much about them and . . . careless about them" (p. 78). These swings between sentimentalism and sophistication are "conditioned reflex" (p. 78) in Fielding and reflect his "complex set of attitudes towards life" (p. 81).

*20 NEUFELD, EVELYN. "The Historical Progression from the Picaresque Novel to the 'Bildungsroman' as shown in 'El Buscón,' 'Gil Blas,' 'Tom Jones,' and 'Wilhelm Meisters Lehrjahre.'" Dissertation, Washington, 1970.

A historical study illustrating the development from the seventeenth-century picaresque to the eighteenth-century Bildungsroman. Tom Jones has the "seeds" of the latter.
Source: Dissertation Abstracts, 31, no. 7 (Jan. 1971), 3514A-15A.

21 OLSHIN, TOBY A. "Pompey the Little: A Study in Fielding's Influence." Revue des Langues Vivantes, 36, no. 2, 117-24.
Sets out Coventry's several technical borrowings from Fielding: the prefatory material; the intrusions; the chapter headings; the pattern of narrative; contextual, structural and tonal parallels. Olshin argues that Coventry's omission of an introductory chapter and his interconnecting of characters in his revision of Pompey (between second and third editions) indicates a growing understanding of Fielding's art.

22 PARK, WILLIAM. "What Was New About the 'New Species of Writing'?" Studies in the Novel, 2, no. 2 (Summer), 112-30.
Argues that Richardson and Fielding founded a new species of writing which made use of familiar scenes, "writing to the moment," moral instruction, a digressive style, and humor. Nineteenth-century critics, stressing realism, saw Defoe as the founder of the novel; twentieth-century critics, trying to see the evolution of the form, attempted to trace it from the seventeenth century. Park constructs a model of the form as devised by Fielding and Richardson and then argues that only in Marianne by Marivaux, among earlier continental and English "novels," had this unique form been attempted.

23 POSTON, CHARLES. "The Novel as 'Exemplum': A Study of Fielding's Amelia." West Virginia University Philological Society Papers, 18:23-29.
In an attempt to "suggest that Amelia is a consistent artistic work . . . that . . . does not evidence a decline in Fielding's artistic sensibility" (p. 23), Poston argues that it is "an exemplum consistent in function with the Wilson and the Man of the Hill narratives" (p. 28). He sees a number of close parallels between the life of William Booth and these earlier exempla: the principal events are determined by chance and imprudence; they share specific subject matter; there is similarity in thematic development (illustrating benevolence). The only significant difference is that "Booth's life is directed solely to a world outside the novel itself. And it is this

methodical presentation of a moral lesson which is likely to disappoint the reader of Joseph Andrews and Tom Jones" (p. 28).

24 PRESTON, JOHN. "Tom Jones: Plot as Irony" and "Tom Jones: The 'Pursuit of True Judgment,'" in his The Created Self: The Reader's Role in Eighteenth Century Fiction. London: Heinemann; New York: Barnes & Noble, pp. 94-132.

Reviewed by John J. Richetti, Criticism, 13 (1971), 427-31; TLS, 5 March 1971, p. 276.

Reprint of 1966.B17 and 1968.B29.

25 RAWSON, C. J. "Nature's Dance of Death: Part I: Urbanity and Strain in Fielding, Swift, and Pope." Eighteenth-Century Studies, 3, no. 3 (Spring), 307-38.

Studies the dance image as the expression of an ideal literary aesthetic. "The patterned forms of 'couplet-rhetoric,' in verse and prose, are probably the most frequent and appropriate expressions of these ideals, as we should expect" (p. 314). After discussing a number of modern uses of the image (Yeats, Eliot, Roethke, Valéry, etc.), Rawson turns to Fielding's "characteristic idiom" (p. 316), couplet-prose "which shows these forms existing under strain, real or potential: the strains of disorderly or 'unnatural' fact, of powerful or unbalancing emotions, and finally of a painful skepticism of order" (pp. 315-16). As he compares Swift and Fielding, he ranges from the citing of "paired opposites" (p. 317) to a discussion of "a mode of statement which pretends to truths of unhesitating completeness, but of somewhat externalized quantity, whose clear outlines are blurred by doubts and by the loose ends of an introspective self-implication" (p. 319). Argues that Fielding's later prose no longer "conveys a confidence that things hang together even when an expected fitness has been betrayed" (p. 328); "all the tones of certainty and the air of overall grasp leave the impression, somehow, of being no longer real but a mere habit of mind, the relic of style" (p. 336).

Reprinted 1972.A9.

26 _____. "Nature's Dance of Death: Part II: Fielding's Amelia (with some comments on Defoe, Smollett, and George Orwell)." Eighteenth-Century Studies, 3, no. 4 (Summer), 491-522.

Argues that there is a radical uncertainty in Amelia between the brutal facts and Fielding's "rage" for order. "It seems instead to be that Fielding's world has ceased to make total sense, so that his reactions have become fragmentary" (p. 522). In order to examine this fundamental ambiguity, Rawson first briefly considers the interrelated ideas about fortune, passion, and fatalism in the novel. He then turns to the Newgate chapters, first looking carefully at the portrait of Thrasher and then at Blear-Eyed Moll (comparing Moll with Moll Flanders, a prostitute in 1984, and a bawd in Ferdinand Count Fathom). The unsettling aspect of Fielding's portraits is the contrast between the extremely grotesque and the reminders of order. Rawson then considers the altered tone of the narrative voice, finding the cool, even severe urbanity in radical imbalance with the reconstituted comic and sentimental material.

Reprinted 1972.A9. See 1969.B21 for a similar view of Fielding's novels.

*27 RAYNAL, MARGARET I. "A Study of Sarah Fielding's Novels." Dissertation, North Carolina-Chapel Hill, 1970.

Compares Sarah Fielding's ideas about human nature with Henry's and finds them similar.

Source: Dissertation Abstracts, 31, no. 5 (Nov. 1970), 2352A-53A.

28 ROBERT, FRÉDERIC. "Tom Jones: de Fielding à Philidor," in Roman et lumières au XVIIIe siècle. Paris: Editions sociales, pp. 360-65.

Describes the initial failure of the French musical comedy Tom Jones in 1765, with music by Philidor and script by Poinsinet, and its success when revised by Sedaine in 1766. The comédie lyrique based on the first sixteen chapters of the novel became as important in Europe as the 1750 de la Place translation of the novel. In French. See 1881.B2, 1960.B19.

29 ROGERS, PAT. "Fielding's Parody of Oldmixon." Philological Quarterly, 49, no. 2 (April), 262-66.

Sets out the parody of John Oldmixon in The Covent-Garden Journal for 29 Jan. 1752 (Fielding calls him Newmixon), written ten years after the hack, Oldmixon, had died. Rogers briefly argues that "Newmixon-Oldmixon exists fictively as an heuristic tool. Fielding uses his imaginary historical narrator to get at certain comic and satiric ends [the self-satisfaction of contemporary society]: but the main centre of attention is never the deficiencies of historiographic craft which are displayed" (p. 265).

30 ROY, G. ROSS. "French Stage Adaptations of Tom Jones." Revue de Littérature Comparée, 44, no. 1, 82-94.

Briefly sets out the popularity of the translated novel (1750) and then reviews the various stage adaptations, some of which were "based more or less on incidents in the novel . . . [and] others . . . placed Fielding's characters in situations wholly unrelated to the novel" (p. 94). Begins with Alexander Poinsinet's comic opera Tom Jones (1764), and includes Desforges' adaptation, as well as George Colman's The Jealous Wife (1761) and Piédefer's Sophie et Francourt (1783). See 1970.B28 and 1974.B22.

31 SELLERY, J'NAN. "Language and Moral Intelligence in the Enlightenment: Fielding's Plays and Pope's Dunciad, Part I." Enlightenment Essays, 1, no. 1 (Spring), 17-26.

Argues that both Pope and Fielding deflate the self-imposed "human impulse to pretentious verbosity" (p. 17) through the use of the theater as a metaphor. Sellery describes their concept of the unresponsive and disorderly audience and their awareness that this audience confused life and art. Specifically, Sellery discusses the ways in which Fielding exploits the aesthetic and moral confusions implicit in the play within a play in The Historical Register, among these the "ironic aural/oral strategies" (p. 24) of his play. See continuation 1970.B32.

32 ______. "Language and Moral Intelligence in the Enlightenment: Fielding's Plays and Pope's Dunciad, Part II." Enlightenment Essays, 1, no. 2 (Summer), 108-19.

In this half of his essay (see 1970.B31), Sellery compares Pope's narrator with the role of Medley in The Historical Register, as well as the imagery of ears (including bestial imagery) in the Dunciad with hearing and perceiving in Fielding's play. He concludes that "both authors consciously recognize the eighteenth-century audience's marked incapacity to hear and make of it a metaphor for the human condition" (p. 118). The "bumbling playwrights and nodding kings" are also controlling images of broken rule "repressive of man's capacity for enlightened thought and action" (p. 119). See 1972.B10.

33 SHERBO, ARTHUR. "Fielding's Dogs." Notes and Queries, 215 (Aug.), 302-303.

Most of the names of the dogs who attacked Parson Adams came from Thomas D'Urfey's "Solon's Song" in Marriage-Hater Match'd.

34 SHESGREEN, SEAN. "The Moral Function of Thwackum, Square, and Allworthy." Studies in the Novel, 2, no. 2 (Summer), 159-67.

Argues that Fielding patterns these three characters on the three motives for benevolence expressed in his "An Essay on the Knowledge of the Characters of Men." Square represents the philosophic love of virtue, Thwackum the allurements and terrors of religion, and Allworthy active sympathy. Only active sympathy is a real basis for "good nature." See 1972.A11 and dissertation 1970.A18.

35 STEVICK, PHILIP. The Chapter in Fiction: Theories of Narrative Division. Syracuse: Syracuse University Press, pp. 23-28 and passim.

Reviewed by E. A. Bloom, JEGP, 70 (1971), 524-26; J. Ricchetti, Criticism, 13 (1971), 427-31.

In this book which examines the psychological, formal, and historical reasons for division in a novel (including chapters on conventions, order, the shaping imagination, and history), Fielding is only briefly discussed. Stevick finds Fielding's theory of chapter division in Joseph Andrews "arch [and] puzzlingly ironic" (p. 25), and his practice determined by the reader's attention span. He also mentions Fielding's use of the anticipatory cadence, repetitive form (contrast and thematic grouping), and epic parallels.

36 STITZEL, JUDITH G. "Blifil and Henry Fielding's Conception of Evil." West Virginia University Bulletin Philological Papers, 17, series 70, nos. 12-17 (June), 16-24.

A careful study of the character of Blifil to illustrate Stitzel's conviction "that Fielding's sexual ethic forms the substratum of his total ethical system" (p. 23). She examines Blifil's total egotism, his inability to love, and his deep ability to hate, which is all hidden in circumspection and deliberation. Thus, for him, sex is power and an unnaturally cultivated decadent appetite. See dissertation 1968.A17.

37 WEINBROT, HOWARD D. "Chastity and Interpolation: Two Aspects of Joseph Andrews." Journal of English and Germanic Philology, 69, no. 1 (Jan.), 14-31.

Argues that, contrary to the accepted critical notion, Joseph is not a comic prig; he is "sexually normative" (p. 15) when he resists Lady Booby, Slipslop, and Betty, and illustrates both the proper control of passion and an admirable faithfulness. The three interpolated tales (Leonora, Wilson, Leonard and Paul), Weinbrot argues, illustrate the alternative to such decent behavior and "to the world of a benevolent God and benevolent narrator" (p. 31). This world is sometimes "grim, savage, and terrifying" (p. 26), and comments on "the pernicious doctrines and moral and artistic confusions that Fielding believed he saw in Pamela" (p. 31).

For another view of Joseph, see 1966.A16 and 1971.B26. For a discussion of the interpolated tales, see 1968.B14 and 1973.B34.

*38 WESS, ROBERT V. "Action, Character, and Thought in Tom Jones, Pride and Prejudice, Emma, and Persuasion." Dissertation, Chicago, 1970.

Source: McNamee, 1969-1973, p. 320. See 1970.B39.

39 _____. "The Probable and the Marvelous in Tom Jones." Modern Philology, 68, no. 1 (Aug.), 32-45.

Using Fielding's chapter on the marvelous in Tom Jones, Wess answers Watt's charges of improbability (1957.B17) by arguing for a new criterion for probability in the novel. Fielding's position ("what is probable is what a given character is likely to do," p. 34) makes the marvelous probable, given unusual characters and unusual incidents. Wess points out the manipulation of readers' moral concerns by Fielding's clearly established hierarchy of values in which only merit and fortune shift. He examines the relation between merit and fortune in Tom and Blifil, Tom and Sophia, and Western/Bridget and Tom, as each character acts out of his own values and as values conflict with each other (and with real moral worth). The denouement is largely brought about by interlocking plausible choices of various characters, and Wess insists that the improbable coincidences of the plot were deliberate plants by Fielding to emphasize that Tom's fortune was partly coincidental and might "never have occurred at all" (p. 44). See 1969.B7, 1970.B1, and dissertation 1970.B38.

40 WOODCOCK, GEORGE. "'Colonel Jack' and 'Tom Jones': Aspects of a Changing Century." Wascana Review, 5, no. 1, 67-73.

An article on cultural history describing Defoe's Colonel Jack as the last of the early stage of picaresque fiction and Tom Jones as "the maturity of the genre" (p. 68). Sees Defoe's novel as retaining "the crude vigour that distinguished the 1680's from the true Augustan age" (p. 70); Tom Jones "suggests the altered social atmosphere" (p. 71). Sees Fielding's world as stable and hierarchical in its sexual mores and its class attitudes.

1971

1971 A BOOKS

*1 BREWERTON, MARTI J. "Henry Fielding's The Mock Doctor: or The Dumb Lady Cur'd and The Miser: A Critical Edition." Dissertation, North Dakota, 1971.
An old spelling text of the two plays and a study of Fielding's adaptation from Molière.
Source: Dissertation Abstracts, 33, no. 1 (July 1972), 269A.

*2 EVANS, JAMES E. "Fielding's Community of Fiction: Fielding's Supporting Characters in Joseph Andrews, Tom Jones, and Amelia." Dissertation, Pennsylvania University, 1971.
Fielding creates communities (families and larger social groups) of supporting characters around his heroes (Adams, Jones, and Booth) to give their actions meaning.
Source: Dissertation Abstracts, 32, no. 8 (Feb. 1972), 4560A.

3 FIELDING, HENRY. The History of the Adventures of Joseph Andrews and of His Friend Mr. Abraham Adams and An Apology for the Life of Mrs. Shamela Andrews. Edited by Douglas Brooks. Oxford Paperbacks. London, Oxford, New York: Oxford University Press, 422 pp.
Reissue of 1970.A8.

*4 LOFTIS, JOHN E., III. "The Moral Art of Henry Fielding." Dissertation, Emory, 1971.
Fielding is neither one of the conservative Augustan satirists nor one of the moderns. He bridges the two, creating new forms and values and using old.
Source: Dissertation Abstracts, 32, no. 11 (May 1972), 6382-A.

*5 NAGOURNEY, PETER. "Law in the Novels of Henry Fielding." Dissertation, Chicago, 1971.
Source: McNamee, 1969-1973, p. 321.

*6 NELSON, JUDITH K. "Fielding and Molière." Dissertation, Rice, 1971.
Studies the influence of Molière on the comic theory and technique of Fielding.
Source: Dissertation Abstracts, 32, no. 4 (Oct. 1971), 2064A.

*7 NEWHOUSE, EDWARD B. "Poetic Theory and Practice in the Novels of Henry Fielding." Dissertation, Ball State, 1971.

The interpolated tales are like Fielding's rehearsals or scene-within-a-scenes in his dramas; they have both a thematic and structural relationship to the whole.
Source: Dissertation Abstracts, 32, no. 9 (March, 1972), 5194-A.

*8 PASSLER, SUSAN M. "Theatricality, The Eighteenth Century, and Fielding's Tom Jones." Dissertation, North Carolina, 1971.
Studies the relationship between the heightened self-awareness of theater, the philosophical aim of self-consciousness, and Fielding's self-conscious form in Tom Jones (obtrusive narrator, etc.).
Source: Dissertation Abstracts, 32, no. 12 (June, 1972), 6941A.

*9 RUDOLPH, VALERIE C. "Theatrical Verisimilitude and Political Belief in the Plays of Henry Fielding." Dissertation, Iowa, 1971.
Fielding's plays of theatrical self-reference (rehearsal plays, burlesques, etc.) became increasingly political and not just a critique of bad art.
Source: Dissertation Abstracts, 32,no. 3 (Sept. 1971), 1485A.

*10 SULLIVAN, WILLIAM A. "Fielding's Dramatic Comedies: The Influence of Congreve and Molière." Dissertation, Louisiana, 1971.
Traces the influence in form and content of Congreve and Molière on Fielding, who is not a slavish follower.
Source: Dissertation Abstracts, 32, no. 7 (Jan. 1972), 3966A.

1971 B SHORTER WRITINGS

1 AMORY, HUGH. "Fielding's Lisbon Letters." Huntington Library Quarterly, 35, no. 1, 65-83.
Reviews the "Dobson" last letters (1911.B2) and a new last letter (offered at Sotheby's in 1962), reprinting the long four page "Dobson" letter. Attempts to date the letter accurately, reargues the biographical information that can be gleaned from it, computes Fielding's growing financial crisis, and briefly sets out Fielding's complex and seemingly harsh attitude toward his wife, children, and Margaret Collier.

1971

2 _____. "Henry Fielding and the Criminal Legislation of 1751-2." Philological Quarterly, 50, no. 2 (April), 175-92.

Careful review of the "Committee of 1751" (for the reform of criminal law) and Fielding's relation to the work of the committee. Amory rejects Radzinowicz's (1948.B8) notion that the committee had any guiding spirit of liberal reform or any theoretical structure at all. They shared with Fielding, and their age, a notion that crime increased as a result of idleness and luxury, neither well defined. Reproducing parallel passages in the Murder Bill, Fielding's Examples of the Interposition of Providence in the Detection and Punishment of Murder, and the King's address at the opening of Parliament in 1752, Amory argues that there was little or no influence but mere shared assumptions. He concludes that the portrait of Fielding as the man behind the scenes is quite inaccurate; "there is little or no evidence that he possessed the widespread influence commonly attributed to him" (p. 189). See 1962.B7, 1966.A26, and 1967.B35. See dissertation 1964.A1.

3 _____. "Shamela as Aesopic Satire." Journal of English Literary History, 38, no. 2 (June), 239-53.

Argues that the ambiguity about the authorship of Shamela was deliberate: the act of a fictional Aesopian slave "too confused, too kind, too uninformed or too unintelligent to analyse the real nature of the satiric subject" (p. 252). This "subject" is the politics of the parvenus, perfectly embodied in Robert Walpole but also reflected in Cibber's Apology, Middleton's Life, and Richardson's Pamela. Amory does not think that Shamela is Fielding's attempt to criticize the sexual morality of Pamela; instead it is an analysis of the victim's complicity in "political" corruption. Amory sees these "politics" worked out in a rather complex, but interrelated, series of literary, religious, and political allusions. See 1965.B7 and 1968.B31.

4 BARNES, JOHN L. "Lady Bellaston: Fielding's Use of Charactonym." South-Central Names Institute Publication 1 (Of Edsels and Marauders). Edited by Fred Tarpley and Ann Moseley. Commerce, Tex.: Names Institute Press, pp. 114-16.

An article arguing that Fielding means to suggest that Lady Bellaston is obese and has a bell-shaped "derrière." Dismisses the suffix "ton" as unimportant to his argument. Largely ignores the English usage of the word "arse."

5 B[ATTESTIN], M[ARTIN] C. "Henry Fielding," in The New Cambridge Bibliography of English Literature, 2 (1660-1800). Edited by George Watson. Cambridge: University Press, pp. 925-48.

Briefly discusses the few surviving manuscripts, lists a few bibliographies (including a Russian one), the important collections of Fielding's works, a few selections, and a fairly complete list of editions of individual works (including translations). Section 2 opens by citing two bibliographies of secondary works on Fielding and then chronologically lists these works from 1744 through 1968, occasionally briefly annotating entries. Chronology is only violated when a critic has written more than once on Fielding; then all of the critic's works are listed when his name first appears.

*6 BEASLEY, JERRY C. "Minor Fiction of the 1740's: A Background Study of the Novels of Richardson, Fielding, and Smollett." Dissertation, Northwestern, 1971.

Describes the minor fiction of the 1740s (270 full length works of fiction) and sets these novelists in this "tradition."

Source: Dissertation Abstracts, 32, no. 6 (Dec. 1971), 3242A. See 1972.B3.

7 BRACK, O. M., JR. and CURT A. ZIMANSKY. "The Charles B. Woods Fielding Collection." Books at Iowa (Nov.), pp. 26-32.

Describes Woods' lifelong work on Fielding and lists Iowa's holdings under three categories: Fielding's published works, works to which Fielding contributed, and works associated with Fielding.

8 BRADBURY, MALCOLM. "The Comic Novel in Sterne and Fielding," in The Winged Skull: Papers from the Laurence Sterne Bicentenary Conference. Edited by Arthur H. Cash and John M. Stedmond. London: Methuen, pp. 124-31.

Briefly argues that Fielding is writing in the central comic mode of the novel (with a special kind of action--a reverse tragedy--and a special kind of universe, in which manners become morals), and that Tristram Shandy is not only technically an anti-novel but also "the working out of a different comic typology" (p. 127), which Bradbury calls the irony of fictiveness. See also 1973.B5.

9 COLMER, DOROTHY. "Fielding's Debt to John Lacy in The Mock Doctor." English Language Notes, 9, no. 1 (Sept.), 35-39.

Granting that Fielding followed Molière's text rather than using John Lacy's adaptation of Le Médecin Malgré Lui as a source, Colmer argues that Fielding's additions may have been influenced by Lacy. Although the spirit of Fielding's play differs sharply from Lacy's, "scenes 13, 14, 15 and 18 of Fielding's Mock Doctor . . . correspond to episodes in The Dumb Lady" (p. 36), and the play may contain other random verbal parallels. Fielding may also have borrowed from Lacy's The Old Troop (1664).

For a more careful analysis, see 1900.B2. For another discussion of sources, see 1952.B5.

10 DEWEY, NICHOLAS. "Fielding: 'Justice Dingo.'" Notes and Queries, 216 (Feb.), 67.

Fielding was once referred to in this uncomplimentary slang way by a contemporary, Thomas Edwards.

11 DONALDSON, IAN. "Drama from 1710 to 1780," in Dryden to Johnson. History of Literature in the English Language, edited by Roger Lonsdale. Vol. 4. London: Barrie & Jenkins, pp. 190-225.

Reviewed in TLS, 3 Dec. 1971, p. 1526.

Discusses the varied nature of Fielding's plays, his development of good-natured comedy, and his plays in the burlesque tradition, particularly his burlesque tragedy (Tom Thumb), and his political plays (Pasquin and The Historical Register). Bibliography for students included.

12 EAVES, T. C. DUNCAN and BEN KIMPEL. Samuel Richardson: A Biography. Oxford: Clarendon Press, passim.

Reviewed by F. W. Hilles, YR, 61 (1971), 109-17; F. R. Leavis, DQR, 1 (1971), 175-79; Ellen Moers, NYRB, 10 Feb. 1972, pp. 27-31; W. B. Warde, SoHR, 6 (1972), 417-18; TLS, 9 July 1971, p. 807; JNL, 31 (1971), 1-2.

Reviews Fielding's relationship with Richardson. Briefly touches on Shamela, which Fielding may have been "none too proud of" (p. 127) and which he probably wrote without knowing "that Richardson was the author of Pamela" (p. 293), and Joseph Andrews; carefully reviews their relationship from 1749 onwards. "There are some signs of friendliness during the publication of Clarissa and many signs of enmity, on Richardson's part at least, after the publication of Tom Jones" (p. 294). They set out Richardson's public and private enmity to Fielding, to Tom Jones and Amelia, and Fielding's last hit at Richardson in The Journal of a Voyage to Lisbon, concluding that Richardson's "bitterness against Fielding in 1749 has done as much as anything to injure his reputation as a person"

(p. 295), that they were not publicly quarreling at the time of Fielding's death, and that they had much in common. See 1948.B5.

13 FREEDMAN, WILLIAM. "Joseph Andrews: Fielding's Garden of the Perverse." Tennessee Studies in Literature, 16:35-45.
Contending that for Fielding good nature is the "essential" nature of man and ill nature a bestial distortion, Freedman examines Fielding's "Jonsonian" bestiary in Joseph Andrews. He examines how, directly and indirectly, Fielding links the relatively ineffectual Mrs. Slipslop and Beau Didapper with a cow and a bird respectively, and the more harmful Parson Trulliber, Mrs. Tow-wouse, and the hunting squire with a pig, a dragon, and a hunting cur. This bestiary metamorphoses them.

*14 GRAF, SUSANNA. Das aussereheliche Kind und die Problematik der Illegitimität in englischen Romanen von 'Tom Jones' bis 'Lady Chatterley's Lover.' Zürich: Juris.
Source: MHRA, 46 (1971), 334.

15 HILSKÝ, MARTIN. "A Note on the Style of Tristram Shandy." Prague Studies in English, 14:41-55.
Comparing Tom Jones and Tristram Shandy, Hilský argues that "the dialogues of the characters and the narrator's discourse are much more 'dialogical' and therefore more dramatic [in Tristram Shandy] than those in Tom Jones" (p. 52). Specifically examines the close-knit subordinate clauses, the synonyms and logical links, the slow and ceremonious introduction of story and character, and the "one way communication of Fielding's narrator to his reader" (p. 51).

16 JENKINS, RALPH E. "A Note on Hogarth and Fielding's 'Shamela.'" Notes and Queries, 216 (Sept.), 335.
Hogarth's two engravings of 1736 entitled "Before" and "After" may have given Fielding the plot and character of Shamela.

17 KISHLER, THOMAS C. "Fielding's Experiments with Fiction in The Champion." Journal of Narrative Technique, 1:95-107.
Demonstrates Fielding's familiarity with the ethos of Augustan satiric fiction by examining his manipulation of persona (in his creation of the Vinegar family) and his use of various satiric functions: the impersonated letter writer, the non-ironic exemplum, the mock serious account of a fictional or semi-fictional situation reported as

fact, and especially Job Vinegar's imaginary journey. Kishler links this specialized use of fantastic fiction to its conventional use in periodic literature and in full-fledged satires like Gulliver's Travels.

18 LONGMIRE, SAMUEL E. "The Critical Significance of Rambler 4." New Rambler, 3:40-47.

Argues that "it is useful to read [Johnson's essay] not only as a covert attack on Fielding, but as a sophisticated argument about the nature of novelistic fiction" (p. 40). Uses Tom Jones to illustrate Johnson's argument: specifically considers the balancing of virtues and vices and Fielding's moral failure, caused by his inability to create psychologically believable characters (greater psychological realism in the Bellaston affair would have made Tom "more guilt-ridden," p. 44). Johnson approved of Amelia because "Fielding takes a harder and generally more realistic view of human shortcomings and social ills than he did in Tom Jones" (p. 46). See 1951.B4.

19 MALHOTRA, K. K. "'The Art of Life'--a study of Fielding's Amelia." Panjab University Research Bulletin (Arts), 2, no. 1 (March), 29-38.

Despite an awareness of modern studies on "prudence" and irony, Malhotra reads the novel autobiographically (Booth is Fielding) and sentimentally (a Richardson-like "gentle" novel). Thinks "the theme . . . the triumph of true love" (p. 31) and "adultery . . . the main target" (p. 34). A study of domestic relationships, of the "fascination and the hold that evil exercises on the wrong-doer" (p. 33), and of the twin ideals of virtue and innocence, this novel is Fielding's Art of Life.

20 MAUROCORDATO, ALEXANDRE. "The Picaresque Novel as a Variation on the 'Game of the Goose,'" in Le Voyage Dans La Litterature Anglo-Saxonne. Actes du Congrès de Nice (1971). Paris: Marcel Didier, pp. 71-80.

Sets up parallels between this ancient game and the picaresque novel, using Joseph Andrews as an illustration of lineal and chronological structure, the unifying element of the hero, and the vertical movement through social strata of the nomad hero. Provides two charts to show how the game can be "integrated into" the picaresque novel, specifically into Joseph Andrews, which he says "boils down to a pilgrimage" (p. 78).

21 MICHON, JACQUES. "Du Beggar's Opera au Grub-Street Opera." Etudes Anglaises, 24 (Jan.-March), 166-70.

Reviews this new genre, the ballad opera, which Michon thinks the predecessor of the German Singspiel and Gilbert and Sullivan. For Michon, Gay is the innovator in this form, which not only parodies the Italian opera but makes song an integral part of the play; Fielding merely imitates The Beggar's Opera. Gay's social and moral satire is also more far-ranging than Fielding's, which is narrowly centered on the Court. Michon even thinks The Grub-Street Opera inappropriately titled, as Gay's opera is not.
In part a review of 1968.A7.

22 MORRISSEY, L. J. "Henry Fielding and the Ballad Opera." Eighteenth-Century Studies, 4, no. 4 (Summer), 386-402.
Attempts to reconstruct the reasons for Fielding's musical choices in The Grub-Street Opera and musical choices for ballad operas in general. Fielding partly relied on the musical taste of his friend James Ralph (a third of the songs in The Grub-Street Opera had been used earlier by Ralph in The Fashionable Lady). Morrissey notes three influences on the writers of ballad operas: the limited number of tunes used (probably reflecting the audience's insistence on "popular" songs), growth of musical repertoires, and John Watt, who not only printed most of the ballad operas, but also owned the only wood block cuts to reproduce ballad opera tunes. See 1966.B19, 1972.B22, and 1973.A11.

*23 NIEHUS, EDWARD L. "The Nature and Development of the Quixote Figure in the Eighteenth-Century Novel." Dissertation, Minnesota, 1971.
Looks at the developing use of the Quixote figure, from the intolerant and satiric view of Swift, through Goldsmith, and including Fielding's innocent idealists.
Source: Dissertation Abstracts, 32, no. 6 (Dec. 1971), 3319A-20A.

24 PALMER, E. TAIWO. "Fielding's Tom Jones Reconsidered." English, 20, no. 107 (Summer), 45-50.
A reading of the novel that grows out of recent criticism. Emphasizes the novel's Cervantic dimension (a corrective satire directed at the world and the hero) and its Christian scheme (sees it as fall, repentance, and redemption). Argues that the keeper of this paradise (Allworthy) is a short-sighted deus figure, and that Tom needs heart, head, and prudence (a complex moral ideal). He briefly considers Tom's various passionate encounters with women (not excusing his behavior with Lady Bellaston), Fielding's

keeping the serious material of the novel comic through farce and the mock-heroic, and Sophia as the middle path of wisdom.

25 _____. "Irony in 'Tom Jones.'" Modern Language Review, 66, no. 3 (July), 497-510.

This precise article begins by identifying and illustrating various kinds of irony in Tom Jones ("the perfection of Fielding's art," p. 497), among them simple "praise/blame inversion," "tonal irony," "linguistic irony" (different from tonal in that the surface meaning is supposed to seem sane and reasonable; ideal for exposing near perfect characters like Allworthy), "rhetorical irony" (exposed in its argument or elaboration), the irony embodied in a falling clause, and finally the irony of characters who expose themselves. Then, using Empson's useful distinction between double and single irony (1958.B6), Palmer discusses double irony as a structural device (the pairing of people and events neither of which is ideal) and "as an element of texture" (p. 505). He examines the character of Allworthy, the passage on prudence, Fielding's ambivalent attitude to Tom (particularly in his relations with Lady Bellaston). Concludes that Fielding's style is not prosaic and straightforward but complex and ironic, and his meaning resides in this irony. See 1965.A15 and 1967.A12.

26 _____. "Fielding's Joseph Andrews: A Comic Epic in Prose." English Studies, 52, no. 4, 331-39.

Briefly argues that Joseph Andrews corresponds to Le Bossu's conception of the epic, then turns to an examination of the blending of Fielding's latitudinarian ideas and his epic conception (discussing the development of the interrelated concepts of charity, married love, and "agape"). Finally Palmer argues that Fielding's comic intention is to show how the two objects of laughter, Joseph ("a ridiculous prig," p. 337) and Adams, experience life, and how Joseph is educated by it. See 1931.A9 and 1970.B37.

27 PALMER, EUSTACE. "Amelia - The Decline of Fielding's Art." Essays in Criticism, 21, no. 2 (April), 135-51.

Sets out to demonstrate that Amelia is an artistic falling off. Though Fielding uses many conventional devices: irony, juxtaposition (Mrs. Atkinson is a foil to Amelia), contrast, burlesque, and mock epic, even adding analogy to underline his theme (Palmer also examines the deliberate parallels with the Aeneid and Othello); Palmer contends that "the morality in this novel is largely stated rather than demonstrated" (p. 144). Dismisses the defense that sees Amelia as different in kind (because it is about more serious matters), and examines Fielding's inadequate use of his traditional devices and "irrelevances, inconsistencies and examples of faulty structuring which point to a serious decline in the author's control over the events of the story" (p. 146). Particularly concerned with the inadequacy of irony and imagery in Amelia.

For other views, see 1960.B23, 1967.B26, 1971.B29, and 1975.B12.

28 PAULSON, RONALD. "The Pilgrimage and the Family: Structures in the Novels of Fielding and Smollett," in Tobias Smollett: Bicentennial Essays Presented to Lewis M. Knapp. Edited by G. S. Rousseau and P.-G. Boucé. New York: Oxford University Press, pp. 57-78.

In this interesting mythic analysis, Paulson first argues that "strange parallels began to occur" (p. 58) between Smollett and Fielding (in the use of third-person narrator, extended background for the hero, etc.), and then shows the way each uses the two forces (the adventures on the road and "the relationships and hereditary pressures" [p. 61] of the family) to organize Tom Jones and Peregrine Pickle. Paulson contends that in both novels the relationships within a family come to dominate, "replacing the shifting relationships of chance encounters on a road" (p. 65). He briefly discusses the tradition of the picaresque and that of the spiritual pilgrimage, discussing each novel as a working out of the Christian myth (fall, expulsion, forgiveness, God or novelist as creator, the reenactment of the parents' sexual sin). "The excesses of Amelia can be traced back to the gradual shifting of responsibility from son to parent and environment in Joseph Andrews and Tom Jones, as well as in Smollett's Peregrine Pickle" (p. 74). Finally Paulson briefly considers this mythic ordering in later novels (Tristram Shandy, Humphry Clinker, Vicar of Wakefield, and Pride and Prejudice).

29 POSTON, CHARLES D. "The Novel as 'Exemplum': A Study of Fielding's Amelia." West Virginia University Bulletin Philological Papers, 18, series 72, nos. 1-3 (Sept.), 23-29.

Argues that Amelia has been undervalued because it has not been seen in its true genre, the exemplum. Poston compares Amelia to two earlier exempla of Fielding's--

Wilson's and the Man of the Hill's narratives--in event and thematic development. Finally argues that Amelia is embedded in "life" as the two narratives are in their novels. See 1971.B27 for another view.

30 RAWSON, C. J. "Fielding and Smollett," in Dryden to Johnson. History of Literature in the English Language, edited by Roger Lonsdale. Vol. 4. London: Barrie & Jenkins, pp. 259-301.

Reviewed in TLS, 3 Dec. 1971, p. 1526.

Considers the influence of Fielding's dramatic career on his novels, noting Fielding's use of stylized genres (which often include commenting or participating authors and call attention to themselves as artifice). Rawson sees Jonathan Wild as Fielding's "real beginning as a comic novelist . . . where parody . . . is systematically transcended and overwhelmed by the comic action" (p. 268). Joseph Andrews is a further development of parody, "the comic," and "the mock-heroic" (used mostly as stylistic ornamentation). Largely ignores 1943.B3, which argues that Wild antedates Joseph Andrews. In Tom Jones, Fielding's "patrician hauteur and moral generosity" (p. 274) create a "distinctly Augustan style" and a new sexual ethic that is sharply unlike Richardson's. Finally, Rawson feels that in Amelia Fielding's developed technique is under an "inward strain" which "stiffens and deadens" the book. Despite his idiomorphic phrases, Rawson mentions conventional themes in Fielding criticism: the intrusive narrator, sexual morality, style, moral seriousness, and the failure of Amelia. Bibliography for students included.

31 ______. "Some Considerations on Authorial Intrusion and Dialogue in Fielding's Novels and Plays." Durham University Journal, n.s. 33, no. 1 (Dec.), 32-44.

Beginning with the assumption that Fielding's "novels seldom attempt a 'dramatic' rendering of character or situation, with a minimum of authorial commentary, as in Richardson" (p. 32), Rawson compares the lifeless dialogue of his plays (where vitality would have to be added by actors and managers) with the lively dialogue in his novels. The vitality of the novel dialogue is often achieved with the subtlest narrative intrusion. By examining brief passages from Shamela, Joseph Andrews, and Tom Jones and comparing some of them to passages of dialogue from Fielding's plays, Rawson argues that through a contrast of styles, a mixing of comic opera farce and vulgar reality, a subtly placed "he said," which breaks a vulgar rhythm, Fielding creates a sense of "realistic notation . . . vitalized by its interplay with the surrounding artifice" (p. 39). He finally examines this process of contrast in a scene in Tom Jones involving Squire Western, Mrs. Western, and Sophia. See 1973.B34 for a conventional discussion of intrusion.

32 ROSENBERG, SONDRA. "Travel Literature and the Picaresque Novel." Enlightenment Essays, 2, no. 1 (Spring), 40-47.

Compares Fielding's The Journal of a Voyage to Lisbon, Smollett's Travels Through France and Italy, and Sterne's A Sentimental Journey Through France and Italy, arguing that Fielding both showed "concern for the travel genre as a genre" (p. 43) and parodied it. The parody is implicit in his inclusion of boring detail, his breaking off when he actually gets to Lisbon, and in tone.

33 RUTHVEN, K. K. "Fielding, Square, and the Fitness of Things." Eighteenth-Century Studies, 5, no. 2 (Winter), 243-55.

Argues for tension between Fielding, the Christian censor, and Fielding, the novelist. First establishes that Square (the deist) is a caricature of Samuel Clarke (who attacked the fallacies of deism) and that the combination of Clarkeian expressions "interlaced with others which were anathema to Clarke" (p. 244) is typical of the way Fielding's "mind worked when he was writing as a novelist and not in propria persona" (p. 245). Ruthven then examines the appropriateness of Square's name ("which evoked not only the Euclidean tropes of recent ethical controversies but also the traditional iconography of Virtue," p. 248), arguing that "Square's pursuit of Molly is a kind of parody of Tom's pursuit of Sophia [wisdom]" (p. 250). Finally Ruthven examines several iconographic and geometric jokes (square into delta) in the scene in Molly's bedroom where Square is "subjected to the ignominy of Tom's Shaftesburyian laughter" and where Fielding illustrates "the limitations of that doctrine of fitness which was one of Clarke's main legacies to eighteenth-century moralists" (p. 254). See 1959.A1 and 1968.B3.

34 STANZEL, FRANZ. "The Authorial Novel: Tom Jones," in his Narrative Situations in the Novel: Tom Jones, Moby Dick, The Ambassadors, Ulysses. Translated by James P. Pusack. Bloomington and London: Indiana University Press, pp. 38-58.

Reviewed by William B. Bache, MFS, 18 (1972), 318-22; Philip Stevick, Novel, 7 (1973), 71-74.

This rhetorical study uses Fielding's Tom Jones as the central illustration of the authorial novel, the novel in which there are two realms of reality (the fictional and the authorial) that are always consciously separated. Stanzel first describes this phenomenon and then discusses its consequences for narrative distance (in time and space), narrative interpolation (commentary that displays the author's superior insight), and point of view (both angle of observation and the nature of the observer). The authorial novel is freer in its use of all of these techniques than is the post-Jamesian novel.

For another view, see 1960.B16.

35 STEWART, MARY M. "Henry Fielding's Letter to the Duke of Richmond." Philological Quarterly, 50, no. 1 (Jan.), 135-40.

Reproduces a letter Fielding wrote to the Duke of Richmond in 1749 in which Fielding expected "some form of patronage from the Duke of Richmond and the Duke of Montagu" (p. 135). Both were loyal to Walpole and both were trying to stop the murdering gangs of smugglers in Sussex. The letter suggests that Fielding helped in this attempt to control the smugglers; Stewart describes the murders committed by them. See 1960.B4.

36 STRATMAN, CARL J., DAVID G. SPENCER, and MARY ELIZABETH DEVINE, eds. Restoration and Eighteenth-Century Theater Research: A Bibliographical Guide, 1900-1968. Carbondale and Edwardsville: Southern Illinois University Press, pp. 280-97.

An annotated list, including theses, chronologically organized. A long section on biography and criticism, very brief sections on editions and bibliography.

Includes the material on Fielding in Stratman, Carl J., ed., Restoration and Eighteenth-Century Theater Research and Bibliography 1961-1968, Troy, New York: Whitson, and in Stratman's "Theses and Dissertations in Restoration and Eighteenth-Century Theater," Restoration and Eighteenth-Century Theater Research, 2, no. 2 (1963), 20-40.

37 WILLIAMS, AUBREY. "Interpositions of Providence and the Design of Fielding's Novels." South Atlantic Quarterly, 70, no. 2, 265-86.

Argues that all of Fielding's novels are "heavily influenced by the prevailing, that is to say, Christian, world-picture of his time. That world-picture was still deeply informed by the conception of a Providence that intervened directly, though usually by means of agents, in human affairs" (pp. 266-67). After discussing Fielding's tract (Examples of the Interposition of Providence . . .) in light of other similar popular religious tracts, Williams turns to Providence in the novels, examining the several providential interferences to save Fanny's innocence in Joseph Andrews, Booth's providential release from prison in Amelia, the providential reward and punishment of Jonathan Wild, and the many providential occurrences in Tom Jones, but particularly those connected with the rescue of Mrs. Waters. Finally, Williams does not think we need to strain to "Christianize" Fielding, because he obviously believed in a system of Christian reward and punishment and organized his fictive worlds around this prevailing belief. See 1959.A1, 1965.B21, 1970.B1.

1972 A BOOKS

*1 BURNETTE, PATRICIA L. "The Polemical Structure of Fielding's Plays." Dissertation, Indiana, 1972.

Examines Fielding's experimentation with form as he tried to find one to fit his didactic concerns; his burlesque rehearsal play finally evolved.

Source: Dissertation Abstracts, 32, no. 12 (June 1972), 6921A.

2 FIELDING, HENRY. Joseph Andrews and Shamela. Edited by Sheridan Baker. Crowell Critical Library. New York: Thomas Y. Crowell, 539 pp.

Reproduces the first edition of Joseph Andrews, including and marking "those changes we can accept as Fielding's in the next three editions he successively touched up for the press. . . . I have used the same system for Shamela" (p. viii). Reprints essays and parts of chapters by Spilka (1953.B10); Taylor (1957.B16); Battestin (1959.A1); Baker (1960.B3); Rothstein (1968.B31); Spacks (1968.B35); Brooks (1967.B13), and Kearney (1968.B22). Includes a chronological outline of Fielding's life and a selected bibliography. Baker's introduction searches Fielding's plays for themes later used in his novels (his political satire, his moral concern, etc.), describes the "political-sexual-religious satire" (p. xix) in Shamela and the parody of Pamela, then examines the way Fielding's growing seriousness is evident in Joseph Andrews. Finally describes the modulation from farcical parody to romance and comic realism in Joseph Andrews.

1972

3 _____. Miscellanies by Henry Fielding, Esq. Edited by Henry K. Miller. Vol. 1. Wesleyan Edition of The Works of Henry Fielding. Middletown, Conn.: Wesleyan University Press; Oxford: Clarendon Press, 344 pp.

Reviewed by Tom Davis, Library, 28, no. 4 (1973), 351-54; Ronald Paulson, PQ, 52 (1973), 501-503; TLS, 29 June 1972, p. 740.

This "critical, unmodernized text" is now the standard text of vol. 1 of the Miscellanies. A long "general introduction" discusses the "circumstances of composition" (his politics and his financial needs), the "contents" (arguing that the serious verse and prose essays are analogous to Cicero's De Oficiis), the date of composition (dating those items that had been published earlier), and the "history of publication" (to the present). The textual introduction by Fredson Bowers discusses the copy text (the 1743 first edition), reconstructing the way in which Fielding prepared the text ("Fielding sent the marked-up pages of the printed versions to the press as copy for the Miscellanies," p. lii), and describing the early "editions."

Vol. 1 includes the "preface" and the following poetry: "Of True Goodness," "Of Good-Nature," "Liberty," "To a Friend on the Choice of a Wife," "To John Hayes, Esq.," "A Description of V-n G-," "To the Right Honourable Sir Robert Walpole," "To the Same," "Written Extempore, on a Half-penny," "The Beggar. A Song," "An Epigram," "The Question," "J-n W-ts at a Play," "To Celia," "On a Lady, Coquetting with a Very Silly Fellow," "On the Same," "Epitaph on Butler's Monument," "Another. On a Wicked Fellow," "Epigram on One Who Invited Many Gentlemen to a Small Dinner," "A Sailor's Song," "Advice to the Nymphs of New S-m," "To Celia. Occasioned by Her Apprehending Her House Would Be Broke Open," "To the Same. On Her Wishing to Have a Lilliputian," "Similes. To the Same," "The Price. To the Same," "Her Christian Name. To the Same. A Rebus," "To the Same; Having Blamed Mr. Gay," "An Epigram," "Another," "To the Master of Salisbury Assembly," "The Cat and Fiddle," "Untitled," "A Parody, from the First Aeneid," "A Simile, from Silius Italicus," "To Euthalia," "Juvenalis Satyra Sexta," "Part of Juvenal's Sixth Satire, Modernized in Burlesque Verse," "To Miss H-and at Bath." It also includes "An Essay on Conversation," "An Essay on the Knowledge of the Characters of Men," "An Essay on Nothing," "Some Papers Proper to be Read Before the R-L Society," "The First Olynthiac of Demosthenes," "Of the Remedy of Affliction for the Loss of our Friends," "A

Dialogue between Alexander the Great and Diogenes the Cynic," and "An Interlude between Jupiter, Juno, Apollo, and Mercury."

Full bibliographical apparatus is included in five appendices.

*4 _____. Tom Jones. Translated by Dattatreya Dhondo Nagarkar. Poona: Continental prakašan, 223 pp.

Marathi translation.

Source: Hugh Amory's working bibliography.

5 HARPER, HENRY H. The Genius of Henry Fielding. Folcroft, Pa.: Folcroft Library Editions, 208 pp.

Reprint of 1919.A2.

*6 HOLMES, E. B. "The Control of Narrative Distance in Tom Jones." Dissertation, Alberta, 1972.

Source: McNamee, 1969-1973, p. 321.

7 HUMPHREY, THEODORE C. "Henry Fielding: An Annotated Bibliography of Studies and Editions: 1895-1970." Dissertation, Arkansas, 1972.

A careful and well annotated bibliography organized by topic ("Law and Legal Writings," "Drama," "Bibliography," etc.) with a long foreword on Fielding's critical reputation.

8 ISER, WOLFGANG, ed. Henry Fielding und der englische Roman des 18. Jahrhunderts. Darmstadt: Wissenschaftliche Buchgesellschaft, 533 pp.

Reprints Sherburn 1936.B10; Humphreys 1942.B5; Mack 1948.A3; Kettle 1951.B3; Crane 1950.B2; Spilka 1953.B10; Van Ghent 1953.B12; Sherburn 1956.B14; Erzgräber 1957.B3; Empson 1958.B6; Coley 1959.B8; Coolidge 1960.B6; Ehrenpreis 1960.B7; Baker 1962.B1; Cazenave 1964.B3; Spilka 1969.B33; R. S. Crane, "Suggestions Toward a Genealogy of the 'Man of Feeling.'" ELH, 1 (1934), 205-30; Mack 1947.B2; Watt 1949.B5; Sherwood 1949.B3; Kermode 1950.B6; Booth 1952.B2; Stanzel 1954.B17; Lange 1958.B9; Iser 1973.B14.

Introduction reviews Fielding's late eighteenth- and nineteenth-century reputation and then classifies the essays in the collection. They deal with Fielding's functional philosophy and morality, his relationship with Richardson, his literary repertoire, the formal organization of his novels (as discovered by "new critics," Chicago critics, or topological critics), and his relationship with his audience. In German.

1972

9 RAWSON, C. J. Henry Fielding and the Augustan Ideal Under Stress: 'Nature's Dance of Death' and Other Studies. London and Boston: Routledge & Kegan Paul, 279 pp.

Reviewed by Benjamin Boyce, ELN, 11 (1973), 142-43; J. Paul Hunter, PQ, 52 (1973), 504-505; Ronald Paulson, MLQ, 34 (1975), 470-73; TLS, 11 May 1972, p. 525.

In this series of related essays, Rawson collects five earlier essays (1967.B30, 1970.B25, 1970.B26, 1972.B21, 1973.B25) and adds two new ones; all illustrate the thesis "that disruptive pressures and radical insecurities became evident in some of the seemingly most confident, and some of the most conservative, writing of the period" (p. ix). Fielding, who occupies an ambiguous position between the older aristocracy and newer forces, is his "chief example" (p. x) of this strain.

The first of the new essays ("Epic vs. History: Jonathan Wild and Augustan Mock-Heroic") argues that Jonathan Wild "marks a step towards a more modern and skeptical kind of mock-heroic, whose positive allegiances are themselves insecure" (p. 158). Rawson first outlines the tension between the mock-historical and the mock-epic allusiveness of the book and then distinguishes it from great Augustan mock-heroics like the Dunciad (where the traditional cultural allegiances are set against modern realities) and from the modern epic fragments of Joyce and Eliot. He concludes that Fielding is distinct from Pope because "he is unable to keep the epic grandeurs entirely separate from the historical evils of the ancient world" (p. 158), and distinct from Eliot and Joyce because, with the epic as a living tradition, he could make "satirical use of the mock-heroic" (p. 164).

In the other new essay ("The World of Wild and Ubu"), Rawson argues that Jonathan Wild, like Ubu (in Jarry's Ubu Roi), "is both arch-villain and childish prankster . . . and (in Fielding's case but not in Jarry's) in spite of the author, vice and folly have become play, a type of play which in its absurd vigor and integrity emancipates us from the values of virtue and sense. . . . As in the Ubu plays, there is a complex and sophisticated reliance on popular art forms and folk drama" (p. 217). Draws comparisons with Auden, Swift, Jonson, Gay, Camus. See 1941.A2.

*10 ROJAHN-DEYK, BARBARA. "Untersuchungen zu Wesen und Funktion der Ironie in der fruehen Prosa von Henry Fielding." Dissertation, Erlangen, 1972.

Source: McNamee, 1969-1973, pp. 321-22. Appears to have been reprinted as No. 48 of Erlanger Beiträge zur Sprach- und Kunstwissenschaft. Nürnberg: H. Carl, 1973. In German.

11 SHESGREEN, SEAN. Literary Portraits in the Novels of Henry Fielding. DeKalb, Ill.: Northern Illinois University Press, 216 pp.

Reviewed by Henry K. Miller, MP, 72 (1975), 321-24; Susan M. Passler, SoHR, 9 (1975), 215-17.

Distinguishes between indirect (dramatic) portraiture and direct portraiture, and emphasizes the importance of direct portraiture (visual impression, moral or psychological analysis, evaluation of disposition, or a combination of these). Shesgreen sets out four traditions or methods of portraiture: biographical sketch, psychological or moral sketch, idealized portrait, caricatures. He also examines the sources for such portraits: rhetoric from Quintilian to Vicars (1721); Theophrastan and English character sketch; classical and English love poetry and French romance; Hogarthian caricature (used "exclusively to portray villains and rogues," p. 40).

In separate chapters on Jonathan Wild, Joseph Andrews, Tom Jones, and Amelia, Shesgreen discusses the balanced archetypes in Jonathan Wild (in which Heartfree is merely an unconvincing counterpart to Wild) and the rhetorical elements in the character of Wild, Fireblood, and Heartfree. He thinks Mrs. Heartfree "least at home in her setting" (p. 62) because she is psychologically and dramatically characterized. Concludes that we cannot see characters in Jonathan Wild as "lifelike" and that "Fielding's character drawing in [Joseph Andrews] maintained a fundamental continuity with his first work of prose fiction" (p. 72). Joseph and Fanny are a paired standard of idealized beauty, Wilson a working out in prose of Hogarth's engraving of "A Harlot's" or "Rake's Progress," Adams an English character sketch. With Adams and Fanny, Fielding also continues to work by contrast with bad parsons or wicked women.

In his discussion of Tom Jones, Shesgreen begins by analyzing the moral function of the three flat, allegorical characters (Allworthy, Thwackum, and Square) and the contrast in characterization between Blifil (merely an antithesis to Tom) and Tom (an English character sketch). Shesgreen then analyzes Sophia, "the most complex formal piece of character drawing Fielding ever attempted" (p. 131), and the contrasting females (Mrs. Western, Lady Bellaston, Bridget). He finds Joseph Andrews' portraiture richer and more varied, but in Tom Jones the characters are "no longer as absolute and cerebral" (p. 151). In Amelia, Shesgreen argues, Fielding virtually abandoned "the classical forms and literary devices for characterization," moving from figures as "ethical embodiments of an absolute, intellectual morality," to characters who represent "a sentimental moral vision" (p. 176). See dissertation 1970.A18.

1972

1972 B SHORTER WRITINGS

1 AMORY, HUGH. "Magistrate or Censor? The Problem of Authority in Fielding's Later Writings." Studies in English Literature, 12, no. 3 (Summer), 503-18.

Argues that in his Enquiry into the Causes of the Late Increase of Robbers (1751) Fielding hesitates between his normal Ciceronian role of censor and his practical role as a utilitarian magistrate offering palliatives. These two roles represent the paradox of impotent authority and of "illegitimated" power. Amory goes on to argue that in Amelia Fielding escapes from the paradox through burlesque (drawn from the genres of romance and farce). In this scheme, Dr. Harrison becomes a more radical and idealized fictive censor than Fielding the magistrate can be, and the world's rejection of his authority is a burlesque demonstration of the effects of luxury.

2 ANDERSON, HOWARD. "Answers to the Author of Clarissa: Theme and Narrative Technique in Tom Jones and Tristram Shandy." Philological Quarterly, 51, no. 4 (Oct.), 859-73.

Argues that Fielding and Sterne reject Richardson's notion of "costly self-reliance" in Clarissa "by developing narrative techniques that establish the possibility and indeed the necessity of mutual trust . . . the narrative method demonstrates directly the reader's reliance upon the narrator to help him correctly comprehend the experience in which he is participating" (p. 859). Anderson first demonstrates the ways in which Fielding and Sterne challenge our ability fully to comprehend the events of the novel on our own (through withheld information, emphasis on selection, complex character motivation, etc.) and then demonstrates how, through the use of metaphors (invitations to meals, etc.) and direct comments (their evaluations are superior to the readers'), both "make us recognize that others may be [more] reliable" (p. 866) perceivers than we are.

3 BEASLEY, JERRY C. A Check List of Prose Fiction Published in England 1740-1749. Charlottesville: University Press of Virginia.

Lists all of the editions of Fielding's novels printed between 1740 and 1749 (with occasional brief comment), as well as The Female Husband, Miscellanies, Journey from this World to the Next, the preface and letters added to Sarah Fielding's Familiar Letters, the preface to David Simple, and the doubtful Apology for the Life of Mr. T- C-. See dissertation 1971.B6.

4 GOLDGAR, BERTRAND A. "Fielding, Sir William Younge, and the 'Grub-Street Journal.'" Notes and Queries, 217 (June), 226-27.

A brief reconstruction of the Grub-Street Journal attack on Henry Fielding in 1732, motivated, Goldgar thinks, by political enmity. The attacker, according to Goldgar, was not Sir William Younge, as Cross (1918.A1) suggests.

5 GOLDKNOPF, DAVID. "The Failure of Plot in Tom Jones," in his The Life of the Novel. Chicago and London: University of Chicago Press, pp. 125-42.

Reprints a shortened version of 1969.B7.

6 GOTTFRIED, LEON. "The Odysseyan Form," in Essays on European Literature: In Honor of Liselotte Dieckmann. Edited by P. U. Hofendahl, H. Lindenberger and E. Schwarz. St. Louis: Washington University Press, pp. 19-43.

After describing "the 'odyssey' as a literary form or sub-genre" (p. 19), Gottfried looks at its use in Don Quixote, Joseph Andrews, and Huckleberry Finn. Calls Joseph Andrews "the most consciously constructed, as well as being historically pivotal" (p. 26). Thinks Joseph develops into a romantic ingénu and Adams is comically quixotic; thus the novel "blends quixotic comedy and comic romance" (p. 28). It follows the Odysseyan form in its three part structure, its digressions which offer thematic contrast, its conflict between "home" and "road" values, its return of a komos of characters. It is modern because it does not have a maturing hero who can find "a substantial reality worth affirming" (p. 41).

7 GRUNDY, ISOBEL M. "New Verses by Henry Fielding." Publications of the Modern Language Association, 87, no. 2 (March), 213-45.

Reprints and annotates 800 lines of MS poetry ("the only MSS remaining from the whole of Fielding's literary career," p. 218) that Grundy has found preserved among Lady Mary Wortley Montagu's papers. "The new verses consist of three parts of an ambitious, unfinished burlesque epic (1729) and a separate verse-epistle (1733)" (p. 213). These poems illuminate Fielding's early political position (he defends Walpole and vigorously attacks Pope) and illustrate both the development of his peculiar mock-heroic burlesque and his verse epistles on literary or philosophic themes. See 1959.B20, 1960.B4, and 1969.B8.

8 HARTWIG, ROBERT J. "Pharsamon and Joseph Andrews." Texas Studies in Literature and Language, 14, no. 1 (Spring), 45-52.

Argues that Marivaux's Pharsamon "contributed to the development of Fielding's distinctive narrative technique" (p. 45). After briefly pointing out parallels in structure and scene, Hartwig examines the use of the intrusive "third-person narrators . . . completely detached from the characters whose stories they are relating" (p. 47). He discusses narrator-reader intimacy, the rhetorical attack on ignorant readers, and digressions on the characters' motives. He also studies Fielding and Marivaux's shared use of irony, attitude toward the comic, and similar moral purpose.

9 HASSALL, ANTHONY J. "Fielding's Amelia: Dramatic and Authorial Narration." Novel, 5, no. 3 (Spring), 225-33.

Argues that the weakness of Amelia is a result of an uncertainty of narrative method. It essentially substitutes a "dramatic narrative method for the earlier authorial method" (p. 233), but it vacillates weakly between the two and thus fails "to establish a consistent and authentic tone" (p. 227). Although Amelia's theme is harsher than Tom Jones', the author establishes no intimacy with the reader, fails to help him in the complex judgments he is asked to make (about Booth's character, for example), and when he does appear he is not functional as he is in Tom Jones. When the old authorial narration does strongly reappear (as in the history of Mr. Trent), it seems incongruous; mostly "authorial commentary [although used persistently] is . . . uneven and much of it is markedly inferior to that of the earlier novels" (p. 232). Fielding is not capable of wholly dramatic narration, and Amelia lacks the coherence the authorial narrator gave to Tom Jones. See 1969.B32 and 1974.B4.

10 HUNTER, J. PAUL. "Fielding's Reflexive Plays and the Rhetoric of Discovery." Studies in the Literary Imagination, 5, no. 2, 65-100.

Argues that in his last plays (those written in the two seasons before 1737) Fielding came close to raising "the potential metaphysics of rehearsal plays into prominent actuality" (p. 99). Hunter discusses several early irregular plays (The Author's Farce, Tom Thumb, The Grub-Street Opera) which either embody the "dialectic between commentary and action" (p. 74) or the potential for multiple levels of meaning (political, social, and fictional). Then, with Pasquin and The Historical Register, Hunter discusses Fielding's self-conscious use of the conventional stage/state and minister/manager metaphors, the "reciprocity between stage and audience" (p. 89), and the aesthetics of creation (his near "preoccupation with art as process," p. 93, his exploration of the judgmental limits of both the senses and interpretation, his joining of the Augustan controversy about the primacy of the word, and his search for the artistic device that makes a whole of good material). See 1970.B31 and B32.

*11 KIEHL, JAMES M. "Epic, Mock Epic, and Novel: 1650-1750." Dissertation, Syracuse, 1972.

This genre study examines the mock epic as a link between the epic and the novel and the specific epic elements in Tom Jones.

Source: Dissertation Abstracts, 33, no. 9 (March 1973), 5182A-83A.

12 KINDER, MARSHA. "The Improved 'Author's Farce': An Analysis of the 1734 Revisions." Costerus, 6:35-43.

Argues that the 1734 revisions "increase the commenting author's reliability [by making both Luckless and Harriot more sensible and shifting the burlesque of romance to Mrs. Moneywood], expand the range of the satire [by moving from an attack on card playing to one on business, law, and government], and introduce a more controlled use of irony [by creating a more controlled syntax]" (p. 42).

13 KNIGHT, CHARLES A. "Multiple Structures and the Unity of 'Tom Jones.'" Criticism, 14, no. 3 (Summer), 227-42.

Argues that if we are to understand the unity of Tom Jones, particularly the middle or journey section, we must abandon an attempt to see the novel as having a single Aristotelian plot. Knight begins by examining the static opening and closing of the novel, with their morally charged locales (country-city antithesis), their contrasting characters, and their causal plot developed by the "judicious introduction of character" (p. 231). The middle section, which he metaphorically sees as "arch-like," has four structural patterns: (1) geographical movement and causal sequence; (2) a non-linear pattern of causation with hidden events and enveloping time (flashbacks); (3) symmetrical narration alternating between Tom and Sophia; (4) symmetrical corresponding events "arranged around the Upton scenes and pointing backwards and forwards towards Somerset and London scenes" (p. 239). He concludes that the novel is not static because the "reader is . . .

perpetually in the process of discovering a form that extends beyond him" (p. 241). See 1950.B2 and 1969.B7.

14 LONGMIRE, SAMUEL E. "Allworthy and Barrow: The Standards of Good Judgment." Texas Studies in Literature and Language, 13, no. 4 (Winter), 629-39.

Examines Allworthy's various judgments in relation to the care recommended by Isaac Barrow in his sermon "Against Rash Censuring and Judging." Longmire concludes that Allworthy is not simply foolish or inadequately characterized but that his character is complex, dramatizing "one of the major themes of the novel--the standards of right judgment" (p. 639). By carefully examining Tom's trials and Allworthy's subsequent judgments of Tom, we see Allworthy struggling with the right correlation between action and motive, with the proper weighing of fact and opinion, and with an awareness of the gravity of an offense.

For another view, see 1966.B17.

15 _____. "Amelia as a Comic Action." Tennessee Studies in Literature, 17:67-79.

Argues that Fielding carefully prepares for the comic resolution of the novel by means of three "narrative patterns." First, Fielding's comic technique, particularly his intrusive narrator, diminishes the serious implications of Booth's three arrests. Second, through narrative and event the potential threat of hindering characters like the Jameses and Miss Matthews is commically disarmed. Third, Fielding portrays Booth as a good man in action whose faults in spirit do not make him undeserving of Amelia's love. See 1974.B4 and dissertation 1968.A10.

*16 MCKEE, JOHN B. "Literary Irony and the Literary Audience: Studies in the Victimization of the Reader in Early English Fiction." Dissertation, Syracuse, 1972.

Studies "reader-victimizing irony" in the narration of Tom Jones, Gulliver's Travels, and Tristram Shandy.

Source: Dissertation Abstracts, 33, no. 9 (1973), 5132A-33A.

17 MILWARD, PETER. "Shakespeare and Fielding." Studies in English Literature (English Literature Society of Japan), 48:33-42.

Milward thinks the influence of Shakespeare on Fielding "no less profound than [that] of Cervantes or of Homer" (p. 35). Sees Fielding half-consciously and nostalgically parodying Shakespeare in Tom Thumb and Joseph Andrews, where he "simply borrows famous lines" (p. 38). In Tom Jones the "influence reaches very far beyond parodies of this kind" (p. 39): thinks the Jones and Sophia relationship borrowed from Romeo and Juliet, the Jones and Blifil contrast from the Edgar/Edmund contrast in Lear, and sees allusions to events in Othello throughout (incident at Upton, Jones' story to Dowling, Fitzpatrick's jealousy).

18 MORRISSEY, L. J. "Fielding's First Political Satire." Anglia, 90, no. 3, 325-48.

Historical article arguing that The Tragedy of Tragedies, Fielding's revision of Tom Thumb, not only sharpened the literary burlesque but made "clear what was, at most, latent political satire in Tom Thumb" (p. 328). The allusions in the play are to Walpole, the Court, other members of the ministry, and the political situation in general. Suggests that the play embodies the Walpole (Tom) and Townshend (Lord Grizzle) rivalry within the ministry, the attempt to get Anne, Princess Royal, married, and the controversy over the signing of the Treaty of Seville. See 1970.B12 and 1972.B7.

19 MOSS, HAROLD G. "A Note on Fielding's Selection of Handel's 'Si Cari' for 'The Lottery.'" Notes and Queries, 217 (June), 225-26.

Fielding wanted to embarrass the royal family when he added a song from his suppressed royal satire, The Grub-Street Opera, to The Lottery.

*20 PHILIPPIDE, AL. "Un strămoş al romanului modern," in Considerații confortabile. Bucharest: Editura Eminescu, II, pp. 130-35.

Romanian article entitled "An ancestor of the modern novel," in Cosy Considerations.

Source: MHRA, 47 (1972), 330.

21 RAWSON, C. J. "Fielding's 'Good' Merchant: The Problem of Heartfree in Jonathan Wild (With Comments on Other 'Good' Characters in Fielding)." Modern Philology, 69, no. 4 (May), 292-313.

Examines the ambiguity Rawson senses in Fielding's treatment of good characters (Joseph, Allworthy, Adams, Dr. Harrison, Amelia, and Sophia) by comparing them with his allegorical treatment of greatness and goodness in Jonathan Wild. Contending that for Fielding true greatness implied "an ideal fusion of virtue and rank" (p. 293) and heroic prowess, Rawson argues that Fielding condescends to Heartfree because he is a tradesman and passively lacks the will to fight. He is foolishly naive and contemptibly passive. Rawson then measures other good characters against Heartfree, sensing condescension in his treatment of Joseph, Dr. Harrison, and Allworthy because all lack rank. The model for Allworthy is a merchant, and Rawson calls Harrison "aldermanly." Each is thus ironically subverted. The strength of Parson Adams is the open comedy of his treatment and his heroic prowess, which Fielding usually describes without parody (he is not undercut with Wildian bombast). Thus Heartfree is Fielding's ambiguous "sentimental tribute to a virtuous tradesman" (p. 311); thereafter, Fielding will avoid writing "a serious novel about a merchant" (p. 313), but his portraits of good middle-class men will often hover near the subversion of unconscious humor.

Reprinted 1972.A9. Anticipated and intelligently argued by Bispham (1909.B1). For another view see 1973.B35.

22 ROBERTS, EDGAR V. "The Songs and Tunes in Henry Fielding's Ballad Opera," in The Eighteenth-Century English Stage. Edited by Kenneth Richards and Peter Thomson. London: Methuen, pp. 29-49.

Lists Fielding's ballad operas, describes several actors and singers who performed in them (Fielding may have rewritten parts for at least one), describes the typical theater orchestra for a ballad opera, offers evidence for Fielding's musical preference, and describes Fielding's skillful use of the ballad tradition ("Fielding's ballad-opera songs depended for their entire meaning not only upon the context of his play, but also upon the context, both topical and musical, of the original street or drawing-room ballads," p. 43). See 1971.B22.

23 ROGERS, PAT. "The Genuine Grub-Street Opera," in his Grub Street: Studies in a Subculture. London: Methuen, pp. 327-49.

Reviewed by C. C. Barfoot, DQR, 3: 86-91; Jean Dierickx, Erasmus, 25:290-92.

Discusses Fielding's plays in the Scriblerian tradition (particularly The Author's Farce). Rogers finds this play written from the point of view of a cultural outsider; "The Author's Farce heralds the breakdown of an incisive critique [The Dunciad] and its replacement by a cosier idiom" (p. 332). It is comic rather than "tragic," and there is some sympathy for the Grub Street hack. Rogers considers Fielding's criminal and reform pamphlets analogous to The Dunciad's implied notions of reform, and he thinks that The Covent-Garden Journal keeps "up a regular fire on the approved targets of the Scriblerus party" (p. 335). He sees Fielding as the last important author for whom the trope of Grub Street had any significant meaning.

24 SOKOLJANSKIJ, MARK G. "Genre Evolution in Fielding's Dramaturgy." Zeitschrift für Anglistik und Amerikanistik, 20, no. 3, 280-95.

Describes Fielding's experiments in various dramatic forms--comedy of manners (Love in Several Masques, etc.), farce (Author's Farce, etc.), and ballad opera (Grub-Street Opera, etc.)--arguing that he never merely followed a form but always added a significant satiric element. After briefly considering Fielding's adaptations from Molière, Sokoljanskij concludes that Molière is the significant influence on Fielding's mature comedies (Don Quixote in England, Pasquin, and The Historical Register). Rather than examining this influence, Sokoljanskij examines the direction and vigor of Fielding's political attacks.

25 STAVES, SUSAN. "Don Quixote in Eighteenth-Century England." Comparative Literature, 24, no. 3 (Summer), 193-215.

Briefly considers Parson Adams as Fielding's quixotic character, along with similar characters created by Mrs. Lennox, Sterne, etc. Argues that Adams "occupies a midpoint between" (p. 207) the quixotic character as contemptible fool and as wholly sympathetic character. Through Adams the "satire is displaced from the Quixote character onto the world and--especially--onto the reader who cooperates by supplying the attitudes of the world" (p. 208). Also suggests that Fielding in Joseph Andrews and Tom Jones "insists on the inadequacy of reason to capture the complexity of experience" (p. 213).

26 STUMPF, THOMAS A. "Tom Jones from the Outside," in The Classic British Novel. Edited by Howard M. Harper, Jr. and Charles Edge. Athens: University of Georgia Press, pp. 3-21.

A consideration of Fielding's conscious "anti-psychologism." Argues that Fielding, who thought it dangerous to divorce oneself from the real world, either refused to enter the minds of his characters or suggested clearly false motives because he believed that human actions should speak for themselves. Stumpf shows that this novel (built around imposition, deceit, and affectation) recommends the clear-sightedness of Sophia, who objectively and comprehensively sees external phenomena (something he had recommended in his "Essay on the . . . Characters of Men"). Briefly examines the episodical development of Tom's character, which we know through his actions, and the failure of Allworthy ("the one character who is not continually revealed by the actions of the plot," p. 17). Finally, he considers Fielding's careful use of externals (countenance, complexion, gesture--in short, physiognomy).

*27 VARCOE, GEORGE. "The Intrusive Narrator: Fielding, Thackeray and the English Novel." Dissertation, Uppsala, 1972.
Source: MHRA, 47 (1972), 126.

*28 VOPAT, JAMES B. "The Denial of Innocence: The Theme of Social Responsibility in the Early British Novel." Dissertation, University of Washington, 1972.
Studies the journey into experience in Robinson Crusoe, Pamela, Tom Jones, Evelina, and Emma.
Source: Dissertation Abstracts, 33, no. 8 (Feb. 1973), 4437A.

*29 WARD, JOHN CHAPMAN. "The Tradition of the Hypocrite in Eighteenth-Century English Literature." Dissertation, Virginia, 1972.
Defines this figure as used by Congreve, Cibber, Fielding, and Sheridan.
Source: Dissertation Abstracts, 34, no. 8 (Feb. 1974), 5128A.

*30 YSKAMP, CLAIRE E. "Character and Voice: First-Person Narrators in Tom Jones, Wuthering Heights, and Second Skin." Dissertation, Brandeis, 1972.
Studies the interaction between narrator as voice and narrator as character in these three novels.
Source: Dissertation Abstracts, 32, no. 12 (June 1972), 6948A.

1973 A BOOKS

*1 BURT, DAVID J. "Henry Fielding's Attitude Toward the Eighteenth-Century Gentleman." Dissertation, Kentucky, 1973.
Argues that Fielding reacts against the eighteenth-century concern for making a gentleman by teaching him charm, elegance, and affability and supports an older notion of personal virtue and civility.
Source: Dissertation Abstracts, 33, no. 9 (March 1973), 5114A.

1973

*2 CASTILLO COFIÑO, ROSA. "Los Conceptos del Amor en la Novelística de Henry Fielding." Dissertation, Madrid, 1973.
In Spanish.
Source: MHRA, 48 (1973), 363.

*3 EVANS, WILLIAM. "Poetic Justice and the Endings of Henry Fielding's Novels." Dissertation, Ohio University, 1973.
Argues that "liberal" poetic justice in the novels acts as the artistic representation of divine providence in the world.
Source: Dissertation Abstracts, 34, no. 5 (Nov. 1973), 2555A-556A.

4 FIELDING, HENRY. A Journey from This World to the Next. Edited by Claude Rawson. Everyman's Library. London: J. M. Dent & Sons; New York: E. P. Dutton, 176 pp.
The introduction discusses Fielding's classical model (Lucian), his use of both the conventions of Augustan satire and of the new sentimental "novels"; and compares Fielding's irony, with its deep ambiguity and its varied tone (from hauteur to festive extravagance), to his later and more mature use of irony, as well as to Swift's and Lucian's use of it. Copy text not indicated.

5 _____. Istorii͡a Toma Dzhonsa, naidenysha. Moscow: Khodozhestvennai͡a literatura.
Russian translation of Tom Jones with introductory essay and commentary by A. Frankovskii.

6 _____. Jonathan Wild and The Journal of a Voyage to Lisbon. Introduction by A. R. Humphreys and notes by Douglas Brooks. Everyman's Library. London: J. M. Dent & Sons; New York: E. P. Dutton, 331 pp.
Essentially a reprint of 1964.A8 with a slightly rewritten introduction and notes added.

7 _____. Joseph Andrews and Shamela. Edited by A. R. Humphreys. Everyman's University Library. London: J. M. Dent & Sons, 381 pp.
Humphreys prints the 1741 (second) edition of Shamela and the Saintsbury (1910.A6) text of Joseph Andrews, emended by the Wesleyan edition (1967.A2). He adds notes to both and a brief addition to his earlier (1962.A5) introduction to Joseph Andrews, in which he discusses the satiric intention of Shamela (an attack on the anonymous Pamela and on Cibber and Middleton).

1973

8 _____. Joseph Andrews. Introduction and notes by James Gordon. A Pan Classic. London: Pan Books, 348 pp.

Gordon provides thirty pages of notes to the text; his introduction sets the novel in its artistic milieu (particularly discussing Fielding's conviction that Richardson betrayed a Christian morality) and briefly discusses the classical influences on the book and Fielding as a humorist. No indication of copy text.

9 _____. Pasquin. Edited by O. M. Brack, Jr., William Kupersmith, and Curt A. Zimansky. Iowa City: University of Iowa Press, 80 pp.

Reviewed by D. Brooks, YES, 5 (1973), 290.

An old spelling edition "set from the first edition" (p. 60) with textual notes collating it with six other editions. There are brief explanatory notes, and the introduction discusses the play's stage history, the play-within-a-play technique, the objects of Fielding's attacks (opera and pantomime), and party politics in the Walpole era.

10 _____. The Adventures of Joseph Andrews. World Classics. London, New York, Toronto: Oxford University Press, 406 pp.

Reprint of 1929.A3.

11 _____. The Grub-Street Opera. Edited by L. J. Morrissey. Fountainwell Drama Series, edited by John Horden. Edinburgh: Oliver and Boyd, 133 pp.

Reviewed by William Kinsley, ESC, 2 (1976), 364-65.

Introduction places Fielding's play within its theatrical context, outlining the "promising time of renewal and experiment" (p. 1) and the "new life and freedom" (p. 2) of the English stage. It discusses the ballad-opera as a form for political satire, Fielding's complex revisions, and the merits of the play. Prints an old spelling text (neither punctuation nor spelling modernized) of The Grub-Street Opera, and carefully examines the bibliographical problems of the play (not printed in its final form until after Fielding's death). Appendix 1 is a record of the substantive textual variants between the copy text (The Grub-Street Opera) and the acting text (The Genuine Grub-Street Opera); appendix 2 discusses the printing of music in ballad-operas and provides the most probable source for each tune in The Grub-Street Opera.

12 _____. The History of Tom Jones. Chatham: The Folio Society, 716 pp.

Reprint of 1959.A8.

13 _____. Die Tragödie der Tragödien oder Leben und Tod Tom Däumlings des Grossen, in Zwei englische Farcen. Translated and edited by Alfred Behrmann. Frankfurt am Main: Athenäum Verlag, pp. 157-292.

A scholarly edition of The Tragedy of Tragedies in English and German (on facing pages), based on Hillhouse (1918.A4).

14 _____. The Tragedy of Tragedies (Tom Thumb). A Scolar Press Facsimile. London: Scolar Press, 62 pp.

A facsimile reproduction of the March 1731 edition of The Tragedy of Tragedies, with a brief bibliographical note by Anthony J. Hassall.

15 _____. Tom Jones: An Authoritative Text. Contemporary Reactions. Criticism. Edited by Sheridan Baker. Norton Critical Editions. New York: W. W. Norton, 942 pp.

An annotated old spelling (unmodernized) edition of "Andrew Miller's fourth and last printing of Tom Jones during Fielding's life" (p. viii).

A brief selection of contemporary reaction (from Captain Lewis Thomas in 1749 to Samuel Johnson in 1772) is appended; a longer section reprints reactions and essays by Coleridge, Goldknopf ("The Failure of Plot in Tom Jones," 1969.B7), Preston ("Plot as Irony: The Reader's Role in Tom Jones," 1968.B29), Battestin ("Fielding's Definition of Wisdom: Some Functions of Ambiguity and Emblem in Tom Jones," 1968.B3), Crane ("The Plot of Tom Jones," 1950.B2), Empson ("Tom Jones," 1958.B6), Booth ("'Fielding,' in Tom Jones," 1961.B4), Powers ("Tom Jones and Jacob de la Vallée," 1962.B14), Rexroth ("Tom Jones," 1967.B33), Baker ("Bridget Allworthy: The Creative Pressures of Fielding's Plot," 1967.B4), and Hilles ("Art and Artifice in Tom Jones," 1968.B21). This edition also includes a brief bibliography, a map of the route Tom travels, and a textual appendix on bibliographical problems. See 1923.A1, 1937.B5, and 1974.A7.

*16 _____. Tom Jones. Translated by Clarice Lispector. São Paolo: Abril, 286 pp. [1973].

Abridged Portuguese translation.

Source: Hugh Amory's working bibliography.

1973

*17 HARMEN, MARGARET M. "Exposition in the Novels of Henry Fielding." Dissertation, Catholic University, 1973.
Studies patterns of exposition (e.g., fictive past and character's past) in Jonathan Wild, Joseph Andrews, Tom Jones, and Amelia.
Source: Dissertation Abstracts, 34, no. 4 (Oct. 1973), 1911A-912A.

*18 HEMINGSON, PETER H. "Fielding and the '45: A Critical Edition of Henry Fielding's Anti-Jacobite Pamphlets." Dissertation, Columbia, 1973.
Edition of A Serious Address . . ., A Calm Address to All Parties . . ., A Dialogue Between the Devil . . ., and The History of the Present Rebellion . . . .
Source: Dissertation Abstracts, 34, no. 8 (Feb. 1974), 5174A.

19 RAWSON, CLAUDE J. Henry Fielding: A Critical Anthology. Penguin Critical Anthologies, edited by Christopher Ricks. Harmondsworth, Baltimore, Victoria (Australia): Penguin Books, 619 pp.
Reviewed by M. A. Doody in DUJ, n.s. 35 (1974), 343-45; M. Butler, EC, 24 (1974), 298-300; H. Erskine-Hall, DUJ, 36 (1975), 246-49.
An excellent anthology of critical remarks on Fielding's work, bringing Blanchard (1926.A1) up to date and supplementing him. Includes a table of important dates in Fielding's life, a selected bibliography with brief annotations, and a very full index. Organized in three parts (contemporary reactions, the developing debate, modern views); each section is introduced by a brief introduction which sums up the critical developments of the period. At a glance one can see what the important (Yeats, Austen, Voltaire, de Sade, Dickens, Gogol, etc.) and the anonymous have said about Fielding in journals, books, letters, and diaries. Non-English extracts are translated. Long extracts from the recent academic debate over Fielding dominate the last section, which is further divided into Plays, Jonathan Wild, Shamela, Comic Epic in Prose, Joseph Andrews, Tom Jones, and Amelia.

20 WILLIAMS, MURIEL BRITTAIN. Marriage: Fielding's Mirror of Morality. Studies in the Humanities: Literature. Alabama: University of Alabama Press, 168 pp.
Reviewed by J. R. Smitten, PQ, 53 (1974), 707-708.
Argues that a "marriage debate" developed in the early eighteenth century: should marriage "be based on romantic love or on prudential considerations; should the parent or the child have the right of picking the marriage partner" (p. 1). Williams contends that the debate was carried on

largely in novels, and Fielding satirically joined it. According to Williams, the prudential Restoration model for marriage dominates Fielding's dramas; only later does he use marriage to test the moral maturity of his heroes. Fielding always balances his approval of prudential marriages in a stratified society with the belief that humane feeling, right reason, and Christian charity should not be violated in the ideal marriage. Williams examines Fielding's own marriages, marriage relationships in his plays, and fictional marriages in his novels, arguing that Fielding's idealism existed before his first marriage, and though there is no development in his treatment of marriage, it is always treated seriously. Williams believes that marriage moves from an incidental concern in Joseph Andrews to "the plot material of primary concern" (p. 70) in Tom Jones and Amelia. She also sees The Modern Husband and the Heartfrees in Jonathan Wild as anticipating the sober statements of Amelia. Although Williams provides appendices on "marriage laws to 1753," "divorce law," "popular attitudes toward marriage and women," this is not a sociological analysis of Fielding's art, nor is it a careful analysis of male-female relationships. See dissertation 1963.A11.

*21 ZAKARAS, LAURA V. "Love and Morality in Tom Jones." Dissertation, Washington-St. Louis, 1973.

Rejects the notion that the prudential ethics of Allworthy are a positive value for Fielding and argues that Tom always acts out of Christian and social love for others.

Source: Dissertation Abstracts, 34, no. 5 (Nov. 1973), 2585A-586A.

1973 B SHORTER WRITINGS

1 AMORY, HUGH. "Henry Fielding," in Poets and Men of Letters. Vol. 7. Sales Catalogues of Libraries of Eminent Persons, edited by A. N. L. Munby. London: Mansell, with Sotheby Parke Bernet, pp. 123-58.

Reprints the sales catalogue of Fielding's library and carefully explains the method of the compiler, the annotations in the British Museum copy, and the nature of Fielding's collection of historical and philosophical works ("Fielding's reading looks back to the famous crise de la conscience européenne," p. 132). See 1895.B1.

2 BAKER, JOHN ROSS. "From Imitation to Rhetoric: The Chicago Critics, Wayne C. Booth, and Tom Jones." Novel, 6, no. 2, (Winter), 197-217.

Theoretical essay which uses Tom Jones to "probe into Neo-Aristotelian 'imitation' [represented by 1950.B2] and 'rhetorical' theory" (p. 216) [represented by 1961.B4]. After contending that Booth's "rhetoric" is largely the result of a quarrel among neo-Aristotelians, Ross examines Crane's "imitative" notion of plot in Tom Jones and Booth's "didactic" notion of narrator. Baker briefly constructs his own "mode," which suggests an unresolved tension among the parts of Tom Jones. Refusing to argue for the primacy of one part or reduce the importance of any part, Baker insists that there is a tension between the strong imitative world of Tom and "the narrator's presence, which reminds us that he has constructed this world" (p. 215), and that tension is lost when either the narrator or the plot is considered more important, reducing the unconsidered element to mere embellishment.

3 BEASLEY, JERRY C. "English Fiction in the 1740s: Some Glances at the Major and Minor Novels." Studies in the Novel, 5, no. 2 (Summer), 155-75.

Sets the novels of Richardson, Fielding, and Smollett among the romances, "novels," "spy" stories, secret histories, feigned "lives," "memoirs," and "histories" of their minor contemporaries. Suggests, in passing, that while they did not borrow directly, they "knew how to exploit these in order to satisfy the heterogeneous tastes of their audience" (p. 172).

4 BLOCH, TUVIA. "Amelia and Booth's Doctrine of The Passions." Studies in English Literature, 13, no. 3 (Summer), 461-73.

Argues that in Amelia Fielding subscribes to George Booth's doctrine that injurious passions are compulsive, uncontrollable even by benevolence. Occasionally in this novel (with Amelia and Atkinson), Fielding dramatizes his earlier belief that reason can control passions and that good nature can prevent vice, but in the characterization of Booth, Colonel James, the Noble Lord, Mrs. Ellison, Miss Bath, Mrs. Bennet, Colonel Bath, and Elizabeth he dramatizes the new doctrine. In each case he first dramatizes their good nature and then unfolds the blameworthy or vicious behavior their overriding passion compels.

For other views, see 1959.A1 and 1966.A16.

5 BRADBURY, MALCOLM. "Fielding, Sterne, and the Comic Modes of Fiction," in his Possibilities: Essays on the State of the Novel. London, Oxford, and New York: Oxford University Press, pp. 31-40.

Reviewed by A. J. Hansen, Novel, 8 (1974/75), 93; TLS, 10 Aug. 1973, p. 925.

A refining of 1971.B8. Bradbury more carefully defines the comic mode ("the hero is characteristically one of us, deviating from sublime or heroic norms . . . because of his capacity to draw misadventure and live by chance . . .," p. 33). Such a mode has anti-heroic diction, is socially inclusive, and has varied incidents and characters. Its social and ethical experience is insubstantial. He defines Fielding's new genre in this mode ("So Tom initiates a very open society and he moves comically about in it . . .," p. 34. "This kind of comic novel . . . tends in the end to stabilize the familiar social reality and throughout to explore the follies within it," p. 35). Fielding is not considered a Melville, a Dickens, or a modern ironist.

For a very different view of Fielding, see 1972.A9.

6 BROOKS, DOUGLAS. "Fielding: Joseph Andrews," in his Number and Pattern in the Eighteenth-Century Novel. London and Boston: Routledge & Kegan Paul, pp. 65-91.

Reviewed by M. Irwin, RES (1974), 479; E. Rothstein, PQ (1974), 587; R. W. Uphaus, ECS (Fall 1974), 116; TLS, 19 Oct. 1973, p. 1268.

Argues that by calling attention to the epic formula, Fielding also called attention to the numerological implications of the epic. Brooks describes four sorts of "mathematical symmetries" (p. 66) in the book. First, the book "is tripartite, since its four books are so arranged that the first and last, largely static, frame two central books of picaresque movement" (p. 67); he also works out the "pervasive pattern of episode-parallelism" (p. 70) in the book. Second, he suggests that the book is organized around the magic numbers 4 ("traditionally regarded as symbolizing concord, friendship, and justice," p. 74) and 16 ("the whole movement of the novel is towards 16 and all that it signifies," p. 76). Third, he sees it as a comic biblical epic-parody of the biblical epic Pamela (with the biblical numerology of 40 and 38). Fourth, he sums up several "minor instances of numerological decorum" (p. 80), e.g., the allusion to 11, the number for grief and mourning, in Book 3, chapter 11 (where Joseph is in despair over Fanny's abduction) and the general midpoint symbolism which Fielding shares with Hogarth.

7 _____. "Fielding: Tom Jones and Amelia," in his Number and Pattern in the Eighteenth-Century Novel. London and Boston: Routledge & Kegan Paul, pp. 92-122.

Argues that there are "two main structural schemes operating in Tom Jones: a large-scale chiasmus, in which each of the books in the first half of the novel is answered in reverse order by the books in the second half . . . and also a bipartite scheme, in which the second half is a direct echo of the first" (p. 101). Brooks also discusses the importance of "the centrality of the Upton episode" (p. 98) with its "implications of moral equilibrium" (p. 104) and the symbolic numbers 7 and 9, which make the novel correspond to "Augustan aesthetic and theological proportional theory" (p. 108). He also briefly discusses the ordering and pairing of episodes in Amelia.

8 CLEARY, THOMAS. "Jacobitism in Tom Jones: The Basis for an Hypothesis." Philological Quarterly, 52, no. 2 (April), 239-51.

Argues on internal evidence that the central chapters of Tom Jones "were significantly revised after the novel was originally completed in draft" and that because there is a "close relationship between the novel and Fielding's political journalism, circa late 1747-early 1748," the "revision probably was accomplished during that period" (p. 239). Points out that the violation in chronology in Tom Jones (1863.B1) is the result of "the sudden introduction of the 'Forty-five' into the novel" (p. 240), that Western, as a Jacobite, is earlier strangely unaware of the 'Forty-five,' that only some of the characters are intermittently aware of it, and that no character in Books 1-6 and 13-18 is aware of it. After examining these anomalies, Cleary briefly compares the satiric concerns of The Jacobite's Journal (6 Dec. 1747-5 Nov. 1748) and the political concerns of the central sections of Tom Jones, including particular allusions to "skirmishes between Fielding and the opposition press between December 1747 and March 1748" (p. 249).

9 COLEY, WILLIAM B. "Notes toward a 'Class Theory' of Augustan Literature: The Example of Fielding," in Literary Theory and Structure: Essays in Honor of William K. Wimsatt, edited by Frank Brady, John Palmer, and Martin Price. New Haven and London: Yale University Press, pp. 131-50.

Looks at two interdependent classes in Augustan society, the writer and the patron (usually the political patron). By examining Fielding's friendship with James Ralph, his changing politics, and his complex relations with Sir

Robert Walpole (the latter as both Fielding and Walpole saw it), Coley concludes that the writer's self-esteem was "a precarious thing, maintained chiefly by indirect means: irony, obliqueness, apology, self-deprecation, parody" (p. 147). By these means he obliquely attacked "the dependency between classes" (p. 148). See 1960.B4.

*10 EMERY, HELEN L. "The Interrelation of Literature and Sociology in the Explication of Three English Novels." Dissertation, Middle Tennessee State, 1973.

Studies Tom Jones, Caleb Williams, and Bleak House as novels that need social explication in the classroom.

Source: Dissertation Abstracts, 34, no. 10 (April 1974), 6588A-89A.

*11 GRAVITT, GARLAND J. "Mockery of the Aesthetic Ideal of Organic Unity in Restoration and Eighteenth-Century Literature." Dissertation, Southern Illinois, 1973.

Considers The Tragedy of Tragedies and other anti-Aristotelian works such as A Tale of a Tub.

Source: Dissertation Abstracts, 34, no. 4 (Oct. 1973), 1910A-11A.

*12 HARRIS, ELIZABETH W. "Fiction and Artifice: Studies in Fielding, Wieland, Sterne, Diderot." Dissertation, Yale, 1973.

Relates the novels of these four novelists to the techniques and aesthetic concerns of their time.

Source: Dissertation Abstracts, 34, no. 11 (May 1974), 7191A-92A.

13 HARRISON, BERNARD. "Fielding and the Moralists." Radical Philosophy, no. 6 (Winter), 7-17.

Later expanded into a book, 1975.A6.

14 ISER, WOLFGANG. "The Role of the Reader in Fielding's 'Joseph Andrews' and 'Tom Jones.'" English Studies Today, 5th. series. Papers Read at the Eighth Conference of the International Association of University Professors of English Held at Istanbul. August 1971, pp. 289-325.

Argues that Fielding provokes the cooperation of the reader to "produce the meaning of the novel" (p. 292) or to bring episodes and character "to life" (p. 305). Specifically examines the gaps in the narration of Lady Booby's and Slipslop's attacks on Joseph and the character of Adams; these challenge our "schematized views" of ourselves and of our social norms. Iser particularly concentrates on the ambiguity of our view of Adams (we both admire him and feel a worldly superiority). To help readers fill in the "vacant spaces" in the text of Tom Jones, a novel of greater complexity, Iser sees a more complex reader-narrator relationship and a system of contrasts (best seen in the Man of the Hill episode). Again the social "norms embodied in the secondary characters act as a restriction which unfolds a whole series of negated possibilities almost like a fan; as far as the hero is concerned, both norms and empirical circumstances act as restrictions, unfolding his good nature" (p. 322).

Reprinted 1972.A8.

15 ITZKOWITZ, MARTIN E. "A Fielding Echo in 'She Stoops to Conquer.'" Notes and Queries, 218 (Jan.), 22.

Goldsmith echoes a passage from Journal of a Voyage to Lisbon.

16 KAPLAN, F. "Fielding's Novel About Novels: The 'Prefaces' and the 'Plot' of Tom Jones." Studies in English Literature, 13, no. 3 (Summer), 535-49.

Argues that the prefaces form a developing explication on the relationship between art, artist, and audience, and that the prefaces are directly related to the plot. Kaplan discusses Fielding's concept of human nature, which is begun in Book 1 and then discussed as it applies to the novel in prefaces 6 to 12. He also discusses the tension between Fielding's desire to recreate reality and his artistic choice of artificial tools like romantic contrivance and self-conscious narration. Kaplan sees Fielding attempting to "emphasize the continuity" (p. 540) between plot and preface throughout Tom Jones. See 1961.A11 and 1973.B2.

17 KEARNEY, ANTHONY. "Tom Jones and the Forty-five." Ariel, 4, no. 2 (April), 68-78.

Arguing that Tom Jones is "a comic working out of the anxieties which disturbed Fielding between 1745 and 1749," Kearney first discusses Partridge's typically English lack of patriotism and the Man of the Hill and gypsy episodes as "cautionary [political] reflections" (p. 70). Then he goes on to discuss the ways in which the Forty-five forms the "basic matrix for the working out of the novel" (p. 72), in which Fielding "gives it the status of myth" (p. 68). In this scheme Blifil becomes the Jacobite pretender, Tom the redemptive hero, the journey to London "a kind of anarchic state" (p. 75), and the end of the novel "celebrates the restoration of order" (p. 76).

*18 KEISER, W. "Die Zeitgenossen Richardsons und Fieldings. Studien im englischen Roman 1740-1760." Dissertation, Hamburg, 1973.

Studies the contemporaries of Richardson and Fielding, including Thomas Amory, Eliza Haywood, Sarah Fielding, and John Cleland. In German.

Source: Dissertation Abstracts (European Abstracts), 37, no. 3 (Spring 1977), 1/3217c.

19 MCDOWELL, ALFRED. "Fielding's Rendering of Speech in Joseph Andrews and Tom Jones." Language and Style, 6, no. 2 (Spring), 83-96.

Argues that, long before Flaubert or Dickens, Fielding used "free indirect speech not only extensively but also expertly" (p. 84). McDowell examines a number of devices of indirect speech in Joseph Andrews and Tom Jones, among them "lexical fillers, expressions of emotion, or vocabulary characteristics of the speaker to suggest direct speech in an indirect string" (p. 92). He examines the effect of such speech on the reader (our belief in Sophia's capacity for sudden bursts of strength is the result of subtle manipulation of free indirect speech) and its part in the reader's detection of the complex irony of the novels (irony expressed by both author and characters).

20 MITANI, NORIO. "Tomu Jonzu ni okeru Nareita." Studies in English Literature (Tokyo), 50:185-98.

Discusses Fielding's limited omniscience, arguing that Fielding, as narrator, both creates an intimate relationship with the reader and manipulates his response. Mitani thinks Fielding's attitude superior, yet skillful and not positively obtrusive. He also suggests that the narrator unifies the novel, instructs the reader, ironically pretends not to know everything (he specifically withholds plot information), and appears to allow fortune and causal sequence to control plot. In Japanese.

21 MOSS, HAROLD G. "'Silvia, My Dearest': A Fielding Ballad-Opera Tune and a Biographical Puzzle." South Atlantic Bulletin, 38, no. 2, 66-71.

Provides some evidence for a fairly close association between Fielding and the publisher John Watts, who may have shown Fielding his Musical Miscellany. See 1971.B22.

22 PAPETTI, VIOLA. "Amor sacro e amor profano in alcuni romanzi settecenteschi." English Miscellany, 24: 105-127.

This study of sacred and profane love in eighteenth-century novels concentrates on Defoe, Fielding, and

Goldsmith. Robinson Crusoe is the best example of the age's ambivalence toward the fundamental opposition between God and money (between mythical signs and economics, charity and social reform). Fielding does not set up this sharp opposition, choosing instead a middle way in which man (the novelist) is also an important directing force. Argues that throughout Tom Jones Fielding advocates the moral formula of returning to the land (to nature) without ignoring the economic vulnerability of man. Thus he helped displace the bourgeois, Puritan ideology of Richardson and Defoe. In Italian.

23 PLUMB, J. H. "Henry Fielding and the Rise of the Novel," in his In the Light of History. Boston: Houghton Mifflin, pp. 37-51.

Brief history of the novel but essentially a sensational biography of virile, manly Fielding in "rip-roaring" London. A reworking of 1964.B10.

24 RAWSON, C. J. "Circles, Catalogues and Conversations: Swift, with Reflections on Fielding, Flaubert, Ionesco," in his Gulliver and the Gentle Reader: Studies in Swift and our Time. London and Boston: Routledge & Kegan Paul, pp. 84-99.

Reviewed by Peter Dixon, Scriblerian, 6 (1974), 90-91; Kathleen Williams, DUJ, 35 (1974), 345-46; TLS, 5 Oct. 1973, p. 1178.

Compares Swift's use of the "rhetorical forms of copia, or variegated repetition" (p. 90), of cant phrases with Fielding's to discover why Fielding's are "comfortingly limited" and Swift's are "imprisoningly infinite." Rawson decides that Fielding limits such copia to comprehensible and "specifiable types" and Swift uses them to illustrate the void and the irrational.

25 _____. "The Hero as Clown: Jonathan Wild, Felix Krull and Others," in Studies in the Eighteenth Century, II, edited by R. F. Brissenden. Toronto: University of Toronto Press, pp. 17-52.

Argues that "Fielding's formulaic harping . . . on Wild's wicked 'greatness' . . . point[s] to a central uncertainty of the novel." Because Fielding failed "to embody his mock-heroic in a live, coherent and self-sustaining fable . . ., the mock-heroic has to be activated largely by verbal insistence" (pp. 17-18). Running counter to this, there is a comic "fiction which is live" (p. 18), and "Wild comes alive . . . as a not unengaging comic figure" (p. 19). Rawson sees Wild as comically self-imprisoned, an "almost invariable failure in crime and in love" (p. 20). He traces this picaresque rogue concept of Wild through the novel and distinguishes it from the role of an "existentialist outsider" like Felix Krull. He distinguishes the tone of Jonathan Wild from The Beggar's Opera and discusses Fielding's concept of "life imitating art" (p. 45). A wide-ranging essay alluding to D. H. Lawrence, Swift, and Brecht.

A slightly expanded version of this essay is reprinted in 1972.A9.

26 RAYNAUD, MARTINE. "Fielding et l'unité dramatique de The Historical Register for the Year 1736." Caliban, 9:41-53.

Objects to Nichols' (1924.B4) notion that the play attacked politics, society, and literature; sees it as entirely political. Raynaud argues that the entertainment prepared by Medley in the first and last scene is entirely political and gives the play a circular structure and a unified action. Offers evidence (key words and allusions) that most of the rest of the play refers to these political scenes. The play is entirely an attack on Walpole; any scenes that don't fit the scheme are seen as there to mask the blatant satire. A graphic representation of the play's construction is provided. In French.

27 ROBINSON, ROGER. "Henry Fielding and the English Rococo," in Studies in the Eighteenth Century, II, edited by R. F. Brissenden. Toronto: University of Toronto Press, pp. 93-112.

Attempts to "reconcile his habitual diversity and virtuosity with the long-established claim of his mastery of composition" (p. 95) by tracing through the novel a set of related ideas, the "myriad demonstrations of acts of judgment and punishment" (p. 96), which often appear to be mere digressions inside digressions. "In this way all the apparently subordinate formal devices--the sub-sub-digression of the horse-thief's trial, [etc.] all help to make possible Sophia's forgiveness of Tom" (p. 103). He briefly demonstrates the same thing with the idea of "the hardships suffered by poor clergymen" (p. 103). This is the ordered exuberance of the English Rococo of Hogarth, with its rich possibilities (allusion, balanced potential, participating minor characters, moral seriousness, etc.).

28 ______. "The Influence of Fielding on 'Barnaby Rudge.'" Journal of the Australasian Universities Language and Literature Association, no. 40 (Nov.), 183-97.

Examines Dickens' borrowings in Barnaby Rudge, beginning with a careful look at the allusion to Sir John Fielding in Dickens' novel. Robinson examines an authorial aside, perhaps borrowed from Amelia, and a scene similar to one in Joseph Andrews; both inspire a shared idea that goodness is an active and "socially eclectic" (p. 188) principle. Robinson points out Dickens' use of the 'bill of fare' conceit and his borrowing of the characteristics of the hunting squire. He suggests that Miss Miggs may have developed out of Mrs. Slipslop and Sim Tappertit out of Beau Didapper. Finally in Dickens' use of "ironic authorial laudation" (p. 191) and in his imagery and attitude toward the mob ("its shift from aggression to acclamation," p. 196), Robinson sees the influence of Fielding.

29 SCHULZ, DIETER. "'Novel,' 'Romance,' and Popular Fiction in the First Half of the Eighteenth Century." Studies in Philology, 70, no. 1 (Jan.), 77-91.

Examines the terms "romance" and "novel," noticing that Defoe, Richardson, and Fielding all attack the "romance" but none of them uses Congreve's term (and his definition), "novel," to distinguish his work. Fielding, in fact, often confused the two because the term "novel" was so often used to designate romantic novellas by Aphra Behn, Mary Manley, and Eliza Haywood.

*30 SOKOLJANSKIJ, MARK G. "Literaturnaya parodiya v romanakh G. Fildinga." Permskii universitet (Perm'), 270: 35-46.

"Literary parody in the novels of H. Fielding." In Russian.

Source: MHRA, 48 (1973), 364.

*31 STEPHENSON, WILLIAM A. "Henry Fielding's Influence on Lord Byron." Dissertation, Texas Tech., 1973.

Studies Fielding's influence on Byron from English Bards . . . to Don Juan.

Source: Dissertation Abstracts, 35, no. 1 (July 1974), 478A-79A.

32 STEWART, MARY M. "A Correction and Further Note Concerning Henry Fielding as Magistrate." Notes and Queries, 218 (Jan.), 13-15.

Corrects her earlier article (1969.B34) and adds more evidence that Fielding did not succeed Poulson as magistrate.

33 TIERNEY, JAMES E. "'Florio'--An Analogue of Tom Jones." Yearbook of English Studies, 3:141-47.

Argues that Joseph Spence's "Florio" (1746) may have been the source for the theme of Tom Jones ("good nature with prudence will lead to a happy life," p. 144) and for some of the incidents. Tierney does not find evidence in Fielding's earlier work for the importance of this dual nature (prudence and good nature) in a hero, and there is circumstantial evidence that Fielding may have read "Florio."

34 WARNER, JOHN M. "The Interpolated Narratives in the Fiction of Fielding and Smollett: An Epistemological View." Studies in the Novel, 5, no. 3 (Fall), 271-83.

Argues that Fielding achieves the epistemological uncertainty (the "ironic oscillation" between the "inductive" and "deductive" view of experience) in Joseph Andrews that Cervantes displays in Don Quixote "largely though not entirely by means of the interpolated stories" (p. 273). Smollett fails to achieve this counterpoint of precept and experience (this "realism of assessment") until Humphry Clinker. In Amelia Fielding abandons his earlier counterpoint (the interpolations are "thematically" and "epistemologically" at one with the main narrative) and creates a Richardson-like realism in which facts speak for themselves.

For some recent views of the digressions and interpolations in Fielding's novels, see 1966.B10, 1968.B9, B14, and B32.

35 WIESENFARTH, JOSEPH. "'High' People and 'Low' in Joseph Andrews: A Study of Structure and Style." College Language Association Journal, 16, no. 3 (March), 357-65.

Argues that "Fielding turns the social ladder upside down and makes his lowest people socially (Abraham, Joseph, and Fanny) his highest people morally" (p. 358). Fielding accomplishes this through structure and style. Wiesenfarth examines the structure of contrasts (Lady Booby and Mrs. Slipslop or the Unfortunate Jilt story framing Adams' fight at the inn) as well as narrative stylistic evaluation (the description of Joseph as the Aeneas and Lady Booby as Surprise) and dialogue (characters exposing themselves through Freudian slip and innuendo). Fielding reduces the upper classes because of their lust and the professions because of their avarice and has "structurally and stylistically destroyed every value that Pamela stood for" (p. 365). See 1972.B21.

36 WILLIAMS, R. W. "Fielding's 'Joseph Andrews.'" Teaching of English, 25 (Aug.), 18-25.

1974

A very general essay which recounts the genesis of Joseph Andrews (growing out of a parody of Pamela), its Augustan qualities (instructing and entertaining, general rather than particular truths), and touches on its comedy, its language, its social satire, and its narrative control.

1974 A BOOKS

1 FIELDING, HENRY. Amelia. Introduction by A. R. Humphreys. Everyman's Library. London: J. M. Dent & Sons; New York: E. P. Dutton, 640 pp.

Reprint of 1962.A4 in one volume.

2 _____. An Apology for the Life of Mrs. Shamela Andrews, in The Life and Times of Seven Major British Writers. Richardsoniana. Vol. 3. New York and London: Garland, 74 pp.

A facsimile of the 1741 edition; printed along with the anonymous Pamela Censured: in a Letter to the Editor.

3 _____. Eurydice, a Farce, in The Ballad Opera. Vol. 7. New York: Garland, 37 pp.

Facsimile of pages 253-290 of vol. 2 of an unidentified edition of Fielding's "Works" in the Bodleian Library. Without music.

4 _____. The Author's Farce; and The Pleasures of the Town, in The Ballad Opera. Vol. 5. New York: Garland, 59 pp.

Facsimile of 1730 edition printed for J. Roberts. Without music.

5 _____. The Genuine Grub-Street Opera, in The Ballad Opera. Vol. 20. New York: Garland, 64 pp.

Facsimile of the 1731 edition "Printed and sold for the benefit of the comedians of the New Theatre in the Hay Market." Without music. See 1973.A11.

6 _____. The Grub-Street Opera, in The Ballad Opera. Vol. 20. New York: Garland, 56 pp.

Facsimile of 1731 edition printed for J. Roberts. Without music. See 1973.A11.

7 _____. The History of Tom Jones, A Foundling. Edited by Fredson Bowers with introduction and commentary by Martin C. Battestin. Wesleyan Edition of The Works of Henry Fielding. 2 vols. Middletown, Conn.: Wesleyan University Press; Oxford: Clarendon Press, 1164 pp.

Reviewed by M. Irwin, RES, n.s. 27 (1976), 473; C. Probyn, TLS, 16 April 1976, p. 472; Frederick W. Hilles, YR, 65 (1975), 128-33.

This must be considered the definitive edition. An eighty-four page introduction provides "circumstances of composition," "date of composition," and a "history of publication." Jensen's (1937.B5) thesis is rejected in the textual introduction and the first edition is established as copy text. Bowers argues that Fielding's revisions for the third edition were confined to Book 8, chapters 13-15, including one block of the Man of the Hill narrative. He also accepts all substantive changes (word changes) in the fourth edition as authorial. There are six appendices of emendations, collations, bibliographical descriptions, and cancellanda. The text has running notes.

For a significant response to the textual problems, see Amory 1977.B1.

8 _____. The History of Tom Jones A Foundling. Introduction by Alan Pryce-Jones. Collins Classics. London and Glasgow: Collins, 798 pp.

Reprint of 1955.A5.

9 _____. The Jacobite's Journal and Related Writings. Edited by William B. Coley. Wesleyan Edition of The Works of Henry Fielding. Middletown, Conn.: Wesleyan University Press; Oxford: Clarendon Press, 604 pp.

Reviewed by G. Curtis, TLS, 12 Sept. 1975, p. 1029; M. Irwin, RES, n.s. 27 (1976), 473; John Cannon, EC, 25 (1975), 452-56.

This volume of the Wesleyan Works "offers a critical unmodernized text of A Dialogue between a Gentleman from London . . . and an Honest Alderman, A Proper Answer, and The Jacobite's Journal" (p. lxxxii). The eighty-two page general introduction sets out the biographical context of "the final phase of Fielding's political journalism" (p. xvii); all three of these "works" are carefully set in their context (largely political); The Jacobite's Journal's indebtedness to Addison's Freeholder and its continuation of the Bickerstaff tradition of literary criticism (the first critical analysis of Thompson's Castle of Indolence was published in it) is discussed, as is the publication history of the three "works" and Fielding's reputation as a political journalist. The textual introduction (by Fredson Bowers) again sets out the editorial procedure (there is no evidence that Fielding ever revised any of this material or even read page proofs); there are succinct but helpful running notes and six appendices, including emendations, bibliographical descriptions, a discussion of Murphy's edition, and a complete reprinting of material from The Jacobite's Journal (largely commenting on material from other journals) that cannot certainly be attributed to Fielding.

10 _____. The Life of Mr. Jonathan Wild. New York and London: Garland, 269 pp.
A facsimile of the 1754 A. Miller edition issued as part of The Flowering of the Novel: Representative Mid-Eighteenth Century Fiction 1740-1775 series and bound together with the anonymous Memoirs of the Love and State-Intrigues of the Court of H-.

11 _____. The Welsh Opera: or, The Grey Mare the better Horse, in The Ballad Opera. Vol. 20. New York: Garland, 39 pp.
Facsimile of 1731 edition printed by "E. Rayner, and sold by H. Cook." Without music. See 1973.A11.

12 _____. Tom Jones. Translated by Carlos González Castresana. Barcelona, Bogota, Buenos Aires, Caracas: Editorial Bruguera, S.A., 890 pp.
Reissue of 1966.A11. This is the sixth edition.

13 _____. Tumble-Down Dick: or, Phaeton in the Suds, in The Ballad Opera. Vol. 9. New York: Garland, 19 pp.
Facsimile of 1736 edition printed for J. Watts. Without music.

*14 HOLLY, GRANT I. "Fielding's Enchanted Glass: A Study of the World as Language in Selected Comic Prose." Dissertation, Rochester, 1974.
Studies the comic interdependence of opposites in Fielding's prose (Wild and Heartfree, Parson Adams and Joseph, etc.).
Source: Dissertation Abstracts, 35, no. 4 (Oct. 1974), 2226A.

*15 KALPAKGIAN, MITCHELL A. "The Idea of the Marvellous or Wonderful in Fielding's Novels." Dissertation, Iowa, 1974.
Studies the marvelous and wonderful "in light of the classical-Christian view of wonder as the beginning of philosophy."
Source: Dissertation Abstracts, 35, no. 4 (Oct. 1974), 2227A-28A.

16 LEIMBACH, BURKHARD and KARL-H. LÖSCHEN. Fieldings "Tom Jones," Bürger und Aristokrat; Socialethik als Indikator sozialgeshichtlicher Widersprüche. Abhandlungen zur

Kunst-, Musik- und Literaturwissenschaft. Vol. 154. Bonn: Bouvier Verlag Herbert Grundmann, 67 pp.

Attempt to discover whether Marxist assumptions about Fielding are accurate. Did he have an insight into the economic relations and contradictions of his society? Specifically they pose and answer three questions: How much did Fielding's social position and eighteenth-century social conditions influence his ethics? What is Shaftesbury's influence on Fielding? Is the new genre an expression of a period of social transition? They answer the first by looking at political-historical, socio-economic conditions around 1750, at Fielding's position in the class structure, and at the reading public and the development of a capitalist book market. They answer the second by comparing Fielding's key concepts of social ethics to Shaftesbury's and then seeing how Fielding confronts reality with these ideas. The final question is answered by an historical discussion of genres and some speculation about the social forces that influenced him. Conclude that Fielding's social ethics (like Shaftesbury's) are ambiguous and that his criticism is directed not toward basic change in the social order but toward a change in individual attitudes. In German. See 1955.B6, 1958.B12, 1966.A26.

*17 MANCIOLI BILLI, MIRELLA. Strutture narrative nel romanzo di Henry Fielding. Milan: Bompiani, 116 pp.

Italian study of narrative structure.

Source: MHRA, 49 (1974), 397.

*18 NISBET, JANICE A. "The Art of Life as Represented in Henry Fielding's Amelia." Dissertation, Ball State, 1974.

Argues that Amelia sets out the art of life as the earlier novels had set out the art of the novel.

Source: Dissertation Abstracts, 35, no. 2 (Aug. 1974), 1057A.

*19 ORF, ROLF-JÜRGEN. "Die Rezeption Henry Fieldings in Frankreich 1744-1812 und ihre Auswirkung." Dissertation, Baienfurt, 1974.

A chronological study of French reviews, etc., of Fielding's works and a collation of French translations with the English texts, all of which suggest that Fielding was more popular and important than Richardson in France. In German.

Source: Review by E. M. Atkinson in N&Q, 221 (Aug. 1976), 370-71.

*20 SELTMAN, KENT D. "Henry Fielding, The Preacher: A Study of the Layman's Sermons in Historical and Rhetorical Context." Dissertation, Nebraska, 1974.

"Examines the extent to which the rhetoric of Henry Fielding is influenced by sermon rhetoric and . . . [whether] the purposes for which he wrote were those of a clergyman."

Source: Dissertation Abstracts, 35, no. 8 (1975), 5425A-26A.

*21 TAKACS, FERENC. Fielding világa. Budapest: Európa, 213 pp.

"Fielding's world." In Hungarian.

Source: MHRA, 49 (1974), 398.

*22 THOMAS, JERRALD P. "Henry Fielding's Comedies of Manners: A Study in the Eighteenth-Century Problem Play." Dissertation, Kansas State, 1974.

Argues that although Love in Several Masques, The Modern Husband and The Universal Gallant are influenced by Restoration comedy of manners and sentimental comedy, they are unique "comic problem plays providing sympathetic, exemplary characters who undergo moral education."

Source: Dissertation Abstracts, 35, no. 8 (1975), 5369A.

*23 WILBUR, FREDERICK. "Henry Fielding's Life in the Theatre and the New Species of Writing." Dissertation, Duke, 1974.

"Deals with some of the less frequently observed influences of the drama on . . . Joseph Andrews," specifically with his metaphor derived from the stage, with his experience as stage manager, etc.

Source: Dissertation Abstracts, 35, no. 9 (1975), 6115A.

1974 B SHORTER WRITINGS

1 BATTESTIN, MARTIN C. "Fielding," in The English Novel: Select Bibliographical Guides. Edited by A. E. Dyson. Oxford and New York: Oxford University Press, pp. 71-89.

A brief but excellent essay that includes discussion of the standard biography (Cross), the best edition of the complete Works (Henley) and of individual works, and discussion of Fielding's critical reputation, with special emphasis on modern studies of Fielding. The list of selected books and articles includes texts, recent criticism, biographies, and background reading.

2 _____. "Fielding: The Argument of Design" and "Fielding: The Definition of Wisdom," in his The Providence of Wit: Aspects of Form in Augustan Literature and the Arts. Oxford: Clarendon Press, pp. 141-92, passim.

Reviewed by Paul Fussell, TLS, 7 Feb. 1975, p. 134; Hoyt Trowbridge, PQ, 54 (1975), 847-50; R. Voitle, MP, 75 (1977), 84-86.

Battestin argues for an eighteenth-century conception of orderly nature ("Nature as Art")--with harmony, symmetry and variety--and of an art imitating this orderly nature; he refines two earlier essays on Fielding (1968.B3 and 1970.B1) in order to illustrate this conjunction of Christian humanism, Newtonian science, and neo-Aristotelian aesthetics.

3 _____. "The Problem of Amelia: Hume, Barrow, and the Conversion of Captain Booth." Journal of English Literary History, 41, no. 4 (Winter), 613-48.

Argues that Amelia is Fielding's anxious response to David Hume's disturbing skeptical challenge to latitudinarian Christianity. Battestin first sets out the philosophical positions of various characters in the book (Booth's Hume-like skeptical stoicism, Robinson's free-thinking, Miss Matthews' Mandevillian cynicism), then goes on to argue that Fielding's own ambivalence is embodied in the novel. Though Booth's conversion and the "exordium" are meant to reaffirm the Christian humanist tradition, the action of the novel "is the expression . . . of a theory of human nature virtually indistinguishable from the psychology it ostensibly repudiates" (p. 635). Battestin discusses the theme of liberty in the novel and the strong dramatization of the passions as a motivating force; these embody the philosophical argument which would dominate the age.

See 1959.A1, and, for a different view, 1971.B37.

4 FOLKENFLIK, ROBERT. "Purpose and Narration in Fielding's Amelia." Novel, 7, no. 2 (Winter), 168-74.

Responding to Hassall (1972.B9), Folkenflik argues that Fielding deliberately chose to avoid the potentially comic authorial narration throughout much of Amelia because he wanted to suggest "the tragic possibilities inherent in [his] comic plot" (p. 168). To support this contention, Folkenflik points "to the extensive allusions to Othello in the second half of Amelia" (p. 168). These allusions are both verbal and structural. While "Amelia is a comic novel, . . . the figured bass of tragedy which plays beneath the surface combines with darker terrors than those in Tom Jones and a far less intrusive narrator to make us feel the possibility of another ending" (p. 174).

5 GREENE, J. LEE. "Fielding's Gypsy Episode and Sancho Panza's Governorship." South Atlantic Bulletin, 39, no. 2 (May), 117-21.

Argues that Fielding's gypsy utopia deliberately parallels Cervantes' utopia under Sancho Panza. Each presents "an ideal political, civil, and social system" (p. 117); each makes a judgment about a "moral question, a supposed or attempted rape" (p. 118); each forms a contrast "with society in general as presented in other parts of the novel" (p. 119), including the inadequate government of Allworthy; each may allude to contemporary politics (Philip II or George II); each ironically comments on the "differences between appearances and reality" (p. 121). See 1967.B8.

6 GUTHRIE, WILLIAM B. "The Comic Celebrant of Life in Tom Jones." Tennessee Studies in Literature, 19:91-105.

Argues that in Tom Jones Fielding suspends his moral judgment and offers a festive celebration of life, similar to the primitive fertility rituals or the comic spirit of Aristophanes and Rabelais. Both the narrator and Tom are celebrants. Guthrie sees the narrator establishing the festive atmosphere by his extensive use of feasting and drinking motifs and especially by his "discussions of love and sexual pleasure" which "combine satire with comic celebration" (p. 95). The narrator's affirmation of sexuality contrasts with Allworthy's moral pronouncements, and Tom displays the goodness and animal spirit of a comic celebrant in his relations throughout the novel.

7 HASSALL, ANTHONY J. "Fielding's Puppet Image." Philological Quarterly, 53, no. 1 (Jan.), 71-83.

Argues that Fielding used the imagery of puppetry to explore "the relationship between an author and his work" (p. 71). Hassall analyzes this imagery that defines "the nature and function of his art at three vital stages of his career: in the play in which he shook off imitation and established his personal voice in the theater [The Author's Farce]; at the point of redirection when, the theater barred to him, he was writing more or less simultaneously his first two novels [particularly Jonathan Wild]; and at the climax of his artistry and achievement in Tom Jones" (p. 83). In the first two he sees Fielding as interested in the nature of the dramatic illusion, in the last in "the moral function and effect of art" (p. 79).

*8 HONHART, CAROL T. "Fielding, Smollett, Sterne, and the Development of the Eighteenth-Century Travel Book." Dissertation, Duke, 1974.

Argues that Fielding burlesques older conventions of travel writing and is the first "to make full use of the personality of the author."

Source: Dissertation Abstracts, 35, no. 8 (1975), 5348A-49A.

9 HUNTER, J. PAUL. "The Lesson of Amelia," in Quick Springs of Sense: Studies in the Eighteenth Century. Edited by Larry S. Champion. Athens: University of Georgia Press, pp. 157-82.

Argues that the "failure" in Amelia "points backward toward some limitations in Fielding's art . . . not plainly to be seen in his earlier novels" (p. 157). First considers some of Amelia's strengths: the allusive richness of the prison setting, the narrative "stasis," the glimpses inside characters (Amelia, like Booth, follows "the orthodox reading of the 'three temptations,'" p. 161). Then considers the critical charges against Amelia: dullness, excessively intricate plot, sentimentality, lack of irony, moral simplicity, awkward characterization. Hunter looks at its similarities to Tom Jones and Joseph Andrews, where he finds intricate, coincidence-laden plots, moral simplicity, and characters subordinate to plot, and a "proximity to sentimentality" (p. 179). He sees the main difference in "Fielding's characteristic didactic strategies" (p. 177), "in attitudes toward [the] action [in the novel] and in the resultant tones" (p. 173).

10 KNOWLES, A. S., JR. "Defoe, Swift, and Fielding. Notes on the Retirement Theme," in Quick Springs of Sense: Studies in the Eighteenth Century. Edited by Larry S. Champion. Athens: University of Georgia Press, pp. 121-36.

Compares the attitudes to retirement ("man without society," p. 125) in Robinson Crusoe, Gulliver's Travels, Joseph Andrews, Jonathan Wild, and Tom Jones. Argues that the Wilson episode and Heartfree's soliloquy "represent . . . the Horatian-Augustan tradition" (p. 129). "The Old Man of the Hill, however, . . . [is] a glimpse of the way in which the retirement tradition will be absorbed . . . beyond the Enlightenment" (p. 129). While his rejection of the city is Horatian, his love of nature and his rejection of mankind and belief in his own singularity is "Romantic" (p. 135). See 1968.B13 and B15.

11 KROPF, C. R. "Educational Theory and Human Nature in Fielding's Works." Publications of the Modern Language Association, 89, no. 1 (Jan.), 113-19.

After setting Fielding's attitude toward education (as a means of modifying human nature) in its contemporary context (David Fordyce, Obadiah Walker, and John Locke), Kropf argues that Fielding changed his mind between Tom Jones and The Fathers ("The Fathers and Tom Jones are informed by opposite theories of education and human nature," p. 117). "The total effect of Tom Jones is to demonstrate the accuracy of Joseph Andrews' observation that character is predetermined and is therefore independent of education" (p. 118). Only in Amelia does Fielding reach Locke's compromise, which believes that character is stamped by God and only capable of partial alteration or improvement. See 1952.B3 and 1968.B17.

12 LEWIS, P. E. "Three Notes on Fielding's Plays." Notes and Queries, 219 (July), 253-55.

Fielding may have used The British Stage; or, The Exploits of Harlequin (1724) for material for three of his dramatic satires (The Author's Farce, Tom Thumb, and Tumble-Down Dick). The reference to Merlin's cave in Pasquin is explained. Lewis thinks that Apollo in The Historical Register is Charles Fleetwood, patentee of Drury Lane, and not Cibber.

13 LONGMIRE, SAMUEL E. "Partridge's Ghost Story." Studies in Short Fiction, 11, no. 4 (Fall), 423-26.

Argues that the ghost story with which Partridge interrupts the Man of the Hill "reveals the character of Partridge and provides a significant ethical perspective on the Man of the Hill" (p. 423). Although Partridge is less egocentric than the Man of the Hill, his superstition and anxiety make him an unreliable narrator. Partridge's conclusions comically parallel the equally unreliable judgments of the Man of the Hill.

14 MCKENZIE, ALAN T. "Processes of Discovery in Tom Jones." Dalhousie Review, 54, no. 4 (Winter), 720-40.

Argues that "discovery" is one of the important words (concepts) in Tom Jones, written in a time in which "as never before or since, the process of discovery was rich with possibilities: dramatic, moral, psychological, sociological, rhetorical, and artistic" (p. 723). Characters, narrator, and reader discover both "things [ideas] that need discovering" and the "abilities of those who will have to discover them" (p. 725). After considering Thwackum,

Wilkins, and Mrs. Western, he examines the "reflexive" (self-discovering) participants, Tom and Sophia, and the inability of Allworthy to discover until he is assisted by Providence. Finally, McKenzie briefly discusses the interaction between omniscient narrator and reader; "Fielding practises the art of discovery teasingly, and . . . his practice of it necessitates ours" (p. 736).

15 MCNAMEE, LAWRENCE F. Dissertations in English and American Literature: Theses Accepted by American, British, British Commonwealth and German Universities, 1969-1973. New York and London: R. R. Bowker, pp. 319-22.
Continuation of 1968.B25.

16 MARESCA, THOMAS E. "Fielding," in his Epic to Novel. Ohio State University Press, pp. 181-233.
Reviewed by J. R. Clark, Novel, 9 (1975/76), 276; M. Irwin, TLS, 12 Sept. 1975, p. 1029; M. Schonhorn, JEGP, 75 (1976), 598.
"Attempts to trace the process by which the novel replaced the epic as the major literary form in English" (p. ix). After studying the mock epics of Dryden, Pope, and Swift, which emphasize the "disjunction between the fragility of contemporary mores and pursuits and the ponderousness of the vehicle" as well as that between the ideal "epic hero and the fragmented, multiplex society he can no longer adequately represent" (p. 181), Maresca turns to Fielding, who combines epic and mock epic with large "sweeps of society" (p. 183) and definitions of wisdom. Maresca examines the allusions, quotations, and parallels in Fielding's novels to the Odyssey, Aeneid, Paradise Lost, and The Faerie Queene ("I want to suggest that in Spenser he could find a versatile structural pattern used to embody a subject matter [constancy] very similar to what he himself had in hand," p. 188). Thus, Joseph Andrews "proceeds by a kind of quasi-allegoresis" (p. 196). By examining the characters of Joseph, Adams, and Fanny, we can see Fielding forcing us "to appraise the littera of his text by juxtapositions that push us to awareness of the values of sameness and difference" (p. 196). Maresca then examines Fielding's comic epic Tom Jones, a step beyond the comic romance of Joseph Andrews, again discussing the theme of constancy and complex simplicity (through which Fielding realizes the figurative, the "iconographic" in the literal). Finally, Maresca briefly discusses the parallels in character and situation between Amelia, "the serious epic in prose [and] Virgil's Aeneid" (p. 216) before setting out in detail the parallels with

Paradise Lost (Booth and others becoming "Satanic," p. 219, and Amelia Eve-like) which allow Fielding to examine Pauline Christianity. See 1931.A9, 1958.B16, and 1969.B33.

17 MOSS, HAROLD G. "Satire and Travesty in Fielding's The Grub-Street Opera." Theatre Survey, 15, no. 1 (May), 38-50.
Reviews the political satire in the play, suggesting that Fielding may have disguised the political satire by making the play appear to be a literary burlesque. Argues that Fielding's use of tunes and his lyrics burlesqued George Lillo's Silvia (1731), imitated Gay's Beggar's Opera (1728) and Polly (1729), and used Ralph's The Fashionable Lady as a guide to hackneyed tunes. See 1971.B22.

18 OLIVIER, THEO. "'Pamela' and 'Shamela': A Reassessment." English Studies in Africa (Johannesburg), 17, no. 2, 59-70.
Reviews the shifting critical attitude toward Richardson --from early approval, through Victorian scorn, to New Critical contempt. By reviewing the growing and developing relationship between Pamela and Mr. B. (full of suspense and understandable complexity), he defends Richardson against the charge of shallow and false morality. Olivier first accuses Fielding of a cynical reading of Pamela in Shamela ("one that simply refuses to believe in the human variability and mixed, changing feelings of that very young girl," p. 68) and then contends that with the creation of Parson Williams Fielding begins a "self-propelling" (p. 70) invention beyond parody that will lead him to Joseph Andrews.

19 PASSLER, SUSAN M. "Coleridge, Fielding and Arthur Murphy." Wordsworth Circle, 5:55-58.
Suggests that Coleridge's river metaphor in "Kubla Khan" may be borrowed from Fielding's description of Allworthy's estate (see 1960.B10) and from Murphy's enthusiastic natural description of Fielding's plotting.

20 RAWSON, C. J. "Language, Dialogue, and Point of View in Fielding: Some Considerations," in Quick Springs of Sense: Studies in the Eighteenth Century. Edited by Larry S. Champion. Athens: University of Georgia Press, pp. 137-56.
Compares Richardson's genius for "render[ing] with great authenticity and vividness" (p. 153) the speech of a maidservant to "Fielding's patrician hauteurs" (p. 151): "Richardson treats . . . [the] 'typical' idiom as part of the vivid flow of spontaneous speech, Fielding stylizes

it . . . isolating it by some act of ironic distancing" (p. 140). After examining Fielding's interest in spoken language and the social attitudes it displays, Rawson looks at "Fielding's familiar procedure of interweaving particular narration with a generalizing awareness of the world's ways" (p. 141). Specifically he looks at "Fielding's special use of indirect, or semi-indirect speech, and of the past tense" (p. 149). Alludes to Moll Flanders, Ulysses, No More Parades, Pamela, and other works when examining these techniques in Joseph Andrews, Tom Jones, and Jonathan Wild.

21 ROGERS, PAT. "Fielding," in his The Augustan Vision. London: Weidenfeld and Nicolson, pp. 275-85, passim.

Reviewed by Paul Fussell, SEL, 15 (1975), 511-12; D. Greene, ECS, 9 (1975/76), 128.

Attempting to trace both the peace and the exuberance of this alien epoch, Rogers emphasizes the vitality of Fielding's burlesque dramas (which dance with "freakish choreography" and shimmer with "intellectual slapstick," p. 168) and the "radically new literary technique" (p. 275) of his fiction. Rogers breezes through Fielding's career as a novelist, ruffling the usual topics (the interpolated tale, the intrusive narrator, the plot of Tom Jones, etc.). Fielding's distinctness seems to come from: "the rich confrontation of men and ideas" (p. 279), and his Augustanism from his "gentle persuasion" (Joseph Andrews "aims not to shock or titillate or convert us," p. 278). Amelia, with its "kind of savage quality, . . . is already a post-Augustan work" (p. 285).

22 RUDUS, RAYMOND J. "Tom Jones in Adaptation: A Chronology of Criticism." Bulletin of the New York Public Library, 77, no. 3 (Spring), 329-41.

Lists and evaluates all of "the adaptations inspired by, and derived from, Henry Fielding's Tom Jones" (p. 329), including a separate list of "non-authenticated adaptations" like Lafficchard's unpublished one act comedy, "Jones; ou, L'Enfant trouvé."

Expands and corrects 1942.B9 and 1970.B30. See dissertation 1969.A19.

23 SCHONHORN, MANUEL. "Heroic Allusions in Tom Jones: Hamlet and the Temptations of Jesus." Studies in the Novel, 6, no. 2 (Summer), 218-27.

Argues that Tom, an "archetypal" hero in an "allusionary" landscape, reembodies two heroes of the Western tradition, Hamlet and Jesus. Suggests that Tom embodies the essential quality of Garrick's Hamlet, filial piety. Argues that Molly, Jenny, and Lady Bellaston represent Tom's temptations in the wilderness beyond Paradise Hall: the flesh, the world, and the devil.

24 SAKUMA, MAKOTO. Laughter as a Weapon: Fielding's Fundamental Theory of Creation. Seijo English Monographs. No. 14. Tokyo: Seijo University, 17 pp.

Distinguishes between the picaresque tradition and Fielding's "symbolic" and satiric use of Joseph in Joseph Andrews. Maintains that throughout his work Fielding uses laughing satire, and not realism, as the shaping aesthetic force.

25 SHESGREEN, SEAN. "Cibber in Fielding's Jonathan Wild." American Notes and Queries, 12, no. 6 (Feb.), 88-90.

After noting the allusive additions that Fielding made to a scene (Book 1, chapters 12-13) in the 1754 edition of Jonathan Wild, Shesgreen concludes that Fielding was continuing the attacks on Cibber begun in Shamela and Joseph Andrews.

26 SOKOLJANSKIJ, MARK G. "Poetics of Fielding's Comic Epics." Zeitschrift für Anglistik und Amerikanistik, 22, no. 3, 251-65.

Argues that if we examine Fielding's "rules" for this new genre in the context of his novels, they become "a system" (p. 252). Sokoljanskij begins with Fielding's theory of character, derived from Joseph Andrews and Tom Jones (that he will depict life in general and include lower-class characters), and then analyzes Fielding's typical "personage-functions" (characters with no existence "outside the artistic system of the novel," p. 254). Specifically, he looks at the complex character oppositions or contrasts in the two novels. Sokoljanskij thinks the theoretical artistic "space" of the new form linear, and he discusses several symmetries (including London, road, and country). "Time" in Fielding's novels he sees as arranged so that "the significance of the depicted event is inversely proportional to the indicated duration of the episode" (p. 260). Finally he sees Fielding's novels as modeled on "the plot development and compositional scheme" (p. 262) of the Odyssey.

27 _____. "Istorizm Fildinga: na materiale 'komicheskikh epopeĭ." Nauchnve doklady vysshei shkoly. Filologcheskie nauki (Moscow), 1, 34-42.

"Fielding's historicism: the evidence of the 'comic epics.'" In Russian.

28 STEVICK, PHILIP. "On Fielding Talking." College Literature, 1, no. 1, 19-33.

Carefully argued stylistic analysis of Fielding's "voice" in Tom Jones. Stevick explicates one passage to illustrate Fielding's exploitation of conventional form, his pairing of syntactic elements, his excessive (even bizarre) demonstration, his use of a family of rhetorical terms "having to do with knowing, understanding, and believing" (p. 21), his conflation of the emotional and the intellectual, and his ingratiating personal tone (achieved in part through personal pronouns, transitional devices, and suprasegmental phonemes). Finally Stevick discusses the "rituals of ingratiation and distance-keeping, of complimenting and taunting, of making loyalties and acknowledging alienation" (p. 26); among these are Fielding's wide-ranging allusions and metaphors. See 1969.B26.

29 VOPAT, JAMES B. "Narrative Technique in Tom Jones: the Balance of Art and Nature." Journal of Narrative Technique, 4:144-54.

A careful examination of some of the metaphoric "structure" of Tom Jones, beginning with the description of Paradise Hall, a moment of "high metaphoric intensity" (p. 144). Vopat thinks this description contains the central theme of the novel, "life as a directed vitality . . . the balance of art and nature" (p. 145). Vopat then examines the images outside Paradise Hall (the world into which Tom is thrust) with their emphasis on the hunt, physical battle, and falling. Finally he argues that the narrator directs his own "bastard offspring" (p. 150), the novel, toward the "controlled metaphor of history" and displays the control of exuberance Tom must learn; as proof Vopat offers the narrator's self-conscious control of style and one arrogant cluster of images of time.

1975 A BOOKS

1 BATTESTIN, MARTIN C. The Moral Basis of Fielding's Art: A Study of Joseph Andrews. Middletown, Conn.: Wesleyan University Press, 207 pp.

Reissue of 1959.A1.

1975

*2 BRADLEY, TOBY S. "The Relationship Between Satire and Sentimentality in the Works of Henry Fielding." Dissertation, California-Santa Barbara, 1975.

Argues that Fielding makes his satire out of sentimental material in his early novels and not just in Amelia.

Source: Dissertation Abstracts, 36, no. 4 (Oct. 1975), 2213A.

3 DUCROCQ, JEAN. Le Théâtre de Fielding: 1728-1737 et ses prolongements dans l'oeuvre romanesque. Études Anglaises 55. Dijon: Didier, 664 pp.

A season by season survey of Fielding's plays, which also briefly reviews Fielding's contemporary theatrical scene (theaters, companies, repertoires, etc.) and types of comic drama (comedy of manners, sentimental comedy, comedy of intrigue and humor). The analysis of individual plays combines description and genre study; characters, events, and plays are essentially identified as being derived from one of the comic types. Ducrocq also discusses Fielding's irregular dramas, the farce satires and parodies (e.g., The Author's Farce, Grub-Street Opera, Pasquin, etc.), asserting that they are in the tradition of Aristophanes, Lucian, Ben Jonson's Bartholomew Fair, and Buckingham's The Rehearsal. These categories lead Ducrocq to summarize the critical views of Dobson, Cross, Bernbaum, Nicoll, rather than to analyze the plays. While the plays are set in their theatrical context of benefit nights, popular actresses, and ministerial harassment, they are not seriously set in their social or political context. This is true despite a final section on grand motifs (in which he reconciles Fielding's attitudes about large ideas, the man-woman relationship, with the demands of conflicting genres, sentimental and manners comedies) and a brief attempt to consider Fielding's radical positions (e.g., his rupture with classical comic conventions). The generic focus of this book is reinforced in the final section in which plays are grouped under various categories (e.g., divers farces, dramatic satires, comedy of manners) and compared (Love in Several Masques, The Temple Beau, and The Modern Husband as sentimental comedies). Ducrocq concludes with a glance at the effect Fielding's satiric dramatic experiments had on the characters, scene making, and the aesthetics of his novels. Selected bibliography in French.

4 FIELDING, HENRY. Enquiry into the Causes of the Late Increase of Robbers. Preface by Nishan Parlakian. Foundations of Criminal Justice series. New York: AMS Press, 165 pp.

Facsimile of 1751 edition printed for A. Miller. Introduction reviews Fielding's legal and judicial career and then points out the solid legal knowledge and social perception of this tract. Asserts that "Fielding's view of criminality is clearly not a 'liberal' one" (p. 11).

5 _____. The True Patriot: and The History of Our Own Times. Edited by Miriam A. Locke. New York: Haskell House, 272 pp.

Reprint of 1964.A17.

6 HARRISON, BERNARD. Henry Fielding's Tom Jones: The Novelist as Moral Philosopher. London: Sussex University Press, Chatto & Windus, 140 pp.

Reviewed by R. Paulson, SEL, 16 (1976), 534-35.

Reviews the charges Fielding's critics and defenders (from Johnson and Hawkins through Kermode, Battestin, and Empson) level against Fielding (moral evasiveness, naive Shaftesburyian morality, the use of wooden allegorical characters, and philosophical naiveté). By carefully analyzing Blifil's release of Sophia's bird (Book 4, chapter 3), Harrison argues for Fielding's complexity, for a concept of character "founded in the notion of the coherence of a man's speech and action when seen from different viewpoints" (p. 45), and for non-Cartesian realism (not of inward but of public consciousness). He then shows how Fielding, through "reconstructive irony" (logical parodies, plays with meaning, complex situations), "gives the alert reader the material he needs to form his own judgments about the characters" (p. 51). Harrison carefully sets Fielding's ideas in their philosophical context (examining both the influence of Hobbes and Mandeville and "Standard Benevolism") and then examines Fielding's ideas (particularly his concept of pure love) in the "dramatic structures" that they dominate. For him the "polarity" of Tom Jones is not between virtue and vice but between the mind that has willed itself into morality and thus feels its emotional force, and the mind which sees morality as a matter of logic. Harrison concludes that Fielding rejects Mandevillian egoism (the rationally self-interested being) and anticipates Kant's imperative (that we should treat every rational being as an end in itself, never as a means) without Kant's coldness. Harrison finally examines the psychological strength Fielding achieved by setting his characters in action so that we can know what a man is by what he does and wants; for instance, Jonathan Wild's flight from morality and finally even from sexual appetite subtly displays his hollow self-sufficiency.

Expands an earlier essay (1973.B13). See also 1950.B6, 1958.B6, and 1959.A1 for other views.

7 HUNTER, J. PAUL. Occasional Form: Henry Fielding and the Chains of Circumstance. Baltimore and London: Johns Hopkins University Press, 277 pp.

Reviewed by S. Baker, MLQ, 38 (1977), 196-200; W. B. Carnochan, JEGP, 76 (1977), 137-41; M. Irwin, RES, 28 (1977), 475-77; R. Paulson, SEL, 16 (1976), 531-34; C. J. Rawson, Criticism, 19 (1977), 99-102.

Hunter attempts to "place Fielding's career and his major works in relation to historical forces operating on his mind and art, chronicling his anxiety and adjustment to circumstances." He sees Fielding as standing "between eras, a reactionary pioneer, and in his restless commuting between rural and urban life he tracked a path from very old values to very new ones, even while he turned the nation's literary energies from the public modes of drama toward the private ones of reflexive fiction" (p. xi). His first chapter ("The Many Masquerades of Henry Fielding") briefly sets out the many tones of voice, personae, and contradictions in ideas in Fielding's works; it also distinguishes him from the perilous rhetorical balance of Augustans like Pope or Swift. In Hunter's view, Fielding and his contemporaries acutely felt the "interaction of external and internal pressures . . . the clash between medieval and modern" (p. 4). By examining echoes and allusions to Shakespeare, Swift, and Pope in The Tragedy of Tragedies (in a chapter called "Fielding Among the Giants"), Hunter distinguishes both Fielding's tentative Augustanism (measuring the present against the past) and his exuberant interest in "the energies of chaos" (p. 45).

In his chapter on "Fielding's Reflexive Plays and the Rhetoric of Discovery," Hunter examines Fielding's use of the rehearsal or the theatrical frame device as it "suggests his conviction that action is not autonomous and that the act of interpretation impinges on the act of perception" (p. 50). Hunter then sets out the "contexts" for Shamela (the Trapp controversy, Cibber's Apology, and Pamela); for Joseph Andrews (the deist controversy and the argument about Christian conduct and charity); and for Tom Jones (the "philosopher" Thomas Chubb and the epic tradition, the Odyssey, and Fénelon's Télémaque). He does this in order to illustrate Fielding's "traffic between the timely and the timeless" (p. 77), as Fielding explored the "limits of traditional exemplary theory" and "the possibilities of bad models and the ability of men to respond, ready to propound a theory of human psychology, of education, of politics, and of art" (p. 120).

In a chapter called "The Conquest of Space," Hunter explores the books as travel analogy, examining various kinds of journey (pilgrimage and quest) and pause (the interpolated tales), and arguing that these illustrate the "experiential" and "perceptual" growth of Tom, Joseph, and the reader. Hunter also studies symmetry and its limits in Tom Jones, arguing that the novel insists on a large order of events (e.g., politics and treatises for the education of a prince) as well as the ordering or balancing of the smallest structural unity (e.g., character or scene). Finally, he considers Amelia's virtues (character interiors, narrative stasis, the classical Christian antithesis) and its defects (sentimental loss of rhetorical control and uncertainty about institutions), arguing that Fielding had changed his mind about reader strategy and had abandoned the "strategies of indirection that were integral to Fielding's didactic method in Joseph Andrews and Tom Jones" (p. 207).

*8 MCCREA, BRIAN R. "Fielding's Political Writings." Dissertation, Virginia, 1975.

Analyzes the social, intellectual, and political background of Fielding's political writings and links them to his "literary efforts."

Source: Dissertation Abstracts, 36, no. 7 (Jan. 1976), 4514A.

*9 MCNAMARA, SUSAN P. "Paradox in the Novels of Henry Fielding." Dissertation, New York University, 1975.

Argues that Fielding's novels are in the tradition of rhetorical paradox (from Plato through Cervantes).

Source: Dissertation Abstracts, 36, no. 4 (Oct. 1975), 2222A-223A.

*10 SIEKER, DON W. "Henry Fielding as Playwright: A Study of Relationships Between Comic Drama and Moral Purpose." Dissertation, California (Davis), 1975.

Argues for the artistic worth of Fielding's dramas and for their moral seriousness.

Source: Dissertation Abstracts, 36, no. 4 (Oct. 1975), 2224A-225A.

*11 SLEVIN, JAMES F. "Morals and Form: A Study of Tradition and Innovation in Joseph Andrews." Dissertation, Virginia, 1975.

Attempts "to show the close interrelation of moral vision, literary form and didactic function in Fielding's art, with particular attention to Joseph Andrews."
Source: Dissertation Abstracts, 36, no. 7 (Jan. 1976), 4517A-18A.

*12 VAN LOON, NELLES H. "The Comic and the Sentimental in the Novels of Henry Fielding." Dissertation, Toronto, 1975.
Examines "the comic and the sentimental elements in Fielding's novels," suggesting that it is the combining of the comic and the sentimental and not the tacked-on morality that makes Tom Jones a superior novel.
Source: Dissertation Abstracts, 38, no. 6 (Dec. 1977), 3461A.

1975 B SHORTER WRITINGS

*1 ALLEN, LOUIS D. "Prose Fiction as Symbolic Form." Dissertation, Nebraska, 1975.
Develops a formalistic criticism based on Ernst Cassirer's theory of symbolic forms and examines "story summary and a binary charting of character alignments to create a framework for further analysis" of Tom Jones.
Source: Dissertation Abstracts, 36, no. 12 (June 1976), 8029A-30A.

2 BATTESTIN, MARTIN C. "Fielding's Novels and the Wesleyan Edition: Some Principles and Problems," in Editing Eighteenth-Century Novels: Papers on Fielding, Lesage, Richardson, Sterne, and Smollett given at the Conference on Editorial Problems (University of Toronto, November 1973). Edited by G. E. Bentley, Jr. Toronto: A. M. Hakkert, pp. 9-30.
Sets out and defends Greg's "classic theory of copy-text" (p. 10), which is being followed in the Wesleyan editions. Argues from the text of Tom Jones and Joseph Andrews that "accidentals" make a "substantive" difference: Fielding uses capitals to personify abstract qualities; italics to indicate linguistic eccentricities (dialect or malapropisms) and stage directions; typographical variations to objectify the qualities he is satirizing, signal allusions, point up crucial thematic analogues, or signal private jokes. Finally argues that from the absence of allusion to the '45 (and any contradictory internal or external evidence) we can conclude that he composed the "first six books (and more) of his narrative" (p. 28) before 1745.

1975

3 BOWLES, STEPHEN E. Index to Critical Film Reviews in British and American Film Periodicals and Index to Critical Reviews of Books About Film. 2 vols. New York: Burt Franklin, 700 pp.

Consult for a more complete bibliography of reviews of the movie Tom Jones.

See also MacCann, Richard D. and Edward S. Perry, New Film Index (New York: E. P. Dutton, 1975).

4 EAVES, T. C. DUNCAN and BEN D. KIMPEL. "Two Names in Joseph Andrews." Modern Philology, 72 (May), 408-409.

Illustrates from earlier literary uses of Slip-Slop (by Ned Ward) and Tow-wouse (in an account of Isaac Atkinson) that the first implies deep passionate kissing and the second "the female pudendum, possibly in a plural form" (p. 409).

5 GORDON, THOMAS K. "The Knight Amid the Dunces." Restoration and Eighteenth Century Theatre Research, 14, no. 1 (May), 10-22.

In an article on the "eight plays based on Cervantes' Don Quixote" (p. 10) written during Pope's lifetime, Gordon briefly considers Don Quixote in England, reporting its stage history and briefly describing the added English scenes and characters.

6 HINES, PHILIP. "'Barathrum' Antedated in Fielding-Young (1742) and Postdated in Randolph (1651)." Notes and Queries, 220 (Jan.), 13.

Fielding and Young, in their translation of Aristophanes' Plutus, used the word 107 years before the source cited in the Oxford English Dictionary.

7 KETTLE, ARNOLD. "The Eighteenth Century Novel in England." Acta Salmanticensia. Filosofia y letras. Estudio Sobre Los Generos Literarios, I: Grecia clasica e Inglaterra, 89: 149-60.

A general survey of the novel that calls Fielding both "the least bourgeois of the English eighteenth century novelists" (p. 157) and a novelist "able to absorb the insights and innovations of the new bourgeois culture into the novel" (p. 159). He also calls Tom Jones both "a profoundly traditional and [a] deeply seditious work" (p. 157).

8 LEWIS, PETER. "Fielding's The Covent-Garden Tragedy and Philip's The Distrest Mother." Durham University Journal, n.s. 37 (Dec.), 33-46.

Argues that this "self-sufficient mock-tragedy . . . stands out as one of the few masterpieces of Augustan dramatic burlesque" (p. 44). Thinks it a specific burlesque of Philip's play, which had already been burlesqued in Gay and Pope's The What D'Ye Call It. As proof Lewis offers parallels and echoes in plot, scene (particularly the opening and denouement scenes in Philip's play), character (Andromache's maternal love is burlesqued by Mother Punchbowl and Blikum), and rhetoric (simile, rhetorical question, set love and honor debates). Lewis compares Fielding to Gay and sets Fielding's later "Prolegomena" defense in its political and social context.

9 LONGMIRE, SAMUEL E. "Fielding's Tom Jones." Explicator, 33, no. 6 (Feb.), item 52.

Argues that Partridge's marriage to Molly is appropriate and comically satisfying because "Partridge is a virile, sexually exuberant male who deserves a girl like Molly." Offers as evidence a close reading of the irony of Mrs. Partridge's suggestion that Partridge is impotent, although he is capable of "fathering bastards."

10 MILLER, HENRY K. "The 'Digressive' Tales in Fielding's Tom Jones and the Perspective of Romance." Philological Quarterly, 54, no. 1 (Winter), 258-74.

Attacking the notion of "art as biological organism," Miller argues that the Man of the Hill and Mrs. Fitzpatrick tales are central to this novel with its Renaissance "art as artifice" (p. 258) structure. He compares the Man of the Hill digression to Greene's Arbasto, Euphues, the Odyssey, etc., arguing that "the Man" is the archetypal hermit and embittered traveler who "extends the range of possible experiences . . . which Jones could . . . undergo without sinking into the character of a picaro" (p. 260). "The Man" tells two brief romances (the loss and regaining of paradise and a tale of exclusion), and Tom (Telemachus-like) instructs him. Miller briefly argues that Mrs. Fitzpatrick's tale is related to comedy of manners and popular "female" novels. Her tale tries Sophia. Tom ("Adamic Jones") and Sophia both "fall from primal innocence" (p. 268). "What is being put to the test is the moral prudence of the youthful initiates . . . and their . . . capacity for love and trust" (p. 270).

*11 MURAKAMI, SHIKO. "Hardy to Igirisu Shosetsu: Hardy to Fielding," in 20 Seiki Bungaku no Senkusha Thomas Hardy. Edited by Mamoru Osawa, Michio Yoshikawa, and Shigeru

Fujita. Tokyo: Shinozaki Shorin, pp. 31-47.
Source: MLA Bibliography, 1 (1977), 102.

12 ROTHSTEIN, ERIC. "Amelia," in his Systems of Order and Inquiry in Later Eighteenth-Century Fiction. Berkeley, Los Angeles and London: University of California Press, pp. 154-207.

Reviewed by W. B. Carnochan, JEGP, 76 (1977), 137-41; M. Irwin, TLS, 9 July 1976, p. 840; R. Paulson, SEL, 16 (1976), 538-40.

Argues that in Amelia Fielding makes "the hiddenness of thought . . . a major concern" (p. 154), thus the narrator retreats and our perceptions of the represented world are frustrated. Rothstein proceeds by comparing episodes in Tom Jones and Amelia (e.g., Jenny's trial and the Robinson episode), by discussing psychological density (revealed in the events of the plot), and by discussing the narrator and the thematic resolution. He examines "the two epistemological poles" (p. 183) of Books 1-7, which he calls Booth's System. In this section, Rothstein thinks Fielding begins with first principles, as the events and the characters' self-perceptions swing between romance (Miss Matthews' story) and arbitrariness (the court and prison yard). The last part of the novel, which Rothstein calls the widening view, offers us an increasing number of perspectives on events and characters, achieved through incremental repetition, shifting context, and through Fielding's handling of sequence, theme (including role-play), and motif. Throughout Rothstein compares Fielding to Sterne, Smollett, and to Johnson's means of epistemological inquiry, with its debunking of systems and its apparent formal negligence.

For another view, see 1971.B27.

1976 A BOOKS

*1 CHANDOR, KENNETH F. "English Inns and Taverns: Their Structural and Thematic Function in Fielding's Novels." Dissertation, Tulane, 1976.

Argues that these resting places help organize the novels, set up character conflicts, and act as microcosms.

Source: Dissertation Abstracts, 37, no. 7 (Jan. 1977), 4364A.

2 FIELDING, HENRY. A Journey from This World to the Next. [New York]: Arno Press, 176 pp.

Facsimile of Golden Cockerel Press edition (1930.A1).

1976

3 _____. An Apology for the Life of Mrs. Shamela Andrews. Edited by R. Brimley Johnson. Folcroft, Pa.: Folcroft Library Editions, 90 pp.

Reprint of 1926.A3. Also issued in 1976 by Norwood Editions.

4 _____. Joseph Andrews and Shamela. Edited by A. R. Humphreys. Everyman's Library. London: J. M. Dent & Sons; New York: E. P. Dutton, 381 pp.

Reprint of 1973.A7.

*5 GLIGOR, EMIL P. "A Study of Fielding's The Opposition: A Vision." Dissertation, Case Western Reserve, 1976.

An old-spelling edition of the pamphlet. Sets it in its milieu and argues that it offers strong evidence for Fielding's movement into Walpole's camp.

Source: Dissertation Abstracts, 37, no. 12 (June 1977), 7761A-762A.

*6 KELLER, ELLEN H. "L'Enfant Trouvé: Tom Jones as an Eighteenth-Century French Novel." Dissertation, Case Western Reserve, 1976.

Study of the de la Place translation of Tom Jones and its reception in France.

Source: Dissertation Abstracts, 38, no. 1 (July 1977), 307A.

7 MILLER, HENRY KNIGHT. Henry Fielding's Tom Jones and the Romance Tradition. English Literary Studies Monograph Series. No. 6. Victoria, British Columbia: University of Victoria, 112 pp.

Contending that "Tom Jones is in all major essentials a 'romance' and vitally profits from earlier modes of fiction, indeed, cannot be adequately interpreted--or 'decoded'--unless the conventions of romance are imaginatively comprehended" (p. 9), Miller briefly reviews the tradition of Anglo-Norman and French romances, as well as those of Spain and Italy, from the middle ages to the eighteenth century, but particularly from the Renaissance to Fielding's day. In five chapters he then deals with elements of the "romance" as they appear in Tom Jones: "Mythos/Questions of Plot and Structure"; "Time and Place/Questions of Setting"; "People/The Characters"; "Ethos/The Dimensions of Meaning"; "Logos/Questions of Style." About time and place, he argues that Fielding, in following the romance tradition, was not creating "a simulacrum of life-by-the-clock nor . . . a sociological emphasis upon environmental conditioning" (p. 43). Discussing "Tom's

Edenic world" (p. 44) and the city/country oppositions, with their allegorical events (e.g., the Upton feast is a "Banquet of Sense"), Miller again attacks the conventional view of Fielding as a "realist." He challenges the usual notion of character "psychology" (in Tom Jones we see not an end-product of "behavioral" or "social determinism" but the "testing of the soul on its pilgrimage"); discusses the multiple levels of style open to the writer in the romance tradition; and illustrates the symbolic, typological, and emblematic morality of Tom Jones as a romance.

*8 PYKARE, NINA C. "The Female Part of the Species: A Study of Women in Fielding." Dissertation, Kent State, 1976.

Argues that Fielding's "good girl" heroines are not full, resourceful women. Only Jenny has a sexually compassionate good nature like Tom's.

Source: Dissertation Abstracts, 37, no. 2 (Aug. 1976), 991A-92A.

*9 SWANSON, GAYLE R. "Henry Fielding and the Psychology of Womanhood." Dissertation, South Carolina, 1976.

Examines Fielding's insight into the conflict in the female psyche between sexuality and public censure. This conflict leads many of his female characters to hypocrisy, vanity, and adultery.

Source: Dissertation Abstracts, 38, no. 1 (July 1977), 291A.

*10 TABBS, BERNARD L. "Fielding's Oedipal Fantasy: A Psychoanalytic Study of the Double in Tom Jones." Dissertation, American University, 1976.

This study looks at Fielding (his Oedipal fear of castration) and at his novel (Tom and Sophia make a psychological whole).

Source: Dissertation Abstracts, 37, no. 3 (Sept. 1976), 1524A.

*11 WARREN, LELAND E. "Henry Fielding and the Search for History: The Historiographical Context of Tom Jones." Dissertation, Illinois (Urbana-Champaign), 1976.

Sets Fielding's novels in the context of eighteenth-century historical theory and practice.

Source: Dissertation Abstracts, 37, no. 5 (Nov. 1976), 2905A-906A.

*12 WILNER, ARLENE F. "Henry Fielding and the Uses of Language: A Study of Joseph Andrews and Tom Jones." Dissertation, Columbia, 1976.

Argues that Fielding shared a skepticism about absolute

knowledge with his contemporaries and that he embodied that skepticism in his deliberate use of ambiguous language.
Source: Dissertation Abstracts, 37, no. 6 (Dec. 1976), 3656A-657A.

*13 WOLFE, GEORGE H. "Lessons in Virtue: Fielding and the Ethical Imperative." Dissertation, North Carolina, 1976.
Source: Dissertation Abstracts, 38, no. 2 (Aug. 1977), 814A. See 1977.B14.

1976 B SHORTER WRITINGS

1 BEASLEY, JERRY C. "Romance and the 'New' Novels of Richardson, Fielding, and Smollett." Studies in English Literature: 1500-1900, 16, no. 3 (Summer), 437-50.
After distinguishing between the heroic romance (out of favor in the 1740s) and the didactic romance (in favor), Beasley looks at "the devices and strategies" borrowed from romance by these three novelists. Discusses Fielding's idealized characters, his use of "fortune" as an element of the marvelous, and his use of sentimental love. See 1962.B1.

2 DUPAS, JEAN-CLAUDE. "Joseph Andrews: L'Excentricité d'un discours carnavalisé," in L'Excentricité en Grand-Bretagne au 18e siècle. Edited by Michèle S. Plaisant. Lille: Eds. univ., Univ. de Lille, pp. 59-82.
Examines eccentric behavior and social eccentricity (carnival spirit from the ancient world to the middle ages). Both are outside the rules, comic, and potentially subversive. After examining eccentric manifestations in character and narrative technique, argues that Fielding was aware of its complex nature and used it to present both a ridiculous comic world and to ridicule masked reality. In French.

3 EVANS, JAMES E. "Fielding's Lady Booby and Fénelon's Calypso." Studies in the Novel, 8, no. 2 (Summer), 210-13.
Argues that Fielding portrays "Lady Booby as an eighteenth-century Calypso" (p. 212), alluding to Fénelon's character in tone and content (i.e., the psychology of the spurned superior woman).

*4 FENSTER, ALAN R. "The Other Tradition: An Essay on Forms of Realism in the Novel." Dissertation, California-Berkeley, 1976.
Calls Tom Jones one of the novels at odds with Jamesian realism (those in F. R. Leavis' Great Tradition). It denies the reader empathic access to character, is not developmental, and emphasizes the novelist's rhetorical

purpose.
Source: Dissertation Abstracts, 38, no. 2 (Aug. 1977), 802A-803A.

5 FOLKENFLIK, ROBERT. "'The Author's Farce' and 'Othello.'" Notes and Queries, 221 (April), 163-64.
By examining speeches that echo Othello III.184, Folkenflik argues that Fielding travesties Othello in order to ridicule the pretensions of Italian opera; this also demonstrates his allusive art.

6 GOLDGAR, BERTRAND A. Walpole and the Wits: The Relation of Politics to Literature, 1722-1742. Lincoln and London: University of Nebraska Press, passim.
Reviewed by Leo Braudy, SEL, 17 (1977), 536-38; D. Greene, TLS, 24 Jan. 1977, p. 752; H. D. Weinbrot, ECS, 11 (1977-78), 263-68.
Fielding is an important figure in this study of "the behavior of literary figures under the immediate pressure of partisan politics . . . [which] in Walpole's day . . . made no bones about its hostility to men of letters and its contempt for their role in society" (p. 6). Goldgar outlines Fielding's early and late relations with Walpole, his political beliefs, and discusses the political satire in his plays, journals, and novels. Argues that Fielding's early plays indicate "a popular playwright cautiously seeking his advantage wherever it lay" (p. 115); that the middle plays (Pasquin and The Historical Register) are not "heavily or bitterly satiric" (p. 151), although they served the opposition cause; finally concludes that "Fielding was primarily a wit rather than an ideologue committed to a specific political program" (p. 207), and that he "not only shifted his allegiances but was probably rewarded for doing so" (p. 205). See 1966.B4.

7 HUNT, RUSSELL A. "Johnson on Fielding and Richardson: A Problem in Literary Moralism." Humanities Association Review, 27, no. 4 (Fall), 412-20.
By illustrating the difference between Johnson's rational and eschatological morality and Fielding's emotional and benevolent one, Hunt argues that "Johnson's condemnation of Tom Jones on ethical grounds, and the severity of that condemnation, are perfectly consistent with his own moral beliefs and critical principles" (pp. 418-19). Sees Richardson, despite his "sentimentality," in essential agreement with the Johnson position.
For another view, see 1951.B4.

8 KERN, JEAN B. Dramatic Satire in the Age of Walpole: 1720-1750. Ames: Iowa State University Press, passim.
Reviewed by R. Paulson, SEL, 16 (1976), 521.

Studying dramatic satire written between 1720-1750, Kern briefly discusses twenty-two of Fielding's plays, along with several hundred other plays, under three headings: political satire (specific events, elections, the Prince of Wales, Walpole), social satire (the middle class, the professions, fashionable society), literary satire (author's world, theory, form). Thus The Grub-Street Opera is discussed under all three headings (as an attack on Walpole, on the clergy, on the social vice of drinking, and on opera). She concludes that in the period topical satire took five dramatic forms: the rehearsal, the mock epic, the satiric allegory, the burlesque parody, and the ballad-opera. Fielding used all of these forms.

9 LOFTIS, JOHN, RICHARD SOUTHERN, MARION JONES and A. H. SCOUTEN. "Henry Fielding," in The Revels History of Drama in English: Volume 5 (1660-1750). General editor T. W. Craik. London: Methuen, pp. 238-40, passim.

Reviewed by Leo Braudy, SEL, 17 (1977), 533-34; J. Kenyon, TLS, 28 Jan. 1977, p. 102; R. Paulson, SEL, 16 (1976), 521.

The section on Fielding briefly argues for his developing competence as a dramatist and repeats positions set out more fully by Bateson (1929.B1). Fielding is also discussed in sections on "drama and the novel," the burlesque tradition (which they think his strongest plays), and repertory companies. His role as theater manager and as provoker of the Licensing Act is also briefly considered, as are thirteen of his plays.

10 OAKMAN, ROBERT L. "The Character of the Hero: A Key to Fielding's Amelia." Studies in English Literature: 1500-1900, 16, no. 3 (Summer), 473-89.

Examines Booth's role as husband and father, spokesman for the author, representative of a bad philosophy of life, and as victim of a corrupt society. In the first role Oakman thinks Booth less admirable than Amelia, but more psychologically believable because of his ambivalence. With the narrator less intrusive in the novel, Booth must speak some of the author's ideas; as a doubter of religion, however, he represents a philosophy of which Fielding disapproved. His conversion, like the fairy tale ending, shows that "Fielding has finished using Booth to prove a point" (p. 483). Many of Booth's difficulties also dramatize the evil institutions and individuals of his age. See 1960.B23.

*11 PÁLFFY, ISTVÁN. "Fielding és a XVIII század angol színpadi paródiái." Kwartalnik Neofilologiczny (Warsaw), 22, 47-55.
"Fielding and 18th-century dramatic poetry." In Hungarian.
Source: MLA: Bibliography, 1 (1977), 83.

12 PAULSON, RONALD. "Models and Paradigms: Joseph Andrews, Hogarth's Good Samaritan, and Fénelon's Télémaque." Modern Language Notes, 91, no. 6 (Dec.), 1186-1207.
Describes eighteenth-century awareness of typology and establishes the complex typology of Hogarth's Good Samaritan, Pool of Bethesda and Harlot's Progress, with their mixing of eros and caritas, arguing that Fielding's use of the Good Samaritan and charity in Joseph Andrews is "based . . . on an existing image of Hogarth, and the context of that image determines in various ways his use of it" (p. 1198). Also argues that the Télémaque is the narrative structure Joseph ought to be typologically following, but doesn't entirely because Joseph is unaware of his real search (for a father). Both of Fielding's models, or paradigms, have demythologized biblical and classical stories in order to create complex new myths. Finally finds Fielding balancing these two levels of allusion to establish his own ways of delivering the truth.

13 POOVEY, MARY. "Journeys from this World to the Next: The Providential Promise in Clarissa and Tom Jones." Journal of English Literary History, 43, no. 3 (Fall), 300-315.
Argues that, though both are Christian epics, Fielding's assumes "the absolute can be perceived through temporal realities" and Richardson's assumes "the two realms [are] contiguous but incompatible" (p. 301). Thus Richardson concentrates on individual spiritual development and Fielding on ethics. Examining Fielding's mixed characters and narrative control, Poovey argues that Fielding metaphorically expresses "the providential pattern in quotidian terms" (p. 301). Action in Tom Jones "does not contribute to internal development" (p. 310); it forms an "iconomatic" impulse in which "actions metaphorically express spiritual states" (p. 312).

14 ROGERS, KATHARINE M. "Sensitive Feminism vs. Conventional Sympathy: Richardson and Fielding on Women." Novel, 9, no. 3 (Spring), 256-70.
Rogers describes Richardson's portrayal of women as "radical feminism," Fielding's as "loving presentation of romantic heroines . . . conditioned by the anti-feminist prejudices of the time" (p. 256). She examines the

one-sided Booth relationship, Fielding's treating Fanny and Sophia as pieces of property (whose lovers have a right to their virginity), the emotional dependence of Fielding's heroines (who ignore the battle of the sexes), and Fielding's crude dismissal of intellectual women. Largely ignores Pamela I.

For another view, see 1907.B1.

15 STOLER, JOHN A. and RICHARD FULTON. "Henry Fielding: A Checklist of Criticism, 1946-1975." Bulletin of Bibliography, 33 (Oct.-Dec.), 193-211.

Lists books on Fielding and editions with critical commentaries; articles and books with sections on Fielding; and dissertations.

16 WOOD, CARL. "Shamela's Subtle Satire: Fielding's Characterization of Mrs. Jewkes and Mrs. Jervis." English Language Notes, 13, no. 4 (June), 266-70.

By examining the ambiguities in two servants in Richardson's novel, illustrated in the Bedfordshire and Lincolnshire bedroom scenes, Wood explains Fielding's inversion of their characters as a satiric insight into Richardson's characterizations.

17 ZIMMERMANN, HEINZ. "Henry Fielding: The Tragedy of Tragedies," in Das englische Drama im 18. und 19. Jahrhundert. Edited by Heinz Kosok. Berlin: Erich Schmidt Verlag, pp. 87-102.

Argues that Fielding sets out to mock current (but archaic) artistic conventions and traditions by using several literary devices in the Tragedy of Tragedies: bathos, doggerel, pretentious scholarly language, etc. Also argues that the play goes beyond ridicule of literary conventions to satirize human "greatness" and the confusion of an age in which the propertied bourgeoisie became the new aristocracy.

1977 A BOOKS

1 FIELDING, HENRY. The Adventures of Joseph Andrews. Illustrated by Haydon Jones. New York: Hart, 554 pp.

A photocopy of 1931.A3 with a two page introduction by Nancy Goldberg.

*2 FLEMING, JOHN P. "The Classical Retirement Theme in the Fiction of Defoe, Fielding, Johnson, and Goldsmith." Dissertation, Bowling Green State, 1977.

Chapter 2 examines the ways in which "Joseph Andrews, Tom Jones, and Amelia qualify the classical theme by employing realistic details to undermine uncritical acceptance of the rural ideal."

Source: Dissertation Abstracts, 38, no. 5 (Nov. 1977), 2804A-805A.

*3 SASS, LORNA J. Dinner with Tom Jones. New York: Metropolitan Museum of Art, p. 208.

Recipes of dishes popular in the eighteenth century like syllabub and sack posset. Sass's introduction surveys culinary styles and eating arrangements with occasional references to Fielding's writings.

Source: Professor A. J. Weitzman.

1977 B SHORTER WRITINGS

1 AMORY, HUGH. "Tom Jones Plus or Minus: Towards a Practical Text." Harvard Library Bulletin, 25:101-113.

Reviews the scholarly history of the first three editions of Tom Jones and the textual studies of the novel. He then argues "that there is an as yet unnoted whole-sheet cancel in the first edition [at Harvard], by which the unexpected and puzzling 'revision' of Book VIII. 13-15 in the third edition may be explained and shown to be unauthorized" (p. 106). Amory contends "that the text of the third-edition 'revision,' the 'short version' as I prefer to call it, descends from a copy of the first edition in which sheet O was accidentally cancelled" (p. 110).

2 BIRKNER, GERD. "Zum Verhältnis von ästhetischer Norm und Funktion in Fieldings Tom Jones und Joseph Andrews." Anglia, 95:359-78.

Asserts that the nineteenth century treated all eighteenth-century novelists as homogeneous creators of "Bildungsromane." But Fielding does not fit the category. Unlike the heroes of Richardson and Defoe, Fielding's heroes do not strive to reach goals, are not responsible for their identity, and do not control their achievements. Instead Fielding stands in opposition to the new aesthetic standards of the bourgeois novel; his novels contain "regressive" traits of the heroic romance and the epic. For example, he places great emphasis on gentility, on the social status of his heroes, and on happy denouements. In German.

3 BURKE, JOHN J. "History Without History: Henry Fielding's Theory of Fiction," in A Provision of Human Nature: Essays on Fielding and Others in Honor of Miriam Austin Locke. Edited by Donald Kay. Alabama: University of Alabama Press, pp. 45-63.

Argues that Fielding moved from an early dialectic with historiographers, in which he argued that "the subjectivity of history was no more reliable than the subjectivity of a fiction" (p. 46), to "idealized autobiography" in Tom Jones, which "represents a considerable retreat from any earlier hopes of creating a new kind of historiography" (pp. 59-60). Burke discusses the contrast between the hero worship and ideal human qualities (embodied in Heartfree in Jonathan Wild), the novel as a new form of history that dramatizes a private world, time in history and fiction, and the shift to autobiography and manners in Tom Jones (where the "national experience [is rendered] through the individual experiences," p. 57). See 1947.B5 and 1964.B14.

4 DURANT, JACK D. "The 'Art of Thriving' in Fielding's Comedies," in A Provision of Human Nature: Essays on Fielding and Others in Honor of Miriam Austin Locke. Edited by Donald Kay. Alabama: University of Alabama Press, pp. 25-35.

"The world of his stage, like that 'greater stage' he refers to in his Essay [on the Knowledge of the Characters of Men], is peopled with thrivers of the most accomplished sort" (p. 25). Durant examines the characters in Fielding's dramas who "people a world fragmented by aggressive self-service" (p. 26). He also examines the comic strategies of the thrivers: comic evasion scenes, in which they run a high risk of exposure; vicious family conflict; institutional corruption, in which "social institutions developed for human safety and comfort fall prey to . . . corrupt people" (p. 29). The dramatization of thriving dictates the various comic resolutions of the plays: the "education" of a corrupt character, good characters morally isolated from strife, good nature fortuitously triumphant, and the "dialectical" form. Durant claims that only the dialectical form is successful, because of its balancing of virtue and vice, good and ill nature.

5 EAVES, T. C. DUNCAN. "Amelia and Clarissa," in A Provision of Human Nature: Essays on Fielding and Others in Honor of Miriam Austin Locke. Edited by Donald Kay. Alabama: University of Alabama Press, pp. 95-110.

Argues that Amelia is not the product of a sick, disillusioned Fielding. On the evidence of a letter by

Richardson, Eaves proposed that Fielding may have begun Amelia "well over a year before Cross and Dudden conjecture he did. He could have started planning the novel even before the publication of Tom Jones" (p. 96). Contends that Amelia was prompted by Fielding's great admiration for Clarissa. After carefully detailing ways in which Amelia is a model of perfection (also examining ways in which she is not), Eaves decides that Fielding intended "to move his readers emotionally" (p. 106) with this model, but failed because she was perfect to begin with rather than growing to perfection as Clarissa does. Fielding also resorted to melodramatic and careless verbal tricks to excite readers (excessive use of the word "poor," a weeping hero, a teary-eyed, swooning heroine).

6 HASSALL, A. J. "Garrick's 'Hamlet' and 'Tom Jones.'" Notes and Queries, 222 (May-June), 247-49.

Sets out Partridge's comments on Garrick's Hamlet, noting that the sequence of the scenes in Act III of Hamlet is reversed. Considering several explanations for this, Hassall thinks Fielding did it to emphasize the effect of the ghost scenes on Partridge.

7 HUTCHENS, ELEANOR N. "O Attic Shape! The Cornering of Square," in A Provision of Human Nature: Essays on Fielding and Others in Honor of Miriam Austin Locke. Edited by Donald Kay. Alabama: University of Alabama Press, pp. 37-44.

Extrapolating on the image of Square crouching in the attic and Jones standing free in the middle, Hutchens concludes that: "from their angular hiding places [the knaves] calculate their own advantage, balance each other in competitive knavery, and cancel each other out" (p. 41). Good characters like Tom, Sophia, and Allworthy appear to be "asymmetrical," autonomous, and free standing. Examines Tom's affair with Lady Bellaston (which balances his father's affair with his mother), Tom's pairing with Blifil, and Allworthy's with Western, saying that such geometry leads characters to do wrong. "Human nature in Tom Jones is what is left after all the logical and formal representations of it have been discarded. Human goodness stands forth spontaneous, natural, and organic, while human badness crouches in the shelter of a rule" (p. 43).

8 KYLE, LINDA D. "'Amelia' by Henry Fielding: A Selective Bibliography." Notes and Queries, 222 (May-June), 255-58.

A sometimes inaccurate list of books and articles reflecting "the major views and contrasting ideas on Fielding's fourth novel from 1751 through 1974."

9 LOFTIS, JOHN E. "Imitation in the Novel: Fielding's Amelia." Rocky Mountain Review of Language and Literature, 31:214-29.

Briefly sets out the epic theory in England from Spenser through Pope (an exemplary portrait of the virtues of the hero and of his society, inverted by Pope). Then examines the "parallels in structure, in setting, in incident, and in character" (p. 218) between Amelia and the Aeneid (e.g., Aeneas' descent into hell is paralleled by Booth's experience at the masquerade). Argues that "the moral value of the family [the "hero" of this novel] and criticism of society, both themes arising from [English] epic expectations . . . both central to the novel, ultimately merge through the theme of adultery" (p. 225) and create a unified, sophisticated imitation adapted to the novel form. See 1936.B10 and 1956.B11.

10 MCCREA, BRIAN R. "Fielding's Role in 'The Champion': A Reminder." South Atlantic Bulletin, 42, no. 1, 19-24.

Argues that "Fielding moved into the Opposition camp hesitantly and indirectly" (p. 23) and observes that: "an allusive, learned, and often non-political essay by Fielding precedes a section of direct, often bellicose, political comment by Ralph" (p. 21). Concludes that it was James Ralph who set the political tone for The Champion, and that Fielding was not an Opposition writer who switched to Walpole's side. See 1960.B4, 1966.B4, 1972.B7, and 1976.B6.

11 MILLER, SUSAN. "Eighteenth-Century Play and the Game of Tom Jones," in A Provision of Human Nature: Essays on Fielding and Others in Honor of Miriam Austin Locke. Edited by Donald Kay. Alabama: University of Alabama Press, pp. 83-93.

Describes "the frequency of eighteenth-century organized merriment" (p. 85) and Fielding's attitudes toward the robust recreations of his society. Argues that Fielding was "in the mainstream of pre-eighteenth-century theories of the educational nature and functions of fun" (p. 87) and that he constructed the "plot, characters, setting, and narration of [Tom Jones] to employ characteristics of actual or metaphoric games" (p. 88). Discusses the "players within Tom's adventures," Tom's "archetypal quest" (p. 89), and Tom's participation in pastimes (poaching,

fighting, etc.) as elements that define the excesses and virtues of Tom's nature. Describes how our reading experience makes us more "perceptive players" (p. 91).
For a similar view, see 1971.B20 and 1976.B2.

12 ROGERS, WINSLOW. "Thackeray and Fielding's 'Amelia.'" Criticism, 19, no. 2 (Spring), 141-57.
Reviews critical attitudes towards Fielding's influence on Thackeray, Thackeray's criticism of Fielding, and Fielding's strengths and weaknesses in Amelia. Argues that Thackeray was deeply influenced by Fielding's mixed, inconsistent narrative voice in Amelia and made use of the technique in his own fiction after 1840. Although Thackeray was aware of other strengths in Fielding, it is in this uncertain technical experiment rather than in character or irony that Fielding's influence is important. Specifically compares the use of narrator in Barry Lyndon, Vanity Fair, The History of Samuel Titmarsh and Amelia. See 1961.B7.

13 WILLIAMSON, EUGENE. "Guiding Principles in Fielding's Criticism of the Critics," in A Provision of Human Nature: Essays on Fielding and Others in Honor of Miriam Austin Locke. Edited by Donald Kay. Alabama: University of Alabama Press, pp. 1-24.
Attempts to understand Fielding's "guiding principles" by reviewing "the kind of critical treatment given to his own dramas and novels" (p. 2) as well as Fielding's "comment on the critical malpractice of his day" (p. 6), which attacked the critics' ignorance, mechanical approach to texts, and unfair dealings with authors. "Infers . . . that he saw the need for a criticism that was informed, genially responsive to creative practice, and fair" (p. 15). Discovers Fielding's critical "desiderata" in direct and satiric statements on his journalism.

14 WOLFE, GEORGE H. "Lessons in Evil: Fielding's Ethics in The Champion Essays," in A Provision of Human Nature: Essays on Fielding and Others in Honor of Miriam Austin Locke. Edited by Donald Kay. Alabama: University of Alabama Press, pp. 65-81.
Examines the essays in The Champion as Fielding's "first attempts, outside the theatre, to order an inchoate but pervasive fascination with ethical problems" (p. 65). Arguing that Fielding's "assaults upon evil are based on the orthodox view that men are born with inherent capacity for sinning, though simultaneously of great good" (p. 67), Wolfe briefly examines Fielding's attitude toward temptation, inherent wickedness (he was not Hobbesian), political

cynicism, human diversity, the balancing forces of good and evil, social responsibility, the ethical basis of judgment, and vigorous virtue. Wolfe concludes that Fielding was an ethical pragmatist and that characters like Tom and Adams "strongly suggest an elementary version of situational ethics" (p. 76). See dissertation 1976.A13.

15 ZAKI, JAFAR. "Sir Robert Walpole and Fielding's Modern Husband." Aligarh Journal of English Studies, 2:60-71.

Argues that the dedication to Walpole "was an act of subterfuge and a palliative to attenuate the causticity of satire on Walpole within the play" (p. 70). Zaki thinks Fielding has "given to Lord Richly the same weaknesses, the same vices which the Opposition writers had detected in Walpole" (p. 63). He cites his "amorous proclivities," his fondness for vulgar entertainment, his inflated sense of greatness; particularly thinks the levee scene "an exact copy of Walpole's . . . weekly levees" (p. 66). Briefly argues that the opposition to Fielding in The Grub-Street Journal did not arise from this play. See 1949.B5 and 1976.B6.

Addendum

The following items have not been indexed

1971

*B3a ARNOLD, ALLEN D. "A Social Ethic in Tom Jones." Horizontes, 26: 53-65.
Source: PMLA. Vol. 1 (1971), p. 70.

*B9a DE BLOIS, PETER. "Ulysses at Upton: A Consideration of the Comic Effect of Fielding's Mock-Heroic Style in Tom Jones." Troth: Syracuse University Graduate Studies in English, 11: 3-8.
Source: PMLA. Vol. 1 (1971), p. 70.

1973

*B7a CLEARY, THOMAS. "Fielding: Style for an Age of Sensibility." Transactions of the Samuel Johnson Society of the North West (Calgary, Canada), 6: 91-96.
Source: PMLA. Vol. 1 (1973), p. 79.

1974

*A20d SIEGEL, SHIRLEY F. "Chivalric comedies: a study of romance elements in 'Tom Jones' and 'Joseph Andrews.'" Dissertation, Southern Illinois, 1974.
Examines the use of 'romantic' conventions: "balanced rhetorical language, heroic, larger than life characters, and archetypal incidents."
Source: Dissertation Abstracts, 36, no. 2 (Aug. 1975), 911A-12A.

*A22a WIECZOREK, ANTHONY P. "Henry Fielding's role as moral arbiter and teacher in the Champion, 1739-1741." Dissertation, Northwestern University, 1974.

Chronological study "in order to discover the author's social and ethical ideas as they emerge in his writing for this periodical."

Source: Dissertation Abstracts, 35, no. 10 (April 1975), 6687A.

*B3a CLEARY, THOMAS R. "Fielding's First Assault on George Whitefield and Parson Adams' 'Good Turk.'" New Rambler: the Journal of the Johnson Society of London (C:15), 40-46.

Source: MHRA, 50 (1975), 371.

*B6a HANES, SARA LOUISE. "Dialect in the Novels of Fielding and Smollett." Dissertation, University of Georgia, 1974.

"Fielding well represents his native Somerset dialect; Smollett carefully portrays his native Scottish speech, as well as the northern dialects; and both authors show some awareness of cockney."

Source: Dissertation Abstracts, 35, no. 10 (April 1975), 6694A.

*B9a JACOBSON, MARGARET CHARLOTTE K. "Women in the Novels of Defoe, Richardson, and Fielding." Dissertation, Connecticut, 1974.

Examines eighteenth-century "conditioning of women" through novels. "Joseph Andrews and Tom Jones, which are set in the countryside, reflect an older sense of community and sexuality; while . . . Amelia shows the new pressures on people who have been uprooted from their rural origins, estranged from their communities, families, and bodies, and isolated in hostile urban surroundings. . . ."

Source: Dissertation Abstracts, 35, no. 11 (May 1975), 7256A-57A.

*B18a ORMOND, JEANNE D. "The Knave with a Hundred Faces: the Guises of Hermes in Nashe, Fielding, Melville and Mann." Dissertation, University of California-Irvine, 1974.

There are two alternatives for a picaresque hero: to marry or repent (Bildungsroman) or to "take on all the ironic capabilities of the archetypal rogue, Hermes. . . . In Tom Jones, the Hermetic perspective emerges during the course of the second reading, when the reader becomes aware that his narrator is a trickster."

Source: Dissertation Abstracts, 35, no. 11 (May 1975), 7320A-21A.

1975

*A11a SOKOLJANSKIJ, MARK G. Tvorchestvo Genri Fildinga: kniga ocherkov [The Works of Henry Fielding: a Book of Sketches]. Kiev: Vishcha shkola, 174 pp.

In Russian.

Source: MHRA, 50 (1975), 372.

B3a BUTLER, MARILYN. "Fielding, Whose Contemporary?" Essays in Criticism, 25, no. 4 (Oct.), 478-79.

Response to 1975.B11b.

*B3b CLEARY, THOMAS R. "The Case for Fielding's Authorship of 'An Address to the Electors of Great Britain' (1740) Reopened." Studies in Bibliography, 28: 308-18.

Source: MHRA, 50 (1975), 371.

*B3c DUCROCQ, JEAN. "Tom Jones (1749)," in Roman et société en Angleterre au XVIIIe siècle. Edited by Jean Ducrocq, Suzy Halimi, and Maurice Lévy. Paris: Presses Univ., pp. 95-102.

Source: PMLA. Vol. 1 (1978), p. 104.

B4a FOLKENFLICK, ROBERT. "Tom Jones, the gypsies, and the Masquerade." University of Toronto Quarterly, 44: 224-37.

Because Tom Jones works by antithesis, the gypsy episode forms a natural contrast with the masquerade (each is the significant event of its book). The morality of Lady Bellaston turns the morality of the gypsies upside-down and the two episodes become masque and anti-masque. Thus the two episodes sum up and symbolize Fielding's complex attitude toward artifice.

*B6a JACOBS, JÜRGEN. "Das Verstummen der Muse: zur Geschichte der epischen Dichtungsgattungen im XVIII. Jahrhundert." Arcadia, 10:126-46.

Source: MHRA, 50 (1975), 371.

B6b KERN, JEAN B. "Fielding's Dramatic Satire." Philological Quarterly, 54, no. 1 (Winter), 239-57.

Argues that three playwrights influenced Fielding's dramatic satire: Molière helped him create ironic and insecure characters; Buckingham gave him the play-within-a-play structure; Gay provided the mixture of song and short scene. His satiric targets were partly determined by the journalistic attacks on Walpole.

Kern discusses Fielding's technical experiments and his mixture of comedy and satire in The Author's Farce,

Tragedy of Tragedies, and The Covent-Garden Tragedy, and the well-focused satire of Pasquin and The Historical Register for the Year 1736. As Fielding became competent in the use of "double focus and multiple meaning" (p. 250), he increasingly began to mix political and theatrical satire. Though "he was a fertile experimenter in form, he never completely settled on a structure for dramatic satire" (p. 254). She concludes that Fielding's satiric plays lack intensity, but they allowed him to hone his irony.

*B7a KLEIN, DE WAYNE. "A Fowl Tom Jones." Bulletin of the West Virginia Association of College English Teachers, 2, no. 2, 29-33.
Source: MHRA, 50 (1975), 371.

*B8a LONGMIRE, SAMUEL E. "Booth's Conversion in 'Amelia.'" South Atlantic Bulletin, 40, no. 4, 12-17.
Source: MHRA, 50 (1975), 371.

*B11a PARK, WILLIAM. "Tom and Oedipus." Hartford Studies in Literature: A Journal of Interdisciplinary Criticism, 7: 207-15.
Source: MHRA, 50 (1975), 372.

B11b RAWSON, C. J. "Fielding, Whose Contemporary?" Essays in Criticism, 25, no. 2 (April), 272-76.
A response to Marilyn Butler's review of his Henry Fielding and the Augustan Ideal Under Stress (1972.A9). See 1975.B3a.

B11c RØSTVIG, MAREN-SOFIE. "Tom Jones and the Choice of Hercules," in Fair Forms: Essays in English Literature from Spenser to Jane Austen. Edited by Maren-Sofie Røstvig. Cambridge: D. S. Brewer, pp. 147-77.
Argues that it is possible to compare Fielding's novel to literary and iconographic versions of the myth of Hercules. The digressions in particular fit this pattern because each turns on choice, "the choice of pleasures subsequently revealed as false or deceptive, and as opposed to virtues" (p. 156). She sees Tom as Hercules after his expulsion from Paradise Hall; Tom at the Inn at Upton is Hercules at the crossroads. The Tom/Hercules choice becomes significant in the mid-section (Books 7 through 12) of the novel.

B13 RUDOLPH, VALERIE C. "People and Puppets: Fielding's Burlesque of the Recognition Scene in The Author's Farce." Papers on Language and Literature, 11, no. 1 (Winter), 31-38.

Argues that Fielding used the "ordered disorder" of the recognition scene in his puppet play to mock such scenes in contemporary theater (e.g., The Conscious Lovers). Fielding mixed "two distinct phases of theatrical illusion --one realistic and one fantastic" (p. 32), so that his audience no longer had a clear indication of what was "real." The interchanges between puppets and Murdertext (underlining that Puritan attacks like Zeal-of-the-Land-Busy in Bartholomews Fair and Collier's were responsible for theatrical decline) and Luckless' transformation into King of Bantam (suggesting that playwrights are puppets of theater management) both call attention to false theater conventions and satirize the forces destroying the theater.

B14 STEWART, MAAJA A. "Techniques of intellectual Comedy in Meredith and Fielding." Genre, 8, no. 3 (Sept.), 233-47.

"By examining these comic techniques Meredith shares with Fielding--a narrator who defines a rational ideal, provides emotional distance, and generalizes characters; the self-deceiving characters whose viewpoints are often exposed by mimicking narrative voices and who are evaluated by the degree of difference between their awareness and the narrator's awareness; and the parody of sentimental fictions to authenticate the novel's 'reality'--we can clarify that part of Meredith"s [Egoist] which is classical and rational" (p. 234).

*B15 WEISGERBER, JEAN. "Nouvelle lecture d'un livre ancien: l'espace dans L'Histoire de Tom Jones, l'enfant trouvé." Cahiers romains d'etudes littéraires, 1: 69-86.

Source: MHRA, 50 (1975), 373.

1977

*B3a DRISKELL, LEON. "Maritornes and Slipslop: Delusion and Dramatic Irony in Cervantes and Fielding." Kentucky Philological Association Bulletin, pp. 15-23.

Source: PMLA. Vol. 1 (1978), p. 104.

B11a RIBBLE, FREDERICK G. "The Constitution of the Mind and the Concept of Emotion in Fielding's Amelia." Philological Quarterly, 56, no. 1 (Winter), 104-22.

An essay on Fielding's "philosophy of mind" (p. 105), asserting that in Amelia "emotion may be regarded as a kind of sensation" (p. 104). Reviews earlier theorists (Locke, Shaftesbury, the Restoration divines) and examines Fielding's metaphor of the mind as a kind of body within the body" (p. 109) in his earlier work. In Amelia, emotion becomes an internal sensation "like a toothache" (p. 115). By examining the behavior of various characters (Booth, Mrs. James, Amelia), Ribble concludes that the reader is given characters who "feel with a violence he knows he could never match, but who performs rather less because of that feeling" (pp. 117-18).

Index

Underscored entry numbers indicate items of particular significance.

Morrissey, L. J.

Henry Fielding, a reference guide

DATE			